Instructional Methods for Secondary Students with Learning and Behavior Problems

FOURTH EDITION

Patrick J. Schloss

Northern State University

Maureen A. Schloss

South Dakota School for the Deaf

Cynthia N. Schloss

late of Bloomsburg State University

PEARSON

Boston • New York • San Francisco
Mexico City • Montreal • Toronto • London • Madrid • Munich • Paris
Hong Kong • Singapore • Tokyo • Cape Town • Sydney

Executive Editor: *Virginia Lanigan*
Series Editorial Assistant: *Matthew Buchholz*
Marketing Manager: *Kris Ellis-Levy*
Production Editor: *Annette Joseph*
Editorial Production Service: *Omegatype Typography, Inc.*
Composition Buyer: *Linda Cox*
Manufacturing Buyer: *Linda Morris*
Electronic Composition: *Omegatype Typography, Inc.*
Cover Administrator: *Elena Sidorova*

For related titles and support materials, visit our online catalogue at www.ablongman.com.

Between the time website information is gathered and then published, it is not unusual for some sites to have closed. Also, the transcription of URLs can result in typographical errors. The publisher would appreciate notification where these errors occur so that they may be corrected in subsequent editions.

Library of Congress Cataloging-in-Publication Data

Schloss, Patrick J.
    Instructional methods for secondary students with learning and behavior problems /
    Patrick J. Schloss, Maureen A. Schloss, Cynthia N. Schloss. — 4th ed.
        p. cm.
    Includes bibliographical references and index.
    ISBN 0-205-44236-6 (alk. paper)
        1. Learning disabled youth—Education. 2. Youth with disabilities—Education
    (Secondary) 3. Special education—Curricula. I. Smith, Maureen A. II. Schloss,
    Cynthia N. III. Title.

LC4704.S35 2007
371.9—dc22

                                                                            2006046008

Printed in the United States of America

10 9 8 7 6 5 4 3 2 1   10 09 08 07 06

In Remembrance

The fourth edition of *Instructional Methods for Secondary Students with Learning and Behavior Problems* is dedicated to the memory of Dr. Cynthia N. Schloss. Cindy was a driving force behind the first three editions of this text. Her professional preparation and experience were centered on the development, refinement, and delivery of education and vocational services to adolescents and young adults with disabilities. Her professional service included the directorship of Missouri Advocacy and Protection and professorships at Penn State University and Bloomsburg University of Pennsylvania. Cindy authored a number of textbooks and articles related to assessment, family interventions, and instructional practices. Students, practitioners, and colleagues who knew Cindy benefited from her knowledge, dedication, and humor. In addition to her professional success, Cindy was a loving wife to Pat and dedicated mother to Patrick, Rebecca, and Tarah. She was grandmother to Mary, Patrick, and Joseph.

Whether directly teaching students with disabilities or preparing other professionals to assume this responsibility, Cindy was tireless in her efforts to ensure that all students had the information and skills they needed to enjoy successful, productive lives. This edition of *Instructional Methods for Secondary Students with Learning and Behavior Problems* is intended to continue her efforts.

Contents

Preface   xiii

PART ONE • *Educational Perspectives in Secondary Special Education*

CHAPTER 1 *Foundations of Secondary Special Education*   **1**

Legislative Foundations   **4**

No Child Left Behind   5   ■   Special Education   7   ■   Vocational Education   11   ■   Implications of NCLB, and Special and Vocational Education Legislation   13

A Transition Perspective   **14**

Curricular Goals and Objectives   14   ■   Transfer of Training   14   ■   Articulation of Services   15

The Goals of Secondary Special Education   **15**

Factors Influencing the Development of Secondary Special Education Programs   **17**

Attitude toward Secondary Special Education   17   ■   Structure of Regular Secondary Education   18   ■   Curricular Emphasis   18   ■   Teacher Preparation Programs   18   ■   Insufficient Database   19   ■   Lack of Appropriate Materials   19

Summary   **20**

CHAPTER 2 *Postsecondary Service Options*   **21**

Postsecondary Educational Programs   **24**

Two-Year Colleges   24   ■   Four-Year Colleges and Universities   27   ■   Postsecondary Technical Programs   32   ■   Business and Industry   33   ■   Vocational Rehabilitation   34   ■   Sheltered Rehabilitation Centers   35   ■   Supported Employment Services   36

Postsecondary Service Selection   **37**

Summary   **38**

CHAPTER **3**   *Challenges of Adolescence*   **39**

by Anjali Misra and Susan Mary Paige

Juvenile Delinquency   **41**

Incidence   41   ■   Causes   41   ■   Intervention Needs   42   ■
Teacher Responsibilities   43

Dropouts   **45**

Incidence   45   ■   Causes   45   ■   Intervention Needs   46   ■
Teacher Responsibilities   46

Substance Abuse   **48**

Incidence   48   ■   Causes   48   ■   Intervention Needs   49   ■
Teacher Responsibilities   49

Depression   **51**

Incidence   51   ■   Causes   52   ■   Intervention Needs   53   ■
Teacher Responsibilities   54

Suicide   **56**

Incidence   56   ■   Causes   57   ■   Intervention Needs   57   ■
Teacher Responsibilities   58

Sexually Transmitted Diseases   **60**

Incidence   60   ■   Causes   62   ■   Intervention Needs   62   ■
Teacher Responsibilities   63

Teenage Pregnancy   **65**

Incidence   65   ■   Causes   65   ■   Intervention Needs   68   ■
Teacher Responsibilities   69

Summary   **71**

PART TWO • *General Instructional Approaches*

CHAPTER **4**   *Instructional Methods for Secondary Learners with Disabilities*   **72**

Learning Standards and the General Education Curriculum   **75**

Direct Instruction   **76**

Direct-Instruction Curriculum Design   77

The Sequence of Direct-Instruction Activities   **79**

Identify Learner Characteristics   79   ■   Establish Goals   81   ■
Identify Objectives   82   ■   Design Instruction   82   ■   Implement
Instruction   92   ■   Evaluate Mastery of the Objectives   93   ■   Determine
Whether the Goals Have Been Achieved   93

Learning Strategies **93**
> Characteristics of a Learning Strategy 95 ■ Teaching a Learning Strategy 96

Constructivism **97**

Grading **100**

Summary **103**

CHAPTER **5** *Assessment for Placement and Instruction* **104**

Norm-Referenced Testing **106**
> Characteristics 106 ■ Placement and Summative Evaluations 107 ■
> Statewide Assessment and Alternative/Accommodative Strategies 108

Curriculum-Based Measurement **112**
> Formative Evaluation 112 ■ Diagnostic Evaluation 113 ■
> Selection of Curriculum-Based Instruments 114

Developing Paper-and-Pencil Tests **114**
> Step 1: Develop the Performance Objective 115 ■
> Step 2: Enumerate Subskills 116 ■ Step 3: Describe the Question-and-Answer
> Format 116 ■ Step 4: Prepare Instructions for the Test 117 ■
> Step 5: Prepare Test Items 117 ■ Step 6: Establish Scoring Procedures 118

Observation Procedures **119**
> Selection of Monitoring Procedures 119 ■ Observation Methods 120 ■
> Interobserver Agreement 125

Graphing Observational Data **126**

Interpreting Graphs **126**
> Mean 127 ■ Level 127 ■ Trend 128 ■ Latency 128

Portfolio-Based Assessment **128**
> Portfolio Content 129 ■ Evaluation of Entries 129

Summary **130**

CHAPTER **6** *Managing the Learning Environment* **132**

Antecedent Control **134**
> Physical Arrangement 135 ■ Rules 136 ■ Routine
> Classroom Procedures 137 ■ Student Schedules 138 ■ Time
> Management 141 ■ Systematic Instruction 144 ■ Functional,
> Age-Appropriate Activities and Materials 144 ■ Rate of Success 149 ■
> Teacher–Student Interactions 150 ■ Interaction with Nondisabled
> Peers 151 ■ Modeling 151 ■ Review of the Educational
> Program 152

Related Personal Characteristics **152**
> Academic Skills 153 ■ Social Skills 153 ■ Emotional Learning 154

***Consequence Control*   155**
    Positive Reinforcers   156   ■   Extinction   157   ■
    Punishment   158   ■   Group Contingencies   162

***Self-Management*   164**

***Schoolwide Systems*   166**
    Detention   166   ■   In-School Suspension   168   ■   Out-of-School
    Suspension and Expulsion   170

***Functional Behavior Assessment*   172**

***Summary*   175**

CHAPTER   **7**   ***Collaboration and the Role of the Consultant Teacher*   176**
    by Maureen A. Schloss and Raquel J. Schmidt

***The Consultant Teacher*   178**
    Principles of Successful Collaboration   179   ■   Advantages of
    Consulting   181   ■   Developing a Consultant Teacher
    Program   182   ■   Characteristics of the Consultant
    Teacher   182   ■   Gaining Acceptance   183   ■   Responsibilities
    of Consultants   184   ■   Barriers to Successful Collaboration   187

***Resource Rooms*   188**
    Defining the Resource Room   189   ■   Advantages of Resource Room
    Placement   189   ■   Staffing the Resource Room   190   ■   Responsibilities
    of Teachers in Resource Rooms   191

***Summary*   193**

PART THREE • *Instruction in Basic and Functional Skills*

CHAPTER   **8**   *Listening and Speaking*   194
    by Daniel C. Tullos

***Listening*   195**

***Speech*   196**

***Language*   196**
    Phonology/Articulation   197   ■   Morphology   197   ■   Semantics   198
    Syntax   199   ■   Pragmatics   200

***Assessment of Listening Skills*   200**

***Assessment of Speaking Skills*   202**
    Form   203   ■   Content/Semantics   204   ■   Use/Pragmatics   205

Strategies to Improve Listening Skills   **205**

Following Directions   206   ■   Remembering What Is Heard   206   ■
Taking Notes   206   ■   Organizing Material   207   ■   Effective
Questioning   207

Strategies to Improve Spoken-Language Skills   **208**

Phonology/Articulation   208   ■   Morphology and
Semantics   209   ■   Syntax   210   ■   Pragmatics   211   ■
Bidialectalism   211   ■   Bilingualism   212

Summary   **212**

CHAPTER 9   *Written Language*   213

by Stephen Isaacson

A Writing Curriculum for Students with Learning Problems   **215**

Assessing the Process   216   ■   Teaching the Process   216   ■   Using Word
Processors to Write   222

Writing as a Successful Product   **223**

Fluency   223   ■   Content   224   ■   Conventions   226   ■
Syntax   226   ■   Vocabulary   228

Writing for Different Purposes   **229**

Answering Chapter Questions   229   ■   Writing Reports   229
Writing for Future Vocations   230

Summary   **231**

CHAPTER 10   *Reading Instruction*   233

by Debi Gartland

Reading Abilities of Adolescents with Disabilities   **235**

Assessing Reading Ability   **236**

Formal Reading Assessment   236   ■   Informal Reading
Assessment   237   ■   The Informal Reading Inventory   237   ■
Oral Reading Error Analysis   239   ■   The Cloze Procedure   239

General Principles of Reading Instruction   **240**

Classroom-Based Reading Instruction   **241**

Vocabulary Instruction   241   ■   Fluency Instruction   244   ■
Comprehension Instruction   245   ■   Study Skills Instruction   249   ■
Textbook Instruction   249

Reading Instruction in Simulation and Community Settings   **252**

Summary   **255**

CHAPTER 11   *Mathematics Instruction*   257

by David Majsterek, Rich Wilson, and Eric D. Jones

Principles of Effective Secondary Math Instruction   **258**

Process of Effective Transition-Oriented Math Instruction   **261**

Step 1: Assessing Instructional Demands   261   ■   Step 2: Planning Specific Instruction   264   ■   Step 3: Implementing Math Instruction   272   ■   Step 4: Measuring Program Success   276

Summary   **276**

CHAPTER 12   *Vocational Instruction*   277

Transition   **279**

Self-Determination   **280**

Assessing Interests and Skills   **281**

Vocational Aptitude Tests   281   ■   Curriculum-Based Vocational Assessment   282   ■   Person-Centered Planning   282

Career Awareness Process   **283**

Vocational Objectives   **285**

Functional Curriculum   **285**

Basic Skills   289   ■   Specific Goal Selection   290

General Principles of Vocational Instruction   **292**

Summary   **293**

CHAPTER 13   *Leisure Education for Positive Leisure Life-Styles*   294

by Phyllis Jones, Diane Lea Ryndak, Barbara P. Sirvis, and Debbie S. Alcouloumre

Concepts of Leisure and Leisure Education   **298**

Leisure Opportunities   **301**

Mechanisms for Developing Leisure Opportunities   **303**

Identifying Appropriate Leisure Options   **304**

Inventories   304   ■   Prioritizing Leisure Options from Inventories   308

Cross-Curriculum Instructional Content Addressed through Leisure Education   **314**

Summary   **316**

CHAPTER **14** *Social Skill Instruction* **317**

Definition of Social Skills **319**

Establishing Objectives **321**

Social Validation of Goals and Objectives **322**

Assessing Social Competence **324**
Self-Reports 325 ■ Self-Monitoring 326 ■ Reports and Ratings by Others 327 ■ Direct Observation 328 ■ Commercial Instruments 328

General Principles of Social Skill Instruction **329**
Social Reinforcement 330 ■ Modeling 330 ■ Behavior Rehearsal 331 ■ Feedback 331 ■ Homework 333 Promoting Generalization and Maintenance 333 ■ Additional Instructional Considerations 335

Summary **336**

CHAPTER **15** *Teaching in the Content Areas* **337**

Science Education **339**
The Science Standards 340 ■ Approaches to Teaching Science 340

Social Studies Education **345**
Social Studies Goals and Curricula 345 ■ Approaches to Teaching Social Studies 346

Content Enhancements **347**
Advanced Organizers 348 ■ Graphic Organizers 348 ■ Study Guides 350 ■ Mnemonic Devices 350 ■ Guided Notes 353 ■ Audio Recordings 355 ■ Peer-Mediated Strategies 355

Summary **357**

References **358**

Author Index **402**

Subject Index **411**

Preface

The educational system in the United States was originally formed to provide for a well-educated citizenry. This country's founders believed that a democracy would operate effectively only if its citizens possessed the skills they needed to contribute to majority governance. Educational efforts to ensure a well-educated citizenry have varied substantially during our country's history, but perhaps never more so than in the last 60 years. We began our elementary school years studying the Three Rs, but experienced firsthand the major shift in curricula that resulted from the launch of Sputnik. Suddenly, development of skills in science and the "new math" became the focus of educational efforts. In the early 1980s, the publication of *A Nation at Risk* raised concerns that American students were not performing satisfactorily on measures of basic skills in areas such as reading, mathematics, and written language. As a result, educational initiatives swung back in the direction of mastering basic skills. More recent reports have presented data comparing the performance of American students to that of students from other countries. Results of these comparisons were dismal, raising grave concerns that students in the United States simply will not be prepared to meet the economic, vocational, and technological challenges of the 21st century. Reform efforts based on these reports have resulted in the development of learning standards by all state education agencies in reading, mathematics, written language, and science; most states have also developed standards in other curricular areas such as social studies, technology, career education, music, art, and foreign language. In addition, state education agencies have mandated that achievement of these standards be assessed periodically throughout students' elementary and secondary educational careers. Performance on these measures has major implications for students, their families, teachers, and officials of local school districts. For example, students who perform poorly may not receive a high school diploma, compromising their ability to enter postsecondary settings such as college or employment. Local schools may be designated as in need of improvement, prompting an examination of curricula, and scrutiny of the qualifications and performance of teachers.

In response to state mandates, local education agencies have developed or revised curricula to ensure *all* students are exposed to the knowledge and skills needed to demonstrate mastery of state standards. The key word in the previous sentence is *all*. Legislation over the past 30 years has emphasized that public education should be made available to all citizens in the country, including those with disabilities. Recent examples include the No Child Left Behind Act (NCLB) and the Individuals with Disabilities Education Improvement Act (IDEA). Special educators have become increasingly aware that exposure to a standards-based curriculum in the general education classroom, with proper support and accommodations, has the potential to prepare even individuals with the most severe disabilities to contribute to society. General educators should also be familiar with this legislation and the impact it has on identification, assessment, and eligibility, given the number of students with special needs who will be enrolled in their classrooms.

Public education has improved the basic skills of individuals with disabilities. For example, individuals who in the past might have gained only a few domestic or manual skills are progressing through elementary curricula in mathematics, reading, and writing. In addition, there have been some gains in the quality and quantity of secondary special education services. NCLB and IDEA support earlier legislative mandates that are the legal foundation for providing quality services to learners with special needs at the secondary level. Problems still exist, however, and it is estimated that six million secondary students, many of whom are disabled, are in danger of being left behind. Evidence indicates that public schools have yet to meet the challenge of preparing students with disabilities to meet the requirements necessary to receive a diploma, and live and work in the 21st century. For example, employment rates for persons with disabilities are substantially below those for the general population. Individuals who have disabilities are likely to spend several years finding stable employment. Only a small number of individuals with disabilities are entering skilled occupations, and once there, they are finding few opportunities for advancement.

The problem is that a gap seems to exist between the acquisition of academic skills and the application of these skills in work, leisure, and independent living. Individuals with disabilities may possess higher levels of basic academic skills, but they appear to be poorly prepared to apply these skills to the demands of community life. There are several reasons for this gap. First, there is an excessive reliance on methods and materials more appropriate for elementary-aged populations than secondary-aged learners. This overreliance is exemplified by the frequent use of the term *children with disabilities,* where "children" includes individuals at intermediate and secondary levels. Second, and on a related note, insufficient attention has been given to the special problems of adolescence and adulthood in general and special secondary education methods courses. Third, while it is recognized that the general education curriculum is appropriate for the majority of students with disabilities, secondary learners with disabilities have specific learning and behavioral characteristics that can undermine progress through general education curriculum. These characteristics include slower rates of acquiring information and skills, deficits in the ability to generalize learned skills to other settings or conditions, and a lack of ability to retain skills. Goals and objectives from other curricula are available, such as a learning strategies curriculum or a social skills curriculum, to address these characteristics.

Instructional Methods for Secondary Students with Learning and Behavior Problems was written to help fill this gap. It describes special education methods that are effective in promoting skills that may generalize to adult life. It has an empirical orientation to special education. The basic teaching model described in the text can be used to evaluate learner characteristics, establish corresponding goals and objectives, implement educational strategies that have been demonstrated to be effective in applied research literature, evaluate the impact of the procedures on the individual learner, and modify educational interventions when sufficient progress is not noted.

The book is unique in its focus on the special needs of intermediate- and secondary-aged learners. It pays special attention to the following topics:

- Unique psychosocial problems of adolescents
- Community resources available to young adults who have disabilities
- Curriculum needs as related to basic skill development and community integration

- Special social and interpersonal skill training priorities of young adults who have disabilities
- Postsecondary educational, leisure, vocational, and residential opportunities
- Validated learning strategies for adolescents and young adults who have disabilities
- Classroom management and motivational strategies that reflect the personal characteristics associated with adolescence

On completing the text, readers will be able to develop and implement educational programs suited to the special needs of adolescents and young adults who have disabilities.

Organization

The fourth edition of *Instructional Methods for Secondary Students with Learning and Behavior Problems* is organized into three main parts. The first deals with educational perspectives of instructional services for youth who have disabilities. The chapters in this part of the book focus on the legislative and social foundations of secondary and postsecondary education, postsecondary service options, and special problems associated with adolescence and adulthood.

Part Two examines general instructional approaches that are effective in teaching secondary-level learners who have disabilities. It opens with a discussion of three instructional models that illustrate how to provide instruction for youth with disabilities. It is followed by a discussion of assessment strategies that will ensure learners progress through instruction. The next chapter presents strategies for managing the learning environment. The concluding chapter of this part presents some consultative and resource functions of educators working with adolescents who have disabilities.

Part Three includes a description of special education methodologies at the secondary level and curricula within each of the major curricular areas. Each chapter reviews specific curriculum concerns, educational approaches, assessment procedures, and instructional materials. The methodology in each of the specific curricular areas is based on the general instructional strategies presented in Part Two. Chapters cover some traditional topics such as listening and speaking, written language, reading, mathematics, science, and social studies. Also covered are nontraditional curricular areas that are particularly appropriate for adolescents making the transition to adult life, including leisure skill training, vocational education, and interpersonal skill development.

Features

We have included several distinctive features that are intended to enhance the value of *Instructional Methods for Secondary Students with Learning and Behavior Problems* as both a course text and a reference.

- *DID YOU KNOW THAT?* The chapters begin with cognitive competencies. These statements outline the scope of the information contained in the chapter. Cognitive competencies are likely to be assessed by college instructors through class discussion and paper-and-pencil measures.

- *CAN YOU?* The chapters also begin with separate performance competencies. These statements identify specific strategies discussed in each chapter. Performance competencies are likely to be assessed by college instructors through direct observations in practical situations or through microteaching simulations.
- *ACTION PLANS.* These features occur throughout the individual chapters. They draw attention to performance by offering a step-by-step guide to implementing educational strategies. In most cases, the action plans summarize activities presented in the text without repeating the underlying rationale.
- *CASES FOR ACTION.* The cases for action provide an opportunity for readers to study and resolve hypothetical instructional problems. They are typically open-ended vignettes that may be resolved through information contained in the text.
- *TECHNICAL WRITING.* Professionals in the discipline of special education employ technical terms to convey particular concepts. It would be inappropriate for a college text to exclude any such terms that are critical to a precise understanding of these concepts. Therefore, when appropriate, technical terms are included and defined. Jargon that does little to communicate the philosophy or strategies associated with secondary special education is excluded.

A Word of Thanks

We are grateful to the people who have made the writing of this text possible. Our appreciation is extended to Virginia Lanigan, editor at Allyn and Bacon. Her leadership has ensured that this book is responsive to the needs of in-service and preservice training programs for secondary special educators. We also thank her assistants, Matt Buchholz and Scott Blaszak, for their dedication and attention to detail.

1 *Foundations of Secondary Special Education*

Did you know that . . .

- Six million secondary students are in danger of being "left behind"?
- Schools are required to demonstrate adequate yearly progress (AYP)?
- Schools that fail to demonstrate AYP must offer options to parents?
- Restructuring a school can include removing some or all staff?
- There are overlapping themes in legislation addressing special and vocational education?
- Students not served under IDEA can still be served by Section 504?

- Of the secondary students receiving special education, 29% graduate or receive a certificate of completion?
- Employment rates of persons with mild disabilities leaving secondary schools range from 50 to 75%?
- Only a minority of individuals with disabilities will enter skilled occupations?
- Students with severe disabilities are less likely than those with mild disabilities to drop out of school?
- Most teachers of secondary students with special needs were trained at the elementary level?
- Many special educators are certified but not qualified to teach at the secondary level?

Can you . . .

- Identify the provisions of the No Child Left Behind Act (NCLB)?
- Define adequate yearly progress?
- Define a highly qualified teacher?
- Define a highly qualified paraprofessional?
- List the information included on a school's report card?

- List parent options if their child's school fails to demonstrate AYP?
- Identify the court cases that contributed to the provisions of IDEA?
- List the provisions of IDEA?
- Define FAPE, LRE, and IEP?
- List the components of an IEP?

- Identify the instructional settings included in Deno's Cascade?

- State the purpose of Sections 503 and 504 of the Rehabilitation Act of 1973?

- Describe the provisions of the Americans with Disabilities Act of 1990?

- Describe the efforts by OSERS to remedy the deficiency in current educational services to persons with disabilities?

- Describe steps to ensure that learning is retained and skills are transferred to life situations beyond the school setting?

- Discuss six factors that hinder the development of secondary special education programs?

- Identify the goals of secondary special education?

The status of regular secondary education is a recurring theme in public and professional circles. Reports and follow-up legislation have focused on the quality of the educational services typically available to students and the impact of these services on their lives. Unfortunately, the picture is bleak. Dunn, Chambers, and Rabren (2004) noted that during the twenty-first century, a high school diploma will be essential if students are to access the additional training and education needed to succeed in the workplace. Their summary of the literature emphasized the implications of the failure to attain a high school diploma, which include estimates from 60 to 228 billion dollars in welfare costs, lost revenue, unemployment, and crime prevention. Individuals who drop out of school earn over $6,000 less than high school graduates.

In 1991, the Secretary's Commission of Achieving Necessary Skills (SCANS) (1991) addressed the adequate preparation of secondary students for the workplace. In its report, the commission stressed the need for higher cognitive skills and learning in the employment setting as essential for meaningful employment and productive lives. SCANS promotes relevance in teaching students in real-life settings versus teaching students in classroom settings (Rusch & Chadsey, 1998). Its framework includes three components: basic skills, thinking skills, and personal skills.

As a result of the SCANS report, the Goals 2000: Educate America Act (1994) was signed into law. Educational reform, being its core purpose, is based on eight national goals:

1. School readiness
2. School completion
3. Student achievement and citizenship
4. Teacher education and professional development
5. Mathematics and science
6. Adult literacy and lifelong learning
7. Safe schools
8. Parental participation

The School-to-Work Opportunities Act (1994) was signed into law during the same year as Goals 2000. Both reinforced the need for education reform (Norman & Bourexis, 1995). Through this act, state systems are to (1) prepare students with skills and knowledge necessary to transition from school to work, (2) prepare students for their first job toward a career, and (3) promote the integration of school and work-based learning.

As Wilcox and Bellamy (1982) have suggested, it would be nice to believe that the impact of elementary special education was so positive that it would enable the vast majority of secondary students with disabilities to enter the regular education classroom and perform at levels comparable to those of their nondisabled peers for the duration of their academic careers. Unfortunately, this has not been the case. Some students are likely to require some form of special education services the entire time they are eligible for public education (Schumaker et al., 2002). Furthermore, the quality and quantity of the special services available at the secondary level are likely to be inferior to those at the elementary level. Indeed, special services available to secondary students may be little more than a repetition or a continuation of elementary-level programs. Special education teachers who are not specifically trained for work at this level may use instructional strategies that have not been validated for use with secondary learners. In addition, the instructional materials frequently used at this level may have been intended either for elementary students with disabilities or for secondary students who do not have disabilities (Meyen, Vergason, & Whelan, 1998).

In their reviews of the literature, Conderman and Katsiyannis (2002) and Dunn and colleagues (2004) reported that outcomes for students with disabilities are dismal. They experience greater difficulties in school, have higher dropout and delinquency rates, do not participate as often in postsecondary education opportunities, have lower employment rates, earn less, and experience less satisfaction with their adult lives. Wehman (2003) summarized the prognosis for young adults with mild disabilities as follows with reference to employment prospects: (1) employment rates of persons with disabilities leaving secondary schools range from 50 to 75%; (2) an overwhelming majority of unemployed persons want to work; (3) those working are employed in a range of occupations; (4) most do not need special equipment or technology to perform effectively at work; (5) many confront discrimination, unfavorable attitudes, and physical barriers in the workplace; and (6) attitudes toward persons with disabilities are more open and positive than in years past.

The prognosis is equally unimpressive for civic outcomes. Individuals with disabilities are thought to commit a disproportionate number of crimes, to vote less often (even though state mandates ensure voting rights for individuals with disabilities), and to be unlikely to perform community service. Large numbers of students not headed for postsecondary settings feel devalued and are phased out of the system without civic outcomes (Edgar & Polloway, 1994). Also, individuals with disabilities are somewhat less likely to marry and have children. Participation in community leisure, social, and religious activities is more limited than it is among individuals who do not have disabilities (Wehman, 2003).

Public education has, in all probability, substantially improved the basic skills of individuals with disabilities (Mangrum & Strichart, 2003). Individuals who in the past might have gained only a few domestic or manual skills are now progressing through elementary levels of mathematics, reading, and writing. Some individuals with mild disabilities even have a strong prognosis for success in postsecondary educational settings (Chadsey-Rusch & Rusch, 1996; Edgar & Polloway, 1994). The main obstacle to further improvement seems to lie in the transfer of training from social service and educational contexts to adult-living environments (Sitlington & Clark, 2006). Individuals with disabilities may possess higher levels of basic academic skills, but they appear to be poorly prepared to apply these skills to the demands of community life.

The Office of Special Education and Rehabilitation Services (OSERS) has provided some guidelines on how to treat this deficiency of current educational efforts. OSERS has defined *transition* as

- A period that includes high school, the point of graduation, additional postsecondary education or adult services, and the initial years of employment.
- A process that requires sound preparation in the secondary school [and] adequate support at the point of school leaving.
- An effort that emphasizes shared responsibility of all involved parties for transition success, and extends beyond traditional notions of service coordination to address the quality and appropriateness of each service area. (Will, 1984, p. 2)

The OSERS definition of *transition* has been criticized by some for being narrow in scope in that it focuses on employment as the major outcome of transition services (Halpern, 1985). This sentiment was reflected in the passage of the Individuals with Disabilities Education Act (IDEA) (Public Law 101-476) in 1990 and reconfirmed in the IDEA Amendments of 1997 (Public Law 105-17), which defined *transition* as

> a coordinated set of activities for a student with a disability that—(a) is designed within an outcome-oriented process, which promotes movement from school to post-school activities, including post-secondary education, vocational training, integrated employment (including supported employment), continuing and adult education, adult services, independent living, or community participation; (b) is based upon the individual student's needs, taking into account the student's preferences and interests; and (c) includes instruction, related services, community experiences, the development of employment and other post-school adult living objectives, and, when appropriate, acquisition of daily living skills and functional vocational evaluation. (Section 602.30)

This legislation calls for a multidimensional definition of transition outcomes, including physical and mental health, mobility and community access, leisure and recreation skills, citizenship, and a sense of general well-being (Halpern, 1993a).

The purpose of this chapter is to review the foundations of secondary special education. We begin with the legislation mandating secondary special education services. We then identify the goals of secondary education for general education students and students with disabilities. Next, we examine factors that have prevented secondary learners with disabilities from attaining these goals. Finally, we identify some of the problems that must be addressed if a free and appropriate education is to be made available to all students at the secondary level.

Legislative Foundations

For a long time, secondary special education was a neglected component of the education system (Heller, 1981; Miller, Sabatino, & Larsen, 1980). Fortunately, in the last 25 years, several pieces of legislation have been enacted that furnish the legal foundation for providing quality services to learners with special needs at the secondary level. These acts reflect federal commitments to general education, special education, and vocational education.

Teachers with special education degrees are likely to be familiar with this legislation; however, general educators should also be familiar with this legislation and the impact it has on identification, assessment, and eligibility, given the number of students with special needs who are enrolled in their classrooms (deBettencourt, 2002).

No Child Left Behind

Estimates are that six million secondary students, many of whom are disabled, are in serious danger of being "left behind." This evidence indicates that public schools have failed to prepare students with disabilities to meet the requirements necessary to receive a diploma and meet the challenge of living and working in the twenty-first century (Schumaker et al., 2002).

Concern for poor high school outcomes has not been limited to students with special needs. Public dissatisfaction associated with the low achievement levels demonstrated by students in the United States and the belief that such performance was the result of low expectations and poor teaching (Johnson, 2000) prompted a variety of reform movements. Most notable was the establishment by many states of learning standards that describe what students should learn. In turn, school districts developed curricula or aligned existing curricula to meet these standards. According to Hoover and Patton (2004), a standards-based curriculum includes three components: (1) the content standards that organize skills and knowledge by content area; (2) performance standards that describe levels of proficiency, and (3) opportunities to learn the standards, including materials and strategies that will enhance student learning. To develop or align the curriculum, school districts must engage in a series of activities. First, they must plan by determining which standards will be included in the alignment, how alignment will be accomplished, and the time lines. Second, school districts must subject the existing curriculum to a needs assessment to measure the extent to which it may already address standards. Third, the district must infuse standards into the curriculum to ensure students have the opportunity to learn essential knowledge and skills. Fourth, schools must pilot a new and revised curriculum to measure the extent to which standards are being met. Fifth, schools make revisions based on pilot data. Sixth, schools implement the curriculum and, finally, make adaptations that will enable students with learning problems to meet standards (Hoover & Patton, 2004). Standards set high expectations for student performance, and proper development and implementation of a standards-based curriculum increase the likelihood that students will have the knowledge and skills needed to perform well on state- and districtwide assessments.

These reform movements culminated in the reenactment of the Elementary and Secondary Education Act (ESEA), which has been more commonly referred to as the No Child Left Behind Act or NCLB. The purpose of NCLB is to close the achievement gap between the general population and four groups of students: students with limited English proficiency, students with disabilities, minority students, and low-income students (Sorrentino & Zirkel, 2004). It is the principal federal law affecting education from kindergarten through secondary education. NCLB address four pillars: accountability for results, an emphasis on the use of strategies that are empirically based, more options for parents, and increased local control and flexibility (Introduction, NCLB, 2004).

Accountability for Results   Each state is to link its assessment to content and achievement standards. Assessments must be conducted every year in grades 3 through 8 and at least once in high school. School officials use test results to make decisions about curricula and teacher preparation. This provision of NCLB has implications for students in special education. NCLB places a cap of one percent of the students at each grade level who will be allowed to meet alternative standards in accordance with their individualized education programs (IEP) (Sorrentino & Zirkel, 2004). Therefore, the overwhelming majority of students in special education must take and pass the test associated with their grade level, which is not necessarily their instructional level. Thus, a student may be making gains toward the goals and objectives included on the IEP yet still fall short of meeting state standards associated with his or her grade level.

NCLB requires states to address adequate yearly progress (AYP) by establishing a minimum level of improvement based on student performance. All schools must establish a plan that ensures all students meet required levels of academic performance by the 2013–14 school year. Districts are allowed to establish a starting point based on the performance of either their lowest-achieving demographic group or their lowest-achieving school (whichever is higher). This starting point can be well below 100% but must increase every year. Each state then identifies a level of student achievement that must be demonstrated every two years until all students in the state are demonstrating proficiency. To demonstrate AYP, schools will have to examine their curriculum and place greater emphasis on testing (Sorrentino & Zirkel, 2004). Schools that fail to show AYP for two consecutive school years are designated as needing improvement. It should be noted that a school can fail to show AYP in any one of the subgroups, provided the number of students included in a subgroup is large enough to produce statistically valid and reliable data (Wiener & Hall, 2004). District officials must develop a plan for increasing student performance. In the meantime, students have the option of transferring to another school in the district. After a third year of no adequate progress, a school must offer supplemental service such as tutoring or remedial classes. After the fourth year of failure to demonstrate adequate yearly progress, a school is designated as needing corrective action, which can include replacing some staff and implementing a new curriculum. Parents can choose to have their child enrolled in supplemental services or transferred to another school. After five years of failing to make adequate yearly progress, a school must be restructured. Most or all of the staff can be replaced, or the school can be turned over to a state or private company with a record of effectiveness (Questions on NCLB, 2004).

Another purpose of NCLB is to enhance the qualifications of teachers and paraprofessionals. NCLB defines a highly qualified teacher as an individual with full certification, a bachelor's degree, and demonstrated competence in core subject knowledge and teaching (Smith, Desimone, & Ueno, 2005). Competence in an academic subject can be demonstrated by passing a rigorous subject matter test or completing an academic major or a graduate degree. Core subjects include English, reading, mathematics, science, foreign language, civics and government, economics, arts, and history and geography. All states were directed to develop plans that will ensure all teachers are highly qualified by the end of the 2005–06 school year. Highly qualified paraprofessionals have either an associates degree or two years of college, or they must pass a state or local assessment (Teacher Quality, 2004).

Emphasis on Empirically Based Strategies   NCLB emphasizes the implementation of teaching practices that are supported by rigorous scientific research.

More Options for Parents   NCLB requires each state to provide parents with information regarding their child's progress in math and reading in grades 3 through 8 and at least once during high school. Science will be added during the 2007–08 school year. In addition to individual reports regarding their child's progress, NCLB requires each state and school district to provide parents with easy-to-read, detailed report cards on schools' and district performance. Report cards can be disseminated via local newspapers and the Internet so that parents will know which schools are succeeding and which are in need of improvement, corrective action, or restructuring, and why. These report cards must include information about student achievement that is sorted according to race, ethnicity, gender, English proficiency, disability, income status, and migrant status. Report cards characterize student performance at three levels: basic, proficient, and advanced. Data are also provided regarding graduation rates and the percentage of students not tested.

Report cards also provide parents with information regarding teacher qualifications. Data are available to describe the percentage of (a) teachers in the state who possess emergency or provisional certification and (b) classes in the state not taught by teachers who are highly qualified. Parents can make comparisons between the qualifications of teachers at high- and low-income schools. In addition, the report card includes information about teachers' baccalaureate degrees and any other graduate degree major or certification.

Options are available to parents whose children are not meeting the standards and/or who are in schools not meeting annual yearly progress. For example, parents can request supplemental educational services such as tutoring, after-school programs, or remedial classes. Parents also have the option of requesting that their child be transferred to a school in the district where adequate yearly progress is being achieved.

Expanded Local Control and Flexibility   NCLB gives states and local agencies more flexibility in how they elect to use federal education funding. For example, local school district officials can choose to allocate resources to fund innovations they believe will enhance student progress. As a result, people in a locality have greater opportunity to affect decisions about educational programs and note the outcomes of these decisions.

Special Education

During the 1970s and 1980s, numerous landmark court decisions were witnessed that affected the education of learners with disabilities. These cases are listed in Table 1.1. The spirit of these court decisions was reflected in Public Law 94-142, the Education for All Handicapped Children Act of 1975 (and its amendments), the most comprehensive law ever enacted on behalf of children and youth with disabilities. PL 94-142 ordered states to provide a free and appropriate public education to all children and youth between 5 and 21 years of age. States could, at their own discretion, provide services for children as young as 3 years of age.

Public Law 94-142 contains five broad measures. The first stipulates that an individualized education program (IEP) is to be developed under the guidance of a team of parents and professionals. The IEP is expected to cover seven major topics: current levels of performance; annual goals; short-term objectives; objective criteria, evaluation procedures, and schedules for annual assessment; degree of participation in general education; special education and related services; and dates for initiating services and their expected duration.

TABLE 1.1   *Special Education Litigation Influencing Secondary Students*

Litigation	Provisions
PARC, Bowman et al. v. Commonwealth of PA (1971)	Guaranteed to students with mental retardation: 1. Free and appropriate public education 2. Least restrictive environment 3. Periodic review 4. Procedural due process
Mills v. Board of Education of the District of Columbia (1972)	Provisions of PARC extend to all students with disabilities.
Diana v. State Board of Education (1970)	Assessment must be in the student's native language.
Wyatt v. Aderholt (1971); *Halderman v. Pennhurst* (1977)	Right to adequate treatment.
Armstrong v. Kline (1980); *Battle v. Commonwealth* (1980)	Extended school year.
Larry P. v. Riles (1981)	IQ tests cannot be used as sole basis for placement into special education.
Smith v. Robinson (1984)	Payment for residential placement. Reimbursement of parents' attorney fees.
Honig v. Doe (1988)	Students with disabilities cannot be excluded for disability-related behaviors from school.
Timothy W. v. Rochester School District (1989)	FAPE must be provided to *all* children with disabilities.

The second measure requires that services be provided in the least restrictive environment (LRE). Service providers are obligated to make available a variety of educational alternatives to students with disabilities. Deno (1970) developed a "cascade of services," ranging from placement in the general classroom to special schools and homebound instruction. This model is presented in Figure 1.1. In addition, Deno suggested that the needs of most learners with disabilities can best be met in less restrictive settings—that is, in settings at the top of the cascade. One ultimate goal of special education is to help the learner move toward the next less restrictive environment; however, educators are advised to monitor a student's performance closely and to promote such movement as needs dictate.

The third measure calls for nondiscriminatory testing and mandates that all contact with the learner, including evaluation, be conducted in that learner's native language. In addition, educators must use the communication mode normally used by students who have sensory impairments or who are unable to read and write.

The fourth measure provides for confidentiality. PL 94-142 guarantees students with disabilities and their parents the right to confidentiality of information and record keeping. Parents must be informed of their rights to (1) review their child's educational records, (2) amend content that is inaccurate or misleading or that violates their right to privacy, and (3) request a hearing to challenge the accuracy of information in the file.

FIGURE 1.1   *Cascade of Services*

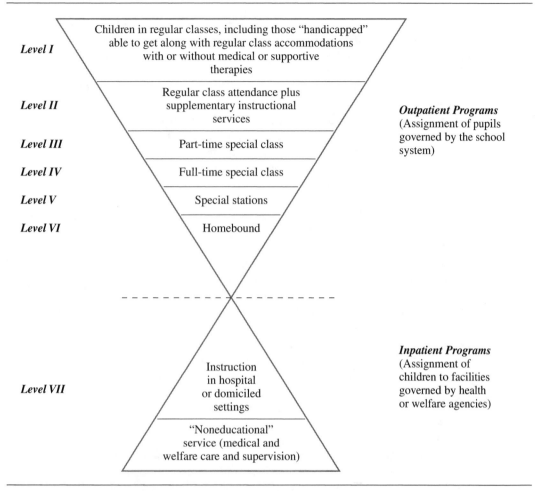

Source: From "Special Education as Developmental Capital" by E. Deno, *Exceptional Children, 37,* 1970, 229–237. Copyright 1970 by The Council for Exceptional Children. Reprinted with permission.

The fifth measure pertains to due process. It guarantees that a learner will not be evaluated or the educational program altered until parent permission has been granted. Parents are entitled to a hearing if they and the educational agency disagree on the need for an evaluation or a change in the child's program.

In 1983 the Education of the Handicapped Amendments (PL 98-199) were enacted by Congress to address major education and employment transition difficulties experienced by youth with disabilities (Rusch & Phelps, 1987). Section 626 of this act, Secondary Education and Transition Services for Handicapped Youth, provides for funds for the development of training programs and related services. Section 626 has two main objectives: (1) to improve and develop secondary special education programs and (2) to facilitate the transition to postsecondary experiences through the careful coordination of education, training, and related services.

In 1986, PL 94-142 was amended by PL 99-457 to extend the rights enjoyed by students between the ages of 5 and 21 years to children between the ages of 3 and 5 years. PL 99-457 also contained provisions formulated specifically for secondary students with disabilities. Congress authorized the allocation of federal funds to activities that would (1) strengthen special education and related services that promote transition of secondary learners to postsecondary environments, (2) improve and develop secondary special education programs, and (3) enhance the vocational and life skills of students with disabilities.

In 1990, PL 101-476 mandated transition services for students with disabilities. It stated that services were to be tailored to a student's individual needs and interests. Such services included career planning, employment options, postsecondary training, financial assistance, community participation, advocacy/legal supports, leisure, transportation, self-advocacy, personal management, living arrangements, medical support, and insurance. The mandate required that transition goals and objectives be developed no later than age 16, and earlier if appropriate. The school, therefore, became a key element in ensuring that adult agencies were aware of particular students with disabilities.

In 1997 the Individuals with Disabilities Act Amendments (PL 105-17) strengthened the transition language throughout the law. The definition of *transition services* remained the same, with the exception of including related services as part of the coordinated set of activities. Transition planning must now begin at age 14 and be updated annually. When a student reaches age 16, a statement of interagency responsibilities is to be included in his or her IEP. Transferring rights at the age of majority must be addressed by those states with this provision. Beginning at least one year prior to the age of majority in a student's state, the student must be informed of his or her rights (IDEA, 1997). Significant changes regarding evaluations, IEPs, and educational placements are also noted.

In 2004 the Individuals with Disabilities Education Improvement Act was signed into law. Changes and improvements addressed five themes. First is greater protection of students' civil rights by granting federal and state agencies the right to impose sanctions if schools do not meet standards; requiring states to develop and implement plans to address free appropriate public education (FAPE), transition services, and the disproportionate number of minority students in special education; making agreements in dispute resolutions binding; and developing standards for training hearing officers. The second theme addresses making IDEA work better for students, parents, teachers, and administrators. Measures include increasing parental involvement by teleconferencing and videoconferencing, and requiring that initial evaluations be conducted within 60 days. Third, this act enhances the quality of services available to students across the age range. In particular for secondary students, it simplifies the rules for transition services and strengthens involvement with vocational rehabilitation while students are still in high school. Fourth, it improves school discipline and promotes safety. Specifically, it requires determining whether a discipline problem is the result of a student's disability or poor IEP implementation and conducting a functional behavioral assessment to prevent future problems. Fifth, IDEA is now integrated with NCLB. It calls for a study of the validity and reliability of alternative assessments and their alignment with state content standards, and clarifies the role of the IEP team in determining whether a student will participate in assessment with accommodations or take alternate assessments. IDEA described highly qualified special education teachers. These qualifications include state certification as a special educator and completion of a bachelor's degree. Teachers working with students meeting alternate achievement standards must meet the standards that apply to elementary teachers or, if working above the elementary level, demonstrate subject matter knowledge as determined by the state. Special education teachers who teach multiple subject matter must demonstrate the same level of competence as that required from an elementary, middle, or high school teacher.

These legislative acts provide ample evidence of federal interest in the educational opportunities available to students with disabilities. Local education agencies are legally obligated to provide a free and appropriate education to all students regardless of the nature or severity of their disability. Timely implementation of appropriate educational programs during the elementary grades may reduce the number of students requiring special education and related services at the secondary level. On the other hand, elementary programs may not last long enough to bring about the desired changes in student performance. Therefore, federal laws have mandated that special education and related services be provided at the secondary level for students who would benefit from them. Additional support for secondary special education programs is found in legislation addressing vocational education.

Vocational Education

Vocational education has been identified as the most realistic means of helping individuals make the transition between education and the world of work (Sarkees-Wircenski & Scott, 1995). Legislation in this area of education reiterates the themes contained in legislation designed to promote special education for individuals with disabilities. These also emphasize free and appropriate educational programming, placement in the least restrictive environment, and cooperative planning by the various parties interested in the student's development (Gartland, 1988).

Sections 503 and 504 of the Rehabilitation Act of 1973 (PL 93-112) mandate that persons with disabilities be given equal access to training and employment opportunities. Section 503 requires employers receiving federal assistance of $2,500 or more to develop an affirmative action plan to recruit, hire, and train individuals with disabilities. This section also requires employers to provide reasonable accommodations for persons with disabilities, such as ramps, curb cuts, and other modifications that make the work environment accessible.

Section 504 is a civil statute (deBettencourt, 2002; Yell & Katsiyannis, 2001). It guarantees that all individuals with disabilities will have equal access to programs, jobs, and housing. Although Section 504 does not include additional funds to serve those individuals to whom it applies, agencies risk losing any federal funds they do receive if they fail to provide individuals with disabilities with services, benefits, and opportunities that are comparable to those afforded to individuals who do not have disabilities. Section 504 can apply to students who are not served under IDEA because their disability falls into something other than one of the 13 categories. These disabilities can include attention deficit disorder, AIDS, and epilepsy (Yell & Katsiyannis, 2001). A student is eligible for services under Section 504 if a major life activity is substantially limited by a physical or mental disability (deBettencourt, 2002). For students in secondary programs, it guarantees access to vocational instruction, counseling, prevocational services, and work-study and job placement programs. They should also be placed in general education programs to the maximum extent possible.

The Americans with Disabilities Act (ADA) of 1990 (PL 101-336) expanded the definitions and intent of the Vocational Rehabilitation Act of 1973 to include all public and private employers, services, and facilities. It prohibited private employers, state and local governments, employment agencies, and labor unions from discriminating against qualified individuals with disabilities in job application procedures; hiring and firing; advancement; compensation; job training; and other terms, conditions, and privileges of employment. A qualified employee or applicant with a disability was defined as any individual who, with or without reasonable accommodation, could perform the essential functions of the job in question. Reasonable accommodation included (1) making existing facilities used by employees readily accessible to and usable by persons with disabilities; (2) restructuring jobs, modifying work schedules, and reassigning to a vacant position; and (3) acquiring or modifying equipment or devices; adjusting or modifying examinations, training materials, or policies; and providing qualified readers or interpreters.

The law required employers to make an accommodation to the known disability of a qualified applicant or employee if it would not impose an "undue hardship" on the operation of the employer's business. *Undue hardship* was defined as an action requiring significant difficulty or expense when considered in light of factors such as an employer's size, financial resources, and the nature and structure of its operation. An employer was not required to lower the quality or production standards to make an accommodation, nor was an employer obligated to provide personal-use items such as glasses or hearing aids.

Public Law 93-380, the Education Amendments of 1974, had implications for individuals with disabilities. Specifically, the act stated that students should be adequately prepared to undertake employment and participate in society according to their abilities. In addition, state and local education agencies were authorized to provide secondary students with a career education program that maximized employment and participation opportunities. Career education should obviously begin early in all academic programs, but its importance for learners with disabilities cannot be overstated. Students with special needs should be exposed to all the opportunities available in employment and community settings from an early age. The secondary school is an ideal place to expand on the foundations laid earlier and to prepare students with disabilities for the challenges that await them on the job and in the community.

Career education received further attention in PL 95-207, the Career Education Incentive Act of 1977. The purpose of this act was to increase career awareness and exploration and to improve career education planning and decision making. Many agencies, including school districts, were allocated funds to develop and implement career exploration and work experience programs, workshops for education personnel, and seminars for community leaders.

The Comprehensive Employment and Training Act of 1978 (CETA) enhanced the employability of youth who were disadvantaged or had disabilities. The act allocated funds to local communities and school districts to disseminate occupational information, develop exploration activities, and provide summer and part-time work experiences. The Job Training Partnership Act (JTPA), known as PL 97-300, replaced CETA in 1982. The purpose of JTPA was to (1) establish programs that prepared youth and unskilled adults for entry into the job market and (2) provide training for individuals facing serious barriers to employment. Private industry councils (PICs) were established and charged with identifying the services to be made available in the service delivery area (SDA). The PIC includes representatives from local businesses, organized labor, rehabilitation, economic development agencies, and education. Individuals eligible for JTPA funds include those who have a mental or physical disability that presents a substantial barrier to employment. A number of services were available to individuals whose eligibility has been established, including job-search assistance, counseling, remedial education, and basic-skills training (Sarkees-Wircenski & Scott, 1995).

The Carl D. Perkins Vocational and Applied Technology Education Act of 1990 provided supplementary services that are essential for members of special populations to participate in vocational programs successfully. Special populations include (1) individuals with disabilities, (2) educationally and economically disadvantaged individuals, (3) individuals of limited English proficiency, (4) individuals who participate in programs designed to eliminate sex bias, and (5) individuals in correctional institutions.

Federal funds were allocated to states to provide information about vocational education, as well as provide support personnel to programs. Funds were also provided for instructional aides and devices, including interpreters for the deaf, bilingual interpreters and tutors, readers and notetakers, materials and supplies, equipment, and other services necessary for success.

Sections of the Perkins Act require that students enrolled in vocational education (1) be assessed to identify their interests, abilities, and special needs; (2) receive special services such as curricular adaptations, instruction, equipment, and facilities; (3) participate in counseling and career guidance activities; and (4) receive counseling to facilitate transition from school to postsecondary opportunities (Sarkees-Wircenski & Scott, 1995).

In 1998 the Carl D. Perkins Vocational and Applied Technology Act Amendments were signed into law. The purpose of this act was to develop the academic, vocational, and technical skills of students enrolled in vocational technical education programs. *Special populations* continues to be a term in the law, which includes students with disabilities.

The School-to-Work Opportunities Act was signed into law in 1994, establishing an educational reform across the country. This reform promotes the practices of school-based learning, work-based learning, and connecting activities (Rusch & Chadsey, 1998) in promoting the transition from school to work. Although this act is often connected to vocational education, its audience is *all* students, grades K–18. This includes students who are in college-bound tracks and those who are not, including students who are at risk or disabled.

The Workplace Investment Act (WIA) was signed into law in 1998, making dramatic changes in the way employment and training services are delivered. One-stop systems are now being developed, streamlining the services being provided by governmental agencies. WIA requires 19 partners in the one-stop system, which includes youth activities, vocational rehabilitation, employment services, and welfare-to-work agencies. Although partners are separately authorized and funded, they appear in WIA rather than as stand-alone legislation. Separate funding streams are provided for target populations, replacing the provisions of JTPA.

Implications of NCLB, and Special and Vocational Education Legislation

The preceding paragraphs have outlined the legislation designed to support secondary education for students with disabilities. As suggested earlier, acts addressing both special and vocational education have many goals in common. Ideally, secondary students with special needs should receive a free and appropriate public education in the least restrictive environment. They should have access to the general education curriculum that is taught by qualified teachers using appropriate supports and accommodations. Students should participate in state- and districtwide assessment that allows documentation of progress toward the achievement of standards. Assessment to determine eligibility for special education should be conducted in each student's native language and should take into account all aspects of the disability. Special education and related services should be tailored to each student's particular needs and should be included in an individualized education program. The IEP should include long-term goals and short-term objectives, which, when mastered, will prepare students to meet the challenges of those environments in which they are currently functioning, as well as those they expect to enter in the near future.

A Transition Perspective

Curricular Goals and Objectives

Bigge (1988) and Bouck (2004) identified six curricular approaches for secondary students with special needs. As will be discussed in Chapter 4, the general education curriculum is appropriate for the majority of students with disabilities. Substantial changes have been made to the general education curriculum to ensure that it reflects learning standards established by state education departments. Adherence to this curriculum ensures that all learners in general will acquire a logical sequence of knowledge, skills, and understandings that will enable them to meet state standards. A second option is a parallel curriculum that reduces the complexity of the general education curriculum. Third is a curriculum that reflects a lower grade. Fourth is a practical curriculum, which makes substitutions in skills to enable students to progress through the general education curriculum. Fifth is a functional curriculum that emphasizes life skills. Finally, there are other curricula that meet the unique needs of students, such as a learning-strategies curriculum or a social skills curriculum. Sabornie and DeBettencourt (1997) outlined six models, some of which overlap those previously listed. Their list includes a basic-skills model, a tutorial model, a compensatory model, a vocational model, a functional skills model, and a learning-strategies model.

Many of these curricular options recognize that children and youth with disabilities have specific learning and behavioral characteristics that can undermine progress through the general education curriculum. Among these are slower rates of acquiring information and skills, deficits in the ability to generalize learned skills to other settings or conditions, and a lack of ability to retain learned material (Schloss & Sedlak, 1986). Therefore, an adolescent with disabilities is likely to master far fewer skills and concepts by the end of formal schooling. The youth may have progressed only to the fourth- to seventh-grade level in basic academic skills.

Transfer of Training

Adolescents with disabilities do not maintain and generalize skills to the same extent as nondisabled learners. Further, youth with disabilities are more likely to have a variety of unsuccessful employment experiences before obtaining a relatively permanent position (Cantrell & Cantrell, 1995). Therefore, a primary goal of educational strategies should be to generalize skills from formal educational settings to community environments. A number of instructional procedures have been devised to promote this transfer (Schloss & Smith, 1998a). The transition orientation would apply these procedures in secondary special education programs.

Altering instructional conditions ensures that the student will do more than just acquire a restricted set of rote skills that cannot be applied beyond the instructional setting. In addition, artificial incentives should be replaced by naturally occurring reinforcers. Reinforcement procedures should be as unobtrusive as possible and yet be sufficiently strong to motivate performance. Finally, self-control skill development can be used to enhance generalization of skills from the classroom to community settings. Self-control is the ability to recognize and manage events that influence one's own behavior (Zarkowska & Clements, 1988).

Articulation of Services

Despite the care and attention that educators may pay to the technology required to promote the transfer of skills, it is unreasonable to expect all students to graduate from high school and enter productive careers. Longitudinal and comprehensive service delivery systems are the most effective means of ensuring that the youth will have skills and abilities needed to adjust to changing community demands (Wehman, 2003).

One individual must be responsible for coordinating services. During the school years, the special educator usually acts as the case manager. After the student reaches the age of 18 or 21, a vocational rehabilitation counselor, a mental health or mental retardation specialist, or the individual's parents may become the case manager.

The Goals of Secondary Special Education

In 1964, Rollins and Unruh reported that the five goals of secondary schools in the United States were to give students an opportunity to do the following:

1. Receive a twelfth-grade education
2. Develop independent critical thinking skills
3. Learn the traditions, ideas, and processes of U.S. democracy
4. Develop an understanding and appreciation of the art, literature, history, science, customs, and people of the United States and other nations
5. Prepare for the roles they will assume after graduation

Experts have also identified goals for students enrolled in secondary special education (Deshler, Schumaker, & Lenz, 1984):

1. To be placed in the least restrictive environment
2. To earn a high school diploma, for which they may have to pass minimum competency exams

3. To develop independent learning skills that will enable them to acquire information in new environments
4. To demonstrate social competence so that they will be able to function in employment and other community settings
5. To prepare for a career

Woodward and Peters (1985) limited their list to the following three goals:

1. Full-time education with nondisabled peers
2. The opportunity to earn the credits required for a high school diploma
3. Vocational training, functional skill development, and job placement for students with a poor prognosis for academic success

In 1994, Goals 2000: Educate America Act (PL 103-227) was enacted to set eight national goals to improve schools:

1. School readiness
2. School completion
3. Student achievement and citizenship
4. Teacher education and professional development
5. Mathematics and science
6. Adult literacy and lifelong learning
7. Safe, disciplined, alcohol- and drug-free schools
8. Parental participation

Although these lists address separate populations, they have some points in common. First, students should be provided with opportunities to maximize their potential. For the majority of special needs students, these opportunities mean satisfactory completion of high school requirements and successful transition to postsecondary settings at school, in the community, or on the job. For others, they will mean participating in an educational program that emphasizes the mastery of functional and vocational skills. Second, to the greatest extent possible, students should receive their education in close approximation to their peers. Third, students should become independent thinkers who are capable of acquiring information outside the school setting. Fourth, students should possess the skills necessary to locate and maintain suitable employment and to meet the challenges of community living. Unfortunately for learners with disabilities, the outcomes of secondary education programs may not match their goals (Deshler et al., 1984).

Services at the secondary level have been expanded as a result of the increased emphasis on transition and the need to preserve gains derived from previous education programs. Despite hopeful signs, an alarming number of secondary students with disabilities do not yet enjoy the benefits extended by special and vocational education legislation. In 1998 the U.S. Department of Education reported that 29% of all students with disabilities, ages 17 to 21, graduate with a diploma or certificate of completion. Of those students, 33% have learning disabilities, 23% mental retardation, and 24% emotional disturbance. Circumstances under which secondary students with special needs leave school appear to have little effect on how they adjust to community settings. Wehman (2003) reported that neither graduates nor dropouts find adequate employment opportunities. Despite federal mandates, secondary students with disabilities appear to be without appropriate programming (Sitlington & Clark, 2006).

Factors Influencing the Development of Secondary Special Education Programs

The statistics cited by the U.S. Department of Education (1998) and Edgar (1987) suggest that many secondary students with disabilities do not take advantage of their rights to an educational program under current legislation. Data may indicate that these students are actually receiving either poor services or no services at all. The professional literature identifies six problems in secondary programming. They are presented in Action Plan 1.1.

Attitude toward Secondary Special Education

Several authors have noted that perhaps the biggest problem limiting the development of appropriate secondary programs is that many professionals do not think students with disabilities require much attention at the secondary level (Lange & Ysseldyke, 1998; Schumaker et al., 2002; Wells, Schmid, Algozzine, & Maher, 1983). This attitude may reflect the amount of professional attention directed toward students receiving special education and related services at the preschool and elementary levels. The importance of providing appropriate services during the elementary years cannot be overstated, as their effectiveness is maximized through early, consistent implementation (Polloway & Patton, 2004; Smith, Polloway, Patton, & Dowdy, 2004). The assumption could be that as a result of early intervention, services at the secondary level are no longer necessary (Schumaker et al., 2002). It is true that many students who complete an elementary special education program may return to general education classes, where they may function appropriately without additional services. The evidence documenting poor outcomes for secondary students, however, suggests that some will continue to require special education and related services for all or part of their high school careers.

Action Plan 1.1 Factors Undermining the Success of Secondary Special Education

Special educators should be aware of six factors that undermine the effectiveness of special education for secondary students:

1. Limited recognition of the need for services at this level
2. The inflexible structure of regular secondary education
3. Curricular emphasis of regular secondary education
4. Inadequate teacher preparation
5. Lack of theoretical and empirical support
6. Lack of appropriate materials

Structure of Regular Secondary Education

Schumaker and colleagues (2002) reported that teachers and principals responding to their survey indicated that in their schools, there were separate general and special education budgets, staff development activities, planning times, roles, and responsibilities. In addition, secondary schools are still organized along traditional lines based on departmental interests and subject matter (Sitlington & Clark, 2006). Obviously, this model limits the use of self-contained classes, a popular service delivery format for special education. Because it is difficult to accommodate self-contained classrooms in secondary schools, students with special needs may have to adapt to a preexisting format that does not fit their needs. The idea of keeping students in the regular class as much as possible is appealing and certainly within the spirit of IDEA; however, true benefits cannot be enjoyed in this setting unless general education teachers are prepared to meet the individualized needs of the students with disabilities who are placed in their care (Stodden, Galloway, & Stodden, 2003). The responsibilities assumed by general education teachers in today's secondary programs are overwhelming, leaving them with little time and perhaps little inclination to deal with the educational demands of special needs students (Kokoszka & Drye, 1981; Smith, Polloway, Patton, & Dowdy, 2004).

Curricular Emphasis

The movement promoting excellence in education has encouraged the public to put more emphasis on academic achievement and to make competency tests a graduation requirement (Thurlow, Ysseldyke, & Anderson, 1995). Many students with special needs enter high school with deficits in background information, vocabulary, reading ability, and social skills (Clark, Field, Patton, Brolin, & Sitlington, 1994). Without the prerequisite skills, they are not likely to master a rigorous high school curriculum. Therefore, students may either be given credit for completing a watered-down version of the general curriculum or be placed in a vocationally oriented curriculum. These scenarios are inappropriate for at least three reasons. First, a watered-down curriculum may render students unable to pass any competency examinations required for graduation. Many students with disabilities fail to meet minimum competency standards even when tests are modified for them (Shriner, Ysseldyke, & Thurlow, 1994). Second, placement in a watered-down curriculum or in a vocational program should not constitute the entire range of programming alternatives available to secondary students with disabilities (Heller, 1981). Third, watered-down curriculums are not in keeping with the intent of FAPE as stated in PL 94-142.

Alternatives or additions to traditional secondary curricula have been proposed in the professional literature. The learning-strategies curriculum, in particular, is exerting a strong influence in education programs for secondary students with special needs (Deshler, Ellis, & Lenz, 1996; Hallahan & Kauffman, 2000; Hoover & Patton, 1995). Also, social skills curricula are being developed that will enable secondary students to enhance their functioning in educational and vocational settings. Learning strategies and social skills are discussed in detail in subsequent chapters.

Teacher Preparation Programs

Another factor limiting the effectiveness of existing programs is the nature of the professional preparation program typically completed by secondary special education teachers

(Bouck, 2004; Langone, Langone, & McLaughlin, 1991; Meyen et al., 1998). Many practitioners are certified to teach kindergarten through twelfth-grade special education classes, regardless of the emphasis of their training program (Meyen et al., 1998). However, there is a big difference between being certified and being qualified to teach at the secondary level. Many secondary special education teachers currently do not have the background or training in various content areas necessary to adequately present subject matter to students with disabilities (King-Sears, 2001; Warner, Cheney, & Pienkowski, 1996). Their college programs may have included a very limited practicum involving secondary students with special needs (Bouck, 2004). Although the interest and dedication of many secondary special education teachers are above reproach, whatever success their students experience may well be the result of the teaching skills acquired through trial and error rather than through the successful completion of preparation programs featuring appropriate course sequences and practicum experiences.

NCLB contains provisions to address this issue; specifically, teachers must now show that they are highly qualified. Certification is changing in some states. For example, in New York a college student who is interested in secondary special education must now complete a comprehensive sequence of study in special education and the equivalent of an undergraduate major (30 credits or 10 classes) in a content area such as history and social studies, mathematics, or English. Although these requirements will certainly increase the qualifications of secondary special educators, it should be noted that more time and tuition will be required to complete degree requirements.

Insufficient Database

The ineffectiveness of existing programs can also be traced to a weak database. The existing secondary special education programs lack strong theoretical and empirical foundations (Fuchs & Fuchs, 1994; McLeskey & Waldron, 1995; Zigmond et al., 1995), a major concern given the strong emphasis on inclusion and the need for greater accountability (Bouck, 2004). Secondary-level teachers who graduated from preparation programs with an elementary emphasis may know little about the needs of secondary students who have disabilities or about the most successful methods for dealing with them. Teachers may also be implementing instructional procedures because they are familiar with them, rather than because they are linked to student progress. Furthermore, they may not be documenting the impact of their programs on the performance of secondary students. Conderman and Katsiyannis (2002) encouraged secondary special educators to consider their classrooms as "a fertile ground for action research" (p. 175) and to contribute systematically to a sound base of knowledge by documenting their own decision-making processes, student progress, and use of instructional practices.

Lack of Appropriate Materials

Secondary special education programs are also plagued by a serious shortage of appropriate materials (Meyen et al., 1998). Two types of problems arise with the materials generally available to secondary teachers and students. First, the instructional materials may have been intended for elementary students with special needs. Whether such materials are appropriate for older students is highly questionable. In any case, secondary learners will already have been exposed to these materials. Second, some material may have been originally designed for regular secondary education students. Therefore, it may not address relevant concepts, be written at an appropriate reading level, or provide the amount of practice required by secondary students with special needs.

Summary

The goals of secondary special education are to provide services that will enable students to acquire the skills they need to function successfully in employment and community settings. Numerous pieces of legislation address special and vocational education and provide ample support for the services needed by secondary students with disabilities. Unfortunately, there are not enough data to document the effectiveness of current endeavors. A number of significant problems appear to hamper the development and delivery of appropriate educational services to secondary students with special needs. Not all professionals recognize the need for special programming at this level. The structure and curricular emphasis of regular secondary education cannot easily be adapted for use with learners with special needs. Teachers whose skills are being developed and refined while on the job are working in programs with limited empirical support using materials not specifically designed and validated for secondary students with disabilities.

Some experts may consider problems of this magnitude to be insurmountable; however, there can be no debate over whether secondary special education services will be provided. Legal mandates and professional ethics will not allow professionals to abandon the cause. The question is, "How can we best deliver such services?" (Wimmer, 1981, p. 610).

The transition perspective underlies the orientation to secondary special education advocated in this volume. If secondary special educators are to achieve lasting performance gains with their students, they must abandon the teaching of isolated skills that have little bearing on future adjustment. Instead, they should focus on educational activities that promote adaptation to future independent residential, work, and leisure settings. Educational objectives based on the developmental expectations of nondisabled youth must be evaluated against the criteria of the individual's potential for future adaptation. These criteria pertain to objectives that are most likely to be practiced and reinforced in home and work environments. Those that are least essential should be eliminated.

2 | *Postsecondary Service Options*

Did you know that . . .

- When compared to typical adults, adults with disabilities are more than twice as likely to live below the poverty line?

- Adults with disabilities who have completed a postsecondary experience are more likely to be employed and require less support?

- PL 94-142 and PL 101-476, known as the Individuals with Disabilities Education Act (IDEA), mandate appropriate educational services and transition planning for individuals up to the age of 21?

- No single federal or state law articulates mandated services to adults with disabilities beyond the age of 21?

- Aside from parents, educators are the primary source of assistance for individuals making the transition to postsecondary settings?

- Programs and services that meet the special needs of young adults with disabilities have proliferated in recent years?

- Rehabilitation programs place over 20,000 individuals with developmental disabilities in competitive employment each year?

- Virtually all colleges and universities provide academic support services for students with disabilities?

- The number of individuals with disabilities entering college has tripled in the last 20 years?

- Students with more significant disabilities are now attending two- and four-year colleges?

- It may be difficult for a student with a disability to obtain a financial aid package to attend college?

- The Rehabilitation Act of 1973 and its 1978 amendments state that no qualified individual with disabilities shall be denied benefits of or be subjected to discrimination under any program or services receiving federal financial assistance?

- The Americans with Disabilities Act (ADA) supports the mandates of the Rehabilitation Act and extends its scope to programs and services not receiving federal support?

- Unlike IDEA, ADA shifts the responsibility for making decisions, disclosing disability status, and requesting accommodations to the student with disabilities?

- The Workforce Investment Act of 1998 authorizes support for educational services provided by technical schools, community colleges, and, to a lesser extent, four-year institutions?

- Vocational rehabilitation services are authorized to assist individuals with disabilities in obtaining or sustaining gainful employment?

Can you . . .

- List the mandates of PL 94-142 and PL 101-476 regarding services to individuals with disabilities?

- Describe common postsecondary obstacles that young adults with disabilities face during the transition to successful employment?

- Identify measures the secondary teacher can take to enhance a student's success in a two- or four-year college?

- List considerations for selecting a two- or four-year college?

- Describe major provisions of the Workforce Investment Act of 1998?

- List the basic elements of the Individualized Written Rehabilitation Program?

- Describe how a sheltered rehabilitation center functions to provide specialized training and work experience in a supportive environment?

- Describe the advantages of programming at enclaves in industry?

- Describe the advantages of programming at sheltered rehabilitation centers?

- Describe the elements of supported employment?

- Identify academic support services available at most colleges and universities?

Educational services available before the age of 21 are mandated by state and federal legislation. Consequently, there is great uniformity in available services regardless of the school district or state that serves the individual. Specifically, before the age of 21, all learners with disabilities are assured of the following:

- A free public education that is appropriate to the learning and behavioral characteristics of the student
- Screening, in an effort to identify those individuals who will benefit from special education services
- Educational services in the least restrictive environment
- Free provision of related services (e.g., counseling, transportation, physical and occupational therapy, etc.) that will enhance the learner's ability to benefit from educational services
- Nondiscriminatory testing conducted in the dominant language of the learner
- Freedom of information for the learner and his or her parents or guardians
- Confidentiality of records
- Annual development and evaluation of an education plan designed to meet the individual needs of the learner
- Due process when disagreements arise regarding the nature of the educational program (Turnbull, Turnbull, Erwin, & Soodak, 2005)
- A clearly articulated transition plan developed before the youth's sixteenth birthday, including postsecondary services that may be needed, service providers, and supports to effect a smooth adjustment into adult life

These mandates indicate what services are available to school-aged individuals with disabilities. During the time that youth with disabilities are in the educational system, they, their parents, and teachers have a clear understanding of the services to be provided in the immediate future. When disputes arise, specific protective safeguards exist to ensure that the best interests of the learner are served. These provisions allow educators to design current services in a way that will promote the learner's transition into future educational programs.

Unfortunately, the picture becomes clouded when the learner leaves the public school system. Outside elementary and secondary educational services, no single federal or state law spells out all the mandated services available to adults with disabilities (Bursuch, Rose, Cowen, & Yahaya, 1989; Dukes & Shaw, 1998; Hill, Seyfarth, Banks, Wehman, & Orelove, 1987). This situation has given rise to a number of problems:

- Other than making reasonable accommodations in admissions, there is no mandate for enrolling young adults with disabilities into educational, residential, or rehabilitation programs (Blanck & Braddock, 1998; Brinckerhoff, 1996; McDonnell, Wilcox, & Boles, 1986).
- Many programs that do exist do little to prepare the individual for community work and living (Bellamy, Rhodes, Bourdeau, & Mank, 1986; Blackorby & Wagner, 1996; Lakin & Bruininks, 1985; Patton, Polloway, Smith, Edgar, Clark, & Lee, 1996; Sample, 1998).
- Agencies may deny services to young adults because of the severity of the individual's condition, the lack of resources, or the great demand for limited services, among other factors (McDonnell & Wilcox, 1983; Turnbull et al., 2005).
- Young adults with disabilities and their parents or guardians are required to identify appropriate services and pursue the proper course to enrollment (Brinckerhoff, 1996; Gajar, Goodman, & McAfee, 1993; Hill et al., 1987).
- Young adults with disabilities may avoid postsecondary services that would support vocational and community adjustment (Malmgren et al., 1998).
- No individual or agency is required to speak on behalf of the young adult with disabilities and the question of process is seldom raised among adult service providers (Alper, Schloss, & Schloss, 1994).
- Owing to confidentiality requirements, efforts of discrete agencies (e.g., Office of Vocational Rehabilitation or Private Industry Council) are seldom coordinated, with the result that some services overlap and others are not provided (McGaughey, Kiernan, McNally, Gilmore, & Keith, 1995; Schalock, 1985).
- Eligibility requirements and performance standards for adult service providers are seldom coordinated and often conflicting (Schalock, 1985).
- There is no systematic provision for reenrolling young adults with disabilities into supportive programs when attempts at independent living or work fail (Patton et al., 1996).

Despite these concerns, there has been an increase in the number of students with disabilities who take advantage of postsecondary educational opportunities. In their review of the literature, Mull and Sitlington (2003) reported that in 1986, 29% of persons who were 16 years of age or older and had a disability were enrolled in postsecondary education. Within eight years, this number had increased to 45%, with a learning disability being the disability reported most frequently. Skinner and Lindstrom (2003) attributed this rise to several factors, including the recognition that a disability continues throughout the life span, formalized transition plans, access to assistive technology, and legislation such as the Vocational Rehabilitation Act of 1973 and the Americans with Disabilities Act.

Teachers, parents, guidance counselors, and school administrators will need to work together to identify and address the problems that students will experience by enrolling in postsecondary education. According to Skinner and Lindstrom (2003), these problems include student deficits in study and organizational skills, limited social skills, academic deficits (particularly in reading and writing), low self-esteem, and a higher dropout rate. Not surprisingly, educators are the primary source of assistance for individuals making the transition to postsecondary settings (Alper et al., 1994; Gartin, Rumrill, & Serebreni, 1996; Hill et al., 1987; Test, Keul, & Grossi, 1988). This role may consist of two related functions. First, the teacher may provide direct educational experiences that prepare the learner for success in specific postsecondary settings. Second, the teacher may facilitate the young adult's transition to these settings. To perform in these roles, the educator must be familiar with postsecondary resources leading to independent life (Edgar, Horton, & Maddox, 1984). Therefore, the purpose of this chapter is to identify postsecondary services available to young adults with disabilities. The main topics covered are postsecondary educational programs, postsecondary technical programs, business and industry, vocational rehabilitation, and supported and independent living.

Postsecondary Educational Programs

According to Stodden and Whelley (2004), when compared with nondisabled adults, adults with disabilities are twice as likely to live below the poverty line. In addition, they are more likely to depend on their families or government programs for financial support. One strategy for changing these outcomes is for people with disabilities to complete some type of postsecondary education. Numerous authors have described the benefits of such program completion, including increasing the likelihood of finding gainful and meaningful employment (Hart, Mele-McCarthy, Pasternack, Zimbrich, & Parker, 2004; Zafft, Hart, & Zimbrich, 2004), an increased sense of personal well-being, and greater financial independence (Stodden & Whelley, 2004). More individuals with disabilities are pursuing higher education (Harris & Robertson, 2001; Janiga & Costenbader, 2002), with numbers tripling in the last 20 years (HEATH Resource Center, cited in Stodden & Whelley, 2004). Legislative mandates support options such as enrolling in two- or four-year colleges. For example, IDEA mandates that transition to postsecondary school and employment be addressed while students are still enrolled in secondary programs. The Americans with Disabilities Act (ADA) mandates that people with disabilities be provided reasonable accommodations to ensure equal access in educational and employment settings. Financial support for training that leads to employment is addressed in the Vocational Rehabilitation Act of 1973. Since 2000 a variety of enrollment options have been created to provide better access for students with disabilities to two- and four-year colleges. As will be seen, these options vary along several dimensions.

Two-Year Colleges

The mission of two-year or community college programs has changed a great deal over the past decades. Initially, community colleges served as transfer programs. Students enrolled in these programs to meet the basic educational and liberal arts requirements for baccalaureate degree programs at other institutions. Some state systems of higher education, for example, restrict university enrollment to upper-division undergraduate students and graduate students. Entering first-year students and sophomores enroll in community colleges where credits will automatically transfer to state universities.

Similarly, states have traditionally used two-year community colleges as a proving ground for young adults seeking admission to an upper-division college or university. A number of states allow for open or unrestricted admission for all students with a high school diploma. Students maintaining adequate progress are assured admission into a state college or university, with all credits transferring into the baccalaureate degree program.

Community colleges offer students from diverse backgrounds the opportunity to begin a career in a chosen field. These institutions have developed a wide range of vocational and technical programs. Students completing these programs may be awarded special certificates or associate degrees.

The structure of many certificate and associate degree programs is shaped by the employment opportunities in the geographic area surrounding the college. For example, community colleges in resort areas typically emphasize travel and hospitality programs. Those in mining regions include mineral engineering or mineral processing programs. Those in rural areas feature agricultural and wildlife management programs.

Two-year and community college programs usually receive considerable support from local, state, and federal taxes. Consequently, the cost of these programs to students is very low in comparison with the cost of four-year degree programs. At the national level, for example, the reauthorization of the Vocational Education Bill, HR 4164, allocates a portion of the basic state grants for postsecondary programs (most often community colleges) for youth who are economically disadvantaged or have disabilities.

Aside from basic academic and technical courses, virtually all two-year and community colleges offer substantial academic support. Other features of two-year colleges match the needs and learning characteristics of students with disabilities. Typically, there are more two-year colleges than four-year colleges. They are usually located in urban areas and accessed by the public transportation system available to students with disabilities. Tuition is generally lower for a two-year college; Grigal, Neubert, and Moon (2002) noted that community colleges may even waive tuition for individuals receiving supplemental security income (SSI).

Two-year colleges offer a unique advantage to students with more significant disabilities. Although there has been an increase in the last 20 years in the enrollment of students with disabilities in colleges and universities, Neubert, Moon, and Grigal (2004) noted that the majority of these students had learning disabilities, sensory impairments, or orthopedic impairments. Traditionally, students with more significant disabilities either met graduation requirements as specified on their IEPs and completed school around their eighteenth birthday, or took advantage of their right to a public school education until they were 21 years old. It is not uncommon, then, for these students to be in close proximity to high school students who may no longer be their peers. This has changed within the last five years, as students with more significant disabilities are participating in postsecondary opportunities such as those available at two-year colleges. This development is in response to parental and student desire to attend classes in settings that are more age appropriate. Actually, some authors have recommended consideration of dual enrollment in high school and a two-year college (Hart et al., 2004), that is, students participating in postsecondary experiences while still in secondary schools. Thus, students use college credits to complete a high school diploma, using IDEA funds. Dual enrollment offers the advantage of allowing students to complete high school requirements by taking classes related to academic or vocational goals in an inclusive setting with same-aged peers.

Grigal, Nuebert, and Moon (2002) identified several goals for providing services for students with significant disabilities at community colleges. They include improved employment opportunities; inclusion in college classrooms; increased community mobility; access to adult service agencies; improved social, communication, and self-determination skills; friendship opportunities; and enhanced recreational opportunities. Different models of service and support have evolved to enable students with significant disabilities to participate in and benefit from enrollment at two-year colleges. Hart and colleagues (2004) and Stodden and Whelley (2004) described three such models. The first model is a substantially separate model in which the curriculum is separate from that provided to other students attending the college; thus, interactions with typical college students are absent or limited. Students with disabilities follow different schedules, focus on instruction that addresses life skills, participate in community-based instruction, rotate through a limited number of job slots, and take courses that do not lead to completion of a certificate or a degree. This program is staffed by special educators or adult disability service providers. Funding is from a local education agency or through a family or corporate trust.

The second model is a mixed program model. Some features of the separate model may be present, such as an emphasis on life skills, but students may also have opportunities to obtain information and skills in integrated college courses in which typical college students are enrolled. Students can also gain work experience by rotating through a variety of employment slots. These programs are staffed by special education personnel working with members of the community college staff. Funding can be from the local education agency and postsecondary program.

The third model is the individualized support model. Students participate in a range of college courses, certificate programs, internships, and degree programs that will result in employment or enhanced career opportunities. This approach is student centered and reflects student choice. They receive individualized services, accommodations, and supports. For example, educational coaches may be available to attend class with the student, take notes, tutor, and assist the student in accessing the full range of campus resources. Note that an educational coach may be considered a personal service, not an accommodation routinely provided by colleges and universities (Zafft et al., 2004). Typically, this model is funded by the local education agency and local businesses. Exemplifying this approach is the College Career Connection described by Zafft and colleagues, a program designed to help students with significant disabilities gain admission to and complete an educational experience at their local community college. Central to accomplishing this goal are (1) using a student-centered framework that identifies strengths and preferences and (2) establishing a student support team to develop services and supports for individual students. Five principles are followed: (1) program direction and decisions reflect the characteristics and needs of individual students, (2) all options are inclusive in that there is a natural proportion of students with and without disabilities in courses, (3) there are no segregated classes, (4) supports match individual student needs, and (5) there is intersystem collaboration. Readers are referred to Zafft and colleagues (2004) for a complete description of the College Career Connection.

Four-Year Colleges and Universities

Colleges and universities offer a wide range of degrees and certificates. Successful matriculation may yield a bachelor of arts or bachelor of science degree. Typical degree programs require two years of full-time equivalent study in the liberal arts (e.g., social sciences, mathematics, physical sciences, humanities, and the arts). The remaining two years are devoted to specific programs of study such as consumer studies, criminal justice, information systems, food science, journalism, broadcasting and speech, math, geosciences, psychology, and so on.

Programs and services that meet the special needs of young adults with disabilities have proliferated in recent years (see deBettencourt, Bonaro, & Sabornie, 1995; Gajar et al., 1993; Grigal et al., 2002; Taymans, West, Sullivan, & Scheiber, 2000). The number of buildings accessible to individuals with physical disabilities has also increased (Burbach & Babbitt, 1988). Despite some evidence that college students with disabilities are unlikely to seek assistance (Cowen, 1988), a growing number of academic support services are now available.

Gartin, Rumrill, and Serebreni (1996) have conceptualized these supports as falling under three major headings. First, *psychosocial adjustment* includes development of self-advocacy skills, frustration tolerances, problem solving, social skills, and mentor relations. Second, *academic development* includes entrance and course-related exam preparation, learning strategies, and transition and college services. Third, *college/community orientation* includes college linkages, buddy systems, college choices, college resources/activities, college orientation, campus support groups, and community services.

The Association on Higher Education and Disability (AHEAD) represents postsecondary personnel who are responsible for ensuring equal access to higher education for persons with disabilities. The organization was chartered in 1978 with 32 members and has grown to include personnel from over 2,000 colleges and universities. AHEAD professional standards provide insights into necessary and available services for college students with disabilities, such as the following:

- Program administration, including clearly articulated policies and procedures, services, knowledge of emerging issues, program goals, program/staff evaluation and resource management, communication, staff development, and legal affairs
- Direct service on behalf of students with disabilities, including notification of available programs and services, records management and confidentiality, advocacy, eligibility determination, faculty support, aides and accommodations, counseling, due process and grievance adjudication, academic scheduling, and program monitoring
- Consultation with campus and community personnel, including rehabilitation agency personnel, physical plant employees, high school students and professionals, and media
- Training and technical support for members of the campus community, including staff, faculty, and administrators (this role may include review of campus policy and procedures)
- Maintaining current professional knowledge and skill through attending conferences and workshops, reading professional literature, and holding membership in professional organizations (Shaw, 1997)

The Rehabilitation Act of 1973 (U.S. Public Law 93-112, 1973) and its 1978 amendments have provided the impetus for a majority of these programs. Under the act, "No otherwise qualified handicapped individual in the United States shall, solely by reason of his handicap, be excluded in participation, be denied benefits of, or be subjected to discrimination under any program or activity receiving Federal financial assistance" (p. 39).

Of course, much of the support received by public institutions of higher education comes from the federal government. Consequently, the Rehabilitation Act requires these institutions to provide equal opportunity to youth with disabilities. Action Plan 2.1 identifies standards that publicly supported colleges must meet in order to comply with the Rehabilitation Act.

Passage of the Americans with Disabilities Act (ADA) in 1990 extended the Rehabilitation Act to private colleges and universities. Subsequent legal challenges have affirmed that all institutions of higher education must accommodate otherwise qualified students with disabilities (Dukes & Shaw, 1998).

The cost of a four-year college education is likely to be substantially more than the cost of other postsecondary programs. Unfortunately, federal vocational education legislation excludes programs that award baccalaureate degrees from reimbursement for occupational and technical training. Consequently, community colleges and technical schools that are eligible for federal support may provide better value.

Despite their cost, four-year colleges and universities offer several advantages to students with disabilities. They provide a variety of courses from which to choose that students may not have had access to in high school. Similarly, extracurricular activities are more extensive, increasing the likelihood of interactions with typical students. Most four-year colleges and universities are residential, so students with disabilities may be able to take advantage of an independent living experience at a dormitory. These colleges and universities generally have professional schools or departments of social science or education. College students enrolled in majors such as education, special education, vocational rehabilitation, social work, speech-language pathology, occupational therapy, and physical

---

Action Plan 2.1   Standards for College and University Compliance with the Rehabilitation Act and the Americans with Disabilities Act

The Rehabilitation Act and the Americans with Disabilities Act require colleges and universities to comply with the following standards:

1. Admissions tests cannot discriminate against qualified individuals who have disabilities.
2. Auxiliary aids must be provided when impaired sensory, manual, motor, or speaking skills limit an individual's ability to adapt to collegiate programs.
3. Academic requirements must often be modified (e.g., deadlines extended, course formats adapted, alternative competency measures provided) to help individuals with disabilities succeed.
4. Alternative, but not necessarily segregated, physical education programs must be provided to meet the needs of individuals with physical or sensory limitations.
5. Infirmary services must be provided that are comparable to those used by nondisabled young adults.

therapy need practicum experiences to meet course requirements or may want to volunteer their time to work with students with disabilities. There are additional disadvantages, however. Four-year institutions may be located in areas not as easily accessed by public transportation. They may have more stringent admission requirements. Finally, college faculty may have a limited understanding of disabilities and may question why a person with a disability is attending.

There are special considerations, regardless of whether a student with disabilities is considering a two- or a four-year college. While students with disabilities are in public schools, IDEA holds school districts responsible for identifying students with disabilities, establishing a multidisciplinary team, and developing an appropriate educational program that includes supports and accommodations. IDEA defines *reasonable accommodations* more clearly than ADA does (Janiga & Costenbader, 2002). However, after students complete public school requirements, IDEA no longer applies. ADA shifts the responsibilities of identification and developing accommodations to students; thus, students are now expected to advocate for themselves. Another consideration identified by Stodden and Whelley (2004) is tuition costs. All college students or their families are responsible for paying tuition, but this responsibility may be more challenging for students with disabilities and their families. Students who are dually enrolled have not yet earned a high school diploma, making them ineligible for financial aid packages. Even with high school diplomas, students may choose to limit the number of college credits they take to increase their chance of success; however, their schedules may not meet the minimum credit number required for financial aid. Because they take fewer credits each semester, they take more semesters to complete certificate or degree programs, thereby increasing costs (Hart et al. 2004). Also, as noted by Stodden and Whelley, students with more severe disabilities may require services not typically available in college settings, such as occupational or physical therapy. Finally, Janiga and Costenbader (2002) noted that students with disabilities encounter difficulty staying in and completing postsecondary education programs. Factors contributing to noncompletion include larger class sizes with less contact with the instructor, college courses that include long-term projects and fewer opportunities for evaluation and feedback, more unstructured time, and reduced contact with a support network of family and friends.

Despite these issues, the advantages of two- and four-year programs warrant their consideration by students with disabilities. Educators can take specific measures to assist students in making the transition to two- or four-year colleges, beginning with the individualized education program (IEP). Legislation mandates that IEP teams begin to address postsecondary goals and outcomes for students when they turn 14 years of age (Janiga & Costenbader, 2002). Several authors have identified goals and programming that should be developed as a result of the IEP process (Babbitt & White, 2002; Lehmann, Davies, & Laurin, 2000; Lock & Layton, 2001; Lodge Rogers & Rogers, 2001; Skinner & Lindstrom, 2003; Stodden & Whelley, 2004), including the following:

1. Students must know and understand what their disability is. They should be able to describe their strengths and weakness and what accommodations and modifications will assist them.
2. To the maximum extent possible, students must know about IDEA, ADA, and the Vocational Rehabilitation Act. They must understand that their status changes once

they complete high school, and they must be prepared with the knowledge required to self-advocate.

3. Students must know their responsibilities. Once in a postsecondary setting, it is their choice to self-identify, but they must provide documentation of their disability and identify accommodations needed.

4. Students must develop the social skills necessary to communicate their needs, express their rights, and negotiate accommodations.

5. Students should be taught learning strategies, mnemonics, notetaking skills, money skills, and organizational skills.

Skinner and Lindstrom (2003), Harris and Robertson (2001), Janiga and Costenbader (2002), and Weir (2004) recommended several ideas to students, their families, and teachers as students consider which two- or four-year college to attend.

1. There should be a meeting to identify the student's academic and career goals.

2. The academic programs offered at available two- and four-year colleges should be reviewed to identify those that match the student's academic and career goals.

3. Carefully consider admission requirements. Some schools are very selective and all students must meet the same eligibility requirements; other schools may have a separate process for admitting students with disabilities. Still other schools have an open admissions policy that requires only a high school diploma. Dual enrollment may be problematic for students' admission to some programs that require a high school diploma.

4. Examine courses the student may be interested in taking. Courses could be taken through a specific department but could also be taken through a continuing education program. This latter option allows students to be nonmatriculated, facilitating dual enrollment.

5. Examine the cost. A variety of issues related to tuition have already been described. These concerns must be balanced against the realization that students who participate in postsecondary experiences are less likely to need continuing support as employees (Zafft et al., 2004).

6. Consider the size of the university. Smaller colleges may be easier to navigate and able to provide more individualized assistance. A larger campus may offer a greater variety of courses and extracurricular activities. Larger colleges may have programs in which majors would be interested in assisting students with disabilities, but the larger classes typically encountered early in a course of study may provide less teacher–student contact.

7. Contact the director of the Office for Students with Disabilities to discuss services the student anticipates needing, and the policies and procedures for documenting the disability and requesting/receiving accommodations.

8. Arrange for the student to shadow other students who are currently enrolled.

Weir (2004) identified strategies for increasing the success experienced by students with disabilities once they are enrolled in courses at a two- or four-year program. They include the following:

1. The student should meet with his or her advisor on a regular basis and carefully consider course options.
2. Once enrolled in the course, students should become thoroughly acquainted with course requirements. They may need to meet individually with the instructor to review the syllabus.
3. Students should be encouraged to self-identify as a person with a disability and seek assistance as soon as possible or they set the stage for failure. Janiga and Costenbader (2002) noted that students with learning disabilities (LD) have a hidden disability. Their needs may not be as apparent, understood, and accepted as those of students whose disabilities are more obvious, such as those students with a vision or hearing loss.
4. Use services available through a learning assistance center such as readers, notetakers, academic support, tutoring, and workshops to improve study skills, social skills, and organization skills. Students are advised to consider taking advantage of assistive technology to compensate for areas of difficulty. Mull and Sitlington (2003) listed the areas in which students with disabilities most frequently encountered difficulty, including written language, reading, spelling, and organization. Action Plan 2.2 lists some of the recommendations offered by Mull and Sitlington. Some assistive technology can be expensive, a concern for college officials. Recommendations must be based on a careful assessment of students and their needs. Action Plan 2.3 lists questions to be considered before investing in assistive technology.

Action Plan 2.2   Recommendations for Assistive Technology

Mull and Sitlington (2003) identified areas of difficulty encountered by students with disabilities and recommended assistive technology that may be helpful.

Spelling

Spell check programs and software
Word prediction software
Online dictionary and thesauruses

Written Language

Voice recognition systems
Word prediction programs
Speech synthesis
Proofreading programs
Scanners

Reading

Large-screen monitors
Voice recognition
Scanner
Talking dictionaries

Organization/Memory

Electronic outlining
Concept mapping
Word processor with word expansion

Time Management

Online calendars and planners

Math

Talking calculators

Action Plan 2.3   Recommendations for Assistive Technology

Before investing resources in assistive technology, consider the following questions:

1. Will students and possibly their instructors need training in the proper use of the device?
2. Will the device increase the student's independence?
3. Is it easy to use?
4. Is it inexpensive to repair?
5. Can it be used without the assistance of another person?
6. Does it require a long or complicated series of demands?
7. Is is reliable?

Postsecondary Technical Programs

Technical schools are similar to community colleges in a number of ways. Both institutions are located in the community in which a majority of applicants reside. Also, both community colleges and technical schools are closer in size to area high schools than to comprehensive universities. Both types of institutions offer a wide range of specialized training programs and certificates. In addition, technical school programs, like the programs in community colleges, are by and large supported by federal, state, and local taxes. As a result, tuition and fee schedules are generally modest.

The main difference between technical schools and community colleges is the breadth of their program offerings. As already mentioned, community colleges offer a variety of academic, preprofessional, and technical programs. Students frequently use these programs to enter advanced training at other institutions.

For the past two decades, support for the educational services of technical schools, community colleges, and, to a lesser extent, four-year colleges has been provided through the Job Training Partnership Act (JTPA) and its predecessor, the Comprehensive Job Training Partnership Act (CETA). The JTPA expired at the end of 1999 and was replaced by the Workforce Investment Act of 1998 (Public Law 105-202). The JTPA required that 70% of available funds must be targeted for preservice and in-service training support. The remaining 30% was dedicated to support for program administration. Though the precise level of training support available through the Workforce Investment Act is unclear, there is little doubt that career and vocational education will be minimally supported. Regardless, the act will provide substantial resources for individuals making the transition from school to work.

The Workforce Investment Act is intended to provide for national workforce preparation and employment systems. The legislation includes the following major provisions:

- Education and employment programs must be developed and operated in local communities and be responsive to area clientele and businesses.
- Area businesses are expected to provide information and play a leadership role in ensuring that programs prepare recipients for employment.
- All services must be provided through a single location in the community. This location must provide preliminary vocational assessment, comprehensive information

regarding available services, support in filing claims for unemployment insurance, job search and placement assistance, and counseling pertaining to labor market trends and essential skills.

- Program recipients should be provided choices through a variety of organizations and operations identified at the community center. Recipients should be able to develop and control their own career development plans. Personal decision making is enhanced through the use of "individual training accounts" that allow recipients to select and pay for the most effective services.
- Program recipients must be provided information about the success of training providers in securing employment for clients.

The Workforce Investment Act authorizes core services that are available to all citizens regardless of eligibility. Core services include employment search and placement assistance, labor market appraisal, worker assessment, and follow-up services that support job retention. Intensive services are provided for recipients who are not able to maintain employment through core services.

A major provision of the legislation is special support to low-income youth between the ages of 14 and 21. To be eligible, youth must face the following challenges to employment: absence of a diploma, limited literacy skills, homelessness, pregnancy, status as an adjudicated offender, or previous difficulty in completing educational programs or securing/maintaining employment (over 30% of funds must be directed to youth not in school).

Youth programs must be directed toward opportunities for employment and link academic and vocational training. Organizations providing services must have strong ties to local employers. Programs are likely to include:

- Tutorial support
- Study skill development related to dropout prevention
- Alternative school services, including summer employment opportunities
- Adult mentoring
- Work experience, including internships and job shadowing
- Occupational training and leadership development
- Necessary supportive services

Business and Industry

More and more private companies are initiating their own intensive and specialized training programs. The large fast-food companies, for example, provide advanced corporate

---

Case for Action 2.1

In your role as guidance counselor for secondary students who have learning disabilities, you have been asked to prepare a brochure describing postsecondary educational opportunities. Provide the essential content. Include a description of possible educational programs, funding sources, special accommodations, and possible employment outcomes.

training. The largest program of this type is McDonald's Restaurant Corporation's extensive training system, which leads to graduate degrees in hamburgerology at Hamburger University. Of course, this is not an actual academic degree—or university. However, many colleges and universities will apply a limited number of credits from McDonald's program to associate or baccalaureate degree requirements.

Despite the effect of the Americans with Disabilities Act in enhancing access to the workplace, the strongest predictor of the extent to which opportunities are made available to individuals with disabilities may be the employer's attitude. For this reason, education and rehabilitation agency personnel have launched vigorous campaigns to encourage business and industry to employ adults with disabilities.

Vocational Rehabilitation

Vocational rehabilitation services are authorized by the Rehabilitation Service Administration of the U.S. Department of Education. Services are administered out of the Office of Special Education and Rehabilitative Services through the Rehabilitative Services Administration (RSA). In turn, the RSA funds state vocational rehabilitation agencies, with each state having several local offices (Neubert & Moon, 2000). Vocational rehabilitation services are intended to help individuals with disabilities obtain or sustain gainful employment so that they can become economically self-sufficient, independent, and integrated into their communities (Mellard & Lancaster, 2003). Eligible individuals include persons with mental, physical, or learning problems that constitute a substantial obstacle to employment. An additional eligibility criterion is that the individual must demonstrate the potential to benefit from rehabilitation services to the extent that he or she can be gainfully employed in business or industry.

Specific rehabilitation services include career information and exploration, vocational evaluation and occupational training, referral, guidance and counseling, mentoring, on-the-job evaluation and training, transportation and commuting expenses, job placement, restoration services (such as surgery), and assistive devices and services (Mellard & Lancaster, 2003). Rehabilitation services may also include psychological counseling; medical evaluation and treatment; support in independent living; licensing fees; and special therapeutic, prosthetic, or occupational equipment.

Federal law requires each state to identify one or more agencies to provide vocational rehabilitation programs for individuals with disabilities. Two typical designations for these agencies are *Office of Vocational Rehabilitation* and *Bureau of Vocational Rehabilitation.* The state agencies, in turn, establish regional offices that serve clients within the immediate area.

Regional offices are staffed by vocational rehabilitation counselors. These professionals are assigned to individual clients. Their basic responsibility is to develop and supervise an individualized written rehabilitation program (IWRP). The IWRP parallels the individualized education program mandated by PL 94-142. It forms a written contract between the rehabilitation agency and the client. The basic elements of an IWRP are presented in Action Plan 2.4.

Any number of services may be made available to a young adult through the state vocational rehabilitation agency. In most cases, the actual services will not be provided by the rehabilitation counselor. The counselor is primarily a broker of services. For example, rather than actually providing on-the-job evaluation and training, the counselor may obtain

Action Plan 2.4   Elements of the Individualized Written Rehabilitation Program (IWRP)

The following are the basic elements of the IWRP:

1. A statement of the eligibility for either direct service or extended evaluation
2. The individual's rights and responsibilities under the rehabilitation program (these include the right to confidentiality, periodic evaluations of progress toward program goals, and annual reviews of the program)
3. Long-range goals and a justification for goal selection
4. Intermediate objectives, direct services to be provided, time limits, and a justification for how these procedures will resolve the vocational disability
5. The extent of participation and benefits
6. Responsibilities of the client in meeting his or her own rehabilitation goals

the services through a contract with a private nonprofit agency, such as a chapter of the Association for Retarded Citizens or the United Cerebral Palsy Association. Occupational education services may be provided through contracts with a technical school or community college. Psychological and medical services may be provided through contracts with local clinics and hospitals. Two of the services most frequently contracted for are placement and training in sheltered rehabilitation centers and supported employment.

Sheltered Rehabilitation Centers

Rehabilitation facilities are staffed by individuals who offer specialized training and work experience in a supportive environment outside of the private workforce. Sheltered rehabilitation centers are best suited for individuals who are not able to succeed in competitive employment. However, many such centers are beginning to provide specialized training (e.g., simulations and on-the-job training) that will lead to competitive employment. Therefore, client goals may range from long-term adjustment as an employee of the center to short-term preparation for placement in a private business or industry.

Most of the work in sheltered rehabilitation centers is provided through subcontracts from business and industry. These contracts usually call for the assembly of small parts, repair, labeling, or packaging of units. Sheltered rehabilitation centers obtain contracts through a competitive bidding process. The centers may also enter into independent manufacture, service, or sales operations. For example, some centers employ clients to construct shipping pallets, picnic tables, storage sheds, or other products. Centers may also employ clients to clean and service automobiles, clean homes and businesses, launder linens and clothing, provide lawn and garden maintenance, and so on.

A more recent development is the provision of *enclaves in industry,* which serve sheltered rehabilitation clients within the facilities of private businesses or industries. The individual with disabilities is placed in an occupational setting with nondisabled competitively employed individuals. In most situations, the client remains under the general supervision of rehabilitation center personnel and is paid on the basis of the ratio of his or her productivity to that of an individual who does not have disabilities. Primary advantages of

Action Plan 2.5   Advantages of Enclaves in Industry

For the following reasons, we recommend the enclaves-in-industry approach for many young adults who have disabilities. In contrast to services provided within a sheltered workshop, it offers several advantages, such as:

1. The young adult is able to interact with nondisabled individuals within a fairly typical work environment. This opportunity may enable the individual to model appropriate work behaviors demonstrated by the competitive workers.
2. The individual who has disabilities may acquire the exact skills necessary for success in the competitive placement. He or she has the benefit of the same tools, work space, materials, and social expectations as nondisabled workers in the setting.
3. Once specific performance criteria are achieved, the young adult is more likely to be accepted as an employee of the specific business or a related business.
4. Young adults employed by a business or industry in which they worked in an enclave are less likely to have difficulty generalizing skills.
5. Salary and benefits to an enclave worker are more likely to be on par with those of nondisabled coworkers.

this approach include the prospect of making higher wages, increased social contact, and broader career choices (McGaughey et al., 1995). Additional advantages of this approach are identified in Action Plan 2.5.

Most individuals with mild and moderate disabilities would find long-term placement in a sheltered work setting excessively restrictive. Consequently, most transition specialists agree that sheltered rehabilitation centers should act mainly as ancillary services and should provide general and special training programs. Ancillary services are generally designed to correct cognitive, social, or motor problems that interfere with work adjustment. They may consist of vocational and personal adjustment counseling, social services, occupational and physical therapy, mobility training, and speech and language training.

General training programs may prepare the participants to obtain and sustain employment. These training programs may include experiences that lead to career exploration and awareness, self-appraisal, employment application skills, interviewing skills, vocational-related social skills, community mobility skills, and the like.

Special training programs may be similar to occupational training programs offered by community colleges or postsecondary technical schools. The main difference is that technical training provided by sheltered rehabilitation centers is conducted by rehabilitation and special education personnel. These professionals are skilled in adapting instruction to the needs of individuals with exceptional characteristics. Conversely, community college and technical school personnel are generally well qualified in a particular trade but may not be as skilled in the methodology of teaching young adults who have special needs.

Supported Employment Services

Advocacy groups, educational units, state developmental disabilities services, and sheltered rehabilitation programs are becoming increasingly interested in providing supported employment services. *Supported employment* is defined as employment within a business or industry that is under the direct supervision of the business's management staff and that receives normal compensation and benefits. Another characteristic of supported employment is that extraordinary guidance or assistance is offered to help individuals succeed in given positions. This may include the use of prosthetic devices, specialized training, or extra supervision.

Postsecondary Service Selection

The preceding sections describe a range of postsecondary services that may be appropriate for learners who have disabilities. Actual services provided must match the needs and interests of the learner. Students with more severe disabilities are likely to require more restrictive services, such as placement in sheltered rehabilitation centers. More capable learners may be served in less restrictive settings, such as community colleges and technical schools.

To some extent, postsecondary services parallel educational services provided in grade schools and secondary schools. Similar to the Cascade of Services Model proposed by Deno (1970), these opportunities fall on a continuum based on restrictiveness. Figure 2.1 contains the Keystone of Postsecondary Placements Model adapted from Schloss (1985).

FIGURE 2.1 *Keystone of Postsecondary Placements Model*

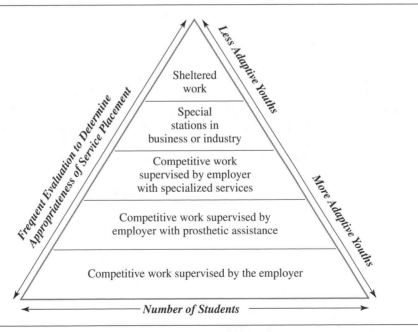

Source: From "Postsecondary Opportunities: The Role of Secondary Educators in Advocating for Handicapped Young Adults," by Patrick J. Schloss, 1985, *The Journal of Vocational Special Needs Education, 7*(2), 18. Copyright 1985 by the National Association of Vocational Education Special Needs Personnel affiliated with the American Vocational Association.

Case for Action 2.2

You have been asked to prepare a policy statement indicating appropriate vocational options for students with varying disability levels. Use the Keystone of Postsecondary Placements Model to formulate your policy.

The keystone model demonstrates the relationship between these postsecondary offerings. Services identified in the keystone range from the most to least restrictive: sheltered work, enclaves in industry, competitive work supervised by the employer with specialized services (e.g., job coach), competitive work supervised by the employer with prosthetic assistance (e.g., calculator, color-coded operations, etc.), and competitive work supervised by the employer. It is likely that postsecondary educational services in the form of technical school, community college, and four-year college educational programs would be preparatory for placements at a higher level on the keystone.

The proportion of graduates with disabilities expected to be placed at any given position in the keystone is represented by the area within the cell. The largest percentage of young adults with disabilities is expected to enter competitive work supervised by the employer. The smallest percentage with disabilities is expected to be served in sheltered rehabilitation settings.

Education and training opportunities that occur after young adults complete high school are likely to lead to a more restrictive placement and eventually to a less restrictive setting. This pattern is depicted by arrows on the side of the keystone in Figure 2.1.

Summary

The Keystone of Postsecondary Placements Model suggests a general orientation to the articulation of services for students graduating from secondary programs. Postsecondary services are not uniformly provided from one region of the country to another. Federal law does not provide for a comprehensive and logical array of resources for young adults who have disabilities. Consequently, new educational services must be identified within the context of the resources available in local communities.

3 *Challenges of Adolescence*

ANJALI MISRA
SUSAN MARY PAIGE

Did you know that . . .

- The number of formally processed delinquency cases increased 62% between 1989 and 1998?

- Individuals with disabilities are disproportionately overrepresented among the juvenile population?

- Very few juvenile offenders who have disabilities receive a legally mandated, appropriate special education program?

- Offenders who have mental retardation are likely to be incarcerated at an earlier age and for a longer period of time than youth without retardation?

- Economically disadvantaged adolescents are more likely than middle-class adolescents to be officially reported for delinquent acts?

- The age at which delinquents commit their first unsocial act is related to future criminal activities?

- School failure and dropout contribute to delinquency?

- A high proportion of delinquents come from nonintact and abusive families?

- The juvenile justice system was established in 1899?

- About 4.3 million, or 13%, of 16- to 24-year-old students drop out of school?

- The dropout rate among students who are seriously emotionally disturbed is approximately 50%?

- School failure is the most common reason for leaving school?

- Only 51% of those who drop out of school are employed?

- Half (51%) of high school seniors use illicit drugs?

- The United States has the highest rate of substance abuse?

- The most commonly used drugs are marijuana and alcohol?

- Approximately 2,000 15- to 19-year-olds commit suicide every year?

- Suicide is the third most common reason for death among adolescents?

- Females attempt suicide more often than males, but fewer females are successful?

Anjali Misra is professor in the Department of Teacher Education, State University of New York at Potsdam, New York. Susan Mary Paige is Lecturer in the Exceptional Education Department, Buffalo State College, New York.

- School failure is related to suicide attempts?
- Youth are experiencing sexual intercourse at an increasingly younger age?
- The United States has the highest rate of sexually transmitted diseases in the world?
- Most students with disabilities are grossly uninformed or misinformed about sex?
- One in every nine women becomes pregnant premaritally?

- HIV/AIDS is the sixth leading cause of death among 15- to 24-year-olds?
- Many teachers have little or no training in developing or implementing a sex education curriculum?
- Estimates of depression are higher for students with learning and/or behavioral problems than for nondisabled youth?
- Depression can become life-threatening?

Can you . . .

- List problems in program implementation for adolescents with disabilities in correctional facilities?
- Identify acts that signify delinquent behaviors to isolate high-risk students?
- Develop a curriculum for use with delinquents?
- Highlight ways of obtaining parental involvement for rehabilitation of delinquent adolescents?
- Describe characteristics of students who are likely to drop out of school?
- Plan school-based experiences to reduce dropout rates?
- Enlist parent support to increase school attendance?
- State different drug categories and their impact on behavior?
- Recognize signs of drug abuse among adolescents?

- Incorporate methods in your curriculum to reduce or prevent drug use?
- Spot distress signals indicative of depression and suicidal thoughts?
- Create an environment that increases communication and prevents suicide?
- Provide sex education to adolescents with disabilities?
- Identify ways in which sex education may be provided through schools?
- Identify and correct myths associated with HIV/AIDS?
- Develop strategies to collaborate with relevant community personnel and agencies?
- Enlist parental support in dealing with the challenges of adolescents?

Adolescence is often portrayed as the most turbulent period of human development. The physical and social changes that occur during this time place challenging demands on the adolescent. Adolescents must face these challenges to make rational decisions regarding their career prospects and life goals. However, a number of formidable obstacles threaten their ability to make appropriate decisions. These obstacles include delinquency, school dropout, substance abuse, depression, suicide, sexually transmitted diseases, and teenage pregnancy. Adolescents with disabilities face similar obstacles; however, their ability to overcome difficulties may be hampered by their disabilities. Young individuals with disabilities require special assistance and education to enable them to select the most constructive course of action. This chapter describes some of the challenges adolescents face and steps they can take to deal effectively with these challenges.

Juvenile Delinquency

The legal definition of a *juvenile delinquent* is "a person under a specific age who violates any state or local law, or commits any act that would be considered a crime if committed by an adult" (Kvaraceus, 1971, pp. 7–8). Delinquent acts include crimes against a person, crimes against property, crimes against society, and status offenses.

Incidence

The number of formally processed delinquency cases increased 62% between 1989 and 1998. In the same period, the number of adjudicated delinquency cases resulting in (a) residential placement increased 37%, (b) formal probation increased 73%, and (c) court-ordered sanctions increased 85% (Cohen & Gies, 2002). In addition, 300,000 juveniles are in adult facilities, and 84,000 juveniles spend time in pretrial detention centers and jails. Although juveniles constitute 20% of the total population, they commit over 40% of all violent crimes and nearly 50% of all property offenses (Snarr & Wolford, 1995).

A disproportionate number of these youth (30 to 60%), when compared to the prevalence of students with disabilities in public schools (6.5 to 13.7%), require special education services (Rutherford, Nelson, & Wolford, 1985). Researchers who have studied the prevalence of specific disabilities among the delinquent population have found variable results. This variability can be attributed in part to inconsistencies in definitions of disabilities and also to discrepant criteria employed by states to classify individuals as "juvenile." Pervasive emotional or behavioral problems have been associated with most delinquent youth (Eisenmann, 1991), especially attention deficits with hyperactivity disorders (Kauffman, 2001). Estimates by administrators from 13 states regarding the prevalence of mental retardation among delinquents have ranged from 0 to 26% (Nelson & Rutherford, 1989). Estimates of prevalence of learning disabilities among juvenile offenders have ranged from 9 to 76% (Nelson & Rutherford, 1989).

Causes

Several factors are associated with delinquency among adolescents. A disproportionate number of delinquent youth are African American or Hispanic and come from economically disadvantaged backgrounds (Farrington, 1980). One reason may be that economically disadvantaged adolescents are more likely to be officially reported and recorded, whereas middle-class youth are more likely to be bailed out by parents and not included in police records. Inadequate family and peer relationships also contribute to delinquency. Juvenile delinquents are more likely to come from backgrounds that include nonintact families, poverty, low educational level, incarceration of a parent, drug use or peddling (Zabel & Nigro, 1999), early sexual activity, and weapon ownership (Daley & Onwuegbuzie, 1995).

Adolescent males outnumber females in the rate of delinquent crimes committed (Cairns & Cairns, 1983). The peak ages for offenders are 15 to 17 years in both sexes. The offenses for which males and females are arrested vary. Females are more likely to be apprehended for running away from home, sexual behavior, or drug abuse, whereas males are arrested for crimes against property, theft, and vandalism.

Repeated school failure may motivate delinquent activities. Delinquents reportedly function two to four years behind grade level (Hill, Parker, Corbett, & Miano, 1980), experience repeated academic failure (Maguin & Loeber, 1996), and have high rates of suspension and expulsion (Daley & Onwuegbuzie, 1995). School failure and dropout also contribute to the likelihood of delinquency among students with learning disabilities, along with social-cognitive problem-solving deficits (Briney & Satcher, 1996). It has been suggested that offenders who have mental retardation are likely to be incarcerated at an earlier age and for a longer period of time than youth without retardation. Contributing factors include their inability to communicate; likelihood to plead guilty; and reduced chances for appeal, parole, or rehabilitation.

Participation in gangs also culminates in delinquent acts. Gangs exert a strong influence over members and provide the direction and reinforcement to engage in illegal actions. For example, use of drugs and alcohol, which is prevalent in gangs, is associated with delinquency (Kauffman, 2001). Adolescents with disabilities are especially susceptible to such pressures because of characteristics such as impulsivity, inability to foresee consequences, failure to recognize social cues, suggestibility to peer instigations, and poor decision-making skills.

Appropriate interpersonal school connections in the school environment are essential in preventing gang involvement. Special education students feel powerless and estranged from their general education peers (Brown, Higgins, Pierce, Hong, & Thoma, 2003). DeHotman, Hughes, and Green-Burns (2000) report that gangs are often able to successfully recruit students with disabilities with offers of friendship, attention, and protection. This condition impacts all students who are alienated, bullied, and/or otherwise "invisible" in school and puts them at high risk for involvement in gang activity (Bender, Shubert, & McLaughlin, 2001).

Intervention Needs

In accordance with Public Law 94-142 and Section 504 of the Rehabilitation Act (1973), correctional programs are mandated to provide a free and appropriate public education to adjudicated adolescents with disabilities. Unfortunately, several programmatic failures in the development and implementation of educational plans for adolescents with disabilities in correctional facilities have been identified by Leone, Price, and Vitolo (1986). First, variability in state laws results in educational laws that exclude correctional and social service agencies. Second, lack of specific standards for curriculum and course content for incarcerated youth makes provision of a specialized program difficult. Third, adjudicated juveniles are frequently moved from one institution to another, which is a major impediment to continuity of educational programming. Fourth, there is not enough information on the educational background of adolescents, most of whom are placed in correctional institutions without individualized education programs (IEPs). Assessment methods are not refined and are conducted in group testing situations by test administrators who are unfamiliar with issues governing assessment of youth who have disabilities. Fifth, most correctional facilities do not work in collaboration with the school district attended by the youth. Judges, court officers, and probation officers are not trained to recognize or provide for the special needs of adjudicated youth with disabilities. Finally, there are ethical problems associated with provision of special educational services to a particular group when other youth, although not labeled, evidence a definite need for similar services.

Different community agencies must collaborate to address these failures in programming and develop the most appropriate service delivery model for delinquent youth, keeping in mind their unique needs and circumstances. Apart from basic academics, these programs must emphasize functional living skills, vocational education, behavior management, and family therapy. Education must be based on needs assessment and collaborative goal development. The Juvenile Corrections Interagency Transition Model (Webb, Maddox, & Edgar, 1985) provides a transition model to help local agencies integrate delinquent youth into public schools and reduce recidivism. This model assumes that there is a need for (1) accurate information about services available to these adolescents, (2) efficient transfer of records, (3) preplacement planning to avoid failure due to improper placement, and (4) clear communication between all involved in the process. Comprehensive information on delinquency prevention and programming may be obtained from the Office of Juvenile and Delinquency Prevention, Department of Justice in Washington, D.C. Action Plan 3.1 identifies additional juvenile justice resources.

Teacher Responsibilities

Teachers must be willing to work with the juvenile justice system to provide an appropriate education to delinquents with disabilities. They must recognize their role as pivotal in preventing the recurrence of criminal actions among this population. To do so, teachers must acquire the skills required in working with the police, courts, correctional officers, and other agents of the criminal justice system. Visits to juvenile facilities, detention centers,

---

Action Plan 3.1   Sources of Juvenile Deliquency Information for Students with Disabilities

Juvenile Accountability Incentive Block
   Grant (JAIBG)
Technical Assistance Toolkit
Development Services Group
7317 Wisconsin Avenue; Suite 700E
Bethesda, MD 20814
301-951-0056   877-GO-JAIBG
www.dsgonline.com

National Center on Education Disability
   and Juvenile Justice (EDJJ)
Department of Special Education
University of Maryland
College Park, MD 20742
301-405-6462   301-314-5757 (FAX)
www.edjj.org
email: edjj@umail.umd.edu

PACER Center
Parent Advocacy Coalitition for
   Educational Rights
8161 Normandale Blvd.
Minneapolis, MN 55437
952-838-9000
www.pacer.org
email: pacer@pacer.org

group homes, and prisons must be an essential component of their training program. Both special and general educators need training to improve instructional skills and classroom management practices to prevent escalation of conduct problems (Shores, Gunter, & Jack, 1993). Alternatives to expulsion and out-of-school suspensions are critical because these methods contribute to delinquency (Allen & Edwards-Kyle, 1995). In fact, 80% of daytime burglaries in the United States are committed by youth who are not in school (Crowe, 1995). Specific efforts need to be directed toward the following areas.

Identifying the Problem   Teachers must be cognizant of factors associated with delin-quency and identify students who may succumb easily to the lures of negative influences. Teachers can work with these youth by channeling their energies toward positive and re-warding activities in and out of school. Teachers must also involve other staff members, such as the counselor or school psychologist, and work with them to develop suitable programs for these youngsters. Timely identification is especially important given that youth with behavior disorders and learning disabilities usually encounter problems early in their school years. To avoid student isolation, teachers should include a discussion of each student's involvement with adults and peers as part of year-end evaluations. This evaluation should have the specific outcome of identifying the adult(s) the student has connected with emotionally as well as his or her peer relationships (Bender et al., 2001).

Preventing the Problem   Programmatic efforts in the prevention of delinquency have been only partly successful, and there are no model programs that provide an absolute so-lution to this problem. Collaborative efforts among all relevant agencies seem to be key. In collaboration with social service and mental health agencies, schools can help in preventive measures for at-risk students and their families. Programs must focus on counseling, social skills training, and transition planning (Maag & Katsiyannis, 1998) and follow an early and sustained model of delivery (Zabel & Nigro, 1999). Crime-prevention curricula must be in-corporated into the education of students with disabilities from elementary through second-ary levels. School shootings provide troubling evidence of the pervasive violence and social breakdown impinging on the minds of the nation's youth. Special education teachers could team up with police officers, lawyers, judges, and correctional facility personnel to provide instruction to students regarding crime, delinquency, consequences of delinquent acts, and other relevant information. Juvenile officers could be a useful resource because they are likely to be more familiar with the community than representatives from other agencies. Walker and Sprague (1999) have offered three levels of prevention: primary prevention that includes effective instruction and schoolwide discipline, secondary prevention that focuses on skill deficits among students displaying early signs of delinquency, and tertiary preven-tion for severely at-risk youth who require interagency partnerships to accommodate their needs and those of their families.

Within the classroom, teachers must attempt to make learning highly motivating, relevant, and successful for students. Concerted efforts that develop academic skills of at-risk youth are essential, given that school failure, especially reading difficulties, is strongly linked to delinquency (Maguin & Loeber, 1996). It is important to have a structured, clearly defined, noncompetitive environment that is positive and nonthreatening. Furthermore, teachers must be familiar with culture-specific behavioral patterns, values, and expecta-tions. Lack of understanding of cultural differences in behavior may create conflict and further exacerbate discipline problems (Misra, 1994). A positive, successful learning environment that caters to individual student differences can be powerful in influencing change. Furthermore, teachers must be willing to be mentors and role models for at-risk youth (Freedman, 1993).

Involving Parents   Parents of delinquents may require school support for information about the legal system and their role in the process. School personnel must be ready to provide this service and encourage parents to take an active role in future proceedings regarding their child. Interested and involved parents could be an important asset in the rehabilitation of an adolescent with a disability.

Dropouts

Incidence

Dunn, Chambers, and Rabren (2004) stated that students who drop out of school present serious problems on local, state, and national levels because of implications for the individual's well-being and the economic and social ramifications for society. These authors noted that individuals who drop out of school earn $6,415 less per year than those individuals who finish school. In addition, dropouts cost the nation from 60 to 228 million dollars because of lost income, unemployment, and crime prevention. The National Center for Education Statistics (2003) reported that the dropout rate among 16- to 24-year-olds (including grade-equivalent diploma [GED] recipients and special needs students) for 2001 was 10.7%—lower than the 1985 figure of 12.6%. The dropout rate for white students was 7.3% (10.4% in 1985), for blacks the rate was 10.9% (15.2% in 1985), and for Hispanic students the rate was 27% (27.6% in 1985). Adolescents receiving special education services drop out of school at a higher rate than their general education peers. The Office of Special Education Programs reported a dropout rate that is double that in general education (Capital Publications, 1997). In the *Twenty-third Annual Report to Congress,* the U.S. Department of Education (2002) indicated that 28.9% of students with disabilities 14 years of age and older dropped out of school. Estimates of the dropout rate among youth with behavior disorders range from over 40.0% (Kortering, Braziel, & Tompkins, 2002) to 50.6% (U.S. Department of Education, 2002). Estimates of the dropout rate among students with learning disabilities range from 27.1% (U.S. Department of Education, 2002) to 63% (Council for Exceptional Children, 1994). The Department of Education (2002) reported that dropout rates among students with retardation, vision impairments, and autism were 24.9%, 11.8%, and 9.5%, respectively.

Causes

The association between school failure and dropping out has been well documented (Harvey, 2001; Gierl & Harnisch, 1995). Negative experiences filled with failure and academic problems, poor grades, or alienation from peers often contribute to dropping out. Such experiences may cause an aversion to school-related activities and may result in poor self-perception and lowered self-esteem. Compared to students with learning disabilities who completed school, dropouts with learning disabilities perceived more social aberration (Seidal & Vaughn, 1991). In their review of the literature, Dunn and colleagues (2004) identified several factors that may contribute to dropping out, including low grades and prior academic failure, the family's low socioeconomic status, the parents' education, substance abuse, absenteeism, and discipline problems.

Negative peer group influences and participation in antisocial activities with other dropouts may encourage dropout behaviors. A high correlation exists between delinquency and dropping out of school; however, which comes first is not entirely clear (Farrington, Gallagher, Morley, St. Ledger, & West, 1986). Marriage, pregnancy, and employment are other contributing variables. Unwed pregnant women and those who get married during adolescent years often drop out of school. McCabe (1992) delineated five characteristics of early dropouts: being a loner, home-supported absences, unique dress codes, full-time employment, and drug use and/or erratic hostile behavior.

Intervention Needs

Programming to prevent dropping out combines several components, such as mentorships and sustained counseling, social services, individualized instruction and competency-based curricula, effective school–business collaboration for placement, incentives for completing high school, year-round schools and alternative schools, increased school accountability for dropout rates, and involvement of parents and community in dropout prevention (Hahn, 1987).

Analysis of the National Longitudinal Transistor Study of Special-Education Students (NLTS) database revealed that counseling and vocational education were significantly associated with graduation rates (Rylance, 1997). A need exists to increase the number of counselors, establish health and family planning programs, develop infant care facilities for teenage mothers, provide remedial instruction, increase student employability skills, and work in collaboration with community social service agencies (Hahn, 1987). Programs must be initiated early because patterns of truancy develop gradually and before high school. Martin, Tobin, and Sugai (2002) reported that students were more likely to stay in school if they were involved in athletic and vocational extracurricular activities rather than dropout prevention programs. Extracurricular activities counteract the isolation of students (Bender et al., 2001) and help them develop conventional social support networks.

Teacher Responsibilities

Teachers must play an important role in reducing dropout among students if the national education goal of 90% high school graduation rate (Goals 2000, 1994) is to become reality. All teachers must become familiar with the special problems associated with dropping out and with the methods and resources that can help students overcome such problems. This knowledge is especially important because of increasing inclusion of adolescents with disabilities in regular education and limited adaptations to accommodate these students in such environments (Meadows, Neel, Scott, & Parker, 1994). Teachers can help in several ways.

Identifying the Problem   Students who are likely to drop out are those who are behind their grade level and older than their classmates, exhibit poor academic performance, lack

Action Plan 3.2   Risk Factors Associated with Dropping Out

Teachers need to be aware of factors that contribute to dropping out of school. They include:

School failure	Frequent suspension/detention
Poor grades	Pregnancy
Lack of basic skills	Single-parent families
Older age than the average student	Lower socioeconomic status
Poor peer relationships	Limited extracurricular activities

basic skills, and have been frequently suspended or given detention. Action Plan 3.2 identifies risk factors. If teachers can identify these youngsters at an early stage, prevention is a possibility.

Preventing the Problem   To prevent youngsters from dropping out, teachers must be actively involved with students and aware of their problems. They should involve students in classroom and school activities and establish clear standards and rules. Teachers must also design a learning environment that is relevant, motivating, and encourages success among students with disabilities. Curricula for adolescents must focus on functional living needs in the workplace, in the community, at home, and within social settings. The mandate for an individualized transition plan at age 14 further emphasizes the need for improved postschool readiness skills. Career education must be infused into the curriculum. Isolated work experiences are not enough to keep secondary students in school. Harvey (2001) suggests that links need to be established among job skills taught, student interest, and community needs. Follow-up activities are needed to help in job search, placement, problem resolution, and support services, including the consideration of vocational education.

Youth with disabilities express the need for teachers to change their attitudes and treatment toward them (Dunn et al., 2002; Kortering & Braziel, 1999). These youth also recognize the need for self-change in attitude and behavior. In addition, they want more support from teachers, changes in attendance and discipline policies, and better textbooks and teaching methods.

Involving Parents   Parent involvement from the initial stages of school truancy is very important. Schools should intervene before the student reaches high school because a well-established pattern is more difficult to break. Parent involvement can be increased if teachers send positive and encouraging reports home about their students. Such reports may serve to motivate parents and may also result in positive feedback for the student. Conferences focusing on both progress and problems should be scheduled on a regular basis. Such conferences should be scheduled at times that allow parent attendance and participation. It may also be extremely beneficial to have the youth present during these meetings. If both teachers and parents monitor student activities, dropout rates may be reduced. Finally, students and parents need to establish ownership of the transition planning process and develop attainable vocational goals (Harvey, 2001).

Substance Abuse

Incidence

According to a National Center for Education Statistics (2001) report, 16.7% of 12- to 17-year-olds used illicit drugs in 1996, compared to 20.3% in 1999. However, there was a decline in alcohol consumption; in 1982, 34.9% of 12- to 17-year-olds used alcohol in the previous 30 days, compared to 18.6% in 1999. Alcohol is the most commonly used drug. Illicit drugs used by teenagers include marijuana, followed by stimulants, inhalants, hallucinogens, sedatives, and tranquilizers. The Office of National Drug Control Policy (2000) reported that despite the fact that federal spending on the drug war increased from $1.65 billion in 1982 to $17.7 billion in 1999, more than half the students in the United States in 1999 tried an illegal drug before they graduated from high school.

Of all the studies and surveys conducted to gather information regarding drug use among adolescents, only a handful have focused on youth with disabilities, and of those the primary focus was on adolescents with learning disabilities (LD) and attention deficit hyperactivity disorder (ADHD). The technical adequacy of research targeting individuals with disabilities is questionable (Leone, 1991). Based on the results of the Substance Abuse Subtle Screening Inventory (Karacostas & Fisher, 1993), significantly more adolescents with LD were classified as chemically dependent than were peers without learning disabilities. Devlin and Elliot (1992) found that 51% of students with behavior disorders displayed patterns of drug use, whereas only 14% of students without disorders showed similar drug use. Also, individuals with ADHD tend to be at risk for alcohol and substance abuse (Stokeld, 1995).

However, the complexity of the issue should not be underestimated. For example, adolescents with LD may not have a higher incidence of substance use disorder (SUD) in later years, but they may have a higher incidence of SUD than the general population, especially if LD problems persist into adulthood (Beitchman, Wilson, Douglas, Young, & Adlaf, 2001). LD, though considered a risk factor for SUD, should not be thought of as a causal factor but rather as a mediator or variable in the overall life experiences of the individual (Weinberg, 2001). The issue is further compounded by the fact that it is often difficult to distinguish between the symptoms of LD and those of SUD (Cosden, 2001).

Causes

There is no single or most common cause for substance abuse. Numerous factors play a role in the adolescent's use of alcohol and drugs. Family disorganization and stress (Stern, Northman, & Van-Slyck, 1984), lack of parental direction and supervision, the need to rebel against authority (Jessor & Jessor, 1980), or the desire to explore new experiences often lead adolescents to seek chemical solutions to problems. Adolescents are more likely to engage in drug- and alcohol-related activities if their peers and parents do so (Brook, Whiteman, & Gordon, 1985). Youth from low economic groups or different ethnic and minority groups may be introduced to drugs early in their lives as a consequence of community conditions, gang-type liaisons (Wright & Fitzpatrick, 2004), and minimal parental supervision. Advertisements and media link alcohol with enjoyment and good living, conveying a strong message to impressionable adolescents and encouraging substance abuse (Gitlin, 1990).

Intervention Needs

Schools must develop drug and alcohol policies. These policies must focus on preventive programming, include students with disabilities, and provide resources to individuals working to help adolescents overcome drug and alcohol dependency (Leone, 1991). School-based programs routinely exclude youth with disabilities, often pulling them out during prevention program implementation (Morgan, Cancio, & Likins, 1992). Efforts must be made to involve this population consistently in all ongoing prevention programs, which must be tailored to meet their behavioral and learning needs (Lamarine, 1993). It has been suggested that the impact of substance abuse on students with disabilities may be more debilitating than it is for their peers (LaGreca & Stone, 1990).

Schools must also have ongoing drug and alcohol education through which students receive honest and accurate information. Support services—such as counseling for students and families, information dissemination, emergency centers, and parent groups—must be established. Schools must establish firm rules and guidelines regarding the use, trade, or possession of illegal substances. These guidelines must be detailed and precise so that the consequences of drug-related activities are clear to all students and can be implemented consistently and effectively by all personnel. Police involvement reinforces the illegal nature of the act and may serve as a deterrent to future occurrences.

Teacher Responsibilities

Substance abuse has a direct and serious impact on student performance within the educational environment. Teacher attention and involvement, then, are an absolute necessity. Reports suggest that teachers are reluctant to get entangled in problems related to substance abuse among their students, especially if the students have disabilities (Shannon, 1986). Most teachers report limited knowledge about substance abuse prevention and treatment (Genaux, Morgan, & Friedman, 1995). Teachers can provide a valuable service by identifying current or potential substance users and must be targeted for both in-service and preservice training. Teachers can also assist students in improving their self-understanding of the nature of their disability. It has been suggested that this information may affect their risk for substance abuse (Cosden, 2001).

Identifying the Problem Action Plan 3.3 lists four major categories of drugs, each having different physiological and behavioral manifestations. Teachers may be first to notice the existence of a problem through changes in student behavior. These changes are listed in Action Plan 3.4. Teachers must refer students displaying such behaviors for evaluation. Personnel conducting assessments must be trained to evaluate students for the possibility of substance abuse, be able to distinguish occasional users from drug abusers, and be able to recognize progressive patterns of substance abuse. An assessment protocol for use by school psychologists has been developed by Fisher and Harrison (1992).

Teachers of students with disabilities must be warned not to make hasty judgments on the basis of a few signs, because several students will probably be on medication that produces similar symptoms. Furthermore, many of these signs are characteristic of behavior variances evident among special populations. The teacher who suspects a serious problem

Action Plan 3.3   Drug Categories and Their Effects

Teachers should be familiar with the effects of different classes of drugs:

Stimulants	Increase alertness
	Reduce hunger
Depressants	Reduce activity
	Induce relaxation and sleep
Hallucinogens	Create perceptual disorders
	Create mood variances
Narcotics	Relieve pain
	Increase euphoria

Action Plan 3.4   Signs of Drug Use

Elmquist (1991) recommended that teachers remain alert to the following signs of drug use:

1. Sleeping in class
2. Mood swings
3. Incomplete work
4. Absence from school
5. Hostile or argumentative
6. Negative self-attitude
7. Dislike of school
8. Poor academic performance
9. Lack of interest in extracurricular activities
10. Poor family communication
11. Secrecy about activities
12. Change in friends
13. Decrease in energy
14. Weight change
15. Poor physical appearance
16. Memory loss
17. Persistent cold symptoms

should make a referral to the appropriate person in the school. Once the problem has been clearly defined, remedial steps can be initiated with the cooperation of the school system.

Preventing the Problem   The best way to prevent substance abuse is to inform students about drug and alcohol abuse and its harmful effects. Effective school-based prevention programs must be comprehensive. They must (1) include information dissemination about drugs and their effects through participation in clubs such as Students Against Driving Drunk (SADD), Just Say No clubs, and adventure-based programs (Putnam, 1995); (2) build on affective skills such as self-understanding, self-esteem, and responsible decision making; and (3) teach social and life skills such as assertiveness, refusal skills, and selecting appropriate friends.

Extracurricular activities, in sports and vocation-oriented clubs, support strong peer relations and reduce student isolation (Martin et al., 2002). Students with disabilities must be active participants in lessons focusing on drug-free living skills because they may rely on a smaller social network (U.S. Department of Health and Human Service, 2003). Teachers can create awareness among adolescents by engaging them in problem-solving activities. For example, teachers might hold brainstorming sessions on the positive outcomes of quitting alcohol and drug use. Students could be presented with scenarios regarding death resulting from drunk driving and be required to appraise such situations. Such activities encourage thoughtful decisions and responsible behavior. Teachers need to convey the idea that drug and alcohol use is not associated with adult status or glamour. Teaching students to ignore peer pressures and providing alternative coping strategies for stressful situations give students a means of avoiding negative consequences. Teachers must identify the positive consequences students derive through drug use and teach acceptable alternatives to experiencing similar gratification. For example, drug use may provide a student with access to a peer group; however, the student could be taught positive social skills that would help him or her develop relationships with peers through more positive social activities.

Considering the relationship between substance abuse and school failure, teachers have the responsibility of providing an enriching and positive classroom environment for all students. Teachers are advised to familiarize themselves with the agencies and curricula related to substance abuse prevention and treatment listed in Action Plan 3.5. Some curricular materials have been specifically developed for students with sensory impairments, mental retardation, learning disabilities, and behavior disorders. Teachers can seek additional assistance and information from the resources listed in Action Plan 3.6.

Involving Parents   Parent involvement is essential for successful drug rehabilitation efforts. Parents are an important source of information regarding family, neighborhood, and community dynamics that perpetuate drug use. School-based programs are unlikely to succeed without parent cooperation, given the strong influence of environmental influences on drug use. Unfortunately, few programs systematically include parents (Dielman, Butchart, & Shope, 1993). Parents must be told of the importance of their support and of the availability of school assistance at all times. Parents need encouragement because they often perceive themselves as helpless or are completely frustrated in their attempts to resolve their child's problem. Adolescents, too, must be encouraged to participate. Research has indicated that parent involvement in prevention programs with their behaviorally disordered adolescents has positive outcomes (Elmquist, 1992). Parents also need information regarding the nature of their child's problem, treatment options, resources available, and monetary issues.

Depression

Incidence

Depression in the school-aged population has been estimated to range from 2 to 21% (Magg & Reid, 1994). Incidence figures for depression among students with disabilities is between 14 and 54% (Newcomer, Borenbaum, & Pearson, 1995). Depression has been identified as characteristic of youth with emotional problems (Cullinan, Schloss, & Epstein, 1987; Maag & Forness, 1991), learning disabilities (Cohen, 1992; Gorman, 1995; Hammen & Campas, 1994; Maag & Forness, 1993; Wenner, 1993), mild mental retardation, and conduct disorders (Gorman, 1995; Hammen & Campus, 1994). Estimates of depression

Action Plan 3.5   Sources of Substance Abuse Prevention Curricula for Students with Disabilities

Teachers can contact the following agencies for information about substance abuse and how to prevent or address it:

Addiction Intervention with the Disabled
    Resource Center
Department of Sociology
Kent State University
Kent, OH 44242
216-672-2440

James Stanfield Co., Inc.
P. O. Box 41058
Santa Barbara, CA 93140
800-421-6534   805-897-1187 (FAX)
www.stanfield.com
email: maindesk@stanfield.com

National Association on Alcohol, Drugs,
    and Disability (NAADD)
2165 Bunker Hill Drive
San Mateo, CA 94402-3801
950-578-8047   950-286-9205 (FAX)
www.naadd.org

National Clearinghouse for Alcohol and
    Drug Information (NCADI)
P. O. Box 2345
Rockville, MD 20847
800-729-6686
(Order No. BKD-288)
www.health.org

National Council on Alcoholism and Drug
    Dependence (NCADD)
20 Exchange Place
Suite 2902
New York, NY 10005
212-269-7797
www.ncadd.org
email: national@ncadd.org

Project OZ
502 South Morris Avenue
Bloomington, IL 61701
309-827-0377
www.projectoz.org

Substance Abuse Resources and Disability
    Issues
Wright State University School of
    Medicine
P. O. Box 927
Dayton, OH 45435
513-259-1384   513-259-1395 (FAX)

Substance and Alcohol Intervention
    Services for the Deaf (SAISD)
Rochester Institute of Technology/
    August Center
115 Lomb Memorial Drive
Rochester, NY 14623-5608
716-475-4978   716-475-7375 (FAX)
www.rit.edu

among youth with learning and/or behavior problems are higher than reported for nondisabled youth, ranging from 50 to 60% (Forness, 1988), and depressive symptoms are higher among those who were physically or sexually abused. Females are more likely than males to experience severe depressive symptomatology because of more negative interpretation of events and harsher self-evaluations (Maag & Forness, 1993).

Causes

Depression may result from medical, psychological, environmental, and situational factors. Low levels of brain chemicals such as serotonin have been linked to clinical depression

Action Plan 3.6   General Resources

Teachers interested in obtaining more information regarding the problems facing adolescents are advised to contact the following agencies:

The Addiction Research Foundation
   (ARF)
33 Russell Street
Toronto, Canada M5S 2S1
www.peele.net

National Families in Action (NFIA)
3854 North Druid Hills Road
Suite 300
Decatur, GA 30033
www.nationalfamilies.org

National Information Center for Youth
   with Disabilities (NICHCY)
P. O. Box 1492
Washington, DC 20013
800-695-0285   202-884-8441 (FAX)
www.nichey.org
email: nichey@aed.org

National Clearinghouse for Alcohol and
   Drug Information (NCADI)
P. O. Box 2345
Rockville, MD 20847
800-729-6686
www.niaaa.nih.gov

National Institute on Drug Abuse (NIDA)
National Institutes of Health
6001 Executive Blvd., Rm. 5213
Bethesda, MD 20892-9561
301-443-1124
www.drugabuse.gov

Resource Center on Substance Abuse
   Prevention and Disability
1819 L Street, NW
Suite 300
Washington, DC 20036
202-628-8080

U.S. Department of Education,
Office of Safe and Drug Free Schools
   (OSDFS)
400 Maryland Avenue, SW
Washington, DC 20202
877-4-ED-PUBS
www.ed.gov/about/offices/list/osdfs/
   index.html

---

by recent biopsychiatric research (Gorman, 1995). Psychological factors include loss of motivation and interest, pervasive sadness, low self-esteem, and poor social relationships (Smolowe, 1995). Depressionogenic ways of thinking, which include a tendency to be pessimistic in interpreting life events, are most associated with depression. Environmental variables of dysfunctional families, death or divorce, abuse, and chronic illness may also cause depression (Goleman, 1995). In addition, depression may result from severe self-criticism due to an inability to cope with excessive school demands among youth with learning disabilities (Geisthardt & Munsch, 1996; Resnick et al., 1997). Lack of social support further increases the risk status of adolescents with learning disabilities. Self-injurious behaviors, aggression, and/or severe withdrawal may be symptomatic of depression among students with severe mental retardation (Mattes & Amsell, 1993).

Intervention Needs

Research linking depression with suicide highlights the need for immediate intervention by the schools and the community. Teachers must be trained to recognize symptoms and be knowledgeable about intervention methods for depression. Special education teachers need to be aware that they have been prepared to develop and implement classroom interventions (social skills training, self-evaluation, etc.) that have also been used to treat depression (Maag, 2002). Preparation of teachers of students with disabilities should focus on both the academic and the social skills/problem-solving value of these strategies to provide coping mechanisms for depressed adolescents. School support staff such as counselors, social workers, and school psychologists must work in collaboration with one another and with teachers of students who are depressed.

Teacher Responsibilities

Depression can be severely debilitating, and it affects student learning. Teachers have the responsibility of identifying and referring students who need intervention in a timely manner. Teachers must also present themselves as approachable and concerned individuals who are willing to listen and offer support to their students (Bender et al., 2001). Garmezy (1991) proposed the resiliency concept, which is the ability to overcome negative outcomes associated with risk factors. Effective, healthy relationships between the youth and a "mentor" role model are key to resiliency. According to Katz (1997), school environments can become critical "resiliency fostering" environments that enable youth to reverse the effects of risk factors. Teachers are key players in such efforts. They can provide encouragement, patience, and affection for students undergoing stress. The likelihood of student outcomes can be greatly influenced by how teachers communicate with their students. Teachers must engage in the activities discussed in the following paragraphs.

Identifying the Problem   Teachers must be alert to symptoms of depression typically displayed by adolescents. According to the Diagnostic and Statistical Manual of Mental Disorders (*DSM-IV*), these symptoms include (a) persistent sad, anxious, or empty mood; (b) feelings of hopelessness and/or pessimism; (c) feelings of guilt and worthlessness; (d) loss of interest in pleasurable activities; (e) insomnia or oversleeping; (f) fatigue; (g) decreased energy; (h) suicidal ideation or attempts; (i) difficulty in concentration and memory; (j) restlessness or irritability; and (k) persistent physical symptoms such as headaches, digestive disorders, and/or chronic pain. The *DSM-IV* also describes behaviors of adolescents that may signal underlying depression. These behaviors are listed in Action Plan 3.7.

Action Plan 3.7   *DSM-IV* Features of Depressive Disorder

The following feelings or behaviors are characteristic of depression:

Poor appetite or overeating	Insomnia or hypersomnia
Low energy or fatigue	Poor concentration
Feelings of hopelessness	Self-criticism
Loss of interest	Irritability
Pessimism	School difficulties
Substance abuse	Aggression
Inattention to personal appearance	Increased emotionality

Prompt action on detection of signs of depression is imperative because depression is linked to suicide. Teachers play a critical role in making referrals within the school and in securing assistance from support staff. Teacher responsibilities also include classroom follow-up of referred students by practicing strategies to alleviate factors related to depression. Teachers may have to monitor the side effects of antidepressant drugs on behavior.

Preventing the Problem   Depression and school failure often result in a vicious cycle that must be broken. Immediate intervention efforts focusing on providing success experiences to students may hinder the onset of depression. Because poor peer relationships are linked to depression, strategies promoting social competence must be an integral part of the curriculum. Success in improving peer relationships as well as personal attitudes about the future has been achieved through peer-mediated programs that address depressed students' negative thought processes (Goleman, 1995; Rice & Meyer, 1994). Teachers can also influence and renew student interest in school activities. To maintain a positive classroom environment, teachers must avoid use of punishment techniques and use positive behavior management strategies. Programs that enhance skill acquisition and increase school success and self-concept are especially beneficial for adolescents with learning disabilities and behavior problems. Teachers may get further information from organizations listed in Action Plan 3.8.

Action Plan 3.8   Organizations Providing Information on Depression among Youth

Teachers may contact the following agencies for information about depression:

American Academy of Child and
   Adolescent Psychiatry (AACAP)
3615 Wisconsin Avenue, NW
Washington, DC 20016
202-966-7300   202-966-2891 (FAX)
www.aacap.org

American Psychological Association
   (APA)
750 First Street, NE
Washington, DC 20002-4242
800-374-2721   202-336-5500
www.apa.org

The Council for Exceptional Children
   (CEC)
1110 N. Glebe Road/Suite 300
Arlington, VA 22210-5704
1-800-CEC-SPED   763-264-9494 (FAX)
www.cec.sped.org

National Alliance for the Mentally Ill
   (NAMI)
Colonial Place Three
2107 Wilson Blvd., Suite 300
Arlington, VA 22201-3042
703-524-7600   703-524-9094 (FAX)
www.nami.org

Depression and Bipolar Support Alliance
   (DBSA)
730 North Franklin Street,
Suite 501
Chicago, IL 60610-7224
800-826-3632   312-642-7243 (FAX)
www.dbsalliance.org

National Mental Health Association
   (NMHA)
2001 Beauregard Street; 12th floor
Alexandria, VA 22311
703-684-7722
www.nmha.org

For students who are not responsive to classroom interventions, a referral to the counselor and/or social worker may be necessary for intensive remediation. The counselor could be invited to the classroom to conduct problem-solving sessions with all students. Too often, depressed adolescents blame themselves for negative events in their lives. Students who are depressed must be made to believe that they have control over personal success and failure. Providing opportunities to discuss and generate alternatives within the classroom will make counseling more realistic to students at risk for depression and at the same time benefit all students.

Involving Parents   Depression among adolescents may have its roots in impaired family dynamics. Furthermore, there is evidence of significant correlation between parents' depression and depression in children (Forehand, McCombs, & Brody, 1987). Therefore, the family's role is critical in any attempts at remediation made by school personnel. The teacher might initiate a referral for family therapy after discussions with the family. Parents require support from school personnel because living with a depressed adolescent can be emotionally stressful. Furthermore, parents may feel helpless in resolving their child's feelings because they blame themselves. Cooperation from the school during the time they are undergoing treatment is essential for accelerating the recovery process.

Suicide

Incidence

In 1997, 5,114 individuals between the ages of 10 to 24 committed suicide, and an estimated 750,000 in this age group attempted suicide (McIntosh & Guest, 2000). The rate of suicide is approximately 10 in 100,000 youth. Suicides are more frequent at age 14 and increase in frequency with subsequent age groups (Blum & Rinehart, 1997; Resnick et al., 1997). Youth who have attempted suicide before are at a higher risk for attempting suicide again (Shaughnessy, Doshi, & Jones, 2004). Suicide is the third leading cause of death among youth who are 15 to 24 years old, ranking only below accidents and homicide (Aseltine & DeMartino, 2004). According to Gould and colleagues (2004), approximately 20% of all teens consider committing suicide and 8% attempt it. Females attempt suicide more frequently than males (Shaughnessy et al., 2004), yet males are three times more likely to be successful (Centers for Disease Control, 2003). This is attributed to use by males of more effective methods such as shooting or hanging, compared to the drugs or poisons typically used by females.

These shocking statistics misrepresent the actual number of suicides, which may be two or three times greater (American Psychiatric Association, 1985). Some reasons for misreporting suicides as accidental deaths or attributing cause of death to undetermined factors include (a) avoidance of social stigma related to suicide, (b) belief that youngsters do not attempt to take their own life, and/or (c) religious beliefs of a group of people (Hawton, 1986).

There is scant information regarding suicide by youth with disabilities. Some evidence indicates a higher rate of suicide among adolescents who have learning disabilities than adolescents without disabilities (Huntington & Bender, 1993). Analysis of suicide notes of 27 adolescents revealed significant deficits in spelling and handwriting similar to those of adolescents with learning disabilities (McBride & Siegel, 1997). Adolescents with behavioral/emotional disorders reported higher frequencies in both suicide ideation and suicide attempts compared to nondisabled youth, with females reporting higher suicidality than males (Miller, 1994). In another study, suicide was found to be an under-recognized but significant phenomenon among adolescents with mental retardation (Walters, 1995).

Causes

Suicidal adolescents usually have a history of personal, familial, or medical difficulties. Personality traits such as aggression, impulsivity, perfectionism, hopelessness (Kuper, 1991), low self-esteem, interpersonal problems, and poor problem-solving skills (Kirk, 1993) have been associated with those who attempted suicide. Depression is considered to be a contributing factor in 60% of suicides (Shaughnessy et al., 1990). Children of parents who suffer from depression disorders and alcohol abuse appear to be at high risk for committing suicide. Physically abused adolescents are five times more likely to attempt suicide than those with no history of abuse (Riggs, Alario, & McHorney, 1990). Other family problems include poor communication, conflicting values, and insufficient affection and support (Dukes & Lorch, 1989). School adjustment problems and poor school performance have been found to be related to adolescent suicide attempts (Kosky, Silburn, & Zubrick, 1990). Drug and alcohol abuse also has been linked to suicide (Hawton, 1986; Shaughnessy et al., 2004).

It appears that suicide can be "contagious," because research shows that suicides often occur in clusters in terms of time or location. A possible reason for this occurrence is the media attention to suicide. Pfeffer (1989) summarized information presented at the American Association of Suicidology (AAS) regarding the link between suicide and media coverage. Factors such as location of the story in a newspaper (front page versus inside page), specificity of news coverage, and romanticized descriptions of reasons for committing suicide appear to have a significant impact on the rate of suicide.

Intervention Needs

Teachers must prepare themselves through education, resources, and related literature to be ready to deal with crisis situations. They must remain alert to the emotional environment in their classroom and investigate irregularities in student behavior. They should know each student as an individual and be alert to behavioral changes. Finally, they should immediately contact school district personnel responsible for contacting parents (McIntosh & Guest, 2000).

Schools must be equipped with services to provide frequent student counseling and family therapy as needed. Schools can also offer professional development activities involving mental health professionals, school psychologists, and social workers. Information dissemination, emergency help, and formation of support groups are services that must be given serious consideration by every school. Schools must also develop a crisis intervention plan with a continuum of procedures ranging from a mental health curriculum to suicide intervention strategies (Wright-Strawderman, Lindsey, Navarette, & Flippo, 1996).

Teacher Responsibilities

Suicide prevention and support for adolescents who display suicidal tendencies are areas in which teachers can make a positive difference. The teacher's role cannot be stressed enough, given that school problems often contribute to adolescent suicide. In the case of adolescents with disabilities, teachers are often singled out as primary adult caregivers and may significantly influence adolescent actions. Some suggestions for teachers that may help them identify and prevent suicide are given in the following paragraphs.

Identifying the Problem   It is not always apparent that a student is experiencing suicidal feelings or displaying associated symptoms. It has been suggested that adolescent suicide attempts are not impulsive actions but occur after numerous appeals for help and support have been ignored (Weiner, 1980). Some warning signs are included in Action Plan 3.9. Teachers must be aware of distress signals that may be verbally expressed in statements such as "You'll be sorry when I'm gone" or "All this will not matter soon." Such verbalizations must not be ignored. Depressed adolescents, harboring suicidal thoughts, may express themselves through excessive fatigue and hypochondria or through restless, unproductive activity (Capuzzi, 1986). Themes or preoccupations in thinking may be yet another indicator of suicidal thoughts—for example, a sudden interest in religion related to life after death or an undue absorption in a recent personal loss. It is possible that parents and teachers may attribute these signs to normal adolescent problems; however, warning signs must never be cursorily dismissed.

Teachers must not take on counseling responsibilities, because they are not trained to prevent suicide. Their responsibility is to identify and make a referral to appropriate professionals and agencies.

Preventing the Problem   Within the educational setting, young individuals who are apprehensive or anxious often need support from peers so they can communicate and learn to cope with their feelings. Open communication may also promote feelings of commonality among peers experiencing similar problems and subvert fears related to feelings of personal differences. An important first step is the willingness to verbalize anxieties and discuss problems that may become dangerous if ignored. Discussions should not, however, directly

---

Action Plan 3.9   Warning Signs of Suicide

Guetzloe (1989) summarized the most commonly cited warning signs of suicide as follows:

1. Extreme changes in behavior
2. Signs of depression
3. Suicidal threat or statement
4. Previous suicide attempt
5. Substance abuse
6. Presence of suicide plan
7. Actions related to making final arrangements (e.g., giving away possessions)
8. Signs of procuring the means (e.g., purchasing a weapon or pills)

Action Plan 3.10   Organizations Providing Information on Suicide among Youth

Teachers can obtain information about suicide from the following agencies:

American Academy of Child and
  Adolescent Psychiatry (AACAP)
3615 Wisconsin Avenue, NW
Washington, DC 20016
202-966-7300
www.aacap.org

American Association of Suicidology
  (AAS)
4201 Connecticut Avenue, NW, Suite 408
Washington, DC 20008
202-237-2280
www.suicidology.org

Council for Children with Behavioral
  Disorders (CCBD)
A Division of the Council for Exceptional
  Children
1110 N. Glebe Road
Arlington, VA 22210
1-800-224-6830
www.ccbd.net

National Institute of Mental Health
  (NIMH)
Office of Communications
6001 Executive Blvd.
Room 8184
Bethesda, MD 20892-9663
866-615-6464   301-443-4279 (FAX)
www.nimh.nih.gov

Center for Suicide Prevention
1202 Center Street, Suite 320
Calgary, Alberta, Canada T2G5A5
403-245-3900   403-245-0299 (FAX)
www.suicideinfo.ca

Suicide Prevention Resource Center
  (SPRC)
55 Chapel Street
Newton, MA 02458-1060
877-438-7772
www.sprc.org
email: info@sprc.org

revolve around issues related to suicide. Use of suicide curricula, including presentation of materials on suicide, has been discouraged by Shaffer and colleagues (1990) due to their "contagious" effects. These researchers found that talking about suicide may result in suicide attempts by youth who are at risk. Providing individual help to those who require it is preferable. However, information regarding suicide prevention agencies and emergency hot lines can be provided to students. See Action Plan 3.10 for a list of agencies that can help.

Teachers must develop a nonthreatening classroom atmosphere that is conducive to student learning. Reducing anxiety associated with learning is crucial, given that school-related stress is one factor that can contribute to suicide. A curriculum increases social skills and communication among students can facilitate suicide prevention. Teachers must build positive rapport and maintain open lines of communication with students. They must take all problems seriously and directly tell their students that they care about what happens to them. Students must be shown how to obtain help in an emergency when they are not in school. The exact procedures for making a telephone call and giving information may be practiced within the school setting.

Special education teachers who work with adolescents who are emotionally disturbed must be prepared to provide support during crisis situations. Although they are not expected to provide counseling or intervention during such times, they could be instrumental in

Action Plan 3.11   Dos and Don'ts for Interacting with Suicidal Adolescents

McGee and Guetzloe (1998) proposed the following recommendations:

Do

1. Identify the causal factors.
2. Ask specific questions about the suicide plan.
3. Encourage the student to get support from parents, friends, church leaders, and so on.
4. Create interest in upcoming school or community events.
5. Ensure the student has a crisis hot line number.
6. Dispose of any weapon in the environment.
7. Attempt to obtain commitment that the student will not hurt himself or herself.
8. Make the appropriate referral.

Don't

1. Downplay the student's feelings.
2. Debate the morality of suicide or create guilt.
3. Leave the student alone.
4. Promise to keep the student's suicidal feelings a secret.

ensuring that such services are made available. If teachers do encounter a situation in which a teenager is suicidal, they can follow the recommendations provided in Action Plan 3.11.

Involving Parents   Parents must become familiar with the signs of suicide and precipitating events, such as parents' prohibiting the adolescent from going out, the breakup of a relationship, school failure, family altercations, pregnancy, and so on. Teachers play an important role in parent education. It is crucial that the suitability of any parent training program, in accordance with family dynamics, needs, and culture, is ensured (Keogh & Weisner, 1993). Involvement with parents not only will enable teachers to become familiar with family circumstances and high-risk students but could also prevent tragedies from occurring. Parent counseling could be included in student IEPs.

Sexually Transmitted Diseases

Incidence

Martin and colleagues (2005) report that youth are experiencing sexual intercourse at an increasingly younger age, heightening the risk of pregnancy and sexually transmitted diseases. The United States has the highest rate of sexually transmitted diseases (STDs) in the industrialized world, accounting for more than 85% of the most common infectious diseases. An estimated 3 million new cases of STD occur in persons aged 13 to 19 each year. By the age of 24, one in three people will have an STD (Kaiser Family Foundation, 1998b). This statistic has led to use of the term *hidden epidemic* for STDs (Eng & Butler, 1997).

Among women, 15- to 19-year-olds had the highest rate of gonorrhea in 2000 compared to all other age groups (Centers for Disease Control, 2002). Women suffer more severe and long-term consequences than men (Alan Guttmacher Institute, 1993).

Action Plan 3.12 lists STDs, including chlamydia, gonorrhea, herpes, human immunodeficiency virus (HIV), and syphilis, and provides information on how an individual gets the disease, when symptoms appear, and available treatments. Sexually transmitted diseases can lead to pelvic inflammatory diseases, infertility, heart disease, arthritis, brain damage, blindness, spontaneous abortion, premature birth, bone deformities, mental retardation, and even death if a timely cure is not available. The life-threatening characteristic of HIV, which causes AIDS, has resulted in a deluge of statistical information on that disease. Reported AIDS cases in 13- to 19-year-olds in the United States peaked in 1993 at 578 and declined to 372 cases in 2001. Of the 372 cases reported in 2001, 44% were male and 56% were female (Centers for Disease Control, 2002). Through June 1999, 387,671 adults and adolescents over 13 years of age were reported to have HIV and AIDS (Centers for Disease Control & Prevention, 1999). Cumulative totals in the 13 to 18 age group through 1998 were 3,589 and among 20- to 24-year-olds were 25,343. These figures suggest that transmission of the virus occurred during adolescent years, because the HIV virus can remain

Action Plan 3.12   Sexually Transmitted Diseases

Teachers should be aware of sexually transmitted diseases, how they are transmitted, when symptoms appear, and treatment options.

Disease	Mode of Transmission	Onset of Symptoms	Treatment
Chlamydia	Sexual intercourse Oral or anal sex During birth	Women have no early symptoms. Men have symptoms in 1 to 3 weeks.	Antibiotics
Gonorrhea	Sexual intercourse Oral or anal sex During birth	Women have no early symptoms. Men have symptoms in 2 to 10 days.	Antibiotics
Herpes	Sexual intercourse Oral or anal sex Kissing someone with herpes blister	4 days to 2 weeks	No cure; pills and creams reduce pain and sores.
HIV	Sexual intercourse Anal sex Infected blood Babies in the womb During birth Breast milk Infected needles and syringes	Blood test shows virus 2 weeks to 6 months after infection. No symptoms for years in some people.	No cure
Syphilis	Sexual intercourse Oral or anal sex Babies in the womb During birth	10 to 90 days for first stage 6 weeks to 6 months for second stage Years for the third stage	Penicillin

Source: Adapted from *Sexually Transmitted Diseases* (Family Planning Council of Iowa, 1991).

undetected for 8 to 12 years. Presence of HIV/AIDS in people with disabilities remains virtually uninvestigated. One survey reported that 45 adults with mental retardation tested positive for HIV, 7 of whom were symptomatic of AIDS (Marchetti, Nathanson, Kastner, & Owens, 1990). A two-year follow-up indicated doubling of these figures (Kastner, Nathanson, & Marchetti, 1992).

Causes

It is important to focus specifically on the cause and transmission of HIV. The virus prevents the body from fighting diseases and infections that may become life threatening. It is transmitted through sexual intercourse, either vaginal or rectal; bodily secretions; intravenous drug use; the placenta; and possibly breast milk. The virus does not survive outside the human body for long and cannot be transmitted through air. Adolescents engage in several behaviors that put them at a high risk for contracting HIV. Surveys reveal that adolescents possess a high degree of HIV-related information, but they continue to engage in sexual behaviors without using protection (Boswell, Fox, Hubbard, & Coyle, 1992). In a telephone survey of 500 teenagers, 55% of 16- to 17-year-olds reported having had sex, 61% had multiple partners, and 39% seldom to never used protection (Gibbs, 1993).

Statistics on drug use indicate that 61% of adolescents have experimented with drugs by high school graduation (Bennett, 1986). Approximately 0.9 to 1.5% of high school seniors use heroin (Johnston, O'Malley, & Bachman, 1985). According to researchers, over 200,000 teenagers have tried injecting drugs (Brooks-Gunn, Boyer, & Hein, 1988), and countless others share needles for piercing ears, tattooing, and becoming blood brothers. Surveys also indicate that there exist differences in knowledge based on sex, religion, ethnicity, and socioeconomic status (Anderson & Christenson, 1991).

Intervention Needs

It is imperative that schools foster a caring and supportive climate in which adolescents with HIV feel welcome. Their health and safety must be ensured and confidentiality safeguarded. Information regarding HIV needs to be excluded from student records that are accessible to unauthorized personnel (Crocker et al., 1994). The National Commission on AIDS (1994) has recommended four components as important to a comprehensive AIDS education program: (1) information, (2) exploration of personal attitudes, (3) skill building, and (4) access to services. Colson and Carlson (1993) have provided scope and sequence for eight areas in HIV/AIDS education: (1) general knowledge, (2) affective development, (3) sexuality, (4) self-esteem, (5) personal relationships, (6) sexual abuse, (7) drug abuse, and (8) sexual responsibility.

Training for special education and secondary school health education teachers is essential. Preservice and in-service training must include legal, ethical, religious, and medical issues as well as topics such as death and dying and family support (Evans, Melville, & Cass, 1992). In addition, the universal precautions for handling body fluids should be part of the core knowledge of all teaching professionals (Edens, Murdick, & Gartin, 2003).

Strategy instruction must address the needs of special populations. Students with disabilities are in greater need of useful sex education because they have fewer opportunities to learn sex-related facts and are at greater risk of exploitation. Programs for this population must include direct skills training and ongoing support for use of those skills (Scotti, Speaks, Masia, & Drabman, 1996).

Teacher Responsibilities

The increasing interdisciplinary nature of treatment of adolescents with HIV requires full teacher participation in intervention and education. The National Forum on HIV/AIDS Prevention recommends that special educators collaborate with health educators to do this (Byrom & Katz, 1991). In addition, special educators need to adapt and modify the existing juvenile teaching resources dealing with the topic of HIV/AIDS for students with disabilities (Prater & Sileo, 2001). The overwhelming fear and prejudice associated with HIV and the tendency to blame the victim must be dispelled. Imparting factual information in an open, honest manner is imperative. Facts about HIV and AIDS are given in Action Plan 3.13.

Identifying the Problem   There are no easily identifiable signs to alert the teacher that students need help for sexually transmitted diseases. If a student confides in the teacher that he or she has an STD, the teacher must immediately refer the student for testing, counseling, and treatment immediately. Teachers may recommend testing to students who appear to be at high risk because of their sexual behaviors and/or drug-related problems. However, every effort must be made to ensure confidentiality. Identification and referral may be facilitated if teachers keep the lines of communication open so students feel comfortable in approaching them and seeking assistance.

Preventing the Problem   Discussion must focus on HIV prevention because of its seriousness and because the same measures can prevent other STDs as well. Abstinence, mutual monogamy in uninfected couples, and no intravenous drug use are the only sure

---

Action Plan 3.13   Some Facts about HIV and AIDS

Teachers must make sure students know the following facts about HIV and its implications:

- AIDS stands for acquired immunodeficiency syndrome.
- There is no cure for AIDS.
- The human immunodeficiency virus (HIV) causes AIDS.
- AIDS does not discriminate among sex, race, profession, geographic location, sexual orientation, or socioeconomic status.
- People infected with HIV look and feel healthy for years.
- HIV is transmitted through sexual intercourse, sharing syringes, blood transfusion, the placenta, and breast milk.
- It is possible, but not likely, to get HIV if infected blood enters the body through cuts, sores, or other breaks in the skin.
- There is no risk of transmission through contact with stool, nasal fluids, urine, or vomit unless these fluids contain visible blood.
- Simple first aid steps and cleaning of equipment provide protection against HIV.

ways to prevent AIDS. Information on STDs and AIDS must be integrated into health or sex education programs. Ideally, an interdisciplinary program will be integrated across the curriculum through the cooperation of health teachers, content area teachers, special educators, social workers, and speech, vocational, and occupational therapists (Oliver, Anthony, Leimkuhl, & Skillman, 2002). Teachers must familiarize themselves with curricula adopted by schools on these topics and share this knowledge with their students. Wolfe and Blanchett (2003) have developed an evaluation guide to analyze the components of sex education curricula for students with disabilities. Teachers should determine that (1) the publisher designed the materials for students with disabilities, (2) the reading level is appropriate, and (3) the material can be adequately modified. Curricula may vary in coverage, and school district policies may dictate what information can be given to students.

Teachers can aid in prevention of STDs by conducting classroom discussion on topics critical to issues surrounding the sexual activities of adolescents. During such discussions, students should be encouraged to delay sexual activity and to practice safe sex when they decide to become sexually active. Distribution of condoms in school is controversial. Information regarding condom purchase and use may be provided. Discussion should also focus on AIDS in relation to homosexuality, sharing needles for drug use, and contact with blood and other body fluids. Researchers have found that, in the past, teachers, parents, and other caregivers were often reluctant to engage in frank and open conversations about sexuality with students with disabilities. The failure to prepare for adult sexuality, however, often leads to inappropriate behavior, misconceptions, and sexual exploitation of adults with disabilities (Hingsburger & Tough, 2001; Lesseliers & Van Hove, 2001; Stinson, Christian, & Dotson, 2001).

Misconceptions must be dispelled (see Action Plan 3.14) as well as irrational fears and rumors. Teachers must conduct social skills training sessions focusing on how to say no, negotiating mutually acceptable solutions, and making decisions regarding safe sex. Students will benefit from practice related to skills acquired in the classroom. They can be

---

Action Plan 3.14   Misconceptions Regarding Transmission of the AIDS Virus (HIV)

Students may believe that one can get the AIDS virus (HIV) through:

- Hugging, touching, cuddling, shaking hands
- Sneezing, coughing, sweat, and tears
- Sharing forks, knives, spoons
- Eating meals cooked and/or served by someone with AIDS
- Sharing toilet or shower facilities
- Swimming pools
- Telephones
- Sports equipment
- Chairs, computers, desks, or bus seats
- Mosquitoes, bed bugs, lice, flies, or other insects
- Pets

Teachers must provide students with accurate information.

given assignments that involve purchasing a contraceptive and discussing birth control with a dating partner. Several curricular materials are available that describe how teachers might teach these skills. Agencies listed in Action Plan 3.15 may be useful.

Involving Parents   Parents of all students need to know the facts related to STDs so they can make informed decisions. The National Commission on AIDS (1994) recommended involving parents in the development of AIDS policies and curricula, which could help empower them and alleviate some of their concerns. Families of adolescents with HIV consistently report feelings of isolation, stigmatization, fear, depression, anger, and guilt (Johnson, 1991). Teachers must understand parental fears and emotions and help establish support networks for both the student and the family. They must also be aware that some parents may display limited participation due to physical, financial, and emotional stresses of dealing with HIV.

Parents may also seek information and education from school personnel. Miller and Downer (1988) demonstrated that a 50-minute training session significantly increased AIDS awareness and resulted in higher levels of tolerance and compassion for people with AIDS.

Parents may need advice on how to talk to their children. Most parents do not feel comfortable approaching the topic of sex and sexuality. Adolescents sometimes require explicit information. Cultural views regarding sexual issues and levels of comfort in discussing such issues must be studied and considered before discussion with parents. Teachers can refer parents to sources of information, including the agencies, publications, and materials provided in Action Plan 3.15.

Teenage Pregnancy

Incidence

In 1991 the pregnancy rate for women aged 15 to 19 years was 61.8%, and in 2002 the rate fell to 43.0%. During the same period, the teen pregnancy rates for unmarried black teenagers fell 40%. This decline in teen pregnancy is attributed to (1) postponement of sexual activity by teens and (2) improved contraceptive use (Centers for Disease Control, 2003). In spite of the progress illustrated by these figures, there is still room for improvement. Although exact numbers on the pregnancy rate among teenagers with disabilities are not available, unwanted pregnancies among this population occur frequently (Kerr, Nelson, & Lambert, 1987).

Causes

Klein (1978) identified several factors contributing to teenage pregnancy, including societal attitudes that popularize sexual activity; the failure of sex and family education; and the failure to provide birth control, early pregnancy detection, and prenatal care. Some adolescents fulfill their need for love, self-esteem, peer acceptance, and independence by sexual promiscuity (Muccigrosso, Scavarda, Simpson-Brown, & Thalacker, 1991). Rebellion against family norms or the lack of family control or direction are other contributing factors. Adolescents from single-parent families and those with working mothers are more likely to be sexually

Action Plan 3.15   Resources for AIDS Education

Teachers may contact the following resources for information regarding AIDS:

Websites

Centers for Disease Control and
  Prevention
www.cdc.gov

Planned Parenthood
www.plannedparenthood.org

U.S. Department of Education
www.ed.gov

Hot Lines

The Minority Task Force on AIDS
Information for women
212-563-8340

National AIDS Information Hot Line
800-342-AIDS
In Spanish
800-344-SIDA
TTY/TDD users
800-AIDS-TTY

CDC Sexually Transmitted Diseases
  National Hotline
800-227-8922
In Spanish
800-344-7432 (8 AM to 2 PM)
TTY/TDD users
800-243-7889 (Mon to Fri 10 AM to 10 PM)

Agencies and Organizations

AIDS Resource Center/National PTA
700 North Rush Street
Chicago, IL 60611
312-787-0977

American Foundation for AIDS Research
  (amfAR)
120 Wall Street; 13th Floor
New York, NY 10005-3908
212-806-1600   212-806-1601 (FAX)
www.amfAR.org

CDC National Prevention Information
  Network (NPIN)
P. O. Box 6003
Rockville, MD 20849-6003
800-458-5231
www.cdcnpin.org
email: info@cdcnpin.org

Kaiser Family Foundation (KFF)
2400 Sand Hill Road
Menlo Park, CA 94025
650-854-9400   650-854-4800 (FAX)
www.kff.org

Publications

AIDS: What Young Adults Should Know
The American Alliance for Health,
  Physical Education, Recreation,
  and Dance
1900 Association Drive
Reston, VA 22091
800-321-0789

*Learning AIDS: An Information Resources
  Directory*
American Foundation for AIDS Research
  (amfAR)
120 Wall Street; 13th Floor
New York, NY 10005-3908
212-806-1600   212-806-1601 (FAX)
www.amfAR.org

U.S. Center for Disease Control
  Publications
  *Guidelines for School Health
    Education to Prevent the Spread
    of AIDS*
  *STD: A Guide for Today's Young
    Adults*
  *AIDS: What Young Adults Should
    Know*
  Teens and AIDS: Playing It Safe

Database

U.S. Public Health Services
  Combined Health Information
  Database (CHID)

Includes:
  AIDS resources bibliography
  School programs
  Policies
  Films, videotapes, audiotapes,
    books, journal articles
  Parent materials
  Teacher training programs
www.chid.nih.gov

Training Programs

Abstinence-Based Programs
Postponing Sexual Involvement
Cincinnati Children's Hospital
  Medical Center
Postponing Sexual Involvement
  Office
c/o Hughes Center, Suite 334
2515 Clifton Avenue
Cincinnati, OH 45219
513-363-7795
www.cincinnatichildrens.org/svc/
email: christopher.kraus@cchmc.org

Choosing the Best
Choosing the Best Publishing
2625 Comberland Pkwy., Suite 200
Atlanta, GA 30339
800-774-2378
770-803-3110 (FAX)
www.choosingthebest.org

Books and Magazines

Jeanne Blake, *Risky Times: How to Be
  AIDS-Smart and Stay Healthy.* New
  York: Workman, 1990.

K. Hein and T. F. DiGeronimo,
  *AIDS: Trading Fears for Facts:
  A Guide for Teens.* New York:
  Consumer Union of the United
  States, 1989.

E. M. Johnson. *What You Can Do to
  Avoid AIDS.* New York: Random
  House, 1992.

Straight Talk
Magazine for teenagers
Rodale Press
33 East Minor Street
Emmaus, PA 18098

Curricula

*AIDS Education—Supplemental Teaching
  Guide*
Columbus Health Department, AIDS
  Program
181 Washington Blvd.
Columbus, OH 43215

*AIDS Instructional Guide,
  Grades K–12*
New York State Education Department
State University of New York
Bureau of Curriculum Development
Albany, NY 12234
www.emsc.nysed.gov/rscs/chaps/
  HIV/HIV

*SAFE: Stopping AIDS through
  Functional Education*
For adolescents with mental
  retardation
University Affiliated Programs
Oregon Health Sciences University
Child Development and Rehabilitation
  Center
Portland, OR 97203

(continued)

Action Plan 3.15   Resources for AIDS Education *(continued)*

Videos	*Materials*
It Can Happen to You: Adolescents and AIDS Ohio Department of Health 35 East Chestnut St. Columbus, OH 43215 614-644-1838	Body Charts Planned Parenthood of Minnesota 1965 Ford Parkway St. Paul, MN 55116

*Saving a Generation: Successful Teaching
    Strategies for HIV Education in Grades
    4–12*
Select Media
74 Varick Street
Third Floor
New York, NY 10013
212-431-8923
	Effie Dolls
	Anatomically correct cloth dolls
	Judith Franning
	4812 48th Avenue
	Moline, IL 61265
	
	Wrap It Up!
	Rock and roll message for safer sex
	Tulare County Children's Mental Health
	    Services Consortium
	3350 South Fairway, Suite A
	Visalia, CA 93227
	209-733-6944

Teen AIDS in Focus San Francisco Study Center P. O. Box 425646 San Francisco, CA 94142-5646 800-484-4173	

active (Fick, 1984). Disillusionment about personal future may motivate other youngsters to seek pleasure (Gibbs, 1993). Exploitation by strangers, acquaintances, or even family members or caregivers may also occur, especially among adolescents with intellectual disabilities, who are vulnerable to sexual abuse and pregnancy (Levy, Perhats, & Johnson, 1992).

Numerous other factors contribute to improper sexual behavior. Several myths surround the sexuality of adolescents with disabilities that make it difficult to dispel misconceptions and promote their education. Myths attribute either asexuality or oversexuality to adolescents with disabilities. There is an unspoken yet prevalent belief among nondisabled members of society that only physically fit, young, intelligent, vocationally able individuals are entitled to express sexual feelings (Thorn-Gray & Kern, 1983). Opportunities for sexual expression are severely limited among individuals with disabilities who lack interpersonal skills, physical attributes, financial resources, dating options, and contacts with potential partners. Furthermore, adolescents with disabilities have few if any occasions to observe sexual interchange among others and thus have no models of appropriate behavior. This limited knowledge of sociosexual skills has contributed to the inappropriate sexual behavior exhibited by adults with disabilities and has become a challenge for community service providers (Ward, Trigler, & Pfeiffer, 2001)

Intervention Needs

Reducing teenage pregnancy must be given prime consideration. Pregnant teenagers are at serious socioeconomic disadvantage throughout their lives. They are generally less educated, have larger families (National Research Council, 1987), and are at risk for health complications. Only one-half of the women who have their first child before age 17 will graduate from high school, compared to 96% of those who do not have children before age 20 (National Organization on Adolescent Pregnancy, Parenting, and Prevention, 1995). Nearly 60% of teenage mothers live in poverty at the time of the birth (Alan Guttmacher Institute, 1994). These statistics highlight the necessity of immediate attention to this national concern.

Sex education programming in the nation's schools is currently insufficient; 13 states do not require sexuality education in their schools, and 15 states require only STD/HIV education (NARAL Foundation, 1995). Furthermore, in many states, this mandate may be fulfilled by a 45-minute class. Opponents of sex education fear increase in sexual behavior due to exposure to such programs. However, this fear is not supported through research, which showed no increase in early onset of intercourse (Kirby, 1997). Similarly, condom availability does not result in increased sexual activity among high school students but does affect condom use (Guttmacher et al., 1997). Sex education for students with disabilities is even more neglected. Secondary students with mild mental retardation have been found to be grossly uninformed and/or seriously misinformed (Brantlinger, 1984). These sexual attitudes and the lack of knowledge could lead to irresponsible sexual behavior. Relevant education must be provided to avoid sexual ignorance among adolescents, especially those with disabilities, in light of the movement toward inclusion of these individuals in every aspect of life.

Special education teachers need preservice and in-service training. Fewer than half of the special education teachers responding to a survey included sex education in their curriculum, and the rest covered it cursorily (Brantlinger, 1984). At the same time, these teachers expressed concerns over problematic sexual information, sexual activity, and misinformation prevalent among their students. Providing guidance and information to students with disabilities represents a proactive approach to reducing teen pregnancy and sexual exploitation; however, barriers remain in the reluctance to honestly face the issue of sexuality in individuals with disabilities (Wolfe & Blanchett, 2003).

Teacher Responsibilities

Teachers must recognize that the only effective way to avoid long-term negative outcomes for their teenage students is through education. More important, teachers can be instrumental in promoting a positive and hopeful outlook among students regarding their future, which will motivate them to become responsible and to avoid unwanted pregnancy. The following paragraphs suggest some ways in which teachers can help students.

Identifying the Problem Teachers must be sensitive to the interpersonal dynamics among students in the classroom. A display of interest and concern regarding sexuality may motivate students to seek help and advice. Students should feel free to discuss any problems, fears about diseases, anxieties about relationships, or undesirable experiences with an adult at school or home. This sensitivity may ensure early intervention in cases requiring immediate medical attention and may also prevent future emotional problems. Teachers must be prepared to help those who ask for assistance and direction without letting their moral opinions and values govern their actions. They must be ready to make arrangements for referral to health care agencies and counseling services. The PLISST model program, developed by Jack Annon (in Muccigrosso et al., 1991), outlines four levels of intervention and is designed to assist the teacher in determining when a referral to another professional is necessary. *P* represents giving permission to recognizing sexuality concerns; *LI* stands for expanding limited information; *SS* stands for providing specific suggestions; and *T* represents seeking therapy.

Preventing the Problem   Teachers might stress the following topics during sex education. First, masturbation is normal at any age or with any frequency, provided it occurs in private. This issue is important, as it may be the main channel of release for individuals with disabilities and, if ignored, may result in incidents in inappropriate settings. Second, students must be taught that pregnancy is always a possibility during intercourse and that birth control is mandatory. Third, adolescents can be taught that they do not have to engage in sexual acts if urged to do so and that it is wrong to force someone else to perform sexual acts. The likelihood of legal consequences can be stressed. Fourth, students must be told not to accept offers of money or other goods in exchange for sexual favors. Fifth, students need information on STDs owing to the increasing risk of AIDS. Role-play situations, films, and demonstrations may be helpful in teaching adolescents how to react under certain circumstances. A social skills curriculum must include opportunities to interact with the opposite sex during social situations.

Teenage girls with disabilities may require extended education using instructional techniques and materials suited to their functional abilities. An assessment of their awareness of giving birth and raising a family must be conducted. Youth with disabilities may have misconceptions about the hardships involved in bringing up a child. They have to be given a realistic picture of different aspects of child rearing through films, role-play, or simple questioning techniques. A visit to a nursery or a daycare center may make them more aware of skills and resources necessary for a parent.

Involving Parents   Parents are often ambivalent and confused about the sexuality of their teenaged children with disabilities. They feel inadequate when it comes to providing sexual information, although they agree, more frequently than parents of nondisabled youth, that their children should receive education in this area. Haavik and Menninger (1981) found that most parents who sought professional advice did so to help their adolescent with issues related to sexuality. Parents' personal feelings and beliefs regarding behaviors such as masturbation and other sexual issues must be explored. Some parents may have misconceptions about certain behaviors and may react to the situation by punishment that may be unnecessary or even potentially harmful. They may be referred to a counselor or therapist to help resolve the problem.

If teachers suspect that a student is pregnant, parents must be contacted and solutions identified to secure the well-being of all involved. Teachers can make referrals to agencies that can consult with the teenager and parents on the best course of action. Several issues have to be addressed, including the young woman's ability to carry, give birth, and raise a child; economic factors; the possibility of adoption; parental support; and genetic factors. Parent participation is essential if these problems are to be resolved.

Summary

Adolescence places several challenging demands on youngsters who are faced with major decisions concerning their future. Societal and physiological demands requiring adaptations in personal development, social roles, and parental and peer expectations often result in confusion, loss of self-confidence, and frustration among adolescents. Most emerge from the experience with new skills and motivations; however, others are unable to cope as effectively and may undergo intense feelings of hopelessness, insecurity, and depression. Obstacles such as drugs and alcohol, pregnancy, suicide, or participation in delinquent acts further complicate their lives. Most adolescents are able to cope with potentially harmful influences, although young individuals with disabilities may require special help and guidance.

Incidence figures on juvenile delinquency, dropping out, substance abuse, suicide, and sexual behavior related to individuals with disabilities provide a dismal picture of the scope of these problems and highlight the immediate need for collaborative programmatic efforts. Teachers can help to identify and prevent these problems. In particular, they should learn to look for the specific signs of different problems and learn how to minimize their impact on youth with disabilities.

4

Instructional Methods for Secondary Learners with Disabilities

Did you know that . . .

- Students with disabilities are more likely to forget recently acquired knowledge and skills?

- All students, including those with disabilities, are expected to master state standards and participate in state- and districtwide assessments?

- There are two types of curricular orientations that should be considered when selecting goals for secondary students with disabilities?

- Age is a key factor in making the shift from a developmental to a functional orientation?

- Annual goals must be included on the IEP?

- Short-term objectives are derived from annual goals?

- A short-term objective has four components?

- Teachers rarely deviate from their written lesson plan?

- Including contingency plans increases teacher flexibility?

- Materials for secondary learners with disabilities are scarce?

- Specific teacher behaviors are associated with student achievement?

- Both large and small group instruction can be individualized?

- There are six levels of prompts?

- Homework should be given only to strengthen knowledge or skills already presented in class?

- Learning strategies are used primarily with secondary students who have learning disabilities?

- There are strategies for specific content areas and strategies that cut across content areas?

- Critics of direct instruction and the strategies intervention model argue that such approaches make students passive learners?

- Constructivism has its roots in the works of Piaget and Vygotsky?

- Constructivists believe students should be active learners who create their own knowledge?

- Teachers are not completely convinced of the appropriateness of grading adaptations?

- Pass/fail options, checklists, and comments may be more appropriate grade formats for students with disabilities?

Can you . . .

- Define a standard?
- Describe the link between a standard and the curriculum?
- Identify the features of an appropriately written standard?
- Define direct instruction?
- Write an annual goal?
- Derive short-term objectives from an annual goal?
- Develop a task sequence from a short-term goal?
- Differentiate between advance planning and contingency planning?
- Write a lesson plan that includes a contingency plan?
- Write a lesson plan that reflects guidelines for presenting new information?
- Develop prompting hierarchies for academic and motor skills?

- Determine how much time an eleventh-grader should spend doing homework?
- Describe a learning strategy?
- Explain the goals of a learning-strategies curriculum?
- Define constructivism?
- Identify the basic premises of constructivism?
- Describe the role of proximal development?
- Explain how constructivism differs with respect to the role of the learner and the teacher, content, context, motivation, and assessment?
- Identify the purpose of grades?
- Identify four standards for effective grading practices for students with disabilities?
- Use a decision model to collaborate with another professional when assigning grades to students with disabilities?

The Individuals with Disabilities Education Act of 1997 clearly mandates that consideration be given to placing students with disabilities in the general education setting. Therefore, secondary educators who previously were used to having students with disabilities served elsewhere now face the challenge of meeting the needs of these students in the general classroom. Increased numbers of secondary students with special needs have added to the responsibilities already shouldered by high school teachers in the general classroom. They must select which instructional techniques can be used to facilitate skill development by students with disabilities and their nondisabled peers. Even if the nature or severity of the disability warrants placement in a more restrictive setting, such as a self-contained classroom, special educators will need to use instructional methods that will maximize student gains. Educators in both settings need to be aware of the fact that time is running out for secondary students with disabilities. Most students will arrive in the secondary setting with deficits in skills and background knowledge and with a limited amount of time remaining in their academic career. Practitioners have much to do and very little time in which to do it. They need to identify important, relevant areas of the curriculum; teach in exciting, interesting ways; and provide several opportunities for students to practice and demonstrate mastery.

A major goal for adolescent learners is to acquire the tremendous amount of information presented in the secondary general education curriculum. Students with disabilities will need to master a secondary curriculum that is organized according to departments or subject matter, unlike the elementary school system with which they are familiar. Students are expected to be more independent. They must learn to deal with several teachers over the course of the school day. They must deal with a curriculum that is supposed to be preparing all students to meet common standards. They are expected to attain high standards with grading requirements that seem less clearly defined. The method of instruction may no longer reflect the way they learn. For example, students may not do as well in high school classrooms in which the teacher uses a lecture format as the primary method of instruction. In addition, several factors limit the extent to which secondary learners with disabilities can accomplish this task. These factors reflect general learning and behavioral characteristics of individuals with disabilities, which are presented in Action Plan 4.1. First, according to Schloss and Sedlak (1986), many of these learners acquire information and skills at a slower rate than their nondisabled peers. They simply require more time to learn things. Second, youth with disabilities are less likely to benefit from incidental information. Many of the skills mastered informally by their nondisabled peers, such as social skills and leisure skills, will have to be directly taught to them. Third, knowledge and skills mastered in one setting may not be used in other settings by students with disabilities. For example, the study skill taught by the consulting teacher may not automatically be used by the student with disabilities who is preparing for a biology test. Finally, students with disabilities are less likely to retain newly acquired information following instruction. Teachers will have to provide review and practice activities to make sure these students maintain their skill levels.

As a result of these characteristics, secondary students with disabilities may not bring to the learning situation all the prerequisite skills necessary for success in the secondary school. Teaching content clearly and appropriately to secondary students with disabilities is not an easy task. High school teachers may be responsible for teaching content material across different grade levels. They may need to switch classrooms as often as their students do. Their instructional year may be broken up into semesters, quarters, or even shorter periods of time, leaving them little time to get to know their students and address unique learning problems.

Conderman and Katsiyannis (2002) surveyed secondary special educators to identify the roles these professionals assume, how they spend their time, and their perceptions of various instructional approaches. Results indicated that special educators fulfill a variety of roles and have diverse responsibilities. They consulted with general education, co-taught in general education settings, coordinated work experiences, provided vocational education, developed IEPs, and conducted assessments. They used more than one instructional orien-

---

Action Plan 4.1   Learning and Behavioral Characteristics of Students with Disabilities

Teachers should be aware that the following characteristics can influence the knowledge and skills acquired by students with disabilities:

1. Information and skills are acquired at a slower rate.
2. Information and skills are less likely to be acquired through experiences incidental to the learning task.
3. Information and skills acquired in one setting are less likely to generalize to other settings or conditions.
4. Information and skills are less likely to be retained following instruction.

tation to provide content area instruction and to teach learning strategies and transition, social/emotional development, and functional living skills. In their discussion, Conderman and Katsiyannis emphasized the importance of using best practices and balancing instructional approaches to ensure students complete required courses and develop functional skills needed for graduation and successful transition.

Learning Standards and the General Education Curriculum

All states have moved toward the establishment of standards that serve as the basis for (1) organizing and designing curriculum and instruction and (2) evaluating the performance of all students, including those with disabilities. Developed by national, state, and local curriculum groups and by subject area experts, the purpose of a standard is to identify clearly the knowledge, skill, or understanding a student should have in a particular subject. Standards are what state and local education agencies value, and what teachers must teach and assess. All states have developed standards for reading and mathematics, and the overwhelming majority have developed standards for written language and science. Students with disabilities are expected to achieve the same standards as their typical peers and earn high school diplomas (Boyle et al., 2003; Conderman & Katsiyannis, 2002; Schumaker & Deshler, 2003; Schumaker, Deshler, Bulgren, Davis, Lenz, & Grossen, 2003). According to Munroe and Smith (cited in King-Sears, 2001), curricular standards are characterized by the following:

1. They are clearly written and jargon free.
2. They are specific in that they identify the knowledge students must acquire and the skills they must demonstrate.
3. They are balanced in that they do not direct students toward one moral or social perspective.
4. They use action verbs that describe what students must know or do, such as *analyze, compare, explain, make,* and *use.*
5. They include benchmarks, that is, specific activities by which students can demonstrate mastery of a standard.
6. They guide teachers in the development or selection of appropriate activities, materials, and teaching methods.

Standards are translated into national, state, or local general education curricula. A *curriculum* is defined as "an overall plan for instruction adopted by a school or a district" (Hitchcock, Meyer, Rose, Jackson, 2002, p. 10) that guides teachers in what to teach yearly, by semester, quarterly, and on a day-to-day basis. IDEA mandates participation of students with disabilities in the general education curriculum and in district- and statewide assessments. Therefore, all professionals working with secondary special needs students must obtain and review these curriculum guides. They should familiarize themselves with what students are expected to learn and do to indicate they can meet standards (King-Sears, 2001).

A curriculum can reflect a universal design to meet the needs of all learners, including those with disabilities (Pisha & Coyne, 2001). The concept behind universal design is to include elements or features within a system so that it has more widespread application. Applied to architecture, universal design ensures the construction of buildings that feature ramps and wider doors. Thus, these buildings are accessed with relative ease by able-bodied individuals and people who use wheelchairs. A curriculum reflects the concept of universal design by recognizing the diversity of today's students and providing options to support learning difference from the start of an educational career. Hitchcock and colleagues (2002) said that a curriculum that incorporates universal design has several design features. It includes (1) goals that challenge all students, (2) materials that have a flexible format to support all students' learning, (3) flexible instructional methods that challenge but support all learners, and (4) assessment that enables teachers to make instructional adjustments. Teachers can use these design features to evaluate the general education curriculum and supplement when one or more of these features is missing or incomplete. For example, the teacher may need to identify additional review activities to ensure that students develop skill fluency. Some supplements may be more challenging to develop. For example, a special educator may have limited background in social studies and not be able to identify the goals associated with that curriculum. To solve this problem, the special educator should collaborate with a general educator with expertise in that area. With such supplements, many students with special needs may be able to proceed with general education curriculum instruction with little or no problem. Still others may need changes such as accommodations, adaptations, parallel construction, and overlapping curriculum outcomes (King-Sears, 2001). Accommodations can include use of audio recordings (Boyle et al., 2003), graphic organizers, and outlines (discussed in Chapter 15). An example of an adaptation is to allow the student to complete fewer math problems that are comparable in difficulty. In a parallel curriculum, the content is the same but the outcome is not. King-Sears (2001) described an example in which a student with a disability reads the same novel as typical peers but writes a brief report that describes one character instead of writing a lengthy analysis of the entire book. Finally, implementation of an overlapping curriculum enables students to use general education activities to meet goals selected from a functional curriculum.

General and special educators cannot and should not automatically assume that secondary students with disabilities will not benefit from exposure to the general education curriculum. In the absence of solid attempts to make the general education curriculum accessible, teachers may select and use another curriculum that may not challenge students. More important, use of another curriculum may undermine success and hurt performance on district- and statewide assessments.

Despite the importance of participating in mainstream schooling, it is likely that secondary students with disabilities will struggle to meet the demands of the general education curriculum due to poor reading skills and a lack of effective learning strategies (Boyle et al., 2003). They will require considerable instruction by a skilled teacher. Fortunately, there are instructional methods suitable for use with secondary learners with special needs regardless of the setting in which they are placed. This chapter describes three major instructional approaches, including direct instruction, the learning-strategies model, and constructivism.

Direct Instruction

The direct-instruction model "is a comprehensive system of instruction that integrates effective teaching practices with sophisticated curriculum design, classroom organization and management, and careful monitoring of student progress, as well as extensive staff development" (Stein, Carnine, & Dixon, 1998, p. 227). The model considers the fact that many students who enter school have academically less relevant background information when compared to their peers. It uses explicit, teacher-directed instruction to increase the quality and quantity of student learning by developing background knowledge, applying it, and linking it to new knowledge.

Direct-Instruction Curriculum Design

Engelmann and Carnine (1991) and Stein, Carnine, and Dixon (1998) emphasized that the heart of direct instruction (DI) lies in an analysis of the curriculum. They have identified five key curriculum design principles, listed in Action Plan 4.2, that serve as the foundation for direct-instructional programs. The first principle is to use "big ideas" to organize content. A big idea is a concept within a content area that makes it possible for students to acquire a substantial amount of knowledge in an efficient manner. For example, rather than teach students that the Revolutionary War resulted from a series of acts imposed by the British, students might be taught the relationship between the war and England's need to solve economic problems. Similarly, rather than teaching a series of facts, concepts, and rules about the earth, the oceans, and the atmosphere, teachers could focus on how convection links phenomena related to the earth, the oceans, and the atmosphere.

The second curriculum design idea is to teach explicit, generalizable strategies that can be applied to a broad range of problem types. For example, Stein and colleagues (1998) noted that younger learners are frequently introduced to fractions through activities that require them to mark part of a single object, such as one-half of a pie or one-quarter of a

---

Action Plan 4.2   Five Principles of Curriculum Design

Engelmann and Carnine (1991) and Stein, Carnine, and Dixon (1998) identified the following five principles of curriculum design:

1. Organize content around "big ideas." Big ideas can be found by:
   - Looking for concepts that frequently appear in a specific grade level
   - Identifying concepts that are allocated more time
   - Determining whether concepts that are allocated more time are important to teach at a specific grade level
2. Teach explicit, generalizable strategies that will enable students to solve problems.
3. Scaffold instruction so that students are supported by coaching, prompts, and feedback as they are learning strategies and materials. Support is gradually reduced as students complete tasks independently.
4. Integrate skills and concepts so that students know when to apply their knowledge and skills.
5. Provide an adequate review. Make sure it is:
   - Sufficient to maintain skills
   - Distributed over time
   - Cumulative
   - Varied to promote generalization and transfer of training

pizza. The problem is that these examples are less than or equal to one, which may cause difficulties when introducing improper fractions. A more generalizable strategy is to teach students to decode fractions. Students will have no problem with improper fractions if, from the beginning, they are taught that the denominator is the number of parts in each group and the numerator is the number of parts that are "shaded." Examples of proper and improper fractions are provided early in instruction, and students learn very quickly that $\frac{3}{2}$ means there are 1½ pizzas. In addition, it should be noted that direct instruction requires use of explicit strategies, as only a small number of students may be able to infer strategies from implicit instruction. Use of implicit strategies can be time consuming and inefficient for students with little time remaining in their academic careers.

Third, teachers are encouraged to scaffold instruction by providing students with support as they learn new strategies. This support can include coaching, prompting, and feedback from teachers, and use of peer activities, such as cooperative learning. Curriculum materials can be developed or selected that require students to complete tasks with decreasing levels of assistance.

The fourth principle of curriculum design is to integrate skills and concepts so that students learn when to apply their knowledge. Rather than teaching skills in isolation, teachers should provide a meaningful context. Students should learn basic punctuation skills, for example, but they should learn them in a context that emphasizes the role of punctuation in the process of editing a report for a content area.

Finally, the fifth principle of curriculum design requires teachers to provide an adequate review. This principle assumes that the quality of instruction was adequate in the first place, which will be the case if the previous four principles have been addressed.

The effectiveness of direct instruction has been well documented. Early studies involved regular elementary and intermediate students (Anderson, Evertson, & Brophy, 1979; Evertson et al., 1981; Fisher et al., 1978; Good & Grouws, 1979); the suitability of these techniques for elementary students with special needs has also been demonstrated (Chow, 1981; Leinhardt, Zigmond, & Cooley, 1981; Sindelar, Smith, Harriman, Hale, & Wilson, 1986) and extended to the secondary level (Stallings, Needles, & Stayrook, 1979). *Direct instruction* has been defined as the direct measurement of a student's performance on a learning task and the accompanying arrangement of instructional programs and procedures for each child (Haring & Gentry, 1976). Haring and Schiefelbusch (1976) identified the following phases of direct instruction:

1. Assessment of student characteristics
2. Establishment of instructional goals
3. Systematic planning of instruction
4. Use of instructional materials
5. Use of replicable instructional procedures
6. Use of motivating consequences
7. Monitoring of student progress

Secondary teachers who use direct-instruction procedures target a specific body of objectives they believe the learner should master. Usually, these objectives correspond to academic skills. For example, a history unit on civic responsibilities might include the procedures for nominating and electing candidates for the office of president of the United

States. Secondary special educators might also target another body of objectives addressing functional life skills, such as establishing and maintaining a checking account. After students demonstrate mastery of each body of objectives, the teacher targets another set and the process is repeated.

In summary, direct instruction is a comprehensive set of instructional practices that requires the teacher to evaluate the learning environment, define objectives, select and implement teaching techniques that reflect student characteristics, and apply motivating consequences (Schloss & Sedlak, 1986). The next section discusses each phase of direct instruction in detail.

The Sequence of Direct-Instruction Activities

As suggested earlier, direct instruction has been used successfully with students of all ages who display various disabilities. A number of experts have developed graphic representations of the sequence of activities they followed. These activities have been incorporated into the Sequence of Instructional Activities by Schloss and Sedlak (1986). A copy of their sequence is presented in Figure 4.1. Note that the information in the rectangles on the left side of the figure refers to the steps the practitioner takes in developing and delivering instruction. The vertical arrows connecting the rectangles indicate that instructional planning and delivery are proceeding normally. When difficulties are encountered, the practitioner is directed by the horizontal lines to the questions in the diamonds. Rather than assume that problems are the result of student flaws, the practitioner focuses attention on how the instructional program can be modified when resumed. Once the goal has been achieved, the entire sequence is repeated. This section describes each step of the sequence, with illustrations from the secondary special education literature.

Identify Learner Characteristics

The first step in the sequence is to identify the learner's characteristics. Practitioners need to conduct a thorough analysis of the strengths and weaknesses a student brings to the learning situation. Traditionally, this assessment is conducted by all members of the multidisciplinary team on a student's entry into the special educational program. Assessing a student's strengths, accomplishments, and weaknesses in all areas helps educators identify the current levels of instruction. This information is particularly important to have before placing the student in specific curricular programs. Such an assessment is also used to establish preintervention baselines against which subsequent achievement gains can be measured. Assessment data can also include information about students' motivation and reinforcement histories. This information will be valuable when selecting motivational techniques for use during the fourth step in this sequence.

Several formal and informal instruments are available to help practitioners assess secondary students. Formal measures include norm-referenced devices; informal measures include commercially produced criterion-referenced tests, curriculum-based measurement (CBM), systematic observation, trial teaching, skill checklists, student interviews, and rating scales. Houck (1987) suggested that secondary educators examine student records and interview significant others to determine the nature of previous educational interventions.

FIGURE 4.1 *The Sequence of Instructional Activities*

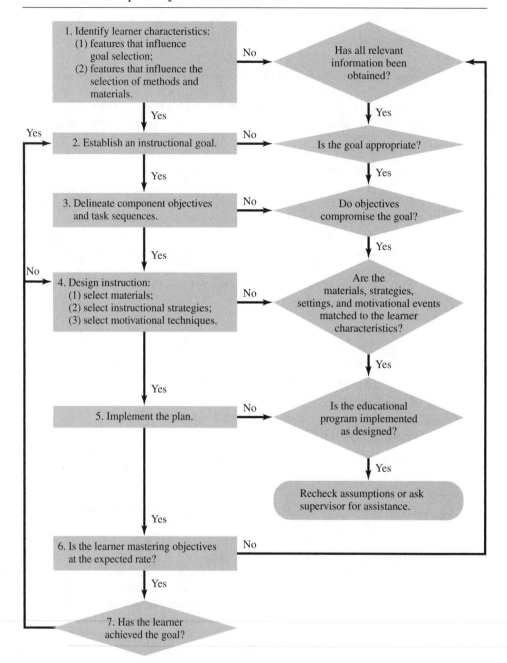

Source: From Patrick J. Schloss and Robert A. Sedlak, *Instructional Methods for Students with Learning and Behavior Disorders.* Published by Allyn and Bacon, Boston, MA. Copyright © 1986 by Pearson Education. Adapted by permission of the publisher.

Action Plan 4.3   Annual Goals and Related Instructional Objectives

Practitioners need to develop short-term objectives from long-range goals. The following example may be helpful:

Mark is a senior who is moderately retarded. Although he is living at home, he will be moving to a group home shortly after he graduates from high school. The multidisciplinary team has targeted the following goal:

Mark will develop independent living skills.

In addition, the team has decided that Mark should be placed in a functional curriculum. His teacher has developed the following objectives:

Given a destination time and place, Mark will use public transportation to arrive in a timely manner without assistance.

Given a recipe, Mark will locate the ingredients and follow the directions to prepare a nutritious dinner with no assistance.

During free time, Mark will identify and engage in a recreational activity with the peer of his choice.

Case for Action 4.1

Ramona is a senior with a mild learning disability. She has expressed an interest in attending a local community college to study hotel and restaurant management. Members of her multidisciplinary team have identified the following goal:

Ramona will improve her written language.

Develop the short-term objectives.

of authors have identified components of an advanced written lesson plan (Academy for Effective Instruction, 1987; Cohen, 1986). Action Plan 4.4 presents a lesson plan outline suitable for use with secondary learners.

During contingency planning, the practitioner reviews the advanced plan, identifies potential areas of student difficulty, and plans alternative instructional procedures. Although this process increases the amount of time practitioners must commit to planning, it has the advantage of building flexibility into the lesson plan. The practitioner can better respond to student difficulty because he or she will already have preplanned instructional alternatives to implement. Figure 4.2 presents portions of a direct-instruction lesson plan that incorporates contingency plans.

As suggested earlier, effective lessons are those that pay attention to materials, techniques, and motivation. Although these factors are discussed separately, it is important to remember that they are related. For example, selecting age-appropriate materials for use during the body of the lesson may motivate students to participate in the activity.

Action Plan 4.4   Components of a Written Lesson Plan for Use with Secondary Learners with Disabilities

Practitioners developing a lesson plan for secondary students should include the following components when using direct instruction:

1. Basic information
   a. Curricular area and skill
   b. Nature of lesson (e.g., mathematics/subtraction; introduction)
2. Objective
   a. Linked to the state standards
   b. Components
      i. Student orientation
      ii. Condition
      iii. Behavior
      iv. Criterion
3. Materials
4. Procedures
   a. Introduction: review previous material, motivate, establish purpose of current lesson
   b. Body: steps in the correct sequence, questions to ask students
   c. Conclusion: review, summarize main points
5. Evaluation
   a. Student performance: checklist, worksheet, systematic observation
   b. Teacher performance: strengths, weaknesses
6. Follow-up activities
   a. Review
   b. Extend
   c. Provide independent practice

Materials   As indicated in Chapter 1, educational programs for secondary students with special needs are seriously in need of suitable instructional materials. Although special education legislation has encouraged educators to produce more materials for learners with disabilities, the majority of commercially available material is designed for younger learners. Generally, secondary educators must choose between material that is intended for younger learners with disabilities and material for nondisabled secondary students. The materials that accompany a learning-strategies curriculum are different. Typically, the packets of instructional material and procedures include whatever the teacher needs to implement the program.

Practitioners should always be cautious in their selection of suitable materials. The importance of using relevant, age-appropriate materials that are attractive and well organized has been emphasized by many authors (Mercer & Mercer, 2005). Secondary teachers may need to look beyond traditional sources. For example, a few publishers offer high-interest low-vocabulary items that appeal to secondary students without overwhelming them; however, such materials may be expensive. Before purchasing any new materials, practitioners are advised to identify materials to which students have been exposed. This

FIGURE 4.2 *Contingency Plans Included in a Written Lesson Plan*

Objective

Given 10 word problems involving addition and subtraction, the student will use a calculator to compute the answer with 100% accuracy.

Procedures

1. Review previous work, describe today's activity, and emphasize how this skill will be useful to students.
2. Read a sample problem with the class. Determine the correct operation. Turn on the calculator. Show how to enter the first number, the operation sign, the second number, and the equal sign. Identify and record the answer.
3. Repeat with another problem requiring a different operation.
4. Show the class a third problem using a transparency on the overhead projector.
   a. Call on a student to read the problem out loud.
      Contingency: For a student unable to read parts of the problem, read it for him or her; then have the student repeat it.
   b. Determine the correct operation.
      Contingency: Students unable to determine the operation will be provided a list of key words and phrases that provide hints. For example, "How much more?" indicates subtraction.
   c. Turn on the calculator.
      Contingency: Use a red marker to highlight the "on" button for students unable to locate it.
   d. Enter the first digit of the first number.
      Contingency 1: Students unable to determine which number should be entered first will be assisted in setting up the problem on paper first.
      Contingency 2: Students unable to determine which digit of a number should be entered first will be told to enter the digits as they are softly repeated out loud.
   e. Enter the operation sign.
      Contingency: Students unable to locate the operation sign will be referred to a sample problem on the board and asked to match the sign written on the board with the button on the calculator.
   f. Enter the equal sign.
      Contingency: Use a blue marker to highlight the "=" button for students unable to locate it.
   g. Record the answer.
5. Repeat with another problem presented to the entire group.
6. Provide a worksheet with 10 word problems to those who needed no assistance during the teacher-directed activity.
   Contingency: Continue to work in a small group with those who experienced difficulty.
7. If time permits, allow students who have mastered the skill to go "Christmas shopping" using a catalog from a department store. Tell them they have $200 to spend. They must keep track of their expenses.
   Contingency: Have students previously engaged in small group instruction complete the worksheet containing 10 problems. Be available to provide assistance.

information can be obtained by reviewing the students' previous IEPs, checking with former teachers, and talking with the students themselves. In addition, practitioners are encouraged to consider nontraditional sources of material, such as the newspaper, music trade magazines, computers, and the library. Practitioners who need to minimize reading as the primary vehicle for acquiring new information might consider audiotapes, videotapes, and talking books. Chapter 6 presents additional information on the selection, adaptation, and development of appropriate materials for secondary students with disabilities.

Instructional Techniques   A substantial body of literature attests to the positive relationship between several instructional procedures and student achievement. Although the majority of these studies have involved younger learners (Anderson et al., 1979; Fisher et al., 1978; Good & Grouws, 1979), some have addressed the older student with disabilities (Stallings et al., 1979). These instructional procedures fall into three categories: presentation of new information, guided practice, and independent practice. A fourth category, review and reteach, is also discussed.

Presenting the Information.   The first phase of direct instruction consists of presenting new information and demonstrating a new skill. Although this seems to be a rather obvious step, a demonstration of the concept or skill students are expected to master is often omitted from the instructional activity or is poorly managed. Guidelines for demonstrating a concept or skill are listed in Action Plan 4.5.

The first guideline states that it is important to cue the students that instruction is about to begin. Students may be distracted because they have just arrived and are settling down for the day or have just completed another activity. Practitioners need to use a consistent, discrete cue signaling that instruction is about to begin and, therefore, the students should pay attention. For example, practitioners might flicker the lights or they might consistently use a phrase as simple as "All eyes up front" or "We are ready to start working." Eventually, students will learn that instruction will not proceed until they are all paying attention to the teacher. Practitioners are also advised to teach their students to capitalize on attentional cues the teacher may use during the presentation of new information. These cues include changes in intonation, volume, or pitch or the use of pauses or common phrases (e.g., "Now listen," "This is important"). These cues should signal that the learner is expected to pay close attention and take notes because this information is particularly important.

The second guideline suggests that during the presentation of information the learners should be motivated to participate in the planned activity. Sikorski, Niemiec, and Walberg (1996) suggested that teachers present a brief overview of any new concepts, relate these

---

Action Plan 4.5   Guidelines for Presenting New Information

Practitioners should present new information using the following guidelines:

1. Use a discrete cue to gain student attention.
2. Motivate the learners to participate in the activity.
3. Teach to large and small groups.
4. Model the skill or concept.

5. Use precise language.
6. Ask questions frequently.
7. Provide feedback.
8. Review material.

concepts to previous knowledge, inform students about critical questions they will need to answer, identify objectives, provide a schedule or sequence of instructional activities, explain their expectations, set standards for behavior, and pretest, if necessary.

The third guideline pertains to the size of the group being taught. Special educators have long held the belief that instruction is most effective when it is conducted on a one-to-one basis. Stevens and Rosenshine (1981) defined individualization from a different perspective. Rather than working one to one with a teacher, *individualization* refers to maximizing each student's success and confidence by providing activities that allow a high percentage of correct responses. Well-planned and carefully implemented group lessons can certainly accomplish this goal. Although some unique situations may warrant one-to-one instruction, it is generally not feasible for daily instruction in the secondary classroom. Many secondary students with disabilities are included in general classrooms; therefore, group size will reflect the number of students typically assigned to the class. In self-contained classrooms, it is possible that the teacher will be working with the entire group.

The fourth guideline states that practitioners should model the skill or concept to be mastered by the students. Modeling allows students to observe the correct performance of a skill they are expected to acquire by the end of the lesson. If the skill can only be acquired through a number of steps, then the practitioner should model and verbally describe each component in sequence. Several demonstrations or examples of the concept may have to be provided, depending on the learning characteristics of the students.

The fifth guideline for presenting new information calls for the use of precise language (Chilcoat, 1987). Students with special needs may be confused by statements that are vague, uncertain, or include irrelevant language. Teacher statements to the students should be grammatically correct, clear, specific, and expressive. They should provide students with the exact details needed to master the skill or concept.

Sixth, the practitioner should ask numerous challenging, higher-order questions while presenting information to determine the extent to which students are comprehending the material. Asking frequent questions keeps students alert, accountable, and on task. In addition, Stallings and colleagues (1979) recommended that questions be directed to specific students rather than to volunteers. Although volunteers usually raise their hands because they know the answer, their performance may not be representative of the entire group. Students' answers to questions allow the practitioner to detect and correct problems at an earlier stage and thus help students avoid repeating errors.

The seventh guideline is to provide feedback. Practitioners can enhance students' performance by explaining what was correct and incorrect about their responses. Feedback for a correct response can include a repetition of the answer and a compliment when appropriate. In the event of an inaccurate response, the practitioner can use corrective feedback. The exact nature of corrective feedback can vary. Stallings and colleagues (1979) recommended that the teacher respond to an incorrect answer with guides and probing questions. Stevens and Rosenshine (1981) suggested that the practitioner provide a hint, a rule, or a process that will enable the student to respond correctly. Feedback helps not only the individual who is

---

Case for Action 4.2

You are about to start a science lecture. How will you gain your students' attention?

receiving it directly but also other members of the instructional group. Those who were not called on but already knew the correct answer receive indirect confirmation of their responses. Those who did not know the answer can benefit from the instruction being given to a peer.

Finally, practitioners should review material at the end of the lesson or as they move from one part of the lesson to the next. They should encourage students to paraphrase or summarize new information and relate it to previous knowledge. They can review or highlight key points and help students relate one part of the lesson to another. Teachers can also suggest how new information can be applied to problem solving (Sikorski et al., 1996).

General secondary educators who have students with disabilities included in their content area classes will find that direct instruction will benefit *all* of their students, not just those with disabilities. Instruction that adheres to these guidelines helps students acquire new information in a systematic, efficient way. Having mastered the material under close teacher supervision, students are now ready to proceed to the guided practice phase of direct instruction.

Guided Practice.   The purpose of guided practice is to allow students to practice newly acquired skills under successively less structured conditions. This phase of instruction allows students to commit items to memory. Heward (2003) emphasized the role of guided practice in developing a student's fluency with the knowledge and skills they have just acquired. Students who can perform skills fluently and automatically can apply them to more complex tasks and problem solving. Guided practice activities foster automaticity (Carnine, 1989)—that is, the ability to access information and respond quickly. A student who can process information quickly can focus more of his or her attention on higher-order skills that require critical thinking. Creativity is enhanced as students develop competence and confidence (Heward, 2003).

Specifically, the practitioner fades out cues or prompts that may have been available to students during teacher-directed instruction. Prompts are events that help the student initiate a correct response. Schloss and Sedlak (1986) have arranged prompts in a hierarchy from least to most intrusive, as follows:

1. *Cue:* The teacher simply instructs the student to perform the behavior.
2. *Graphic product:* Students are shown an illustration of the product.
3. *Graphic process:* Students are shown an illustration of how a behavior is accomplished.
4. *Oral:* The teacher describes how a task is accomplished.
5. *Modeling:* The teacher identifies the correct answer or shows the student how to perform the behavior.
6. *Manual:* The teacher physically guides the student through the task.

The nature of the task determines which prompts are available to students during guided practice. Action Plans 4.6 and 4.7 present prompting hierarchies for academic and motor tasks. Prompts can be made more effective if the teacher takes the following five steps (Schloss & Sedlak, 1986):

1. Preplan the use of prompts. Compare the hierarchies in Action Plans 4.6 and 4.7 to see the impact that the target behavior has on the prompts selected for use. For example, motor activities readily lend themselves to graphic-process prompts; therefore, the teacher

Action Plan 4.6   A Prompting Hierarchy for an Academic Task

Prompts are more effective if their use is planned in advance, as in the following example:

The student is spelling words orally. The teacher has preplanned the following prompts:

1. *Cue:* Tell the student to spell the word *employer.*
2. *Graphic product:* Present a flash card for the student to read.
3. *Modeling:* Say, "e-m-p-l-o-y-e-r."

Action Plan 4.7   A Prompting Hierarchy for a Motor Skill

Prompts can be used to promote motor skills, as in the following example:

The student is laying out a pattern to make a pair of shorts. The teacher has preplanned the following prompts:

1. *Cue:* Lay out the pattern.
2. *Graphic product:* Show the student a bulletin board displaying a correctly laid out pattern.
3. *Graphic process:* Give the student a sheet listing the steps in order.
4. *Oral:* Describe how to lay out the pattern.
5. *Modeling:* Show the student how to lay out the pattern.
6. *Manual:* Physically guide the student's hands as the pattern is laid out.

---

who elects to use this level of prompt should have a bulletin board or illustration available for the student to look at.

   2. Begin with the least intrusive prompt and move up the hierarchy only as student responses warrant. For example, the teacher cues a student to begin a science experiment and waits three seconds for the student to initiate a response. If the student does not respond, the teacher should provide an oral prompt, describing the task to the student. After three more seconds, if the student is still unable to respond, the teacher should model the task for the student.

   3. Use only the least intrusive prompt necessary to ensure a high success rate. In the previous example, the teacher should stop progressing through the hierarchy if the modeling prompt is successful in producing the desired response. A manual prompt will undoubtedly be successful; however, its use may not be warranted.

   4. Always pair intrusive prompts with less intrusive prompts to facilitate fading. For example, the teacher pairs oral and modeling prompts when he or she describes how to conduct the experiment while demonstrating it. Eventually, the student's behavior will be prompted by the use of the less restrictive verbal prompt.

   5. Interrupt nontarget behaviors as soon as possible to reduce the amount of time students spend practicing errors. Schloss and Sedlak (1986) pointed out that if practice can strengthen appropriate behaviors, it can also strengthen inappropriate behaviors.

Case for Action 4.3

You are planning a lesson on check completion. What prompts will you have preplanned?

The basic point to remember is that guided practice activities give students access to a teacher. Should they encounter any difficulty, the teacher is immediately available to interrupt and correct any errors using the appropriate prompt. When students no longer require a prompt to produce the correct response, they are ready to try the independent practice activities.

Independent Practice.   At this phase of instruction, students can perform the skill correctly; however, they may need additional practice until the skill becomes automatic. Automaticity allows students to direct their efforts toward the acquisition of other concepts, skills, or strategies. Independent practice activities frequently involve the use of seatwork. Students complete drill sheets, workbooks, or chapter reviews. During school they may also use computer-assisted instruction, videotapes, and audiotapes. Stevens and Rosenshine (1981) suggested that teachers remain available to students in the event they need assistance; however, they warned that teacher contact of more than 30 seconds could indicate that students are not ready for independent practice activities on this particular skill.

One of the most widely used independent practice activities is homework (Mims, Harper, Armstrong, & Savage, 1991). Polloway, Epstein, Bursuck, Jayanthi, and Cumblad (1994) reported that of the 67 high school teachers they surveyed, 70.1% assigned homework two to four times a week, 13.4% assigned homework five times a week, 10.5% assigned it once a week, and 6% did not assign any homework. When teachers follow good policies, homework can be an effective learning tool, especially for students with disabilities (Epstein, Polloway, Foley, & Patton, 1993). It is assigned only after the teacher is sure that knowledge or a skill has been learned with approximately 90% accuracy. Homework can be assigned by both general and special educators as a way to ensure mastery and retention

Action Plan 4.8   Ways to Adapt Homework

Polloway, Epstein, Bursuck, Jayantni, and colleagues (1994) identified the following ways to adapt homework assignments:

1. Adjust the length of the assignment.
2. Adjust due dates.
3. Provide additional teacher assistance.
4. Provide a peer tutor.
5. Arrange a study group.
6. Include effort as part of the grading criteria.
7. Provide assistive devices, such as calculators and computers.
8. Give fewer assignments.
9. Provide extra credit options.
10. Modify the response format.

of a newly learned skill and its application to new situations. However, Salend and Schliff (1989) surveyed 88 teachers of students with learning disabilities and reported that the biggest problem with homework assignments was that the students did not complete them. Obviously, students will not benefit from work they do not do. To increase the effectiveness of homework and the likelihood that students will complete it, Bryan and Sullivan-Burstein (1997), Epstein and colleagues (1993), Hodapp and Hodapp (1992), Jayanthi, Bursuck, Epstein, and Polloway (1998), Mims and colleagues (1991), and Oppenheim (1989) have recommended the following teacher guidelines:

1. At the start of the school year, provide parents with information regarding course assignments, possible adaptations, the policy governing missed assignments, and extra credit. Polloway, Epstein, Bursuck, Roderique, and colleagues (1994) identified several homework adaptations, included in Action Plan 4.8.
2. Develop a method of record keeping, such as a homework notebook. Many school districts provide each student with an agenda that includes a school calendar, codes for dress and behavior, and a record of assignments. The assignment section or notebook can serve as an avenue for communication between the school and the home.
3. Encourage students to build time for homework into their daily routines.
4. Make sure that homework assignments are a review of skills or knowledge that has been presented and practiced in class.
5. Make sure that homework assignments are relevant to the long- and short-term goals of students with special needs.
6. When giving an assignment, state its purpose, review directions, complete an example, provide a time estimate, give a deadline for its completion, and describe how it will be graded.
7. Give assignments that can be completed within a reasonable time frame. Epstein and colleagues (1993) noted that a minimum of two hours should be required from high school students. Oppenheim (1989) recommended 10 minutes times the grade level as the amount of time a student should spend doing homework each weeknight.
8. Evaluate all assignments so that students know they are accountable for the work. In addition, teachers can determine whether knowledge or a skill is being applied correctly.
9. Consider the attention span and functional level of the student when developing assignments. Less able students will require longer amounts of time to do less homework.
10. Understand that homework may take a backseat to such issues as attendance and unusual family circumstances. Obviously, these issues must be addressed first.
11. Use a homework hot line or answering machine so that students and parents have access to information about homework. If possible, have a special section on the school website that students can access to find out information about assignments.
12. Consider teaching study skills.

Review and Reteach.   Experienced practitioners are familiar with the problems that secondary students with disabilities demonstrate in maintaining a level of skill or concept development. Concepts that are not immediately relevant to the students' needs, or skills that are not frequently practiced, may be lost after a period of time. Therefore, it is important to select carefully the concepts and skills that will be targeted for development. It is also important to provide periodic reviews of previously mastered material. Schloss and Sedlak (1986) have recommended that newly acquired concepts be reviewed daily, then weekly, then monthly.

Motivational Techniques   The third factor that should be considered while practitioners are planning for instruction is motivation. Practitioners need to motivate secondary students with disabilities to participate in activities similar to the ones in which they may have experienced little or no success. The previous sections have occasionally alluded to methods for accomplishing this task. First, teachers should select their goals and objectives with great care. These must reflect the students' interests and abilities. It was suggested earlier that secondary learners may be more motivated to participate in educational programs they have helped to develop; therefore, to the greatest extent possible, secondary students should attend and participate in multidisciplinary team meetings. Second, teachers are advised to explain the purpose of acquiring specific information or developing a skill. They should explain why this information or skill is important. Students who understand how knowledge or skills will contribute to their competence are more likely to participate in the instructional activity. Third, practitioners should pay close attention to the materials they incorporate into the lesson. Functional, age-appropriate materials that are bright, attractive, and novel will be more appealing to secondary learners with disabilities. Fourth, practitioners are advised to plan to use reinforcement when providing feedback for a correct response. This reinforcement may be a simple compliment or an elaborate contingency plan such as a token economy. Finally, at the end of a lesson, practitioners may need to reinforce student participation and achievement (see Chapter 6).

Implement Instruction

Having attended to materials, techniques, and motivation, the practitioner is now ready to implement the lesson plan. Brophy (1983) and Kounin (1970) have identified five behaviors displayed by effective teachers as they implement a lesson plan.

The first two behaviors are related: continuity and momentum. *Continuity* is displayed by the practitioner who builds one instructional sequence on another without omitting information or steps in the skill. *Momentum* refers to the ability to make quick, smooth transitions from one phase of the lesson plan to the next. Teachers who display these behaviors during their lessons keep their students attentive and on task.

Third, effective teachers have the ability to *overlap*. They must implement and monitor several activities simultaneously. For example, a practitioner who is directing a small-group lesson may also need to supervise two students engaged in peer tutoring. In addition, another student may be experiencing difficulty with seatwork while a fourth is completely off task and teasing a peer. In a situation of this type, the practitioner has to teach, supervise, assist, and correct—all within a narrow time frame.

Fourth, effective implementation of the lesson plan also depends on the teacher's *with-it-ness,* or the ability to anticipate problems and intervene before the situation gets out of hand. Consider the case of the secondary learner identified as behavior disordered who began to tap and then stomp his foot when a task became too frustrating. When these warning signs were ignored, the student progressed to even more disruptive behaviors. Of course, careful consideration of the nature of the independent task would have prevented the problem in the first place. In any case, attending to the student early in the chain of disruptive events minimizes its negative impact on other students and the flow of the lesson. Practitioners can be more "with it" by spending time developing contingency plans. They can also circulate among students engaged in guided and independent activities or, if directing a small group lesson, they can frequently scan the room to observe student activity.

Fifth, effective teachers hold their students *accountable* for their own learning. They direct frequent questions to both specific students and volunteers to keep all learners interested and attentive.

Evaluate Mastery of the Objectives

At this point, the practitioner determines the extent to which the students have mastered the objectives established earlier in the direct-instruction sequence. Although practitioners may choose from any number of assessment devices to make this determination, they are more likely to choose informal measures, such as paper-and-pencil tests, checklists, and systematic observations. Ideally, these devices will indicate the effectiveness of the instructional program by documenting gains in student achievement, and thus allow the practitioner to move on to the next set of objectives. However, as the horizontal arrows in Figure 4.1 indicate, the students may not master the objectives at the anticipated rate. Practitioners are then directed back through the sequence to generate hypotheses about factors that may have contributed to student difficulty. For example, the goals may have been inappropriate or the instructional objectives out of sequence. Perhaps the materials failed to motivate. After examining and ranking these hypotheses, the practitioner systematically alters one condition at a time, implementing instruction again until the culprit is identified and modified. This process keeps practitioners from automatically blaming the student for his or her inability to learn.

Determine Whether the Goals Have Been Achieved

Consistent, appropriate use of the sequence of instructional activities should enable students to master the objectives derived from each annual goal. Students now possess a specific body of skills that previously eluded them. Practitioners have documented the effectiveness of a specific set of techniques that promote skill development. These techniques will be used in the future to help students with similar characteristics acquire new skills.

Learning Strategies

Many secondary students with disabilities are included in general classes for a substantial part of the school day and are expected to master the same curriculum as their nondisabled peers (Lenz & Hughes, 1990; Schumaker & Deshler, 2003). Their success in these settings may be hindered by limited reading and writing abilities. They may not be able to obtain information from textbooks, write an essay, take notes, or study for a test. An instructional method involving the use of learning strategies was developed in response to the needs of secondary students with disabilities, particularly learning disabilities.

Deshler, Ellis, and Lenz (1996) stated that "an individual's approach to a task is called a strategy. Strategies include how a person thinks and acts when planning, executing, and evaluating performance on a task and its subsequent outcomes" (p. 12). Rogan, LaJeunesse, McCann, McFarland, and Miller (1995) defined *learning strategies* very simply as "ways of thinking, acting, and performing that enhance student learning" (p. 36). Over the last several years, many specific learning strategies have been developed, tested, and reported in the professional literature. The University of Kansas Center for Research on Learning (CRL) has organized this research into an instructional model called the *strategies intervention model (SIM)*. The model is based on the idea that practitioners should develop three instructional areas for effective instruction. First, some strategies can be applied to all content areas. For example, there are generic strategies for writing an opinion essay, taking notes, studying, and taking tests. Although each of these strategies makes an individual contribution to student achievement, they can be combined by students who must complete a complex task, such as a midterm examination. Some strategies are for specific content areas. Examples of generic and content-related strategies are listed in Action Plans 4.9 and 4.10. Ultimately, mastery of these strategies facilitates secondary students' ability to meet classroom demands for acquiring, storing, and expressing knowledge and skills within and across content areas. Second, SIM provides teachers with explicit instructional routines to assist students in mastering strategies that will enable them to learn content. Finally, SIM

Action Plan 4.9   Sample Generic Learning Strategies

A secondary teacher can teach learning strategies to students with disabilities so that they can complete generic tasks that are required across the curriculum. Such strategies include the following (Desher, Ellis, & Lenz, 1996):

1. To teach notetaking, teachers can use LINKS:
   L—Listen
   I—Identify verbal
   N—Note
   K—Key words
   S—Stack the information into outline form

2. To teach students how to study, teachers can use CRAM:
   C—Create an image
   R—Relate something
   A—Arrange boxes
   M—Make a code

3. To teach students how to respond to essay items on a test, teachers can use ANSWER:
   A—Analyze the situation
   N—Notice requirements
   S—Set up an outline
   W—Work in details
   E—Engineer your answer
   R—Review your answer

Action Plan 4.10   Sample Content Area Learning Strategies

A secondary teacher can teach learning strategies to students with disabilities so that they can master information within a specific content area, such as mathematics. Such strategies include the following (Desher, Ellis, & Lenz, 1996):

1. To compute basic facts, use DRAW:
   D—Discover the sign
   R—Read the problem
   A—Answer or draw and check
   W—Write the answer

2. To solve word problems, use FAST:
   F—Find what you are solving for
   A—Ask, "What are the parts of the problem?"
   S—Set up the numbers
   T—Tie down the sign

provides a strategic environment that will enable students to learn and generalize strategy use across a variety of settings.

The strategies intervention model is very different from other instructional models that may be available in a secondary classroom (Rogan et al., 1995). It requires students to assume responsibility for their own learning and performance, make a commitment to learning the strategies and generalizing their use, and, ultimately, become independent learners. Second, SIM provides enough information for students to use the strategies independently. They will learn when and where it is necessary to use a strategy, how to select from several options the strategy that is most appropriate for meeting task demands, how to complete the cognitive and physical demands required by the strategy, and how to monitor strategy use and outcomes. Third, SIM emphasizes generalization, so that students will use appropriate strategies correctly outside the instructional setting.

Characteristics of a Learning Strategy

An examination of the strategies provided in Action Plans 4.9 and 4.10 may highlight some of the features of a learning strategy. First, each strategy includes a mnemonic to help students remember the strategy. Many people use mnemonics to remember pieces of information. For example, HOMES is used to help students remember that Huron, Ontario, Michigan, Erie, and Superior are the names of the Great Lakes (mnemonics are discussed in Chapter 15). The mnemonic that represents a learning strategy is carefully constructed in that each letter represents an action word that cues the student to do something. The action may be covert, in that the student is required to engage in a cognitive effort, or overt, in that a student must physically do something. Typically, a mnemonic includes no more than seven steps, and the wording of each step is simple and to the point. The steps are carefully sequenced; following them should enable students to complete a specific outcome successfully.

Teaching a Learning Strategy

The ultimate goal of a learning-strategies curriculum is to develop skills that will enable the individual to analyze and solve novel problems encountered in academic and nonacademic settings. The individual will not only be able to meet the challenge presented by the immediate situation, but he or she will also be able to generalize these skills to other situations over time.

Bos and Vaughn (2002) noted that strategy instruction is actually a combination of techniques from behavior, cognitive, and social learning theories. These techniques promote a change in cognitive behavior through a specific series of steps that involve modeling, guided instruction, and self-regulation. Ellis, Deshler, Lenz, Schumaker, and Clark (1991) and Schumaker and Deshler (2003) described the following eight-stage sequence for teaching a learning strategy.

1. *Stage 1—Pretest and make commitments:* The teacher motivates students to learn a new strategy by making them aware of the specific task demands of their classes, how well they are currently doing, and how a strategy that is learned accurately and applied consistently can help them be successful. The teacher also assesses current levels of performance and then shares the results. He or she describes the requirements of mastering the strategy in terms of time and energy, and encourages students to make a commitment to learn and use it.

2. *Stage 2—Describe the strategy:* The teacher tells the students what the new strategy is all about and how it can alter learning and performing. The teacher needs to describe the overt and covert processes included in the strategy.

3. *Stage 3—Model the strategy:* An important part of teaching the strategy is showing students how to "self-talk" effectively to guide their performance. Rather than simply telling the students what to do, the teacher will need to demonstrate cognitive behaviors. This activity may feel strange because most teachers have not been trained to demonstrate their thought processes by thinking aloud. While thinking aloud, the teacher can demonstrate self-instruction, model how to do problem solving, and demonstrate monitoring.

4. *Stage 4—Verbally elaborate and rehearse the strategy:* Students should name the strategy steps automatically and in their own words.

5. *Stage 5—Allow for controlled practice and feedback:* Students need ample opportunity to practice using the new strategy with materials or in situations in which the demands of the general class setting are reduced. This way, students can focus attention on learning the strategy and building confidence and fluency. As students become more proficient, the teacher can make the materials and task more complex. The teacher provides students with feedback about their performance and offers suggestions for improvement. Cues are faded out over time until students no longer need assistance.

6. *Stage 6—Allow for advanced practice and feedback:* This stage is a milestone for students as they start to apply newly learned strategies to more complex assignments and materials typically found in the general education classroom. These assignments may be items students were previously unable to do well, if at all.

Case for Action 4.4

You are the consulting teacher in a secondary school. A secondary English educator is curious about the concepts of learning strategies and asks for an explanation. What will you tell her? How can you work with her to implement a learning-strategies curriculum?

7. *Stage 7—Confirm acquisition and make generalization commitments:* Stages 1 through 6 are critical to the learning process; stage 7 is critical to the application process. The teacher provides the students with an appropriate task and allows them to complete it under typical classroom conditions. The teacher emphasizes that the true measure of success will be the students' ability to use the strategy to meet the demands in other instructional settings.

8. *Stage 8—Generalize:* This stage requires students to apply and adapt the strategy independently across settings and tasks that vary in complexity and purpose. Students need to determine when to use the strategy, develop methods for remembering the strategy, and adapt the strategy as needed to meet additional problems and demands.

Constructivism

Critics argue that explicit instructional approaches such as direct instruction may not be the most effective way to enhance student achievement. It is argued that students are passive participants in such instructional formats because important information is transmitted to them from adults and textbooks. An alternative set of instructional procedures has been suggested that reflects a constructivist perspective. Constructivism has its roots in the works of Piaget (1970) and Vygotsky (1978). According to Harris and Graham (1994), Riedesel, Schwartz, and Clements (1996), and Reys, Lindquist, Lambdin, Suydam, and Smith (2003), constructivism is based on the following premises:

1. Knowledge is created or invented by a naturally active learner, not passively absorbed from the environment. Learners who construct their own knowledge learn it, understand it, and can apply it.
2. Ideas are constructed when learners have the opportunity to reflect on their physical and mental actions. They should be encouraged to observe, recognize patterns, and make generalizations so that new knowledge can be integrated into their existing knowledge base.
3. Learning is a social process that occurs in functional, meaningful, and authentic contexts. Ideas and truth are established by a community of learners who manipulate materials, discover patterns, and generate solutions, and then explain, negotiate, and share ideas and truth. The teacher does not teach discrete skills in a linear sequence, nor does he or she assume that mastery of basic skills is essential before students move on to more advanced, higher-order thinking skills. Rather, his or her role is to structure situations so learners use what they already know to discover knowledge.

A teacher assists with performance and in the construction of knowledge rather than explicitly providing students with knowledge and information.

Constructivists argue that rather than simply accepting new information, students interpret what they see, hear, and do and relate these interpretations to what they already know. Many leading associations support constructivism and advocate strongly for the use of constructivist-based approaches. For example, the National Research Council (1989) stated: "In reality, no one can teach mathematics. Effective teachers are those who can stimulate students to learn mathematics. Educational research offers compelling evidence that students learn mathematics well only after they construct their own mathematical understanding" (p. 58).

Constructivists believe that learning a set of isolated facts does not contribute to retention and comprehension of important information. The content should make sense to students so that they will understand that a body of knowledge has order, structure, and relationships and be able to use it to solve problems. Developmental theorists, such as Piaget (1970), suggest individuals proceed through several stages of development, starting at birth and continuing through adulthood. Each stage provides a learner with the opportunity to experience a range of learning activities (Reys et al., 2003). The lower limit of this window of opportunity rests on previously established concepts and skills, whereas the upper limit is determined by successful completion of tasks. The learning activities and experiences within this range have been described by Vygotsky as being within the student's *zone of proximal development* (Reys et al., 2003). The zone of proximal development can vary, with more able students having wider zones than less able students (Pressley, Hogan, Wharton-McDonald, Mistretta, & Ettenberger, 1996). Teachers must have a solid understanding of these zones and be able to provide activities for students that have a high probability of enhancing student success (Reys et al., 2003). The size of the zone of proximal development can vary and should not be construed to mean that not all students can learn.

Many different instructional approaches and perspectives have their roots in constructivism, including whole language, cognitively guided instruction, scaffolded instruction, literacy-based instruction, and directed discovery (Harris & Graham, 1994). In general, constructivists have views of the student, the task, the role of the teacher, student motivation, and assessment that are different from those who favor more explicit instructional methods. Mercer, Jordan, and Miller (1994) summarized these differences, starting with how the learner is viewed. Students are perceived as active participants in the learning process. They do not merely sit and absorb material and information from their teachers or their textbooks. As active learners, they make connections between their prior knowledge and the knowledge they have discovered. They have a deeper understanding of the knowledge and are better able to apply it in problem-solving situations.

Constructivists have a different view of the content to which students are exposed. Content to be mastered must come from authentic and purposeful contexts. Instruction in basic skills or mechanical skills is important but must occur in an authentic, real-world setting. For example, skills in sound–symbol relationships must be acquired if students are to become successful readers, but authentic children's literature should serve as the context for their development.

The nature of teacher–student interactions is perceived differently among constructivists. Rather than present explicit instruction, constructivists representing an endogenous perspective believe that the teacher should structure challenging activities that allow students to explore and discover new knowledge. Constructivists from an exogenous perspective believe the teacher should describe, explain, model, and provide students with feedback. In the middle are dialectical constructivists who believe teachers and students should collaborate. For example, the teacher can ask questions as needed to guide students in the discovery process.

Constructivists believe that students are motivated by "an intrinsic need to reflect on one's self, behavior, and knowledge" (Mercer et al., 1994, p. 294). Motivation is increased by a student's ability to self-appraise (i.e., examine a task) and self-manage to monitor and evaluate performance and make any necessary revisions. The student who constructs new knowledge successfully will realize the importance of self-regulation and self-management in becoming an active, independent learner, increasing his or her use and refinement of these skills.

Finally, constructivists' perspective on assessment reflects their concern that instruction should occur in a student's zone of proximal development. Preassessment involves determining what the student's current needs are, whether the student has the necessary preskills, and his or her motivation. During learning activities, assessment becomes more dynamic, with the teacher monitoring student performance and offering assistance in the form of cueing, questioning, prompting, providing feedback, modeling, or providing explicit instruction.

According to Reys and colleagues (2003), constructivism takes time and reflects developmental stages. Constructivism from a Piagetian perspective suggests that there may be limits to what students can learn, based on their progression through developmental stages. For example, students between the ages of 7 to 12 years are in the concrete operations stage and can think logically, classify, order, reverse their thinking, take others' perspectives, and consider several aspects of a situation. The knowledge these students construct will be substantially different from that of younger learners at the preoperational stage who have not developed these skills. Reys and colleagues (2003) pointed out that constructed knowledge is not always correct. They described an example in which a learner rationalizes that "0.285 is greater than 0.4 because 0.285 has more digits." The learner is basing this conclusion on the fact that as whole numbers, 285 is bigger than 4. He or she is interpreting information about decimals in light of this previous knowledge but has reached the wrong conclusion.

These two concerns have implications for secondary students with disabilities. No one argues against the idea that students should be active, motivated learners who develop higher-order thinking skills using authentic materials and should be able to apply skills in novel settings. However, it must be noted that cognitive deficits may mean some secondary students with disabilities may never "be ready"—that is, arrive at a developmental stage at which more sophisticated levels of knowledge can be created. In addition, students with disabilities are likely to enter the secondary classroom with deficits in knowledge and skills and with a limited amount of time to acquire them. It can be argued that instruction must be explicit and precise so that students learn efficiently with a minimum number of errors. As Harris and Graham (1994) noted, "Explicitness and structure need not equate with decontextualized learning of meaningless skills, passive learning, or the teaching of basic skills as a pre-requisite to higher-order thinking and skills" (p. 238).

Grading

One measure of the effectiveness of the instructional techniques a teacher uses is the grade a student receives. Grades are an integral part of the U.S. educational system and a critical area of concern for all students (Munk & Bursuck, 2001). This concern is further heightened as more students with disabilities are integrated into general education classrooms (Espin, Busch, Shin, & Kruschwitz, 2001; Polloway, Epstein, Bursuck, Roderique, et al., 1994; Salend & Garrick Duhaney, 2002). Action Plan 4.11 lists purposes for grading identified by Munk and Bursuck (2001) and Salend and Garrick Duhaney (2002). In the short run, grades reflect the achievement of goals and mastery of specific content, motivate students to continue to perform or strive to improve performance, compare one student to others, assist teachers with planning, and identify students who could benefit from special courses or programs (Bradley & Calvin, 1998). In the long run, grades can serve as the basis for securing employment and postsecondary educational opportunities.

Bursuck and colleagues (1996) noted that "classroom grades earned by students with disabilities provide a direct measure of the successful performance of the students and an indirect measure of the success of integration efforts in general" (p. 301). They also noted that students with disabilities who are in general education classrooms are "trying to meet increasing academic standards despite below average skills" and "may be desperately in need of some grading adaptations" (p. 303). Empirical data tend to support this concern. Donahue and Zigmond (1990) studied grading patterns for students with learning disabilities who had been integrated into high school classrooms. From 60 to 75% of the students received passing grades, although their grade-point averages (GPAs) were consistently below average, suggesting a persistent lack of success. Further clouding the issue is when grading practices for students with disabilities vary as a function of placement. Valdes, Williamson, and Wagner (1990) reported that 62.4% of students with disabilities who were served in secondary classrooms were graded against the same standard as their general education peers; however, 74.3% of students in special education classrooms were graded on different

---

Action Plan 4.11   Purposes of Grading

Munk and Bursuck (2001) and Salend and Garrick Duhaney (2002) identified 11 purposes for grading.

1. Achievement of curricular goals and specific skills
2. Progress over a period of time
3. Effort put into learning
4. Comparions among students
5. Instructional planning to identify student strengths and needs
6. Program effectiveness
7. Motivation to learn and succeed
8. Communication and feedback to students and families
9. Educational and career planning
10. Eligibility for programs and awards, promotion, and graduation
11. Accountability to the community, employers, legislators, and educational policymakers

standards. Should grading standards be the same for everyone or can they be adapted for students with disabilities? Christiansen and Vogel (1998) reported that some teachers are reluctant to make grade accommodations because of the belief that such accommodations compromise academic standards, violate grading policies, and are unfair to students who do not have a disability. In fact, Schumm and Vaughn (1991) reported that teachers considered adaptations in grading practices as least desirable of 30 possible adaptations for students with special needs. These data are interesting in light of the results of a survey completed by Bursuck and colleagues (1996). Approximately 50% of the secondary teachers they surveyed reported using some modifications for students without disabilities; in fact, 73.4% indicated that limiting adaptations to students with disabilities was not fair. When asked to rationalize what is fair for students with disabilities, teachers responded with comments such as, "Students with disabilities are fighting an uphill battle," "Effort should be rewarded," and "Disabled students should not be punished for handicapping conditions" (p. 311).

Specific grading practices are a function of teacher preparation, philosophical beliefs, school district policies and procedures, and the information that teachers believe should be shared about student performance. Polloway, Epstein, Bursuck, Roderique, and colleagues (1994) surveyed the grading policies of 225 schools representing independent and cooperative urban, suburban, and rural districts within nine census regions of the United States. Of the respondents, 146 had a formal grading policy and 107 reported that teachers were required to use it. In all, 88 respondents had a policy for students with disabilities. Types of grades included letter grades, number grades, narratives, achievement scores, pass/fail, checklists, and class ranks. Information regarding grading policies was communicated to parents by means of a school handbook or a district handbook, and to teachers by means of a school handbook, a district handbook, or faculty meetings. Ninety-four districts had policies that specified grades be assigned on the basis of tests, homework, projects, attendance, behavior, and extra credit. Nearly all districts reported that the grading policy was reviewed periodically. Of the districts with grading policies, 60 indicated there were modifications in grading practices for students with disabilities. The two most common ways in which modifications were determined were through the development of the IEP or through decisions generated by an existing committee structure such as a pupil evaluation team.

In a follow-up study of 368 teachers, Bursuck and colleagues (1996) reported that letter grades and number/percentage grades were more useful for students without disabilities. Pass/fail grades, checklist-type grades, and written comments were more useful for students with disabilities. Based on the work of Bursuck and colleagues, possible grading adaptations for students with disabilities are listed in Action Plan 4.12. Action Plan 4.13 identifies how various requirements contributed to a grade. Finally, Bursuck and coauthors advised that letter and number grades could be made more useful for students with disabilities by basing them on the process rather than the product, considering the amount of improvement and progress made toward IEP goals, adjusting grade weights based on assignment and ability, and assigning grades on the basis of completing an individual contract that specifies the quantity and quality of work and the time lines for completion.

Christiansen and Vogel (1998) identified four standards for effective grading practices for students with disabilities. They must "be consistent with school policy, meet the communication needs of the grading process, reflect the theoretical orientation of the teachers involved, and be consistent with the individual education program" (p. 34). The grades that result from these standards meet four criteria: (1) a grade should be the result of frequent

Action Plan 4.12   Grading Accommodations for Students with Disabilities

Bursuck and colleagues (1996) surveyed secondary teachers and rated the following grading adaptations for students with disabilities on a four-point scale of acceptability:

1. Giving separate grades for a process (effort) and for products (tests)   3.37
2. Grades based on the amount of improvement a student demonstrates   3.32
3. Assigning grades on the basis of an academic or behavioral contract   3.14
4. Grades reflect whether the student has met IEP objectives   3.18
5. Adjusting grades according to student ability   3.08
6. Weighting items so that effort and projects count more than tests   3.04
7. Modifying the scale so that an A that required 93 to 100% now requires 90 to 100% mastery   2.91
8. Grades reflect less content coverage   2.70
9. Passing students who make an effort to pass   2.52
10. Assigning passing grades no matter what the student does   1.22

Action Plan 4.13   The Basis for Grades

Bursuck and colleagues (1996) identified the following percentages of each of several assignment types as they contributed to grades for high school students with disabilities:

1. Test/quizzes   41.1%
2. In class/homework   26.4%
3. Reports/papers   11.3%
4. Class participation   6.5%
5. Effort/attitude   3.5%
6. Notebooks   3.5%
7. Attendance   1.9%
8. Preparedness/organization   1.1%
9. Progress   1.0%
10. Level of ability   0.9%

assessment; (2) it should reflect important elements, such as product quality, progress made, effort, and work habits; (3) it should convey accurate information about achievement to students and parents; and (4) a grade should provide students with direction for improvement.

The question remains as to who should be responsible for assigning grades to students with disabilities. Bursuck and colleagues (1996) reported that 49% of their survey respondents indicated general education teachers took full responsibility for assigning grades, which can be problematic if they have had little or no special training; 42% reported that the general educator and special educator shared in this responsibility; and 8.9% reported the special educator assumed primary responsibility for grading. Christiansen and Vogel (1998) recommended that grades for students with disabilities result from a collaborative effort between general and special educators. They developed a four-step model to facilitate the grading process, which is summarized in Action Plan 4.14.

Action Plan 4.14   Determining Grades for Students with Disabilities

Christiansen and Vogel (1998) recommended that general and special educators follow these four steps to determining grades for students with disabilities:

1. Review district, state, and federal policies and guidelines regarding grading.
2. Each teacher should determine his or her own theoretical approach to grading, which can include:
   - A criterion-referenced viewpoint that assumes grades reflect a mastery of objectives
   - A self-referenced viewpoint based on growth by the student
   - A norm-referenced viewpoint based on an assessment of student strengths and weaknesses in relation to others
3. Each teacher should identify his or her colleague's theoretical approach.
4. Jointly determine the grading practices for an individual student:
   - Know the student's goals, objectives, and accommodations.
   - Keep personalities out of the discussion and focus instead on the student's interests.
   - If necessary, seek assistance from a colleague or administrator whom both parties respect.

Summary

Both general and special educators need to select and use instructional methods that will allow secondary students with disabilities to acquire important information efficiently and apply it to situations outside of the instructional setting. This chapter described three sets of methods that will be useful to teachers. First was direct instruction, which addresses curriculum design, classroom organization and management, delivery of explicit instruction, and careful monitoring of student progress.

There are times, however, when teachers are more interested in developing their students' ability to use one or more generic skills that can be applied across the secondary curriculum. Such skills include how to paraphrase, take notes, study, and take an exam. The strategies intervention model (SIM) is useful in such circumstances. Implementation of this model can enable students to meet classroom demands for acquiring, storing, and expressing knowledge and skills across and within content areas.

The third method of instructional delivery involves approaches that reflect the philosophy of constructivism. Based on the work of Piaget and Vygotsky, constructivism says that learning is a social process in which students are active learners who construct their own knowledge and integrate it into their existing knowledge base.

Finally, this chapter addressed the issue of grading. Secondary general and special educators need to report progress to students, parents, and school district officials, yet standard grading methods may not be appropriate for learners with disabilities who are in inclusive placements. General and special educators should collaborate when assigning grades, bearing in mind district grading policies; their own theoretical approach to grading; and the student's goals, objectives, and accommodations.

chapter

5

Assessment for Placement and Instruction

Did you know that . . .

- The quality of an educational program depends largely on the accuracy of educators' instructional decisions?
- Norm-referenced tests provide little information from which to design, conduct, or evaluate educational interventions?
- Many norm-referenced tests discriminate against minority students?
- Uniform assessment programs conducted in all states may not exclude students with disabilities, and, depending on the student's needs, accommodations or alternative measures must be used?

- An accommodation can "level the playing field" for a student taking a statewide assessment?
- Curriculum-based tests are useful not only for identifying skills that adolescents have acquired but also for measuring the efficiency and effectiveness of instructional procedures?
- Special behavioral objectives should serve as the basis for constructing curriculum-based tests?
- Direct-observation procedures must be consistent with the behavioral objective being evaluated?
- Portfolio-based measures are used by teachers and students as an integral part of instruction?

Can you . . .

- List the steps required to implement instruction for adolescents with disabilities?
- Describe the characteristics of the two general types of assessment procedures?
- Describe the limitations of norm-referenced tests in the assessment of students with disabilities?
- Describe the two principal uses for norm-referenced tests?

- Identify problems associated with the participation of students with disabilities in statewide assessments?
- Define an accommodation?
- Identify steps for ensuring the proper use of testing accommodations?
- Describe the two principal uses for curriculum-based tests?

- List the seven steps used to develop paper-and-pencil tests?
- Describe the factors that influence the reliability and validity of a test?
- List three criteria for judging the consistency of the observation procedure and behavioral objective?

- Develop a paper-and-pencil curriculum-based measure?
- Develop an observational measure?
- Develop a portfolio-based assessment method?

It should be apparent from Action Plan 5.1 that assessment occupies a central role in the direct-instruction sequence. The quality of an educational program depends largely on the accuracy of educators' instructional decisions. The most effective way to ensure accurate decision making is to base judgments on reliable observations of student performance. The purpose of this chapter is to describe assessment procedures that can serve this function.

Two general types of assessment are discussed. The first, norm-referenced assessment, compares a student's performance on a standardized test to the performance of a large group of students. Recent studies have drawn attention to limitations of norm-referenced tests in the instruction of youth with disabilities (Brandt, 1992; Fuchs & Deno, 1994). Despite the limitations, a major use of norm-referenced tests is in statewide assessment programs. Because federal law requires that individuals with disabilities participate in these programs, special emphasis is placed on alternative assessment that accommodates students' performance characteristics. The second type of assessment discussed in this chapter is curriculum-based measurement. Curriculum-based methods include paper-and-pencil criterion-referenced measures, observational procedures, and portfolio assessment. These approaches compare the student's performance within the curriculum to a performance

Action Plan 5.1   Assessment Procedures in the Direct-Instruction Model

Identifying instructional goals: Tests are used to match instructional goals to the learning and behavioral characteristics of the student.

Establishing component objectives: Tests are used to determine that objectives can be attained by the student in a reasonable period of time.

Designing instruction: Tests are used to identify or refine efficient individualized instructional strategies.

Maintaining accountability during instruction: Assessment probes are used during instruction to keep the student accountable for the mastery of information and skills.

Evaluating instruction: Assessment data are collected during instruction to ensure that adequate progress will be made toward objectives.

Revising the instructional plan: Assessment data are used to alter the instructional plan when satisfactory progress is not noted.

Determining that the goals and objectives have been achieved: Data are used to summarize the student's progress.

standard or objective. These curriculum-based methods are most consistent with the instructional design process that underlies this text. Therefore, a majority of the chapter will focus on these methods.

Norm-Referenced Testing

As already mentioned, norm-referenced tests allow an examiner to compare the performance of an individual to the performance of a group of individuals. The norm-referenced test evaluates interindividual differences, or differences between learners. A norm-referenced achievement test may indicate that a student's mathematics performance is superior to 57% of the students in the standardization sample or reference group. An intelligence test may indicate that a student's IQ is two standard deviations below the mean established by the standardization sample. This also indicates that approximately 2% of the students taking the test obtained IQ scores lower than the given student.

Characteristics

Well-designed norm-referenced tests have several characteristics in common. First, the test procedures are standardized so that there is one and only one way to administer and complete the test. Obviously, valid comparisons could not be made between students if the nature of the evaluation task was different.

Second, test items are designed so that a wide range of scores are obtained from individuals in the standardization sample. A test that produced comparable scores from one individual to the next would not be effective in accentuating individual differences.

Third, a student's performance on a test item is a function of his or her competence relative to the attribute being assessed rather than to other factors. There should be only one legitimate interpretation of a student's final score. This explanation should relate to the student's ability in the area being studied. Alternative explanations (e.g., the student was unable to understand the directions, he or she did not fill in the answer sheet correctly, etc.) should be ruled out by the administration procedure.

Fourth, members of the standardization sample and the individual taking the test have similar characteristics. It is illogical to make comparisons between a student and the standardization sample if differences exist beyond those under study (e.g., dominant language, age, sex, ethnicity, specific disabilities, etc.).

Finally, the results of the test must correspond with other evidence of the student's capability in the area being studied. Low scores on a norm-referenced reading achievement test should correspond with poor performance in daily reading activities. Similarly, high career preference data in manual skills should be supported by evidence that others with similar scores eventually assumed positions in manual trades.

Unfortunately, the same characteristics that make norm-referenced measures appealing in general often detract from their usefulness for people with disabilities. Foremost, although it may be useful to know a student's relative standing in a group, teachers are often better served by the data referencing a student's abilities to community standards. Norm-referenced math scores, for example, do not indicate the extent to which a student can balance a checkbook, shop at a supermarket, or work as a shipping clerk. Norm-referenced reading scores give no idea of whether a student can use classified ads, participate in table games, or shelve books in a library.

Norm-referenced tests also provide little information that can be used to design, conduct, or evaluate educational interventions. Most of the early research studies that attempted to base instructional decisions on norm-referenced test data produced unimpressive results (Sedlak & Weener, 1973). Because it is important to follow the standard test administration procedures, teachers cannot modify the test to evaluate instructional hypotheses (e.g., Would a student's math performance improve if a horizontal format were used rather than a vertical format? Can a student's difficulties with word problems be explained by reading-comprehension deficits rather than math-skill deficits?). Moreover, if a norm-referenced test were administered several times a year, as would be required to evaluate the effectiveness of instruction, the results would be invalid. One would not know whether the student's performance improved because the items had become familiar or because skills had developed.

As mentioned earlier, the student being tested must be represented in the standardization sample. Unfortunately, many standardized tests fail to include in their standardization sample a representative number of individuals who have disabilities or who are bilingual or educationally disadvantaged (McLoughlin & Lewis, 1994). It is therefore inappropriate to use normative data when interpreting their scores.

Still another drawback is that many norm-referenced tests discriminate against minority students (Taylor, 2006). A student's cultural background, rather than learning or behavioral problems, may account for low performance. For example, the Native American culture values cooperative and careful work while rejecting independent and fast production. Therefore, students raised in this culture may be at a disadvantage when taking timed tests requiring solitary effort.

Placement and Summative Evaluations

The limitations outlined in the preceding section have led some authors to call for the total abolition of norm-referenced testing (for a comprehensive discussion, see Reynolds & Brown, 1984). In addition, litigation (*Larry P. v. Riles,* 1972; *Lora v. Board of Education of City of New York,* 1984; *Matti T. v. Holladay,* 1979) has placed strict controls on the use and reporting of norm-referenced test results. There is a similar impetus for states to draft legislation restricting norm-referenced testing. One example is New York's "truth-in-testing" legislation.

Nonetheless, many authors believe that norm-referenced tests can serve a valuable but limited function in educational programs for adolescents with disabilities (Meehan & Hodell, 1986; Peterson, 1986; Salvia & Ysseldyke, 2003; Sattler, 2001; Stodden, 1986; Ysseldyke & Olsen, 1999). In particular, they can be used as tools of placement evaluation and summative evaluation (Taylor, 2006).

Placement Evaluation   Well-developed aptitude tests, achievement tests, intelligence tests, and other norm-referenced tests produce scores that have universal meaning. For example, a report may indicate that a student obtained scores above the mean on all subtests of the Peabody Individual Achievement Test (PIAT), with the exception of the mathematics subtest, in which he scored significantly below the mean. The same report may reveal that the student's score on the Wechsler Intelligence Scale for Children—III (WISC—III) (Wechsler, 1992) is within the normal range. Because the PIAT and WISC—III involve standardized application procedures with uniform norms and scoring, the data can be interpreted by any qualified professional across the country.

More important, because the tests compare the student to a group of individuals, the tests, coupled with other information, may provide strong evidence regarding the potential for success when that student is placed with particular students in a given curriculum (McLoughlin & Lewis, 1994). It is important to note that many placement classifications are tied by state law to performance on norm-referenced tests. The learning disabilities classification and placement, for example, is tied to performance on intelligence and achievement tests (Mercer & Pullen, 2004); mental retardation is tied to performance on intelligence tests and adaptive behavior scales (Hallahan & Kauffman, 2006); and visual impairment is tied to performance on the Snellen chart (Hatfield, 1975).

Summative Evaluation   Norm-referenced tests are also widely used to evaluate the long-term performance of a student (Nunnally & Bernstein, 1994). To serve this purpose, the test items must be matched to the curriculum content. A geography achievement test that includes items pertaining to all inhabited continents will produce little evidence of student performance in a geography course focusing on North America. Similarly, an adaptive behavior scale that includes social, independent living, vocational, communication, and academic adjustment domains will produce only a vague reflection of gains in a curriculum designed to increase self-control skills.

Likewise, norm-referenced tests used for summative evaluation purposes should be used only to sample skills in a broader curriculum domain. It is not appropriate to identify specific items on a test and provide instruction only on those discrete items. This approach would not provide an accurate reflection of competence in the general subject, but would reflect only a student's ability to successfully complete the specific items.

Statewide Assessment and Alternative/Accommodative Strategies

The No Child Left Behind Act requires all states to establish standards and ensure that all students, including those with disabilities, meet these standards. State legislatures have required periodic assessment of student performance; such assessment has been referred to as "high-stakes testing." Departments of education, charged with this task, have developed and evaluated a wide range of achievement measures. In many cases, these are norm-referenced instruments that encourage comparison of performance from one student, class, and/or district to another (Roeber, Bond, & Braskamp, 1997).

The major purpose of statewide assessment programs is to ensure accountability of school systems. According to Bolt and Thurlow (2004), the results of high-stakes testing

---

Case for Action 5.1

You have been asked by your superintendent to chair a committee on the use of norm-referenced assessment devices in your district. What are the main questions your committee needs to address? Provide an outline for the final report that your group will submit.

are used to make decisions about student promotion and graduation, teacher salaries, and allocation of school resources. To this end, legislatures use student performance in a number of ways. Some issue a public "report card" for each school or school district. Parents use this report as a consumer guide that may influence relocation decisions, support of tax increases, and election of school boards. Others use statewide assessment data to guide program and revenue-enhancement decisions. In one example, the Kentucky legislature allows for cash awards to schools who meet performance targets. Those who fail must engage in mandated steps for improving student performance, including technical assistance from state-appointed consultants. Teachers and administrators can be dismissed if problems are sufficiently severe or persistent.

Statewide assessment programs may also be used informally as a prereferral measure for individuals suspected of having disabilities. Students who score poorly despite well-conceived and implemented general education programs may be provided a more comprehensive case study evaluation. The case study may include intelligence testing, achievement testing, adaptive behavior monitoring, and social adjustment rating. Depending on the outcome, the multidisciplinary team may recommend eligibility for special education services.

Previously, students with disabilities had been excluded from high-stakes testing. This practice was questioned by several authors (Johnson, 2000) who noted that excluding students with disabilities from assessment programs undermined the quality of instruction. Without assessment data, state and local school officials will not have the information they need to make decisions regarding the effectiveness of instructional programs. Passage of the 1997 amendments to the Individuals with Disabilities Education Act (IDEA) required states to include students with disabilities in assessment programs so that ultimately all students can benefit from state reform initiatives. Espin, Busch, Shin, and Kruschwitz (2001), Johnson, Kimball, Olson Brown, and Anderson (2001), Sorrentino and Zirkel (2004), and Washburn-Moses (2003) identified concerns when using statewide assessment instruments with students with disabilities. First, standards, and the measures used to assess progress toward achieving them, were developed without the involvement of special educators. Involvement was most likely a review of documents prepared by others whose expertise in special education is limited. Second, while these tests may assist with the identification of students who do and do not meet state standards, they may be of little use in providing information about students who are low achievers. Third, the reliability of these instruments is affected by the relatively small number of students with disabilities included in the testing sample. Fourth, accommodations (discussed shortly) may affect the validity of results. Fifth, state assessments are conducted once a year and therefore do not provide teachers with sufficient and immediate feedback regarding student performance. Sixth, with very few exceptions, students who are disabled must take and pass the test that matches their grade level, not the level at which they are receiving instruction. Finally, consequences of high-stakes testing should be considered and shared with students. Washburn-Moses (2003) urged consideration of the following questions: What options do students have for remediation? What are the options and requirements for retaking the exam? Is there an appeals or waiver process? How does test performance influence the diploma or certificate a student receives? How are students with nonstandard diplomas perceived by employers or college admissions officers?

Bolt and Thurlow (2004) indicated that while nearly all students with disabilities can participate in statewide assessments, up to 10% will require accommodations or alternatives. This is consistent with statistics reported by the National Center on Educational Outcomes (NCEO) (cited in Johnson, Kimball, et al., 2001) that 85% of the students with special needs should be able to participate in statewide assessments without accommodations. When indicated by the students' learning and behavioral characteristics, states must provide appropriate testing accommodations or alternative measures so that students are able to demonstrate what they truly know and can do (Bolt & Thurlow, 2004). An accommodation can "level the playing field" (Washburn-Moses, 2003, p. 12); it is defined as a change in the way a test is administered under standardized conditions. For example, the test could be presented or scheduled differently, response formats could be altered, the setting can be changed, or the use of special equipment could be permitted (Bolt & Thurlow; 2004; Fuchs, Fuchs, Eaton, Hamlett, & Karns, 2000; Washburn-Moses, 2003). The question remains: Which accommodations are appropriate? There is concern that some accommodations may in fact change the nature of the skills being assessed (Bolt & Thurlow, 2004). In many states, the selection of appropriate accommodation is left to the student's IEP team, which should consider the student's strengths, weaknesses, and learning characteristics (Washburn-Moses, 2003). Elliot, Kratochwill, and Schulte (1998) have offered comprehensive guidelines for accommodating special learners in statewide assessment programs. Their Assessment Accommodation Checklist includes recommendations that might be considered based on the unique characteristics of the student. In each case, the recommendations should be selected only if they allow the student to compete with others despite the presence of a disability. The accommodations are not provided to obscure academic deficiencies that are independent of the presence of a disability. Guidelines are as follows (Elliot et al., 1998):

- *Motivation:* Provide extrinsic motivation to students who may not be personally able to perform their best in the standard testing context. This might take the form of providing special privileges or treats for completing each item thoughtfully and in a timely manner.
- *Pretest assistance:* Provide guidance in navigating through the test and practice in responding to items. Desensitize students to stressful aspects of the testing situation.
- *Scheduling:* Provide flexible scheduling for students whose disabilities suggest difficulty in remaining on task for extended periods, whose disabilities result in them working at a slower rate, or who use adaptive equipment that requires additional time.
- *Setting:* Provide a testing setting that is free from distractions. When necessitated by health concerns, provide testing in a sheltered setting.
- *Assessment directions:* Provide modified test instructions for students unable to read or interpret directions without support.
- *Provide assistance during the test:* Provide additional information during the test that helps students understand test questions or response expectations.
- *Using aids:* Provide equipment or adaptive technology that allows students with disabilities to compete on equal footing with nondisabled learners.
- *Changes in test format and content:* Provide large-print formats or other modifications as indicated by the sensory or cognitive characteristics of the learner.

Bolt and Thurlow (2004) identified several considerations that could maximize the appropriateness of accommodations and the impact on student performance:

1. Before selecting an accommodation, identify clearly those skills that the assessment is supposed to measure. If the purpose of a written language assessment is to measure a student's ability to express thoughts in an organized, coherent way, then the use of a scribe is appropriate. However, if the purpose of the test is to measure the student's knowledge and use of writing mechanics, then it is inappropriate to provide a scribe who capitalizes, supplies punctuation, and spells correctly.
2. Examine all options carefully and choose the one that is least intrusive. For example, a student who reads slowly but comprehends should receive extended time limits rather than a reader.
3. The day of the statewide assessment must not be the first time a particular accommodation is used with the students. Make sure students have had the opportunity to use accommodations in instructional settings.
4. Train those individuals who provide the accommodations. For example, a scribe should understand that he or she is only to write what the student dictates and not provide any prompts or cues.
5. Be aware that an accommodation may produce additional difficulties. For example, the use of large print can change the ways items are arranged on a page, confusing the test-taker.
6. Monitor the effects of accommodations to ensure that they increase student performance.

Regardless of the amount of accommodative support, students with more severe disabilities may not be able to participate in statewide assessments. NCLB regulations specify that no more than 1% of the students tested at a grade level can be allowed to take alternative assessments or meet alternative standards in accordance with their IEPs (Sorrentino & Zirkel, 2004). According to IDEA regulations, the state or local education agency must develop alternate assessments and guidelines for participation by students who cannot take the statewide assessment. Browder, Spooner, Algozzine, Ahlgrim-Delzell, Flowers, and Karvonen (2003) identified the "promise of alternate assessment" (p. 46). First, such assessment would encourage greater consideration of these students at local and state levels; at the very least, it would be known whether students were meeting learning expectations. Second, including students whose level of disability warranted participation in alternative assessments would increase overall expectations. All students would be included in the accountability system. Third, alternate assessment would increase the possibility that students would have access to the same curriculum. Alternate assessment does not necessarily mean different standards. Fourth, as is the case for all assessment outcomes, it is anticipated that the results of alternate assessments would be used to improve educational programs for students with disabilities.

Unfortunately, IDEA does not stipulate what form alternate assessment should take or how it should be administered, scored, or reported (Tindall, McDonald, Tedesco, Glasgow, Almond, Crawford, & Hollenbeck, 2003). Browder and colleagues (2003) identified best practices for alternate assessment. First, they recommended that states clarify what standards should be addressed on alternate assessments and how performance indicators should be adapted. For example, a state standard may address the ability to communicate ideas by speaking. This standard could be met by the student who uses assistive technology to communicate. Second, alternate assessments should be used only with students with the most significant disabilities. Third, paper-and-pencil methods should be discarded in favor of techniques such as observations, record reviews, and portfolio assessment. Finally, consideration must be given to how alternate assessments are scored. For example, holistic scoring that uses a three- or four-point scale can be used to evaluate a portfolio.

Portfolio assessment (discussed shortly) has been identified as the most common alternate assessment (Tindall et al., 2003). Another option is curriculum-based measurement (presented below), which includes direct observations of gains achieved through a functional curriculum as opposed to the standard written format. Ysseldyke and Olsen (1999) proposed the following data-collection methods that may be an alternative to standardized instruments:

- *Direct observation of critical skills:* These may be systematic, as described later in this chapter, or nonsystematic, such as anecdotal comments and log entries.
- *Recollection of critical events:* Individuals familiar with the learner may be asked to describe past events associated with skill development or failure. Rating scales may be used with this form of assessment.
- *Record review:* Data may be collected from cumulative school records, student products collected in portfolios, anecdotal records, and nonschool records.
- *Testing:* Alternate tests that measure similar competencies but in a format more sensitive to the students' characteristics can be used. An oral achievement test, such as the PIAT-R, may be substituted for the state's written test.

Curriculum-Based Measurement

Curriculum-based measurement (CBM) can be used by general and special educators to collect data about the performance of secondary students and then make decisions about instructional programs (Heward, 2003). CBM provides the type of data needed to reach decisions on most daily instructional questions. Students are assessed on a weekly or biweekly basis; data are graphed and student progress is analyzed to ensure improvements are made. If the data indicate students are not progressing, the teacher changes the instructional program. Unlike the results of high-stakes testing discussed previously or the use of grades (discussed in Chapter 4), CBM allows teachers to examine and, if necessary, change instruction before students fail (Espin et al., 2001). CBM is distinguished from norm-referenced tests in that rather than comparing a student's performance to the performance of a norm group, a student's performance is compared to an objective standard. The standard is typically the short-term objective of a specific lesson or group of lessons. Curriculum-based tests are used primarily in formative and diagnostic evaluations.

Formative Evaluation

The instruction model described in the previous chapter emphasizes the direct and continuous measurement of progress toward objectives. This evaluation function is referred to as *formative evaluation.*

Formative data are used to determine the rate at which new skills are presented. The direct-instruction model suggests that the major objective be broken down into logically sequenced subskills. The subskills are presented in order, from the last to the first (backward chaining) or from the first to the last (forward chaining), until all of the subskills are mastered. Formative evaluation during instruction in each subskill indicates whether mastery has occurred. Instruction should progress to the next subskill only when mastery is demonstrated. If the student moves too quickly, "holes" are likely to develop in his or her repertoire. These deficiencies will limit the extent to which the objective is achieved. Conversely, if instruction continues on a subskill that has been mastered, less instructional time will be available for subsequent skill development at a more advanced level.

Diagnostic Evaluation

Educators need information not only on whether subskills have been mastered but also on what specific aspects of a subskill are causing the learner difficulty. A criterion-referenced test may indicate that the student has not mastered multiplication with two-digit multipliers. Diagnostic evaluation may determine that the student has difficulty with replacement, zero as a place holder, specific math facts, and so on. Subsequent instruction addressing the subskill may focus on the specific errors uncovered in the diagnostic evaluation.

Diagnostic evaluation may also indicate which instructional methods are best suited for an individual learner. The teacher may note that the student performs better on curriculum-based tests that follow instruction with a high ratio of guided-to-independent practice. Similarly, test data may indicate that morning instruction is more effective than afternoon instruction. This information may lead the teacher to reschedule the day so that essential academic skills can be developed during morning periods.

Action Plan 5.2 outlines the main reasons for engaging in curriculum-based and norm-referenced testing.

Action Plan 5.2   Uses of Curriculum-Based and Norm-Referenced Tests

We recommend the following uses for each general assessment approach:

Norm-Referenced Tests

- Provide information that contributes to placement decisions
- Assist in determining a student's current performance level
- Determine a student's long-term progress

Curriculum-Based Tests

- Select the most efficient and effective instructional procedure for an individual student
- Provide a formative assessment of progress toward objectives during instruction
- Identify specific performance problems during instruction
- Maintain student accountability for skill and concept mastery

---

Selection of Curriculum-Based Instruments

A curriculum-based test is any instrument that compares a student's performance to an objective standard. Consequently, these measures may vary greatly in form. Ideally, CBM techniques are simple, direct, easy to administer, time efficient, can be used repeatedly, and are reliable and valid (Espin et al., 2001). For example, a paper-and-pencil test may compare a student's spelling ability with an objective indicating mastery of words commonly found on employment application forms. A task-analytic assessment may compare a student's actual performance in wiring an electrical circuit with an objective indicating that each step of the process will be completed without error. Observational assessment may indicate that a student will increase the amount of time spent on academic tasks. Duration data may be used to measure the amount of time a student spends on seatwork. This may be compared with a standard indicating that the learner will be engaged in academic activities for 30 minutes during a 45-minute period. Finally, a portfolio of a student's work may demonstrate quality gains over a semester.

It has been emphasized that the behavioral objective establishes the standard by which a learner's performance is judged. The objective also provides information that is used to select or design the testing instrument. Any statement regarding a student's performance level must be qualified by the conditions under which the measure of performance was obtained. For example, a statement indicating that a student was able to identify five European countries cannot be interpreted unless the testing conditions are known. Did the student fill in the names on an unlabeled map? Did the student match the five names with the five countries? Did the student provide the name of a country on the basis of a description of each country's culture?

As a general rule, objectives indicating that a student will identify, describe, or select can be assessed using paper-and-pencil (or verbal report) measures. Objectives indicating that a student will construct, perform, or demonstrate can be assessed using observational procedures. The manner in which these tests are designed and administered varies greatly. Both paper-and-pencil tests and records of observations may be included in a portfolio.

Developing Paper-and-Pencil Tests

Schloss and Sedlak (1986) have suggested six steps that are used to develop curriculum-based tests. These steps are included in Action Plan 5.3. They are also described in this section.

Action Plan 5.3

We recommend the following procedure for constructing a curriculum-based test:

1. Develop the performance objective.
2. Enumerate subskills.
3. Describe the question-and-answer format.
4. Prepare instructions for the test.
5. Prepare test items.
6. Establish scoring procedures.

Step 1: Develop the Performance Objective

The obvious first step in developing a curriculum-based test is to establish the standard by which the student's performance will be judged. As indicated in the preceding chapters, the adolescent's multidisciplinary team is responsible for establishing annual goals. We have argued that goal selection must be based on a comprehensive analysis of the learning and behavioral characteristics of the youth. It is also important to take into account future environments in which the learner is expected to participate. In short, goals selected for a youth with disabilities should prepare the individual to participate in future community settings (e.g., work, leisure, social, and independent living).

The objectives are logically sequenced subsets of each goal. The goal "increase participation in community recreational activities" might include the following objectives:

- Given a specially designed map and time schedule, Bill will use the bus without error to go to three recreational settings.
- Without assistance, Bill will pay for community recreational events without miscalculating the cost or change expected.
- Bill will bowl one of three games over 80 points at the public lanes with the assistance of a friend only for scoring and no other assistance for selecting shoes, ball, lane assignment, etc.
- Bill will play three video games without assistance to the level of competence that he passes the initial screen.
- Bill will perform all tasks necessary without error to use a mechanical batting cage without assistance.

The behavioral objectives include four elements that have considerable bearing on the design of paper-and-pencil curriculum-based tests:

1. *The student's name:* The direct-instruction approach emphasized in this text matches instruction to the characteristics and needs of individual learners. Including the student's name in the behavioral objective serves notice that instruction is designed for the individual adolescent.
2. *The actual skill or skills to be demonstrated by the student:* The target response portion of the objective indicates the response features to be included in the curriculum-based test. An objective may indicate that Keesha will state in writing the consequences that result from drinking and driving. To be consistent, the curriculum-based test must provide an opportunity for Keesha to write down the consequences associated with drinking and driving. Similarly, an objective might state that Keesha will select the fastening device most frequently used in home construction. The word *select* indicates that Keesha must be provided the opportunity to choose the correct response from a set of options.
3. *The conditions under which the student is expected to demonstrate the target skills:* The condition statement indicates the context in which performance is expected to occur. An objective might indicate that Philip will write the correct answer to all one-digit math facts. The condition statement might include phrases such as "given an untimed math facts worksheet" and "given three seconds to respond verbally to math

facts flash cards." Another objective might be that Philip will plan menus for a week. The condition statement might be "given a set of foods representing each of the basic food groups."

4. *The performance criteria:* This element of the behavioral objective sets the actual performance standard expected, given the preceding response and condition statement. The criteria may indicate quantitative aspects of the youth's performance such as, "Ricardo will accurately complete 8 of 10 math facts." It may also indicate qualitative aspects of performance such as, "sufficiently loud to be heard at a distance of 20 feet." It should be clear that changes in any of the components of the objective may substantially alter what is expected of the student. For this reason, careful attention must be given to defining specifications for all aspects of the objective.

Step 2: Enumerate Subskills

Just as performance objectives constitute the annual goal, subskills are logically sequenced subsets of the performance objective. Performance objectives are typically too broad to produce useful formative and diagnostic data. Knowing that Bill was unable to use the bus to go to three recreational settings provides little information that is of direct instructional value. It would be important to have additional information. To what settings, if any, was he able to go? What common mistakes did he make on the way to each setting? Was he early or late for the bus? Was he able to locate the initial and terminal bus stops? Was he able to signal the bus driver to stop? Did he use the appropriate change?

To provide a more refined analysis of the student's performance, the initial objective is broken down into its component subskills. The test then indicates a student's competence in each of the subskills. For example, one objective might be that Wanda will be able to prepare a personal résumé. The subskills for résumé preparation include the ability to report personal information, educational history, employment history, and employment objectives. Test data may reveal adequate performance in each of the subskills except for reporting employment objectives. Of course, this information is far more useful than simply knowing that Wanda has failed to meet the criteria expected for preparing a résumé.

Step 3: Describe the Question-and-Answer Format

The teacher should produce a blueprint for the test before actually preparing items for it. This blueprint should follow the question-and-answer format for the test. Careful attention must be given to matching the question-and-answer format with the initial objective and subskills to ensure that the assessment results are valid.

Question formats can include the following measures:

- *Construct* objects to demonstrate important aspects of the instructions or questions. An objective that includes the condition "given a demonstration of mouth-to-mouth resuscitation" should be tested with items that include the construct dimension.
- *Present* a fixed visual display of instructions or questions. An objective that includes the condition "given a picture of a deciduous forest" should be tested with items that include the present dimension.

Action Plan 5.4   Criteria for Evaluating a Paper-and-Pencil Curriculum-Based Test

The following criteria are recommended for evaluating the reliability, validity, and usability of a curriculum-based test:

1. Did a behavioral objective serve as the basis for the construction of the test?
2. Were the subskills that make up the objective identified?
3. Were 5 to 20 items used to evaluate mastery of each subskill?
4. Were the test items matched to the condition statement, the target behavior, and performance criteria of the initial objective?
5. Did the recording and scoring procedure allow the teacher to identify specific subskill deficiencies?

Case for Action 5.2

You are teaching a modern history unit on the presidents of the past three decades. Identify the goal of your unit. Identify six component objectives. Prepare five test items that assess each of the component objectives. Develop a diagnostic scoring procedure to use with your test. What instructional decisions can be made from your test data?

The next section focuses on systematic observation, another curriculum-based measurement strategy. This approach is appropriate for evaluating progress toward objectives indicating that a student will construct, perform, or demonstrate specific skills.

Observation Procedures

A number of methods for monitoring overt behavior of adolescents have been described in the literature. These strategies have three elements in common. First, the monitoring procedures must be objective. The feelings of the observer or other factors must not influence data that result from the observation. Second, observations must result in valid statements about the learner's performance. That is, the teacher must provide a direct report of performance without unsupported inferences about motive or internal causation. Finally, monitoring procedures must be reliable. A reliable monitoring system produces the same results, regardless of who makes the observations.

Selection of Monitoring Procedures

Like paper-and-pencil measures, direct observation procedures must be consistent with the behavioral objective being evaluated. The consistency of the observation procedure and behavioral objective is bridged using three criteria. First, *the setting and conditions under which the observations are conducted must match the condition statement of the behavioral objective.* The condition statement indicates the situation in which the target behavior is expected to occur (or not occur). To be consistent, the observation must be conducted under the same conditions that are specified in the objective. If an objective indicates that the student will identify the shortest route from New York City to Los Angeles using a road atlas, pencil, paper, and ruler, observations must be conducted while the learner is using these instruments. If an objective indicates a youth will rebuild a two-cycle engine using a repair manual, mechanic's tool set, and working model, these same elements should be available during observation.

The second principle for ensuring consistency is that *the target behavior statement of the objective should correspond with the precise behavior being observed.* An objective indicating that a youth will remain in his seat for a 40-minute period must correspond with observation of the time spent in seat. An objective indicating that the youth will be punctual for class each morning must be measured through observations of the time the student arrives at class each day.

The third principle is that *the level of performance expected following intervention corresponds with the measure of behavior strength used in the observation procedure.* An objective that indicates the learner will increase the time on task by 50% must involve the use of rate data. An objective that indicates a youth will reduce the number of verbal attacks must involve the use of a frequency measure. The final sections of this chapter review four observational measures that correspond to most criterion statements: (1) frequency and rate, (2) permanent product, (3) duration and latency, and (4) interval. Before discussing observation methods, we should review the procedures for defining the behaviors being observed.

Observation Methods

Frequency recording requires the least amount of time and is often the most useful of the observation methods. The frequency of a student's behavior is established by tallying each occurrence of the target behavior over a specified period of time. Frequency recording is appropriate when several conditions are met.

First, the response must have a distinct start time and stop time. If the onset and termination of the response are unclear, the recorder may not be able to distinguish between an episode and a series of episodes. For example, it may not be clear whether a student was unhappy for one period lasting over an hour or was unhappy a number of times within the hour.

Second, the response must have a relatively consistent duration. A behavior that lasts from one second to over an hour (e.g., walking, crying, or writing) cannot be measured accurately with frequency recording. One walking tally may not be comparable to another because the actual time spent walking was substantially different.

Third, the time during which observations occurred must be consistent. A youth might be observed for three class periods one day and only one class period the next. Frequency data may indicate that the youth was aggressive three times each day. Because he was observed for different periods of time, it would be misleading to indicate that he was equally aggressive on the two days.

To take into account varying observation periods, frequency counts may be converted to rate data. This is accomplished by dividing the frequency tally by the amount of time in which the individual was observed. For example, if William wrote 12 sentences in a period of 30 minutes, the rate of sentence writing would be computed by dividing the frequency of occurrences (12) by the amount of time observed (30). The resulting rate would be four-tenths of a sentence per minute, or 24 sentences per hour. Figure 5.1 shows a standard form for collecting frequency and rate data.

Permanent product recording means evaluating the tangible result of a student's behavior. Permanent product recording may be appropriate for monitoring homework completion, property damage resulting from aggression, or production units assembled; such data are frequently included in portfolios (described later in this chapter). Permanent

FIGURE 5.1 *Standard Form for Recording Frequency and Rate Data*

Adolescent _____ Instructor _____

Setting(s) _____

_____

Response and definition _____

_____

_____

DATE	FREQUENCY	PERIOD OBSERVED			RATE
		Beginning	*End*	*Total*	

product recording is similar to frequency and rate recording, except that the observer tallies products of the behavior rather than the actual behavior.

As with frequency data, several conditions must apply if the recording method is to produce accurate information. First, the task or setting demands must be relatively constant from one observation to the next. For example, data on the number of assignments completed accurately are useful if the assignments are equally difficult. Second, the amount of time during which the permanent products are created must be constant. If this condition is not met, permanent product data can be transformed to "products over time." Finally, the standards for judging whether the product was completed must be clear and complete. Writing assignments, for example, may be considered completed only if certain standards are achieved. These may include the quality of penmanship, spelling, sentence structure, and so on.

Duration and latency measurement is useful for determining the amount of time a youth spends in an activity. It is also useful for determining the amount of time that elapses between an event and the initiation of a response. A teacher might use duration recording to discover the amount of time a student spends cleaning the shop. Duration recording might also be used to monitor the amount of time spent practicing specific skills. Latency recording might be used to determine the amount of time a student is tardy. It can also be used to discover the amount of time required for a student to comply with specific instructions.

Duration and latency recording are appropriate when several conditions are met. First, as in frequency recording, the response must have a distinct start time and stop time. If the start and stop times are not clear, the recorder will not know when to begin or stop timing. Second, the overall period of time during which observations occurred must be consistent. A student may appear to have been more productive on one certain day. However, in fact, he or she may simply have had more time to work during the first day. As with other recording methods, varying times available for observation can be accounted for by computing a rate; that is, the number of minutes the student was observed engaging in the behavior is divided by the amount of time available.

Duration and latency data may be difficult to collect in most instructional situations. Not only must the teacher watch the student to determine the start and stop times for responses, but he or she must also keep an eye on a clock or stopwatch, which is difficult to do while conducting a lesson. Consequently, many teachers select other measures of behavior that can be used more efficiently.

Figure 5.2 illustrates a form that can be used to collect duration data. The teacher records the day of the observations in the left column, and then records the times the behavior begins and ends next to the day. The duration for each episode is added for the day and entered in the far right column. This form can be altered to collect latency data by changing the center columns to read "time of cue" and "time of student response." The far right column would be changed to read "latency from cue to response."

Interval measurement avoids many of the special conditions required for frequency, latency, and duration measurement. Responses measured with interval recording need not have discrete start and stop times. In addition, interval recording standardizes the amount of time available for observation. Interval data accurately reflect the strength of behaviors that are of variable duration. Interval data are obtained by sampling a student's behavior within a portion of the school day. Behavior that occurs in a seven-hour day might be observed

FIGURE 5.2 *Standard Form for Recording Duration or Latency Data*

Adolescent _____   Instructor _____

Setting(s) _____

_____

Response and definition _____

_____

_____

| DATE | TIME | | DURATION/LATENCY |
	Begin	End	

during three 10-minute intervals. These 10-minute periods might be divided into twenty 30-second intervals. A response is scored as occurring or not occurring throughout each interval. The resulting measure is the percentage of intervals that contained the uninterrupted occurrence of the target behavior.

Interval data can be collected using three types of procedures. The first, *whole interval,* requires the behavior to occur throughout the interval (e.g., 30 seconds of writing during a 30-second period). The second, *partial interval,* requires the behavior to occur any time during the interval (e.g., an amount of writing during the 30-second period). The third, *momentary-interval recording,* requires the behavior to occur at the precise time the interval begins or ends (e.g., writing during the start of the interval).

Figure 5.3 depicts a form that can be used to collect interval data. The teacher marks a + or – to signify that the behavior occurred or failed to occur during the interval (partial interval), throughout the entire interval (whole interval), or at the start of

FIGURE 5.3   *Standard Form for Recording Interval Data*

Adolescent _____   Instructor _____

Setting(s) _____

_____

Response and definition _____

_____

Interval length _____

+ = occurrence

– = nonoccurrence

DATE	TIME	1	2	3	4	5	6	7	8	9	10	% SCORED +

the interval (momentary interval). Data are translated to the percentage of intervals in which the behavior occurred by dividing the number of occurrences by the number of intervals.

Interobserver Agreement

The preceding methods of observation are useful only to the extent that they produce accurate reflections of the learner's actual behavior. Interobserver agreement is usually the preferred method for determining the accuracy of observational data. *Interobserver agreement* is the extent to which two independent observers agree or disagree that the responses occurred. The procedure for determining the level of agreement differs for each of the observation methods:

- *Frequency and rate reliability* are judged by two individuals observing a student over the same period of time. The lowest tally reported by the two observers is divided by the highest to produce the reliability coefficient.
- *Permanent product reliability* is judged by two individuals independently judging the same products. The smaller score is divided by the larger score to produce the reliability coefficient.
- *Duration and latency reliability* is determined by dividing the shorter time by the longer time reported by the independent observers.
- *Interval reliability* is established by dividing the number of intervals in which both observers agreed on the occurrence or nonoccurrence of the behavior by the total number of intervals observed. Intervals in which both observers scored a nonoccurrence may be excluded from the analysis to produce a more conservative measure.

A reliability check should be conducted before initiating a formal baseline. Reliability should also be evaluated periodically throughout baseline and each intervention phase. Fewer reliability checks may be made when high reliability levels are obtained (e.g., 0.95 to 1.0). Low but adequate reliability levels (e.g., 0.75 to 0.80) should signal the need for more frequent checks.

The criteria for adequate reliability levels are based on target behavior, the observation method, and the purpose for which data are being collected. Affective behaviors may necessarily yield lower reliability levels. Conversely, permanent product data should yield high levels of reliability. Reliability of data gathered by independent observers who do not have instructional responsibilities should be higher than data collected by individuals implementing instructions. Finally, data used for minor instructional/behavior management decisions may be less reliable than data used for placement decisions. In general, reliability levels exceeding 0.75 can be considered to be acceptable for most instructional purposes.

When it is necessary to obtain higher reliability coefficients, the teacher should consider the following: Is the target behavior clearly and completely defined? Is the definition unambiguous? Are the observers well trained? Do they understand the definition and use the observation method accurately? Would another observation method produce more reliable data?

Graphing Observational Data

Data obtained on recording sheets are transferred to a line graph so that comparisons can be made over a period of time. As demonstrated in Figure 5.4 and summarized in Action Plan 5.5, there are five major conventions for graphing observational data. First, the horizontal axis should record the period of each observation. This may be in days, weeks, sessions, periods, and so on. Second, the vertical axis indicates the measure of behavior strength. This may include frequency, rate, and permanent product. Third, vertical lines in the graph represent the onset of intervention or changes in the program. These lines should be accompanied by a brief description of the program change (e.g., addition of a response cost, use of an extraordinary aide, etc.). Fourth, solid points are used to denote the level of behavioral strength in each observation. These points are joined by a solid line, except when separated by missing observations or phase changes. Finally, missing observations are denoted by connecting available points on either side of the missing observation with a broken line.

Interpreting Graphs

Four principal criteria are used to analyze observational data: mean, level, trend, and latency (Kazdin, 1982). Although we discuss these criteria separately, it is important to recognize that they are best used in combination when judging the effectiveness of an intervention.

FIGURE 5.4   *Sample Graph Illustrating Conventions for Reporting Observational Data*

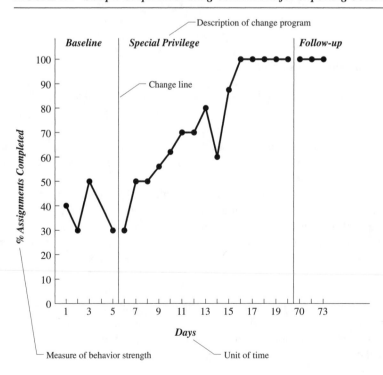

Action Plan 5.5   Major Conventions for Graphing Observational Data

The following elements are usually included in graphic reports of observational data:

A horizontal axis reports the period of each observation.

A vertical axis indicates the measure of behavior strength.

Vertical lines in the graph represent the onset of intervention or changes in the program.

Solid points are used to denote behavior strength in each observation.

Solid lines join individual observations, except when separated by missing observations or phase changes.

Missing observations are denoted by connecting points on either side of the missing observation with a broken line.

Case for Action 5.3

You have collected observational data that indicate a substantial improvement in the social behavior displayed by one of your students while in a work placement. Some of your colleagues question whether so much attention should be placed on his interpersonal skills. How can you use social validation techniques to support your focus on social skills?

Mean

This is the average measure of behavior during a baseline or program phase. The mean is determined by adding the measures of behavior strength for each of the sessions in the baseline or intervention period. This sum is then divided by the number of measures added together.

Demonstrating a mean increase from 15 words written per minute for the baseline to 28 for intervention suggests that the instructional procedure was effective. Similarly, demonstrating a mean decrease from 12 aggressive acts per week when planned ignoring was used to 3 aggressive acts per week when a response cost was used suggests the effectiveness of the response cost over planned ignoring.

Level

Next to mean, level may be the most frequently used criterion for evaluating program effectiveness. Level is determined by comparing measures of behavior strength for observations immediately before and after the phase change. Level differs from mean in that mean uses all of the data in the phase, whereas level uses only the data points near or adjacent to phase changes.

The level may shift from 4 and 5 assignments completed before using a token economy to 8 and 12 assignments completed immediately after using the token economy. This suggests that the token economy had an immediate and direct effect on assignment completion.

Trend

This criterion indicates the extent to which the behavior was improving, stable, or deteriorating before and after intervention. One would expect the behavior to be stable or deteriorating during baseline. One would also expect the behavior to improve following intervention. The more drastic the change in slope from baseline to intervention, the more effective the educational or behavior management procedure.

Suppose, for example, that during a typical class period a teacher observes a youth respond when called on from 0 to 10% of the time. This level remains constant over a period of weeks. One week after counseling begins, the rate moves to 20%. As the youth gains increased insight into the importance of the class, her performance increases to 40%, 60%, and eventually 100%. This performance pattern suggests that counseling has gradually modified the student's response.

Latency

This is the period of time between the start of intervention and the time that the adolescent's behavior begins to change. Direct and intrusive procedures—such as punishment, physical management, and some reinforcement procedures—result in little or no latency. When told that a youth will be fined $20 for parking his car illegally, the youth may immediately discontinue this activity. Less direct and intrusive procedures such as counseling and instruction may produce a longer latency period. For example, progressive muscle relaxation may have actually begun a month before one actually sees an improvement in the youth's ability to remain calm during the testing situation.

Portfolio-Based Assessment

Portfolio-based assessment is a curriculum-based assessment method that directly indicates a student's progress during instruction. A student's portfolio results from the systematic collection of his or her work during an academic period. The portfolio can reflect a number of academic domains by including sections on reading, math, art, history, and so on. Or it can be highly specialized with a more extensive and detailed account of work in one curriculum area. As noted by Swicegood (1994), portfolios include outcomes sampled from authentic tasks completed in natural instructional contexts. Assessment is ongoing and a natural outcome of teaching and learning.

A number of advocates emphasize that portfolio-based assessment is unique in involving the student in the design of the assessment process. Paulson, Paulson, and Meyer (1991), for example, indicate that "the collection must include student participation in selecting contents, the criteria for selection, the criteria for judging merit, and evidence of student reflection" (p. 60). This approach is suggested because of the anticipated effect in motivating students and developing self-management skills. Another advantage is its effect in promoting collaboration between teachers and students.

Highlighting these views, Swicegood (1994) identified five major advantages of portfolio-based assessment:

1. The portfolio method involves collaboration among teachers, other professionals, students, and family members.

2. Greater weight is given to classroom-based assessment, including informal, qualitative, and ecological methods.
3. Portfolios distinguish each student's unique characteristics.
4. A wide range of measures is used to confirm decisions previously based on a single input.
5. The portfolio method recognizes that literacy growth, academic achievement, and social functioning are interrelated domains and are mutually influential.

Portfolio assessment can serve a number of purposes in secondary special education programs. Virtually all domains in the curriculum may be tapped directly or indirectly through a portfolio method. Math, science, history, writing, and other basic skill areas can be assessed directly by including periodic assignments, quizzes, or projects in the portfolio. Examples might include lab reports, themes, sketches, and problem sets. Indirect assessment might apply to interpersonal skills development, athletic performance, and other motor skills. In these cases, the portfolio entry would be a reflection of authentic tasks. For example, the student might record bench press totals, reflections on interpersonal interactions, or attitudes toward events occurring in the classroom.

Portfolio Content

Work samples contained in a portfolio are determined by the purpose for which the portfolio is being used. As a general rule, the closer the portfolio's content to authentic performance, the better (Saland, 1998b). To this end, math problem sets may be preferred to occasional quizzes if being used to judge time spent engaged in instruction. Photographs of projects are preferred to descriptions or summary evaluations of projects if the goal is to assess the appearance of the project. An audio recording of social skills used through the day is preferred to completion of a social skills inventory. If direct and authentic performance measures are not available, secondary evidence may be used. Examples include performance ratings, test scores, awards, and anecdotal reports. It is important to note that these elements may be less valid and reliable than materials that are a direct result of the student's behavior. As such, the student, and others, may disagree when assessing their value.

The selection method for material contained in a portfolio may vary depending on the instructional context. Carpenter, Ray, and Bloom (1995) suggested that selection can be made independently by the teacher or student, through collaboration between the teacher and student, or by an external authority, such as the principal or a subject specialist. In any case, standards for selection should be introduced before portfolio material is produced. These standards might indicate the frequency with which materials are selected ("one assignment each week"), the scope of materials ("only assignments completed as homework"), and the purpose for which each entry is collected ("to produce an optimum estimate of your ability to run the quarter mile").

Evaluation of Entries

As with all assessment methods, two major concerns are reliability and validity. *Reliability* refers to the consistency or accuracy of measurement. The major question is whether the evaluation produces constant results from appraisal to appraisal. Limited reliability in a portfolio would indicate changes in performance scores where no change in performance actually occurred. *Validity* refers to the truthfulness of the interpretation of the scores. Is the conclusion drawn from the assessment accurate?

Both reliability and validity are enhanced by the preparation of a clear, objective, and complete scoring scheme. Examples might include the following:

- Each problem set will be scored against the answer key in the teacher's guide. The percentage correct will be indicated for each set. The overall portfolio score will be the average for all sets.
- The ceramics portfolio will contain five works completed during the course and selected by the student. Each piece will receive a qualitative rating of 0 to 5 for the following criteria: originality, technical competence, complexity/difficulty, and aesthetic appeal. The overall rating for each piece will be determined by adding the ratings for each criterion. There is a maximum score of 20 and a minimum score of 0. The overall portfolio score will be the sum of the ratings for the five works, with a grade A portfolio scoring over 90, a grade B scoring over 80, and so on.
- The language arts portfolio will include 10 papers selected by the student but including at least one of the following products: a newspaper article, a technical report, a fictional story, an autobiography, and a poem.
- Letter grades from A to F will be based on spelling, grammar, organization, originality (for fiction and poetry), accuracy (for technical reports, newspaper articles, and autobiographies), and content clarity. The portfolio grade will be the average grade for all entries minus the two lowest grades.

Reliability is judged by the extent to which two independent evaluators produce comparable scores. In general, a 20% error in numeric scores is acceptable. The percent error is determined by subtracting the lower raw score from the higher and dividing by 100. In the case of one teacher scoring 95 and another scoring 80, the error score would be 15% ($95 - 80 = 15$, $15 \div 100 = .15$). Fractional letter grade differences are also considered acceptable (e.g., B+ v. B–, or A v. B+). Differences in independent ratings may be reconciled through conventions or rules established before the evaluation. For example, the actual grade may be the highest of the independent raters, the average of the raters, or the rating provided by the major authority (e.g., teacher over student) as long as the level of agreement is within the standard of 20% error.

Validity is supported by the relationship between the portfolio content and decision being made. A math portfolio that contains periodic tests and assignments has reasonable validity against a judgment on the quality of a student's math performance through the academic period. Validity may be diminished if products from a critical period or reflecting critical content are not included. Validity may also be diminished if nonessential materials are given excessive weight.

Summary

Assessment data are used to establish placements, diagnose instructional difficulties, monitor the short-term effectiveness of instruction, and establish the long-term effectiveness of instruction.

There are two main types of assessment. One is norm-referenced assessment, which is an evaluation procedure that compares an individual's performance on a standardized instrument to the performance of a group of individuals. Norm-referenced assessment is considered to be most appropriate for supporting placement decisions and for determining the long-term effectiveness of instruction. The other is curriculum-based assessment, which includes both paper-and-pencil and observational measures; it compares an individual's performance with an objective standard. Curriculum-based measures are most appropriate for conducting diagnostic evaluations and establishing the short-term effectiveness of instruction.

In conclusion, all aspects of educational service for adolescents with disabilities depend on the careful analysis of learner characteristics. Placement decisions, specific goals and objectives, the instructional procedures, and the method used to determine the effectiveness of instruction hinge on the secondary educator's ability to evaluate youth.

6 *Managing the Learning Environment*

Did you know that . . .

- Student learning is maximized by an effective classroom management system?

- There are many different ways to prevent inappropriate behavior?

- Only a few publishing companies sell materials suitable for secondary students with disabilities?

- There are three alternatives to purchasing instructional material?

- Arrangement of the classroom can influence student behavior?

- The school day is generally broken into four categories of time?

- Antecedents precede a behavior and influence the probability of future occurrences?

- Consequences can be arranged on a continuum that reflects their intrusiveness?

- Token reinforcers are more appropriate for secondary learners with more severe disabilities?

- There is a link between poor academic performance and inappropriate behavior?

- Punishment techniques should never be used in isolation?

- There are different forms of time-out?

- Group contingencies can reduce jealousy among peers?

- Self-management can be used before other, teacher-directed behavior management techniques are implemented?

- IDEA now requires a functional behavior assessment be conducted when a student displays a long-standing, serious problem for unknown reasons?

- Students with disabilities cannot be suspended or expelled for demonstrating behaviors related to their disabilities?

- There are few data documenting the effectiveness of suspension and expulsion, despite the fact that these techniques are used frequently?

- In-school suspension was developed to circumvent the problems associated with out-of-school suspension?

Can you . . .

- Identify methods for preventing inappropriate behavior?
- Identify the steps required to obtain and validate new materials?
- Modify a complicated set of directions for secondary learners with special needs?
- Explain the importance of a seating chart?
- Identify basic equipment for the secondary classroom?
- Explain the importance of minimizing transition time?
- Describe how to minimize transition time?
- Describe how to maximize engaged time during teacher-directed and guided practice activities?
- Explain why some antecedent control techniques must be faded out?
- Set up rules for a secondary special education classroom?
- Devise a schedule for secondary students with special needs?

- Develop a systematic desensitization hierarchy?
- Arrange consequent techniques on a continuum?
- Deliver appropriate reprimands?
- Distinguish between three types of group contingencies?
- Arrange a group contingency?
- Develop a self-management program?
- Make a manifest determination?
- Conduct a functional behavior assessment?
- Distinguish between detention and in-school suspension?
- Identify inappropriate behaviors that warrant detention, in-school suspension, out-of-school suspension, or expulsion?
- Identify the disadvantages associated with suspension and expulsion?

Maag (2001) pointed out a common misconception about "discipline": most people associate the word with punitive procedures used to correct unacceptable behaviors. Maag highlighted the surprisingly positive aspect of the word by citing how it is defined in the American Heritage Dictionary. Specifically, *discipline* refers to "training that is expected to produce a specific character or pattern of behavior, especially training that produces moral or mental improvement" (p. 178). His perspective echoed that of Schloss and Smith (1998) and Yell, Rozalski, and Drasgow (2001), who noted that teachers who discipline are creating a pleasant and safe environment in which they can teach and students can learn. In such an environment, students learn the effects of their behavior on others and develop the ability to control and manage their behavior. Therefore, a *discipline problem* is any psychologically or physically unsafe behavior that destroys property or interferes with either the teaching act or the rights of others to learn. Teachers have long identified discipline problems with students as a major concern. Their concerns are reflected in federal legislation such as IDEA, which in 1997 was amended to address discipline. Specifically, disciplinary measures were to ensure that schools (a) provide students and staff with a learning environment that is safe and orderly, (b) enable staff to prevent and address discipline problems, (c) balance the need for the safety of all students and staff while ensuring the rights of students with disabilities, and (d) provide an appropriate education for students with disabilities including effective behavior interventions plans (Katsiyannis & Smith, 2003; Yell et al., 2001). Teachers are challenged to meet the needs of an increasingly diverse population of students (Hester, 2002), and they must manage the learning environment effectively if the teaching process is to meet its objectives. They must create learning environments that support all students' academic and social development while preventing discipline problems or minimizing their impact (Hester, 2002).

The practitioner can invest precious time and effort in assessing student characteristics. He or she can plan interesting lessons to demonstrate new concepts and provide students with creative practice activities. Practitioners hope to accomplish these tasks in a positive classroom atmosphere that allows them to work and their students to learn in a pleasant, safe environment. Teachers are advised to use a three-pronged approach consistently (Hester, 2002) to prevent discipline problems or minimize their effects. The three points of interest are antecedent control, the development of related personal characteristics, and consequence control. This chapter presents techniques within each category that contribute to effective management of the secondary classroom environment.

Antecedent Control

The term *antecedent* is synonymous with *prevention* (Schloss & Smith, 1998). An antecedent precedes a behavior and influences the probability of future occurrences. In addition, an antecedent can cue either appropriate or disruptive behaviors. For example, a student who enjoys math will smile and quickly prepare for the lesson when instructed to do so by the teacher. A student who dislikes math may procrastinate or become disruptive on hearing the teacher's directive.

Antecedents that cue student behaviors vary with the characteristics of the students in the class. Some are predictable—most students are pleased by good grades and are upset by low grades. Other antecedents are unique, as in the case of a secondary student identified as emotionally disturbed who engages in both self-abuse and physical aggression against others whenever he is told "no," "don't," "stop," can't," or "won't."

Antecedents that prompt appropriate and inappropriate behaviors should be identified and controlled by practitioners; however, a word of caution is in order. It is important to realize that some antecedents to disruptive behavior should always be eliminated or controlled by the teacher because to do so is simply good teaching. For example, good teachers provide their students with schedules and establish procedures for completing routine events in the classroom. These antecedent control techniques will remain intact throughout the school year. Other antecedent control techniques, however, should be in place only for a short time and should be used in combination with techniques that address related personal characteristics and consequences. For example, exposure to words with negative connotations should be minimized for the student described earlier. At the same time, the student participates in carefully structured social skill lessons that enhance his ability to respond appropriately to critical remarks. The frequency of his exposure to negative words increases as his social skills improve. In the long run, it would be unethical to shield the student from negative words. It is unnatural to have an environment in which every wish is granted and there are no disappointments. Similar treatment could not be guaranteed in future environments; indeed, it is extremely likely the student would not have moved to a

Action Plan 6.1   Antecedent Control Techniques

Attention to the following areas can minimize classroom disruption:

1. Physical arrangement
2. Rules
3. Routine classroom procedures
4. Student schedules
5. Time management
6. Systematic instruction
7. Functional, age-appropriate activities and materials
8. Rate of success
9. Teacher–student interactions
10. Interaction with nondisabled peers
11. Modeling
12. Review of the educational program

less restrictive setting at all if he were unable to respond appropriately to critical remarks from peers and authority figures.

Twelve useful antecedent control techniques are listed in Action Plan 6.1. Each is discussed separately.

Physical Arrangement

Most general secondary teachers are assigned one classroom in which they conduct their lessons or a few classrooms they move to throughout the day. Similarly, secondary special education teachers, whether self-contained or consulting, have little control over the location of their classrooms. However, students whose disabilities warrant placement in a separate setting should be served in a classroom located near rooms for typical secondary students. The room should also have easy access to the main office, the guidance counselor's office, and restrooms.

Teachers will want to set up an environment that will allow them to carry out various teaching activities more efficiently and encourage students to do their best in school. A carefully arranged classroom that decreases student noise and disruption can increase student achievement. Standard equipment in most classrooms includes a teacher desk and chair, preferably located off to the side of the room, a desk and chair for the paraprofessional, desks or tables and chairs of an appropriate size for the students, file and storage space, bulletin boards, chalkboards, audiovisual equipment, computers, textbooks, and supplies. Ideally, materials should be in good shape.

Everything should be arranged attractively, appropriately, and neatly. Although teachers have little control over the physical condition of walls and floors, they can decorate to compensate for old paint and encourage students to keep their work areas clean. Arrangement can affect how students behave. Poor seating arrangements or congested traffic patterns can increase misbehavior. For example, students may talk to one another out of turn. Noisy work areas located near quiet areas can increase distractibility and off-task behavior.

When considering the physical arrangement, a teacher should look at traffic patterns and make sure that areas of the room are easily accessed by students. Note and plan for high-frequency areas, such as group work areas, pencil sharpeners, trash cans, the water fountain, certain books, and storage areas. Separate these areas from one another, allowing plenty of space, and make them easy to get to. Keep work areas separate—that is, separate areas in which only work behaviors are reinforced from those in which more informal behavior is permitted. Try to give students as much personal space as possible. Never let "difficult" students sit near one another; they should be seated closer to the teacher. Classroom attractiveness can be enhanced by bulletin boards, plants, displays, aquariums, and student projects, but not so much material as to be distracting. The classroom should send the message that this is a place of business (and the business is learning). The room should be neat and uncluttered. In addition to being more attractive, a neat room enables teachers and students to find things more quickly and devote more time to instruction. Finally, teachers should be able to see everyone and everything in the room when they are scanning, and they should scan frequently.

Rules

Teachers are required to develop and maintain order in their classrooms; one way to achieve this goal is to require students to obey reasonable rules (Yell et al., 2001). A *rule* is a verbal statement regarding behavior; it tells students that a specific behavior will pay off in a particular situation. Thus, students know exactly what is expected of them (Hester, 2002). They will know what behaviors will and will not be accepted in the classroom and that they will be held accountable for following them (Yell et al., 2001). Rules are truly an important part of overall classroom management, but to be effective, they cannot be posted and then forgotten. They should serve as a framework for both the students' and the teacher's behavior throughout the year. They are the backbone of any proactive strategy to prevent discipline problems; they are also the backbone of any reactive strategy to respond to discipline problems as they occur. Rules are necessary because expectations for acceptable behavior differ in and outside of school. Students need to get used to the idea that standards vary across settings. What is acceptable in the cafeteria is not acceptable in the classroom; what is acceptable in the gym may not be acceptable in the music room. Establishing rules offers distinct advantages to teachers and students. They communicate the teacher's expectations regarding student behavior. Once rules are established and agreed on, students cannot then say they did not know about a rule or that it is unfair. If students participate in the rule-making process, their involvement establishes their expectations for one another as well.

It is unfair to criticize behavior when students do not know what is expected of them; therefore, the earlier the rules are developed, the better. The sooner students know the rules, the sooner they will start following them. Students are also more receptive to rules at the beginning of the year. Schloss and Smith (1998) have presented several guidelines for rule development:

1. Keep the list of rules relatively short. Opinions about the exact number of rules vary, but too few may not cover all the needs of the class. Having too many rules is inefficient and time consuming to enforce. Schloss and Smith recommended that up to seven rules that address academic and behavioral expectations may be necessary for efficient instruction. On a related note, teachers should check to see what rules exist for the building and make sure schoolwide policies are reflected on their list. Look for duplication in rules. Many times, two or three rules will address the same problem. For example, two rules such as "Bring your pencils" and "Bring your books" could be combined to state "Bring necessary supplies to class." Rhode, Jenson, and Reavis (1993) recommended including a compliance rule, such as "Do what the teacher says immediately."

2. Depending on the nature of the students, consider soliciting student opinion regarding the specific rules to be established. At times, however, student input results in more rules or more serious consequences for violations than the practitioner had originally intended. Seek student input, but have a good idea of what you want before starting this discussion and then shape the discussion.

3. Be precise. Students may have their own interpretation of what it means to "be po-lite," and it may not reflect the practitioner's perceptions. Yell and colleagues (2001) noted that vague or general rules may lead to the violation of students' rights simply because they did not understand exactly what was expected of them.

4. State rules positively and use observable terms. Rules should tell students what they *should* do rather than what they *should not* do. Following this guideline can be problematic at times because positively stated rules can be so convoluted that they do not make sense or seem ludicrous. It is more efficient to say "Don't spit" rather than "Keep saliva in your mouth" (Grossman, 2003). Nonetheless, rules do need to be observable so that an unequivo-cal decision can be made as to whether the rule has been broken.

5. Have consequences for rule infractions and be prepared to implement them. Conse-quences should be rational and fair (Yell et al., 2001).

6. Post the rules in a visible location using an age-appropriate format. It is not enough simply to establish classroom rules. They must be permanently on display in a prominent place in the room.

7. Teach the rules (Hester, 2002). Action Plan 6.2 lists steps for teaching rules to second-ary students.

8. Monitor adherence, for rules do no good if they are not enforced. Bear in mind that rules apply to everyone in the class, with no exception. Once exceptions are made, teachers have permitted a double standard and all rules become worthless.

Routine Classroom Procedures

Routines are procedures for handling regularly occurring events. They are what students need to know to meet their own personal needs and perform routine instructional and "housekeeping" activities. Students who know the routines are more likely to behave (Witt, LaFleur, Naquin, & Gilbertson, 1999) and less dependent on their teacher, leaving him or her free to devote time to instruction. Like rules, routines also communicate expectations for behavior, but they are applied to a specific activity and are directed at accomplishing

Action Plan 6.2   Teaching Rules

Teach rules the same as you would any other subject matter.

1. Establish rules the first day of school to let students know that rules are important. An introductory discussion can note that people have rules about obeying traffic, paying taxes, and so on.
2. Identify the importance of having rules; specifically, they promote learning and are necessary for the safety and comfort of all students.
3. Use group discussion. Allow students to question the usefulness or fairness of a rule, but the final decision about whether to include a rule rests with the teacher.
4. Identify how the teacher will know students are following and breaking each rule. Use the idea of "I will know you are following the rule when you . . ." and "I will know you are breaking the rule when you . . ."
5. Discuss what will happen by following the rules. For instance, discuss global benefits, such as getting along, making school a more pleasant place to be, getting more done, keeping all privileges, and so on.
6. Discuss what will happen when a rule is broken.
7. Provide teacher demonstrations of following and breaking rules, and have students identify the difference. When the teacher demonstrates a rule violation, the students should identify the consequences and appropriate alternatives. Always end with a positive demonstration.

something rather than defining a standard of behavior (Evertson, Emmer, & Worsham, 2005). They can be written and posted, especially if they are complex, but they do not have to be. Routines fall into two major categories: academic and nonacademic. Academic routines relate to ongoing lessons and include tasks such as obtaining and returning materials, getting assistance, providing headings for written work, and communicating assignments. Nonacademic routines contribute to the efficient management of the classroom but are not directly related to the ongoing lesson. They include getting a hall pass, using lockers, obtaining permission to use the bathroom, turning in homework or independent assignments, executing fire drills, and cleaning up at the end of the day. Routines need to be taught as systematically as academic content or rules. Action Plan 6.3 lists the steps for teaching routines.

Student Schedules

Another factor contributing to a successful secondary experience is the ability to follow a schedule. A *schedule* can be considered a set of instructional activities that delineates the organization of every school day, providing consistency and structure for students and staff (Hester, 2002). There are two advantages to developing a student schedule. First, it allows the practitioner to translate IEP goals and objectives into practice. Ideally, there should be an exact correspondence between goals stated on the IEP and the subject matter included in the students' schedules. This practice ensures that sufficient attention is being given to all prioritized areas. Second, a schedule permits the student, the teacher, and ancillary per-

Action Plan 6.3   Teaching Routines

Practitioners can teach routines as systematically as they teach rules or academic content by using these steps recommended by Jones and Jones (2001):

1. Discuss the importance of the routine.
2. Solicit ideas (but have a few in mind).
3. Finalize the procedure.
4. Demonstrate the routine.
5. Have students practice the routine.
6. Reinforce when the students adhere to the procedures.
7. Ask students who are having difficulty to state the correct procedure and then demonstrate it.
8. Consider posting routines such as fire drill routes and how to write a heading on a paper.
9. Revisit routines to ensure they are working as smoothly as anticipated and to add new routines as warranted.

Case for Action 6.1

It is September and your principal has advised the faculty that all students will be required to carry hall passes except when classes are changing. What procedure for obtaining passes will you develop and teach to your secondary students?

sonnel to predict what will happen during the school day. In some cases, predictability will minimize disruptions. For example, a thoughtfully planned schedule will help the student who dislikes science to maintain an appropriate attitude because he or she knows exactly how long the lesson will last. In other cases, a schedule allows staff members to anticipate and prepare for student difficulty. The teacher can arrange for other staff members to provide management assistance for a student who has a history of becoming disruptive just before physical education.

Schloss and Smith (1998) also identified eight guidelines for schedule development:

1. When possible, seek student input. General secondary education students will probably receive a completed schedule the first day of class. Schedules of secondary students with special needs may be more flexible if they include both some content area instruction and resource room assistance. Whereas some items, such as lunch or physical education, may have already been scheduled, a list of negotiable items can be presented to students for discussion.

2. Schedules should be available for quick reference. The schedule, like rules, should be on permanent display in a format that is consistent with the age and ability of the students. Some students might tape their schedules inside textbooks or in their appointment books.

3. Use the Premack principle. Students are more likely to engage in a less-preferred activity when they expect it to be followed by an activity they do enjoy. With 25 students in a general education class, or even 18 students in a special education class, teachers cannot plan a schedule that takes everyone's preferences into account. However, the sensitive teacher will probably have some good guesses about what most of them do and do not like and should plan accordingly.

4. The duration of the activity should reflect students' abilities. Older, more able students should engage in activities for lengths of time that correspond to those found in classrooms for nondisabled students. Secondary schools typically have instructional periods that last 40 minutes. Students with special needs who are included in content area classes should be able to participate for this length of time. If a student has difficulty maintaining attention this long, the teacher can break the period into chunks of time during which the student is doing different things. For example, the teacher can review homework, discuss the purpose of the lesson, demonstrate a skill, ask questions, and allow students to practice the skill in a variety of novel ways. All students, not just those with special needs, will benefit from this format. As the students' attention span develops, the teacher can gradually lengthen the amount of time the class is participating in any one activity.

5. Avoid revision. Inform students of holidays, staff personal days, assemblies, and field trips as soon as possible. Some secondary school officials vary the time when assemblies or other special events occur so that the same time period is not always lost. Other officials keep the time of special events constant but shave off five minutes from each instructional period. This accommodation allows all students to complete each item on their schedule while leaving sufficient time for the special event. Do not disrupt the schedule any more than necessary, because revisions undermine the students' ability to anticipate pleasant activities. In addition, a student may use disruptive behaviors to avoid or escape a scheduled activity. As soon as the student is ready to resume work, he or she should reenter the schedule at the point of disruption. The student will learn that manipulation of the schedule through inappropriate behaviors will not be tolerated. Ideally, the student should complete every class included on his or her schedule, but that may not be practical in secondary settings in which classes change or transportation schedules are inflexible. As a compromise, the student who became disruptive should complete the activity during which misbehavior occurred and then progress through an abbreviated schedule that includes sample activities from every class until he or she is caught up.

6. Motivate students. Occasionally, students will complete an activity earlier than expected. Practitioners should have a variety of related activities available so that students are appropriately engaged for the time scheduled.

7. Reinforce effort. Occasionally, the practitioner may overplan and assign more work than can be finished in the time allocated to instruction. Through no fault of their own, students do not finish their assignments. As the class draws to a close, summarize what has been completed, advise students of material that will be covered in the next lesson, and reinforce their efforts to complete assigned tasks.

8. Include parents. Send a copy of the schedule home to parents. In addition, schedules can be placed in students' permanent files.

Time Management

In general, time can be assigned to one of four categories: allocated time, engaged time, academic learning time, and transition time. The amount of time spent in these categories influences student achievement.

Allocated Time   *Allocated time* refers to periods during the school day in which specific activities are scheduled. Each period reflects the maximum amount of time for which students will be receiving instruction in a subject area. Unlike their colleagues at the elementary school level, secondary educators may have little or no flexibility in scheduling the length of instructional periods, as these may be dictated by administrative concerns. Practitioners may simply be told that they will have eight 40-minute instructional periods each day, for a total of 40 per week. Similarly, state regulations may dictate that minimum amounts of time are to be devoted to instruction in specific areas such as health or physical education. It is the practitioner's responsibility to ensure that the time allocated to instruction at the secondary level reflects state requirements and goals included on students' IEPs.

Engaged Time   The rate at which students acquire knowledge and skills depends on how effectively their teachers use the time that has been allocated to instructional areas. *Engaged time* refers to the time students are on task, performing the work that has been assigned to them. Several teacher behaviors maximize students' engaged time during teacher-directed and guided practice activities.

Practitioners should have all their materials and supplies ready before the lesson begins. They should use specific signals, called *discrete cues,* to obtain student attention at the beginning of the lesson. Teachers should also ask questions frequently during a lesson. Posing the question, then pausing, and then calling on a student randomly keeps the entire class alert. Using techniques such as think-pair-share and response cards can provide students with more opportunities to respond. These techniques and their advantages are described in Action Plans 6.4 and 6.5.

Teachers should also scan the room frequently and establish eye contact with students. Such visual contact may keep students on task, even those who are doing independent assignments rather than participating in the teacher's lesson. Obviously, disruptions seriously undermine the amount of engaged time for the misbehaving student and his or her classmates; therefore, practitioners should use effective behavior management techniques.

Finally, practitioners can increase their engaged time by examining their seating arrangement. Teachers spend nearly 70% of their time in front of the classroom, so it is no surprise that students at the back of the room contribute less to the discussion, pay less attention, are on task less, and achieve less. Interestingly enough, the brightest students tend to sit closer to the teacher; therefore, they are the ones the teacher attends to and reinforces. Dispersing higher-achieving students throughout the room directs teacher attention everywhere, increasing the likelihood that teachers will note when all students are appropriate and reinforce them.

During guided practice activities, teachers can provide specific instructions for completing interesting and challenging activities. They can also monitor student performance to ensure that students are not practicing errors. These and other suggestions are included in Action Plan 6.6.

Action Plan 6.4   A Combination of Think-Pair-Share and Response Cards

Maximize engaged time by combining the use of think-pair-share (Sacca & Raimondi, 1996) and response cards (Cavanaugh, Heward, & Donelson, 1996):

1. Randomly divide the class into equally and evenly numbered (if possible) groups of four.
2. Each group member is assigned 1, 2, 3, or 4.
3. Each group receives a small dry erase board (to serve as a response card), a marker, and something to use as a wipe (paper towel or tissue).
3. The "pairs" will be members 1 and 2, and members 3 and 4.
4. Ask a question and give every person some time to think about an answer. No one calls out or is called on.
5. When the time is up, pairs should share their answers and their rationale. One answer is selected.
6. All the pairs in the group share their answers and rationale.
7. The group selects and writes one response on a response card. Everyone should know and be able to explain the answer.
8. Response cards are held up on cue. The teacher may ask, "Number ___, raise your hands," and choose one person with that number to provide an explanation.
9. Erase the response cards and repeat.

Action Plan 6.5   Advantages of Think-Pair-Share and Response Cards

The advantages of think-pair-share include:

1. A reduction of the occurrence of impulsive responses
2. The requirement that everyone must think
3. The opportunity to work with peers
4. The opportunity for active responding
5. The fact that every student must be prepared with a response because he or she does not know which number the teacher will call out

The advantages of response cards include:

1. Obtaining responses from everyone
2. Obtaining feedback on the effectiveness of instruction
3. Keeping track of the accuracy of responses

Academic Learning Time   Students in classrooms can often be found completing a worksheet or writing answers to questions in a chapter review; however, their work is likely to contain several errors. Practitioners need to avoid this scenario by presenting instructional activities that challenge students without frustrating them. *Academic learning time* refers to the time in which students are engaged in an instructional activity and are experiencing a high rate of success. Teachers can increase academic learning time by

Action Plan 6.6   Effective Use of Time during Guided Practice

Teachers can maximize students' engaged time during guided practice activities by following these practices:

1. Use novel activities that motivate the students.
2. Give precise instructions for completing the task.
3. Reward correct responses with praise and other forms of reinforcement.
4. Monitor the time required to answer students' questions or explain errors. If it takes more than 30 seconds, the activity may be too difficult.
5. Organize practice activities so that students who finish earlier than anticipated know they should engage in another activity such as silent reading, peer tutoring, or computerized instruction.

presenting information in small steps, giving frequent feedback, and providing practice on materials that will be used on a test.

Transition Time   Time devoted to getting materials or putting them away, lining up for lunch, or moving from one subject or room to another is called *transition time*. Transition time is unavoidable; most middle schools and high schools plan for it specifically by having a brief time period during which students and teachers move to their next class. If there are 4 minutes between classes and eight classes a day, then the average secondary student uses over 150 minutes, or 2 hours, a week just moving between classes. Student disruption during transition often leads to extended periods of off-task behavior, which drains teacher energy and reduces student achievement. Transition time within or between lessons can be minimized with careful planning. Action Plan 6.7 offers specific suggestions.

Action Plan 6.7   Minimizing Transition Time

Teachers can do the following to reduce transition time:

1. Arrange the room for efficient movement. It may help to walk through the activities that are likely to occur. Furniture and equipment may be relocated to allow for smooth, unobstructed travel.
2. Have a schedule and adhere to it. If there are any anticipated changes, discuss them first thing in the morning.
3. Have all materials and supplies ready in advance. This tip not only increases engaged time but also reduces transition time. Teachers who are prepared can move more quickly and smoothly from one lesson to the next. Also, teachers who are not spending all their transition time getting ready can keep better track of what the students are doing.
4. Warn students of an impending transition. Teachers should keep an eye on the clock. Two minutes before the bell rings, advise students that they have two minutes to finish what they are doing and get ready.

Case for Action 6.2

You notice that the students in your secondary class are noisy and late coming to your class. They frequently forget items and return to their lockers, disrupting your lesson with questions about the location of their materials. What can you do to improve the situation?

Systematic Instruction

Classroom disruptions are minimized or prevented when students are actively engaged in teacher-directed lessons. (See Chapter 4 for a review of teacher behaviors that contribute to student achievement.)

Functional, Age-Appropriate Activities and Materials

Activities should be functional; that is, there should be a direct relationship between the skills acquired and the demands of the environment in which students must function. For example, students who need to practice their addition and subtraction skills would find it more appropriate to work on balancing a checking account than on completing drill sheets. Practitioners working with students with special needs in the regular classroom are advised to use the introductory phase of a lesson to emphasize the relationship between the target objective and environmental demands.

It is likely that the materials found in secondary special education classrooms were intended for either elementary students with disabilities or typical secondary students. Although materials designed for elementary students may emphasize skills that the secondary student should master, their format may be highly unsuitable for this level. For example, they may feature large illustrations or cartoon characters that appeal to younger learners but embarrass older learners. Materials designed for general secondary students also present a variety of problems. First, the material is more difficult to read because of the vocabulary level and the use of complex sentences. Textbooks may also lack transition words and cues (such as italics, boldface print, and introductory and summary paragraphs) to highlight key concepts (Deshler, Putnam, & Bulgren, 1985). Second, the material in some textbooks may require the student to have a knowledge base that secondary students with special needs do not possess. Third, the concepts presented in typical secondary materials may not be functionally related to the needs of youth with disabilities. For example, a text on consumerism that devotes a chapter to the law of supply and demand may not be relevant to a student who is having trouble managing checking and savings accounts. Fourth, even if typical secondary materials do address concepts relevant to students with special needs, they may not provide sufficient practice to ensure that students will master the concept. Although the consumerism text may mention checking and savings accounts, for example, it may provide only one or two practice activities.

Although there are commercial materials suitable for students with disabilities, most focus on elementary students. Some publishing companies are now supplying items suitable for older students who have disabilities. Some of these companies are listed in Action Plan 6.8.

Action Plan 6.8   Publishers of Materials Suitable for Use with Secondary Students with Disabilities

Teachers seeking materials suitable for secondary learners with special needs can contact the following companies:

Academic Communication Associates
4001 Avenida de la Plata
P. O. Box 4279
Oceanside, CA 92058
www.acadcom.com

Attainment Company
P. O. Box 930160
Verona, WI 53593
www.attainment-inc.com

Boys Town Press
Father Flanigan's Boys Home
14100 Crawford St.
Boys Town, NE 68010
www.boystown.org

Cambridge Development Laboratory
86 West Street
Waltham, MA 02451
www.edumatch.com/special

High Noon Books
20 Commercial Blvd.
Novato, CA 94949
www.HighNoonBooks.com

PRO-Ed
8700 Shoal Creek Blvd.
Austin, TX 78757
www.proedinc.com

Sopris West
4093 Specialty Place
Longmont, CA 80504
www.sopriswest.com

Steck-Vaughn Company
Harcourt Achieve
Attn: Customer Service 5th Fl.
6277 Sea Harbor
Orlando, FL 32881
www.steckvaughn,harcourtachieve.com

Edmark Associates
6727 185th Ave. NE
P. O. Box 3903
Redmond, WA 98052
www.edmark.com

Research Press
Dept. 20
P. O. Box 9177
Champaign, IL 61826
www.researchpress.com

Special Education Exchange
P. O. Box 948
Saratoga Springs, NY 12866
www.spedx.com

James Stanfield Company
P. O. Box 41058
Santa Barbara, CA 93140
www.stanfield.com

Secondary special educators could also serve on committees established to review and purchase materials for the secondary school (Deshler et al., 1985). Colleagues in general education who have been sensitized to the unique needs of secondary students with disabilities can make more thoughtful, appropriate decisions. Practitioners should take the following steps if the opportunity to purchase new materials for the secondary classroom

The following guidelines help teachers measure the suitability of commercial materials. Positive answers to the following questions support the appropriateness of commercial materials being considered for use with secondary learners:

A. General Information

1. *Publisher*
    a. Is it a reputable company that you or your colleagues have successfully dealt with in the past?
2. *Major Skill Area*
    a. Does this material represent a neglected skill area in your classroom?
    b. Can the major goals of the material be easily identified?
    c. Is the material relevant to your students' current or anticipated needs?
3. *Cost and Durability*
    a. Is the cost of the material within the budget?
    b. Are supplemental materials inexpensive and easily obtainable?
    c. Is the material well constructed and built to last?
4. *Target Age*
    a. How old are your students?
    b. Was this material designed for students of a similar age?
5. *Research and Field Test Data*
    a. Are data available to support the effectiveness of this material with secondary students with special needs?

B. Characteristics Related to Teaching

1. *Sequence of Skills*
    a. Is the sequence complete?
    b. Is it logically arranged?
    c. Do students have the necessary background experiences?
2. *Directions*
    a. Are directions to the teacher complete and clear?
    b. Are directions to the student complete and clear?
3. *Task Levels*
    a. Does the material contain activities for students who are at concrete or abstract levels of ability?
    b. Is the reading level appropriate for secondary students with special needs?
    c. Is the language level appropriate?
4. *Stimulus-Response Modality*
    a. Are a variety of modalities used to present new information?
    b. Can students respond to activities using a variety of formats (written responses, motoric responses)?
    c. Can the material be used without disrupting peers?
5. *Pace*
    a. Is the rate at which information is presented appropriate?
    b. Is there frequent review of key concepts?
    c. Is there a sufficient number of practice activities?
6. *Motivation*
    a. Will the materials increase the students' desire to learn the subject matter?

C. Characteristics Relating to Classroom Management

1. *Evaluation and Record Keeping*
   a. Are methods for measuring student progress included?
   b. Are data sheets included?
   c. Can students or peers measure and record progress?
2. *Space Requirements*
   a. Can the material be stored easily?
3. *Time Requirements*
   a. Can the material be set up and taken down quickly?
4. *Teacher Involvement*
   a. After initial instruction, can the material be used independently?
5. *Interest Level*
   a. Will secondary learners enjoy using this material?

---

arises (Mercer & Mercer, 2005): (1) Identify all the curricular areas in which new materials are needed, (2) rank the curricular areas in terms of priority, (3) identify affordable materials in the curricular area(s) receiving the highest priority, and (4) obtain and evaluate the material using the criteria included in Action Plan 6.9. Publishers may send specimen sets for practitioners to examine. A nearby resource or curriculum materials center may have the item in its collection.

Of particular concern is the textbook selected for use in secondary content classes (Schumm & Strickler, 1991). In most instances, teachers do not have the opportunity to select a textbook; rather, they choose texts from brief lists of district- or state-adopted books. These books may not meet the needs of secondary students with disabilities. Armbruster and Anderson (1988) identified steps teachers can take to choose the most "considerate" text from those available. The recommendations include looking for books that are well structured, coherent, and appropriate for the audience. Specific strategies for carrying out these recommendations are included in Action Plan 6.10.

Some practitioners may elect not to purchase any new materials because those available do not meet their students' needs. Instead, they may try to adapt existing materials to their needs, use material from nontraditional sources, or make their own materials.

When adapting materials for learners with special needs, the teacher usually has to modify the reading level, format, pace, or directions. The reading level can be modified in a variety of ways. For instance, students can be encouraged to develop and maintain their own glossaries of vocabulary words. Practitioners can highlight essential information in a text or block out extraneous information by covering parts of a page and then copying it. They can also provide students with an outline, an overview, study questions, and a summary.

A paraprofessional or a volunteer can record the book on tape (Meese, 1992). Recorded segments should be short and clear. The reader might also provide a preview before beginning the section, provide signals indicating page location, and stop occasionally to summarize important information. A secondary educator can also design a graphic

Action Plan 6.10   Choosing a "Considerate" Textbook

Armbruster and Anderson (1988) have suggested the following guidelines for identifying a considerate textbook:

1. *Look for structure.*
   a. Make an outline of the headings and subheadings. How reasonable is the structure that is revealed? Does it reflect your understanding of the content?
   b. Look for signals. Are the headings and subheadings informative? Are there marginal notations, graphic aids, boldface, italics, or underlining? Are there signal words that designate patterns of organization, such as *on the other hand* or *first, . . . second, . . . third, . . . ?*
2. *Look for coherence.*
   a. Are pronoun referents clear?
   b. Are there too many vague quantifiers, such as *some, many,* or *few*?
   c. Are transition statements used?
   d. Is there a chronological sequence that is easy to follow?
   e. Are the graphic aids important, clearly referenced to the text, easy to read and interpret, and clearly labeled?
3. *Is it appropriate for the target audience?*
   a. How adequate are explanations? Select a topic you know well and then read about it in the book. Determine whether its treatment was too light or too heavy.
   b. Check for the salience of main ideas. Are topic sentences the first sentences of the paragraphs? Does the text provide previews or summary statements? Are main ideas underlined, italicized, boldfaced, or highlighted in any other way?

organizer, which is a diagram depicting relationships in text material. This diagram provides students with a visual overview of reading material before they actually read it (Horton, Lovitt, & Bergerud, 1990; Meese, 1992). Chapter 15 includes more information on how graphic organizers can be used to teach secondary students with disabilities who are included in content area classes.

A more complex method of modifying the reading level is to rewrite the text. Some guidelines to assist the secondary educator who elects to rewrite materials are presented in Action Plan 6.11. Bear in mind that rewritten material will be longer than the original work and therefore may seem threatening to an insecure reader. Practitioners who do rewrite are advised to allocate more sessions to instructional units in which rewritten materials are incorporated.

A confusing format can be improved by "cutting and pasting." The practitioner can arrange materials in a more reasonable sequence, insert new headings, and eliminate distractors. The pace of instructional materials can be adjusted by providing additional practice in the form of games, peer teaching, and computer technology. In addition, the practitioner can modify the directions accompanying instructional material by pairing oral and written instructions, defining and explaining terms, giving one or two directions at a time, or asking students to repeat directions.

Action Plan 6.11   Rewriting Materials

We recommend the following suggestions made by Osterag and Rambeau (1982) for rewriting materials for secondary students with special needs:

1. Identify the current readability level.
2. Try to retain most of the material. Keep essential facts.
3. Reorganize the original sequence of ideas only if it is unnecessarily complex.
4. Rewrite materials that will be used again.
5. Shorten sentences by dividing them and deleting adjectives or adverbs.
6. Reduce the number of difficult words.
7. Use action verbs as much as possible.
8. Team up with other teachers to reduce the workload.
9. Read the revised story to someone else and revise as needed.

Case for Action 6.3

A new student refuses to use the supplemental reading series you have in your classroom. He says his other teacher used it in his other classroom and he hated every minute of it. What can you do?

A secondary educator might also want to consider using high-interest low-vocabulary materials. Many of these materials are available from the publishers listed in Action Plan 6.8. Educators are encouraged to review these materials to make sure they have proper content coverage (Mercer & Mercer, 2005).

If materials cannot be purchased or modified, practitioners may need to use items from nontraditional sources. Community settings in which secondary students are functioning or expected to function should contain a variety of materials suitable for use in the classroom. Items from nontraditional sources include newspapers, catalogs, bills, receipts, magazines, food labels, and employment applications. Nontraditional materials might even contribute to the maintenance and generalization of students' skills because of their functional relevance.

Rate of Success

If students experience a rate of success that is too high, they may become bored and disinterested in the task. If the assignment is too difficult, they may become frustrated. In both cases, students may engage in behaviors that are disruptive to the rest of the class. Schloss and Sedlak (1986) identified four levels of mastery to guide practitioners in the selection of student assignments:

1. Tasks that have been completed with 100% accuracy have been mastered and should only be reviewed occasionally. Tasks that lend themselves to paper-and-pencil activities can

be kept in a review folder for use when students complete other activities ahead of schedule. These activities should be interesting in nature, not simply a review. For example, a student who has mastered calculator skills could be assigned an activity that requires him or her to simulate purchase of catalog items necessary to attend the prom.

2. Tasks completed with 90 to 99% accuracy are considered learned, although the student occasionally makes an error. The teacher needs to provide guided practice activities such as games and drill-and-practice sheets. As noted in Chapter 4, homework assignments can be given for material learned to this level of accuracy.

3. Students completing activities with 70 to 90% accuracy should still be receiving teacher-directed instruction. Left to their own devices, they will make and practice errors. Instruction should occur in large or small groups and should be characterized by teacher behaviors that include a discrete cue, a logical sequence, minimal digressions, several examples, and many teacher questions (see Chapter 4).

4. Performance that is less than 70% accurate indicates the student is working at the frustration level. Practitioners are advised to break the instructional objective into smaller steps and teach them using the techniques suggested earlier. These activities should never be assigned as independent work, because they will lead to frustration and disruptive student behaviors. As noted in Chapter 4 and repeated in Chapter 7, the secondary teacher needs to make at least two well-documented attempts to assist the learner with special needs who is having difficulty. If a problem persists, the teacher is encouraged to contact a consulting teacher.

Teacher–Student Interactions

Secondary learners with severe disabilities frequently approach academic tasks with some degree of trepidation because they have experienced limited or no success in earlier endeavors. Practitioners can minimize this anxiety by developing positive, stable relationships that provide students with encouragement and warmth and increase their comfort in learning situations. Teachers need to be responsive and sensitive (Hester, 2002), yet firm and consistent in their interactions with students. The following guidelines proposed by Schloss and Sedlak (1986) indicate how to enhance teacher–student interactions:

1. Speak in concrete terms. Students with disabilities may be confused by frequent references to past or future events. Practitioners are advised to speak about concerns of immediate importance, using vocabulary and syntax that are sensitive to their students' level of comprehension.
2. Talk with students in a manner that indicates respect for their age and abilities. Although it may be necessary to modify vocabulary and syntax to accommodate the language characteristics of some learners, avoid talking down to them. Secondary students may resent the teacher who uses intonation patterns, facial expressions, or postures that are appropriate for conversations with much younger children.
3. Balance praise with corrective feedback. Secondary students with disabilities may display a number of problem behaviors that make them easy targets for criticism from their teachers. It may be necessary to limit critical remarks to a short list of inappropriate student behaviors. Additional behaviors can be added as old behaviors improve

and are displayed less often. Practitioners are also encouraged to identify and comment on any positive behaviors that students display. They should strive for a ratio of four or five positive comments for each reprimand or criticism (Hester, 2002).

4. Provide objective feedback. Praise or criticism that is immediate and specific can enhance student performance. Practitioners need to get the student's attention and deliver a complimentary or critical remark in objective terms. Feedback of this nature helps students identify precise aspects of their performance that should be repeated or modified.

5. Encourage students to develop their own solutions to problems. Students are more likely to assume responsibility for changing problem behaviors if they identify appropriate alternatives. Practitioners are advised that not all students with special needs will be able to identify appropriate solutions.

6. Redirect irrational or dysfunctional lines of thought. Sometimes students may not have all the information they need to identify valid explanations for, and suitable alternatives to, inappropriate behaviors. Practitioners may need to challenge and question the statements students make or identify reasonable alternatives for them.

Interaction with Nondisabled Peers

Consideration must first be given to how to meet secondary students' academic and social challenges in an appropriate manner. The nature and extent of participation in a less restrictive environment with typically learning peers are a reflection of the degree of a student's disability. Carefully sequenced instruction and the use of consulting teachers can increase the amount of time that secondary students with more severe disabilities are included in the general program.

Modeling

Modeling can have a powerful effect on secondary students with disabilities. Two sources of models should be considered: the teacher and peers. Most teachers are models for their students whether they plan to be or not. The ways a teacher acts, addresses others, dresses, or even wears his or her hair can influence these same aspects of student behavior. Bearing this in mind, it is important that secondary teachers model acceptable standards of behavior at all times.

Obviously, peers serve as models for secondary students with disabilities. Closer proximity to models of typical behavior is one reason for including students with disabilities in general education classrooms. Be advised, however, that proximity does not ensure students with disabilities will emulate appropriate academic and social behavior of their peers. Students who do not possess skills in the first place are unlikely to produce them regardless of their level of motivation; therefore, teachers will need to identify and teach academic and social skills to their students. Placement in a general education setting will then allow students to observe the benefits of displaying such behaviors as they see how their peers are rewarded, increasing the likelihood that these behaviors will be emulated.

Teachers can do more than just rely on proximity and incidental modeling to influence the likelihood that their students will demonstrate appropriate behavior. More proactive measures can draw students' attention to appropriate models and increase their desire to emulate them. Secondary teachers who have students with disabilities included in their content area classes have an ideal opportunity to use modeling to motivate use of acceptable behavior. Some suggestions for using modeling appropriately follow:

1. Because motivation to perform a skill is an essential but not sufficient condition for modeling to succeed (Schloss & Smith, 1998), make sure that the student with a disability is able to perform the targeted skill.
2. Identify students in class who are admired and respected by their peers. Choose carefully; some students are admired for the wrong reasons.
3. Praise these students for appropriate behavior in the presence of others. (It is assumed that these models do not object to overt teacher praise.)
4. Make sure that praise statements specify the appropriate behavior and its consequences, thereby highlighting the connection between the behavior and the reward.
5. Be sure to praise the student with disabilities when he or she demonstrates the desired behavior.

Review of the Educational Program

Ideally, practitioners should provide their secondary students with information and activities that facilitate mastery of IEP goals and objectives. An educational program can become out of date sooner than anticipated. Legally, IEPs must be reviewed once a year; however, practitioners are advised to *review them on a more frequent, informal basis.* This will ensure that goals and objectives are still appropriate and are being met at the expected rate. Practitioners experiencing concerns over existing programs can arrange for a meeting with all interested parties to formally review and update students' educational programs.

Related Personal Characteristics

As suggested earlier, practitioners must use antecedent control techniques carefully. They must decide which techniques should be permanent and which should be used only until students develop skills that will enable them to respond appropriately to previously pro-

---

Case for Action 6.4

Identify antecedents and antecedent control techniques for the student described below:

Louis is a 17-year-old who has been dually diagnosed as having moderate mental retardation and serious emotional disturbance. He becomes frustrated when confronted with academic tasks he cannot do. This frustration leads to object aggression on his part. Louis becomes physically aggressive toward anyone who attempts to halt his object aggression. Recently, Louis has been allowed to leave the room when feeling upset. This has been followed by one-to-one informal counseling by the teacher in the hall. This procedure has decreased the number of aggressive outbursts, but Louis continues to do poorly on his academic work.

voking events. *Related personal characteristics* refer to those skills that enable students to behave appropriately. Schloss and Smith (1998b) defined them as the observed and inferred characteristics of the individual that influence the target behavior. Once developed, these skills mediate between a provoking antecedent and a disruptive response. Previously, students may have acted inappropriately because it was the only response they had in their skill repertoires. After appropriate instruction, students no longer need to be disruptive; they will have in their repertoires a number of socially acceptable alternatives. Three strategies are available for improving students' related personal characteristics (for a more detailed discussion, see Schloss & Smith [1998]). They can be classified under academic skills, social skills, and emotional learning.

Academic Skills

Certainly many secondary students with disabilities display inappropriate behaviors when requested to participate in academic activities. Hester (2002) noted the link between poor academic performance and discipline problems. She maintained that students who perform poorly have fewer opportunities to respond, are praised less often, and earn lower grades. Given the frustration and anger students must feel after experiencing years of poor achievement, it is no surprise that poor academic performance can contribute to discipline problems. Practitioners will probably have to examine the secondary curriculum carefully or develop a functional curriculum from which to select skills that will have an immediate and positive impact on students' functioning. Secondary students with disabilities are more likely to respond appropriately to academic demands if the content is relevant and they believe they can master it. (See Chapter 4 for information on how to select and teach academic skills to secondary students with disabilities.)

Social Skills

Many secondary students with disabilities use disruptive behaviors in social settings because they are unaware of the socially appropriate methods for attaining their goals. Suppose that an individual receives a paycheck that is less than expected because of a clerical error. He proceeds to the payroll office, locates a clerk, and, using abusive language, demands a new check. He probably will get a new check; however, it is equally likely that he will get a reprimand from his employer criticizing his behavior and warning him that the firm will not tolerate similar outbursts in the future.

The difficulties that individuals with disabilities encounter in employment and community settings may be as much a function of social skill deficit as of the lack of academic or vocational competence. Consequently, it is important to include social skill instruction in educational programs developed for secondary students with disabilities. Social skills may need to be taught in separate small groups by a speech-language pathologist, the classroom teacher, or the consultant teacher. However, it is essential that these skills be practiced in general settings. Including students with disabilities in typical secondary programs will give them the opportunity to use newly acquired social skills and experience the reinforcement that occurs naturally as a result of their use. Inclusion will also expose them to appropriate models of socially skillful behavior. (See Chapter 14 for a detailed discussion of social skill development.)

Emotional Learning

Emotional learning techniques are based on respondent learning in which the environment acts on an individual to produce an uncontrollable emotional response. For example, a pop quiz produces anxiety, a good grade produces happiness, and a sarcastic remark produces anger. Students who have been exposed to supportive environments in which they have observed and participated in satisfactory relationships acquire and demonstrate appropriate emotional behaviors. In contrast, students who have been exposed to unpleasant events or who have interacted with punitive adults may acquire and display less desirable emotional characteristics. Unfortunately, many secondary students with disabilities fall into the latter category. Their teachers may have to develop and implement techniques that promote positive emotional development.

A new emotional response can be developed through pairing. The practitioner (1) identifies the event that fails to produce a positive response, (2) identifies an event that does produce the positive response, and (3) pairs the two events. For example, Ann may not display positive responses during interactions with peers. Her teacher, knowing how much she enjoys going to the mall, may arrange a field trip for Ann and some of her peers. A new emotional response may also be developed through vicarious conditioning. The practitioner (1) identifies the event that fails to produce a positive response, (2) identifies situations in which other individuals display the response, and (3) arranges for the learner to observe these situations. For example, a student who is afraid to raise his hand in class needs to see other students being reinforced for doing so.

Emotional learning can also help practitioners reduce excessive responses demonstrated by their students. Counterconditioning can be conducted by (1) identifying the event that produces the excessive response, (2) identifying an event that produces a stronger response, and (3) pairing them. For example, students who are anxious about taking an exam can eat homemade chocolate chip cookies during the test. Another technique for reducing excessive emotionality is desensitization. All the events related to an excessive response are identified and listed in order, from least to most provoking. An incompatible response is identified and repeatedly paired with the least provoking event until the individual no longer exhibits the response. Gradually, more provoking events from the hierarchy are introduced. An example of a desensitization hierarchy is presented in Action Plan 6.12.

Of course, an incompatible response may not be in the student's repertoire and therefore may have to be developed before a systematic desensitization program can be implemented. Bernstein and Borkovec (1973) have suggested a progressive muscle relaxation technique that requires the systematic tensing and relaxing of major muscle groups, including the arms, neck and shoulders, face, and legs. As each muscle is relaxed, the learner is asked to focus on the contrast between relaxed and tensed muscles. (For more information on progressive muscle relaxation, see Bernstein & Borkovec [1973]; Schloss & Smith [1998]).

Case for Action 6.5

What related personal characteristics would you target for development by Louis (in Case for Action 6.4)? How would you develop them?

Action Plan 6.12   A Systematic Desensitization Hierarchy

Eric becomes extremely agitated when his peers tease him. He and his teacher have developed a plan to help Eric control his feelings. They believe that his peers will stop after they see that their teasing no longer affects him.

Eric loves the beach. Therefore, while his teacher describes a peer who is teasing him, Eric will pretend to be relaxing on the sand, basking in the warmth of the sun. Eric and his teacher have developed the following hierarchy:

1. A peer is at the end of a long hall.
2. A peer is at the end of a long hall and is teasing Eric in a quiet voice.
3. A peer is about one-third of the way down the hall.
4. A peer is about one-third of the way down the hall and is teasing Eric in a voice at normal volume.
5. A peer is two-thirds of the way down the hall.
6. A peer is two-thirds of the way down the hall and is teasing Eric in a loud voice.
7. A peer is standing next to Eric.
8. A peer is standing next to Eric and is shouting teasing remarks.

Consequence Control

A *consequence* is an event that follows a behavior and influences the probability of future occurrences. A behavior has been reinforced if it increases in strength or frequency; similarly, it has been punished if its strength or frequency decreases. Consequent control techniques have received a great deal of professional attention; indeed, entire books have been devoted to the topic. The following section highlights some of the techniques suitable for secondary learners with disabilities. (For more elaborate discussions, see Alberto & Troutman [2003]; Schloss & Smith [1998]; Zirpoli [2005]).

Consequent control techniques exist on a continuum. This continuum is presented in Figure 6.1. On the left end are techniques that enhance the development of new behaviors.

FIGURE 6.1   *The Continuum of Consequent Control Techniques*

Primary Reinforcers	*Secondary Reinforcers*	*Extinction*	*Punishment*
Food Drinks	Social Activity Token Contracts	Planned ignoring	Reprimands Response cost Time-out Detention In-school suspension Suspension Expulsion

On the right end are techniques that reduce or eliminate inappropriate behaviors. Movement from the left end to the right end represents a shift away from positive techniques that are fairly common in educational practice toward techniques that are less natural and used cautiously only after less intrusive procedures have failed to produce desired results. The main points on the continuum are discussed in the following subsections.

Positive Reinforcers

Positive reinforcers are administered contingently and immediately on the display of the desired response, and they increase the probability that the response will be repeated in the future. They are used to shape the development of a skill and to increase or maintain the use of a skill already in the learner's repertoire. There are two types of positive reinforcers: primary and secondary. Primary reinforcers are biologically important to the individual and include food and liquid. In classrooms they are typically used with younger, less able learners because they are highly motivating and quickly affect behavior.

Secondary reinforcers are not biologically important—students have learned to appreciate their value. There are four types of secondary reinforcers, and all are suitable for use with high school students. The first type is the social reinforcer, which includes many techniques practitioners use almost unconsciously, such as praise, facial expressions, hugs, body gestures, and teacher proximity. Social reinforcers have many advantages. They take little of the practitioner's time and effort, they occur frequently in the natural environment, they can be paired with other techniques, and their use with one student may have a positive impact on the behavior of peers. Most teachers praise so often that they give little thought to exactly how it should be done. It is recommended that they included four items in a praise statement. First, identify the student by name so that he or she is attending. Second, identify what the student has done (the process) and then, third, the benefits of engaging in that behavior (the product). Fourth, provide a sincere compliment. Heward (2003) emphasized the importance of using praise. It would be unfair of a teacher to expect a student to work hard to acquire challenging skills without some formal recognition. In addition, rather than taking time away from the teaching process, praising students who have previously enjoyed little academic success is a very effective teaching practice.

Two words of caution are in order when using social reinforcement with secondary students. First, some students perceive teacher attention, even when positive, as unpleasant because it makes them look like the teacher's pet. A teacher who uses overt praise may in fact be punishing the very student he or she intended to reinforce. The teacher may find the behavior decreasing rather than increasing in occurrence. In such cases, the teacher is advised to use facial expressions (such as a smile), a nod of the head, or a gesture (such as a thumbs-up sign). These examples of social reinforcers communicate to students, albeit subtly, that their work or behavior is appropriate. Second, it is unfortunate but true that a very small number of individuals with inappropriate motives choose professions, such as teaching, that provide relatively easy access to children and youth. The media has publicized the highly inappropriate relationships in which some teachers have engaged. Therefore, in this day and age, some forms of social reinforcement used casually by teachers, such as hugs and pats on the back, may be construed as sexual advances. Teachers are advised to carefully select specific social reinforcement techniques that will safely and professionally convey their satisfaction with a student's academic and social progress.

The second type of secondary reinforcer is the activity reinforcer. It is based on the Premack principle, which was discussed previously with regard to schedule development. The practitioner can use any activity in which a student voluntarily engages to reinforce participation in an activity in which the student is reluctant to engage. A variety of activities are reinforcing to secondary students. They include free time and time to play computer games or listen to a portable stereo.

A secondary reinforcer appropriate for high school students with more severe disabilities is the token reinforcer. A token reinforcer is comparable to money in that it can be exchanged for something considered valuable by the students. As with all reinforcers, a token is delivered immediately and contingently on the display of the target behavior. Typically, it is small, portable, durable, and easy to handle. Practitioners may use poker chips, buttons, or play money; however, they are cautioned against using objects that students can easily obtain elsewhere. "Counterfeit" tokens will undermine the effectiveness of a token economy. Tokens are exchanged at predetermined intervals for any one of a variety of items that are age appropriate for secondary learners. Examples of appropriate items include coupons for fast-food restaurants, cosmetics, movie passes, key chains, and comic books.

The fourth secondary reinforcer is a contingency contract. A contract is a written document developed and signed by the teacher and a student that identifies the relationship between specific behaviors and consequences. Consider the case of Mike, a secondary learner who displayed high rates of physical aggression against authority figures. Figure 6.2 presents the contract used to bring Mike's behavior under control. Mike's contract contains the components of a good contract. First, it was the result of mutual negotiation. Second, it clearly described the behaviors being targeted for development and reduction. Third, it identified the pleasant consequence for displaying appropriate behavior for a specific period of time. Fourth, it also identified the consequences of not living up to the agreement. Fifth, it required the signatures of Mike and his teacher.

The consequent control techniques just described are all designed to promote the development of new skills or to increase the use of skills already in the learner's repertoire. In all likelihood, secondary special educators will not only have to develop new skills, but they will also have to reduce or eliminate inappropriate behaviors. Other points on the continuum assist practitioners with this task.

Extinction

The next point on the continuum of consequent control techniques is extinction. *Extinction* has been referred to as planned ignoring. An inappropriate behavior is extinguished by removing the positive reinforcement that maintained it. For example, Carlos uses profanity every time the practitioner announces a homework assignment. The practitioner reprimands Carlos, not realizing he is using this language to get her attention and possibly postpone the assignment. By no longer taking notice of it, the teacher can extinguish Carlos's swearing. Unfortunately, this is not as easy as it sounds. There could be an extinction burst—that is, Carlos's behavior might escalate as he swears more vehemently to get his teacher's attention. In addition, he might find the laughter of his peers reinforcing. Nonetheless, Carlos's behavior will eventually subside as the teacher continues to ignore him and praise other students for their cooperation.

FIGURE 6.2   *A Contingency Contract for a Secondary Student with Severe Behavior Disabilities*

Name: Mike S.   Date: September 8, 2005
Teacher: Mrs. Klein

Part A

Mike must pay attention to the teacher. He must follow her directions. When the teacher
gives a direction, Mike will

1. look at her and listen,
2. begin following the direction within 10 seconds, and
3. finish the task on time.

Part B

Mike will follow every teacher's direction for three days. On September 11, Mike and his
teacher will go to McDonald's for lunch.

Part C

When the teacher gives a direction, Mike will not

1. swear or shout,
2. refuse to comply,
3. try to leave the room, or
4. try to hit the teacher.

If these behaviors occur, Mike will

1. not go out to lunch,
2. lose points for noncompliance, and
3. go to the time-out room if necessary.

Student signature   Date   Teacher signature   Date

Punishment

The third major point on the continuum is *punishment,* defined as an event delivered immediately and contingently on the display of a targeted behavior that reduces the probability of
future occurrences. The use of punishment has distinct advantages. First, it is quick; that is,
there should be an immediate change in the student's behavior. Second, it facilitates learning by providing a clear discrimination between behaviors that are and are not acceptable.
Third, it illustrates for other students the consequences of displaying the behavior. Punishment procedures also have their drawbacks. First, the student who is being punished may
escalate his or her behavior. For example, the student who is being punished for swearing
may become physically aggressive. Second, it is possible that the student who has been

Action Plan 6.13   Guidelines for Using Punishment Techniques

Secondary special educators are advised to use punishment techniques cautiously. The following guidelines may be useful:

1. Use the procedure only in extreme instances, such as for behavior that is of a long-standing nature or that threatens personal safety.
2. Document the ineffectiveness of less intrusive consequent control techniques.
3. Plan everything in advance, share the program, and obtain permission from the parents or legal guardians.
4. Observe safety guidelines.
5. State the contingency when you need to use it.
6. Do not threaten or warn—do what you said you were going to do.
7. Deliver the punishment consistently, immediately, and in a nonemotional, matter-of-fact manner.
8. Use the procedure at an intensity expected to be effective. Do not let the student develop a tolerance for it.
9. Make sure that everyone who will come into contact with the student is trained in the use of the procedure.
10. Target the development of appropriate alternatives and reinforce their use.
11. Document the effectiveness of the punishment. Its effects should be immediately noticeable and should be maintained over a period of time.
12. Identify in writing the steps for using positive procedures and punishment procedures. Have another person observe and check off steps on the list to make sure the steps were followed in the right order, at the right time, and at the right intensity.

punished may withdraw. Secondary students may "get sick," cut class, or even drop out of school. Third, a student being punished may try to escape the situation. Fourth, the teacher who punishes may serve as a model for other students in the class. Finally, the use of some punishment procedures has been challenged in the courts (*Gary W. v. Louisiana,* 1976; *Ingraham v. Wright,* 1977; *Romeo v. Youngberg,* 1982; *Wood v. Strickland,* 1975). Practitioners who use aversive behavior management techniques risk legal complications if they are unfamiliar with their conceptual bases, correct applications, and legal implications. These disadvantages show how important it is to adhere to the guidelines presented in Action Plan 6.13 when developing a punishment program.

Reprimand   One of the least intrusive techniques a secondary teacher can use to stop inappropriate behavior is a reprimand. Reprimands are used frequently in all public school classrooms, but teachers can increase their effectiveness by following the guidelines established by Misra (1991). These guidelines are listed in Action Plan 6.14. First, make the reprimand a brief and specific statement, focusing on one behavior at a time. Identify the student by name, pinpoint the target behavior, briefly explain why the behavior is not acceptable, and then describe an alternative. Using statements rather than questions clearly identifies what the student should be doing yet minimizes the likelihood that the student will talk back or try to answer sarcastically. Second, avoid judgmental words such as *bad* or

Action Plan 6.14   Reprimanding

Misra (1991) offered the following guidelines for using reprimands:

1. Be brief and specific.
2. Avoid judgmental language.
3. Use concrete terms and appropriate vocabulary and syntax.
4. Do not repeat ineffective reprimands.
5. Be courteous.

stupid. Such language has no place in the classroom. Third, use concrete terms that reflect age-appropriate vocabulary and syntax. As suggested earlier in this chapter, students with disabilities may have difficulty understanding abstract vocabulary and complex syntactic structures. Concrete, measurable terms increase the likelihood that students will follow through with the suggestions provided in a reprimand. Fourth, do not repeat a reprimand that has failed to produce desired changes in student behaviors. Repetition does not increase the likelihood that students will comply. Students may in fact learn that they can stall the teacher and prolong the delivery of more intrusive consequences. Fifth, be courteous and talk in an age-appropriate manner. A teacher's tone of voice and facial expression should always convey respect for students, even when they are misbehaving. Action Plan 6.15 provides sample reprimands.

Response Cost   Response cost procedures involve the immediate removal of a reinforcer contingent on the display of an inappropriate behavior. Secondary learners may already

Action Plan 6.15   Appropriate versus Inappropriate Reprimands

Fifteen-year-old Kate is in health class, staring out the window rather than watching the filmstrip.

Appropriate:

"Kate, don't look out the window. You are missing the filmstrip. You need to watch carefully."

Inappropriate:

"Kate, stop looking outside." (Lacks specificity; does not provide an appropriate alternative)

"Kate, how many times do I have to tell you to pay attention?" (Asks a question; does not provide an appropriate alternative)

"Kate, how many times do I have to tell you to pay attention? You are always looking out the window. You will be really sorry when it's time to take the quiz. All of your answers will be dumb." (Asks a question; does not provide an appropriate alternative; is too long and judgmental)

Action Plan 6.16   Steps in Developing a Response Cost System

Secondary special educators should follow these steps when developing a response cost system:

1. Target the behavior to be reduced.
2. Identify the type and amount of reinforcer to be withdrawn contingent on the display of the targeted behavior.
3. Teach and reinforce the use of appropriate alternatives to the targeted behavior.
4. Explain the response cost procedures to the students.
5. Document the effectiveness of the program.
6. Prepare a backup procedure in the event that a disruptive behavior escalates.

be familiar with the concept of response cost. For example, they may have paid a fine for keeping a library book past the due date, or they may have been docked a portion of their allowance for not complying with a parental request. The fact that response costs occur frequently in the natural environment makes them particularly useful in the classroom. Unfortunately, they have their disadvantages as well. Response cost procedures do not necessarily motivate students to use appropriate behavior. As a result, response cost procedures must be used in conjunction with reinforcement techniques that promote skill development and use. Another disadvantage is that a response cost may produce a negative emotional reaction that leads to more disruptive behavior. A student who is upset because he lost points for refusing to open his textbook, for example, may throw the book across the room. Practitioners who need to develop a response cost system for their students should follow the procedures listed in Action Plan 6.16.

Time-Out   Time-out denies students the opportunity to receive reinforcers for a specific period of time. There are different forms of time-out: contingent observation, exclusion, and seclusion (Yell, 1990). Contingent observation involves the removal of the disruptive student to some peripheral area of the classroom. The student can still observe activities occurring in the classroom; however, he or she cannot participate for a period of time. During exclusion time-out, the student is removed from the immediate setting for a period of time. For example, the student is removed to a corner of the room sectioned off by partitions or to the hall. This form of time-out is less drastic than total seclusion, and it protects the rights and interests of other students in the classroom. Seclusion time-out requires the removal of the student from the classroom to an isolation room. This type of time-out ensures the safety of others in the classroom and affords the disruptive student the opportunity to learn and to practice more appropriate behavior. Procedures for using seclusion time-out are listed in Action Plan 6.17. Be advised that the room used for seclusion time-out must adhere to certain standards (Alberto & Troutman, 2003). These include using a room that measures at least 6 feet by 6 feet, has adequate lighting and ventilation, and does not contain any potentially harmful objects. In addition, the room must not be locked, and it must be monitored by staff members when in use. Central to all forms of time-out is the premise that the secondary classroom and the activities occurring in it are appropriate and

Action Plan 6.17   Using Seclusion Time-Out

School officials who elect to use seclusion time-out should adhere to the following guidelines:

1. Determine in advance disruptive behaviors that will result in seclusion time-out and clearly explain them to all students.
2. Develop procedures for being released from seclusion time-out and explain them to all students. These include the demonstration of appropriate, nondisruptive behavior for a specified period of time, restitution for destroyed property, identifying and role-playing alternatives to disruptive behavior, and a return to the activity during which the disruptive behavior occurred.
3. Attempt other, less intrusive procedures first.
4. Use seclusion time-out in conjunction with positive procedures such as social reinforcement of appropriate behavior.
5. Minimize all verbal communication with the disruptive student. Only encourage him or her to calm down.
6. Document its use.
7. Evaluate its effectiveness.
8. Become familiar with any district policies regarding the use of seclusion time-out.
9. Ensure that the time-out room meets specifications.

---

interesting. Time-out will not be an effective punishment technique if time-in does not have any reinforcing properties.

Group Contingencies

The consequences just described will allow secondary teachers to increase student use of appropriate behavior and decrease or eliminate the use of behaviors that are unacceptable. Teachers who are concerned about the time and energy required to develop and implement behavior change programs are reminded that it takes even more time and energy to deal with inappropriate behavior ineffectively. Despite the advantages these techniques offer to teachers, it is acknowledged that their use may not take group dynamics into account. It is likely that use of a special program with one student may spark a note of jealousy among peers. This is a valid concern. Why should a student who misbehaves have the opportunity to earn special events or items that are unavailable to students whose behavior is appropriate most of the time? In addition, many management techniques are based on the assumption that there is only one student in the class rather than 30.

The inclusion movement has increased the likelihood that more students with greater behavior management needs are receiving educational services in the typical secondary classroom. Teachers who need a behavior management program may prefer to use one that will efficiently address the needs of more than one student and allow them to devote more time to meeting the academic needs of all the students in their class. A technique that addresses these issues is a group contingency. The basic premise of a group contingency is that desired rewards will be provided to the group as a whole if students within that group demonstrate a set of appropriate behaviors. Group contingencies exert more control over student behavior by capitalizing on peers as an important influence on classroom behavior. Teachers are advised that a group contingency can also penalize all students on the basis of the behavior of one or two students. Therefore, it is not surprising that the fairness of a group contingency has been debated. Rhode and colleagues (1993) suggested that use of group contingencies in educational settings is indeed fair if peers are contributing to the inappropriate behavior committed by one or two students. According to Smith and Misra (1994), group contingencies are a fact of life. Insurance premiums reflect the cost of fraudulent claims. Shoplifting increases the cost of department store items. On a positive note, everyone benefits when a single person's medical or technological breakthrough enhances the quality of life.

Generally, there are three types of group contingencies: dependent, independent, and interdependent (Litow & Pumroy, 1975). The major difference between them is the manner in which students earn the reinforcement. In a dependent group contingency, the same contingency is in effect for all students; however, the performance of one student or a small group of students determines the consequences received by the entire group. For example, Tim is out of his seat a lot, chatting with his neighbors. He is not getting his work done and is falling behind academically, as are the peers he visits. The teacher arranges for Tim to receive a point after completing each assignment. At the end of the week, if Tim has five points, the whole class can have free time. This contingency is public in that all the students know the reward is contingent on Tim's behavior. Peers are less likely to allow Tim to be out of his seat chatting with them. Perhaps Tim is one of several students who display this behavior and the teacher thinks it is unfair to put too much pressure on Tim to perform. Under these circumstances, the teacher can select one or more student names at random and keep them confidential. All are more motivated to remain in their seats and finish their work because they do not know whose name has been selected.

In an independent group contingency, the contingency that is in effect for all group members is applied on an individual basis. Thus, each student in the class can earn reinforcement based on his or her own appropriate behavior without affecting the consequences experienced by other group members. Although this type of group contingency does not single out any particular student from his or her peers, it may not be a true group contingency because students do not depend on one another's behavior to earn rewards.

In an interdependent group contingency, the same contingency applies to all students, but final evaluation is based on a specified level of group performance. For example, a class might be divided into two or three smaller groups or teams, with each team treated as though it were a single person. Points for appropriate behaviors are awarded to team members and totaled up at the end of the day. The group with the most points earns a special reward. Conversely, a team can receive a mark each time any one of its members misbehaves. At the end of the day, the team with fewest marks earns the reinforcers. Finally, an interdependent group contingency may involve a comparison of each group's total to a predetermined criterion. All groups who meet or exceed the criterion receive the reinforcement. Procedures for implementing a group contingency are presented in Action Plan 6.18.

There are several advantages to using group contingencies for teachers and students. The emphasis on group behavior means that individual students are not singled out for teacher attention. Group contingencies are also very efficient because secondary teachers can plan, implement, and monitor one program rather than several individualized programs. Finally, they can be used to address a wide variety of behavior. There is a disadvantage,

Action Plan 6.18   Implementing a Group Contingency

Teachers can use group contingencies to manage behavior from one student that is being reinforced by peers or to handle a problem being demonstrated by more than one student in the same class. Teachers should follow these steps recommended by Smith and Misra (1994) and Schloss and Smith (1998b):

1. Clearly define the target behavior.
2. Collect data on target behaviors.
3. Determine which type of group contingency to use. When using the interdependent group contingency, arrange groups with individuals who have similar behavioral and academic characteristics.
4. Define the criterion for performance. The teacher may use the total number of behaviors, a classroom average, or the performance of a particular student or a student selected at random. The criterion can become more stringent as student performance improves.
5. Encourage student participation through activities such as setting goals, monitoring behaviors, awarding points, tutoring, and keeping records.
6. Make sure students possess the skills needed to meet the criterion. Address skill deficits through instruction in academics or social skills.
7. Identify items or events that are reinforcing to students.
8. Explain the contingency to students.
9. Assign students to groups.
10. Implement the contingency and collect data to monitor its effectiveness.

---

however. One or more students may undermine the group's efforts; specifically, rather than earning the predetermined reinforcer, these students may find it more rewarding to spoil others' opportunity to earn the reward. Rhode and colleagues (1993) recommended that such students be assigned to their own group, even if it is a group of one, to eliminate the satisfaction they feel.

Self-Management

In an ideal world, by the time students enter high school they are able to manage their own behavior. Several techniques have been recommended for assisting students who demonstrate difficulty in controlling their behavior. As effective as they are, however, techniques such as praise, token economies, reprimands, and response cost have one disadvantage in that they are externally driven; that is, they are heavily dependent on teacher implementation if they are to have the desired effect. Having assisted students in gaining control over their own behavior, teachers can now turn to a set of techniques known as *self-management* to encourage students to maintain and generalize newly learned skills.

   Self-management refers to an individual's ability to maintain or change his or her own behavior. It includes several behaviors, such as self-determination of criteria, self-determination of reinforcement, self-evaluation, self-instruction, self-monitoring, self-punishment, self-reinforcement, and self-scheduling (Carter, 1993; Schloss & Smith, 1998). Self-management offers several advantages over traditional externally managed systems of reinforcement. It increases students' independence by making them accountable for their own behavior. It allows the teacher more time to deal with other school matters. It can easily be adapted to meet a wide variety of students' behavioral needs across a range of settings. Finally, self-management is a powerful tool for promoting generalization and transfer of training of newly acquired knowledge and skills. These advantages make self-management ideal for use by students in the secondary school. In fact, King-Sears and Bonfils (1999) recommended that teachers consider using self-management before developing an external reinforcement system.

Whether using it as the starting point or after applying externally managed techniques, most students with disabilities will need to be taught to self-manage their behavior. King-Sears and Bonfils (1999) described an instructional sequence called SPIN, which is summarized in Action Plan 6.19. Phase I is called *Select,* which first requires the teacher to operationally define the target behavior to be changed and illustrate it with examples and nonexamples. Perhaps the teacher is targeting the development of in-seat behavior. Examples include specific behaviors that indicate to the teacher and the students that they are displaying in-seat behaviors. Nonexamples include specific behaviors that indicate students are out of their seats. Next, the teacher determines the criteria for acceptable performance. Also, systematic observation procedures are used to measure students' current level of performance. Phase II is called *Prepare,* during which the teacher develops lessons for teaching self-management and creates a self-monitoring device. This device typically consists

---

Action Plan 6.19   SPIN

King-Sears and Bonfils (1999) described the following self-management instruction sequence called SPIN:

Select the target behavior the students will self-manage.
- Identify and define the target behavior.
- Identify the criteria for mastery.
- Measure the students' current level of performance.

Prepare materials and lesson plans.
- Select the type of self-management system.
- Develop the system.

Instruct the students.
- Introduce the behavior.
- Introduce the self-management program.
- Provide practice opportunities and measure student progress.

Note effectiveness.
- Measure the short-term effects on the target behavior.
- Assess long-term use of the program.
- Encourage generalization.

Action Plan 6.20   Steps in the Instruct Phase of SPIN

King-Sears and Bonfils (1999) used the following steps to instruct students in the use of self-management:

- Introduce the target behavior.
  1. Identify and demonstrate examples and nonexamples of the target behavior.
  2. Discuss why the target behavior is important.
  3. Practice the target behavior.

- Introduce the self-management program.
  4. Describe the self-management program and its advantages.
  5. Model how to use the self-management recording device.

- Provide practice and assess student performance.
  6. Incorporate the target behavior and use of the recording device into role-play.
  7. Assess student performance during role-play.
  8. Discuss real situations in which self-management will be used.
  9. Provide independent practice in real settings.
  10. Assess student performance in real settings.

of a method the students can use for recording whether the target behavior occurred. The recording method may include a section students can use to identify goals they have set for themselves. The teacher will also use this time to create a timing device so that students will know when to record their own behavior. This device might be as simple as a tape that plays a tone at a regular interval. Phase III is called *Instruct* and the teacher uses a 10-step sequence to teach students how to self-manage. These steps are listed in Action Plan 6.20. During Phase IV, *Note,* the teacher uses systematic observation procedures to assess the short-term effects of the self-management program on the target behavior. The teacher also determines whether students are continuing to use the program independently and in settings other than those originally selected for intervention.

Schoolwide Systems

Most schools have procedures for dealing with misbehavior typically demonstrated by secondary students. These procedures include detention, in-school suspension, out-of-school suspension, and expulsion. The last two items have special implications for learners who are disabled.

Detention

Detention refers to a period of time before or after school during which students report to a separate room because they have committed rule infractions. Kerr and Nelson (1998) indicated that this time period can range from 30 to 90 minutes. They also recommended

Action Plan 6.21   Using Detention

Kerr and Nelson (1998) recommended several guidelines for developing and implementing a detention policy:

1. Assign staff to monitor the detention room.
2. Clearly specify behaviors that will result in detention.
3. Consider transportation options.
4. Schedule detention for certain days and times.
5. Assign detention in writing.
6. Notify parents.
7. Have assignments ready.
8. Establish, post, and review rules for the detention room.
9. Evaluate the effectiveness of detention.

that school officials carefully plan a detention policy using guidelines presented in Action Plan 6.21.

1. Develop a schedule for staff who will be responsible for monitoring the detention room. School officials might consider having a coordinator who is responsible for scheduling detention and contacting parents.
2. Clearly specify the behaviors that will result in detention and share them with staff, students, and parents. These behaviors should be less serious than those that would result in in-school suspension.
3. Consider transportation options. For example, parents may be contacted and asked to make transportation arrangements; however, the need for most parents to work may undermine their ability to transport their children to and from school. Therefore, a late bus might be arranged for students who are transported to and from school.
4. Set aside certain days and times for detention days. For example, detention might be scheduled for every Tuesday, Wednesday, and Thursday. This guideline has the disadvantage of postponing the delivery of punitive consequences, which could undermine its effectiveness. However, scheduling detention in this manner makes it more enforceable. It allows time for parents to be informed and for transportation arrangements to be made. In addition, such advanced notice enables school staff to make adjustments to their schedules to cover detention duty. Finally, regularly scheduled detention days should provide teachers and students with sufficient time to identify and prepare appropriate independent assignments.
5. Assign detention in writing. A detention slip, preferably several carbonless copies, should note the rule violation, the date of detention, and the name and phone number of a school official parents can contact if they have any questions.
6. Notify parents in writing that their son or daughter has been assigned to detention. Adjustments can be made to accommodate any reasonable, verifiable excuses for absences (such as a doctor's appointment).

7. Have teacher-made assignments ready in the detention room for students to complete. Students who fail to bring their own assignments, having previously been instructed to do so, should be given another detention.
8. Establish, post, and review firm rules for behavior in the detention room.
9. Regularly review the impact of detention on student behavior. School officials may want to keep track of repeat offenders, the nature of their offenses, and which teachers are abusing the system.

In-School Suspension

More intrusive than detention is the use of in-school suspension (ISS). It is being used more frequently in public schools as an alternative to the disadvantages associated with out-of-school suspension and expulsion, which will be discussed shortly (Yell, 1990). Kerr and Nelson (1998) identified three assumptions of effective in-school suspension programs. First, like time-out, it is assumed that the setting from which the student is removed is reinforcing. Second, it is assumed that the ISS room is nonreinforcing. Third, it is assumed that the student moves to and from in-school suspension on the basis of carefully constructed contingencies. Used correctly, ISS offers many advantages to secondary school officials. Disruptive students are separated from the rest of the school population yet are still in school, rather than roaming about the community unsupervised. In addition, ISS does not deprive students of their right to an appropriate education (Yell, 1990).

Kerr and Nelson (1998) identified specific guidelines to increase the effectiveness of in-school suspension. These guidelines are listed in Action Plan 6.22.

1. School officials can either select one individual to assume ISS responsibilities on a permanent basis or rotate this responsibility among different staff members. Regardless of which option is chosen, those who assume this responsibility must be able to manage disruptive behavior.
2. Students can enter ISS only at the beginning of the school day. Those who arrive late or during the day may create additional problems by being disruptive.

Action Plan 6.22   Guidelines for In-School Suspension (ISS)

The following guidelines for ISS were adapted from Kerr and Nelson (1998):

1. The staff member in charge of ISS should be a skilled behavior manager.
2. Students must enter ISS at the beginning of the school day.
3. Before entering ISS, students should meet at a central location where their offenses and ISS rules are discussed.
4. Assignments should be ready at the beginning of ISS.
5. Opportunities to leave the ISS room should be minimized.
6. Additional ISS days should be required for students who violate rules in the ISS room.
7. At the end of ISS, alternatives to inappropriate behavior should be reviewed.
8. Teachers should be kept advised of student behavior during ISS.

---

3. Students assigned to ISS should meet in a central location at the beginning of the school day. At this location, they can be reminded of both their offenses and the rules governing the ISS room.

4. The staff member in charge of ISS should already have students' assignments prepared. These assignments should come from teachers whose courses will be missed as a result of the student being sent to ISS. It is most helpful if classroom teachers provide work that students can complete independently or with minimal assistance. This will minimize the likelihood that the inappropriate behavior that resulted in ISS is inadvertently reinforced by teacher attention.

5. Students should have only limited opportunities to leave the ISS room. For example, only one or two students should be allowed to use the restroom at a time. Also, students should eat their lunch in the ISS room to minimize disruptive behavior in the cafeteria.

6. Additional days should be assigned to students who violate rules governing behavior in the ISS room.

7. When the student has completed ISS time, the staff member in charge should review appropriate alternatives to the behavior that resulted in being sent to ISS.

8. The staff member in charge of ISS should ensure that the teacher who requested ISS placement is aware of how the student behaved during this time.

The major advantage of ISS is that it allows for the provision of instructional time and support services to students whose behavior is disruptive to teachers and classmates. Kerr and Nelson (1998) warned that ISS could be easily misused and recommended several troubleshooting ideas, which are listed in Action Plan 6.23.

1. They suggested that ISS rules be shared with all staff, students, and parents. Yell (1990) advised establishing a written ISS policy.

2. Any violation of these rules should result in firm negative consequences.

3. Parents must be informed on each occasion that their son or daughter has been assigned to ISS.

4. Disruptive behaviors that will result in ISS assignment must be considered carefully. They should be behaviors of a more serious nature that require more severe consequences than time-out or detention. For example, Rose (1988) reported that ISS was

---

Action Plan 6.23   Troubleshooting In-School Suspension (ISS) Procedures

Kerr and Nelson (1998) identified the following ways school officials can reduce misuse of the ISS room:

1. Share ISS policies with staff, students, and parents.
2. Establish firm consequences for violating rules in ISS.
3. Inform parents when their children are assigned to ISS.
4. Clearly define those behaviors that warrant a referral to ISS.
5. Monitor referrals to ISS.
6. Evaluate the impact of ISS and make necessary revisions.

used with students with disabilities who were disruptive, fighting, displaying repeated violations of a behavior code, late for or cutting classes or detention, showing lack of respect, using profanity, smoking, or stealing. These behaviors should be clearly defined and thoroughly explained to staff, students, and parents at the beginning of the school year. Such specificity and clarity keep the ISS room from being overrun by students who have committed minor rule violations.

5. Student assignments to ISS should be monitored to ensure that a teacher is not making unnecessary referrals.
6. As is true for any intervention program, ISS should be monitored and reviewed to ensure that it is effective. Staff, students, and parents should be informed of any revisions.

Out-of-School Suspension and Expulsion

Other disciplinary techniques that may be available to secondary school officials include out-of-school suspension and expulsion. *Out-of-school suspension* is a short-term exclusion from school for a period of time, usually between 1 and 10 days. *Expulsion* is exclusion from school for an indeterminate amount of time. Suspension and expulsion are the most frequently litigated punishment procedures used with students who have disabilities (Hartwig & Ruesch, 2000; Yell, 1990).

The rulings resulting from these court cases have clarified the use of out-of-school suspension for students with disabilities (*Board of Education of Peoria v. Illinois State Board of Education,* 1982; *Goss v. Lopez,* 1975; *Honig v. Doe,* 1988). Learners with disabilities may be suspended for up to 10 days, using the same procedures as those used for nondisabled learners. These short-term suspensions are not viewed as changing the learner's educational placement; however, the student must be assured of due process protections. Specifically, the students must be notified of the charges either in writing or orally, be provided with an explanation of the charges and supporting evidence, and be provided with an opportunity to present his or her side (Yell et al., 2001). Typically, these events occur before that student is suspended unless there is an emergency that warrants the student's immediate removal.

Out-of-school suspensions for more than 10 days may be used if the student with disabilities is posing a danger to himself or herself or others. It may require adherence to more extensive due process procedures, including a written notice of a hearing; the evidence; and a formal hearing during which the student has representation and can introduce additional evidence and witnesses, confront accusers, and make an appeal (Yell et al., 2001). A student can be suspended only after the multidisciplinary team has determined whether the behavior was related to the student's disability and that due process rights have been protected. The process for determining whether there is a causal relationship between a student's disability and the behavior being subject to disciplinary action occurs during a manifest determination review. This review must be conducted within 10 school days after the date of the disciplinary action. The IEP team reviews all relevant information, information provided by the parents, observations of the student, the IEP, and the placement. The team must answer the following four questions: (1) At the time of the incident, did the student have a disability? (2) Are the student's IEP and placement appropriate? (3) Did the disability impair the student's ability to understand the impact and consequences of his or her behavior? and (4) Did the disability impair the student's ability to control the behavior? If the IEP team finds that the behavior was not a manifestation of the disability, all appropriate disciplinary measures can be taken (Hartwig & Ruesch, 2000).

Yell (1990) stated that the decision in *Honig v. Doe* clearly indicated that students with disabilities cannot be expelled from public schools. Expulsion for more than 10 consecutive days constitutes a change of placement; therefore, change of placement procedures described in IDEA apply. School officials who are considering expulsion must convene a meeting of the IEP team to conduct a functional behavior assessment (described next in this chapter) and make a manifestation determination (Hartwig & Ruesch, 2000). A manifest determination is an examination of any relationship between a disability and a misbehavior. The meeting at which the manifest determination is made must include all members of the IEP team. Yell and colleagues (2001) identified the steps that must be followed. First, this group gathers all relevant information about the misbehavior and considers additional information offered by parents. The team then uses the data to determine whether the student understood the consequences of his or her actions and was capable of controlling those actions. Second, the team reviews the IEP and the placement to rule out the possibility that they caused the misbehavior. If the misbehavior is linked to an inappropriate IEP or placement, corrective action must be taken immediately. Finally, the team determines whether the misbehavior was a function of the student's disability. Specifically, did the disability limit the student's ability to understand the effect of the behavior and its consequences? Did the disability undermine his or her ability to control the behavior? If the answer is yes to either of these questions, the behavior is considered a result of the student's disability. If the answer to both of these questions is no, the predetermined consequences may be used.

Parents must be informed of their rights to demand an impartial hearing. If parents and school officials disagree regarding placement, the student must remain in the current placement until administrative and judicial reviews have been completed.

There are disadvantages associated with both out-of-school suspension and expulsion. They include the loss of instructional time, isolation from peers, encouragement of dropping out, a loss of parent and community support, a loss of state aid if based on average daily attendance, and an increase in daytime juvenile delinquency (Rose, 1988). In addition, some students may prefer being away from school and all of its demands; therefore, suspension and expulsion may reinforce inappropriate behavior rather than deter it. Finally, it should be noted that procedures such as detention, ISS, suspension, and expulsion are used in many schools; however, few data support their efficacy. School officials who use these procedures are reminded to evaluate the effect they have on the frequency and severity of disruptive behavior. Practices that do not contribute to the development and use of appropriate behaviors should be modified or discontinued in favor of those that do.

IDEA allows for the removal of a student with disabilities from school for up to 45 days if the student, while at school or a school-sponsored event (such as a field trip) (a) brings, has, or acquires a weapon; or (b) knowingly has, uses, or sells controlled substances or illegal drugs. This consequence can occur even if these behaviors are linked to the student's disability. In addition, the student who is perceived as a threat to himself or herself or to others can be removed for 45 days if a hearing officer believes that (a) the student poses such a threat, (b) the district has attempted to minimize the risk of harm, (c) the IEP and placement are appropriate, and (d) the school has identified an interim alternative educational setting (IAES) (Yell et al., 2001).

Case for Action 6.6

What consequent control techniques would you select for use with Louis (in Case for Action 6.4)? How would you reinforce appropriate behaviors? How would you punish inappropriate behaviors?

Functional Behavior Assessment

It is possible that a student will not learn or use appropriate behavior despite a secondary teacher's best efforts to provide solid instruction and a positive learning environment. In the past, it was likely that students with long-standing, challenging behaviors would have been referred for special education services; if they were already receiving special education services, then perhaps a more restrictive placement would have been considered. However, the Individuals with Disabilities Education Act has mandated that consideration first be given to placement in the least restrictive environment, such as the general education classroom. General education teachers will no longer be able to automatically refer students for placement in special settings. Even with a referral, it can no longer be assumed that students will be removed from an inclusive general education setting until their behavior is under control. Nor is it as easy for special education teachers to refer students with more severe problems to even more segregated settings. Both general and special educators will need to address the problem behaviors demonstrated by their students while still meeting the academic needs of other students in their class (Weigle, 1997). IDEA described the use of specific procedures to ensure that the rights of students with disabilities were safeguarded, including the use of functional behavioral assessment, manifest determination hearings, and alternative educational placements (Katsiyannis & Smith, 2003; Peck & Scarpati, 2003).

Challenging behaviors can serve a function for the individuals who demonstrate them (Ryan, Halsey, & Matthews, 2003). For example, the inappropriate behavior might be used to obtain something the student desires, or it might allow the student to escape or avoid an event that is unpleasant (Artesani, 2001; Shippen, Simpson, & Crites, 2003). The law now mandates that teachers use a functional behavior assessment (FBA) to determine the function that a challenging behavior might serve and to develop a behavior intervention plan (BIP) to address student needs. An FBA is a behavioral assessment method used to identify the functional relationship between behaviors, antecedents, and consequences. The professional develops and tests hypotheses about conditions that lead to or maintain a problem behavior. An FBA can identify a replacement skill that can serve the same function for the individual (Weigle, 1997).

Given the changes in the law, much attention has been devoted to functional behavior assessment in the professional literature. An FBA is a set of strategies that allows parents and professionals to gather information about factors that predict and maintain an inappropriate behavior (Yell et al., 2001) and to form a hypothesis about a behavior and an environmental event. The goal of engaging in this process is to "enhance the effectiveness and efficiency of behavioral support for students" (Ryan et al., 2003, p. 9) by helping IEP team members to determine student needs and develop a program to meet them. Despite its

Action Plan 6.24   Functional Behavior Assessment (FBA)

IDEA now mandates that teachers conduct a functional behavior assessment for students with challenging behaviors that are resistant to change. The steps in an FBA include the following:

1. Verify the seriousness of the problem.
2. Complete behavior checklists and rating scales.
3. Conduct interviews with all significant parties.
4. Conduct anecdotal recording using a narrative format and/or an anecdotal-behavior-consequence (A-B-C) recording.
5. Collect data in the natural setting using systematic observation.
6. Review data from all sources.
7. Develop a hypothesis about the function a behavior serves and/or environmental variables that control it.
8. Test the hypothesis.
9. Develop and implement a behavior intervention plan (BIP) that includes functional equivalency training.
10. Measure the effectiveness of the BIP and make any necessary changes.

importance and the advantages it can offer, an FBA is a time-consuming and labor-intensive process to complete. The process for conducting an FBA is briefly presented here and summarized in Action Plan 6.24, but secondary teachers are referred to other, more comprehensive discussions presented by Chandler and Dahlquist (2002); Gable, Quinn, Rutherford, and Howell (1998); Larson and Maag (1998), McConnell (2001); McConnell, Hilvitz, and Cox (1998); and O'Neill, Horner, Albin, Sprague, Storey, and Newton (1997).

A functional behavior assessment is a collaborative process between the classroom teacher and all the other school personnel involved with the student. As Larson and Maag (1998) pointed out, it is unlikely that highly trained consultants will be available; therefore, the teachers, both special and general education, will need to develop skills in conducting an FBA. Even though an FBA is mandated, IDEA does not identify the steps to be followed when an FBA is conducted. Yell and colleagues (2001) suggested that Congress intended an FBA to be consistent with the meaning described in the professional literature. Gable and colleagues (1998) encouraged teachers to start the process by verifying the seriousness of the problem. They also encouraged school personnel to try one of the more universal strategies before conducting an FBA. Only after making sure that the behavior is resistant to conventional interventions should a teacher proceed with a functional behavior assessment. Next, the teacher needs to complete an indirect assessment using checklists, rating scales, and interviews. These methods are indirect because they do not require direct contact with the student in the setting of interest. Several checklists are available, including the Motivation Assessment Scale (Durand, 1990). Interviews can be conducted using protocols developed by O'Neill and colleagues (1997).

Having conducted indirect assessments, the teacher now has a better understanding of the student's behavior. Larson and Maag (1998) noted that it may be possible to generate some hypotheses about what is going on; however, they also advise that the results of the FBA will be more reliable if direct assessments take place in the natural environment. Whereas checklists, ratings scales, and interviews constitute indirect assessment, observations of problem behavior in the inclusive settings in which it occurs are a direct method of assessment. There are two major categories of observation within a functional behavior assessment: anecdotal and systematic. An anecdotal observation allows the professional to become acquainted with the student and the behavior in the natural environment. It is useful when a teacher is not sure exactly what is happening in the setting. An anecdotal report conducted early in the assessment process can have a narrative format or it can be an antecedent-behavior-consequence (A-B-C) recording. A narrative report describes environmental and setting demands and any critical events that occurred during the observation period. An A-B-C recording enables the teacher to generate a hypothesis about the relationship between each inappropriate behavior and environmental events surrounding its occurrence. For example, the behavior might enable the individual to escape task demands, obtain attention, communicate physical status, entertain himself or herself, receive sensory stimulation, or gain access to desired objects.

The results of an FBA will be more reliable if the teacher gathers more information about how often or how long the behavior happens. Therefore, the next step in an FBA involves the use of systematic observation techniques such as frequency recording, interval recording, and time sampling.

Next, the teacher needs to analyze the data that have been gathered through indirect and direct assessments from several sources. Gable and colleagues (1998) suggested triangulating the data so that the teacher can compare information collected through various means, including checklists, rating scales, interviews, anecdotal reports, and systematic observation. The goal is to identify or hypothesize what variable is maintaining a challenging behavior and the function that behavior serves for the student. The teacher should then test the hypothesis by systematically manipulating the behavior and environmental factors believed to be maintaining the behavior. The basic model for arranging the manipulation is to place the student in two or more conditions. For example, if the student becomes aggressive in the presence of task demands, the teacher should first remove the task demands, note what happens to the behavior, and then reintroduce the task demands.

Next, the teacher needs to develop and implement the behavior intervention plan. The BIP is a logical extension of the FBA process (Shippen et al., 2003). As was the case for the FBA, IDEA did not specify the components of a BIP, other than indicating it must be individualized to meet student needs (Yell et al., 2001). Typically, a BIP includes all the details regarding the strategies that will be used to assist the student in developing and using appropriate behavior. The BIP includes assessment strategies; multiple, positive techniques that promote appropriate behaviors and prevent target behavior; procedures to be followed if inappropriate behavior is demonstrated; program modifications; and supplementary aids and supports to address the behavior. It should identify a replacement behavior or functional equivalent that serves the same purpose as the misbehavior (Hester, 2002), and methods for teaching it. The teacher may have to use functional equivalency training to teach an appropriate replacement skill that will allow the student to satisfy needs and wants. Finally, the teacher implements the program, continuing to conduct evaluations of the student's behavior and making programmatic changes as necessary.

Summary

Practitioners can be easily overwhelmed with the curricular demands associated with teaching in a secondary classroom. As important as teacher mastery of the content area and the use of effective teaching strategies are, teachers will find it necessary to use behavior management techniques to ensure that they can work and students can learn in a safe, pleasant environment. In this chapter, teachers were advised to consider three entry points in the development of classroom discipline. The first entry point involved antecedent control, through which teachers could promote appropriate behavior and prevent unacceptable behaviors that interfere with student learning. Twelve techniques were described, many of which can be in place on the first day of school and that can set the tone for the entire school year. Whereas antecedents focused on the classroom and the teacher, related personal characteristics, the second entry point, focused attention on the students. Specifically, if the teacher and the classroom are less than ideal, academic skills, social skills, and emotional development can be fostered in students to ensure that they are able to stay in control and achieve. The third entry point is consequence control, through which teachers can motivate and reward acceptable behaviors and decrease or eliminate behaviors that undermine students' academic and social development. Many of these techniques are ideal for use with one or a small number of students; however, secondary teachers typically deal with greater numbers of students. To meet their needs, group contingencies and self-management were described. Finally, teachers were advised to consider how schoolwide policies such as detention, in-school suspension, out-of-school suspension, and expulsion can be used with secondary students with disabilities. Because of IDEA, suspension and expulsion can be used only after specific procedures, such as a manifestation determination review and a functional behavior assessment, have been followed.

Managing student behavior requires substantial investment of teacher time and effort; however, dealing with student misbehavior ineffectively contributes to teacher job dissatisfaction and the likelihood that students will not make anticipated academic and social gains. It is important that teachers be fluent with these techniques and be prepared to implement a comprehensive approach to discipline.

7

Collaboration and the Role of the Consultant Teacher

MAUREEN A. SCHLOSS
RAQUEL J. SCHMIDT

Did you know that . . .

- The IDEA increased the number of students with special needs who are enrolled in general classrooms?

- General education teachers *must* be members of the IEP team since the 1997 reauthorization of the IDEA?

- Consultation, in its strictest sense, involves indirect services to students?

- Students should be active partners in the consultation/collaboration process?

- Many factors must be considered when developing a consultant teacher program?

- The caseload for a consultant teacher should be no more than 35 students?

- Many general educators may be hesitant to use the services of a consultant teacher?

- Effective use of a resource room requires the cooperation of the consultant teacher and the general educator?

- The responsibilities of consultant teachers are not uniform across school districts?

- The consultant teacher's job description may be developed without the cooperation of the general or special education teacher?

- There are many similarities between the responsibilities of resource teachers and those of consulting teachers?

- An effective consulting–teaching relationship can enhance the learning outcomes of students with and without disabilities?

Can you . . .

- Identify three potential barriers to inclusion in secondary schools?

- Define *consultation*?

- Differentiate between direct and indirect consultation?

- Identify responsibilities associated with direct consultation?

Raquel Schmidt, Ph.D., is an assistant professor in the Exceptional Education Department of Buffalo State College.

- Identify responsibilities associated with indirect consultation?

- Identify the advantages of collaborative consultation?

- Describe the process of consultation?

- Identify factors that can or may undermine the effectiveness of the consulting teacher?

- Identify ways to decrease the resistance of general educators to participating in the consulting process?

- Describe the advantages of placement in a resource room?

- Explain why the consultant teacher "wears many hats"?

- List the responsibilities of the secondary consultant teacher?

- Set up a schedule for a secondary resource room?

In the past, special education was perceived as a vehicle by which specific academic deficits were remediated and the negative impact of a disability reduced. Special education professionals believed their primary responsibility was to develop and provide direct services for children with disabilities. Traditionally, instructional objectives were selected from a separate curriculum and occurred in settings other than the general education classroom. In essence, regular and special education were perceived as mutually exclusive categories, with little or no interaction at either the professional or the student level.

Times have changed. The Regular Education Initiative (REI) proposed by Will (1986) was based on data suggesting that students with mild disabilities appeared to do at least as well in regular education classrooms. The widespread implementation of inclusion programs, which can be correlated to changes in federal education funding and school cost reimbursement, has resulted in a rethinking of the full continuum of special education services—inclusion is based on the notion that all students should have the opportunity to achieve success in the regular education classroom (Schulte, Osborne, & Erchul, 1998). The potential benefits of inclusion include decreased segregation of students with diverse learning needs (Huefner, 1988) and a stronger focus on individual student strengths rather than weaknesses. Unfortunately, unless all teachers are adequately trained to collaborate with their peers and receive additional supports for the challenge of working with diverse needs, research on inclusive programs reinforces the notion that these programs are likely to fail. General education teachers have expressed attitudes toward inclusion that include feeling underprepared, ineffective, and unwilling to accommodate students with needs that differ from the mainstream (Schumm & Vaughn, 1991; Whinnery, Fuchs, & Fuchs, 1991).

Legislation such as the Individuals with Disabilities Education Act (IDEA) has mandated that students with special needs receive appropriate educational services in the least restrictive environment. As a result, greater numbers of secondary students with disabilities are currently spending some, if not most, of their school day in a general education setting. Although there is limited research available on successful inclusive programs at the secondary level (Keefe & Moore, 2004), it is clear that the formal structure of most secondary classrooms, content-driven instruction, and high-stakes assessments all present unique challenges to successful consultation. Rather than relying on a separate method of service delivery, general education teachers will need to choose instructional methods and service delivery options that will maximize the development of skills needed for success in secondary and postsecondary environments for students with and without disabilities.

Despite legal mandates, there are still three challenges to successful inclusion in secondary settings. First, secondary students with disabilities traditionally enter high school without the skills necessary to ensure success in this setting. The gap between their skill levels and the skills needed in the secondary environment widens as students progress through the curriculum. Second, the tremendous workload already demanded of secondary educators may leave them with little time and motivation to provide the intensive, empirically based instruction required to overcome skill deficits. Third, major changes may be difficult to initiate because of secondary education organizational structures, such as teacher-centered didactic instruction, limited teacher–student contact time, and autonomous curriculum planning (Friend & Cook, 2003).

Professionals at the secondary level need to develop and implement methods of service delivery to secondary students with special needs that can circumvent these barriers. Although secondary general educators have expertise in a content area and have developed techniques for conveying important knowledge and skills to their students, meeting the unique needs of students with disabilities may pose several challenges. A solution to their problems lies with the assistance that is available through a consultant teacher, if they are able and willing to access special education support. Although a school may embrace inclusion and provide a scheduling structure for teachers to work together, teacher characteristics and beliefs about effective teaching appear to play a crucial role in the success of the consultative relationship (Austin, 2001; Mastropieri et al., 2005). Secondary teachers have been traditionally characterized as resistant to inclusion and unreceptive to consultation, although some studies illustrate that successful professional collaborations do exist, and, more important, these relationships appear to enhance student outcomes (Dieker, 2001; Keefe & Moore, 2004; Mastropieri et al., 2005).

The purpose of this chapter is to discuss the characteristics and skills of the consultant teacher and describe how the indirect and direct services he or she provides in a secondary class or in a resource room can assist secondary teachers and the students they serve.

The Consultant Teacher

According to Idol (1988), special education is a process for providing special education services for students with special needs who are enrolled in general education classes. This process involves many professionals, including special educators, general educators, ancillary professionals, and parents. These individuals cooperatively plan, implement, and evaluate instruction conducted in the general classrooms so that educational problems can be prevented or remediated.

This definition emphasizes a collaborative relationship that is based on mutual consent and commitment to a goal, joint development of an intervention plan, and shared responsibility for the implementation and evaluation of that plan (West & Idol, 1990). Idol, Paolucci-Whitcomb, and Nevin (1994) developed the following broad definition of *consultation*:

Collaborative consultation is an interactive process that enables teams of people with diverse expertise to generate creative solutions to mutually defined problems. The outcome is enhanced, altered, and produces solutions that are different from those that the individual team member would have produced independently. (p. 1)

The consulting teacher can provide services to secondary teachers and their students in two ways. The first way is through the provision of indirect services. In this capacity, the consultant and secondary teacher work jointly to clarify a problem, assess the student, develop an instructional approach, and monitor its effects. However, the secondary teacher assumes primary responsibility for actual program implementation; the consultant teacher does not teach the student experiencing difficulty. Indirect services offer several advantages. Professionals can work with and learn from each other. Any stigma associated with a special education classification can be reduced, as students are not singled out for separate instruction. Finally, the secondary teacher can implement an instructional program whose features benefit not only the special education student but also any student who might be experiencing difficulty. Continued use of such effective practices can minimize student problems in the future.

The second way the consultant teacher can assist secondary teachers and their students is through the provision of direct services. In such situations, the consultant and the secondary teacher still work together to clarify the problem, conduct assessment, and plan an intervention; however, the consultant is responsible for teaching the student. He or she can take over a class for one or more instructional periods, work with the student and some peers in a small group within the secondary class, tutor the student in the classroom, or work with the student in a resource setting (discussed later in this chapter). Direct service also offers distinct advantages. When delivered in the secondary classroom, the target student and peers receive quality instruction that enhances skill development. The consultant teacher can model the use of a new teaching technique for the secondary educator, who can observe and incorporate it into his or her repertoire.

For teachers, the consultation process has two goals. The first goal is to maximize the interaction between students with disabilities and their peers through the development and implementation of comprehensive, effective educational programs (Idol et al., 1994). The second goal is to enhance each teacher's skills to facilitate subsequent problem solving.

Principles of Successful Collaboration

Friend and Cook (2003) and Idol and colleagues (1994) identified key elements or principles of successful collaboration. First, true collaboration requires willing participants; therefore, it should be a voluntary process. With special education's long history of providing services in separate settings, general and special educators may not be used to working voluntarily side by side. General education teachers are reminded that placement of students with disabilities into inclusive settings is not conducted on a voluntary basis. Secondary teachers do have to work with all students but they may be able to choose whether to work with a consultant teacher. They are strongly encouraged to do so. Research supports the positive effect on the relationship between the special and general education teachers when participation in the relationship is voluntary. Unfortunately, the majority of secondary teachers report that they were not given the choice of working with another professional (Austin,

2001). This situation can be frustrating for teachers who want support but aren't getting it, or those uncomfortable with an unwanted colleague in their class (Keefe & Moore, 2004).

It is understandable if teachers are intimidated by the idea of having another professional in the classroom for part or all of the instructional day. They may feel as if their every move is being closely monitored by an outsider. Special educators have some issues of their own to deal with, too. Many may have originally prepared to have their own classrooms for students with special needs. Changes in the delivery of special education services has required them to rethink how they can best serve students. To maximize a student's potential for academic and social gains in inclusive settings, general and special education teachers will need to set aside any preconceived notions about territoriality. This change in orientation is facilitated by the second principle of successful collaboration, which requires participants to have a sense of equality. It is likely that each member of the collaborative team has knowledge or skills that others do not; however, each person's knowledge and expertise are considered equal in value to everyone else's. A sense of equality allows all participants to share their ideas but also makes them responsible for respectfully listening to and learning from others. The knowledge base of special education teachers must be respected and valued as much as the general education teacher's knowledge of the content area. Some experts suggest that secondary special education teachers specialize in one or two content areas to support systematic adaptations of a challenging curriculum (Friend & Cook, 2003; Keefe & Moore, 2004). Third, all parties must mutually agree on a set of goals. For example, one important goal that may require a substantial investment over a period of time is to improve a student's level of competence to promote success in inclusive settings. Another goal can address the practitioners' commitment to increase their knowledge base and enhance their ability to use teaching techniques that benefit all students, regardless of disability status. Even under ideal circumstances, effective consultative relationships appear to take anywhere from three to five years to develop. Mutual goals can be revised to reflect changes in the teachers' relationship and the unique characteristics of the students they are working with. A special education teacher may feel uncomfortable co-teaching a whole class lesson, but can model adaptive teaching strategies for the general education teacher by means of flexible small group instructional arrangements such as cooperative grouping or station teaching.

The fourth principle of successful collaboration is that all parties must "own" or share responsibility for the problem that a student is experiencing. Practitioners demonstrate ownership by dedicating time and resources to identifying and clarifying the problem and by developing, implementing, and evaluating a plan to address it. It would be inappropriate for the secondary teacher who notices that a student with disabilities is having difficulty taking notes in class to assume that his or her responsibilities end once the consultant teacher has been contacted. Similarly, it would be inappropriate for a consultant teacher to refuse to become involved with a general education student who, according to the secondary teacher, is having difficulty mastering content. In each situation, the student should have access to a team of professionals whose members are committed to pooling their time, energy, and skills to achieve problem resolution. The fifth element requires the team to be collectively responsible for the success or failure of the intervention that is used to address the student's problem. An important feature of this principle involves having regularly scheduled time to discuss student progress and plan interventions (Friend & Cook, 2003). Flexible scheduling is a must for secondary consultants, who may have students with disabilities in the classrooms of a dozen (or more) different teachers. In buildings with limited resources to support costly planning time, teachers have developed innovative ways to maintain regular contact, including early morning breakfast meetings, email listserves, and informational checklists. An advantage of working with older students is that they can be taught to assume increased responsibility for their learning experience—they can and should be an active part of the consultative process.

Advantages of Consulting

Collaborating with a consultant teacher using the principles just described offers many advantages to secondary educators (Gutkin, 1996). They are summarized in Action Plan 7.1.

1. Outcome effectiveness data summarized by Idol (1988) have indicated that consultation is an effective means of increasing the skill levels of students with disabilities.

2. The teamwork promoted by effective consultation makes general and special educators more effective because their combined impact is greater for students than special education services alone.

3. The title "consultant teacher" dissociates students from the label *disabled.* In its purest sense, consultation offers indirect services to students through their teachers; therefore, students with disabilities can remain in the general classroom and benefit from instruction provided by the secondary teacher.

4. The general classroom provides appropriate peer role models to be emulated by students with disabilities.

5. Nondisabled peers have the opportunity to understand and appreciate students with disabilities.

6. Consultation enhances the skill repertoires of the general educator by providing on-the-job training in areas such as task analysis, behavior management, diagnostic

---

Action Plan 7.1   Advantages of the Consulting Teacher

The following advantages are associated with the use of the consulting teacher:

1. Students' skill level is increased.
2. Teamwork is promoted.
3. The need to label students is minimized.
4. Access to peer models is available.
5. Nondisabled students can develop an understanding of and appreciation for students with disabilities.
6. General educators get on-the-job training.
7. The cost of special education is reduced.
8. The mystique surrounding special education is dispelled.
9. It is especially suited to the secondary school.
10. Suitable topics for in-service education are identified.

assessment, curricular adaptation, and continuous measurement. The joint efforts of the secondary teacher and the consultant teacher can ensure the delivery of quality instruction to all low-achieving students in the classroom, not just those formally identified as needing special education services (Gersten, Darch, Davis, & George, 1990).

7. Consulting teachers can reduce the cost of special education services. Students can remain in regular classes in their neighborhood schools, thus reducing the costs associated with both busing and the establishment and maintenance of more restrictive educational alternatives. Cost effectiveness is also enhanced when potential academic and behavior problems are prevented, thereby reducing the number of referrals to special education.

8. The communication required to implement the consultant model can dispel the mystique associated with special education. General and special educators can develop a better understanding of and appreciation for the talents each brings to an educational program.

9. The consultant model is uniquely suited to the secondary school.

10. Use of consultation facilitates the identification of staff development needs that can be addressed through in-service education.

Developing a Consultant Teacher Program

Careful consideration must be given to several factors if a consultant teacher program is to provide the benefits previously identified (Idol, 1988). First, it must be adequately funded. When implemented properly, inclusion can be one of the most expensive service delivery models (Friend & Cook, 2003). Teacher training, modified curriculum materials, and reduced student to teacher ratio can add significant cost to a model program but will not guarantee the success of that program. Second, preferral and referral strategies must be formulated and should include making a request of consultation and conducting observations and conferences. Third, performance standards should be established for the individual who will serve as the consultant teacher. Idol (1988) recommended that this individual have at least three years of experience as either a regular or a special educator and possess a credential or certification. Fourth, an appropriate caseload for consultant teachers should be determined. The pupil–teacher ratio should reflect the responsibilities of the consultant. For example, consultant teachers who provide some direct services should have a lower ratio than those who assume only indirect responsibilities. Idol (1988) has recommended a maximum load of no more than 35 students. Fifth, a workload schedule must be developed that allows the consultant teacher to meet all the responsibilities of direct and indirect services. Sixth, an evaluation program with formative and summative measures must be designed and implemented to ensure that the consultation program is having the desired impact on students and their teachers.

Characteristics of the Consultant Teacher

Several authors have identified the qualifications needed to be a consultant (Gersten et al., 1990; Huefner, 1988; Mastropieri et al., 2005; Tindall, Shinn, & Rodden-Nord, 1990; West & Idol, 1990). First, consultants must be excellent teachers, highly skilled in diagnosis, prescription, and evaluation. Second, they must be able to communicate effectively. That is,

Case for Action 7.1

You have just received a bachelor's degree in special education and are considering apply-ing for a position as a consultant. What factors should figure in your decision?

they must be able to paraphrase, negotiate, conduct an interview that elicits information and actions, identify and empathize with the perspectives of others, interpret nonverbal com-munication, give and receive feedback, and minimize the use of jargon. The combination of effective teaching and communication skills appears to be the most important features of effective collaborative consultation relationships (Mastropieri et al., 2005). Third, consul-tants must be able to solve problems. This characteristic means consultants must be able to identify learning and adjustment problems accurately and precisely, including antecedents and consequences, and to develop, implement, evaluate, and revise an appropriate inter-vention plan and coordinate the efforts of contributing professionals. Fourth, consultants must be experts in systematic observation procedures. They must be able to choose and use the procedure most sensitive to the nature of the learning or adjustment problem. Fifth, they must make every endeavor to follow through on interactions with staff and students. Follow-through could be as simple as following up on a suggestion made during an initial interview or as complex as conducting periodic checks on the success of a maintenance and generalization program. Sixth, consultants must manage time efficiently. They are dealing with a variety of teacher and student schedules and must be able to accommodate their needs in a timely manner. Seventh, consultants must be skilled at planning and implement-ing in-service training that enhances the skill level of their colleagues. In-service sessions can be designed to provide content information or practice with a new skill. Eighth, they must possess administrative skills. They will be involved in student referrals, multidisci-plinary team meetings, IEP development, and record keeping.

Gaining Acceptance

In an earlier section, the possibility was raised that working with a consultant teacher could be an intimidating process. Such feelings can be mitigated if the consultant teacher actively works to make other professionals feel comfortable expressing concerns and sharing ideas. Idol and colleagues (1994) identified several strategies a consultant teacher can use to gain acceptance. The first strategy is showing respect. The consultant who listens to oth-ers, acknowledges and capitalizes on the expertise and experience of other practitioners, works willingly with others to solve problems, and maintains confidentiality is demonstrat-ing respect and increasing the likelihood that respect will be mutual. Idol and colleagues noted that listening can be passive in that the consultant stays quiet and closely attends to what others have to say. Listening can also involve paraphrasing what others have said to ensure the message has been understood. Next, a consultant should share clear, concise descriptions about the nature of the skills he or she is bringing to the partnership. Teachers who are aware that the consultant possesses skills in the areas of assessment, instruction, adaptations, and modifications are more likely to take advantage of such assistance. On a related note, whether verbally or in writing, these descriptions should incorporate terms that are familiar to other practitioners. Any new terminology should be accompanied by an explanation. A consultant also increases the likelihood of acceptance through the use of good interview skills, which helps in gaining information from teachers, exploring feelings about collaboration, solving problems, and planning interventions.

Bearing in mind that collaboration is a two-way process, the consultant should demonstrate a willingness to learn from others. He or she is not the only person who brings knowledge and a set of skills to the process. Secondary educators are experts in their content areas, have valuable teaching experience, and have direct experience working with the student who is having difficulty. The consultant and the secondary educator have much to learn from each other. The consultant can enhance acceptance further by paying close attention to how feedback is given and received. Idol and colleagues (1994) suggested that feedback include the identification of one area that needs improvement and two areas of strength. They also suggested that the consultant begin the process of feedback with an honest evaluation of his or her skill level. The consultant who self-evaluates to identify two sources of strength and one weakness shows that he or she is willing to develop new skills. The consultant should also give others credit for the contributions they make to the success of an intervention. Teachers who know their efforts are acknowledged and appreciated are more willing to accept the consultant and collaborate in the future. Ideally, the collaboration process should directly result in a successful resolution to a student's problem and indirectly enhance practitioner competence, but it is not uncommon for collaborators to run into problems. When problems do occur, the consultant is more likely to gain and maintain acceptance by using confrontation skills appropriately. Use of these skills requires all teachers to listen to others; to express needs, feelings, opinions, and concerns; to avoid assigning blame; and to work together to develop alternative solutions. The role of good people skills in a productive consultative partnership cannot be overemphasized. Although it is easier for teachers to collaborate when they like each other and have volunteered to work together, studies also show that teachers with very little in common and involuntary participation can work together effectively (Keefe & Moore, 2004; Mastropieri et al., 2005).

Responsibilities of Consultants

Consultants may need to address any number of issues, including academic problems, individualized instruction, large- and small-group instruction, classroom management, resequencing curriculum materials, large-group management problems, and in-service training.

As Gutkin (1996) pointed out, although there are minor variations across consultant models (Idol et al., 1994; Hobbs & Westling, 1998), each incorporates a problem-solving process. Figure 7.1 summarizes the steps typically followed by the consultant teacher and the classroom teacher during the collaboration process. Each step is described separately here.

Identify the Problem Behavior   A consultant teacher may be assigned to a cadre of secondary teachers with whom he or she works collaboratively. Thus, he or she may already be familiar with a group of students, some of whom have disabilities. Either the secondary teachers or the consulting teacher may suspect that a particular student within the group is having difficulty. It is also possible that one or more consulting teachers are assigned to a building and are available to teachers and students on an as-needed basis. The consultant

FIGURE 7.1   *The Steps in the Consultation Process*

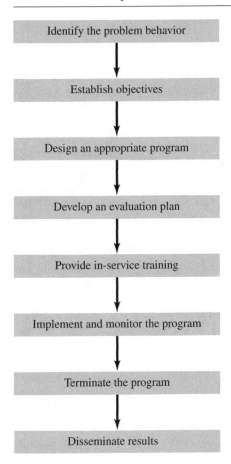

teacher may not be aware of a student's difficulty until he or she is contacted by the second-ary teacher. Regardless of how the consultant teacher learns of the problem, the first step in the collaboration process is to identify the problem clearly and objectively. The team can identify any possible causes or antecedents to explain why the student is having dif-ficulty. They should consider academic, behavioral, and social factors. Such information can be obtained from a comprehensive assessment of all areas believed to be related to the student's problem.

Assessment may involve formal and informal measures such as norm- and criterion-referenced tests and systematic observations of student behavior in the classroom. Addi-tional observations and interviews can be scheduled with the teacher, the student, and peers. Current levels of performance are measured, and factors contributing to the development and maintenance of the problem are identified. Next, the consultant and teacher determine the standard for acceptable performance. They may sample the behavior or skill levels of other students in the class to establish minimal standards of acceptable performance. By comparing the target student's performance with that of his or her peers, they will get an idea of the seriousness of the problem. In the event that there is more than one problem, the team will have to rank the issues in terms of intervention priority. These priorities may be reflected in the goals included on an IEP and should be established in cooperation with parents.

Establish Objectives   The team translates goals into short-term objectives that clearly define both the targeted behavior in measurable terms and the criterion for acceptable performance. Hobbs and Westling (1998) stated that teachers could ask, "What are the preferred outcomes regarding these problems?" and "How would we like this situation to look a year from now?" (p. 14).

Design an Appropriate Program   The consultant and teacher next design an intervention program that addresses the targeted skill and that can be implemented by the general educator in the general education classroom. An appropriate plan should have the potential for addressing the problem, be acceptable to all members of the team, and be suitable for implementation in the secondary classroom. Having developed a plan, the consultant is advised to describe all aspects of the intervention program in technological terms—that is, in terms that allow a knowledgeable reader to apply the procedures with few or no questions. Finally, Gutkin (1996) advised that each team member's responsibilities during plan implementation be specified clearly. Poorly defined roles may cause some aspects of the intervention to be poorly implemented or neglected altogether, leading to failure. Ultimately, a plan that could have been effective in producing desired changes may be discontinued prematurely, and valuable time and energy will have been wasted.

Develop an Evaluation Plan   The team needs to consider how the impact of the program will be measured. This step ensures that all necessary sets of data are gathered.

Provide In-Service Training   It is possible that the individual(s) responsible for daily implementation of the intervention program will require training. The consultant may need to provide a demonstration lesson or opportunities to role-play.

Implement and Monitor the Program   After sufficient practice during in-service training, the teacher implements the program and monitors it on a daily basis. Monitoring is extremely important for two reasons. First, the team needs to ensure that the program is being consistently implemented in the manner intended so that any discrepancies or confusion can be addressed in a timely manner. Second, the team needs to measure the impact of the program on student behavior and make adjustments accordingly.

Terminate the Program   After the student has met the criteria, the program may be faded out and eventually dismantled. A team member should conduct periodic follow-up to ensure that new skill levels are being maintained.

Disseminate Results   All relevant parties should be notified of the results of the intervention program. Secondary students may find progress reports motivating, and this response can enhance generalization and maintenance. In keeping with the law, parents should be informed of their child's performance throughout the program. Other professional staff

Action Plan 7.2   Factors Undermining the Effectiveness of the Consulting Teacher

The following factors can limit the effectiveness of the consulting teacher:

1. Heavy caseload of more than 35 students
2. Role primarily that of tutor/aide
3. Unrealistic administrative expectations
4. Regular educators who resent having a troubled student removed from the room for a reduced time
5. Too much time spent in direct service
6. Lack of appropriate training

members should be notified of results. They can watch for and reinforce the student's new appropriate academic and social behavior. In addition, it may be politically savvy to make others aware of the positive impact of the consultation program.

This sequence of consulting activities has two advantages. First, the student has acquired a skill that was previously unfamiliar. Furthermore, this was accomplished without removing the student from the general education class. Second, the teacher has also acquired new skills that may benefit either the same student or his or her peers in the future.

Unfortunately, consultation may not proceed as smoothly as the preceding discussion suggests. A number of factors can adversely influence the effectiveness of the consulting teacher. These factors, which are presented in Action Plan 7.2, include case overload, misunderstanding of the consultant's responsibilities, and the lack of appropriate training.

Barriers to Successful Collaboration

The problem most likely to undermine the success of collaborative efforts is the lack of time for professionals to meet (Idol, 1997; Olson, Chalmers, & Hoover, 1997). Practitioners should not be expected to collaborate if they are not given time. It is unfair to expect collaboration to occur before or after school hours or during the time allocated to curriculum planning or lesson preparation. West and Idol (1990) offered some suggestions for increasing the amount of time devoted to collaboration. School principals can designate a specific time each day or week for collaboration—perhaps even one day each grading period could be designated as "Collaboration Day." Principals and other support staff can teach for a specific period a day on a regular basis so that teachers can be released to collaborate. School district officials can hire a permanent "floating" substitute teacher so that teachers can be released from their classroom at a specific time.

Another problem is resistance to the consultant teacher and the collaborative model. Consultants have the potential to have a positive impact on secondary students with disabilities and their teachers. Despite this potential, some secondary educators are reluctant to avail themselves of a consultant teacher's services. It is possible that some secondary educators would simply rather have students with special needs served elsewhere. It is also likely that the autonomous nature of secondary educators keeps them from requesting assistance. Although the desire to solve problems with a minimum amount

---

Case for Action 7.2

A school district is considering implementing a consultant teacher program. What arguments in favor of this move would you offer to the superintendent?

---

of fuss is commendable, working cooperatively with a consultant teacher can result in problems being solved easily and more quickly, leaving the busy secondary educator more time to deal with other responsibilities. Margolis and McGettigan (1988) offered some specific suggestions consultant teachers can use to increase the possibility that reluctant teachers will work cooperatively to implement programs that increase student success.

First, the consultant teacher is advised to involve the general educator as much as possible in all facets of the consultation process. As directly stated in the definition offered earlier, consultation requires cooperation. Just as students are more likely to follow a plan they helped create, so too are secondary educators more likely to support a decision in which they had input. Therefore, it is essential that secondary educators be present and have influence at meetings in which programming decisions are made. Another suggestion is to make sure that the consultant teacher recommends instructional modifications that are practical, concrete, easy to use, minimally disruptive, and likely to yield positive results. On a related note, the secondary educator may need assurances that the recommendation can work. A teacher who does not expect a course of action to succeed is not likely to invest valuable time and energy implementing it. A teacher who is unsure of the effectiveness of a modification can be encouraged to use it provisionally. If it works, it can be implemented as long as needed. If it does not produce anticipated results, adjustments can be made. In addition, the secondary educator must believe that he or she is receiving adequate support. Therefore, the consultant teacher must provide whatever assistance is necessary to implement an instructional modification. Next, a consultant teacher should listen carefully to the secondary educator's personal concerns and perceptions. Finally, the consultant teacher can involve the secondary teacher in gathering instructionally useful information. Such information can increase his or her knowledge of the problem and ability to identify possible solutions. This information may also foster the secondary educator's perception that his or her knowledge is comparable to that of the consultant teacher, thus increasing confidence and the willingness to participate in the consultation process.

Resource Rooms

As mentioned earlier, a consultant teacher may provide direct services to students with disabilities in secondary settings. It is possible, however, that a student's multidisciplinary team may choose to utilize the support available in a resource room. The resource room is the most common method of service delivery for secondary students with mild disabilities (Ellett, 1993). It is also the most abused. Properly organized and implemented, however, it can assist educators in meeting the educational needs of secondary students with disabilities.

Defining the Resource Room

Friend and McNutt (1984) have defined a *resource room* as a structural arrangement in which students with disabilities receive some instructional assistance, although most of their educational program takes place in the general education setting. A resource room is most frequently multicategorical; therefore, it can accommodate students displaying mild or moderate disabilities. The time each student spends in the resource room is based on his or her needs and usually ranges from three hours a week to half of the school day. Traditionally, instruction focuses on academic areas in which students display severe skill deficits; however, nonacademic areas can be addressed, including social skills, job finding and maintenance, and appropriate use of leisure time. Regardless of the skill being addressed, instruction will be more effective if it reflects the cooperative efforts of secondary teachers and the consultant.

Advantages of Resource Room Placement

The resource room has six advantages in particular for secondary students with disabilities (Weiderholt, Hammill, & Brown, 1983), which are summarized in Action Plan 7.3. First, most students who receive resource room services remain integrated with their nondisabled peers for most of the school day. This arrangement is less stigmatizing than placement in a self-contained secondary special education classroom. Second, more students can receive special education assistance. Indeed, some students who need assistance may not be getting it because their problems are not severe enough to warrant a more intrusive form of service delivery. Third, some students assigned to full-time special classes might be included in less restrictive settings if resource support were available. They could be included in a general secondary class for select subjects and receive resource room assistance where necessary, with the goal being full-time inclusion as soon as possible. Thus, self-contained secondary special education classrooms would be reserved for the small number of students who truly needed them. This arrangement would have the added benefit of keeping students with disabilities in their neighborhood schools. Fourth, the flexible scheduling that is characteristic of the resource room enables resource personnel to quickly meet the changing needs of students and their teachers. Fifth, in addition to providing direct services for students, the consultant teacher can continue to assist other professionals. For example, he or she can keep colleagues apprised of the latest developments in curricula, materials, effective

---

Action Plan 7.3   The Advantages of Resource Room Placement

Secondary students who receive resource room services may benefit in the following ways:

1. They may remain in the classroom with their nondisabled peers.
2. They may receive services that are more intense than those available in the general classroom.
3. They may avoid being placed in a self-contained class.
4. New problems may be more easily addressed because of flexible scheduling.
5. Their general education teachers may continue to receive support from a consultant.
6. They may receive increased parental support.

Case for Action 7.3

You are at a multidisciplinary meeting where a secondary student's placement is being discussed. The parents have expressed concern about scheduling resource room services for their child. They would prefer a self-contained setting. How will you argue for resource room services?

teaching, and classroom management. Sixth, placement in a resource room may be more acceptable to parents of secondary students with disabilities.

Staffing the Resource Room

The success of resource rooms depends to a large extent on the professionals who manage it. The resource room may be staffed by the consultant teacher who also provides direct and indirect services to teachers and students in secondary classrooms. It might also be staffed by a teacher whose sole responsibility is to provide services in this setting. Either way, individuals who assume the responsibility must be effective teachers, because much of their time is devoted to providing direct services to students with mild and moderate disabilities. As such, they must be skilled in the use of teaching strategies that enhance student competence in a variety of domains. Unlike their elementary counterparts, the teachers in a resource room also need to be highly skilled in the content areas. Students assigned to the resource room may display deficits in subject areas as discrete as algebra, geometry, biology, and chemistry. A solid background in one or more content area improves the effectiveness of secondary resource teachers.

The teachers in a resource room must also be curriculum specialists, thoroughly familiar with all aspects of the curriculum being used in the secondary school. In addition, they need to be aware of and able to locate alternative curricula for students who need them. On a related note, teachers must be skilled in curriculum development. They may need to assume leadership roles in the development of a functional curriculum in the event that an appropriate one cannot be located.

Teachers in resource rooms must also be competent administrators. They are responsible for processing referrals, writing reports, maintaining records, arranging schedules, ordering materials, attending meetings, and organizing and managing the learning environment.

They may also need to be counselors. In addition to academic difficulties, or perhaps as a result of them, secondary students with disabilities frequently experience problems in their relationships with peers and authority figures. Students may also demonstrate limited confidence in their ability to achieve academic, interpersonal, or vocational goals. In addition, colleagues may need to vent their frustrations or be reassured that they are capable of handling challenging students and unique situations. Teachers in resource rooms should be skilled in counseling techniques suitable for use with both of these groups.

Furthermore, teachers who provide resource room services need to be public and human relations experts. They are in frequent contact with administrators, colleagues, students, parents, public officials, and representatives of outside agencies. They may be called on to teach, explain, confront, counsel, request, or advocate. Regardless of the nature of the interaction, they must conduct themselves in a professional manner.

Case for Action 7.4

You have been asked by your principal to consider a professional reassignment to a resource room from a self-contained classroom for secondary special needs students. What skills should you possess to assume such responsibilities?

Responsibilities of Teachers in Resource Rooms

Although teachers in resource rooms are known to have a great many responsibilities, the exact nature of these responsibilities remains open to debate. To complicate matters, at times school officials develop job descriptions outlining specific responsibilities without consulting the professional involved. There are several key areas of responsibility.

Program Planning   Personnel who manage a resource room are responsible for developing programs that meet the needs of secondary students and their teachers. They need to consider several factors early in the establishment of a secondary resource room. When possible, they should begin by securing a room that is located close to regular education classrooms. Such a location will have two advantages. First, it may reduce the negative feelings and stigma students and other educators attach to a "special" room. It is more likely to be used if it is viewed as an integral part of the general education setting. The second advantage is convenience. An accessible location minimizes the amount of the student's instructional day that is lost in transition time. Related to the location of the room is its name. "Resource room" or "learning lab" are titles appropriate for use in the secondary school.

When planning a program, teachers should locate materials that are suitable for secondary learners. Chapters 1 and 4 pointed out how difficult it can be for secondary special educators to obtain appropriate materials. Chapter 6 presented techniques for purchasing, adapting, and modifying materials. Practitioners are again reminded of the importance of obtaining and using relevant, age-appropriate materials with secondary students with disabilities. In addition to being more appropriate to the students' skill levels, these materials may encourage them to enter and use the resource room.

A fourth aspect of program planning is public relations. Merely setting up shop in proximity to general secondary classrooms may be an ineffective way of advertising the room and its functions. Informal invitations to administrators, colleagues, students, and parents to visit the room would allow the teacher to explain the program and establish rapport. In addition, teachers in resource rooms should be highly visible and should assume duties assigned to other educators, such as supervising the cafeteria, the detention room, and after-school activities.

Direct Service   Secondary teachers who use the instruction techniques described in Chapter 4 will probably find that most of their students with disabilities are progressing toward the goals that have been established for them. However, if an instructional difficulty persists after two well-documented attempts have been made to resolve them, secondary educators may seek outside assistance. This assistance may take the form of either direct or indirect services.

Much of the day is devoted to direct service to secondary students with disabilities. Instruction may address any of the academic content areas typically encountered in the secondary school curriculum. For some students, especially those with mild learning disabilities, instruction will focus on the development of learning strategies. In addition, teachers may use resource time to help some secondary students develop social skills in small-group settings.

Indirect Service   For a variety of reasons, the teacher in a resource room is likely to provide indirect services to secondary education personnel on a daily or weekly basis. These services are indirect in the sense that direct work with general education colleagues indirectly benefits secondary students with special needs. For example, a secondary teacher may report that a student with disabilities is experiencing difficulties mastering the goals of a particular instructional unit. Assistance from the teacher in a resource room can assume a variety of forms. He or she may examine the goals of the unit and make suggestions for modifications that more closely approximate the student's needs. Additional materials can be located and utilized. The teacher can also observe the classroom during the scheduled activity and identify strategies that will facilitate student learning. The teacher may even offer to conduct a sample lesson for the group of which the special needs student is a member.

Behavior management is another area that may require the cooperative effort of general educators and consultants. A secondary teacher might seek assistance in managing a problem that quantitatively or qualitatively exceeds the norm typical of secondary classrooms. The teacher in a resource room can assist in defining the behavior; identifying current antecedents and consequences; gathering baseline data; and designing, implementing, and evaluating an intervention program.

There are two advantages to providing indirect services to secondary teachers. First, with such support, secondary teachers can give students with disabilities the assistance they need to maintain the academic and behavioral standards of the mainstream classroom, and thus eliminate the need to consider a more restrictive placement. Second, general educators may acquire or fine-tune specific techniques for teaching academic skills and managing behavior that may prove useful in other situations with other students.

In-Service Education   Closely related to indirect services are the in-service sessions that can be conducted occasionally by the teacher in a resource room. Secondary teachers in a particular building may have a common need for specific information or skills. The teacher can organize and present an in-service solution to this problem. Topics of potential interest include recent legislation, current research regarding the characteristics and educational needs of students with disabilities, technological developments, behavior management techniques, and learning strategies. In-service time should be reserved for presenting new information or demonstrating new materials or techniques, with sufficient time budgeted for discussing the implications for secondary teachers.

Administration   Teachers in a resource room have a number of administrative responsibilities. They develop and monitor IEPs, arrange and participate in multidisciplinary team

Case for Action 7.5

A secondary teacher is experiencing difficulty in getting a student with special needs to complete his homework and to hand it in on time. She asks for your advice. What will you suggest?

Case for Action 7.6

You are establishing a resource room program in a secondary school where no such program has ever been available. Your principal has asked that you provide four 30-minute in-service sessions for the faculty. Identify your topics and outline the content of each.

meetings, keep records, process referrals, schedule in-service sessions, and maintain contact with other public and private agencies serving students with disabilities.

Resource room programs can play a valuable role in the delivery of educational services to students with disabilities. Their most notable advantage is that they keep students in a less restrictive environment without compromising the integrity of their educational programs. The success of a resource room obviously depends on the skills of the practitioner assigned to this setting. The roles and responsibilities in this setting can be carried out only by a well-trained, dedicated professional.

Summary

Consideration must be given first to placing a student with a disability in the general classroom; thus, in addition to their typical learners, general education teachers are responsible for meeting the needs of one or more students with special needs. Despite the fact that secondary educators are experts in their content areas and have considerable teaching experience, the responsibility for meeting the academic, social, or behavioral needs of some students may appear overwhelming, particularly in this era of standards-based reform and high-stakes assessments (Austin, 2001; Mastropieri et al., 2005). Fortunately, assistance is available, and there are benefits to a team approach in transforming traditional teaching and enhancing the learning experience of all students.

In recent years, consultant teachers have been available to work collaboratively with secondary teachers to develop and implement programs for students who have disabilities or who are low achievers. Collaboration between secondary educators and consultant teachers has many advantages. Both sets of practitioners develop new skills, and students are better able to develop the skills they need to succeed in inclusive high school placements. These advantages can be realized if the consultant teacher has the appropriate training and if all practitioners are willing to set aside territorial issues and preconceived notions about their roles (Friend & Cook, 2003).

It is also possible that the needs of a student with a disability can be met appropriately in a resource room. This room can be staffed by the consultant teacher who will provide direct services to small groups of students. Other responsibilities include indirect service, in-service education, parent education, and administration.

Both of these arrangements make it possible for students to develop important skills in the least restrictive setting. In addition, professionals who participate in collaborative efforts increase their ability to meet the needs of all the students in their classroom. Areas of difficulty can be identified and addressed effectively and quickly, reducing the need for more expensive and intrusive options.

Listening and Speaking

DANIEL C. TULLOS

Did you know that . . .

- People spend approximately 75% of their time speaking and listening?
- The primary goal of listening is understanding?
- All speakers are occasionally dysfluent?
- There are 43 phonemes in American English?
- All phonemes are acquired by 8 years of age?
- Semantics may be the most important aspect of language functioning?
- By the age of 6 years, children understand nearly 20,000 words?
- Social skills and pragmatics are similar?

- Listening is best assessed through informal measures?
- Syntax is most effectively evaluated by a language sample?
- Listening instruction should be infused into other curricular areas?
- Instruction in spoken-language skills needs to be provided separately and integrated with other curricular areas?
- Techniques for assessing and teaching pragmatic skills resemble those used to assess and teach social skills?

Can you . . .

- Define language?
- Identify the components of language?
- Identify four types of voice disorders?
- Differentiate between two types of phonological problems?

- Identify morphological endings that pose difficulties for secondary students?
- Develop a listening skills assessment?
- Construct sentences to informally assess morphological skills?

Daniel C. Tullos is professor and director of the Communication Disorders Program at Harding University, Searcy, Arkansas.

If asked to list all the activities in which they participated during a given day, most individuals would neglect to mention communication. However, a careful consideration of these activities would reveal that two dimensions of communication—speaking and listening—are important characteristics of most activities. Researchers have found that people spend between 33% (Weinrauch & Swanda, 1975) and 60% of their time listening (Purdy, 1997) and about 26% of their time speaking (Weinrauch & Swanda, 1975). These data mean that individuals may spend up to 75% of their time in speaking and listening.

This chapter examines some of the basic characteristics of speaking and listening necessary for normal interaction within a secondary school program. Emphasis is on the testing of speaking and listening skills as well as the remediation of speaking and listening deficits among secondary students who have disabilities. Note that many of the skills involved in successful speaking and listening are mastered before and during the elementary school years. Therefore, the age at which specified skills are usually mastered is presented. The goal of primary school speech, language, and hearing screening programs is to identify and provide remediation for deficits in normally acquired communication skills before a student participates in a secondary program. Also included in this chapter are sections on bidialectalism and bilingualism. No discussion of speaking and listening would be complete without an awareness of issues inherent in our multicultural society.

Listening

Listening is a selective process that involves both the reception of auditory cues and the interpretation of information contained in those cues. Listening is effective only when the listener is participating actively in the listening process and the primary objective is understanding. "Listening is the basic language skill that is used the highest percentage of time" (Larson & McKinley, 2003, p. 52). For secondary students with disabilities, listening is particularly important (Deshler, Ellis, & Lenz, 1996). First, these students can gain a great deal of information through the auditory channel. Second, new information and a variety of leisure activities become accessible by means of devices that require listening skills, such as television, radio, cell phone, and telephone. Third, employment and social situations demand efficient listening skills.

A student who seems to be having listening problems may actually have one of several basic disabilities: a hearing problem, an attention deficit, or a language comprehension deficit. To rule out a hearing problem, the student should be referred to an audiologist for a hearing screening or an audiological evaluation. If a school does not have an audiologist, the speech-language pathologist can screen the hearing of the student and, if necessary, refer him or her to a local audiologist for a more extensive assessment. If no hearing problems are indicated, then an attention or a language comprehension deficit should be suspected.

Attention deficits are often caused by mental and physical distractions. Physical distractions draw the student's attention away from the teacher and the information/instructions being presented to the class. Physical distractions can often be identified. Some examples are a brightly colored and moving screen saver, fish in a classroom aquarium, and a blinking neon light. Mental distractions are more difficult to identify. The student might be planning a party, rehearsing how to ask "Mr. or Ms. Perfect" out on a date, or thinking about what the teacher would look like without any hair. In any case, the information communicated by the teacher is not received by the student. Note, however, that it is difficult to separate an attention deficit from an interfering language-comprehension problem.

Speech

In the past, an effort was made to clearly differentiate aspects of communication related to speech from those related to language. *Speech* was taken to mean the production of the sounds of language (articulation) and the quality (voice) and smoothness (fluency) with which those sounds are produced. Articulation is no longer as clearly differentiated. Researchers (Bauman-Waengler, 2000; Bleile, 2004; Yavas, 1998) have indicated that some sound-production or articulation errors that have been labeled speech problems actually have to do with the rules governing how speech sounds are produced or combined (phonology). In this chapter, there is no attempt to differentiate rule-governed or phonological errors from sound-production errors caused by other factors. For the sake of convenience, all errors of sound production are discussed under phonology/articulation.

A person is said to be "dysfluent" if the rhythm or smoothness of his or her communication is abnormally disrupted. This difficulty is frequently referred to as *stuttering*. Stuttering is often considered a disorder of childhood (Bloodstein, 1995), although some students continue to be dysfluent during their secondary school and adult years. The student who appears to be struggling to say something, expresses concern about blocks or repetitions, or is criticized by peers for abnormal rate or rhythm of communication should be referred to the speech-language pathologist. The speech-language pathologist will observe the student in various speaking situations and compare fluency to that of peers. It should be noted that all speakers are dysfluent, depending on the circumstances, and only dysfluent speakers who fall outside the range considered normal need therapy. The speech-language pathologist then meets with the teacher to discuss ways in which the pressures surrounding communication for the student can be reduced. The causes of and most effective treatment programs for fluency disorders continue to be widely debated.

Voice disorders can be divided into four types: pitch, loudness, quality, and duration. A secondary teacher would be most likely to observe students with disorders of voice quality, such as the hoarseness caused by vocal nodules. Unfortunately, many students with such nodules are never referred for proper management. The student who has persistent hoarseness and continually sounds as though he or she has a cold should be referred to an otolaryngologist for a visual inspection of the vocal cords to determine whether nodules are present. The school speech-language pathologist can assist with the consultation and referral. Another voice disorder is hypernasality (nasal-sounding voice). The speech-language pathologist can evaluate and determine possible causes and then either provide therapy or refer the student to someone for appropriate medical intervention.

Language

Language has been defined as a socially shared, arbitrary, rule-governed code through which people share ideas and maintain contact. The words used to communicate are arbitrary signals in that they possess no inherent meaning. That is to say, their meanings have been arbitrarily assigned by the members of that language community. For communication to take place, the person sending the message must place the idea into code form (encode) and transmit that code to another person, who will translate that code into an idea (decode).

Language is rule governed in that it is predictable and, to a large extent, consistent throughout a language community. The system of rules governing a language can be divided into *form* (phonology, morphology, and syntax), *content* (semantics), and *use* (pragmatics). Although these concepts can be defined and discussed separately, in the speaking process they are all combined.

Phonology/Articulation

Every language can be divided into a specific number of sounds. When combined, they form the words of that language. These small, distinctive, individual units of sound are called *phonemes,* and the system of rules that governs their combination or sequencing is termed *phonology.* Although the English alphabet contains only 26 letters, the sound system of American English contains approximately 43 phonemes, 24 of which are consonants and the remaining 19 vowels (Small, 2005). By the age of 3, a child can produce many of these sounds, especially the vowel sounds, in the standard way accepted by the community. Native English speakers do not usually have difficulty producing English vowel sounds unless they have a significant hearing loss. Most individuals have acquired all 43 phonemes by the age of 8. Certainly, by the time an individual has reached a secondary program, no abnormalities in sound production should be noted.

Errors in producing or articulating the phonemes of American English fall into three main categories: substitution, distortion, and omission. When a student uses another recognizable American English sound for the target sound, a substitution has occurred. For example, a student who labels an object flying in the sky as a "tite" instead of "kite" is making a substitution error. A distortion error occurs when a student uses a sound not considered an English sound, or not an American English sound, for the target sound. For example, a student who forces air out of one side of her mouth when producing an "s" is distorting the sound. In an omission error, a student simply omits the target sound in words, as in "bo" for "boat" and "o" for "toe."

Other errors in sound production may be rule based (phonological). For example, a student may exhibit final consonant deletion. She can produce /t/, /b/, and /s/ and says words such as "tea," "bee," and "stay." However, all consonants occurring at the end of words are dropped. Thus, she says "e" for "eat," "ca" for "cab," and "pa" for "pass." The difference between rule-based phonological errors and the errors of articulation is that the former involves systematic application of rules governing sounds the student may be able to produce; for example, the student can produce all the consonants but does not use them if they appear at the end of a word. Articulation disorders render a student unable to produce a particular sound regardless of where it appears in the word. Neither of these categories includes sound-production differences that are dialectal in nature. These differences are not considered disorders.

Morphology

Morphology refers to the way the sounds of American English are combined into meaningful units and to the rules governing this process. The smallest meaningful units produced as a result of this combination of sounds are called *morphemes.* Root words, as well as prefixes, suffixes, and both parts of compound words, are classified as individual morphemes. The word *cars,* for example, contains two morphemes. "Car" is called the root or free morpheme and the "s" the marker of plurality or bound morpheme. Readers interested in the types of morphemes that occur in English and the developmental order in which they would normally be acquired are referred to in Cole and Cole (1989). Students who have experienced developmental delays, as well as students from language environments using different dialectal variations, may have difficulty with morphological constructs. For example, a teacher, asking whether anyone has seen Mary and Sue, might receive a reply such as "I seed them" instead of the expected "I saw them." Or consider the student who described a picture in which a dog is obviously pregnant by saying, "Her's having puppies."

Semantics

The aspect of language that has to do with the meaning of words is referred to as *semantics.* Semantics is considered to be extremely important because "the communication of meaning is the central function of language" (Crystal, 1981, p. 131). Children learn through experience that whatever occurs around them can be described or controlled by using words. They hear significant individuals within their environment use certain words, and they begin to associate those words with specific objects, actions, and events. Understanding the meaning of a word (reception) precedes the use of that word (expression). By the age of 6, a child is capable of understanding approximately 20,000 words but actually uses significantly fewer (McLaughlin, 1998). This pattern, with isolated exceptions, continues throughout life.

Two aspects of semantics have great bearing on secondary education. The first is the type of words used by the student. Weiss and Lillywhite (1976) have stated that word acquisition normally follows this sequence:

    nouns–verbs–adjectives–pronouns–adverbs
    prepositions–articles–conjunctions–interjections

By the time students enter a secondary program, they should be using all of these types with the same frequency as their peers. Because vocabulary is so closely linked with experience, and experiences vary from location to location as well as from person to person, the vocabulary used in an individual school should be a primary consideration for secondary educators. Cultural and dialectal factors must also be considered as a significant influence in the development of semantics.

Semantics also has to do with the way words are combined in sentences to convey complex meaning. A student must be aware of the meaning of words to be able to combine them into meaningful sentences. The significant classes of words in semantics are not the same as those in syntax, discussed in the following section. Semantically, words are grouped into specific areas or fields of meaning. In a limited study of adults, Crystal (1981) found that 12 classes accounted for 55% of the words used by the sample group: time, leisure, possession, people, cognitive activity, quantity, location, coming and going, sensory perception, animals, foods and meals, and house and furniture. In the agent–action–object sentence "The ____ sees the ____," semantic rules dictate that only words from the people or animal class can fill the agent position, whereas words from additional classes such as foods and meals can be used in the object position. Semantic rules also dictate that the words chosen to fill specific positions must match the actual situation. In the sentence "The *tall* man is eating the apple," the word *short* could not be used even though it would still produce an acceptable sentence. In this context, the meaning of the word *short* does not describe the 6-foot man eating the apple.

Vocabulary development is an ongoing process. People normally continue to add words to their receptive and expressive vocabularies on the basis of their experiences. Students participating in a science experiment, for example, may first learn the meaning of the word *reaction* when the teacher talks about and demonstrates a chemical reaction. The students begin to notice and understand *reaction* as the word is used in different situations. Gradually, *reaction* begins to appear in the students' expressive vocabularies as they describe specific situations. Words may also disappear from expressive vocabularies as experiences change. Remember that words do not have inherent meaning. The meaning of a word depends on how the word is used by the majority of people within a specific environment or by the communicator and receiver. Words may have a denotative or dictionary meaning, as well as a connotative or personalized meaning. The word *phat* (pronounced *fat*), for example, has a negative denotative meaning but is frequently used with a positive connotative meaning. The sentence "That student was phat!" could have two totally opposite meanings when expressed by a teacher and a teenager. Teachers must be aware of this potential problem in semantics.

Syntax

The rules of syntax determine the way in which words are put together to form phrases and sentences. What is commonly referred to as *grammar* is actually a combination of the rules of syntax and morphology. Listeners may not be able to list English syntactic rules, but they can detect when one has been violated. Developmentally, syntax becomes a factor in communication at around 18 months of age, when an infant begins to combine single words into two-word phrases. Initially, these phrases are made up of functional words and are telegraphic in nature (telegraphic speech). Gradually, these phrases and sentences become more complex until a child is able to master all patterns of sentence structure, usually about the age of 7 or 8.

Syntactic rules are grasped through repeated exposure to language. Children are surrounded by adults and older siblings who are using language to control their environment through interaction. These children begin to notice that words are always placed in a certain sequence. In an English-speaking environment, they notice that the subject usually precedes the verb, and the verb usually precedes the object. When they begin to produce two- and three-word combinations, these combinations follow the rules picked up from their environment in a progressive sequence.

After learning to construct simple or kernel sentences, children begin to transform them into more complex sentences. A transformation is the rule-based altering of a sentence. For example, the active construction "The boy hit the ball" can be transformed into a passive construction, "The ball was hit by the boy." Another type of transformation involves embedded sentences. This type of sentence consists of two kernel sentences that have been combined in such a way that one depends on the other. An example is "We can eat if Dan gets here." The first part is called the *independent clause* and the second part the *dependent clause.* As a general rule, students in a secondary program should understand and be able to generate all types of complex and embedded sentences. However, this area of syntax is the most likely to present difficulties for secondary students who have experienced developmental delays or disorders.

Pragmatics

The rules underlying the functional use of language are collectively referred to as *pragmatics.* The social context in which language is produced and the way in which that context affects meaning are closely tied to pragmatic rules. An individual exhibiting problems with the pragmatics of language would also be exhibiting social skill deficits. Pragmatics takes in several aspects of communication, including nonverbal codes, discourse, and shifts in style. Cultural background significantly affects the development and interpretation of pragmatic aspects of communication.

A nonverbal code can be any form of communication that does not consist of words. Gestures, facial expressions, tone of voice, and even clothing can be considered pragmatic factors in communication. A student sent to the principal's office for fighting might say, "I will never cause any more trouble." However, if she is slouched in a chair in the office, has a bored look on her face, and is using a sarcastic tone of voice, the message being sent is the opposite of the words used. The message the principal receives is "I will fight if I want to." Clothing, too, can influence the message transmitted. An individual who wears torn blue jeans and a dirty T-shirt to an interview for a summer job at a local clothing store is communicating that this job is not important. The fact that he really wants the job is not the message being conveyed.

Discourse refers to conversation in which individuals function as both speakers and listeners. To participate in a conversation, students need to be skilled in taking turns; initiating, maintaining, and terminating dialogue; and making repairs in the event of a communication breakdown.

To communicate successfully, a person must be able to evaluate a specific speaking situation and determine the style of language that would be most effective or appropriate at that time. For example, a student offering a peer a candy bar might say, "Here, pig out on this." However, the same student offering the candy bar to a teacher needs to change the style to "Would you like this candy bar?" Some students with learning disabilities have difficulty recognizing the situational factors (pragmatics) necessary to shift to the appropriate style.

Assessment of Listening Skills

Listening skills can be assessed formally or informally. In a formal assessment, one measures the student's ability to retain and comprehend information presented auditorily. Few formal measures have been developed to assess listening skills alone; therefore, the teacher/ examiner will have to use subtests of more comprehensive language assessment techniques. The *Clinical Evaluation of Language Fundamentals,* Fourth Edition (CELF–4) (Semel, Wiig, & Secord, 2003), *Comprehensive Assessment of Spoken Language* (CASL) (Carrow-Woolfolk, 1998), *Comprehensive Receptive and Expressive Vocabulary Test,* Second Edition (CREVT–2) (Wallace & Hammill, 1994), *Detroit Tests of Learning Aptitude,* Fourth Edition (DTLA–4) (Hammill, 1998), and the *Fullerton Language Test for Adolescents* (Thorum, 1986) are norm-referenced measures with listening components.

The teacher may find informal assessment a more appropriate and readily available method for measuring the listening skills of secondary learners with disabilities. Wallace, Cohen, and Polloway (1987) described two methods of informal assessment: teacher checklists and skills assessment. A teacher checklist is used to document listening skills in areas that occur frequently and naturally throughout the day. A sample checklist charting various aspects of listening across a variety of settings is presented in Figure 8.1. This technique offers two advantages. First, it is easily adapted to other settings. For example, the teacher may develop separate lists for regular and special education environments. Second, teacher checklists are easy to use and interpret.

Larson and McKinley (2003) present a listening questionnaire developed by Schreiber and McKinley for secondary students to complete. This questionnaire provides additional information about how the student approaches listening tasks. This information would then be combined with the results of the checklists.

FIGURE 8.1 *A Teacher Checklist for Measuring Secondary Students' Listening Skills*

Name: _____   Date: _____

Observer: _____   Setting: _____

Listening Skill	*S #1*	*S #2*	*S #3*	*S #4*	*S #5*
1. Responds to discrete cue signaling the beginning of instruction.					
2. Responds to bells signaling the end of class.					
3. Attends to announcements over the public address system.					
4. Participates in class discussions.					
5. Sequences events.					
6. Participates in informal conversations with peers.					
7. Appears to be listening: e.g., watches teacher and establishes eye contact, looks at maps, etc.					
8. Answers questions.					

A skill assessment is a more structured method of measuring listening abilities. Rather than waiting for opportunities to occur in the natural environment, the teacher structures situations in which the student must respond. A skill assessment can be conducted to measure discrimination, recall, and comprehension skills. For example, the teacher might notice that a student frequently mispronounces common words. She develops a skill assessment to measure how well a student can discriminate sounds. The teacher then establishes a criterion level, pronounces one item at a time from material within the student's listening comprehension, has the student repeat it, and records the accuracy of the response. For a thorough evaluation of sound-discrimination skills, the student should be referred to a speech-language pathologist (see Locke, 1980). Larson and McKinley (2003) provide a Secondary-Level Referral Form that would be useful in supplying information to the speech-language pathologist. Although this method requires more preparation time, it does allow the teacher to identify listening skills that need to be developed.

Assessment of Speaking Skills

The skills necessary for age-appropriate speaking are assessed according to the *form, content,* and *use* of language. Methods are available to evaluate skills in each of these areas; however, as indicated earlier, all of these components must work together to produce effective and appropriate communication. These components can be assessed by formal and informal measures, both of which provide valuable information for the remediation process.

Formal measures of language functioning are designed to assess language skills in a designated area(s) and are usually conducted by the teacher or speech-language pathologist. These tests sample skills by examining specific items that research and standardization studies have shown to be typical of the performance of peers in the designated area(s). Formal language assessment measures focus attention on specific deficit areas but do not describe the language system used by the student. Several of the norm-referenced measures that are currently used to assess spoken language include the *Clinical Evaluation of Language Fundamentals,* Fourth Edition (CELF–4) (Semel et al., 2003), *Comprehensive Assessment of Spoken Language* (CASL) (Carrow-Woolfolk, 1998), *Comprehensive Receptive and Expressive Vocabulary Test,* Second Edition (CREVT–2) (Wallace & Hammill, 1994), *Detroit Tests of Learning Aptitude,* Fourth Edition (DTLA–4) (Hammill, 1998), *Expressive One Word Picture Vocabulary Test* (EOWPVT–2000) (Gardner, 2000), *Expressive Vocabulary Test* (EVT) (Williams, 1997), and *Fullerton Language Test for Adolescents* (Thorum, 1986).

Unfortunately, a student may have no problems with the items sampled on a formal test but still exhibit significant problems in that particular area. The *Peabody Picture Vocabulary Test–III* (Dunn & Dunn, 1997), for example, presents 204 vocabulary items and provides an age-equivalency score based on the number of items correctly identified. A student may obtain an appropriate age score because he is familiar with many of the items on the test but still have a significant receptive/expressive vocabulary (*content*/semantic) problem. The reverse is also true. A student may obtain a low age-equivalent score because she is unfamiliar with the vocabulary items included on the test; however, she may have no difficulty with the vocabulary used in her dialectal (including her home) and educational environments.

Informal measures of language functioning usually consist of structured or unstructured observations. Suppose the teacher becomes concerned about a student who has trouble participating in class discussions. When he does respond, he uses several short, simple sentences rather than a complex sentence more typical of the responses from other students. The teacher has an aide make a list of all of this student's verbal utterances during a specified period of time. This observation will produce a better and clearer picture of how this student is forming sentences (syntax) and more specific information for developing a treatment program. Informal testing can provide ample information regarding the *content, form,* and *use* rules that are being used by a student, even if that information is not sufficient for referral for special services.

There is a place for both formal and informal spoken-language assessment in secondary programs. Many of the formal tests of speech and language functioning are administered by the speech-language pathologist within each school. A teacher who suspects that a student is having difficulty with speaking should refer that student to the speech-language pathologist. A speech and language evaluation, which usually includes formal and informal measures, would then be conducted and the results discussed with the student, parents, and teacher. Note, however, that the classroom teacher is usually in a better position to conduct informal observations. He or she is around the students and can observe their verbal and nonverbal interactions more successfully than the speech-language pathologist (see Chapter 5). The speech-language pathologist might help the teacher identify specific behaviors that need to be observed and thus may enhance the teacher's contribution to the assessment process.

As already pointed out, it would be impossible to cover all of the assessment procedures that are used, or that are necessary, for a thorough evaluation of speech and language functioning. These suggestions are only some ways that the components of language can be assessed. Again, the specific areas of language will be considered individually, although in reality each must be considered within the framework of the others. It is strongly recommended that students exhibiting any speech or language difficulties be referred to a speech-language pathologist for a complete evaluation of functional skills. Additional sources should also be consulted for complete information on normal and abnormal space and language (e.g., Bleile, 2004; Cole & Cole, 1989; Larson & McKinley, 2003; McLaughlin, 1998; Owens, 2005; Shames & Anderson, 2002).

Form

A secondary student who is exhibiting any sound production (phonology/articulation) errors should be referred to a speech-language pathologist. One speech-language pathologist in a university program receives several referrals of incoming first-year students each year who are exhibiting easily correctable, nondialectal sound-production errors. The majority of these students have never received therapy and report that they have never been informed that their articulation is abnormal. A disservice is done to these students if they have not been referred for services that are routinely provided within elementary and secondary school programs.

The speech-language pathologist will conduct an inventory of all sounds used in American English and determine any sound with which a student is having difficulty and whether there are any organic causes such as a hearing loss or poorly aligned teeth or jaw.

Students with organic problems will be referred for appropriate management, perhaps to a dentist, or a treatment plan will be developed to remediate the errors in sound production. Sound-production differences related to dialects are also identified, and options dealing with bidialectalism and "language education" may be discussed.

Few commercial measures are available to diagnose morphological difficulties. Therefore, information regarding morphological functioning must be based on informal observation and testing. A teacher should take note of those students who seem to be having trouble with these endings and compare them with the other students in the class or school program. Morphological prefixes such as "de-," "ex-," and "un-" are more likely to present problems at the secondary level. A written or oral exercise would be one way for a teacher to evaluate a student's use of prefixes. This exercise could include a list of prefixes (see Wiig & Semel, 1984) with instructions for the students to describe the meaning and give an example of words containing certain prefixes.

Similarly, there are few formal measures of syntactic ability available for secondary students. The *Detroit Tests of Learning Aptitude* (DTLA–4) Sentence Imitation (Hammill, 1998) subtest requires the student to verbally repeat increasingly complex and lengthy sentences. This test is designed for individuals between 6 and 17 years of age. As with any formal test, the results assist a teacher in identifying deficit areas that need to be assessed informally.

A spontaneously produced sample of oral language is again the most effective way of assessing syntactic functioning. A large sample of spontaneous language should be collected along with the context in which the sentences were produced. The number of sentences in this sample would range from at least 50 to well over 100 utterances. This record of the oral sample can then be analyzed according to the type of sentence used, such as noun + copula + noun/adjective simple sentences (*The boy is very sick.*) and complex adverbial embedded sentences (*You don't mind if I eat this apple.*). Some syntactic problems will be obvious, such as inappropriate word order and lack of agreement between subject and verb. A deeper analysis may indicate that a student is using very few complex sentences or is producing incorrect compound sentences. Although a language sample yields a great deal of useful information, it takes a great deal of time and substantial skill to collect and analyze (see Retherford, 1993). Time constraints may limit its use; however, a speech-language pathologist might elect to use this procedure.

An analysis of an adolescent's ability to produce narratives is a more efficient way of evaluating language development at this stage. Narratives involve the telling of events that the student has experienced, the telling of fictionalized stories, and the explanation of procedural activities (such as applying for a driver's license). Hughes, McGillivray, and Schmidek (1997) have stated that "production of narratives is a rigorous test of many levels and aspects of language *content, form,* and *use*" (p. 7). Students exhibiting difficulty with any of the components of language would profit from an evaluation of their narrative skills by a speech-language pathologist.

Content/Semantics

Semantic development can also be assessed informally. The most effective informal evaluation of semantic functioning works from a sample of the student's language in specific contexts. Semantic concepts are linked with experiences; therefore, the language that is used to relate characteristics of an experience should reflect ongoing semantic development. Ask each student to share a recent experience, such as a concert, with the class for about five minutes. Make a list of the concepts and vocabulary items expressed. Then generate a discussion and compare the vocabulary items and concepts to those used by the rest of the class. Introduce new semantic concepts to the class and note whether those concepts were understood and used by the students participating in the group. This same approach can be used in semantic training.

Use/Pragmatics

Most pragmatic measures that are currently available look at the skills of children. Little is currently available for the assessment of adolescent pragmatic functioning. Following are some examples of pragmatic difficulties that would be noticeable in secondary students:

1. Utterances that lack adequate referential clarity and therefore confuse or mislead the listener
2. Difficulty in initiating topics, maintaining topic relevance, switching and returning to the main issue or topic, and terminating a conversation
3. Frequently impolite, interrupting points in the conversation

Speech-language pathologists would assess through observational analysis or narrative evaluations discussed under language form. What speech-language pathologists refer to as *pragmatics,* special educators often refer to as *social skills.* Larson and McKinley (2003) have developed an excellent Social Skills Rating Scale for both the student and the adults commenting on student behaviors. Providing these as an aspect of pragmatic assessment would elicit valuable information. A review of social skills literature provides a variety of formal and informal techniques for measuring this aspect of spoken language. These techniques are reviewed in detail in Chapter 14.

Strategies to Improve Listening Skills

Although teachers cannot confer on students the ability to listen, they can provide experiences that will help them listen more effectively (Wallace et al., 1987). In other words, listening skills can be taught. Individuals should listen for a purpose. Teachers are advised to instruct their students to listen *for* something rather than listen *to* something. Rather than treat listening skills separately, teachers should develop them through activities conducted during instruction in other curricular areas.

Larson and McKinley (2003) divided listening into three remedial areas: comprehension of linguistic features, informational listening, and critical listening. As is required in remedial situations, these authors stressed the need to establish goals before beginning intervention and presented an extensive list of intervention goals for the development of listening skills. The reader is referred to their excellent materials for detailed information. The remainder of this chapter deals with a general classroom approach to improving listening skills.

Wallace and colleagues (1987) identified five general categories of listening that can be addressed throughout the curriculum: distinguishing nonlanguage sounds, discriminating voices, following directions, remembering what is heard, and organizing material. The last three categories are relevant to secondary students with disabilities. Wallace and colleagues (1987) also described a number of activities to promote listening skills in each of these categories.

Following Directions

The following activities can be useful in helping secondary students follow directions:

1. Assign a partner to each student. Give one student a picture to describe to his or her partner. The description should be given as a set of directions. The partner must draw the picture described without asking any questions.
2. Explain the potential uses of a new piece of equipment and provide directions for its use to one student. Have that student explain to a peer how to operate the device.
3. Give students working on map skills a set of directions that takes them on a special trip.

Remembering What Is Heard

Being able to remember what is heard is vital if the secondary learner is to experience success in school and in community environments. Wallace and colleagues (1987) suggested the following activities to strengthen listening skills:

1. During class discussion, have students summarize the comments made by the individual who spoke immediately before them. They may follow up with their own comments.
2. Read an article from the newspaper aloud and instruct students to remember as many of the details as possible.
3. Give comprehension questions just before students listen to a selection from a social studies or science textbook.
4. Have students listen to a radio news broadcast. Ask each student to write a headline for every story remembered.

Taking Notes

Notetaking is a necessary skill for effective participation in secondary education. Students who have trouble taking notes usually try to write too much, thereby missing many of

---

Case for Action 8.1

A secondary teacher working with a student with special needs in social studies reports that the learner has difficulty following directions. The student never appears to be on the correct page, does not follow along during oral reading, and frequently turns in the wrong homework assignment. What suggestions can you make?

the important points. Students should be encouraged to write down only key words and phrases. Usually the important information in a sentence could be captured by writing only the subject and verb. As the important words or phrases are written down, they should be organized in some way. Notes about the Civil War could take the following form with the major subject mentioned first and related information indented:

Civil War
- 1861–1865
- Union/Confederacy

Secondary teachers could develop notetaking activities for the entire class. Most students could use some assistance in this area. Chapter 15 includes a discussion of notetaking and the use of guided notes.

Organizing Material

Teachers can use the following activities to help secondary students organize the information they acquire by listening:

1. Have students predict the outcome of historical accounts and scientific experiments.
2. Use the cloze technique. Read a series of sentences from which key words have occasionally been omitted. Students must decide which words can be inserted appropriately.
3. Develop a time line for a series of historical events or the events described in a story.
4. Prequestion students before an oral presentation. Students should be instructed to listen for the answers and take notes on what they are hearing.
5. Have students develop an outline to organize important information.

Finally, secondary teachers are advised to capitalize on opportunities for listening instruction that occur in real-life situations. These include listening to music on the radio or stereo headphones, watching a movie, talking with friends, and using the cell or telephone.

Effective Questioning

Another important listening skill involves asking effective questions. Many secondary students hesitate to ask questions, even if important information has been missed. Students should be encouraged to ask questions. A checklist of questions can be developed that would include "who," "is doing or did what," "where," and "when."

A classroom activity can be developed that will assist students in asking questions. The teacher can divide students into groups of five and present one student in each group with a short story. The rest of the group must obtain information only by asking questions of that one student. Each student must write down the question before it is asked and then write down the answer. Following a specified period of time, the teacher randomly selects students from each group to re-create the story. The group that best re-creates the story then presents their sequence of questions to the class. These questions are then analyzed to determine why they yielded the most information.

Strategies to Improve Spoken-Language Skills

As mentioned when discussing listening strategies, Larson and McKinley (2003) have developed an excellent resource that gives detailed information about speaking skill development. Readers wanting more detailed information about the development of speaking skills are referred to their excellent text. The following strategies are designed to easily integrate with existing classroom activities.

Wallace and colleagues (1987) identified some guidelines for providing instruction in spoken-language skills. First, although students may display weaknesses in the reception or expression of one component of language, intervention techniques should highlight the integration of all components at both receptive and expressive levels. Second, language intervention should be scheduled and taught on a regular basis. Teachers should remember, however, to expect and reinforce newly acquired skills when they are demonstrated during the course of the school day. Third, teachers should always serve as models for the appropriate use of language.

Phonology/Articulation

Secondary students who make *form* errors in sound production should be referred to the speech-language pathologist for a complete phonological/articulation evaluation. This evaluation will produce a complete inventory of the sound-production errors exhibited by the student. In addition, the speech-language pathologist will attempt to determine whether the sound-production errors are caused by an abnormality in the oral structure, confusion with phonological rules, or some other factor. This information is used to develop a remediation program. Generally, the speech-language pathologist provides therapy and identifies specific approaches that can be taken by the teacher in the classroom. A thorough discussion of the cause, identification, and remediation of sound-production errors is available in other sources (cf., Bauman-Waengler, 2000; Bleile, 2004; Yavas, 1998).

Although the speech-language pathologist provides direct intervention in the area of sound production, classroom teachers will continue to interact with students in their classrooms and thus have many opportunities to assist with the therapy process. With this in mind, Sedlak and Sedlak (1985) have suggested several behaviors for a classroom teacher:

1. Do not embarrass or reprimand the learner for speaking poorly, because such negative behavior could be modeled by classmates. Do establish an atmosphere in which students feel free to experiment with speech.
2. Do become a good speech model, but do not overarticulate, because such behavior will call undue attention to the student's speech problems.
3. Do set aside time in the schedule for specific practice in speech development. Tape recorders, the Language Master, telephones, TalkBack, and similar types of materials and devices can be used for these periods.

Case for Action 8.2

A student in your class has speech that is very garbled. You and his peers find it difficult to understand him. You have to ask him to repeat things frequently, which you suspect causes him a great deal of embarrassment. What can you do to help?

Morphology and Semantics

Students exhibiting difficulties in the areas of morphology and semantics may profit from participating in a communicative environment. This type of environment is created when classroom material is presented in a discussion or interactive format. A teacher makes a list of vocabulary words that relate to a specific experience, such as a classroom science experiment. The list includes not only the scientific words but also the words related to the topic. The teacher conducts the lesson by stating what he or she is doing or has done and then asking students specific questions. For example, "First I dropped the red dye in the test tube, then shook it vigorously. Mary, what happened?" This type of interaction allows the teacher to direct the responses of the students and even correct their responses without appearing to concentrate on the errors. Other activities include oral reports, informal class presentations, and role-playing. In each of these situations, the teacher selects the topic or helps the student do so. Emphasis is placed on morphological endings and prefixes, as well as on vocabulary and semantic placement of vocabulary words.

The following strategies could be applied to the previously presented activities after a list of key vocabulary words is developed:

1. Present the object or action in combination with the vocabulary item (e.g., dye).
2. Each student should repeat the word in combination with an observation. (*The dye is red. The dye is a powder.*)
3. Each student should ask a question using the new vocabulary word. (*What would happen if you put less dye in the water?*)

A thorough analysis of semantics and its role in communication is available in other sources (e.g., McLaughlin, 1998; Owens, 2005).

Wallace and colleagues (1987) also suggested that revision be used to enhance semantic skills. The teacher provides students with a sentence or group of sentences and asks them to restate it or them in their own words. "Mary will not ride with Tom because he drives too fast" could be a revision of "Mary will not ride with Tom. Tom likes to drive his car very fast. Mary will not ride with anyone who drives fast."

Teachers at the secondary level also should make their students aware of the multiple meanings of some words. For example, the word *run* can refer to a motor act, competition for political office, a snag in a pair of panty hose, the operation of machinery, and a host of other meanings. Teachers may wish to screen reading material and present various meanings of words students might encounter. On a related note, teachers may need to familiarize students with the meaning of idioms such as "You can't tell a book by its cover." Excellent resources for idioms are currently available (Oliver, 2005; Terban, 1998).

Teachers can capitalize on sentences students produce throughout the school day. For example, during a social studies activity, a student might correctly answer a teacher's question by saying, "Columbus discover America in 1492." The teacher might respond, "Yes, Columbus discovered America in 1492," an expansion that reinforces the student's correct answer but also provides a model of appropriate language by including the verb marker. This technique is also useful for promoting syntax skills.

Syntax

If a student is exhibiting a serious problem with sentence structure, it is helpful to illustrate graphically the appropriate ordering of the words within sentences. The Fitzgerald key, developed by Fitzgerald (1954), is used to illustrate some types of appropriate sentence structure (see Figure 8.2). The Fitzgerald key shows the standard location of particular words in a sentence. This key can be displayed somewhere in the class for students who need visual aids.

The *Fokes Sentence Builder* (Fokes, 1976) was a commercially developed program for training students to recognize acceptable sentence structure. This program was designed to teach "grammatical rules, such as the inclusion of articles, auxiliary verbs, and prepositions" (p. 3) and to help students understand "different types of sentence constructions" (p. 3). Although it was designed for younger students, it may be useful for secondary students with significant syntactic difficulties. Use of a teacher-made slot filler approach will also be useful to address syntax problems. With the slot filler approach, the teacher provides spaces (either on the board, using index cards, or with blank lines on a page) that the student must complete with the appropriate words. The Fitzgerald key could be used as a basis for selecting the appropriate words.

Teachers can also help students improve their syntax skills by using the combination approach. Students are presented with a series of short sentences that they must combine into longer, more complex sentences. For example, a set of sentences might include "Sue had $20. She went to the store. She bought a new blouse. The blouse is for her mother. It is her birthday." The students can combine these sentences to produce "Sue went to the store with $20. She bought her mother a blouse because it was her birthday." It should be pointed out that there is no "correct" way to combine these elements into a more complex sentence. Several alternative methods of combining these simple sentences into more complex sentences should be discussed.

FIGURE 8.2   *The Fitzgerald Key*

What or Who	**Verb**	**Whom or What**	**Where**	**When**

Pragmatics

An excellent resource is currently available for pragmatic training. Marquis (1990) developed *Pragmatic-Language Trivia for Thinking Skills,* a pragmatic interaction game for older children and adolescents. This game approaches these skills in a practical, nonthreatening manner.

Schloss and Sedlak (1986) have listed six factors that should be considered when training students in pragmatic skills:

1. Taking turns in conversation
2. Initiating conversations
3. Clarifying a point made in a conversation
4. Following the sequential organization of a conversation
5. Making coherent contributions to a conversation
6. Maintaining a reasonable social distance

All of these factors must be modeled by the teacher during the daily activities of the class. In addition, the teacher can structure both simulation and independent activities in which students practice these skills. There are several social situations in which older learners must display pragmatic competence, such as using the telephone, making formal and informal introductions, participating in employment interviews, requesting assistance in consumer and employment settings, and sharing personal interests, hobbies, and experiences with peers and authority figures (Mandell & Gold, 1984). As noted earlier, activities that promote pragmatic competence closely resemble those designed to enhance social skills. These activities are described in detail in a subsequent chapter.

Bidialectalism

The view that there is an "ideal standard dialect" of American English is no longer accepted. According to Owens (1996), "a preference represents only the bias of the listener" (p. 402). The issue of dialects and whether the characteristics of nonstandard spoken English should be considered differences, deficiencies, or disorders has been widely debated (e.g., Owens, 2005; Schloss & Sedlak, 1986; Wallace et al., 1987). However, one point on which experts agree is that all speakers tend to shift between a formal and an informal level of language. Therefore, speakers of dialects should strive to learn how to shift from informal English to formal English.

Schloss and Sedlak (1986, p. 232) have suggested the following guidelines for teaching the speaker of informal English:

1. Accept the nonstandard English form, especially in the elementary grades, and build linguistic competence on into high school.
2. Restate a nonstandard English phrase in standard English, but do not call attention to the nonstandard form. That is, if a student responds with a phrase such as "John be goin' to the store," the teacher should follow with "That's right. John is going to the store."
3. Teach styles and have students discriminate among different situations in which each style is appropriate.
4. After the student is able to discriminate style, teach the variant forms and the appropriate situations for each.
5. Be a good speech model.

Bilingualism

The issue of bilingual or multicultural secondary education for the student with special needs is a complicated one that is beyond the scope of this chapter. However, by the time a bilingual student reaches a secondary program, he or she may be proficient in one language and exhibit difficulties with the second. In this situation, language use must be evaluated. The following issues must be considered:

1. Is the student proficient in the language of the home and social environment? If so, the student may need to approach the second language through a systematic learning program such as those connected with ESL curricula.
2. Does the student have trouble with both languages? If so, deficits should be identified and targeted.

In bilingual environments, opportunities exist to stress multicultural education issues for all students in the classroom. Each of the language areas mentioned earlier can be emphasized in both languages. Syntactic differences can be presented together. Content differences can be stressed in all class activities and lessons.

Summary

Listening and speaking skills are essential if students with special needs are to succeed in secondary settings. Whether a student is enrolled in a regular or a special class, the primary means of receiving directions or content-related instruction is through listening to the teacher. Similarly, the primary means of participating during instruction is speaking. Unfortunately, students with disabilities may be at risk for incomplete development of listening and speaking skills. Therefore, secondary educators must be aware of normal patterns of development and be alert for signs of delay or deviance among secondary learners. This chapter presented an overview of many factors involved in listening and speaking. Three aspects of language were discussed, including *form* (phonology, morphology, and syntax), *content* (semantics), and *use* (pragmatics). Also presented was a brief discussion of the assessment and treatment of speech and language disorders as they affect secondary students. Finally, cultural and linguistic differences were considered. These differences are not considered to be deficits; nonetheless, they have implications for working effectively with secondary students.

Although typical professional preparation courses describe normal and abnormal patterns of development in listening and speaking, it is unlikely that teachers possess the skills necessary to diagnose and remediate problem areas. This task is better left to speech-language pathologists. Nonetheless, general and special secondary educators are in ideal positions to observe student performance, note any irregularities, and request assistance. This assistance can take many forms, including the provision of therapy in a separate setting or the presence of the speech-language pathologist in the student's classroom during delivery of content-related instruction. Collaboration between speech-language pathologists and general and special educators can enhance students' listening and speaking skills, thereby increasing the chance for success in secondary settings.

9

Written Language

STEPHEN ISAACSON

— *Did you know that . . .*

- Written expression is probably the most difficult skill to teach?

- The vast majority of states mandate assessments in written language?

- Twenty-two percent of twelfth-grade students are not able to write at even the most basic level?

- There are three facets to a complete written language curriculum: process, product, and purpose?

- Most descriptions of the writing process include three operations: planning, sentence generation, and revising?

- A student's process can be assessed informally through observation or interview?

- The teacher models the cognitive processes in writing by thinking aloud as he or she demonstrates the task?

- Writing can involve collaboration with peers as well as the teacher?

- The writing process can be prompted through the use of "think sheets"?

- Self-instructional strategies allow the student to use the process independently?

- Word processors are effective only if students have been taught the necessary computer skills and composition strategies?

- The writing product has five components: fluency, content, conventions, syntax, and vocabulary?

- Conventions, the features of a text that reflect mechanical concerns, are the product component that instructors should approach with the greatest caution?

- The writing curriculum should take into account various school-related and job-related *purposes* for writing?

Stephen Isaacson is professor of special education and chairperson of the Department of Special Education and Counselor Education, Portland State University, Portland, Oregon.

Can you . . .

- State the four principles related to teaching the process of writing?

- Describe one way in which a teacher can model the subprocess of planning for writing?

- Describe one way to entice a student to revise and write a second draft?

- State the guidelines you would teach to student response groups?

- Give an example of a self-instructional strategy for writing?

- Distinguish between revising and editing?

- Give an example of how to informally assess each of the five product components?

- Give an example of how to improve a student's skills in each of the five product components?

- State two school writing tasks that students should be taught in order to succeed in content area classes?

- State three job-related writing tasks that students should be taught in order to succeed in the workplace?

The Individuals with Disabilities Education Act (IDEA) mandated that students with disabilities participate in the general education curriculum and that they be included in district- and statewide assessment programs. Nearly all states assess student performance in the areas of reading and math, and the majority of states have added written language assessments. Passing scores on assessments are not the sole goal of written language curricula; it is essential that students develop the written language skills necessary for the complex tasks they face in secondary and postsecondary settings, including taking notes, completing essay exams, writing reports and term papers, and handling correspondence (Schumaker & Deshler, 2003). Such task complexity can be challenging for students who may have already developed an aversion to writing long before they entered secondary school (Hallenbeck, 2002; Harris, Graham, & Mason, 2003). Many students in the United States, regardless of the presence of a disability, have difficulty with written expression. The National Center for Education Statistics (Greenwald, Persky, Campbell, & Mazzeo, 1999) indicated that 22% of the twelfth-grade students who participated in the National Assessment of Educational Progress were unable to write at even the most basic level. Unfortunately, numerous reports have shown that students in special education programs have problems with written expression (Marchisan & Alber, 2001). Algozzine, O'Shea, Stoddard, and Crews (1988) and Klein (1990) confirm that students with learning disabilities score much lower in writing on state competency assessments than students with no learning disabilities. Egelko (2002) reported that 82% of students with disabilities failed the language arts portion of their California high school exit examination. Specific areas of weakness include mechanical skills (Newcomer & Barenbaum, 1991) such as spelling, sentence formation, capitalization, and handwriting (Graham, Harris, MacArthur, & Schwartz, 1991), and cognitive processes such as planning, organizing, and revising (Bui, 2002). In all, when compared to the writing produced by typical peers, the writing of students with disabilities can be characterized as "less polished, expansive, coherent, and effective" (Harris et al., 2003, p. 1).

Marchisan and Alber (2001) suggested that written language is "probably the most difficult skill to teach because it is the most complex form of communication" (p. 155). All is not lost, however. Schumaker and Deschler (2003) noted that the outcomes of several studies indicate that the use of well-designed instructional methods can have a positive effect on students' written language performance. When planning writing instruction and assessing writing skills, it is useful to keep in mind the three facets of written language: process, product, and purpose. First, writing is a complex *process* that begins with generating and organizing ideas. The process requires the author to coordinate decisions about mechanical concerns such as spelling and punctuation at the same time that thoughts are being converted into written words. The process ends with editing and producing the final draft.

Second, writing results in a *product.* The process is successful only if the product clearly conveys the author's message. The product is most often judged by the writer's success in meeting the widely accepted standards of spelling, grammar, and punctuation, but other aspects of the product are also important, such as variation and economy in the use of syntax, appropriate word choices, and clear organization of ideas.

Third, people write for different *purposes.* The mode of writing (e.g., persuasive) usually depends on the purpose. The product will be judged according to the degree to which it fulfills its intended purpose. This chapter examines all three facets. Indeed, process, product, and purpose should all be considered when assessing any writing.

A Writing Curriculum for Students with Learning Problems

Through the 1980s, instruction in written language reflected a product-oriented model that focused on the development of mechanics and grammar. Writing time was limited, working independently was emphasized, and first drafts were often the only draft. Assignments were reviewed only by the teacher, whose grade reflected attention to handwriting, spelling, and punctuation. More recently, there has been a shift toward a process-oriented model that allows students more choice in topic selection; provides more time to think about what they are writing; encourages students to help one another; emphasizes writing for real purposes; and involves the use of teacher modeling, writing conferences, peer collaboration, and mini-lessons (Harris et al., 2003).

Writing instruction needs to originate from a well-thought-out curriculum that takes into account process, product, and purpose. First, what kind of explicit writing process should teachers present to students? The composition process consists of coordinating three major operations: planning (prewriting), sentence generation (writing), and revising (Hayes & Flower, 1987; Marchisan & Alber, 2001). First, the writer develops an implicit or explicit writing plan, generating ideas and organizing them in some fashion. The writer identifies the purpose for writing, the topic, content, voice, and audience. During the writing stage, the writer translates the ideas into sentences designed to be read by someone else. The writer produces a first draft and is primarily concerned with clear, logical expression rather than mechanics. In revising, the writer reads what has been written, evaluates the strengths and weaknesses, and attempts to improve it (Marchisan & Alber, 2001).

Hayes and Flower (1987) emphasized that these processes are *interleaved;* that is, the cycle—planning, generating sentences, revising—may occur repeatedly throughout relatively short periods of composition. They also may be applied recursively (Baker, Gersten, & Graham, 2003; Strassman & D'Amore, 2002); that is, one operation may interrupt and influence another. For example, a writer may write a sentence or two, plan what he or she is going to say next, write some more, reread, plan, revise, and so forth until the last word is written on the final draft.

However, a spontaneous, recursive process is not the best way to make the process clear to inexperienced writers. Students can best be taught how to handle the writing task by dividing the process into specific operations, beginning with prewriting planning activities (Graham et al., 1991). The resulting plans can then guide the writing of the draft. Throughout the guided composition lesson, the act of generating text is kept separate from that of revising the text, and revising content is kept separate from editing for mechanical errors. Kellogg (1988) made a useful distinction between the recursive operations of the *process* (planning, sentence generation, revising) and the linear *phases* of product development, which include prewriting activities, first draft, and subsequent draft(s).

Assessing the Process

Informal assessment of the student's progress during each step of the writing process can be made through observation or interview. If students are observed as they write in class, a checklist can be used that includes steps from initial choice of topic to final editing. The teacher should keep in mind that progress through all phases of the assignment may take more than one day to accomplish and, therefore, to observe. The purpose of this type of assessment is to determine which corresponding strategies need to be taught to the adolescent with writing problems.

Students also can assess the degree to which they have remembered the steps of the process. Action Plan 9.1 presents a self-assessment based on an explicit, easy-to-remember conceptual model of the writing process developed by Englert, Raphael, Anderson, Anthony, and Stevens (1991).

Teaching the Process

Writing instruction cannot focus only on isolated skills such as sentence grammar, spelling, and punctuation. Students in early writing programs that emphasized mechanics and grammar achieved significantly lower qualitative gains in writing than students receiving instruction that emphasized the organization of ideas and the problem-solving process of writing (Hillocks, 1984). The teacher must introduce the student to the entire process of writing, from initial idea generation to editing of the final draft. A process approach has four characteristics.

The Process Should Be Modeled   The teacher should model planning strategies by leading students in carefully prepared prewriting discussions. Preparing to write is the most essential step in helping students make decisions about content. Planning can begin with the teacher leading the class in a prewriting discussion of the topic. The critical skill for the teacher may be knowing when to cut off discussion (Rubin, 1987). If students have spent their ideas in talk, they may no longer experience the dissonance created by an incomplete idea that motivates them to write.

Planning might begin by raising questions of the WH type (Marchisan & Alber, 2001): *who, what, where, when,* and *how* (*Who* were the first people to explore the territory? *What* dangers did they encounter? *Where* did they first settle?). Questions also can be

Action Plan 9.1   POWER: Looking at How I Write

	My Comments		Teacher Comments

Plan

I chose a good topic.	Yes	No	
I read about my topic.	Yes	No	
I thought about what the readers will want to know.	Yes	No	
I wrote down all my ideas on a "think sheet."	Yes	No	

Organize

I put similar ideas together.	Yes	No	
I chose the best ideas for my composition.	Yes	No	
I numbered my ideas in logical order.	Yes	No	

Write

I wrote down my ideas in sentences.	Yes	No	

When I needed help, I
___ did the best I could.
___ looked in a book.
___ asked my partner.
___ asked the teacher.

Edit

I read my first draft to myself.	Yes	No	
I marked the parts I like.	Yes	No	
I marked the parts I might want to change.	Yes	No	
I read my first draft to my partner.	Yes	No	
I listened to my partner's suggestions.	Yes	No	

Rewrite

I made changes to my composition.	Yes	No	
I edited for correctness.	Yes	No	
I wrote the final draft in my best writing.	Yes	No	

generated by listing "What We Know" and "What We Don't Know" about the topic. As the students contribute information, everything is written down—accurate or not. Verification of the "What We Know" facts comes as students research the topic.

Some students may not yet have the prerequisite research skills to use references on their own. In this case, the teacher can provide sets of data (e.g., tools used by pioneers, sources of energy) and model ways to organize the data in order to write something about it. Often, the teacher might demonstrate the use of a grid (Figure 9.1), chart, or semantic map (Figure 9.2) as a way of organizing information.

FIGURE 9.1   Compare/Contrast Grid

Building Stones

	Limestone	Marble
Hardness		
Difficulty of use		
Surface texture		
Color		
Expense		
Where found		

FIGURE 9.2   Semantic Map

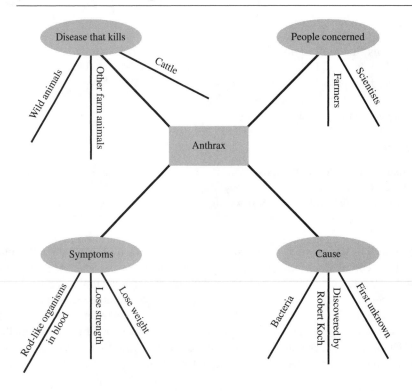

The teacher should also demonstrate how to convert planning notes into written sentences. Expert and average writers construct sentences in much the same way (Hayes & Flower, 1987). Sentences are composed of parts containing about 7 to 12 words in length, with thinking pauses in between. One important teaching function is to model *self-regulatory* thoughts that occur in the thinking pauses and assist in controlling the writing process. The teacher models these by thinking aloud while performing the task (Hallenbeck, 2002; Marchisan & Alber, 2001), using a verbal style matched to the student's own vocabulary (Harris & Graham, 1992). For example, as the teacher generates sentences, he or she might think aloud by saying things such as, "I'm thinking: What is the best way to introduce this topic to make it interesting to the reader? We should add an example here to make the point clearer. I'm stuck here, but I won't panic. I'm going to look at my notes and let my mind play around with that a little more."

The teacher should model reviewing and revising strategies. The more expert the writer, the greater the proportion of writing time he or she will spend on revision (Hayes & Flower, 1987).

Many times, students balk at having to rewrite something they considered finished. This resistance can be overcome by making first drafts obviously different from a completed product. One method of doing this is to use colored paper for first drafts (Raphael, Kirschner, & Englert, 1986). Students can be instructed to write on every other line, leaving a space between lines to make corrections and insertions. Teachers can have students do their first drafts in writing and then allow final drafts to be typed on the word processor and printed. In each case, first drafts have a form much different from the finished copy, and students realize that the form of the first draft is not adequate for the finished copy.

Hull (1987) drew the distinction between *revision*—reworking the text in such a way as to alter its content or structure—and *editing,* the process of correcting errors in grammar, syntax, punctuation, and spelling. Reading aloud helps some writers correct a few of their grammatical errors, but many others will read their compositions without realizing that their correct oral reading differs from the faulty version in the text. Hull stressed that editing requires a special kind of reading that students must develop.

The Process Can Be Collaborative   Writing can be undertaken in collaboration with either the teacher or peers. Writing with the teacher is sometimes a good starting point for the student with learning disabilities. The teacher can assist in coordinating the various processes and functions of writing and, when necessary, alleviate the mechanical demands by transcribing the text as the student dictates. Collaboration provides the teacher with an opportunity to model the process and guide the student through its steps.

Collaboration can also involve other students (Baker et al., 2003). Students can collaborate in the planning process by jointly brainstorming ideas, contributing needed information, or organizing information into an outline, comparison grid, or semantic map. Students can work in pairs, one transcribing what has been rehearsed first verbally while the other serves as a "scribal auditor" (Zoellner, 1969, p. 299). Students also can work together as teams, listening to one another's first drafts, giving constructive feedback, and editing one another's work for mechanical errors.

Collaboration can occur when planning ideas are first being copied down. Zoellner (1969) proposed a *talk–write* model of composition in which students could work as pairs or teams in front of chalkboards or writing easels with large pads of newsprint. The most important rule for this routine is this: Whatever is written must be spoken first. The intent of the talk–write procedure is to disinhibit students who have good ideas but have a hard time translating them into written form. When confronted with an example of their own unclear writing and asked what they meant, many students often can *say* what they had intended to write. Once the utterance has been made, the student is instructed to write it down exactly as he or she said it. Saying aloud the idea or thought to a teacher or a peer functions as a form of verbal rehearsal that helps students to find their voices as authors.

Collaboration is particularly beneficial during the reviewing and revising stages of the process. Several authors (e.g., Gere, 1987) have recommended interactive writing groups for the purpose of sharing writing and developing ideas. Peer review has several benefits. First, when students know that they will be reading what they have written to an audience of peers, they become aware of the expected audience as they write. Sharing writing with others increases student motivation to write and particularly to revise. Participating in writing groups also fosters students' critical capacities (Gere, 1987). As Hayes and Flower (1987) have pointed out, writers' knowledge of their own texts often makes it difficult for them to detect faults in those texts. Feedback from others teaches the writer principles of good writing that can be applied to the next composition.

The peer team is also a good arrangement for editing written work. By reading aloud, some inexperienced writers can correct a few of their errors. However, writers may be too close to their texts to detect faults. Indeed, students have been found to detect a larger proportion of faults in another's text than in their own (Hayes & Flower, 1987). One way to make editing more palatable is to teach students to use proofreader's marks when editing one another's work and, later, when editing their own drafts. The proofreading marks recommended by Tompkins and Friend (1988) are shown in Figure 9.3.

The Process Can Be Prompted   Bereiter and Scardamalia (1982) described *procedural facilitation* as any reduction in the executive demands of a task that permits learners to make fuller use of the knowledge and skills they already have. In the case of writing, the teacher can provide facilitative assistance by prompting the steps of the process or helping students with the many decisions that have to be made throughout the complex process. Procedural facilitation can apply to planning, generating sentences, or revising.

An example of a prompt procedure related to planning is to have the students list, before writing on a topic, isolated words related to the topic that might be of use in the composition. Generating a list of words prompts a memory search for topic ideas as well.

Hull (1987) made three recommendations for making the editing process more manageable for the inexperienced writer. First, as mentioned before, editing should be separated from revision when taught to inexperienced writers. Attention should first be directed to the content of the composition, and editing should be the last step in the process. Second,

---

Case for Action 9.1

A ninth-grade student comes to you for help in writing a social studies report due in a week and a half. What approach would you take to assist the student in the process of writing his report? What are the specific ways in which you would address the three phases of the process?

FIGURE 9.3 *Proofreader's Marks*

Function	Mark	Example
Delete	ℐ	A pirate ~~who~~ attacks and robs ships.
Insert	∧	Blackbeard was a ∧ *famous* pirate.
Capitalize	≡	The pirate flag was known as the jolly Roger.
Change to lower case	/	The flag had a white skull and Crossbones on a black background.
Add period	⊙	People became pirates because they wanted to get rich quickly ⊙
Insert comma	⋏	A pirate carried a pistol ∧ dagger ∧ and a long sword in his belt.
Possible misspelling	⬭	Pirates (probable) didn't make their victims "walk the plank."

Source: From "After Your Students Write: What's Next?" by G. E. Tompkins & M. Friend, *Teaching Exceptional Children, 20,* 1988, 4–9. Copyright 1988 by The Council for Exceptional Children. Reprinted with permission.

teachers can structure the search process by pointing out the general location of the errors. The teacher can write in the margin a code for the type of error the student should look for in that same line: *sp* for spelling, *cap* for capitalization, *v* for verb form, and so on. This procedure still leaves to the student the responsibility for finding and correcting the error. Third, the task can be made simpler by focusing the student's search on one category of error at a time. An example of an error-correcting strategy that guides the search one category at a time is "COPS," a mnemonic for *c*apitals, *o*verall appearance, *p*unctuation, and *s*pelling (Schumaker, Nolan, & Deshler, 1985).

The Process Should Become Self-Initiated and Self-Monitored Eventually, students should be able to instruct themselves successfully in the processes necessary for writing. At this stage of skill development, the teacher gives students specific writing strategies, ideas for self-instruction statements, and explicit instruction in how to employ them. Cognitive strategy instruction reflects aspects of behavioral, cognitive, and social learning theories (Hallenbeck, 2002). As discussed in Chapter 4, a strategy is a set of steps that, when followed, allows students to complete a task quickly and accurately. Each step in the strategy has a short name that provides students with a cue as to what to do. When the first letter of each step is combined, a mnemonic is formed that helps students remember all the steps. Several writing strategies were developed for secondary students at the Kansas Institute for Research in Learning Disabilities (Schumaker, Deshler, Alley, & Warner, 1983), including the error-correcting procedure (COPS).

Action Plan 9.2   Teaching a Writing Strategy

Harris and Graham (1992) recommended the following steps for teaching a writing strategy:

Step 1   *Preskill Development*
The teacher instructs the student in any preskills (including new vocabulary and concepts) not yet acquired but necessary for successful use of the strategy.

Step 2   *Initial Conference—Instructional Goals and Significance*
The teacher and student discuss the importance of the strategy, examine the student's current performance level, and set a training goal.

Step 3   *Discussion of the Composition Strategy*
The teacher describes the composition strategy and discusses how and when to use it.

Step 4   *Modeling of the Composition Strategy and Self-Instruction*
The teacher models the strategy while writing an actual composition and thinking aloud self-instructional commands.

Step 5   *Mastery of the Strategy*
The student memorizes and rehearses the strategy steps.

Step 6   *Collaborative Practice*
The student applies the strategy while writing a composition. The teacher encourages, prompts as necessary, and provides feedback.

Step 7   *Independent Performance*
The student applies the strategy independently, using self-instructional commands covertly.

A successful procedure for teaching a writing strategy is described in Action Plan 9.2. The procedure has been used to teach students a strategy to increase the vocabulary diversity of their compositions (Harris & Graham, 1985). Action Plan 9.2 illustrates how to encourage students to use more action verbs in their writing. The five steps of the strategy are (1) look at the picture stimulus and write down good action words; (2) think of a good story to use the words in; (3) write the story while concentrating on making sense and using good action words; (4) read the story, asking yourself "Is this good? Did I use action words?"; and (5) fix the story if it needs changes.

Using Word Processors to Write

Many authors have claimed that word processors can help students improve their writing skills. Word processors are said to have motivational appeal, in part because typing is easier than handwriting for many students, revisions can be made easily, and there is no need for tedious recopying (Marchisan & Alber, 2001). Although word processors may have advantages for certain students, research has not yet confirmed that this is the case for all students with learning problems (Hunt-Berg, Rankin & Beukelman, 1994).

Case for Action 9.2

A student's IEP stipulates that he do his written work on a computer to help him compensate for poor fine motor skills. What do you need to teach him in order to maximize the benefits of using the computer?

When using word processors, many students produce slightly longer, neater, and more error-free texts (Sturm, Rankin, Beukelman, & Shutz-Muehling, 1997). However, they tend to make surface-level revisions rather than content changes to their compositions (as they also do in handwritten work). Clearly, computers have a motivational benefit for many students. Although they may not produce qualitatively better written products, students often *believe* they are better writers.

Sturm and colleagues (1997) recommended a decision-making model that focuses on a student's writing needs, the writing requirements, and assistive software features when integrating technology with student writing. They suggested that writing through word processing should be viewed as one of many tools that can be used in the writing curriculum. MacArthur, Schwartz, and Graham (1991) found that students need to have some keyboarding skills, producing an average of 8 to 10 words per minute in order to benefit from word processing.

Simply providing word processors without teaching students how to use them will not improve the writing of those with learning problems. Composing on a word processor is most effective when paired with strategy instruction (Ellis & Sabornie, 1986; MacArthur, 1988).

In summary, word processors and publishing programs can enhance writing instruction. However, for these resources to contribute to the development of writing skills, teachers must teach the necessary subskills (e.g., keyboarding) and self-monitoring strategies for writing that take advantage of computers' full capabilities.

Writing as a Successful Product

A writing process is successful only if it results in a good composition. Teachers must consider all aspects of the written product. When various theories of writing are compared (Isaacson, 1984), five principal components emerge: *fluency* (the amount written); *content* (originality of ideas, organization of thought, and maturity of style); *conventions* (the mechanical aspects such as spelling, punctuation, and correct verb endings that teachers expect students to use); *syntax* (construction of the sentences); and *vocabulary* (originality and maturity in the student's choice of words).

Fluency

Fluency usually is assessed by the number of words a student has written. Although this may seem to be a superficial measure of a student's writing ability, several studies have revealed a significant correlation between fluency and other measures of writing skill (Anderson, 1982; Daiute, 1986; Grobe, 1981). A student who is able to write more words is likely to be more fluent in generating ideas as well. Although there is no fixed standard for how many words a secondary student should write, the student who always writes relatively few words should be expected to gradually increase composition length with frequent opportunities to write and teacher encouragement and prompting.

Fluency is usually the first writing goal for the beginning writer. The single best method of prompting fluency is prewriting discussion. One high school English teacher in Tucson, Arizona, used fire drills to stimulate ideas and provide opportunities for students to write daily. A fire drill is a short (one-minute) writing session in response to a quotation or, sometimes, a single word. The students quickly write any images or ideas generated by the stimulus. The only rule enforced is that during the designated writing time, pencils must be moving, if only to write "I can't think of anything to say." After everyone has written one or two sentences, ideas are shared and discussed as a way of generating and organizing additional writing ideas. Students then write paragraphs or short compositions that elaborate the ideas discussed. Fisher and Frey (2003) described power writing as another method for building fluency. The teacher identifies a topic or choice of topics and then gives students one minute to write everything they can about that topic. When time is up, students count and then record the number of words they wrote.

Content

The ideas, style, and organization of student compositions are best assessed with an analytical scale such as the one shown in Figure 9.4. The checklist was developed from Mary Gleason and the author's analysis of expository and persuasive writing samples collected from middle school students with learning problems.

Inexperienced writers sometimes are too preoccupied with the mechanics of writing to give much thought to the prospective reader. Several authors (Englert et al., 1988; Gere, 1987; Perl, 1983) have recommended group interaction and feedback for remediating writers' difficulties in making their message clear to their readers. In small groups, students can read their works in progress to their peers and use the feedback to make changes in their composition. Initially, teachers should begin by forming small groups (two or three members only) and directly teaching group processes and rules for interaction. A teacher must do four things to establish successful feedback groups:

1. Disallow put-downs. Teach students to replace criticism with questions or "I want to know" statements. For example, a listener might respond by saying, "I would like to know about the *differences* between squash and racquetball." On another theme, a student might respond with the question, "How did your friend manage to write the letter if both of his arms were in a cast?"
2. Reinforce helping behaviors through praise or group points, first in nonacademic tasks that require group cooperation, and then in group writing tasks. After the teacher models for the whole class the kind of feedback that is appropriate, a small role-playing group can be selected to demonstrate how the interaction should work while the teacher prompts and reinforces helpful remarks.
3. Model respect. Provide opportunities throughout the week for positive sharing activities in which all feelings and opinions are accepted.

FIGURE 9.4 *Analytical Checklist for Evaluating the Content of a Composition*

Assessment Questions	Circle here if satisfactory	Circle here if need work
Clarity		
• Can the reader readily identify the topic or main idea?	S	N
• Is the author's purpose clear to the reader (to inform, persuade, describe, or tell a story)?	S	N
• Does the writer include sufficient detail to support topic ideas?	S	N
Accuracy		
• Is supporting information accurate and credible?	S	N
Organization		
• Is there a clear beginning, middle, and ending?	S	N
• Does the composition contain all important elements of the appropriate text structure?	S	N
• Are the ideas presented in a logical sequence?	S	N
Cohesion		
• Do all sentences relate to the topic or main idea and include relevant details?	S	N
• Do related ideas fit together?	S	N
• Do key words or linking phrases assist with the flow of ideas (*First, second, third; therefore; on the other hand*)?	S	N
Voice		
• Does the writer demonstrate commitment to or interest in his or her theme, topic, or point of view?	S	N
• Does the writer stay consistent with his or her point of view?	S	N
• Does the writer use an original or engaging approach for representing the ideas or point of view?	S	N
• Does the writer demonstrate a sense of appropriate distance from or closeness to the audience?	S	N

4. Ignore mechanical errors when focusing on content. Misspellings, grammatical errors, and incorrect punctuation can be addressed later, in a final editing activity, but these concerns will interfere with concentration on ideas, organization, and clarity.

The content of student compositions also can be improved by teaching organization strategies. As described on preceding pages, the teacher provides sets of data (e.g., tools used by pioneers) and models ways to organize the data in order to write something about it. Organization strategies are often linked to prescribed text structures appropriate for different writing purposes. For example, a persuasive essay usually follows this structure:

(1) state the problem; (2) state the position you support and summarize the reasons; (3) reason number 1: statement followed by *proof, information,* or *examples* support ("Statement-PIE"); (4) reason number 2: Statement-PIE; (5) continue with the same structure for other reasons; and (6) conclude by summarizing your position and reasons.

A comparison/contrast text addresses the questions (1) What is being compared? (2) On what factors or attributes? (3) First factor: How are they alike? How are they different? (4) Second factor: How are they alike? How are they different? (5) and so forth (Englert et al., 1988). In addition, the teacher should model the use of key words that signal the important information being addressed. For example, in a comparison/contrast essay, key words such as *similarly, in contrast to,* and *however* are used frequently.

Conventions

Writing conventions—spelling, punctuation, correct usage, and handwriting—can be assessed in terms of specific errors that interfere with successful communication of the message. For example, Howell and Morehead (1987) described the problems of poor handwriting under the categories of letter formation, spacing, consistent slant, line quality, alignment, letter size, and fluency (the relative speed at which a person can write). Grammatical errors made by students with learning problems fall in the categories of subject–predicate agreement, tense, plurals, possessive endings, word order, omissions, and incomplete sentences or fragments. Error patterns for spelling, punctuation, and capitalization can be analyzed in a similar manner through the use of error checklists.

Writing conventions are the elements of writing most frequently taught, but they are also the elements that should be approached with the most caution in the context of composition. Students in writing programs that emphasize mechanics and grammar achieve significantly lower gains in writing quality than students receiving instruction in which mechanics and grammar are not stressed (Hillocks, 1984). The teaching of spelling, punctuation, and handwriting should be separated from and not interfere with a beginning writer's composition attempts. There is no evidence that the teaching of grammar rules, at least as it has been traditionally done, has any significant effect on either oral or written language (Glatthorn, 1981; Hillocks, 1984; Straw, 1981). Grammar, it seems, is best learned through practice in expression and exposure to good language models.

Syntax

Although there are quantitative measures of syntactic maturity based on the length of clauses (Isaacson, 1988), teachers can make their own qualitative assessment by examining the types of sentence a student uses most frequently. The following patterns are adapted from Powers and Wilgus (1983):

Level I   Use simple sentence forms (kernel sentences) repetitively, such as:

> I like Burger King.
> I like Pizza Hut.
> I don't like McDonald's.
> I don't like their burgers.

Level 2   Vary the use of simple sentence patterns. There are five basic types of simple sentences (Phelps-Gunn & Phelps-Terasaki, 1982): (1) subject + verb (*The man jumped*); (2) subject + verb + object (*He threw the football*); (3) subject + state of being or linking verb + adjective (*The girl is sunburned*); (4) subject + state of being or linking verb + predicate nominative (*The girl was a pianist*); and (5) subject + state of being or linking verb + adverbial phrase (*The queen was in the castle*).

Level 3   Expand each basic form by adding adverbial phrases, infinitives, and object complements, such as:

The baby *always* goes to sleep *after her lunch.*
The man wants to live *here in the city.*
Then later the city grew *bigger.*

The student may also use compound sentences, such as:

The guy was tall *and* the girl was short.
Mr. Smith is a nice guy *but* his wife is a witch.

Level 4   Combine kernel sentences into longer sentences with relative clauses and subordinate clauses, such as:

He gave a rose to the girl *who kissed him.*
Mrs. Green trusted him *because he was always nice to her.*

Sentence-combining practice is an effective way to increase a student's syntactic maturity. These three sentences

Microwaves do not heat the cookware.
Dishes can get hot.
Heat is generated by the food.

can be combined into this longer, more complex sentence:

Microwaves do not heat the cookware, although dishes can get hot from the heat generated by the food.

The purpose of sentence-combining exercises is to make students more conscious of the transformational choices available to them for expressing their ideas (Mellon, 1981).

In his sentence-combining program, Strong (1983) began with just two kernel sentences in each problem, and then gradually increased the number into problems that would result in whole paragraphs. If a student favors one type of combination almost exclusively, other transformations can be encouraged through patterned models such as those proposed by Hunt and O'Donnell (1970):

Model: The monkey eats bananas.
The monkey is in the tree.

Solution: The monkey in the tree eats bananas.

The model was followed by problems that required the same transformation. Mellon (1969) went even further in prompting the combining task. His curriculum consisted of a series of short sentences to be combined in a certain way signaled both by indentation and by symbols, such as:

Mother wondered SOMETHING.
Sally would come home from school sometime. (WHEN)

Solution: Mother wondered *when* Sally would come home from school.

Studies conducted from the mid-1960s until the present consistently have shown the beneficial effects of sentence combining on students of various ages and ability levels (Hillocks, 1984; Mellon, 1979; Stotsky, 1975). Few literacy teaching methods are better supported by research.

Vocabulary

Vocabulary can be assessed according to the uniqueness or maturity of words used in the composition. In a qualitative analysis, the teacher can pick out unusual but appropriate words that suggest a mature vocabulary, as well as inappropriate or overused words that suggest a word-finding problem. Quantitative measures of written vocabulary (Isaacson, 1988) usually calculate the proportion of large words used (generally defined as seven or more letters), proportion of mature words (those not found on a list of common, frequently used words), and proportion of unrepeated words.

A direct way to teach vocabulary is to teach synonyms for overused words. Synonym and antonym charts can be hung in the room for reference during writing periods. Mercer and Mercer (2005) recommended giving the student a short passage in which several words are underlined. The teacher then asks the student to substitute for the underlined word a more colorful or interesting word or phrase. After fluency has increased and the student is attending to text structure and other aspects of content, the teacher can use the same underlining routine on drafts of the student's own work.

Varied and colorful word choices can be prompted by word brainstorming in the planning stages of the process as described earlier in the chapter. The Harris and Graham (1985) strategy can be applied to adjectives and adverbs, as well as action verbs used in the previous example.

Case for Action 9.3

An eleventh-grade student has just moved to your district and has been assigned to your class. You were given no assessment information related to the student's written expression. How would you informally assess the student's writing skills, taking into account process and product factors?

Writing for Different Purposes

In a functional writing curriculum, students need to learn writing skills required for success in classes and, most important, success in future occupations. Writing tasks in content area classes include taking notes, answering chapter questions, and writing reports or essays. Job-related tasks may include writing business letters, progress reports, requisitions, technical descriptions, résumés, contracts, advertisements, brochures, and project proposals.

Answering Chapter Questions

A written assignment given in content area classes is answering chapter questions. A student with learning problems might have difficulties in completing such an assignment because of failing to read the material before attempting the questions, not reading questions carefully, writing answers that have little relation to the question, and writing incomplete answers. Archer and Gleason (1993) field-tested a strategy that addresses all these concerns. The steps are included in Action Plan 9.3.

Writing Reports

The process of writing a research report consists of four stages (Moore et al., 1986): identifying questions to be answered, locating information, organizing the information, and reporting the information. Questions can be generated from the five question words or the lists of "what we know, what we don't know" mentioned earlier in the chapter (Moore et al., 1986). The teacher might assist students by directing them to materials in which they could find relevant information. Organizing the material could be facilitated through comparison grids, think sheets, or self-initiated planning strategies. The first draft of the report is written in paragraph form, to be followed by one or more revised drafts.

Teachers often have unstated expectations for students' written assignments. They expect the work to be legible and reasonably neat in appearance, to be completed according to

---

Action Plan 9.3

The following strategy, proposed by Archer and Gleason (1993), is recommended to assist students in writing in the content areas:

1. Read the question carefully. (e.g., What are the three purposes of roots?)
2. Change the question into part of the answer. (Student writes, "The three purposes of roots are_____.")
3. Locate the section of the chapter that talks about the topic. (Student finds subtopic "Roots.")
4. Read the section of the chapter until you find the answer. (Chapter section says: "Roots have three purposes.")
5. Complete the answer. (Student fills in: "The three purposes of roots are *to anchor the plant, to absorb water and minerals,* and *to store food.*")

Source: Archer, A., and Gleason, M. (1993). *Advanced Skills for School Success.* Reproduced by permission of the publisher.

directions, and to meet a certain standard of accuracy. Many teachers unconsciously judge students by the appearance of their papers. For this reason, Archer and Gleason (1993) also devised a strategy to improve the appearance of a student's written work, using the acronym HOW (HOW your paper should look):

> H = Heading, which should include name, date, subject, and page number if needed.
>
> O = Organized, which means started on the front of the paper (holes on the left), includes a left margin and right margin, has at least one blank line on top and on the bottom, and is well spaced.
>
> W = Written neatly, which means words or numbers are on the line, they are neatly formed, and errors are neatly erased or crossed out.

Many students also need a strategy for planning and completing work according to written directions. Common problems are failing to read directions carefully, not getting prepared before they begin, and not completing all the items. Archer and Gleason (1993) recommended a four-step approach for planning and completing written work. This approach is included in Action Plan 9.4.

Writing for Future Vocations

Algozzine and colleagues (1988) surveyed 249 employers from different communities in the state of Florida to determine critical job-related reading and writing skills. The researchers selected corporations and businesses that were most likely to hire recent high school graduates. Writing accurate messages and requests, noting work assignments, and

---

Action Plan 9.4

The following approach was recommended by Archer and Gleason (1993) for helping youth with learning problems to complete written work:

Step 1   *Plan it.*
Read the directions and circle the words that tell you what to do. Get out the materials you need. Tell yourself what you are going to do.

Step 2   *Complete it.*
Do all the items. If you can't do an item, ask for help. Use HOW (the neat-paper strategy).

Step 3   *Check it.*
Did you do everything? Did you get the right answer? Did you proofread? (*Note:* Here the student could use Schumaker, Nolan, and Deshler's [1985] COPS strategy; the mnemonic reminds the student to look for errors in capitalization, overall appearance, punctuation, and spelling, one at a time.)

Step 4   *Turn it in.*

Source: Archer, A., and Gleason, M. (1993). *Advanced Skills for School Success.* Reproduced by permission of the publisher.

Case for Action 9.4

A student's IEP stipulates that you prepare her for transition from school to life after graduation. She currently has many problems writing reports and producing other extended compositions. What writing skills will you need to teach her to prepare her for work?

completing forms were the writing tasks employers ranked as most important. Therefore, a curriculum for students with learning problems should include functional writing skills such as writing short messages and completing forms.

As with other writing skills, the process of writing office messages or completing application forms should be modeled. The teacher can model the planning stage of messages through the use of the *who, what, where, when,* and *how* questions. The teacher can model the transcription of messages using common abbreviations when appropriate to promote fluent transcription. The teacher should model the reviewing of the message to make sure all necessary information is there, again using the five WH questions. Teaching students how to complete a job application begins with teaching the necessary prerequisite skills, such as accurately reading the questions on the form, knowing the information requested, and being able to spell the words required to answer the questions. As with messages, the teacher should explain and show how to complete the form. Modeling should be followed by guided practice on controlled materials—forms specifically designed to include items found on nearly all application forms. In addition, the students' skills should be checked by giving them real application forms that vary from those used in guided practice to fill in by themselves.

Summary

A writing curriculum should reflect three facets of writing: process, product, and purpose. First, writing is a complex *process* in which the writer coordinates three major operations: planning, sentence generation, and revising. Informal assessment of the student's attention to each step in the writing process can be made through observation or interview. Four principles should be followed when teaching the process to students: (1) The process should be modeled, from the planning stage to final revision and editing tasks; (2) the process can be collaborative, the student receiving assistance from either the teacher or peers; (3) the process can be prompted through word lists, think sheets, or self-evaluation cards; and (4) the process should become self-initiated and self-monitored through instruction in self-control strategies. If word processors are used to facilitate the process, attention must be given to teaching the necessary computer skills.

Second, attention should be given to all aspects of the written *product,* not just obvious surface features. When various theories of writing are compared, five principal components emerge: fluency, content, conventions, syntax, and vocabulary. Several methods can be used to assess and teach the skills related to each product component. Conventions—or the mechanical aspects of producing text—are the component that should be approached most cautiously. Content is the aspect of writing that should receive the most emphasis in instruction.

Third, a writing curriculum should take into account the various *purposes* of writing. School writing tasks include answering chapter questions and writing reports or essays. Students can be taught strategies for planning, completing, and checking written work. Job-related writing tasks include writing accurate messages and requests, noting work assignments, and completing forms. The most important form a high school graduate will have to complete is a job application.

Teachers have three important functions in providing instruction in written expression. First, teachers must allocate sufficient time for writing in the classroom curriculum. Writing will not improve unless students have an opportunity to write. Second, teachers must actively be involved with students, guiding the process, teaching necessary subskills, and giving specific feedback on first drafts. Third, teachers must work from a complete model of writing that encompasses all stages of the process and skills related to the product. Writing is an important aspect of literacy and therefore deserves careful, systematic instruction.

10

Reading Instruction

DEBI GARTLAND

Did you know that . . .

- Reading ability can be likened to the performance of a symphony orchestra?
- Adjusting the rate of reading affects comprehension?
- Teachers should use a combination of formal and informal reading measures?
- Each student has four reading levels?

- Study skills are important reading objectives for secondary students?
- Instructional strategies are linked to the assessment process?
- There are commercially published high-interest, low-vocabulary reading materials?

Can you . . .

- Describe the two basic processes in reading ability?
- Explain the importance of literacy in today's society?
- Identify and describe the four levels of reading comprehension?
- Explain how the cloze procedure can be used as an informal assessment measure?

- Contrast direct instruction and functional instruction?
- Identify three strategies used in vocabulary instruction?
- Identify the components of a directed reading activity?

Debi Gartland is professor of special education at Towson University in Towson, Maryland.

Of all the academic skills students acquire in U.S. schools, reading ability is the most highly valued. Despite its importance, considerable controversy still shrouds the reading process. Numerous conceptualizations of reading exist. Reading is a highly complex activity in which the individual constructs meaningful interpretations of written symbols. Rather than defining reading as simply reading words and coming to a single, shared idea of what the text said, professionals talk about multiple literacies that acknowledge personal interpretations and cultural differences.

Reading involves two basic processes: a decoding or word recognition process and a comprehension process. Word recognition skills contribute to the reading-comprehension process. Word recognition is the means to comprehension, the all-important end. The skills enable the individual to pronounce the words correctly. Word recognition skills evolve from subskills in the following five areas:

1. *Phonetic analysis:* In phonetic analysis, the student employs specific sound–symbol associations to pronounce each part of the word. To perform this skill, the student must know the phonemes of the language and the rules governing them.
2. *Structural analysis:* In structural analysis, the student uses the meaningful parts of words as an aid to pronouncing and discerning the meaning of the whole word. Structural analysis permits a faster rate of reading than the phonetic analysis of individual sounds.
3. *Sight words:* Sight words are words that the student recognizes without applying phonic skills. Many words with irregular spelling are taught in this whole-word fashion.
4. *Clues:* There are three types of word analysis clues: context clues, picture clues, and configuration clues. The student uses the surrounding words and their meanings, accompanying pictures, and the shape of the unknown word to determine its identity.
5. *Vocabulary:* At the secondary level, three types of vocabulary exist. *General* vocabulary consists of common words with generally accepted word meanings. *Special* vocabulary contains words that have both general and specialized meaning, depending on the context. *Technical* vocabulary comprises words representing a specific concept applicable to a specified content area.

The comprehension process enables the reader to understand the meaning of the text. Without comprehension, reading is reduced to little more than word calling. Written material cannot be comprehended until word recognition skills are learned. The secondary student who has not mastered word recognition skills faces the insurmountable task of memorizing every word. The skilled reader uses word recognition skills and knowledge about people, places, and things to determine the intended meaning of the passage. Knowledge possessed by the reader and information from the text interact to produce full comprehension. As a student's language experience increases, comprehension of increasingly difficult reading material also increases.

Barrett (1968) formulated a four-level taxonomy of reading comprehension:

1. *Literal recognition or recall:* Literal comprehension means the reader recognizes or recalls information, ideas, and happenings that are explicitly stated in the reading materials.

2. *Inference:* Inferential comprehension can be defined as the hypotheses or conjectures arrived at from a synthesis of the literal content of a selection and the products of intuition, personal knowledge, and imagination.
3. *Evaluation:* Evaluation refers to the judgments a reader makes about the content of the written material by comparing it with external criteria.
4. *Appreciation:* Appreciation refers to the student's awareness of the forms, styles, literary techniques, and structures employed by authors to stimulate emotional responses in their readers.

Modern society appears to thrive on technological information. Many of its rewards require increasing levels of literacy (Hammill, 2004; Snow, Burns, & Griffin, 1998). The level of literacy deemed satisfactory in 1950 is considered marginal today. The complex society of today requires not just basic literacy but an unprecedented level of literacy (McLaughlin & DeVoogd, 2004; Vacca & Alvermann, 1998). As Moore, Bean, Birdyshaw, and Rycik (1999) pointed out, adolescents entering adulthood in the twenty-first century will read and write more than at any other time in history.

Children begin to receive formal reading instruction in kindergarten or earlier. Learning to read in the elementary grades sets the stage for later learning. However, secondary students with reading problems are at high risk for school failure (Fischer, 1999/2000; Wilhelm & Smith, 2005). As Donahue (2003) pointed out, secondary teachers find themselves charged with teaching subject matter but are challenged by their students' difficulties with reading texts that are central to content area instruction. Faced with persistent failure and disapproval from family and peers and subjected to discrimination by employers, poor readers experience less self-satisfaction and a lower opinion of themselves.

Reading Abilities of Adolescents with Disabilities

Reading is the most frequently mentioned academic difficulty among adolescents. Whereas scores for the high-performing students have improved over time, those of the low-performing students have declined (U.S. Department of Education, 2003a, 2003b). Consensus has not been reached on the prevalence of reading disability (Badian, 1999), yet estimates of the number of students who experience reading failure remain high (Archer, Gleason, & Vachon, 2003; Stein, Johnson, & Gutlohn, 1999). Also, most students identified for special education and related services experience difficulties in learning to read (Ahrens, 2005; Gardill & Jitendra, 1999). This is particularly problematic, given that the academic demands in secondary content course work increase dramatically, requiring a large amount of reading, with textbooks and supplementary materials the major sources of information (Salembier, 1999).

Because the reading process is complex and reading problems can stem from numerous causes, secondary students have difficulty grasping the importance of school literacy and subject matter learning (Hinchman, Alvermann, Boyd, Brozo, & Vacca, 2003/2004) and manifest various types of reading difficulties, depending on the nature and severity of their disabilities. They may fail to attain adequate sight vocabulary, a problem compounded by the fact that they are not consistent in applying phonetic or structural analysis and do not make adequate use of contextual, picture, or configuration clues. In oral reading, these students tend to skip or reverse letters, words, or sentences; omit words or substitute words of similar phonetic characterization; exhibit more hesitations and repetitions; fail to observe, or misinterpret, punctuation; and read with poor phrasing and a lack of expression.

Secondary students with disabilities are also limited in their comprehension abilities. They are more successful with the literal level than with comprehension of an inferential, evaluation, or appreciation level. They do not adequately comprehend content area reading materials, which constitute much of the information presented at the secondary level. In addition, they fail to develop appropriate study skills and fail to adjust their rate of reading according to purpose, both of which affect overall comprehension.

The sections that follow present information designed to give the secondary teacher insight into the demands of reading instruction for students with disabilities. No single approach to the teaching of reading is superior to all other approaches in accommodating all individual differences (Cowen, 2003). Kameenui (1993) argued against a single right method or approach to literacy instruction, asserting that such a search is misguided and takes its greatest toll on students who have diverse learning and curricular needs. The secondary teacher must be knowledgeable about general principles of reading instruction and a good consumer of evidence-based or scientifically based reading instruction (Odom et al., 2005; Stanovich & Stanovich, 2003; U.S. Department of Education, 2004), which means that the program or instructional practice has a record of success (International Reading Association, 2002).

Assessing Reading Ability

Of all the academic skill areas, reading ability is probably the one most studied as part of special education assessment. For students with disabilities, assessments often present both needed opportunities and serious challenges (National Joint Committee on Learning Disabilities, 2004; Reutzel & Mitchell, 2005). Because reading ability is such a complex phenomenon, composed of numerous integrated subskills, no single test can encompass all of its aspects. Confusion and debate continue regarding the goals of reading assessment and the types of tests and other assessments needed to achieve those goals. The bottom line in selecting and using any assessment, however, should be whether it helps the student (Dewitz & Dewitz, 2003; Johnston, 2005; Swanson & Howard, 2005). Literacy instruction should be informed by and based on meaningful reading assessment (Duffy-Hester, 1999; Johnston, 2003; Johnston & Costello, 2005). Of particular importance at the secondary level, students should also be involved in their assessments (Au, 1997; Skillings & Ferrell, 2000).

Formal Reading Assessment

A variety of formal measures and techniques are available to assess the reading performance of learners with disabilities. These tests differ in many respects, including the skills assessed, task demands, ease of administration, curriculum match, technical qualities, and scoring and interpreting procedures. However, there are limitations inherent in formal assessment used to measure student achievement, particularly with students with disabilities.

Although formal reading tests may be superior to general achievement tests in identifying general reading skills, as Sternberg (1991) pointed out, they measure reading in a very narrow range of reading tasks and situations. Professional ethics dictate that before any standardized measure is selected, the test consumer should research the test to arrive at informed judgments about the technical adequacy of the specific test in the given classroom situation. Unfortunately, because the field abounds with technically inadequate reading measures, it is up to consumers to select the most appropriate tests for their purposes.

Informal Reading Assessment

In this era of increased accountability through assessments, it is clear that individually appropriate reading instruction is anchored in assessments of individuals and programs (Conley & Hinchman, 2004). Assessment for planning instructional strategies relies more heavily on informal procedures, including teacher-made tests, checklists, questionnaires, criterion-referenced measures, and clinical reading interviews. Wolf (1993) coined the phrase "informed assessment" to describe the situation in which teachers have meaningful goals for instruction and clear purposes for assessment and when they use multiple methods to systematically observe and selectively document their students' performances across diverse contexts and over time. Several reading professionals are calling for more authentic assessment in the form of student portfolios (Cleland, 1999; Courtney & Abodeeb, 1999). The use of portfolios represents a major shift in the practices and goals of assessment, emphasizing formative rather than summative evaluation (Tierney et al., 1998). Mitchell, Abernathy, and Gowans (1998) offered a four-step portfolio plan that takes into consideration the reliability and validity of literacy portfolios as measurement tools. The plan includes planning the focus, selecting the content, adding materials to build a portfolio, and providing feedback. At the secondary level, three widely used procedures involve the use of informal reading inventories, oral reading error analysis, and the cloze procedure.

The Informal Reading Inventory

The informal reading inventory is a widely used method to determine a student's reading level and to assess the student's specific skills in word recognition and comprehension (Paris & Carpenter, 2003). At the secondary level, informal reading inventories (IRIs) are helpful in determining what materials in a reading series, as well as in various content areas, a student can read independently and the appropriate level of difficulty for assigned readings used as instructional materials. IRIs consist of a series of passages below, at, and above various grade placements. A student's independent, instructional, frustration, and listening levels are determined on the basis of the number of words recognized and the percentage of correct answers to comprehension questions. Oral reading errors (see the next subsection) can also be tallied. At the secondary level, it may be preferable to use IRIs rather than standardized measures for learners with disabilities because IRIs provide information about the students' skills in relation to the grade-level system of the regular school curriculum. Because IRIs provide only an estimate of reading levels, teachers must use their professional judgment in interpreting the results.

Sedlak and Sedlak (1985) suggested several procedures for constructing an IRI. Their recommendations are included in Action Plan 10.1. They also suggested strategies for administering IRIs. These are included in Action Plan 10.2.

Action Plan 10.1   Constructing an Informal Reading Inventory

Sedlak and Sedlak (1985) have suggested the following procedures for constructing an IRI.

1. Select two passages of approximately 200 words from each level of a series, and type each passage on a separate sheet of paper.
2. Develop five comprehension questions for each passage. Questions should deal with vocabulary, factual information, sequencing, main ideas, and inferences, and should not elicit merely a yes or no response.
3. Construct a list of vocabulary words for each level by selecting every fifth new word, and type the words on a sheet of paper.
4. Develop a scoring sheet. (Often this is just a teacher's copy of the passages and vocabulary words on which errors can be tallied.)

Action Plan 10.2   Administering and Scoring an Informal Reading Inventory

Sedlak and Sedlak (1985) have recommended the following procedures for administering and scoring an IRI:

1. Have the student read the vocabulary words in isolation while the teacher records all errors, tallying them by type (e.g., omission, repetition). Stop the student when 25% of the words on one level are missed. (*Note:* Self-corrections are not errors.)
2. Allow the student to silently read the first passage at the highest level for which vocabulary recognition was 100%, recording start and finish times. Orally ask the comprehension questions and record responses.
3. Ask the student to read the passage aloud while the teacher records all errors. The second passage can be used as a reliability check when needed. The student should be stopped when comprehension drops to less than 50% and oral reading is characterized by meaningless substitutions, word recognition difficulties, and a lack of rhythm.
4. Orally read the parallel passage for the last completed level and ask the student to respond to the comprehension questions. Continue this process until the comprehension question errors drop below 75%.
5. Use the following criteria as guidelines for establishing a student's independent, instructional, frustration, and listening levels:
   - *Independent:* The level at which comprehension is at least 90% and the student reads in a natural, rhythmical, conversational tone, free from tension and with few oral recognition errors
   - *Instructional:* The level at which comprehension is at least 75% and the student reads with good phrasing and no more than one word recognition error per 20 words after silently reading the passage
   - *Frustration:* The level at which comprehension is less than 60% and word recognition is less than 90%; the student shows extreme difficulty in reading, making meaningless word substitutions, and reads with a lack of rhythm
   - *Listening:* The level at which the student responds correctly to at least 60% of the comprehension questions after listening to the teacher read; the listening level indicates that the student understands the syntactic structure and vocabulary

Oral Reading Error Analysis

Oral reading error analysis is another frequently used technique in the informal assessment of secondary students with disabilities. The focus of analysis here is the mistakes students make. The student orally reads a text or a passage on the IRI form while the teacher notes the kinds of errors that occur in the student's reading. In addition, the teacher may also note the instructionally important behaviors that typify the student's oral reading. These behaviors might include a lack of intonation or expression, the use of finger guides, word-by-word reading, or other inappropriate phrasing. The teacher should remember that although error analysis is a time-consuming scrutiny of a student's oral reading accuracy, information from this process yields valuable information needed to determine the appropriate direction of instructional interventions.

Before the assessment session, the teacher must decide which errors are instructionally important and therefore need to be tallied. The following are 10 categories of errors that may be considered when assessing oral reading accuracy:

1. *Hesitations:* The student pauses for two or more seconds before attempting the word.
2. *Insertions:* The student adds one or more words into the sentence being read.
3. *Inversions:* The student changes the order of the words in the sentences being read.
4. *Mispronunciations:* A *gross* mispronunciation of a word is scored when the student's rendition bears little resemblance to the correct pronunciation. A *partial* mispronunciation of a word is scored when the student omits part of a word, makes errors in syllabication or accent, or phonetically mispronounces part of the word.
5. *Omissions:* The student deletes a word or group of words while reading.
6. *Omissions or disregard of punctuation:* The student does not observe the punctuation marks. For example, the student fails to pause at a comma or stop at a period.
7. *Repetitions:* The student repeats a word, phrase, or sentence while reading.
8. *Self-corrections:* An error is scored if the student fails to correct himself or herself within three seconds.
9. *Substitutions:* The student replaces the printed word with another word. For example, the student reads *house* instead of *home.*
10. *Unknown or aided words:* The student does not attempt the word within five seconds and the teacher supplies the word.

The Cloze Procedure

The cloze procedure is both an instructional technique and an informal measure of comprehension used to determine whether content area or reading materials are appropriate for a particular secondary student. As an informal measure, it is relatively easy to construct, administer, and score. The teacher selects a passage of approximately 250 words and retypes the passage on a sheet of paper, keeping the first and last sentences intact. In each of the other sentences, every fifth word is deleted and replaced with a uniform-length blank. In administering the cloze procedure, the student silently reads the entire passage and then rereads it, filling in words for those that have been deleted. The student must rely on context clues within the passage to comprehend the story in order to close each sentence correctly. So the assumption is that if a student can supply the exact word or a synonym or other reasonable substitution, the student must adequately comprehend the sentence and the overall meaning of the passage. The following criteria can be used to determine the secondary student's reading levels:

Reading Level	Accuracy (%)
Independent	57 or greater
Instructional	44–57
Frustration	Below 44

General Principles of Reading Instruction

As is true with any solid educational program, reading instruction for secondary students with disabilities is based on information from the assessment process. General instructional strategies can be planned only after the teacher has identified a student's strengths, weaknesses, and needs in the area of reading skills (Gaskins, 1999; Strommen & Mates, 2004; Winn & Otis-Wilborn, 1999). Reading instruction then begins from what the student knows, building on strengths and working toward improving weaknesses. The instructional methods and materials selected should be of an appropriate level of difficulty while arousing interest and maintaining effort (Elbaum, Vaughn, Hughes, & Moody, 1999; Katims, 2000; Kliewer & Landis, 1999; Williams, 2004/2005).

The reading curriculum at the secondary level is traditionally organized around direct and functional instruction. *Direct instruction* focuses on skills arranged according to scope-and-sequence charts and proceeds systematically. Emphasis is on developing these reading skills so they can eventually be applied to various reading situations. In *functional instruction,* however, reading skills are not taught or practiced in drill, in isolation from their actual use in a real reading situation. Functional instruction centers on the application of skills to real-life tasks. In elementary school, reading instruction is mostly of a direct nature. At the secondary level, the teacher integrates the teaching of content with the teaching of skills required to learn the content. Although some reading instruction is direct instruction, the main thrust is on functional instruction.

In recent years, school literacy practices have been the target of unprecedented public scrutiny (Dillon, O'Brien, & Heilman, 2000; Henk, Moore, Marinak, & Tomasetti, 2000; Shannon, 2000), and, as Dressman (1999) pointed out, the disagreements have seldom been as heated or as fraught with issues of power and control as in the 1990s. The historic argument between advocates of the phonics approach and advocates of the whole-word approach about how best to teach reading, dubbed "The Great Debate" by Chall (1967), has been replaced by a debate between phonics advocates and whole-language advocates (Moustafa & Maldonado-Colon, 1999; Willis & Harris, 2000), dubbed "The Reading Wars" (Carson, 1999; Denton, 1999; Goodman, 1998; Swanson, 2000). At issue is whether students learn to read best from a *bottom-up* or parts-to-whole approach, whereby students learn the nuts and bolts of reading and assemble them into a whole, or from a *top-down* or whole-to-parts approach, whereby students start at the top of the reading process and proceed downward to letters and sounds. However, most teachers opt for a balanced approach, recognizing there is no single, right approach to teaching reading (Babbitt & Byrne, 1999/2000; Duffy & Hoffman, 1999; Fitzgerald, 1999; Freppon & Dahl, 1998; Manset-Williamson & Nelson,

2005; Tyner, 2004; Villaume & Brandt, 1999/2000), a generalization that holds especially true for secondary students with disabilities. In fact, Cassidy and Wenrich (1998/1999), in their review of literacy research and practice, reported that "balanced reading instruction" was voted "hot" by all respondents for a second year in a row, probably indicating a compromise in the so-called reading wars.

In light of early literacy development debate, there has been much less debate about the parallel crisis in adolescent literacy development (Deshler, 2005; Vacca, 1998). Hence, the International Reading Association's Commission on Adolescent Literacy developed a position statement (Moore et al., 1999) containing the following principles for supporting adolescents' literacy growth:

1. Adolescents deserve access to a wide variety of reading material that they can and want to read.
2. Adolescents deserve instruction that builds both the skill and the desire to read increasingly complex materials.
3. Adolescents deserve assessment that shows them their strengths as well as their needs and that guides their teachers to design instruction that will best help them grow as readers.
4. Adolescents deserve expert teachers who model and provide explicit instruction in reading comprehension and study strategies across the curriculum.
5. Adolescents deserve reading specialists who assist individual students having difficulty learning how to read.
6. Adolescents deserve teachers who understand the complexities of individual adolescent readers, respect their differences, and respond to their characteristics.
7. Adolescents deserve homes, communities, and a nation that will support their efforts to achieve advanced levels of literacy and provide the support necessary for them to succeed.

Classroom-Based Reading Instruction

Vocabulary Instruction

Vocabulary instruction focuses on words and word meanings. A cyclical effect exists between vocabulary, reading comprehension, and knowledge: Word knowledge affects reading comprehension, which in turn helps students expand their knowledge bases, which in turn facilitates vocabulary growth and reading comprehension (Bloodgood & Pacifici, 2004; Francis & Simpson, 2003; Johnson & Rasmussen, 1998). Because students who know many words are more likely to be competent readers than those with limited vocabularies, vocabulary is an important area of concern for teachers (Harmon, 1998; Jitenda, Edwards, Sacks, & Jacobson, 2004). As Lubliner (2004) points out, when students confront the complex vocabulary that characterizes upper-grade texts, reading problems are often first revealed. The need for a rich vocabulary base then becomes even more critical during secondary school years. Hence, vocabulary instruction for secondary students with disabilities is an essential aspect of the educational program in both English and the content areas.

Many students with disabilities do not benefit from incidental learning of words through wide reading and therefore need teacher-directed instruction (Rupley, Logan, & Nichols, 1998/1999).

No one method for acquiring new vocabulary has been singled out as most effective (Bryant, Goodwin, Bryant, & Higgins, 2003). However, Watts (1995) outlined the following six features of effective vocabulary instruction:

1. Students are provided multiple exposures to words in a variety of contexts over time.
2. Words are taught in the context of a story, theme, or content area unit.
3. Teachers help students activate prior knowledge when learning new words.
4. Relationships are drawn between new words and known words and concepts.
5. Students are taught to use context clues and dictionaries to enhance their word knowledge.
6. Students are encouraged to interact with the words so they are able to process them deeply.

Although instruction in general vocabulary and special vocabulary is necessary at the secondary level, a majority of the words encountered in content area reading materials are of a technical nature related to a specific subject. Words and concepts are interrelated, so understanding vocabulary helps to lay the foundation for understanding concepts, especially in the content areas.

There are three major differences between the vocabulary of reading lessons and that of content area lessons (Armbruster & Nagy, 1992). First, in reading lessons, knowing the new words may not be necessary for understanding the gist of the story, whereas content area vocabulary often represents major concepts that are essential for comprehension and learning. Second, learning new vocabulary in reading lessons often involves simply learning a new label for a concept the student already possesses (e.g., learning a synonym). In contrast, new vocabulary in content areas is mostly associated with unfamiliar concepts. As students learn new content area vocabulary, they are also learning whole new concepts. Third, new vocabulary words associated with reading lessons are typically unrelated to one another, whereas vocabulary words in content areas often are related in meaning. The implication for instruction, therefore, is that it is important to distinguish between *target vocabulary* (i.e., concepts that are introduced and explained in the text) and *prerequisite vocabulary* (i.e., words and concepts needed for understanding the text) and adjust instruction accordingly.

The number of words in printed school English is estimated to be about 88,500 (Nagy & Anderson, 1984). On average, adolescents acquire about 3,000 new words each year as they read numerous materials as part of content area and independent reading (Bryant, Ugel, Thompson, & Hamff, 1999). Teachers should focus on teaching key vocabulary words because it may be impossible to teach every unknown word, given the high proportion of unknown words contained in content materials. The following is a summary of strategies used in vocabulary instruction at the secondary level:

1. Teachers should preview reading materials to identify potentially difficult vocabulary words and introduce those words before students begin to read. The appropriate word recognition skill for a particular word will depend on the given word.

- *Phonetic analysis* may be used to help students pronounce unknown words. Teachers can introduce the word along with its phonetic spelling, complete with diacritical markings.
- Teachers might use *structural analysis* to emphasize the word's meaningful elements. The procedure may involve examining the root word and various prefixes and suffixes.
- Before assigning the reading, the teacher can introduce a core list of *sight words* using chalkboards, charts, overhead projectors, handouts, flash cards, tachistoscopes, or computers. When appropriate, the real object or a reasonable facsimile can be used to introduce the word.
- The *cloze procedure,* described earlier as an assessment technique, can also be used as an instructional method.

Teachers should also teach students to preview the text independently, identify unfamiliar vocabulary, and discern their meanings (Moore et al., 1999). Students can then develop and maintain personal word lists or banks.

2. Context clue instruction will improve overall comprehension because it helps students read between the lines and process text on a deeper level. Teaching vocabulary through syntactic and semantic clues will give students thinking tools necessary to deal with the wide range of reading material they will encounter (Sinatra & Dowd, 1991). Students' ability to use naturally occurring context to learn the meanings of unknown words markedly increases when they work in pairs to problem solve (Buikema & Graves, 1993).

3. Vocabulary instruction should focus on functional words. Numerous studies of textbooks indicate that they are loaded with unnecessary rare and technical words (Harris & Sipay, 1990). Teachers should teach those words that will be important to the students' future environments or, according to Carr and Wilson (1986), words that will help students figure out related words.

4. Word meanings are best taught in context rather than in isolation. Rupley and colleagues (1998/1999) believe that any instructional practice must be called into question that neglects the teaching of words in meaningful context and fails to immerse the students in vocabulary-rich activities. Teachers should provide examples in which the vocabulary word is used correctly as well as provide multiple opportunities for students to apply the word's meaning (Gipe & Arnold, 1979). According to McKeown (1993), simply learning definitions is not a potent route to vocabulary development; instead, teachers might promote their students' learning by transforming definitions into explanations that characterize a word's prototypical use in readily comprehensible language.

5. Teachers must decide to what extent the new vocabulary should be part of students' listening, reading, speaking, or writing vocabulary and adjust instruction accordingly. Vocabulary instruction should provide opportunities for students to expand word meanings. After students understand the word in its given context, discussions of synonyms and antonyms for the word can take place.

6. Word meanings are best taught through concept development (Blachowicz, 1985), whereby mere surface understanding is replaced with a deeper level of understanding.

Concepts might be developed by providing examples, associations, or relationships and a background of experience.

Schwartz (1988) suggested concept maps, graphic organizers that aid the student by literally mapping out what the student knows about the vocabulary word. Concept maps can be used to aid the student's understanding of a vocabulary word by having the student identify the concept to be defined, a subordinate phrase that helps the student to understand what it is, traits, and examples. Another technique that can be used is semantic mapping, promoting categorical structuring of information in graphic form by displaying known and new words under labeled categories or conceptual subtopics (Johnson, Pittelman, & Heimlich, 1986).

7. Teachers can make use of sources of information that fall outside the passage in which the new vocabulary word appears. These external references might include dictionaries, encyclopedias, glossaries, and thesauri. Captioned television can be used as a supplement to reading instruction (Koskinen, Wilson, Gambrell, & Neuman, 1993). Captions place words in a motivating environment in which the audio and video context helps students understand printed words they might not know how to read. Of the many uses of captioned video in the development of literacy skills, vocabulary learning is one of the most valuable. It allows viewers to focus attention on both definitional and contextual information, enhancing word meaning by providing a visual context that includes both printed words and pictorial images.

8. Teachers should help students acquire vocabulary words by being enthusiastic models and by reinforcing their use of newly acquired terms. Motivation, active involvement, relevance, and repetition lead to independent word learning, the goal of vocabulary instruction (Towell, 1997/1998).

Fluency Instruction

The National Reading Panel (National Institute of Child Health and Human Development, 2000) identified reading fluency as a key ingredient in successful reading instruction. Poor readers read less because it is such a struggle (Pikulski & Chard, 2005). Thereby, reading less, poor readers fall further behind, creating what Stanovich (1986) has referred to as the Matthew effect. These students do not engage in essential wide reading of easy materials, which would in turn lead to increased fluency and reading comprehension. Reading fluency problems have long been considered to be among the most common characteristics of students with disabilities. However, fluency is often not addressed at the secondary level (Griffith & Rasinski, 2004; Kuhn, 2004/2005). Mastropieri, Leinart, and Scruggs (1999) stated that reading dysfluency inhibits good reading performance in several ways. By definition, a *reduced reading rate* means that students read less text in the same amount of time as more fluent readers and will therefore have processed less text to remember, comprehend, or appreciate. Moreover, slower reading rates suggest that students may be putting more cognitive effort into identifying individual words than are students who read with automaticity and therefore may have fewer cognitive resources available to process meaning.

Although most teachers have fluency as one of their goals for students' reading, they frequently find it a struggle to explain what fluency is. The two key aspects of fluency are accuracy in word recognition and rate of reading, with the ultimate goal of fluency to enhance readers' comprehension of the text (Hudson, Lane, & Pullen, 2005; Markell & Deno, 1997). Students are fluent readers when they reach automaticity (LaBerge & Samuels, 1974), recognizing printed words quickly and effortlessly. Teachers could guide readers in making videotapes so that students can evaluate their own oral reading (Dwyer & Bain, 1999). Teachers may use several strategies to assist students in becoming more fluent readers. In *repeated readings* (Samuels, 1979), a student reads short, meaningful passages repeatedly until he or she reaches a satisfactory fluency level. *Paired reading* has two students reading in unison, whereas in *choral reading* (Yopp & Yopp, 2003) the whole group reads in unison. In *echo reading,* the teacher reads each line and the group repeats it, matching emphasis and fluency. *Shared reading* is the process in which the teacher and student read together, and in *guided reading,* the teacher explains and/or demonstrates for the students the important things to be done while reading. Green (1997/1998) had middle schoolers actively engaged in content area reading through *rapid retrieval of information,* a strategy of oral rereading to answer a question, prove a point, or provide an example from the text after silent reading. Friedland and Truesdell (2004) suggested using *peer buddies* to increase amount of practice time with a listener; *computer-assisted instruction* with the student reading along with the computer program; and *previewing,* in which the students read aloud or silently or just listen first to the teacher (live or taped).

Comprehension Instruction

Comprehension is the essence of the reading act. The National Reading Panel's synthesis of the research on effective comprehension instruction (National Institute of Child Health and Human Development, 2000) found that students' comprehension improves when students are taught to monitor their comprehension while reading. There is no shortage of instructional methods for teaching secondary students to comprehend. Professional journals and reading texts routinely feature teaching strategies designed to increase students' ability to understand printed matter, although not all strategies are equally effective in promoting all types of comprehension. A number of practices have been proposed for helping secondary students read content materials. These methods help students develop background knowledge, understand unfamiliar text organizational patterns, learn new vocabulary associated with the content, and overcome other challenges associated with content materials.

Secondary students with disabilities need assistance in content area reading to integrate new information with their prior knowledge, to obtain important information from text, and to remember what they have read (Adams, 2003; Bryant et al., 1999; Mathes et al., 2005). Secondary content area teachers often feel unable or unwilling to teach reading (Bintz, 1997; Massey & Heafner, 2004). However, content reading is the domain of all teachers. Although most secondary teachers view themselves as content experts, they still must integrate content instruction with the teaching of reading skills that are essential for acquiring the content (Gartland, 1994).

Content area teachers are in a strategic position to influence adolescents' uses of literacy for academic learning. Yet Vacca and Vacca (1999) reported that even those content area teachers who have taken preservice or in-service reading courses generally avoid incorporating literacy practices into their lessons, thereby hindering the learning of the poor readers in their classes. To assist students with disabilities in achieving in the general curriculum, secondary teachers might be required to make accommodations. For example, teachers might use multiple texts rather than rely only on a single textbook (Hynd, 1999). Through collaboration, content area teachers, special education teachers, and reading specialists can work together to effectively support adolescents' development of advanced reading strategies (Henwood, 1999/2000; Moore et al., 1999; Swiderek, 1997).

The following is a summary of strategies used in comprehension instruction at the secondary level:

Directed Reading Activity   The directed reading activity (DRA) is an instructional method for guiding secondary students through readings in English and other content area materials. Directed reading approaches vary in the number of steps involved, depending on the source, but follow basically the same pattern of (1) developing readiness, (2) guiding reading, (3) skill instruction, and (4) follow-up activities. The DRA is a sound approach used by many teachers to develop reading-comprehension skills in students at all levels (Johnston, 1993).

Instructional Scaffolding   As students make progress as readers, teachers should provide instructional scaffolding (Brown, 1999/2000; Mesmer, 1999) that supports and extends that progress. In the classroom, scaffolding takes the form of reciprocal teaching (Hashey & Connors, 2003), modeling, think-alouds (Block & Israel, 2004), reminding, and coaching, each of which helps learners accomplish what they are almost, but not quite, able to do independently.

Research in reading identifies modeling as an effective way to increase comprehension of text. Dole, Duffy, Roehler, and Pearson (1991) emphasized using modeling to help teachers explain the reasoning involved in performing various reading tasks. Norton (1992a) described a modeling lesson to gain meaning through inferred characterization. It requires readers to go beyond the information provided in the text by using clues from the text to hypothesize about the character's feelings, actions, beliefs, or values and ultimately gain better reading comprehension. The think-aloud technique (Caldwell & Leslie, 2003/2004) is a teacher-modeling technique in which the teacher reads aloud from the text and verbalizes whatever comes to mind to demonstrate how to reason during reading. Secondary students' oral reading, writing, and listening skills improve dramatically using modeling of reading aloud (Fisher, Flood, Lapp, & Frey, 2004; Ivey, 2003; Lenihan, 2003) as students follow along.

Discussion Groups   Using student discussion groups is an engaging method to increase reading comprehension of English and other content area materials (Cena & Mitchell, 1998; Chandler, 1997; Lewis, 1998b; Lloyd, 2004; Martinez-Roldan & Lopez-Robertson, 1999/2000, O'Byrne, 2003). Leal (1993) found that peer group discussions of all types of texts had the potential to be a powerful tool for enriching classroom learning. Such discussions provide teachers with a wealth of information about their students' prior knowledge as well as providing a place for students to negotiate textual meaning through collaboration.

Literature circles (Daniels, 2002; Livingston & Kurkjian, 2005) can change the classroom climate to be more supportive for taking greater academic risks. In her model, Burns (1998) offered students a choice of book, homework pace, and group roles. Jewell and Pratt (1999) noted that discussions were not based on teacher-directed questions but rather on students' responses to books, with the teacher moving into a more facilitative role. They found a greater degree of inferential thinking and an overall increase in motivation. Eldridge (1998) reported success with the "quick book share," in which students are randomly assigned to groups of three, each talking for two minutes to recommend which books had been a good read.

Inferences   Teaching students to make inferences (Richards & Anderson, 2003) and to self-question (Gill, 2000; Gillespie, 1990; Manzo, 1969) while reading allows them to take a more active role in their learning. To facilitate comprehension, secondary content area teachers can train students in question generation as a basis for higher-level thinking about subject matter. The generation of student questions is one area of cognitive strategy instruction that has received major research input. Cognitive strategy instruction combines elements of explicit teaching with scaffolding procedures (Ciardiello, 1998). Question generation is a comprehension-fostering strategy that requires students to search or inspect the text, identify main ideas, and make connections among ideas as a basis for raising a relevant question (Rosenshine, Meister, & Chapman, 1996). Fisk and Hurst (2003) espoused the use of paraphrasing.

Reading Materials   Secondary students with disabilities often are frustrated because books geared to their interest level are often beyond their reading ability. High-interest, low-vocabulary materials provide these adolescents with a relatively easy vocabulary while maintaining an interest level appropriate for the more mature learner. High-interest, low-vocabulary materials (Coleman & Vaugh, 2000; Graves & Philippot, 2002; Kasten & Wilfong, 2005; Liang, 2002) are available from numerous publishers. Teachers can select books on a wide range of topics, estimate the reading level of such books by using various readability formulas, and match up more appropriate materials to these students. Leal and Chamberlain-Solecki (1998) examined the level of difficulty of each Newbery Award–winning book from 1922 to 1997 and found the overall grade-level average to be 6.8, potentially making these books an excellent choice for secondary classrooms.

Visual Imagery   Enhancing students' use of visual imagery will increase comprehension (Hibbing & Rankin-Erickson, 2003). Graphic organizers are visual representations of knowledge and make learning more meaningful (Egan, 1999; Farris & Downey, 2004/2005; Hagood, 1997) across content areas. Gardill and Jitendra (1999) evidenced positive effects on the reading comprehension of middle school students with learning disabilities using story maps. First developed by Beck and McKeown (1981), the story map is a technique by which stories are mapped out by identifying important information about the characters and events of the story.

Norton (1992b) has suggested that older students benefit from drawing plot diagrams for person-against-person and person-against-self plots and relating the plot diagrams to developing characterizations and themes. Webbing (Norton, 1993) is another method for graphically displaying relationships among ideas and concepts. This technique encourages higher thought processes, stimulates oral interactions, and fosters ideas. Webbing helps students understand important characteristics of story structure, increases their appreciation of literature, and improves their reading competencies. The teacher draws a web on the board with the title of the book in the center. On the spokes are placed setting, characterization, conflicts, and themes. The web can also include names of leading characters and types of conflicts that are found in the book. Thematic unit webs are popular in literature-based programs as well as in programs that integrate various content areas. Armbruster, Anderson, and Meyer (1991) have suggested the use of a particular type of instructional graphic called a *frame*. Frames are a visual representation of the organization of important ideas in informational texts intended to help the student focus attention on important information and perceive the organization of that information in content area reading.

Character Interviews   Swindall and Cantrell (1999) used "character interviews" to help students who have experienced difficulty with reading begin to see themselves as readers, active participants in discussions, and even experts on the motives of characters. This technique helps make literature memorable by bringing characters to life. Students generate questions for characters in the books after a book is read, choose a character to portray, and take turns being interviewed. Similarly, Shanahan and Shanahan (1997) used character perspective charts as a strategy when different story structures can be identified, depending on who is identified as the main character. These activities lend themselves to figurative language interpretation instruction (Palmer & Brooks, 2004), including metaphors, similes, personification, hyperboles, idioms, proverbs, and allusions, to increase students' comprehension.

Technology   Use of technology is a pragmatic way of developing emergent literacy skills (Labbo, 2004; Leu & Kinzer, 2000; Smolin & Lawless, 2003). Barnitz and Speaker (1999) described several uses technology has in literacy lessons, including computer use for electronic mail and direct instruction on specific skills for reading. Hypermedia is a computer format in which several media can be viewed in an order chosen by the user. Dillner (1993/1994) described its success in an American history class in which computer-aided reading lessons were designed by the classroom teacher to increase content area comprehension. The Internet is also a wonderful resource (Anderson-Inman, 1998; Forbes, 2004; Fresch, 1999; Gambrell, 2005; Leu, 2000). Rekrut (1999) offered some practical guidelines for teachers who would like to incorporate use of the Internet in their instruction:

1. Determine your instructional objectives and do enough research to know whether the Internet will be a good source for what you want your students to learn.
2. Set Internet lessons in the context of ongoing instruction as part of the general curriculum.
3. Understand the literacy demands the assignment makes as students access various websites, be aware of the vocabulary they may see, and monitor their comprehension.
4. Formulate specific objectives for each Internet session and include a written component in each lesson to become part of the final outcome.
5. Help students publicize their findings and ask them to evaluate their Internet experience.

Writing Journals   The use of writing journals (Bromley & Powell, 1999; Swiderek, 1997; Wollman-Bonilla & Werchadlo, 1999) has been successful in increasing reading comprehension of secondary students (Livdahl, 1993). Hancock (1993) used character journals and found that when adolescent readers comment on a story repeatedly in the voice of one of the characters, they think more about what they are reading. When they disagree with a character's actions or attitudes, they come away with a better sense of their own identity. Bromley and Powell (1999) used a novel type of interactive writing called "interest journals" to promote persuasive writing. Students wrote entries about topics of interest and read entries written by their peers. The middle school students learned that an opinion needs to be supported by evidence and that to persuade, one needs to be logical and use vivid and specific vocabulary. The interest journals motivated reluctant readers and fostered conversations and friendships among students.

Learning Strategies   It is essential that secondary students with disabilities become proficient in the use of learning strategies (Alfassi, 1998; Fischbaugh, 2004; Jongsma, 1999/2000; Rabren, Darch, & Eaves, 1999). Strategies allow readers to be autonomous and in control of the comprehension process, and good readers use them effectively (Baumann, Hooten, & White, 1999; Dowhower, 1999). However, poor readers do not acquire strategic reading behaviors by themselves and must be explicitly taught how, where, and when to consistently carry out such procedures (Swanson & De La Paz, 1998; Welker, 1999). Additionally, it is important to teach students to apply strategies across the content areas (Gaskins, 1998). Information about learning strategies was presented in Chapter 4.

Study Skills Instruction

Study skills instruction is intended to teach basic learning tools that, when developed and appropriately applied, will enable the secondary student to acquire information effectively, efficiently, and independently. Learning on one's own is particularly important today, given the wealth of media sources that make vast amounts of information easily accessible. Students who have not been specifically taught study skills do not pick them up on their own. So for secondary students with disabilities who have difficulty in acquiring content area knowledge, instruction in study skills is a particularly important component of their educational program. There is a lack of agreement among educators concerning which study system is most effective in facilitating long-term learning. Therefore, effective instruction at the secondary level should focus on enhancing students' awareness of the components of their own study style and increasing students' ability to select appropriate strategies for various study tasks (Archambeault, 1992).

Textbook Instruction

Many secondary students with disabilities have difficulty in reading from content area textbooks (Hiebert, 2002; Mastropieri, Scruggs, & Graetz, 2003). Walpole (1998/1999) examined science texts and concluded that new texts in the content areas and a constructivist understanding of comprehension demand new emphases in instruction in the content areas. Textbooks cannot make the curriculum (Shutes & Peterson, 1994), but, at the secondary level, teachers rely heavily on them, providing even more reason to make sure the content is accessible to all students with disabilities.

Readence, Bean, and Baldwin (1989) pointed out that students often lack experiential background and are unfamiliar with the vocabulary and concepts in social studies, science, or any other content areas. Therefore, one of the content area teacher's roles is to facilitate learning from text. This can be accomplished by adapting lessons to match students' abilities and experiential background, helping link prior knowledge to what they are to learn, motivating them to attend to selected pieces of the text, and monitoring comprehension by checking to see whether they understand important parts of a text presentation. Lester and Cheek (1997/1998) surveyed high school students to offer useful insights to those individuals who make decisions about textbook use in secondary classrooms. Serious consideration of student opinion might improve the selection of textbooks, resulting in better use of them (Guzzetti, Hynd, Skeels, & Williams, 1995).

The following is a summary of strategies used in textbook instruction at the secondary level:

1. Because textbooks play such an important role in learning in the content areas at the secondary level, the teacher should carefully evaluate the quantitative and qualitative factors before selecting a text for use with secondary students. The following should be considered in the evaluation: readability; quality of writing; use of abstract concepts and technical vocabulary; appropriateness and quantity of graphics; advanced organizers; headings/subheadings; introductory and summary statements; glossary; end-of-chapter self-quizzes; and whether the text is nondiscriminatory, accurate, and up-to-date.

2. The teacher should also consider the use of illustrations. Purnell and Solman (1991) found that technical content that lends itself to presentation as an illustration will be comprehended better as an illustration than as text, and it will be comprehended best of all if presented in both forms.

3. Sammons and Davey (1993/1994) described an interview procedure that teachers or reading specialists can use to gain information about how middle or high school students learn from textbooks. This procedure can aid in identifying a student's areas of strength and need when the student undertakes tasks requiring textbook reading.

4. Grant (1993) devised SCROL, a strategy to show students how to use text headings to improve their reading and learning from content area texts:

S—Survey: Read the headings and subheadings in the assigned text selection and ask, "What do I already know about this topic? What information might the writer present?"
C—Connect: Ask, "How do the headings relate to one another?" and write down key words from the headings that might provide connections.
R—Read: Read the heading segment, paying particular attention to words and phrases that express important information about the heading.
O—Outline: Write the heading and outline the major ideas and supporting details in the heading segment without looking back to the text.
L—Look back: Look back at the heading segment, checking the outline for accuracy and correcting inaccuracies.

5. Because they believe that secondary students must be able to analyze an academic task and plan actions appropriate for completing it, Schumm and Mangrum (1991) devised FLIP, a framework for content area reading. The student asks the following questions and then decides whether asking for assistance is necessary:

F—Friendliness: How friendly is my reading assignment (i.e., text features)?
L—Language: How difficult is the language in my reading assignment?
I—Interest: How interesting is my reading assignment?
P—Prior knowledge: What do I already know about the material covered in my reading assignment?

6. Ellis (1994) designed a text-perusal strategy (PARTS) to help adolescents with content area books:

P—Perform goal setting. Clarify why you are analyzing the chapter parts and identify a goal related to this reason.
A—Analyze little parts, such as the title, headings, and visuals.
R—Review big parts, such as the introduction and summary.
T—Think of questions you hope will be answered. Check questions provided by the chapter and formulate your own.
S—State relationships, such as how the chapter relates to the unit and how the chapter relates to what you already know.

7. Graphic displays (Gillespie, 1993) improve comprehension and provide a mnemonic in a way that the narrative text cannot. The dominant types of graphic displays in content area textbooks are maps, which show relationships among areas; charts and tables, which focus on relationships between items; and graphs, which compare things and show quantitative information (Harris & Sipay, 1990). However, many students with disabilities have difficulty in reading and interpreting graphics. In today's technological world, graphic displays are widely used not only in textbooks but also in newspapers and magazines. Therefore, it is important that content area teachers draw students' attention to the graphic displays found in textbooks and explicitly teach them how to read the displays.

8. Dreher (1992) emphasized the increasingly important literacy task of searching for information in textbooks. The goal is to locate specific information for a specific purpose, using features such as headings and indexes to avoid irrelevant information while targeting critical portions. Because it involves different processes from those used in reading to learn an entire passage, explicit instruction in searching for information is suggested.

9. Teachers can create anticipation guides (Merkley, 1997) to help students with textbook material. Anticipation guides, also referred to as reaction or prediction guides, assist students in integrating new knowledge and concepts with existing knowledge and concepts. Students react to a series of statements related to the content in the text before reading, stimulating students to read with greater purpose and interest.

10. Beck, McKeown, Hamilton, and Kucan (1997) devised the questioning-the-author technique to enhance student engagement with texts. This technique is a teacher-led procedure that encourages students to build understanding of text through direct teacher questions, such as "What is the author telling us in that illustration?" and "Why does the author use that special typeface there?"

11. Collaborative strategic reading (Vaughn & Klingner, 1999) is a four-step strategy to help students read content area textbooks. Students in large, heterogeneous classrooms work in small groups, helping one another comprehend textbook materials. First, students preview the assignment. Then, after reading short segments, students discuss information that "clicked" and information that "clunked," formulating explanations for confusing words or ideas. Next, students collaborate to "get the gist" by stating what was important, before finally summarizing what they learned.

Reading Instruction in Simulation and Community Settings

Reading is a basic life skill. Literacy is the cornerstone of an individual's success in school and the foundation of lifelong learning. As is evident from the reading objectives based on community demands presented earlier in this chapter, reading is a valuable means of acquiring knowledge and learning new skills, a source of entertainment, and a means of expanding understanding and fulfilling personal goals. Secondary students with reading difficulties generally tend to read only assigned materials and rarely read supplemental or recreational materials. In the past, they had little or no opportunities to develop reading skills in functional or recreational reading materials. The addition of a functional component to the secondary reading curriculum is intended to help the adolescent make the transition into adulthood. These skills are seldom taught in the community setting for individuals with disabilities. Poor readers shy away from employment requiring reading skills. Therefore, it is particularly important to include this functional component in classroom-based reading instruction.

In their 1998/1999 review of "what's hot" and "what's not" in literacy research and practice, Cassidy and Wenrich reported that motivation was voted "hot." Although much of the reading research has focused on cognitive aspects such as word recognition and comprehension, because reading is an effortful activity that students often can choose to do or not to do, it also requires motivation (Baker & Wigfield, 1999). The 1996 National Assessment of Educational Progress findings indicated that approximately one-half of the 9-year-old students tested reported reading for fun on a daily basis, whereas only about one-quarter of the 17-year-old students reported doing so (Campbell, Voelkl, & Donahue, 1998). This is a concern, given that time spent in reading is related to reading success and associated with attitudes toward additional reading (Moore et al., 1999).

Several researchers have suggested that by the time students reach middle school, they become disinterested in reading (Ley, Schaer, & Dismukes, 1994; McKenna, Kear, & Ellsworth, 1995), whereas others (Bintz, 1993; Ivey, 1999; Worthy, 1998) assert it may not be that middle schoolers lose interest in reading per se but rather that they lose interest in the kinds of reading they are required to do in school. Worthy (1996) stressed the importance of "hooking" reluctant readers by making available to them interesting reading materials. Teachers should model their passion for literacy, giving choices whenever possible, encouraging students to read widely, and reminding them that reading is a recreational choice (Powell-Brown, 2003/2004)

The following is a summary of strategies used to motivate reluctant readers at the secondary level:

1. Sustained silent reading (SSR) (Brozo & Hargis, 2003; Fisher, 2004) requires a regular reading time to provide students with an opportunity to practice their reading skills using pleasurable and self-selected content-related materials silently and without interruption.

The purpose of SSR is to promote independent reading and provide opportunities to extend reading skills through practice. Clary (1991) described DEAR, the "drop everything and read" technique.

2. Reading workshop (Atwell, 1987; Kletzien & Hushion, 1992; Swift, 1993) is a method to provide students with greater choice in reading selections and response opportunities. Although there is wide variation in its format, it generally consists of a substantial block of time each day during which self-selected literature is read and used as a vehicle for learning. Sanacore (1992) suggested cluttering up the classroom, surrounding students with various reading materials that will tempt them to browse and read.

3. In a survey conducted by Bintz (1993), secondary students reported assigned reading as not meaningful or relevant to their personal lives. They believed that it required little use of sophisticated reading processes or higher-level thinking skills. The students understood the benefits of using shortcut strategies in the short term, but it did not appear that they understood the implications of using these strategies in the long term to become more proficient readers. The survey implies, therefore, that teachers should use relevant material and explicitly teach the relevance of assigned readings. In the same vein, Frager (1993) suggested teaching students to monitor and express their affective responses to the content text along with their cognitive responses. Kong and Fitch (2002/2003) found success with book clubs.

4. Nilsson (2005) and Vyas (2004) believe that making ethnic-specific literature integral to the literature program enhances a sense of community. Hansen-Krening and Mizokawa (1997) provide criteria for selecting books and lists of literature and sources. Hudley (1992) used successful Hispanic or African American women as role models to help motivate high school girls to stay in school, use school and community resources, and develop an interest in recreational reading.

Diller's (1999) African American students responded positively to books by and about African Americans. Barry (1998) offered reasons and possible solutions to the underrepresentation of Hispanics in literature for young adults, citing that if materials that allow students to see themselves presented in a positive light do not exist, it is much more difficult for teachers to make the curriculum exciting and relevant. The Children's Literature and Reading Special Interest Group (2000) of the International Reading Association is a good resource for teachers. Each year the committee selects quality literature that is culturally authentic and rich in cultural details and that celebrates diversity and common bonds.

5. Sentence collecting (Speaker & Speaker, 1991) is planned discussion based on the sentences displayed on charts. Learner excitement mounts as students discuss where they found their sentences and the merits of each. Menon and Mirabito (1999) created "Hooked on Books" time during which students meet to read and talk about books to develop habits and pleasures associated with reading. The students learned to listen, respond, enjoy reading, and share the joy with others. Lewis (1998a) suggested that, under the guise of sharing their responses to books they have chosen for student "free choice" reading, instead of persuading students to revere all that has been deemed "great literature," teachers not forsake the movies, books, and television shows students love but rather engage students in conversations about the uses they have for a wide range of texts in their lives.

6. Although teachers are always looking for ways to help all students succeed, they often overlook literature, which can enhance the success of all students through broadening their attitudes and perceptions of self and others (Andrews, 1998; Williams, 2004). Kazemek (1998) found that using books that described the roles women played in the Vietnam War can help adolescents become more sensitive to and appreciative of the courage displayed and sacrifices made by these women. Landrum (1998/1999) provided an annotated bibliography of adolescent literature from 1990 to 1997, featuring in her article characters with disabilities as well as criteria for evaluating novels that feature characters with disabilities. Others (Prater & Dyches, 2005; Richardson & Boyle, 1998) described a read-aloud activity to create an awareness of what disabilities are and how to acknowledge them.

7. Working in pairs (Walker, 2003) or using cross-age peers (Coleman & Vaugh, 2000; Friedland & Truscott, 2005; Kreuger & Braun, 1998/1999; Mathes, Howard, Allen, & Fuchs, 1998; Matthews & Kesner, 2000) can be an effective method to increase motivation to read as well as to improve reading skills. Fischer (1999/2000) described an intervention model for at-risk high school readers requiring the students to read to elementary-aged students, thereby addressing the high schoolers' need for increased self-esteem, recognition, and practice in fluency.

8. Parents are still key partners in motivating secondary students (Darling & Lee, 2003/2004; Hughes, Schumm, & Vaughn, 1999; Koskinen et al., 1999; Leslie & Allen, 1999; Neuman, Caperelli, & Kee, 1998). Although a literacy-rich home is a prime factor in reading success (Carson, 1999), frustration and failure can result for secondary students whose home literacy practices differ from those valued as "school literacy" (Nagle, 1999). It is important, even at the secondary level, that teachers keep parents involved in students' literacy learning (Au, 1997). Sanacore (1998) offered proactive suggestions to parents to help students become literate and productive members of society. Volunteers and tutors (Gupta, 2000; Hopkins, 1998; Wasik, 1998, 1999) can also be enlisted to help motivate secondary students.

9. Interactive play increases literacy learning in secondary classrooms by fostering a community atmosphere and encouraging teamwork (Fredericksen, 1999). Teachers can develop noncompetitive games and simulations or have students enter contests (Karnes & Riley, 1997) that require literacy skills practice to help students see school as a place to have fun and learn at the same time. Davis (1997) had middle schoolers go on a scavenger hunt using the newspaper.

10. Opitz (1998) suggested the use of text sets, collections of different books related to a common element or topic. Each student reads a different book related to the topic, enabling students of varying abilities to be grouped together but exposed to "real" books. Sharing of the teacher's own literacy with students (Au, 1997), reading of autobiographies (Spires, Williams, Jackson, & Huffman, 1998/1999), and pairing fiction and nonfiction books on the same topic can boost students' understanding and enjoyment (Camp, 2000; Dreher, 1998/1999).

11. The print that is found in neighborhoods (Lovie, 2005; Neuman, 1999) can provide an excellent source of literacy conversation and learning. Orellana and Hernandez (1999) suggested that by taking literacy walks with students in their community, teachers can learn much about students' everyday literacy in their worlds. Ramos and Krashen (1998) found a positive impact by taking students to their neighborhood public library in the morning before it opened to the public.

12. Role-playing (Erb & Moore, 2003) and drama (Clyde, 2003; Macy, 2004) can be used as a teaching tool to promote student interest in literacy across content areas. Morrison and Chilcoat (1998) reported that the use of drama increases student recall of stories, reading comprehension, and communications skills. It is especially effective when students create their own scripts and perform them as classroom theater (Wolf, 1998). Adding music (Towell, 1999/2000) has also been motivating. Others (Flynn, 2004/2005; Ivey, 1999; Martinez, Roser, & Strecker, 1998/1999; Morado, Koenig, & Wilson, 1999), through readers' theater, used literature, drama, music, and movement to develop literacy learning in what they called "mini-performances," in which students were immersed in a process that explored story elements and reenactments.

13. With the emergence of more sophisticated wordless books, picture books, and short, illustrated books in the last 25 years, such resources are beginning to appear in secondary classrooms (Hadaway & Mundy, 1999). In working with middle school students, Cassady (1998) found success with wordless books because there are no "right" words. The books enhance creativity, vocabulary, and language development for readers of all ages. Miller (1998) had similar results, noting the appeal of independent reading options and a strong visible statement valuing diversity. His article offers lists of quality picture books across the curriculum.

14. It is a difficult task to encourage secondary students with disabilities to read, as they are often more enamored with television or video games than books (Norton-Meier, 2005). However, Shiflett (1998) found success in borrowing marketing techniques and suggested that teachers read a book, find the hook (identify what characteristics of the book would be appealing to adolescents), and reel students in (taking three to five minutes to present the book). Polder (2000) suggested schoolwide literacy days, in which the goal of the activities is to make reading fun and purposeful while developing a sense of community through shared experiences.

15. Kluth and Darmody-Latham (2003) and Worthy, Moorman, and Turner (1999) concluded from their research that perhaps the answer to motivating students to read is as simple as encouraging them to follow their interests. The most preferred materials among secondary students are comics (Norton, 2003) and cartoons, magazines about popular culture, books and magazines about sports, and scary books and stories. In studying the proliferation of and fascination with series horror stories, Richards, Thatcher, Shreeves, Timmons, and Barker (1999) stated that although educators and parents may be torn between wanting to see children reading and not wanting them reading certain kinds of books, reading scary stories does not seem to harm children and may instead provide them opportunities to explore and conquer their fears.

Summary

Reading ability is the most highly valued academic skill that students acquire in schools today. Despite its importance, considerable controversy shrouds the reading process. We do know that reading is a highly complex activity in which the individual constructs meaningful interpretations of written symbols. Reading involves two basic purposes: a decoding or word recognition process and a comprehension process. Word recognition skills enable the individual to pronounce the words correctly. These skills include phonetic analysis; structural analysis; sight words; context, picture, and configuration clues; and general, special, and technical vocabulary. The comprehension process enables the individual to understand the meaning of the text. Comprehension becomes possible only after word recognition skills are learned. Barrett (1968) formulated a taxonomy of comprehension having four levels: literal recognition or recall, inference, evaluation, and appreciation.

Success in secondary school programs and beyond is contingent on the ability to read. Unfortunately, many middle and senior high school students with disabilities are deficient in reading skills. However, aids are available for the secondary teacher attempting to instruct students with disabilities in reading. Formal and informal reading assessment procedures can be used in combination to identify and remedy reading deficits in learners with disabilities. Because these learners may not be working within a traditional age- or grade-referenced scheme, teachers should follow a sequence of developmentally based reading objectives in word recognition, comprehension, and study skills. They should also introduce reading objectives based on community demands, particularly those related to following directions, gaining information, understanding forms, and recreation and leisure-time activity. This functional component of the reading curriculum ensures that students will acquire the reading skill necessary for survival and independence in the community.

11

Mathematics Instruction

DAVID MAJSTEREK
RICH WILSON
ERIC D. JONES

Did you know that . . .

- Students who have failed to learn by traditional means can often learn to compensate for their weaknesses?

- Students with disabilities learn skills best when they are taught directly?

- Increases in teacher-led instruction are associated with higher student achievement?

- Many students with disabilities will receive math instruction in the regular classroom?

- Most students with learning disabilities are served in resource rooms?

- Several types of problem-solving strategies must be directly taught?

- Fluency involves both speed and accuracy?

- Students may not be able to use in the community the skills they exhibit in the classroom?

- Connecting math instruction to real-life experiences promotes generalization?

Can you . . .

- Construct criterion-referenced tests in fractions and decimals?

- Identify a student's optimal instructional level?

- Set overall mastery goals for learning?

- Create an instructional file system?

- Model and demonstrate as you teach?

- Test for student acquisition?

- Deliver effective prompts?

- Develop effective drill-and-practice lessons?

- Deliver appropriate feedback to students?

- Motivate your students?

- Decide when to modify an instructional program?

- Determine whether your program has been successful?

- Plan for generalization of math skills?

David Majsterek is professor of education in the Department of Education, Central Washington University, Ellensburg, Washington. Rich Wilson and Eric Jones are professors of special education in the Division of Intervention Services, Bowling Green State University, Bowling Green, Ohio.

Many students with learning difficulties require additional assistance in the area of mathematics (Geary, 2004). Teachers of these students are faced with a difficult task (Fuchs, Roberts, Fuchs, & Bowers, 1996). Whether their students are identified for services in regular classrooms (Fuchs & Fuchs, 1998), resource rooms, or special classes, they have all been referred for services because they have failed to make average-level academic gains (Cawley, Parmar, Yan, & Miller, 1998). They frequently also have negative attitudes toward themselves and their abilities (Morgan & Jenson, 1988). For adolescents these reduced academic self-perceptions have developed over many years of below-average achievement. The presence of both low self-efficacy and below-average achievement is often negatively related to students' motivation to learn (Dyer, 1978; Seegers, Van Putten, & Vermeer, 2004) and can lead students to think that they are no longer capable of mastering grade-level material as well as their peers. The net effect is that teachers of students with learning and behavior problems must not only focus on remediating significant academic failure, but they must also frequently expend great energies to motivate and improve the self-confidence of their students.

Teachers who lower their expectations to match student perceptions can make matters worse. The fact that students with disabilities have not performed as well as their nondisabled peers can cause teachers to water down the curriculum because they expect their students to continue learning at below-average rates (Mancini & Hughes, 1997). There is evidence that teachers adjust instruction on the basis of the "effort, ability, and personal-social characteristics" of their students (Shavelson & Stern, 1981, p. 467). If the academic level and demand of instruction are reduced because of affective variables rather than prior academic achievement or cognitive abilities, students' opportunities to make maximum academic gains will be reduced. Sustaining high academic expectations for students with disabilities may cause some frustration for teachers, but in order to halt and reverse the trend toward greater failure and loss of self-efficacy, students with disabilities must not only learn as much as the average student (in which case, achievement deficits would stabilize at below-average levels), but they must also learn at an above-average rate in order to eventually achieve age- or grade-level performance. In short, teachers must teach more in a shorter amount of time for students with learning difficulties to overcome their academic deficits.

As difficult as it sounds, students with mild disabilities can often master regular class material if they are provided with an extra allotment of intensive learning strategies by effective teachers using empirically validated techniques (Deshler, Schumaker, Lenz, & Ellis, 1984), and they can become well established in the mainstream (Larrivee, 1986). Students with more moderate or severe disabilities for whom average performance is a more distant goal can greatly improve their performance on many of the complex tasks required for success in general education classrooms (Brown, Campione, & Day, 1981; Horton, 1985). Therefore, there are hopeful indications and compelling reasons for teachers to use well-designed methods and materials with students with disabilities. This chapter describes instructional practices in math that have, for the most part, been empirically supported for use with secondary students experiencing learning and behavior problems.

Principles of Effective Secondary Math Instruction

To be truly effective, instruction must be adapted to meet the constantly evolving needs of the learner. This educational process is most successful if it is founded on a sound theoretical basis. In addition, teachers who develop and articulate a theoretical foundation will find that the resulting principles will help them select more wisely from among currently available methods and materials, and enable them to adapt teaching techniques and instructional programs for students for whom existing methods or materials are ineffective. The tenets presented here are offered in the belief that programs designed from this set of principles are most likely to assist students with disabilities in reaching their potential in academic, personal, and social activities in secondary schools and in making a successful transition to the after-school world.

1. *Ensure that the student experiences success:* "Education" implies that all students deserve an opportunity to develop both competence and confidence in their abilities. One of the best ways teachers can enhance student self-competence is to provide a program designed to ensure success and increase attainment (Whelan, Mendez, deSaman, & Fortmeyer, 1984). The fact that math achievement and self-concept are interrelated provides additional support for this assertion (Kruger & Wandle, 1992).

2. *Provide functional academic instruction:* Instructional objectives taught in the school setting should be directly tied to the skills necessary to succeed in life and career activities (Langone, 1981; Polloway & Epstein, 1985; Schwartz & Budd, 1981). Many things presented in school curricula would be fine to learn, but students with disabilities gain very little from brief instructional exposures. Instead, they learn more and make better adaptations with the mastery of skills and knowledge that have the greatest potential for later application (Patton, Cronin, Bassett, & Koppel, 1997). Because secondary-level students will shortly be leaving school, it is important that the teacher be careful to select the skills that will have the greatest value as students adapt to life outside of school. Thus, basic math fact drill, an activity that consumes considerable instructional time in elementary school, needs to be supplanted with relevant consumer math and purchasing competency. Further, contextualizing instruction in real-world settings (Jitendra et al., 2005) and using simulations or games (Shaftel, Pass, & Schnabel, 2005) can increase the meaningfulness of these lessons and the likelihood that instructed skills will be implemented outside the school setting. Teachers should continually be asking themselves whether the tasks they are teaching will be important once their students leave the classroom.

3. *Provide age-appropriate instruction:* Teachers must help students with disabilities master as many age- and grade-appropriate tasks as possible (Farey, 1986). This requires a sensitivity to social, academic, and career needs. Achieving age-appropriate objectives is often difficult because commercial materials are written for students whose achievement levels match their age levels. For example, driver's manuals and health texts for adolescents often have ninth-grade or higher readability levels. Because students with disabilities need to master the content in these areas, it is up to the teacher either to adapt the commercial materials or to locate instructional materials that are relevant to an adolescent's interests and have the appropriate level of readability.

4. *Offer compensatory instruction:* If instructional time is limited and students are failing to master traditional academic tasks (e.g., telling time or computing sums of money), teach students to compensate by using a digital timepiece, a calculator (Horton, 1985), a typing keyboard (Calhoun, 1985), or even a cell phone with an alarm function. If teachers fail to permit their students to use compensatory learning methods, valuable instructional time will be used up that could have been better spent teaching advanced skills.

5. *Teach skills in meaningful contexts:* Once skills have been sequenced and students assessed, the teacher must take the most efficient and direct path to instruct the student and not depend on incidental learning, discovery learning, or divergent questioning techniques (Bigler, 1984). Generically, this can be described as a three-step procedure: demonstrate, prompt or lead, and test (Rosenshine, 1983; Silbert, Carnine, & Stein, 1990). Explicit skill instruction has proved to be the most effective format for teaching knowledge and skills to students with disabilities. Skill instruction, however, should be embedded in meaningful contexts (Goldman & Hasselbring, 1997). Once planned, lessons taught in real or simulated settings can promote skill maintenance and generalization (Browder & Grasso, 1999; Xin, Grasso, Dippi-Hoy, & Jitendra, 2005).

6. *Increase teacher-led, active student responding:* Teacher–student interactions should be maximized and independent math seatwork closely controlled and limited, because if seatwork consumes more than 80% of instructional time, student achievement decreases (Fisher et al., 1980). In addition, the teacher should ensure a high rate of active student responding, because the combination of many minutes of teacher-led instructional time, numerous teacher questions, and active student responses creates a powerful means of enhancing achievement (Bennett, 1987). Such instruction provides for success by maximizing student participation and teacher evaluation (Archer, Gleason, & Isaacson, 1995).

7. *Begin with and then fade out teacher control of the program:* The teacher is in large part responsible for selecting the instructional objectives, methods, and materials. Very little instruction should be left to chance. Instead, the teacher should assume the role of program manager and control the setting, method, materials, reinforcement, and other instructional variables. Of course, one of the responsibilities of a good teacher/manager is knowing when to teach self-monitoring, self-correction, and independent student work habits and how to increase student responsibility for and control of learning. Planning for this is essential for student success (Alberto & Troutman, 2006). Secondary school teachers need to create a mathematics program that prepares students to function independently in the after-school world.

8. *Provide structure and rigorous scheduling:* Students learn best when the learning environment is designed for efficient and effective delivery of instruction (Jones, Wilson, & Bhojwani, 1997). This includes classroom design, material selection, teacher talk, and, very important, expression of a "We're here to work hard and learn" attitude. In addition, the teacher-controlled variable most associated with student achievement is the amount of time students spend learning. Teachers can maximize learning time by adhering to a tight schedule, eliminating unneeded transitions, reducing disruptions, and increasing academic learning time (Fisher et al., 1980; Wilson & Wesson, 1986). The key to maximizing instructional time is planning ahead. The more the teacher is prepared, the more the students will learn.

9. *Use empirically supported instructional practices:* Teachers should make every effort to use strategies that research has shown to be effective (Carnine, 1997). They should always use the best way to teach a concept or operation (Cohen & Spenciner, 2005). Students will also learn best when teachers control the task difficulty level of assigned activities. Tasks on which students are working must be neither too easy (if they are already mastered, there is no point in teaching them) nor too difficult (if they are too hard, frustration and resignation are likely to occur). Methods to control and maximize task difficulty are presented later in this chapter. Recent technology applications have demonstrated value in math programs for students with learning disabilities (Babbitt & Miller, 1996; Woodward & Gersten, 1992) and moderate to severe cognitive disabilities (Hutcherson, Langone, Ayres, & Clees, 2004; Mechling & Gast, 2003).

10. *Refrain from criticism:* The temptation when working with adolescent learners who are having academic problems may be to attribute their failure to home conditions or lack of effort. However, refraining from making critical comments is a teacher characteristic associated with effective mainstreaming practices (Larrivee, 1986).

11. *Incorporate cognitive strategy instruction:* Recent research has suggested that students with learning disabilities benefit from targeted cognitive strategy instruction (Miles & Forcht, 1995; Miller, Strawser, & Mercer, 1996; Montague, 1997). In particular, the use of self-instruction (Van Luit & Naglieri, 1999) and explicit teaching of math strategies (Kaufmann, Handl, & Thöny, 2003) appear to be effective instructional foci for students with math difficulties.

Process of Effective Transition-Oriented Math Instruction

This section presents a generic model for planning, delivering, and evaluating effective transition-oriented math instruction for secondary students with disabilities. The model does not contain the exact components of any particular commercial program; rather, it incorporates features from numerous sources and is based on the principles previously described. The process of providing effective transition-oriented math instruction can be divided into the following four categories:

1. Assessing instructional demands as they relate to the learner, task, setting, and program goals
2. Planning specific math instructional activities
3. Implementing math instruction
4. Measuring student performance in a math course of study

Step 1: Assessing Instructional Demands

Assessment of Program Goals   All special education teachers are required by IDEA to develop long-term or *annual goals* for their students. Typically, annual goals are developed within an instructional area (e.g., students with learning disabilities may exhibit performance deficits in listening comprehension, basic reading, reading comprehension, oral expression, written expression, math reasoning, or math computation). During this process, teachers must select which skills they will and will not teach to their students. Because there is always a limited amount of instructional time available, some skill areas will either not be taught at all or given only cursory coverage. The following math areas often represent skill-deficit areas for students with disabilities:

time	basic computations	calculus	estimation
money	decimals	trigonometry	ratios & proportions
geometry	fractions	business math	story problems
algebra	measurement	consumer math	

Special education teachers who teach transition-oriented math to students with disabilities must make decisions about what and how much to teach from within each of these categories (Bryant & Rivera, 1997). By applying the principles described earlier (especially those involving relevance, compensation, and student success), teachers can match student needs to curriculum goals by making individual decisions for every student in a math program. For some students, all of the regular math curriculum goals may be taught, although there may be variations in pace, materials, testing, group size, or instructional time. For most students with disabilities, teachers need to select the most important skills from within a math area, providing added instruction on these objectives while deleting other objectives from the course of study. Case for Action 11.1 is designed to approximate this decision-making process in the area of fractions.

Case for Action 11.1

Listed here are 10 skills from a criterion-referenced instructional hierarchy in fractions. You are a secondary special education teacher of students with mild mental retardation and developmental disabilities. Examine the instructional hierarchy and rate each task according to the relevance and importance it has had in your post–high school life on a scale on which 3 is very important, 2 is somewhat important, 1 is barely important, and 0 is not important.

Of course, when teachers make decisions about what to teach, some other factors must also be considered. List and discuss the questions you would want answered before you would plan to include or exclude objectives from instruction. Would you want to know, for example, what career your student is considering or how much time you can devote to teaching fractions?

Fraction Hierarchy

1. Drawing diagrams to represent fractional parts
2. Adding fractions with like denominators
3. Reducing fractions to lowest terms
4. Changing improper fractions to mixed numbers
5. Subtracting fractions with like denominators
6. Subtracting fractions with mixed numbers
7. Multiplying fractions
8. Working story problems involving the multiplication of fractions
9. Multiplying two mixed numbers
10. Dividing fractions
11. Working story problems involving the division of fractions

---

Assessment of the Learner's Entry-Level Skills   Once teachers know what is to be taught, they must determine exactly which instructional objectives each student has already mastered. Entry skills cannot be assessed effectively in transition-oriented programs unless all activities are focused on relevant, practical instructional goals (Cobb & Larkin, 1985; Forness, Horton, & Horton, 1981).

Typically, math skills are assessed by constructing, administering, and interpreting criterion-referenced (CR) informal tests (Frank & McFarland, 1980). Commercial versions of CR tests are available (e.g., BRIGANCE Diagnostic Inventory of Essential Skills; Brigance, 1980). With practice, teachers can construct CR tests that are more specific to the objectives and content of their instructional programs. To begin, teachers may augment published CR tests based on a locally used curricula. If they are carefully constructed, teacher-made CR tests can be more valid and useful than commercially published tests. Teachers may also assess student performance indirectly. For example, Baxter, Woodward, and Olson (2005) analyzed student journals and found that this written communication indicated student conceptual understanding that was not apparent in their classroom performance. Chapter 5 presents information about constructing and using CR tests.

After the test has been scored and proficiencies and weaknesses have been identified, the teacher must construct and present instructional activities at the student's optimal level of instruction. In functional skill domains, it will be necessary for teachers to give close attention to their individual students' levels of proficiency across a variety of skills that are interrelated in their functional application. To interpret test results, the teacher compares obtained student scores (e.g., 100% correct on adding the sums in the columns of the check register with a calculator) to the student performance guidelines in Table 11.1, and rates student performance at the mastery, instructional, or frustration levels for each assessed task. The results of such a comparison and rating are depicted in Table 11.2 for calculator usage. In this example, tasks 5–7 (adding more than two numbers) represent this student's optimal instructional level task.

Assessment of Relevant Student Characteristics   In addition to program and task demands, relevant student characteristics should be determined before instruction. Over the duration of a transition-oriented secondary school program, students will be expected to learn numerous math-related skills that have physical task demands. Therefore, physical disabilities and the necessary adaptations to materials and programs will be important considerations when teaching cooking, writing, typing, or operating a cash register or calculator. It is important to plan for differences in students that are based on cognitive understanding of numerical prerequisites (Kroesbergen, Nan Luit, & Naglieri, 2003). Kaufmann and colleagues (2003) note that numerical skills that others acquire implicitly may need to

TABLE 11.1   *Student Performance Guidelines*

Level	*Percent*
Mastery or independent	90 or more correct
Instructional	70–90 correct
Frustration	Less than 70 correct

TABLE 11.2   *Calculator Task-Hierarchy Segment*

Task	Description	Percentage Correct	Rating
1	Add two whole numbers	100	M
2	Subtract two whole numbers	100	M
3	Multiple two whole numbers	100	M
4	Divide two whole numbers	100	M
5	Add more than two whole numbers	80	I
6	Subtract more than two whole numbers	80	I
7	Multiply more than two whole numbers	70	I
8	Divide more than two whole numbers	50	F
9	Add two decimal numbers	30	F
10	Subtract two decimal numbers	0	F

Key: M = mastery level; I = instructional level; F = frustration level.

be explicitly taught to students with math disabilities. Consequently, familiarity with the cognitive characteristics of students will determine which math applications and processes are appropriate for mastery given the post school transitional needs that students can be expected to encounter.

Step 2: Planning Specific Instruction

Setting Mastery Goals   After teachers have determined the student's optimal instructional level by identifying the task that will be taught, they need to determine the level of student proficiency to be achieved before the task can be said to be mastered. This process must be done for each individual and involves predicting the complex interaction between two factors: the instructional time needed for a student to master a task and the level of correct performance that defines mastery. Although research in this area is lacking, a number of guidelines are available to help teachers set mastery levels.

Standard Educational Guidelines.   Teachers can apply the widely accepted guidelines developed for special education (Stevens, 1977) that set mastery level at approximately 90% for most academic tasks. Not all tasks, however, should be assigned the same mastery-level criterion. Basic skills (e.g., measuring by inches) that are prerequisites for higher-order tasks (e.g., measuring by eighths of an inch) often need to be mastered at 100% correct before instruction begins on the next task. For other skills (e.g., dividing fractions), teachers can set mastery performance closer to 90% correct. Thus, teachers need to apply the standard educational guidelines in Table 11.1 with a measure of common sense.

Functional Rate.   Setting mastery goals using the principle of functional rate is probably the best strategy to use in transition-oriented math programs (Haring, Lovitt, Eaton, & Hansen, 1978). In this method, the mastery goal is set at the level of math performance a student needs to achieve to be successful either in subsequently taught, higher-order tasks or in real-life activities (e.g., the amount of school-based training needed to run a cash register successfully in a supermarket or the amount of calculator training needed to balance a checkbook). Unfortunately, empirically validated functional rate standards have not been determined for the vast majority of math tasks, and much work remains to be done in this area. To address this paucity of standards, teachers may need to directly observe and time real-life tasks in their natural settings (e.g., a clerk making change in a movie theater concession stand).

Social Validation. Kazdin (1977) introduced the concept of social validation to help teachers and therapists set goals for successful behavior management programs. A socially valid goal is attained if, after treatment, the student's behavior approximates the average performance of normally functioning peers. The social validation principle can be used to set numerous math instructional goals, such as the writing rate needed to complete a math competency exam on time; the on-task rate needed for satisfactory math assignment performance; the attention span needed to complete complex tasks such as reading story problems or setting a digital watch; or the average math skills of successful practicing mechanics, carpenters, or technicians who use math in their occupation. Teachers can apply the principle of social validation to set math goals by following the steps in Action Plan 11.1. One of the side benefits of using social validation data is that, after instruction proves successful, the special education teacher can use the results to demonstrate empirically that the student can perform as well as persons considered to be doing well. These findings can be used to enhance placement in both mainstream classes and the workforce. An example of this might be the following: Teachers who prepare students for local employment (e.g.,

---

Action Plan 11.1   Determining Socially Valid Math Performance Standards

We recommend the following four-step process for establishing socially valid math performance standards:

Generic Steps	*Specific Example*
1. Gather data in order to measure the average performance level of mainstream peers or employees who are doing well.	Test the linear measurement skills of 10 practicing woodworkers at local cabinet-making shops.
2. Measure the performance of a target student on the same task.	Test the linear measurement skills of a class of secondary students with developmental disabilities.
3. Compare the results to determine the instructional need.	Determine which skills the woodworkers have mastered (e.g., using a vernier caliper) and how the students perform on these tasks.
4. Begin instruction and continue until goal is attained.	Begin instruction on the easiest task not mastered by the students (e.g., measuring accurately to within $\frac{1}{32}$ of an inch).

working at weighing and charging for products at a local hardware store) might ask to monitor performance at the work site during a busy time of day to gather data on performance expectations.

Normative Data.   Normative data are gathered by testing large numbers of students and employing descriptive statistics to determine the mean, standard deviation, percentile rank, and other indexes of the group. School districts that have incorporated a curriculum-based methodology (Deno, 1985) routinely assess student math skills to determine how every student is performing on the tasks in the math curriculum. Normative data have already been gathered in many instructional and behavior management areas, including spelling, reading fluency, reading comprehension, math computation, story problems, writing, success rates, and on-task rates (Fisher et al., 1980; Starlin & Starlin, 1973).

Perhaps the easiest way to use normative data to set instructional goals is to determine the average range of student performance on a specific task and to use the lower limit of the average range as the goal for students with disabilities. Consider the following example. Assume that general education students who succeed in a two-year technical school after high school can solve higher-order computational problems (e.g., addition with regrouping in a story problem or long division to three decimal places) at an average rate of 90% correct with a standard deviation of 5%. This means that the average range (i.e., the mean plus and minus one standard deviation, representing the performance of 68% of those students) is from 85% to 95% correct. Students with disabilities who wish to attend and succeed at a technical school could work toward becoming as proficient in computation (i.e., at least 85% correct) as students at the lower end of the average range.

Selecting Instructional Materials and Settings   Teacher management of the instructional setting is a critical consideration (Englemann, Carnine, & Steely, 1991; Hanley-Maxwell, Wilcox, & Heal, 1982), and selecting materials for students with disabilities is an important and time-consuming teacher task. However, as Jitendra and her colleagues (2005) note, commercially produced math curricula inconsistently address National Council of Teachers of Mathematics standards (2000), which tend to be represented in high-stakes testing. Appropriate selection of curriculum products is important because the type of materials used has an impact on student achievement. Choosing is time consuming because appropriate commercially made materials are difficult to locate, especially materials needed to teach functional or compensatory tasks (Lambie, 1980). Even when appropriate math materials are available, teachers must supplement commercial programs because students with disabilities often require additional instruction to attain task mastery. Teachers will find that they often have to make their own or locate materials from several sources in order to provide high-quality instruction.

Although developing this system may appear burdensome, teachers will find that once initial materials are gathered, instruction can be delivered efficiently and the materials can be reused or adapted for any future student who needs to master the same tasks. In addition, teachers who use this type of system will become more familiar with the sequence of steps that are associated with each area of mathematical competence.

Selection of the instructional setting is another important variable to consider. Wood (2002) provides a detailed list of instructional variables that teachers should consider in de-

Action Plan 11.2   Setting Variables

We offer the following recommendations based on setting variables:

Variable	*Recommendation*
1. Group size (Sindelar, Rosenberg, Wilson, & Bursuck, 1984)	Three to eight students
2. Seating (Silbert et al., 1990)	Proximity to and eye contact with teacher
3. Furniture management (Wilson & Wesson, 1986)	Control of traffic patterns to minimize disruptions

signing instruction. Several key setting variables, along with suggestions for practitioners, are contained in Action Plan 11.2.

Selecting Instructional Techniques and Formats   Teachers must select instructional strategies and teaching formats that will maximize student achievement. There is empirical evidence that both teaching strategies and lesson formats are related to student performance (Fisher et al., 1980; Sindelar, Rosenberg, Wilson, & Bursuck, 1984). The strategies that follow are especially relevant for teaching math skills to secondary students in a transition-oriented program.

Demonstrating or Modeling the Correct Task Procedures.   A teaching method that has received much research support was developed by those who employ a "generic direct instruction" approach (Rosenshine, 1983). The basic instructional sequence is made up of three steps: demonstrate, prompt, and test. Because it is important for students to make few errors during skill acquisition, new instruction should begin with a teacher demonstration of correct task performance. Instead of asking Bill, "What key on the calculator do you press if you want to recall a value stored in memory?" begin by telling and showing him the correct behavior. If Bill knows the correct key, he probably should not be part of the acquisition lesson. Instead, provide him with fluency-building activities, practice opportunities, or generalization lessons. If Bill does not know the correct key, he is likely to guess, perhaps using a faulty problem-solving strategy that will need to be displaced later during the teaching of the correct strategy. The purpose of a demonstration step is to show a student how to accomplish an instructional objective successfully.

Testing for Student Acquisition.   If students acquired instructional tasks immediately, the sequence of instructional events would be only two steps: demonstrate and test. Teachers would demonstrate the correct way to measure a series of objects in centimeters, and students would use a metric ruler correctly when asked to do so. Teaching, however, is seldom this simple; for many tasks, teachers can expect mastery to occur only after multiple learning trials and practice sessions over several days. Still, testing student performance is an important component of effective teaching that provides a teacher with information about how well a student has mastered an instructional objective.

As important as testing is, it can be overemphasized—to the detriment of student achievement. Duffy and McIntyre (1982) found that many teachers engaged in very little actual teaching, instead spending most of their time monitoring student work and asking students to recite answers, as if their students already knew the skill before the lesson began. Instead, teachers should use a thoughtful blend and sequence of instructional events known to be positively related to achievement. They should begin with teacher demonstration (Rosenshine, 1983), maximize teacher-led instructional time (Fisher et al., 1980), and follow with numerous, relevant teacher questions (Sindelar, Smith, Harriman, Hale, & Wilson, 1986). Testing student performance should be accomplished in a variety of ways in addition to the standard paper-and-pencil assessment. Tests can be group or individual, oral or written, formal or informal, prompted or unprompted, and administered in the classroom or in the workplace. In all cases, however, the purpose (to assess the degree of student mastery) and the process (systematically presenting teacher questions and monitoring student performance) remain the same. Several guidelines for good testing procedures are listed in Action Plan 11.3.

Prompting Correct Student Responses.   Many teachers deliver prompts (i.e., temporary instructional hints that lead to accurate student response) as part of their everyday teaching. In practice, however, prompting occurs infrequently and unsystematically. Nonetheless, all teachers should be trained and prepared to deliver a variety of prompts in order to ensure high student success rates (Alberto & Troutman, 2006; Schloss, 1986).

During transition-oriented math instruction for students with disabilities, teachers are most likely to deliver three types of prompts: verbal, visual, and manual. Verbal prompts are the least intrusive and can be delivered easily during instruction. Teachers should be prepared to deliver verbal prompts during two phases of instruction—after a demonstration step has been modeled and after a student responds incorrectly. In the first instance, a prompt acts as an intervening instructional technique between a teacher demonstration and an unassisted student response.

Teachers also will employ visual prompts during instruction. Visual prompts can be gestures that cue correct student responses. If the instructional objective involves using the keys on a calculator or keyboard, a teacher might point toward a group of keys, encouraging a student to select a single key from within the group. Most visual prompts, however, are graphic or pictorial in nature. The examples in Action Plan 11.4 illustrate ways that a teacher can use visual prompts to increase the likelihood of student success.

Action Plan 11.3   Guidelines for Effective Testing during Lessons

We recommend the following activities for ensuring effective testing:

1. Test after instruction has occurred.
2. Match the testing method to the teaching method.
3. Ensure a maximum overlap between tasks taught and tasks tested.
4. Test in the classroom for acquisition.
5. Test in the applied setting for generalization.
6. Provide for numerous, active student responses during testing.
7. Conduct direct and frequent measurements.

Action Plan 11.4   Pictorial and Written Prompts

We suggest the following procedures for providing written prompts:

1. Tape a copy of the daily schedule on a student's desk.
2. Provide students with one correctly solved math problem on the top of a drill-and-practice worksheet.
3. Use arrows (McLeskey, 1982) or other symbols to remind students, for example, to add from right to left.

$$\leftarrow$$
$$387$$
$$+\,659$$

4. Provide students with reading problems with a deck of picture cards that illustrate successful task completion. For example, the correct sequence of computer keys needed to access math software could be photographed (along with a representation of what appears on the computer monitor) and posted at the CAI (computer-assisted instruction) learning center.
5. Post in the classroom, in either written or picture format, the following instructions for students who need teacher assistance after encountering task failure:
    a. Relax; take a deep breath.
    b. Reread, review, or rethink the problem.
    c. Try again.
    d. Indicate that you need help—perhaps by raising your hand, taking a number (as in a bakery), raising a red flag attached to your desk, or signing up for assistance.
    e. Get back to work until help arrives (perhaps on the next problem or on a different assignment, or, at the very least, read a book reserved for such occasions).

A teacher uses a manual prompt when physically guiding a student through a task. At this prompting level, the teacher assumes primary responsibility for completion of a task. Examples include guiding a student through the writing stages of a division problem, moving a hand to correctly mark a measured surface using a pencil and tape measure, sorting coins into specific sums, or leading a student through the key sequence required to access a computer-aided design program.

Practicing Task Solution.   Teachers must provide students with numerous opportunities to practice assigned tasks. There are two types of practice lessons—controlled (guided) and independent—and each is defined by the degree of teacher involvement. In a typical controlled practice lesson (the type that occurs immediately after a demonstration lesson), a teacher might write problems on a chalkboard or overhead transparency and check student responses periodically. In a typical independent practice lesson, students work on their own, perhaps on a worksheet or computer-assisted instruction (CAI) program, and teacher feedback is less immediate and less frequent. Teachers who implement the guidelines in Action Plan 11.5 will find that their students will benefit from systematic controlled and independent practice activities. Research on the effective use of practice has revealed two points

Action Plan 11.5   Guidelines for Drill-and-Practice Activities

The following drill-and-practice guidelines are recommended for use with students with disabilities:

1. Match the practice activity to the instructional objective.
2. Require no new learning.
3. Control task difficulty carefully.
4. Provide for numerous *active* student responses.
5. Provide efficient error correction.
6. Program sufficient practice to ensure mastery.
7. Program for the development of fluency.
8. Maximize teacher questions during controlled practice (Sindelar et al., 1986).
9. Limit independent practice to less than 80% of total instructional time (Fisher et al., 1980).

that should be remembered about the relationship between practice and the effectiveness of instructional programs. First, with systematic, well-designed instructional programs, students require less practice to master complex math skills than with less efficiently designed programs (Darch, Carnine, & Gersten, 1984). Second, Fisher and colleagues (1980) found too much practice and too little teaching to be associated with lower levels of student achievement. The use of cooperative homework teams has also been found to be effective (O'Melia & Rosenberg, 1994).

Providing Feedback.   One of the most important instructional variables is teacher feedback. Feedback includes error correction, additional information, and praise. Each of these factors is related to student achievement. Error correction lets students know whether they performed correctly or incorrectly. Additional information is provided either to tell a student how to perform correctly or to elaborate on an instructional objective. Praise serves two functions: It lets a student know that a response was correct and it can provide positive reinforcement for accurate responding. The guidelines in Action Plan 11.6 are designed to help teachers deliver effective feedback to youth with disabilities.

Building Periodic Review into Teaching.   Every instructional lesson should contain some review. As important as this feature is for all learners, it is even more important for youth with disabilities, who seem to forget faster than their nondisabled peers. Teachers should program for at least four types of review:

1. *Review before beginning a math lesson:* Typically, this consists of reviewing the rules for appropriate behavior (Rosenberg, 1986) and providing advanced organizers for upcoming instruction (Lenz, Alley, & Schumaker, 1987). These two practices are associated with better student behavior and higher student achievement.
2. *Review homework:* Math teachers who assign but do not review or correct homework are taking the chance that their students will be practicing error patterns that may be difficult to overcome.

Action Plan 11.6   Feedback Guidelines

We suggest the following guidelines for delivering feedback:

1. Generic praise, "Nice work," is good; content-related praise containing task-specific information, "That's right, the final checkbook balance is $34.35," is better.
2. Avoid extended error correction for one student when the rest of the class is ready to move on. Class achievement suffers. Instead, schedule a later individual help session.
3. Avoid terse "No, that's wrong" responses that do not provide a student with constructive information leading to correct responding.
4. Avoid labeling a student's response as totally incorrect when part or most of an answer is correct. If a student missed only one of the 11 steps in a long division problem, sure, the answer is wrong, but consider how much more effective your teaching would be if you acknowledged the accuracy of the 10 correct steps and provided the prompts necessary for the student to correct the error.
5. Build in peer feedback, which has proved important in algebra instruction (Maccini, McNaughton, & Ruhl, 1999).

3. *Review within every lesson:* Teachers should plan to include periodic reviews of important information while conducting a lesson. This is especially important when there are rules that define accurate responding. Teachers should intersperse and require their students to repeat rules in the division of fractions (invert and multiply), multiplication of bases with like exponents (add the exponents), and general computation (multiply and divide before you add or subtract).
4. *Review across lessons:* Teachers can never assume that students, even those who have attained mastery of an instructional objective, will maintain mastery over time. Periodic, distributed review, in which past instructional objectives are practiced for a few minutes, will enhance maintenance and let the teacher know whether reteaching is necessary.

In summary, teachers who want to maximize student achievement should strive to structure their lessons carefully, including as many of the previously described instructional techniques as possible. Action Plan 11.7 lists techniques known to increase the achievement of students with mild and moderate learning disabilities.

Selecting Motivational Strategies   In addition to the instructional content and format, teachers of youth with disabilities must consider which, if any, motivational strategies they will employ to enhance student achievement. The general rule is to use the minimum motivational techniques required to achieve the objective. If students are internally motivated, then teachers should not implement external reinforcement techniques. However, many secondary students who have experienced failure will require supplemental motivation, at least initially. Teachers can enhance student achievement by applying the guidelines in Action Plan 11.8.

Action Plan 11.7   A Six-Pack of Teaching Variables to Consider When Planning Instruction

The following variables should be considered when planning instruction:

1. Academic time and focus	Maximize the minutes of academic instruction and project a "We're here to work and learn" atmosphere.
2. Task difficulty	Assign activities that maintain a high student success rate.
3. On-task rate	Maintain a high level of attention-to-task behavior.
4. Mastery instruction	Teach until students perform tasks correctly and fluently.
5. Data-based decision making	Gather performance data and use these data to determine how and what to teach.
6. Research-validated techniques	Use teaching methods that have been empirically validated in the professional literature.

Action Plan 11.8   Guidelines for Implementing Motivational Strategies

We suggest the following guidelines for motivating youth:

1. Consult and negotiate reinforcement with students and, if appropriate, with parents.
2. Engage students in charting their own progress.
3. Prepare ahead of time to fade out all external rewards.
4. Deliver reinforcement immediately after a correct response.
5. Consider individual behavioral contracting for older students.
6. Use content-related praise to supplement generic praise.
7. Monitor the effects of all reinforcement procedures.
8. Be consistent.
9. Locate reinforcement present in the natural, real-life setting and use these in the classroom.

Step 3: Implementing Math Instruction

Teachers of students with mild and moderate disabilities will find that, in general, comprehensive commercial math programs cannot be used in their entirety when transition-oriented instruction is being planned (Fine, Welch-Burke, & Fondario, 1985). Instead, teachers should develop their own and obtain materials from a wide variety of sources. Armed with appropriate materials, teachers must be prepared to bring their students up to mastery-level performance in each of the three major stages of learning: acquisition, fluency, and generalization.

Acquisition   The first major learning stage involves student mastery of newly taught instructional objectives. Typically, all students, including those with learning disabilities, are exposed to a large number of concepts and operations during secondary math instruction. The concepts to be learned include vocabulary words associated with consumer purchasing, banking, and measurement (to name a few) and the facts and information objectives associated with the same instructional areas. A large number of operations are also introduced in the secondary curriculum, including all the algorithms that define the correct solution of arithmetic problems (e.g., the steps needed to calculate successfully when subtracting fractions); the steps to balance a checking account, calculate interest, and similar formulas; and many others. Teachers can apply the guidelines in Action Plan 11.9 to enhance mastery of newly introduced tasks.

Fluency   After students have mastered the math concepts and operations, teachers must ensure that students can perform with both speed and accuracy. Thus, during fluency teaching, teachers must retain the high accuracy component of acquisition instruction (e.g., 95% correct) and add criteria that specify the completion of a certain number of tasks within a stated time interval (e.g., 40 digits per minute). By adding speeded task completion criteria, teachers can help students prepare for competency and standardized tests, for jobs that require rapid math response (e.g., supermarket cashier), and for any activity that requires both speed and accuracy. In many cases, successful competitive employment requires more than accurate-but-slow responding.

Action Plan 11.9   Acquisition Guidelines

The following guidelines are suggested for enhancing acquisition:

1. Use concrete materials when introducing abstract concepts (e.g., angles, area, money, volume, and measurement).
2. Maximize use of specific teacher questions (Alper, 1985).
3. Ensure that students are responding actively and frequently.
4. Maximize teacher-directed instructional time (Fisher et al., 1980).
5. Limit lengthy, abstract explanations.
6. Teach tasks directly to students instead of relying on discovery, vicarious, or spontaneous learning to occur.
7. Use teacher prompts to ensure that students respond correctly and make as few errors as possible (Schloss, 1986).
8. Control the context when introducing new math vocabulary words (e.g., use the same key words in all story problems involving division [How many in each?] or subtraction [How many are left over?]).
9. Use mnemonic instructional aids to help students remember concepts, vocabulary, algorithm steps, and formulas (Farb & Throne, 1978; Scruggs & Laufenberg, 1986).
10. If reading is included in the math lesson, use advanced organizers to cue students to remember important information.
11. Employ compensatory teaching methods for students who have specific long-standing weaknesses. For example, teach students who have failed to master arithmetic skills to use a calculator (Horton, 1985).

Following acquisition instruction, the emphasis should be on enhancing fluency. Students who are not able to solve problems accurately during untimed assessment should not be required to work toward fluency (Hasselbring & Goin, 1988). Typically, most fluency-building lessons are drill-and-practice activities designed to provide students with both additional exposure to an instructional objective and a means to increase the rate of response. The guidelines in Action Plan 11.10 will help teachers design and implement effective practice activities.

Generalization   After students have attained fluency in problem solving, teachers must ensure that they can use these skills in applied settings. This type of generalization typically does not occur unless specific planning and instruction are implemented (Alberto & Troutman, 2006; Mascari & Forgnone, 1982). For special education teachers serving secondary students with disabilities, three generalization concerns are paramount: (1) Will students retain skill mastery after instruction has concluded? (2) Will students use the skills acquired in the special education setting in mainstream classrooms? (3) Will students use acquired skills in community and career settings? To enhance maintenance and generalization, teachers should apply the guidelines described in Action Plan 11.11.

Decision Making during Teaching   As students progress through material and assigned tasks, their teachers must be prepared to answer several instructional questions (Colozzi et al., 1986). Has a task been mastered? Has a particular teaching, motivational, or prompting practice been effective? As students progress (or fail to progress) through instructional lessons, the answers to these questions lead teachers to make one of three decisions related

---

Action Plan 11.10   Fluency-Building Guidelines

We recommend the following fluency-building strategies:

1. Because the major shortcoming of commercial math programs is inadequate provision of practice (Silbert et al., 1990), teachers must ensure that sufficient opportunities are provided.
2. Gradually shift from concrete (e.g., real money) to semiconcrete (e.g., pictures of real money) to abstract symbols (e.g., $ or ¢).
3. Use peer tutors during practice sessions (Maheady, Sacca, & Harper, 1988).
4. Use appropriate educational games (Beattie & Algozzine, 1982; Wesson, Wilson, & Mandlebaum, 1988).
5. Increase the amount of self-checking required of students.
6. Teach students to self-monitor their work as they solve problems. For math self-monitoring strategies include estimation, self-questioning, and periodic rechecking.
7. Follow lessons in which students practice large numbers of problems (massed practice) with lessons that provide review spaced out over many lessons (distributed practice).
8. Always control the difficulty level of drill-and-practice problems. High student success rates, approaching 100% correct, should be the rule for review exercises.

Action Plan 11.11 Guidelines to Enhance Maintenance and Generalization

The following guidelines are recommended for enhancing maintenance and generalization:

1. Build lots of review into daily instruction.
2. Periodically retest students to determine whether mastery has been retained. If not, reteach essential skills.
3. Teach in the most relevant applied setting. For example, take students to an auto shop, grocery store, or bowling alley (Ellis, Lenz, & Sabornie, 1987).
4. Use materials and lessons in the classroom that approximate those used in mainstream classes or job sites (Smith & Schloss, 1986).
5. Develop cue cards and other prompting devices (e.g., graphic depictions of appropriate behaviors) to enhance student performance after students have left the special education classroom (Wilson & Wesson, 1986).
6. Incorporate procedures into teaching that fade out teacher control and increase student responsibility. For example, replace teacher evaluation with student evaluation or eliminate tangible reinforcement (Santogrossi, O'Leary, Romanczyk, & Kaufman, 1973; Turkewitz, O'Leary, & Ironsmith, 1975).

to the effectiveness of instruction—*exit* (if a task has been mastered), *continue* (if student progress is at the expected level), or *change* (if a student is not making satisfactory progress).

Teachers who directly and frequently measure student performance and make data-based instructional decisions have at least three types of evaluative methodology available. First are the data-reactive single-subject designs. Although single-subject designs are typically used by researchers who publish in the professional literature, several designs (e.g., alternating-treatments design, changing-conditions design, and changing-criteria design) can be used appropriately by teachers as decision-making aids. Single-subject designs can be used to identify more effective instructional methods.

Another data-based decision-making method is to apply one of two models described in the professional literature: precision teaching (Lovitt & Haring, 1979) or data-based program modification (Deno & Mirkin, 1977). Both decision-making programs provide highly structured techniques and rules that enable teachers to decide to *exit*, *continue*, or *change* instruction in an objective way. Because proficiency in these decision-making methods requires substantial teacher training, interested readers should consult the training manuals (Deno & Mirkin, 1977; Haring et al., 1978; White & Haring, 1976). An interesting footnote in the area of data-based decision making is that even though the technology is present and we know that conducting direct and frequent measurement is related to increased student achievement (Fuchs & Fuchs, 1986), many, if not most, teachers fail to monitor student progress systematically (Wesson, King, & Deno, 1984; Wesson, Skiba, Sevcik, King, & Deno, 1984).

The third available method is curriculum-based measurement (CBM) which was presented in Chapter 5. Teachers can use traditional or computer-based CBM means to analyze student performance (Whinnery & Fuchs, 1992).

Step 4: Measuring Program Success

The final step in the instructional process is to determine how well a teacher's program has produced the desired results. Because the desired result of math programs for secondary students with disabilities involves successful job, community, and leisure performance (rather than the more limited goal of successful classroom performance), effective teachers must design programs that are related to post-school life and follow up on students who finish their programs (Nietupski, Welch, & Wacker, 1983). Teachers must not assume that skills learned in the classroom, such as a unit on fractions (Perkins & Cullinan, 1985), will automatically be performed in a real-life setting (Bourdeau, Close, & Sowers, 1986).

Assessment of generalization should be a straightforward process. Rather than relying on commercial tests that purport to measure job readiness, teachers should observe and evaluate student performance in several real-life settings. Computational, computer, or cash register skills can be assessed directly by observing students performing in a cooperating grocery and hardware store. Leisure math skills can be measured by observing students at bowling, bingo, or card parties. Community math skills can be evaluated during either simulated or actual bus or car trips (map skills), major appliance purchases (consumer math), bank transactions (checking and savings account skills), and a wide variety of additional in situ experiences. The use of curriculum-based measurement techniques with problems selected from functional settings is an excellent choice for program evaluation (Fuchs & Fuchs, 1991).

Teachers should assess student performance on at least three occasions after the initial instruction has brought the student to the mastery level: one or two weeks after the program ends to measure short-term maintenance, several months later to assess long-term maintenance, and in the applied setting to determine generalization. If it is determined that mastery-level performance has been lost or is inconsistent, it is often necessary to reteach the skills. At the very least, teachers will know that some aspect of their instructional program needs to be altered so that future students will have a greater chance of achieving success.

Summary

If teachers follow the guidelines and instructional suggestions described in this chapter, they will be able to design and implement effective math programs for adolescents with mild disabilities. Perhaps the greatest danger for secondary special education teachers is to assume that classroom instruction is an end in itself. It is all too easy for teachers to neglect planning instruction that is designed to enhance student performance in real-life experiences. Rather, teachers should frequently ask themselves if what they are teaching to youth with disabilities will be important and relevant long after secondary school has ended. Students of teachers who answer affirmatively will have received the most effective instructional program.

chapter

12

Vocational Instruction

Did you know that . . .

- Despite participation in special education programs, students have experienced major difficulties in their transition from school to work?

- A vocational program's success is determined by the placement and advancement of students in occupations related to their training?

- Self-determination is important in a student's transition to adult life?

- Aptitude tests are used to determine the likelihood of an individual's success in a given occupation?

- Curriculum-based vocational assessment uses informal procedures based on the individual student's learning needs?

- Career education aids in the vocational instruction process by providing a foundation for specific skills training?

- Vocational goals and objectives should be developed to maximize an individual's potential for independence?

- A student's employment value has become increasingly important to society?

- Vocational programs that are based on business and industry's needs are likely to ensure future success in employment?

- Person-centered planning is an assessment method for transition planning?

- Vocational education should encompass all aspects of successful performance in an occupation?

- Individual vocational goals and objectives should be based on the characteristics and needs of the student?

Can you . . .

- Identify the relationship between vocational education and business and industry?

- Identify the two most important skill areas noted by employers?

- Identify skills associated with self-determination?

- Describe how to help a student be more self-determined?

- Differentiate between vocational skill tests and vocational aptitude tests?

- Observe appropriate safeguards when using or interpreting vocational aptitude tests?

- Identify the common elements of a person-centered plan?
- Conduct a curriculum-based vocational assessment?
- Identify the essential features of life-centered career education?
- Include career education competencies in the educational program of students who have disabilities?

- Establish a vocational curriculum on the basis of the characteristics of a student and his or her community?
- Identify employment opportunities for high school graduates who have disabilities?
- Establish a vocational program that meets the unique needs of a student and his or her community?

Numerous authors have expressed concern about the postsecondary experiences of students with disabilities, particularly the poor employment rates and the lack of functional educational and vocational experiences (Benz, Lindstrom, & Yovanoff, 2000; Johnson, Stodden, Emanuel, Luecking, & Mack, 2002). These are viewed as major detriments to the success of youth with disabilities (Harris Survey of Americans with Disabilities, 1998; Levine & Nourse, 1998; Thoma, 1999). One is therefore led to ask whether there is life after school, and whether individuals with disabilities can be productive citizens.

This chapter is concerned with the manner in which vocational and special educators can provide meaningful experiences leading to successful transition to postsecondary environments. Emphasis is placed on strategies that ensure that youth with disabilities will become productive adult citizens.

The need for preparatory programs for secondary students is evident from the literature (Colley & Jamison, 1998; Malian & Love, 1998; Owens-Johnson & Johnson, 1999). Although vocationally oriented programs are available to school-aged individuals with disabilities, there is still a need. Smaller local education agencies (LEAs) are less likely than larger ones to provide services, and few have actual transition programs. Students who are higher functioning with few to no challenging behaviors are more likely to be enrolled in transition programs than others.

Although many students participate in special education programs, they experience great difficulty in making the transition from school to work (Aspel, Bettis, Test, & Wood, 1998; Collet-Klingenberg, 1998; Knight & Aucoin, 1999; Levine & Nourse, 1998; Malian & Love, 1998; Wehman, West, & Kregel, 1999). Most youth with disabilities (1) are unemployed or underemployed, (2) obtain jobs through family friend connections as opposed to vocational training and placement services, (3) earn only slightly above minimum wage in unskilled or service-related positions, and (4) are unlikely to advance above the entry-level position.

In 1990 the Secretary's Commission on Achieving Necessary Skills (SCANS) was established to investigate the needs of the workplace. The commission reported in 1991 that more than 50% of students who leave school do not have the "knowledge or foundation required to find and hold a job." They reported "globalization of commerce and industry and growth of technology on the job" as the key conditions for their findings. Eight requirements were identified as essential for preparation for all students, including those going to work and those planning further education. These requirements include foundation skills

(Basic Skills, Thinking Skills, and Personal Qualities) and competency areas (Resources, Interpersonal, Information, Systems, and Technology).

Businesses continue to cite difficulties in finding qualified applicants. The gap between the skills needed by business and industry and those available is widening. This situation is also creating a need for vocational preparation among school-aged individuals with disabilities (Knight & Aucoin, 1999; SCANS, 1991; Wagner, Blackorby, Cameto, Hebbeler, & Newman, 1993).

Transition

IDEA mandates for transition planning and services were a response to research that indicated students with disabilities experienced (a) poor integration on graduation, (b) higher dropout and unemployment rates than typical peers, (c) low rates of postsecondary education entrance and completion, (d) low-quality independent living experiences, and (e) limited participation in the community (Baer et al., 2003; Benz et al., 2000). As summarized by Benz and colleagues (2000), research also indicated that postsecondary and employment outcomes are better if students participate in vocational education classes during the last two years of high school; completed paid work experiences in the community during the last two years of high school; were competent in functional skills in academics, community living, personal and social skills, vocational skills, and self-determination skills; participated in transition planning; and graduated from high school. In their summary of the literature, Kohler and Field (2003) reported similar findings, noting that student outcomes were more positive when consideration was given to vocational education, paid work experience, parent involvement, and interagency collaboration.

IDEA and its amendments require state and local agencies to address the school and postsecondary needs of students with disabilities. Recognizing the importance of early planning, IDEA mandates that transition planning begin when a student reaches 14 years of age. At this age, a statement of transition needs must be included in the IEP (Lodge Rogers & Rogers, 2001). By the time the student reaches 16 years of age, the plan must include two items. First is a statement of needed transition services, defined as a coordinated set of activities that promote the movement from school to postschool activities. These services include postsecondary education (discussed in Chapter 2), vocational training, integrated employment (including supported employment), continuing and adult education, adult services, independent living, or community participation (Halpern, 1993b; Lodge Rogers & Rogers, 2001). Services are based on student needs, reflecting student preferences and interests (Kohler & Field, 2003). Second, a transition plan must identify interagency responsibility and community linkages to address students' needs, interests, independent living, community participation, and opportunities in postsecondary education and employment. Transition planning requires the cooperative efforts of students, their parents, special and general educators, and representatives of community service agencies. To ensure that both of these items are addressed, teachers are advised to follow the steps listed in Action Plan 12.1 when developing a transition plan. Secondary teachers assist with transition planning by working with students and families to identify interests and needs. They can assist with plan implementation by providing career education activities; arranging job shadowing, internships, or paid work experiences; examining any vocational

Action Plan 12.1   Transition Plan

We recommend the following steps in developing a transition plan:

1. Infuse a life-centered career education program into the school's academic program, grades K–12.
2. Promote a functional curriculum throughout the student's educational program.
3. Conduct an individual assessment of the student. Include vocational interests, vocational aptitudes, occupational skills, employability skills, and special services.
4. Develop individual goals and objectives to maximize the student's potential in a vocational program.
5. Place the student in a vocational skill-training program appropriate for the student's goals and objectives.
6. Provide the student support services to ensure success in the vocational skill training program.
7. Place the student in a vocational setting appropriate to the training received.
8. Provide support services at the location of placement (e.g., emphasize interagency collaboration).
9. Conduct activities that will make the individual aware of alternative programs, if appropriate (e.g., technical school, military, community college).
10. Promote other services appropriate to the individual's needs (e.g., medical, independent living, recreation, mobility, residential living).

technical offerings that might be available; and having students complete interest inventories (Neubert & Moon, 2000).

The primary goal of transition planning is to "promote and facilitate normalization in post school life" (Kohler & Field, 2003, p. 180). Best practices in transition would allow students to earn a diploma, attain successful employment, succeed in postsecondary settings, and enjoy a suitable quality of life (Mellard & Lancaster, 2003).

Self-Determination

Kohler and Field (2003) noted that students who are more involved in establishing their educational goals are more likely to achieve them. Therefore, self-determination has become important in the transition of a student with disabilities from school to adult life. *Self-determination* refers to "acting as the primary causal agent in one's life and making choices and decisions regarding one's quality of life free from undue external influence or interference" (Wehmeyer, 1996, p. 24). To become self-determined, the student needs to make choices, problem solve, set and attain goals, take risks but still ensure safety, self-regulate, self-advocate, and be self-aware. Thus, the student who shows self-determination has greater control over his or her life, makes more informed decisions and choices, develops objectives to meet personal goals, solves problems, and assumes responsibility. These are the key elements for a successful transition to adult life (Steere & Cavaiuolo, 2002; Wehmeyer & Schwartz, 1998). Students who engage in self-determination are more effective in planning for their futures because they are more aware of their own wishes and aspirations (Steere & Cavaiuolo, 2002).

One way to help a student become self-determined is to increase the student's participation in his or her IEP transition plan. This involvement will be of great value in promoting goal setting, decision making, and problem-solving responsibilities. Wehmeyer, Martin, and Sands (1997) have identified other activities that should also be promoted:

1. Be involved in assessment and planning activities.
2. Participate in structured, individualized instruction on self-determination skills.
3. Model self-determination skills in community settings.
4. Participate in experiences that promote self-determination.

Assessing Interests and Skills

IDEA mandates that transition be considered during IEPs when students reach the age of 14. According to Levinson and Palmer (2005), vocational assessment is a primary component of a transition plan. The assessment process should comprise the combined efforts of several professionals, including teachers, parents, the student, counselors, psychologists, and representatives from a variety of agencies including mental health, vocational rehabilitation, and social services. Rojewski (2002) defined *vocational assessment* as the "data collection methods, usually formal assessment procedures and standardized testing, used to gather information about an individual's interests, abilities, and aptitudes as they pertain specifically to vocational potential" (p. 74). It is an ongoing process that provides information that practitioners can use to design and implement vocational instruction for each student. This information may relate to academic skills, daily living skills, vocational aptitudes, work interests, work habits, social skills, personal care skills, current occupational and vocational skills, and attitudes. The goal is to facilitate educational and vocational planning that enables the students to be successful in community settings and at work or in a postsecondary setting (Levinson & Palmer, 2005).

Vocational Aptitude Tests

Vocational aptitude tests are designed to determine whether an individual has the potential to succeed in a given occupation. A high aptitude score in a quantity foods occupation suggests that the student has the ability to learn the competencies necessary to become a chef, restaurant manager, or owner. A low aptitude score might suggest that the student will have difficulty in acquiring these complex skills. Careful matching of capability to level of potential is important to ensure interest and success in employment.

Rojewski (2002) identified tests that are used to assess the vocational aptitude of students with mild disabilities. They include the Career Ability Placement Survey, the Career Occupational Preference System, the McCarron-Dial System, and the Occupational Aptitude Survey and Interest Schedule. Some authors have questioned the use of vocational aptitude tests when used with special populations (Hagner & Dileo, 1993; Menchetti & Piland, 2000). Because reading and writing are prerequisite to performance on many of these measures, the performance of students with disabilities may not reflect their actual vocational ability. Even when actual performance items are used that do not require reading and writing, it is questionable whether the standardized testing conditions adequately mirror actual work conditions. Furthermore, aptitude tests provide a static indication of current ability. Vocational instruction may alter a person's aptitude. Unfortunately, data from an aptitude test may be used unwisely to deny a student the necessary vocational education.

Schloss and Sedlak (1986) have suggested the following guidelines for applying information from vocational aptitude tests:

1. Ensure that the student has been previously exposed to the test.
2. Ensure that the student is motivated to perform well on the test.
3. Ensure that the student possesses the necessary test-taking abilities (e.g., reading and writing).
4. Ensure that the test format and expected student response accurately reflect work demands in the actual vocational setting.
5. Corroborate results of the test with other measures.

Curriculum-Based Vocational Assessment

Special educators and vocational educators have long recognized the importance of individual assessment services. Congress has confirmed this need by prescribing a full range of services in the Carl D. Perkins Vocational and Applied Technology Education Act of 1985 (PL 98-524) and its reauthorization in 1998. Specifically, students with disabilities who enroll in a secondary vocational education program must receive an "assessment of the interest, abilities, and special needs of such student[s] with respect to completing successfully the vocational education program." Vocational assessment practices must be organized to provide such services. Many commercial products are available, but over time they may not fulfill the assessment services needed by students with disabilities.

Curriculum-based vocational assessment is an alternative approach to commercial assessments. It is a continuous performance-based process that provides information about students' career development and vocational needs (Rojewski, 2002). This approach is characterized by the use of informal assessment procedures (observational checklists, rating scales, critical incident reports) developed and used by local vocational and special service personnel, based on each student's learning needs. Curriculum-based vocational assessment has four distinct characteristics. First, it responds to the information needs of personnel during the beginning stage of planning a student's vocational program. Second, it views assessment as an integral part of a student's vocational education program. Third, it ensures that personnel conducting curriculum-based vocational assessment activities are also responsible for the student's vocational instruction. Fourth, it uses informal and direct methods to determine student achievement in the vocational education program.

Person-Centered Planning

Person-centered planning facilitates the assessment and planning process of students with disabilities. *Person-centered planning* refers to several strategies and techniques that may be used to promote personal choice and empowerment (Menchetti & Piland, in 2000). Although person-centered planning was not designed for transition planning purposes, the

Case for Action 12.1

Students in your classroom have just completed vocational aptitude tests. One student interested in veterinary science has scores that suggest an occupation with limited science and math competence. In talking with the student, you discover that the student's aunt is a veterinarian.

What guidance might you give this student in determining an appropriate career choice? How might you intervene in providing an occupational experience?

methods can be easily adapted and modified. Studies have been reported (Menchetti & Piland, 1998; Murphy & Rogan, 1995) noting adaptations designed for career planning purposes. Five common elements (Menchetti & Piland, 1998) of the person-centered planning process include:

1. Group facilitation and support
2. Capacity-based description
3. Positive vision of the future
4. Plan of action and commitments
5. Respect and empowerment

Person-centered plans and IEP transition plans are very similar. They provide the structure for transition assessment, including the future exploration of the student's strengths, needs, and preferences. Input is gathered and reviewed by the student and his or her person-centered team members. Person-centered plans promote student empowerment, choice, and self-determination (Menchetti & Piland, 2000). The focus is centered on the goals of the student and family and incorporated into the student's IEP planning process (Miner & Bates, 1997).

Curriculum-based vocational assessment is used to conduct formative and summative evaluation. Information can be gathered when determining placement, during participation in the program, and when exiting the program. This approach provides both ongoing information about students as they progress through their current vocational education programs and the information necessary to make decisions about future placements.

Career Awareness Process

Career development is a continuous process, beginning at birth and continuing until death. The development of this lifelong process is crucial to students with disabilities. Students may have severe deficits in academic areas and not be able to understand how these deficits might affect their lives when they leave school. *Career education* is defined as the process of systematically coordinating all school, family, and community components to facilitate each individual's potential for economic, social, and personal fulfillment (Brolin, 1997). Career education not only provides vocational preparation but also promotes awareness, exploration, decision making, entry, and advancement. Career education experiences should be integrated into regular education programs to provide a foundation for specific skills.

Career education makes a unique contribution to the educational system (Brolin, 1997):

1. Education and work interface in career education work.
2. All levels of education and all school personnel are affected by career education.
3. Career education and traditional subject matter coexist.
4. Career education and development occur in stages through carefully planned experiences.
5. Life skills, affective skills, and employability skills are the focus of career education.
6. Schools work more closely with families and community resources through career education.

Career education should also be a significant and integral part of the curriculum for school-aged youth with disabilities (Lloyd & Brolin, 1997). It focuses on the total life plan of an individual, facilitating growth and development in all life roles and settings. This total life plan is best represented in Brolin's (1997), which organizes 22 competencies (see Figure 12.1; p. 286) into three primary curriculum areas: daily living skills, personal social skills, and occupational guidance and preparation. Life-centered career education is designed to enhance and promote transition skills. Instruction for academic competencies in a student's program would support each of these three skill areas. For example, if the academic area to be taught is math and the skill area is daily living skills, the competency might be managing personal finances. Action Plan 12.2 notes six key points to be reviewed when considering such a curriculum.

Each of the 22 competencies and individual subcompetencies can be classified into one of the three curriculum skill areas. This classification can guide the teacher in developing educational objectives for each individual's program. Extensive assessment materials and instructional units are now available to assist educators in teaching students at all educational levels these 22 important competencies (Brolin, 1992).

Action Plan 12.2   Life-Centered Career Education

When infusing a life-centered career education model into your program, keep in mind that the model is

1. Community based	4. Cost effective
2. Competency based	5. Practical
3. Individualized to the student's needs	6. Manageable

Case for Action 12.2

Your school superintendent recently charged all faculty to develop a warranty program on the quality of its graduates. The superintendent stated, "Contractors give warranties on their homes. Car manufacturers give a warranty on their cars. Now, schools must give warranties on their products too." How does this responsibility affect your program and teaching? What action will you take?

Vocational Objectives

The development of goals and objectives that will lead to employment should be a concern of all educators. They should begin to focus on developing students' vocational competence in the preschool years and continue to do so through postsecondary levels, regardless of whether an individual is in an academic or a technical program. Goals should be specific to each individual and should be based on an assessment of what skills the learner needs in order to become an independent citizen. They should specify what skills and behaviors the student will learn in a year to increase the likelihood of achieving anticipated outcomes. Steere and Cavaiuolo (2002) offered several recommendations for developing goals and objectives that contribute to successful transition planning and the attainment of vocational aspirations. First, they suggested that outcomes be sufficiently clear to provide direction for the student's transition plan. Identifying outcomes is facilitated when students have the opportunity to job shadow or to complete job training or situational assessments. Person-centered planning (discussed earlier in this chapter) will assist the IEP team in establishing outcomes. Second, and on a related note, all goals and objectives should be stated clearly and unambiguously, describing exactly what the student will do and the level at which he or she will perform. Third, make sure goals and objectives are realistic. All team members, including the student and family members, need to understand the demands associated with different outcomes. For example, a career in veterinary science may not be a good choice for a student who has a history of poor performance in science classes. Fourth, connect anticipated outcomes to goals and objectives. Steere and Cavaiuolo suggested asking, "Will the attainment of this objective and the larger goal lead to attainment of the desired outcome?" (p. 57). For example, a math objective that addresses multiplication and division of fractions is not connected to the money skills required to use public transportation to get to and from work independently. Fifth, review and revise goals and expectations as students complete academic, social, and work experiences. Sixth, goals and objectives should provide direction for a plan of action that helps students achieve. Identify specific assignments, tasks, and experiences that will facilitate progress.

Functional Curriculum

The instructional strategies used to teach the necessary skills should be taught not only in a classroom but also in the natural environment. Training in natural environments may enhance the transfer of learning.

A *functional curriculum* is one in which students learn community-referenced skills in the most appropriate setting for specific skill acquisition (Wehman & Kregel, 1997). It is considered the conceptual framework for developing learning activities and experiences appropriate to adolescents and adults who are experiencing learning problems (Patton, Cronin, & Jairrels, 1997; Polloway & Patton, 1993). A functional curriculum prepares students for vocational competence and an independent life because it is based on the real-life experiences of individuals.

The functional curriculum approach outlined in Action Plan 12.3 (on p. 288) prepares students to function directly in the natural vocational settings in which they may be employed. This curriculum model served as a basis for Project PROGRESS, a model

FIGURE 12.1 *Life Centered Career Education (LCCE) Curriculum (Revised 1997)*

Curriculum Area	Competency	Subcompetency: The student will be able to:	
Daily Living Skills	1. Managing Personal Finances	1. Count money & make correct change	2. Make responsible expenditures
	2. Selecting & Managing a Household	7. Maintain home exterior/interior	8. Use basic appliances and tools
	3. Caring for Personal Needs	12. Demonstrate knowledge of physical fitness, nutrition & weight	13. Exhibit proper grooming & hygiene
	4. Raising Children & Meeting Marriage Responsibilities	17. Demonstrate physical care for raising children	18. Know psychological aspects of raising children
	5. Buying, Preparing & Consuming Food	20. Purchase food	21. Clean food preparation areas
	6. Buying & Caring for Clothing	26. Wash clean clothing	27. Purchase clothing
	7. Exhibiting Responsible Citizenship	29. Demonstrate knowledge of civil rights & responsibilities	30. Know nature of local, state & federal governments
	8. Utilizing Recreational Facilities & Engaging in Leisure	33. Demonstrate knowledge of available community resources	34. Choose & plan activities
	9. Getting Around the Community	38. Demonstrate knowledge of traffic rules & safety	39. Demonstrate knowledge & use of various means of transportation
Personal Social Skills	10. Achieving Self-Awareness	42. Identify physical & psychological needs	43. Identify interests & abilities
	11. Acquiring Self-Confidence	46. Express feelings of self-worth	47. Describe others' perception of self
	12. Achieving Socially Responsible Behavior	51. Develop respect for the rights & properties of others	52. Recognize authority & follow instructions
	13. Maintaining Good Interpersonal Skills	56. Demonstrate listening & responding skills	57. Establish & maintain close relationships
	14. Achieving Independence	59. Strive toward self-actualization	60. Demonstrate self-organization
	15. Making Adequate Decisions	62. Locate & utilize sources of assistance	63. Anticipate consequences
	16. Communicating with Others	67. Recognize & respond to emergency situations	68. Communicate with understanding
Occupational Guidance and Preparation	17. Knowing & Exploring Occupational Possibilities	70. Identify remunerative aspects of work	71. Locate sources of occupational & training information
	18. Selecting & Planning Occupational Choices	76. Make realistic occupational choices	77. Identify requirements of appropriate & available jobs
	19. Exhibiting Appropriate Work Habits & Behavior	81. Follow directions & observe regulations	82. Recognize importance of attendance & punctuality
	20. Seeking, Securing & Maintaining Employment	88. Search for a job	89. Apply for a job
	21. Exhibiting Sufficient Physical-Manual Skills	94. Demonstrate stamina & endurance	95. Demonstrate satisfactory balance & coordination
	22. Obtaining Specific Occupational Skills		

3. Keep basic financial records	4. Calculate & pay taxes	5. Use credit responsibly	6. Use banking services	
9. Select adequate housing	10. Set up household	11. Maintain home grounds		
14. Dress appropriately	15. Demonstrate knowledge of common illness, prevention & treatment	16. Practice personal safety		
19. Demonstrate marriage responsibilities				
22. Store food	23. Prepare meals	24. Demonstrate appropriate eating habits	25. Plan/eat balanced meals	
28. Iron, mend & store clothing				
31. Demonstrate knowledge of the law & ability to follow the law	32. Demonstrate knowledge of citizen rights & responsibilities			
35. Demonstrate knowledge of the value of recreation	36. Engage in group & individual activities	37. Plan vacation time		
40. Find way around the community	41. Drive a car			
44. Identify emotions	45. Demonstrate knowledge of physical self			
48. Accept & give praise	49. Accept & give criticism	50. Develop confidence in oneself		
53. Demonstrate appropriate behavior in public places	54. Know important character traits	55. Recognize personal roles		
58. Make & maintain friendships				
61. Demonstrate awareness of how one's behavior affects others				
64. Develop & evaluate alternatives	65. Recognize nature of a problem	66. Develop goal seeking behavior		
69. Know subtleties of communication				
72. Identify personal values met through work	73. Identify societal values met through work	74. Classify jobs into occupational categories	75. Investigate local occupational & training opportunities	
78. Identify occupational aptitudes	79. Identify major occupational interests	80. Identify major occupational needs		
83. Recognize importance of supervision	84. Demonstrate knowledge of occupational safety	85. Work with others	86. Meet demands for quality work	87. Work at a satisfactory rate
90. Interview for a job	91. Know how to maintain post-school occupational adjustments	92. Demonstrate knowledge of competitive standards	93. Know how to adjust to changes in employment	
96. Demonstrate manual dexterity	97. Demonstrate sensory discrimination			
There are no specific subcompetencies as they depend on skill being taught				

Action Plan 12.3

We recommend that the following steps be completed when developing a functional curriculum:

1. Identify current and/or future environments in which the learner is expected to participate.
2. Observe others in these settings to determine what skills are needed for successful participation.
3. Develop a skill checklist that assesses learner competence in using the skills required by the setting.
4. Observe the student performing the task and use the checklist to determine what skills the student possesses and what skills are lacking.
5. Determine what skills can be accommodated through prosthetics (e.g., calculators, charts, color codes, amplification).
6. Delineate developmentally sound task sequences to improve skill deficits not covered by prosthetics.
7. Provide educational experiences that promote the acquisition of the skill sequences.
8. Assess the learner using the skill checklist to determine the effectiveness of instruction and the degree to which the learner is prepared to participate in the target environment.

demonstration project for developing vocational skills in youth with mild and moderate disabilities (Schloss, McEwen, Lang, & Schwab, 1986). The first step is to identify future vocational settings in which the youth may be employed. This step may be accomplished through Brolin's (1997) Life Centered Career Education approach. Emphasis should be placed on the assessment of the student's career interests and aptitudes as well as the vocational opportunities available in the community.

The second step is to observe others in the specific vocational setting to determine the specific skills the student will need to succeed in the placement. In this step, all subenvironments of the vocational placement should be considered. For example, observations might reveal that successful workers are able to perform math, utilize social skills, and read the menu while at the customer order station. They are also able to exhibit assertiveness skills while in the employer's office and display specific social and personal skills while on lunch break in the employee's lounge.

The third step is to develop a checklist that can be used to evaluate performance of skills identified in the preceding step. This checklist indicates all skills necessary for success on the job. The skills should be listed in chronological order referenced to each subsetting (e.g., work floor, commissary, employer's office, washroom) in the vocational placement. The skills in the checklist should be based on the capabilities of the learner. Advanced students may benefit from a few more general entries such as "cleans the restroom," "arranges chairs in the seating area," or "takes orders." Less capable students may require a larger number of more precise entries such as "mops the floor," "cleans the sink," or "replaces the tissue paper."

The fifth step is to identify skills that can be developed through assistive devices. As a general rule, a prosthetic should be used any time the cost of training (i.e., time, effort, or actual expense) outweighs the disadvantages of relying on the artificial assistive device.

The sixth step is to establish developmentally sound task sequences. In this step, the educator determines the skills to be taught and the order of instruction. Instruction should be sequenced logically (Schloss et al., 1986). For example, it could be forward-chained from the first task to the last, or backward-chained from the last to the first used on the actual job. Again, the size of the chain should be matched to the capabilities of the student.

The seventh step is to provide instruction. We recommend using concrete materials, multiple modalities, distributed drill and practice, and frequent feedback. In many cases, the most direct and efficient form of instruction may be workstation simulation or actual on-the-job training. In other cases, basic-skills instruction in traditional academic classes may be advisable.

The last step in the functional curriculum sequence is to assess learner competence using the checklist developed in step 3. Success in each area of the checklist should indicate that the student is fully prepared to participate in the vocational setting.

As should be apparent from the preceding curriculum process, basic academic and interpersonal skills are likely to be among the skills required for most positions.

Basic Skills

Academic Skills   Vocational competence cannot be achieved without some basic academic skills. Levinson and Palmer (2005) suggested that academic skills included in vocational training should address reading and writing, math, problem solving, listening comprehension, speaking, and computer skills. At primary school levels, academic subjects are usually taught using worksheet and textbook exercises outside of a vocational context. Once the student advances to the secondary level, activities are directed to everyday living and vocational situations. Math activities might include budgeting and ordering; reading activities might focus on occupational manuals and directions. These activities can then be implemented in a community setting by performing them in a bank, grocery store, or auto shop.

Social Skills   Social skills have been identified as a key factor contributing to the success of individuals with disabilities (Black & Rojewski, 1998; Owens-Johnson & Johnson, 1999; Patton, Cronin, & Jairrels, 1997). Authors have reported that a lack of social skills is a major reason for the termination of employment (Black & Rojewski, 1998; Chadsey-Rusch, 1992; Hanley-Maxwell & Collet-Klingenberg, 1997). Along with basic academic skills, social skills should be taught in the primary grades through a functional approach. Basic skill building is taught in the primary grades, and the skills are implemented in vocational contexts in the secondary grades. Actual guided practice should take place in community and vocational settings. Levinson and Palmer (2005) suggested attention be given to telephone use, appropriate workplace behaviors, discussion of topics appropriate for the workplace, problem solving, protection from victimization, following and giving directions, and requesting and offering assistance. More information about enhancing social skills is presented in Chapter 14.

Personal Care Skills   Employment success also depends on skills related to grooming, hygiene, and dress. If individuals are to live independently, they must be able to care for themselves. Dressing, toileting, personal hygiene, and general nutrition are typical personal care components taught to primary-level students. In the secondary years, students may learn to purchase and care for items. For example, youngsters have their clothing selected for them and they are told when and where to wear it. As adults, they learn (1) how to plan and budget for their wardrobe; (2) what size, colors, and styles are appropriate; (3) when and where to wear specific clothes; and (4) how to care for clothing. Instruction geared to developing personal care skills should eventually take place in natural community settings. In the case of clothing, instruction could begin in the classroom and continue at a shopping center, laundry room, apartment, or employment setting.

Motor Skills   Motor skills will contribute to vocational competencies that rely on strength, speed, dexterity, coordination, and balance. The performance of motor skills will become increasingly refined with age. At the primary levels, fine and gross motor skills are developed through academic and recreational activities. Motor development is then directed to vocational activities in the secondary grades by the use of tools, keyboarding, and the manipulation of large objects. For example, students interested in quantity food production might develop motor skills by learning the proper use of cutlery and the use of large paddles and spoons.

Job Search Skills   Students should be proficient in basic job search skills regardless of the exact job that interests them. Levinson and Palmer (2005) suggested that several job search skills be developed, including using a newspaper to locate suitable positions, developing résumés, writing cover letters, obtaining and completing applications, obtaining appropriate identification, soliciting references, completing forms such as a W2, and participating in an interview.

Specific Goal Selection

As already mentioned, the functional curriculum approach takes into account student and community or industry needs. Therefore, the skills taught are based on those the student will need in real-life situations (Cartwright, Cartwright, & Ward, 1995).

After studying the needs of employers in light industry, Rusch, Schutz, Mithaug, Steward, and Mar (1982) developed an empirically based assessment and curriculum guide for individuals with learning disabilities. This assessment, the Vocational Assessment and Curriculum Guide (VACG), reviews eight performance categories important for employment success: attendance and endurance, independence, production, learning, behavior, communication skills, social skills, and grooming and eating. The results of an individual's performance on the assessment are interpreted on the basis of employers' expectations for each. Areas in which students scored less than expected by employers are suggested as student objectives. The VACG is one example of how community and industrial needs can be incorporated into the curriculum.

A student's success in society is often determined by his or her employment value. The employment value of individuals with disabilities has been stressed by their parents and advocates, as well as by local education agencies (Hutchins & Renzaglia, 1998). Vocational education programs must continue to evaluate the services offered and ensure that individuals with disabilities will acquire the vocational skills they need to adjust to community life. According to Renzaglia and Hutchins (1988), service providers must be able to perform five basic functions:

1. Identify potential employment opportunities.
2. Functionally assess the student or client.
3. Design an individualized vocational curriculum.
4. Select the appropriate training experiences and placements with respect to the abilities and needs of the individual and the prospective employer.
5. Using sound methodological procedures, effectively instruct persons with disabilities to successfully perform all necessary job requirements.

Performing functions 1 and 2 will aid in identifying the vocational programs that need to be provided. Specific skills can then be determined.

Historically, follow-up studies have been conducted in regular and vocational education programs. As noted earlier, these studies aid in measuring the effectiveness of education programs. They also produce a demographic record of educational outcomes. Follow-up studies focus on students' educational needs as well as their in-school experiences. Information received from these studies is an excellent resource for determining current employment trends of graduates and nongraduates, vocational/career awareness information received while enrolled in school, and vocational/career awareness information they might need to be successful in their present occupations.

A number of other resources may be used to determine employment trends and make educators aware of employment opportunities. Two excellent resources for projecting employment trends are publications printed by the U.S. Department of Labor: the *Dictionary of Occupational Titles (DOT)* (1991*)* and the *Occupational Outlook Handbook* (2006). These publications provide information regarding labor growth and opportunity.

This information may not always be applicable to an individual's location and may be inappropriate, owing to regional and economic differences. In this case, local and regional employers should be surveyed regarding projected labor growth, industry concern, turnover data, and identified areas of growth and opportunity. Suggested contacts are the Chamber of Commerce, employment offices, clubs and organizations, local employers, newspapers, telephone book, private industry councils, and school advisory councils. This information should then be reviewed and analyzed, and appropriate vocational programs for the location in question should be identified. Action Plan 12.4 presents some possible resources for various types of educational programs.

Once vocational programs have been identified, the practitioner should select the specific skills to be taught. These should include specific occupational and vocational competencies (e.g., interview skills), which can be identified by conducting on-site job analyses, employer interviews, and reviews of published research, curricula, and job-skill catalogs.

Case for Action 12.3

Two of your students want to participate in your school's vocational graphic arts program. You discussed their requests with the vocational director and were told that you must vouch for their competence after training. The director stated that students cannot be enrolled unless capable of success in their trained area.

You realize that this may be possible for one of the students. How would you pursue this conversation? What direction would you take?

Action Plan 12.4   Developing Vocational Programs

The following resources are useful when developing a vocational program:

School

Follow-up studies
Employer studies
Vocational placements
Advisory board members

Community

Employers
Private industry council
Chamber of Commerce
Small business association
Employment office
Telephone book
Newspaper
Radio/television
Internet

State/Nationwide

U.S. Department of Labor
U.S. Department of Commerce
U.S. Employment Service
Labor/apprenticeship programs
Dictionary of Occupational Titles (DOT)
Occupational Outlook Handbook
Specific occupational references
Newspapers
Periodicals
Reference books
Radio/television
Internet

Vocational education providers can thus obtain validated information that can help them define appropriate goals and objectives. Individuals with disabilities can then be evaluated to determine their level of competence, and appropriate individualized goals and objectives can be determined.

General Principles of Vocational Instruction

Vocational education is defined as an organized educational effort that directly prepares individuals for paid or unpaid employment requiring other than a baccalaureate or advanced degree (Sarkees-Wircenski & Scott, 1995). Vocational education encompasses all aspects of an occupation, including theory, occupational skill components, and nonoccupational skill components. In the teaching of vocational education theory and occupational skill-building components, it is usually assumed that nonoccupational skills are "givens," or are present. In teaching learners with disabilities, however, it is not appropriate to assume any givens. All vocational components should be taught.

Students in vocational programs are expected to be employable after completing a program. To ensure employability, they must meet certain proficiency and employability standards or competencies. Vocational programs should be competency based, with the curriculum and instruction focusing on the specific competencies necessary to successfully perform in a position.

Program competencies that ensure success in an occupation should be adjusted only as a last resort. Alternative intervention strategies should be considered when traditional strategies are not effective. Each student's goals and objectives should reflect his or her particular capabilities. This method enables the vocational teacher to match an individual student's abilities with realistic employment opportunities.

Specialized and integrated transitional services should be provided throughout the vocational program to help students experience a smooth transition from school to work. Special attention should be paid to ensuring that skills acquired in the vocational program are carried over to employment settings. The development of a transition plan by the special educator, vocational rehabilitation personnel, employers, parents, and others may serve this end.

Summary

Vocational education should be designed to provide a meaningful and practical experience for all learners with disabilities. The ultimate goal of vocational education is the successful integration of a student into the workforce. To meet this goal, educators may have to teach both specific occupational skills and basic academic skills. It is also important that students learn to be self-determined, in that they take greater control of their lives by making informed decisions, developing objectives to meet their goals, solving problems, and assuming responsibility.

The vocational evaluation process provides data that can be used to design and monitor the key components of vocational instruction. Aptitude tests are used to determine an individual's prospects for success in a given occupation. Curriculum-based vocational assessment uses informal procedures based on the student's individual learning needs. Person-centered planning refers to strategies and techniques used to promote personal choice and empowerment. These assessment techniques will provide data for determining placement, evaluating a student's progress during placement, and planning future goals.

Career education is a lifelong practice that enhances vocational instruction by providing a foundation for specific skills training. Life-centered career education is a useful approach in this regard because it organizes instruction into three curriculum areas: daily living skills, personal social skills, and occupational guidance and preparation. Academic competencies serve as a support to each of these curriculum areas.

Vocational goals and objectives should be based on an individual's strengths and weaknesses. The goals and objectives should maximize the individual's potential for independence in society. This process begins in primary levels and continues up to placement. It focuses on functional skills curricula leading to employment. These include academic, social, motor, and specific goal selection. A student's employment value has become increasingly important to society. Vocational programs need to continue evaluating their services to ensure that the skills acquired contribute to employment success.

Realistic program goals and objectives should be included in all vocational instruction programs. Investigating local and regional needs of employers and communities, follow-up studies of previous students, and literature reviews are examples of the resources that can help educators plan appropriate vocational programs. Programs based on business and industry's needs in your local or regional area will improve students' chances of success in employment placement.

Students with disabilities need to be taught all vocational skills, particularly non-occupational skills. Individual vocational goals and objectives will vary, but they should be flexible enough so that students can exit at any appropriate point.

13

Leisure Education for Positive Leisure Life-Styles

PHYLLIS JONES
DIANE LEA RYNDAK
BARBARA P. SIRVIS
DEBBIE S. ALCOULOUMRE

Did you know that . . .

- Leisure and a positive leisure life-style make a significant contribution to a person's overall mental health and life satisfaction?

- A person's leisure opportunities and experiences are related to his or her feelings of belonging in the community?

- Developing access to leisure opportunities for adolescents with disabilities can have a long-term impact on their social networks?

- The vast majority of adults without disabilities have not developed a positive leisure life-style?

- Leisure education is a much broader concept than the activity-oriented view familiar to most educators?

- Central to the concept of leisure are freedom of choice and control over your own actions?

- Opportunities for leisure occur in every environment?

- It is critical to include traditional, nontraditional, and contemporary aspects of adult leisure life-styles in leisure education programs for adolescents with disabilities?

- Leisure education must be individualized for adolescents with disabilities?

- For adolescents with disabilities, leisure education must be a distinctive component of the curriculum with specific objectives for each learner?

- Leisure is a means for developing and practicing self-determination?

- Leisure competence is developing a balance between an individual's skills and the demands/challenges of a particular activity or event (Csikszentmihalyi, 1990)?

Phyllis Jones is assistant professor, Department of Special Education, University of South Florida, Sarasota. Diane Lea Ryndak is associate professor, Department of Special Education, University of Florida in Gainesville. Barbara P. Sirvis is president of Southern Vermont College in Bennington. Debbie S. Alcouloumre is a community and vocational instructor for the Orleans Parish Schools in New Orleans, Louisiana.

Can you . . .

- Obtain information from the learner about his or her leisure preferences?

- Support a learner in making informed choices about his or her leisure options and experiences?

- Identify traditional, nontraditional, and contemporary leisure activities at work, at home, or in the community?

- Identify the general principles of leisure instruction?

- Obtain information about leisure options available and appropriate in a learner's environment?

- Identify the opportunities for leisure teaching and learning in a standards-based curriculum?

- Manage leisure instruction in a standards-based curriculum?

- Support the inclusion of a learner into extracurricular or integrated leisure programs with peers who do not have disabilities?

- Assess a learner's ability to participate in specific leisure options outside the school environment?

- Conduct a family inventory to identify leisure options important to teach a learner?

- Obtain information from a learner's peers and coworkers with and without disabilities about available and appropriate leisure options?

- Identify the most important leisure options to include in a learner's leisure education program and individualized transition plan?

- Incorporate content from other curricular areas into leisure instruction?

- Identify barriers to participation?

- Ensure that a learner is addressing and progressing on his or her leisure-related goals and objectives?

> Leisure is freedom to experience what is personally rewarding. The leisure experience reaches to the center of our development; it encourages self actualization. (Carter & Nelson, 1992, p. 25)

Leisure can occur anytime, anywhere. Historically, people thought that leisure could transpire only when they were not working, studying, or participating in activities related to survival. However, leisure can occur in the transition when something people have to do becomes something they want to do. Leisure occurs when a person experiences joy, satisfaction, and contentment; it also occurs as people improve their present skills and master new challenges. Leisure is laughter, pride in accomplishments, pursuit and fulfillment of dreams, and simple connections with others. Leisure pursuits are evolving constantly as society changes, which explains the current emphasis on technological elements of some leisure pursuits. Leisure occurs when people expect and plan for it, as well as when they are open enough to just "let it happen." Leisure is play; it is relationships; it is belonging, doing, and just being. Leisure is an integral part of a quality life-style.

Many individuals do not understand the role and function of leisure in their daily lives and frequently see leisure simply as a reward for surviving the stresses of life at work or at home. However, leisure fulfills a more important role in life. To achieve leisure satisfaction, people must learn to recognize, utilize, and enjoy leisure opportunities. They must discern when they have freedom, know how to make choices, and exert control within their environments to actualize leisure experiences. Participating in positive leisure experiences promotes an individual's feelings of belonging and acceptance in the local community. Leisure is self-defined and relies primarily on what an individual thinks and feels during an activity, rather than the activity itself. The leisure experience cannot be structured or taught; however, the ingredients of leisure can be taught and practiced. Educators can teach skills and behaviors that enable life-style choices concerning physical, social, intellectual, educational, and creative opportunities. These endeavors provide a basis for satisfaction with who a person is; what he or she is doing and with whom; and how to continually develop, change, and grow as an individual. This is a lifelong process that begins in the school years but continues into old age.

Imagine that someone you know was unable to use and enjoy his or her leisure opportunities. Imagine that person's boredom, loneliness, and frustration. Commonly, the more severe a person's disability, the more time the individual has to devote to leisure and the less likely it is that he or she will possess the skills and resources to plan for and use leisure opportunities. Feelings of isolation and segregation are common experiences of young learners with disabilities and their families (Jones, 2005; Jones, in press; Murray & Penman, 2000), and enabling greater participation in leisure opportunities will help to address these issues. Indeed, happiness indexes on persons with significant disabilities demonstrate a higher level of personal well-being in leisure experiences, rather than in work situations (Yu et al., 2002).

Young peoples' choices of leisure activities and the development of a positive leisure life-style are influenced by peers, media images, and personal security. All of these variables can have either a positive or a negative effect, depending on the extent to which each adolescent is prepared for leisure options and independence. The ability, right, and responsibility to choose one's own leisure life-style require active participation and practice. To facilitate choice making, learners must be supported in making choices across their educational experiences.

Leisure-related problems are particularly significant for today's adolescents. Often unsure about their emerging self-images, increasing numbers of children, adolescents, and working adults are using their unobligated time to turn to nonconstructive activities such as substance abuse, vandalism, or gang activities. The accessibility of drugs to all adolescents is high. In a recent report, 87.2% of high school seniors had easy access to marijuana, 57.4% to amphetamines, and 44.6% to cocaine (U.S. Department of Health and Human Services, 2002). The trend in substance abuse is at least as prevalent with learners with disabilities as with their typical peers—approximately 20% (Centre for Addiction and Mental Health, 1996). Newfound freedoms associated with adolescence include driving, more time unsupervised, and more options for personal choices. In addition, some adolescents with disabilities may feel forced to experiment with sexual intimacy before they are ready, or not have opportunities to participate in natural dating experiences, which is an important teenage ritual in learning to develop lifetime partners.

The Individuals with Disabilities Education Act (IDEA) of 1997 and its reauthorization of 2004 continued a national movement to educate learners with disabilities in the least restrictive environment (LRE). Inclusive education demands that both general and special education personnel engage in attitudinal and systemic change efforts that enable learners with diverse learning needs to receive a free and appropriate education in inclusive contexts (Olive & McEvoy, 2004). For this chapter, *inclusion at school* refers to the provision of special education and related services for learners with disabilities within general education settings and general education activities, along with general education classmates of the same chronological age (Ryndak & Alper, 2003). To be effective, an inclusive education program provides the learner both the support and the adaptations required to meet his or her individualized goals successfully within those settings and activities (Ryndak, Alper, Stuart, & Clark, in press; Ryndak, Jackson, & Billingsley, 2000). The success of including learners with disabilities also relies on the identification and removal of specific barriers to a learner's physical, social, and educational access (Frey, Buchanan, & Sandt, 2005), as well as preparation of their classmates with and without disabilities (Jackson, Ryndak, & Billingsley, 2001). Inclusive education presupposes that the learner with disabilities belongs within the school and classroom community, and the feeling of belonging emanates from the learner with disabilities, his or her classmates, each teacher, school staff members, and administrators (Ryndak et al., 2000). Tilton's (2000) description of inclusion encapsulates a wider community emphasis:

> A sense of community pervades the inclusive classroom. This sense of belonging goes beyond the classroom walls to parents and resources in the community itself. Together, adults and children form a partnership of respect for individual differences and a willingness to work together to help all students learn. (p. 16)

Learners with disabilities need to learn to identify and plan for unstructured time while developing the necessary attitudes and skills to engage in self-selected leisure activities. Making and maintaining friendships is an important element of this. Most of all, learners with disabilities need to discover and build their own leisure identity through practicing these skills and incorporating them into their daily lives. The education team and community workers need to (1) recognize the physical and attitudinal barriers that impact negatively on the leisure choices of an individual with disabilities and (2) develop services that address those barriers (Frey et al., 2005). Action Plan 13.1 lists ways that the education team can use the individualized education program (IEP) and the individualized transition program (ITP) to enhance the development of leisure skills by learners with disabilities.

In an era of standards-based education in which the call for accountability is strong (No Child Left Behind, 2002), the consideration of leisure programs can become an area of tension when teachers feel the pressure of high-stakes testing. In addition, leisure education can fall prey to funding cuts and be one of the first electives removed from the curriculum, reducing the choice of leisure-based programs. This situation is exacerbated for some learners with disabilities as, in some states, a regular high school diploma requires a leisure component, whereas a special diploma does not. However, learners with disabilities require a formal leisure education program if they are to implement a positive leisure life-style (Cordes & Howard, 2005). Leisure can provide an educational bridge to the inclusion of learners with disabilities in society. Collaborative working practices between general and special education teachers is essential so that learner- and curriculum-led priorities are considered and integrated into any leisure program. This chapter presents a framework for understanding the importance of leisure for adolescents who have disabilities. It emphasizes the use of information relevant to an individual adolescent to promote self-determination about the most important and relevant leisure education content for that learner. The purpose of this framework is to ensure that each adolescent is provided the opportunity to learn the social and leisure skills necessary to participate successfully, both

---

Action Plan 13.1   Leisure Education Programs and Individualized Education Programs (IEPs)

Educational plans must reflect the support that many learners need in order to engage in meaningful leisure lives both during and beyond the school years. Considerations might include one or more of the following:

1. Learners may need practice in cognitive skills (e.g., deciding, organizing, sequencing, and planning an activity).
2. Learners may experience problems with money or time management.
3. Social dilemmas may require skill development in (a) identifying and inviting friends to participate, (b) using social etiquette and appropriate interpersonal skills, (c) maintaining personal hygiene, (d) participating in social conversations, and/or (e) reacting appropriately to various situations.
4. Learners may experience physical difficulties with mobility, architectural barriers, fine or gross motor problems, and fatigue.
5. Learners may require assistance with (a) adapted leisure equipment; (b) understanding and following rules; (c) methods of participation or partial participation; or (d) emotional support and strategies to weather disappointments, loneliness, and rejection.
6. Learners may need to learn how to access activities, including transportation, locating facilities, and finding and procuring equipment and supplies.

---

immediately and in the future, in leisure options of their choice with peers with and without disabilities, coworkers, neighbors, and community members, thus ensuring a higher quality of life (Sheppard-Jones, Prout, & Kleinert, 2005).

Concepts of Leisure and Leisure Education

Leisure is a much broader concept than the activity-oriented view familiar to most educators. Most people do not realize the significant contribution of leisure and a positive leisure life-style to overall mental health and life satisfaction (Carter & Nelson, 1992). As outlined in Action Plan 13.2, leisure is a complex concept that incorporates opportunity, time, control and choice, activity, and personal satisfaction. Leisure is based on interests, priorities, competencies, and skills. It is a personalized process during which an individual makes choices to determine his or her own leisure life-style, which results in personal satisfaction. However, leisure pursuits can be influenced by the culture of society, including the media. Currently, there is an explosion of technological-based leisure pursuits ranging from Xbox and PlayStation to Web-based chatrooms and instant messaging. All adolescents, including those with disabilities, must be taught to make informed decisions while supporting their own personal safety. Technology can assist adolescents in this endeavor (Cordes & Howard, 2005). For example, Taber, Alberto, Hughes, and Seltzer (2002) demonstrated that adolescents with disabilities can use a cell phone to obtain assistance when lost.

Confusion and a lack of understanding about leisure often result from the inability to recognize the difference between *real* leisure and *enforced* leisure. Real leisure cannot be imposed on an individual (Brightbill, 1966). Rather, it is an activity that an individual

Action Plan 13.2   Concept of Leisure

Leisure is a personalized process in which an individual makes choices to determine his or her own leisure life-style, which will result in personal satisfaction. As such, it includes

1. Opportunity
2. Time
3. Choice
4. Activity
5. Personal satisfaction
6. Responsibility
7. Skills to meet activity challenges

Case for Action 13.1

Because it is outdated, your school district is revising its curriculum for learners with disabilities. As a member of the curriculum revision committee, you are responsible for developing the written narrative describing physical education and leisure education. How do you describe leisure education? How is it different from physical education and recreation?

---

freely chooses at a specific time because it brings personal satisfaction (Kelly, 1982). Freedom of choice, control, and responsibility over individual actions are central to the real issue: No two people, either with or without disabilities, will need or want the same leisure life-style.

Leisure education is the development of sufficient skills, knowledge, attitudes, and "abilities to participate in and be satisfied with leisure and recreation experiences" (Stumbo & Peterson, 1998, p. 83). Leisure education facilitates a learner's holistic growth in a number of ways, including social, emotional, academic, and physical development (Frey et al., 2005). It can be integrated into the curriculum to allow a meaningful outlet for skills taught in an academic program, enabling young people to apply their skills in varied social contexts. Thus, leisure education can provide the means for learning and using a number of applicable skills while also meeting its primary function of assisting learners in the development of concepts of choice, control, and responsibility that are critical to successful leisure (Sheppard-Jones et al., 2005).

For adolescents with and without disabilities, recreational activities can be used as a means to teach academic curriculum content. For adolescents with disabilities, however, leisure education must be an essential part of the curriculum. Leisure education is necessary "to eliminate, reduce, overcome or compensate for leisure barriers" (Stumbo & Peterson, 1998, p. 84) and to develop the necessary leisure skills, knowledge, attitudes, and abilities (Frey et al., 2005; Sheppard-Jones et al., 2005). In this way, leisure education is critical for adolescents with disabilities in developing both leisure skills and positive leisure life-styles. Indeed, leisure experiences for adolescents facilitate the development of social networks that may last long after school has ended. Stumbo and Peterson (1998) presented a clear model for the components of leisure education, including leisure awareness, social interaction skills, leisure activity skills, and identification and use of leisure resources. This model provides the framework for the instructional applications that follow.

Leisure awareness means knowing and understanding the concept of leisure, as well as the relevance of a positive leisure life-style to overall life satisfaction. Leisure life-style develops as an individual learns to assume responsibility for his or her personal behavior. Self-awareness also is an aspect of leisure awareness because individuals must understand their abilities and disabilities, both actual and perceived, in order to engage in successful choices of activities to meet their leisure goals. Recognition of one's personal attitudes toward activities, as well as the societal attitudes toward certain events, will shape options and choices. Personal selection, choice of leisure options, and related participation and decision-making skills are critical variables of this component.

Comfort with social *interactions* is critical for learners with disabilities to access the world, so instruction in social interactions must be incorporated into leisure education. Appropriate social skills are necessary to form and maintain relationships, which require social interactions. Learners need to know how to converse, share, listen, and be a friend, as well as respond during leisure options to (a) the social milieu, (b) the social culture, and (c) the age, number, and relationship of participants. Specific social skills can be taught, but because some learners experience difficulty in generalizing their use across inclusive situations, social skill instruction in inclusive settings must permeate every aspect of life. Learners must be taught not only basic social skills (e.g., eye contact, body spacing, etiquette) but also subtle social responses critical to success in inclusive settings (e.g., how to observe others within social situations to identify how their own behavior should be modified). In addition, learners practicing social interactions must demonstrate the flexibility that is intrinsic to relationships and the negotiation skills required to develop and maintain reciprocal friendships. For successful social interactions, learners must communicate, interact, and behave appropriately within the contexts of activities across inclusive settings.

Leisure activity skills are important to the overall leisure education program and a positive individual leisure life-style. For learners to develop a sense of competence, leisure skills must be taught, practiced, and developed, emphasizing the importance of an individual fully experiencing a leisure activity before deciding whether he or she likes it. This will be helpful when the component of choice is introduced in conjunction with instruction on the skills required to perform a leisure activity. In addition, activities should represent a broad range of leisure options across inclusive settings, not just the activities favored by members of the education team. To accomplish this, the education team may have to seek instructional assistance from others with skills relevant to different leisure options. When selecting leisure activities to be taught, the education team must consider and incorporate the needs and resources of the learner (e.g., transportation, financial resources) because each learner eventually will plan and initiate various leisure options based on his or her available resources. Although interactive activities can be emphasized, solitary leisure activities also should be included as typical adult forms of leisure that are especially useful during transitions (e.g., riding a bus) or during activities that require waiting (e.g., doing laundry).

Leisure resources constitute the fourth area of the leisure education model. If individuals are to have maximum choice and satisfaction, they need to know what leisure options are available. Learners should understand their own personal resources, including skills, finances, education level, and experience. They need to be able to identify resources that

Action Plan 13.3   General Principles of Leisure Instruction

To ensure effective leisure instruction, education teams should do the following:

1. Facilitate the learner's active participation in all aspects of leisure and developing the leisure education plan.
2. Provide the learner opportunities to choose leisure activities and determine the degree to which he or she will participate in that activity.
3. Provide systematic opportunities for practice and role-playing.
4. Develop the learner's competence in leisure activity and associated social skills.
5. Promote the learner's responsibility for self and personal decisions.
6. Facilitate the learner's participation in planning, initiating, and implementing leisure activities.
7. Provide the support needed from the family, peers, and social coach.
8. Provide instruction in real leisure activities of the learner's choice in his or her own environments.
9. Encourage the involvement of persons who are important to the learner, including nondisabled peers.
10. Facilitate the learner's becoming his or her own leisure advocate.

are available in their home and in their immediate community. Are their leisure resources limited, or do they have opportunities for leisure satisfaction at home (e.g., cooperative games with household members, cooking, gardening, reading materials)? What resources are available to assist with any necessary transportation? What portion of their income is available to spend on leisure? What local resources exist (e.g., YMCA/YWCA programs, community leisure service agencies, fitness centers)? Knowledge of the available resources, as well as skill and practice in accessing those resources, will facilitate the learner's acceptance of responsibility for his or her own leisure life-style.

As a learner practices leisure activities, instruction should incorporate choosing, planning, initiating, and implementing those activities, including steps such as making telephone calls, arranging for transportation, inviting a friend, and getting directions. To accomplish this, it is critical that the learner develop the skills to make positive choices and maintain reciprocal relationships, including dating relationships. Education teams can provide practice opportunities by assigning the learner to invite a friend over to participate in an interactive leisure activity. Although role-playing may provide opportunities to develop cursory skills, double dates with responsible and supportive friends also can be effective in providing age-appropriate models of dating behavior. It is important that the learner become his or her own leisure advocate. These principles are summarized in Action Plan 13.3.

Leisure Opportunities

The broad concept of leisure education takes into account the need for all of the components of the model proposed by Stumbo and Peterson (1998). Leisure education must take place in the actual places in which the learner will participate in recreation activities both now and in the future. In the development of programs, it is also important to consider an adolescent's preferences and the nature of the activities that may be part of the leisure life-style of an individual, as well as the contexts and environments in which the leisure occurs.

Opportunities for leisure occur in virtually any environment—at home, in school, in the community, and at work. This concept is often difficult to understand if only the traditional definitions of leisure are accepted, such as:

Sports and games	Computer games	Music
Aquatics and water-related activities	Literature	Dance
Arts and crafts	Mental games and activities	Drama
Outdoor activities	Theater	Hobbies

Stumbo and Peterson (1998), however, have suggested that some nontraditional leisure activities also can represent the *adult* contexts for leisure. These include, but are not limited to, the following:

Social interaction	Maintenance of living things	Fitness
Spectating and appreciating	(pets and plants)	Travel
Leadership and community service	Self-development	Shopping
Food preparation	Education	Eating
Relaxation and meditation	Internet social groups	Self-care
Cognitive and mental activities	Fantasy and daydreaming	

These lists are presented to provide examples of a broad definition of leisure that includes many traditional activities that are enjoyed by, and are appropriate for, adolescents who have disabilities. However, this broad definition also recognizes that leisure extends far beyond traditional activities and encompasses nontraditional and contemporary activities that are seldom consciously considered as leisure options. For example, our technologically advanced world involves leisure pursuits that can be based on the World Wide Web. Adolescents with and without disabilities need to have the skills necessary to participate safely in this aspect of leisure, including technological and personal safety skills. The preparation for a mature leisure life-style must be less structured than the life-style of childhood, adaptable to adult environments, and less time specific. However, many learners will always need a high level of structure and supervision in their leisure. It is critical, then, to consider the traditional, nontraditional, and contemporary aspects of adult leisure life-styles in the development of leisure education programs for adolescents who have disabilities.

In addition to recognizing the diverse nature of the choices that are available for leisure, education teams must recognize the numerous contexts and environments in which leisure might occur. By accepting the more diverse definition of leisure, it becomes easier to understand how leisure choice and satisfaction might occur in the home, at school, in the community, and at work. For example, a break for coffee or lunch at work can become an opportunity for social interaction while eating. Clearly, this experience can provide leisure satisfaction if the individual has the appropriate social and mealtime skills, as well as relationships with coworkers. It also is a good example of a leisure skill that can begin to be developed during lunchtime at school.

The attitudes, knowledge, and skills developed through direct and indirect leisure education can be applied in numerous settings and throughout a learner's life. The remainder of this chapter focuses on the development of a leisure education program for adolescents who have disabilities.

Remember that the ultimate goal is for the learner to develop a positive leisure life-style and personal satisfaction through the expression of free and informed choice. The model presented here has a community-based focus that integrates leisure education into existing curricula. The content should be incorporated into the curriculum in the same way that a positive leisure life-style is incorporated into an individual's life. Leisure education can be found in all areas of the curriculum, from the decision making and mathematics needed to select and pay for a movie to more traditional activities taught in physical education.

Traditional physical education curricula expose learners to activities that typically are not part of an adult leisure life-style; however, with a leisure education focus, physical education can be an opportunity for skill development related to fitness and wellness (Macias, Best, Bigge, & Musante, 2001). A few lifetime leisure activities appropriate for physical education might include bike riding, walking, hiking, jogging, swimming, bowling, dancing, weight lifting, aerobics, yoga, golf, bocce, tennis, or cross-country skiing. Physical education instruction should occur primarily across a variety of inclusive settings to enable learners to practice and generalize leisure skills (Piletic, 1998).

Clearly, leisure education is not solely the domain of physical education; it extends across numerous curricular areas. Reading can include newspapers and telephone books to identify community resources. Mathematics can apply budget management to include money for leisure options. Social studies can explore community structures that include leisure opportunities. Art and music should include participation and appreciation activities that provide potential leisure pursuits. Home economics can provide food preparation skills. Information technology (IT) can develop more technologically based leisure pursuits, as well as crucial life skills that adolescents with and without disabilities need to participate safely in a wide range of contemporary social activities (Davies, Stock, & Wehmeyer, 2002, 2003a, 2003b). The ultimate goal is preparation for a positive leisure life-style based on individual choices after developing a positive attitude, becoming aware of activity opportunities, and developing appropriate social interaction skills.

Mechanisms for Developing Leisure Opportunities

The best way to build a social network and create leisure opportunities is by participating in an ongoing, organized leisure group. Such groups usually meet one to five times a month around a similar interest. For children, groups such as Boy Scouts, Girl Scouts, and 4-H Clubs provide a structured social environment. For adolescents, there are clubs that meet for a whole range of social and physical interests. For example, learners can join religious social groups, book clubs, and political action groups. However, the participation of adolescents with disabilities must be supported because simple attendance at such clubs does not ensure active participation (Minton & Dodder, 2003). Leisure opportunities also can be developed when students volunteer for various community service groups, hospital auxiliaries, or school or church activities. In addition, many high schools have developed social clubs designed to facilitate social interactions and potential friendships between learners with disabilities and their peers with and without disabilities. Such groups provide adolescents with opportunities to meet peers with similar interests that may lead to the development of long-term friendships.

Friendships, however, may not develop automatically. Generally, friendships develop as learners participate in inclusive leisure opportunities with a designated peer who acts as a "social coach." This peer helps the learner with disabilities (a) become aware of how his or her behavior affects others, (b) learn to interpret others' body language, and (c) learn to accept feedback about social behaviors. If the learner does not understand social mores or conduct, the social coach answers questions, models appropriate behavior, and provides relevant feedback. The social coach provides opportunities for the learner to practice behaviors and role-play before the actual social event and provides emotional support as the learner navigates the social scene.

Identifying Appropriate Leisure Options

A *leisure option* is defined as an activity that is appropriate for a specific time and place; it is an activity in which individuals can choose to participate during their free time in order to achieve some level of personal satisfaction. To choose a leisure option, an individual must:

1. Have formed attitudes or preferences about the leisure options.
2. Recognize available time.
3. Know the leisure options that are appropriate and available during that free time.
4. Have the skills to participate in the leisure options.

The initial step in providing effective leisure education for adolescents with disabilities, then, is to determine the specific leisure options that are available and appropriate for each individual learner in an average week. Once the leisure options are identified, each adolescent can be taught the skills required to participate successfully in those options.

Inventories

One effective method of determining available and appropriate leisure options and resources for an adolescent with disabilities is to use inventories of relevant people and places in that adolescent's life (Ryndak & Alper, 2003; Ryndak et al., in press). Inventories can be completed for

1. The environments in which the adolescent currently participates or will participate in the near future, including the home, school, workplace, and community settings
2. The adolescent's family members
3. The adolescent's peers at school, in the community, and at work

Figure 13.1 displays a schema incorporating the procedures required when using numerous inventories to determine potentially appropriate leisure education content for an adolescent.

FIGURE 13.1 *Identifying Leisure Options Appropriate to Teach a Learner*

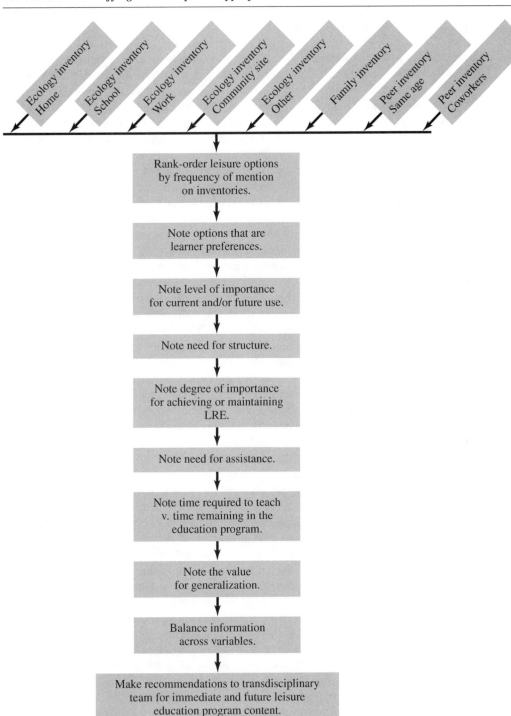

Such inventories allow the education team to change the focus of a program from predetermined content to content based on an individual adolescent's needs and choices (Ryndak & Alper, 2003; Ryndak et al., in press).

Inventories of Environments   Inventories of environments are concerned with the settings in which an adolescent spends time currently or in the near future (Ryndak & Alper, 2003; Ryndak et al., in press). As discussed in previous chapters, it is particularly important to identify both current and future environments for each adolescent to ensure that the learner has all the skills necessary to succeed both now and when leaving the education program. This information can then be used to build a leisure education program for each learner.

Inventories of environments are compiled in four steps by a team of people who are and/or will be involved in the learner's future (i.e., the learner, parents, teachers, and friends). In the first step, all of the environments that are or will be used by an adolescent are identified. These environments should include the adolescent's home, school, workplace, and community settings. Additional community settings might be identified through sources such as the Yellow Pages, local recreation department, community agencies, or youth organizations. In the second step, the environments are divided into subenvironments representing each of the areas of the main environment with which the learner comes into contact. In the next step, the education team identifies the leisure options that are available and appropriate in each of the subenvironments. The fourth step consists of identifying how the learner can participate independently in each of the leisure options.

In the following example, inventories are used to prepare an adolescent to use leisure effectively at home. First, identify both where the adolescent currently resides and the most probable options for homes after leaving the education program (e.g., independent or supported living in an apartment or home). Second, in each of these home settings, identify the subenvironments with which the adolescent will come into contact (e.g., bedroom, laundry area, balcony, entryway). Next, identify the leisure options that naturally occur in these subenvironments (e.g., listening to music, reading, barbecuing, conversing). Fourth, for each of these leisure options, list the steps the adolescent must complete in order to participate successfully in that leisure option. This list frequently is referred to as a *task analysis*. Although it is critical at this point to have a general idea of the skills required for each leisure option, it may not be necessary to complete a detailed task analysis at this time. Rather, it might be more appropriate to do so after identifying the priority leisure options for each learner.

To be effective, the procedure should be carried out for one subenvironment at a time. In this way, all of the leisure options in those subenvironments will be identified, along with the opportunities that regularly occur and the times to participate in those options. Once all of the leisure options have been identified, it is easy to move systematically through the list to determine whether each of the leisure options already has been taught to an adolescent. If it already has been taught, verify that the learner can participate effectively in that leisure option at the appropriate time in that setting. If a leisure option has not been taught to the adolescent, consciously choose either to teach that leisure option or not to teach it. The main reason not to teach a leisure option would be that the adolescent has a greater need or desire to learn another leisure option.

You might ask: How could one leisure option be more important to learn than another when both are appropriate and available in an environment? Here's an example: Adolescents are almost always taught traditional recreation activities, such as those found in almost every recreation curriculum. Frequently, however, educators neglect to teach adolescents how to use their time in situations that are not specifically leisure centered. A commonly neglected leisure opportunity that occurs in a subenvironment in the home is the time spent waiting for the wash cycle to end while doing laundry. Although this leisure opportunity occurs in most home environments, adolescents are seldom taught appropriate leisure options for this time. It might be important for an adolescent to learn a leisure option to fill this time in a positive manner to deter him or her from either wasting time or using the time in a destructive or troublemaking manner. This situation and its leisure options would then be considered more important than teaching the adolescent another leisure option in the home setting.

Family Inventories Numerous authors have described the use of a family inventory to determine the most appropriate curriculum content for learners with disabilities (Ryndak & Alper, 2003; Ryndak et al., in press). Completing a family inventory for an adolescent with disabilities requires a member of the education team to meet with the adolescent and his or her family members or other primary caregivers. During this meeting, a set of structured questions might be asked regarding the leisure options in which both the adolescent and the family members participate, and the leisure life-style already established by the adolescent. Through this set of questions, the education team should be able to determine:

1. The leisure pursuits of the young person
2. Leisure opportunities that occur throughout the adolescent's average week
3. Leisure options in which the adolescent already participates, with or without the family
4. The adolescent's level of performance in each of those leisure options
5. Leisure options in which the family participates, with or without the adolescent
6. Reasons for the adolescent's lack of participation in any of those family leisure options
7. Leisure option(s) that, once learned, would greatly increase the adolescent's participation in the family's leisure
8. The family's preferences regarding the content of the adolescent's leisure education program
9. Plans for future participation in leisure

This information can then be used to determine the most important and relevant leisure education curriculum content for the adolescent, in accordance with individual and family leisure life-styles. Because the adolescent will soon be transitioning out of educational services, consider not only the family with whom the adolescent currently resides, but also the new significant people with whom the adolescent may reside in the future. For instance, if an adolescent is exiting an education program and transitioning to an apartment-living program, obtain information on the following:

1. Leisure opportunities that occur in that apartment
2. Leisure options that are enjoyed by and important to the individuals with whom the adolescent most probably will be sharing the apartment
3. Leisure opportunities that occur in the neighborhood of the apartment

If the specific individuals with whom the adolescent will be residing are not known, comparable information should be obtained from other individuals who participate in the apartment-living program. Either way, this information is useful when determining the leisure life-style for which the adolescent must be prepared.

Peer Inventories   Another set of information that might assist in determining an adolescent's leisure education content involves identifying the leisure options encountered by peers with and without disabilities of the same chronological age and by coworkers (Ryndak & Alper, 2003; Ryndak et al., in press). This information can be obtained most easily by asking the adolescent's current and future peers about their weekly leisure options. For peers of the same chronological age, the questions included in this inventory should relate to the leisure options available at specific times at home, at school, in the community, and at work, as well as the times these options are available. For coworkers in similar positions, the questions should relate to the leisure options and the specific times available before, during, and after work hours. Through the use of information from inventories of peers and coworkers of the same age, adolescents can be prepared to participate in leisure activities with them.

Prioritizing Leisure Options from Inventories

After information is gathered from inventories of environments, family inventories, and inventories of a learner's peers, a summary can be developed. The goal of this process is to identify the leisure options that should be recommended to the learner and education team for immediate and future inclusion on IEPs.

Leisure Options from Inventories   The first step is to determine which leisure options appear on the inventories and how many times each leisure option is considered to be both available and appropriate across environments. It is possible that a leisure option is included in any combination of inventories of environments, family, or peers. When a leisure option is included on more than one inventory, it can be inferred that the learner will be able to participate in that leisure option in more than one environment once it is learned. In addition, the learner will be able to participate in that leisure option with the various people in those environments.

To determine whether a leisure option is a high priority, simply list each leisure option as it is included in the inventories, tally the number of times it appears on different inventories, and rank those options by the number of times they were identified. The more inventories on which a leisure option is included, the higher it will appear on the rank-ordered list. It will, therefore, be considered a higher priority for incorporation into an individual learner's leisure education program.

Figure 13.2 illustrates this process with an adolescent learner named Emily. In reviewing the information on inventories across her environments, family, and peers, six leisure options were mentioned most frequently. These options were listed in order of the frequency with which they were mentioned.

Learner Preference   The second step is to determine which of the identified leisure options are high-preference options for the learner. Because there is a tendency for adults to

FIGURE 13.2 Worksheet Example: Identifying Leisure Options Appropriate to Teach Emily

Rank Order	Leisure Option	Learner Preference	Use		Importance to LRE	Time (months)		Generalization	Prioritized Order
			Current	Future		To Teach	Left		
1	Reading or other leisure option while waiting	2	////	//// ///	Required	3	9	High	1
2	Window-shop alone	1	////	//// //	Required	6	9	High	2
3	Plant care	3	/	/	No effect	6	9	Low	6
4	Use of DVD	3	/	/	Helpful	1	9	Medium	5
5	Going to a movie alone	2	/	/	Helpful	5	9	High	3 or 4
6	Day at beach with friends	1	/	/	Required	4	9	High	3 or 4

overprotect adolescents with disabilities, it is critical that education teams emphasize the learner's self-determination strategies (Duvdevany, Ben-Zur, & Amber, 2002). Accordingly, this step requires the learner to make decisions about his or her leisure preferences, which enhances the potential for leisure satisfaction. The goal is to encourage learners to choose new options that interest them, and not necessarily activities with which they are already familiar. Teachers may need to encourage learners to choose activities in which they need to develop skills for participation. Learners need to be asked if they want, and are willing, to learn the skills necessary for participation in the identified leisure options. For every identified leisure option, complete information about learner preferences, necessary skills, and resources should be included.

List the leisure options selected by the learner from most to least desirable, and include this information on the worksheet. Rank as number one the leisure options that were selected independently by the learner as preferred choices. Rank the leisure options that were noted by the learner as ones he or she would like to learn as number two. Finally, rank the leisure options the learner did not want to learn as number three.

In reviewing our example for Emily in Figure 13.2, note that the preferred choices she selected independently were ranked second and sixth in the frequency with which they appeared on the inventories. With encouragement, Emily indicated that she also would like to learn the options ranked first and fifth. However, she did not show an interest in learning the options ranked third and fourth.

Use in Current and Future Situations   The third step is to identify the number of current and future situations in which the learner most likely could participate in each of the leisure options. Initially, this is done by counting the number of settings listed for each leisure option across the inventories. This information may be incomplete, however, if inventories were not completed across every environment and set of people with which the learner currently comes into contact, or will come into contact in the near future. However, it is important to make predictions about other situations, people, and environments that may be relevant to the learner and to decide which of the listed leisure options will be both available and appropriate. Add these predictions to the tally of current and future situations for each leisure option.

In Emily's case, the options ranked first and second are verified or anticipated as relevant for 10 settings each. The remaining options cannot compare with these options for the number of current and future environments in which they can be used.

Need for Structure   The fourth step is to determine whether each leisure option requires some sort of structure or organizing prior to the learner participating in it. For instance, planning may be required to have the necessary materials ready and available when the learner chooses to participate in a solitary leisure option (e.g., having personal reading material available when anticipating the need to wait; having plant care materials available). Planning also may be required for some of the steps that are part of the actual leisure option (e.g., inviting friends and arranging transportation to and from the beach). The degree to which the leisure option requires structure either before or during the activity, and the type of structure required, should be considered. The least intrusive type of structure should be determined, allowing the learner to maximally use his or her current skills while learning new skills. The need for structure should be noted on the worksheet.

Relevance for Inclusion The fifth step is to identify the degree to which each of the leisure options is required for the learner to become or to remain successful in inclusive settings. Inclusion for learners with disabilities is still an important issue because it is easy for those exiting an education program to revert to unnecessarily overprotective environments (Duvdevany et al., 2002). In the case of learners who are exiting the education program, the least restrictive environments should include (a) competitive jobs that are either supported or not supported; (b) the most independent home setting possible in the learner's community that allows maximum interaction with non-disabled peers; and (c) a self-selected leisure life-style incorporating interactions with peers, neighbors, family members, and coworkers. To prioritize the leisure options according to relevance for inclusion, determine the extent to which each leisure option:

1. Is *required* for achieving or maintaining inclusion in at least one environment (e.g., home or work setting)
2. Would be *helpful* in achieving or maintaining inclusion in at least one environment
3. Would have *no effect* on achieving or maintaining inclusion in any environment

Add this information to the worksheet.

In reviewing the information in the example for Emily, note that three of the options are required for her to either achieve or maintain access to inclusive settings. Two of the options are considered to be helpful, whereas one option would have no effect on her inclusion. There are numerous possible explanations for these rankings. For example, at times Emily may be required to wait calmly for short periods of time and keep herself constructively occupied. At other times, Emily may have free time all day and will need many leisure options to fill her day. The ranking of each option should match the situation in which Emily will be participating.

Need for Assistance The sixth step is to determine whether the learner will need ongoing assistance when participating in each leisure option. Although it may be assumed that the learner will need assistance to learn each leisure option, during this step consider whether the learner will need ongoing assistance once he or she has acquired the skills needed for participation in the leisure option. If the learner will always require assistance, determine what type of assistance will be required and who could provide that assistance. Remember to consider all types of assistance, and focus on the least intrusive form of assistance that allows the learner to be as independent as possible during the leisure option. Resort to person-centered assistance only when necessary, and when doing so, identify the least intrusive provider of assistance (e.g., individual naturally available in the location; friend or member of natural support network).

Instructional Time The seventh step is to determine the amount of time that will be required to teach each leisure option to the learner. Consider both the complexity of each leisure option and the learning rate demonstrated by the learner in the past on other tasks of similar complexity. Remember that the ultimate goal includes the learner's personal choice and independent participation in the leisure option. Therefore, when considering the complexity of each leisure option, include the following:

1. Developing attitudes or preferences about the leisure option
2. Learning to recognize when free time exists for engaging in a leisure option
3. Learning the leisure options that are appropriate and available during the free time
4. Learning the skills required to prepare for the leisure option, including skills such as transportation, preparation of materials, and organizing other participants in the leisure option
5. Learning the skills required to prepare for the next life activity, including skills such as ending the leisure option on time, getting transportation from the leisure option to the next scheduled life activity, and returning or replacing the materials used in the leisure option
6. Acquiring appropriate social, interactional, and behavioral skills for the activity

With this information, estimate the amount of time required for the learner to develop the skills for that leisure option with enough proficiency to participate successfully in the option in its natural environments. Record this time estimate on the worksheet under Time to Teach. The best estimate of the time required for the learner to learn a leisure option then must be compared with the amount of time left in the learner's education program.

In our example, Emily has nine months left for special education services. Because of her past learning rates and the amount of instructional time available for leisure education in her school day, it was estimated that between one and six months would be required to teach each of these leisure options.

Generalization   The final step on the worksheet is to determine whether the leisure option will generalize to other inclusive environments, because it is possible that a leisure option for one inclusive environment also might be appropriate and available in others. For example, the learner could participate in solitary activities (e.g., reading, needlepoint, letter writing) while at home, on break at work, or riding the bus. The skills needed to participate in one leisure option also may be needed for other leisure options. For instance, learners will require appropriate interaction and social skills, ability to take turns, appropriate behavior, transportation skills, and money management skills when participating in many activities.

Whenever overlap occurs, those leisure options should be considered higher priorities than the leisure options that will neither be usable in other environments nor teach skills that are needed for other activities. To complete the worksheet in this area, simply determine whether each leisure option has a high, medium, or low probability of generalizing to other environments or activities. This information can then be added to the worksheet.

In reviewing the example for Emily, four options are noted to have a high probability of generalizing to other environments or activities. Only the third option, plant care, is considered to have a low probability of generalizing for Emily.

Identifying High-Priority Leisure Options   Once the worksheet is completed, the next task is to review all of the information collected. Pay particular attention to the leisure options that were ranked as the highest priorities across the columns. If those leisure options match, it is easy for the education team to select them. If those options do not match, however, weigh the importance of the areas on the worksheet. Decide which of the areas is most critical for the learner's successful participation in current and future environments.

Action Plan 13.4   Variables for Prioritizing Leisure Options

Several variables must be considered when prioritizing leisure options for inclusion in a learner's leisure education program:

1. The number of inventories on which a leisure option is included
2. The extent to which the learner demonstrates preference for a leisure option
3. The number of current and future environments in which the leisure option can appropriately occur
4. The importance of the leisure option for achieving or maintaining access to the learner's least restrictive environments
5. The estimated amount of time required to successfully teach the leisure option to the learner, compared with the amount of educational time remaining for the learner
6. The degree to which the skills learned to enable the learner to participate in the leisure option will generalize to other environments or activities
7. The ability of the learner to participate independently or at least with the amount of support available

Action Plan 13.4 lists variables the education team should consider when prioritizing leisure options.

Careful consideration should be given to the learner's stated preferences. Learner preference provides the motivation for learning all the necessary skills and increases the probability of future participation. Other issues, however, may take priority. For instance, if particular leisure skills are important for the learner to remain employed in an inclusive setting, those leisure skills may become critical to teach, even if the associated leisure option ranked low in generalization and learner preference.

When reviewing the options selected as the highest priorities for Emily, note that the first priority is a leisure option in which she can participate while waiting for short times, such as reading. This option is one that is acceptable to Emily, is relevant to the largest number of inclusive settings, can be taught within her remaining time in education, and has a high probability of generalizing to other environments and activities. In contrast, the third option, plant care, has the lowest priority. Although it can be taught in the time remaining in her education program, it is an option that Emily does not want to learn, is not relevant to many of her environments, will have no effect on her inclusion, and has a low probability of generalizing to other inclusive environments or activities.

The difficult decision for Emily's leisure education program comes when selecting the third-priority option. In her case, careful consideration must be given to the amount of time required to teach the first two options. If three months are required to teach the first prioritized option (i.e., a leisure option while waiting) and six months are required to teach the second prioritized option (i.e., window-shopping alone), Emily's remaining education time has been allocated already. There is a possibility, however, that Emily will learn these two leisure options more quickly than projected. If this occurs and there is a month remaining at the end of the school year, which leisure option should be taught to Emily? Because the second-priority option (i.e., window-shopping) will take about six months, a decision about the third option can wait. This gives Emily's teacher the opportunity to

---

Case for Action 13.2

Your new classroom assignment is in a high school with learners who have mild disabilities. In developing IEPs, you want to be certain to address each learner's leisure educational needs. What steps will you complete to determine the most important leisure education for each learner?

---

see how quickly and how well Emily can learn the skills required for both reading during short periods and window-shopping. Based on this new information, Emily's teacher can reestimate the amount of education time required to teach the other two options and make a better-informed decision.

Cross-Curriculum Instructional Content Addressed through Leisure Education

Leisure education automatically creates opportunities for a learner to practice skills traditionally taught in other curricular areas. With the additional mandates of No Child Left Behind (2002), this opportunity is an important educational element. It is crucial to consider each of the curriculum areas that are relevant for an adolescent with disabilities and to incorporate those areas whenever possible into the leisure education program. Gardner, Wissick, Schweder, Canter, and Smith (2003) described an integrated and thematic teaching model as one that "cuts across subject matter lines, bringing together curriculum and real world situations, which are interactive" (p. 161). For example, money use and management are traditionally taught within the math curriculum. The contents of the math curriculum traditionally are taught during a specific period of the instructional day. When including leisure education in the curriculum, it is possible to incorporate instruction of money use and management skills within leisure instruction. Money skills are needed when learners (a) must determine whether they have the resources to participate in a leisure option, (b) participate in a leisure option that costs money (e.g., admission to a movie), or (c) purchase the items required for the leisure option (e.g., audiocassette tapes). Similar examples can be cited for almost every curriculum area traditionally included in the education program for adolescents with disabilities. Figure 13.3 lists some of these curriculum areas in a worksheet format.

When using this worksheet, list across the top the priority leisure options identified for a learner. For each leisure option, delineate the ways in which various curriculum areas

---

Case for Action 13.3

To maximize the effectiveness of your instructional efforts throughout the year, you want to integrate your instruction for each curricular area into the other areas. How will you determine what other curricular content you can integrate throughout your leisure education program?

FIGURE 13.3 *Worksheet: Cross-Curriculum Content within Identified Priority Leisure Options*

Learner: _____

	Priority Activity 1	*Priority Activity 2*	*Priority Activity 3*
Transportation to, during, or from leisure option			
Social behaviors and interaction			
Self-care and hygiene			
Functional or leisure reading			
Money use and management			
Written communication			
Time use and management			
Leisure option participation			

Time and place
for instruction of
cross-curriculum content

In classroom	Cross-curriculum content	Cross-curriculum content	Cross-curriculum content
(1)	(a)	(a)	(a)
(2)	(b)	(b)	(b)

In school	Cross-curriculum content	Cross-curriculum content	Cross-curriculum content
(1)	(a)	(a)	(a)
(2)	(b)	(b)	(b)

In community	Cross-curriculum content	Cross-curriculum content	Cross-curriculum content
(1)	(a)	(a)	(a)
(2)	(b)	(b)	(b)

can be addressed throughout the leisure education program. In addition, the worksheet provides a place to identify the situations that will be used for instruction in the classroom, school, and community. In each of those locations, identify which of the delineated curriculum areas will be incorporated into the instruction. In this way, education teams can maximize the time and situations in which a learner is able to use the skills addressed throughout the curriculum.

Other curriculum areas can be added easily or substituted on this list (e.g., information technology, self-esteem, personal responsibility, choice making). Each of these is critical to the development of a positive leisure life-style for any adolescent with disabilities. Determine the curriculum areas for a learner on the basis of his or her particular strengths and weaknesses. In this way, the education team can provide each learner with the most opportunities to learn and practice the skills required for success in his or her environment.

Summary

Leisure education should be an important aspect of the curriculum for all adolescent learners, but especially for those learners with disabilities. As leisure is not necessarily a required element of a special diploma in some states, it is crucial to make space for it in the high school curriculum. Leisure provides opportunities for self-satisfaction and individual choice that are important elements of human development. The establishment of a positive leisure life-style will have lifetime benefits in all settings. If left to chance, it is likely that learners with disabilities will develop television watching as their main leisure activity. Although fine in moderation, as a main leisure activity it can lead to a sedentary and unhealthy life-style while further isolating learners with disabilities.

Leisure education should be incorporated into all aspects of curricula for adolescents with disabilities. The skills for decision making, social interaction, and community resource use essential to leisure education are part of the larger life-preparation aspects of education. Although it is important for all adolescents to learn to manage peer pressure and to select appropriate activities for participation, these skills are even more important for adolescents with disabilities. The goal of any leisure education program must be the development of self-determination for adolescents with disabilities.

Social Skill Instruction

Did you know that . . .

- Social competence is a consideration in the determination that a student may have a learning disability, retardation, or emotional disturbance?

- Social competence is a major factor contributing to the success of community integration for individuals who have disabilities?

- Social skill deficits are frequently the cause of terminations from employment for individuals with disabilities?

- Information gained from social skill assessments can be used to identify goals and objectives for individuals who have disabilities?

- Teacher-developed instruments can be used to assess social skills?

- When developing social skill goals and objectives, one should attempt to look at the overall level of social competence and investigate how target behaviors relate to this total picture?

- A functional social skills program will aid in the acquisition of appropriate skills?

- Training procedures can be evaluated to determine their appropriateness for a given individual?

- Teachers can determine when a specific social skill should be taught?

Can you . . .

- Define social skills?

- Distinguish between social competence and social skills?

- Explain why the level of social competence may indicate the least restrictive environment appropriate for youth?

- Describe six assessment procedures that are used to determine social skill deficits?

- Describe the difference between in vivo and analogue observations?

- Explain how social competence and adaptive behaviors relate?

- Explain how prosocial responses will affect an individual's behavior in society?
- Describe a social skills training package?
- Differentiate between affect, cognition, and specific skills training programs?

- Explain why deficits in social skills might promote low self-esteem?

According to Gresham, Sugai, and Horner (2001), the ability to interact successfully with peers and adults is a hallmark of student development. Social competence is gaining increasing attention from professionals seeking to integrate students with disabilities into the mainstream of education and society. Students who are socially successful are more likely to become adults who are socially competent, capable of engaging in positive relationships with others, and contributing to their communities (Smith & Travis, 2001). A lack of social skills has been reported to relate directly to depressed academic achievement (Bender, 1987; Cartledge & Kiarie, 2001; Gresham, 1982; Gresham & Elliott, 1989; Hallahan & Kauffman, 2000). This deficit might be attributed to the importance of student-to-student interactions during instruction and the fact that teachers react more favorably to students who are socially skillful (Adelman, 1998; Mercer & Mercer, 2005; Polloway & Patton, 2004).

A lack of social skills has been found to affect teacher willingness to include students in the general education classroom (Kauffman, Lloyd, & McGee, 1989). One study found that teachers and professionals ranked social skills as being the most important curricular area for students with learning disabilities and moderate developmental disabilities (Baumgart, Filler, & Askvig, 1991). Students with poor social skills experience a higher rate of peer rejection, increasing the likelihood of adjustment problems in adolescence and adulthood (Cartledge & Kiarie, 2001). In their review of the literature, Smith and Traivis (2001) noted that long-range effects of poor social skills include delinquency, dropping out of school, and, as adults, mental health problems.

Intelligence, specific disabling conditions, and academic achievement have not appeared to be the primary factors contributing to the success of an individual's integration in school and the community integration (Smith, Polloway, Patton, & Dowdy, 2004; Schloss & Schloss, 1987). Instead, personal characteristics—including personal adjustment, initiative, self-esteem, and social competence—have been reported to directly affect success in being included in society (Bender, 1987; Goldstein, Sprafkin, Gershaw, & Klein, 1997; Mercer & Mercer, 2005; Salend, 1999, 2004; Schloss & Schloss, 1987; Walker, Schwarz, Nippold, Nippold, Irvin, & Noell, 1994).

Social competence plays a significant role for students with disabilities. First, it has been a consideration in determining whether a student has a disability. The definition for mental retardation emphasizes the role of social competence. It is also one of several criteria used to identify students with emotional or behavior problems. Finally, although not a formal part of the definition for a learning disability, many students with LD have difficulties with social competence (Gresham et al., 2001).

Second, social competence greatly affects the placement of students in the least restrictive environment. A student who is deficient in social skills may find placement in a general education classroom unbearable and restrictive. Deficits in social competence may lead to aggression, withdrawal, or inappropriate adaptive behaviors (Bender & Golden, 1988; Carter & Sugai, 1988; Heavy, Adelman, Nelson, & Smith, 1989) and thus may promote low self-esteem for the individual (Smith & Travis, 2001). An individual student's social skill deficits may also be a principal source of conflict with peers, teachers, and school and community authorities. However, placement in a more restrictive setting may not be the answer as students in self-contained classes may have as peers other students whose social skill repertoires are just as limited. Legislation in the fields of special education, vocational education, and rehabilitation has encouraged people to support the placement of individuals with disabilities in functional community situations. This trend promotes integrated opportunities for individuals with disabilities, allowing them to profit from socially competent models (Blackbourn, 1989; Gresham, 1981). As Smith and Travis (2001) noted, simply placing students in classrooms with typical peers does not result in "spontaneous improvement" (p. 361) of social skills. Individuals who have disabilities do not automatically interact with peers, disabled or nondisabled, and may not acquire social competence vicariously through observation of these individuals (Cartwright, Cartwright, & Ward, 1995; Hughes et al., 1999). Establishing a social skills program has proved to be effective in promoting the acquisition of social competence (Hallahan & Kauffman, 2000; Polloway & Patton, 2004; Walker et al., 1994).

Outside of school, the specific disabling condition and achievement do not appear to be influential variables in the employment success of individuals with disabilities. Those components that do intervene and promote occupational success include personal adjustment, self-assurance, self-esteem, initiative, and social competence (Black & Rojewski, 1998; Chadsey, Linneman, Rusch, & Cimera, 1997; Goldstein et al., 1997; Masters, Mori, & Mori, 1999).

Greenspan and Shoultz (1981) conducted a study to determine why individuals with mental retardation were terminated from competitive employment. Results showed that the inability to interact effectively with other people often causes termination. Occupational skill level was not a major factor. Extending this finding, Schloss and Schloss (1985) have argued that adjustment problems in employment settings often result from an inability to integrate socially in the work setting. The employee with disabilities is often viewed negatively because he or she fails to interact effectively with supervisors, coworkers, and customers. Deficiencies in social functioning are often overgeneralized to correlate with deficiencies in overall performance.

Social skill training programs have had a positive impact on students with disabilities and highlight the importance of integrating social skill objectives into a school's curriculum (Blackbourn, 1989; Moore, Cartledge, & Heckaman, 1995; Walker et al., 1994). Social skill programs should incorporate a positive approach, emphasizing skill building in deficit areas and maximizing the potential of an individual with disabilities for success in school and the community.

Definition of Social Skills

Social skills are complex abilities that a person needs to adjust to changing social demands. They depend on the specific social context (Masters et al., 1999). Individuals must develop flexible social response mechanisms that will allow behavior to change as each situation demands. The inability to change behavior or responses usually results in rejection or failure.

Repeatedly, the term *social skill* has been defined using two different conceptual approaches: (1) a global reference to the domain of social competence and (2) an emphasis on situation-specific responses. Exemplifying the global approach, Hersen and Bellack (1986) defined *social competence* as the effectiveness of an individual to state positive and negative feelings without producing negative feelings in others. Gresham and colleagues (2001) defined *social competence* as the "degree to which students are able to establish and maintain satisfactory interpersonal relationships, gain peer acceptance, establish and maintain friendships, and terminate negative or pernicious interpersonal relationships" (p. 331). Other researchers have supported these definitions, emphasizing that social competence will produce satisfying consequences from the environment (Gresham, 1997; Gresham & MacMillan, 1997; Polloway & Patton, 2004). Smith and Travis (2001) suggested that social competence is a trait. It includes all responses that "produce, maintain, or enhance positive effects for behaviors" (p. 362). Unfortunately, it is possible that this definition could include behaviors most people would regard as socially inappropriate. For example, we were acquainted with a young man who used to obtain cigarettes from his peers by threatening them. Having obtained the cigarettes, he again threatened to hurt his peers if they told any adult about his behavior. Thus, he was able to obtain his goal (i.e., getting cigarettes) through the use of inappropriate behaviors (i.e., threatening) with no negative consequences (punishment from adults). Most of us would agree that this behavior does not constitute social competence.

The specific approach emphasizes the idiosyncratic nature of *social skills.* Smith and Travis (2001) defined *social skills* as discrete, observable behaviors that result in successful social interactions. These skills increase the likelihood that a learner will earn or maintain social reinforcement and decrease the likelihood that the learner will experience punishment. Social skills are isolated and situation specific; different social responses may be demonstrated in various environmental contexts. Appropriate social skill responses during vocational activities will vary from those in consumer or recreational activities. For example, it is desirable to interact freely during leisure skill pursuits. However, frequent interactions may be a cause for terminating employment.

For instructional purposes, the situation-specific approach has greater utility because it allows educators to target and assess specific skills (Fulk, Brigham, & Lohman, 1998; Mathur & Rutherford, 1994; Polloway & Patton, 2004; Storey, 1997; Walker et al., 1994). For example, social–vocational survival skills would include those behaviors that "increase the likelihood of successful competitive employment in any vocational setting" (Rusch, 1979, p. 143). Social–consumer survival skills might include those behaviors that promote the likelihood of successful consumer actions (e.g., purchasing groceries at a grocery store). Instruction can be directed precisely at this objective.

Even greater specificity can be achieved by considering the exact nature of expected responses. Some might include eye gazing, conversational skills, question asking, self-disclosures, and compliments (Hartas & Donahue, 1997; Mathur & Rutherford, 1994; Moore et al., 1995). A specific skill approach can help improve the management of a general skills approach: (1) students are aware of associations with specific interpersonal contexts, (2) responses are available in reliable observations, (3) skills can be matched to the student's chronological age, and (4) specific social skills are constructive in nature, leading directly to the formulation of goals and objectives.

Establishing Objectives

Specific definitions of social competence must be integrated into a larger conceptual system or curriculum. This curriculum should reflect the complexity of the learner as well as his or her social environment. Of specific concern is the interrelationship between variables, including the student's skill deficits, developmentally appropriate skills displayed by the student's cohorts, and social skills expected by significant individuals in the school and community (Hickson, Golden, Khemka, Urv, & Yamusah, 1998; Hughes et al., 1999; Ohtake & Chadsey, 1999). Students with mental disabilities tend to require more sharply focused training in role taking, decision making, discriminating decisions, and understanding what others are perceiving, thinking, and feeling. Vaughn, Ridley, and Cox (1983) have identified several skills necessary for an individual to be socially competent. An instructional program was designed around these skills and includes the following components: (1) fundamental language concepts, (2) cue sensitivity, (3) goal identification, (4) empathy, (5) alternative thinking, (6) consequential thinking, (7) procedural thinking, and (8) integrating skills.

Social competence must be taught to youth in the schools to ensure that they will adjust to the community after school. Specific objectives to be taught should be related to the characteristics of each student. Of specific concern are the student's age and cognitive abilities (Prater, Bruhl, & Serna, 1998; Schloss & Smith, 1998). Sargent (1988, p. 10) developed six questions to aid teachers in determining when a specific social skill should be taught:

1. Is the social skill deficient or inadequate?
2. Does the student have the cognitive ability to learn the skill?
3. Will the student have sufficient opportunity to practice the skill?
4. Will changing the student's behavior affect significant others in the student's life?
5. Is the skill needed in current or anticipated environments?
6. Is acquisition of the skill essential to the individual's ability to remain in [his or her] current environment?

Consistent with this view, Schloss and Smith (1990) have suggested the following considerations for identifying social skill objectives:

1. *Partner:* The relationship of the student to those with whom he or she is interacting is a critical variable. A student might be taught to be informal, brief, irreverent, and so on when interacting with peers. He or she might be instructed to be more formal, respectful, elaborate, and so on when talking to an employment supervisor or school administrator.
2. *Setting:* The environment in which the social interactions are occurring is another variable in determining the specific social skills to be taught. As with the partner variable, more informal interactions might be appropriate in home and leisure settings. Conversely, more elaborate and "proper" interpersonal behavior might be expected in school, work, and consumer settings.

3. *Major skill area:* Another consideration, and possibly the most important, is that the actual purpose for the interaction will have a major influence on the actual skill. Questioning, complimenting, engaging in small talk, and criticizing are all potentially discrete skills. Each may involve different interpersonal responses.

4. *Role (to v. from):* The role of the student is the last element in arriving at final objectives. Asking whether the student is principally receiving the compliment or criticism or delivering the interaction will help the teacher determine the role the student should be trained to perform.

Schloss and Smith (1990) have provided the table in Figure 14.1 to illustrate the manner in which these considerations are interdependent. Using the preceding variables, 280 cells are constructed. The first cell, indicating one potential objective, is teaching how to ask questions in order to obtain information from an adult at home. The final cell is teaching how to criticize a peer for damaging property in a leisure setting.

Social Validation of Goals and Objectives

A question that constantly arises when developing social skills programs is that of social validation: To what extent does this program affect one's social behavior in society? Will this new behavior promote positive reinforcers? Validation of a social skills program will help students with disabilities gain prosocial responses (Gresham et al., 2001; Matson & DiLorenzo, 1986; Mathur & Rutherford, 1996; Schloss & Smith, 1998; Smith & Travis, 2001). These responses will (1) enlarge the number of people with whom they interact, (2) increase the number of positive social reinforcers they receive, (3) decrease the number of aversive events, and (4) promote self-control when they are confronted by environmental situations. Socially validated criteria must be developed before a skills program is implemented.

Implementing a social skills program depends on three measures of social validity (Wolf, 1978): (1) the significance of the goals, (2) the importance of the effects of the program, and (3) the appropriateness of the procedures used to implement the program. Measuring the significance of a program's goals is to ask: Is this the prosocial response society wants? To find the answer, it is important to socially compare responses (Maag, 1989; Matson & DiLorenzo, 1986; Schloss & Smith, 1998) by observing a group of individuals under a range of natural conditions. For example, when determining criteria for complimenting a person of the opposite sex, several individuals (of both sexes) are observed complimenting individuals of the opposite sex in work, school, and social settings. Another strategy would be to ask individuals for feedback specific to a setting. For example, interview a teacher when observing in a school setting. This strategy, although subjective, will help to establish the social importance of the program's effect.

Measuring the appropriateness of training procedures can be accomplished by answering one of three questions: (1) Is the intensity of each training procedure justified by the program's final outcome? (2) Are the training procedures the most appropriate means to achieve the final outcome? and (3) Is the program cost-effective? These questions can be answered easily and will provide socially validating information for a social skills program before it is implemented. Justifying the intensity of objectives can be done by collecting relevant information pertaining to the students' reaction to the impact of the program. This

FIGURE 14.1 *Table Showing Interdependence of Social Skills*

Setting		Home				School				Work				Consumer				Leisure			
Major Skill Area / **Subareas**	Partner	from adult	from peer	to adult	to peer	from adult	from peer	to adult	to peer	from adult	from peer	to adult	to peer	from adult	from peer	to adult	to peer	from adult	from peer	to adult	to peer
Questions — Requesting information																					
Favor																					
Assistance																					
Invitation																					
Compliments — Global																					
Appearance																					
Skill level																					
Possession																					
Small Talk — Initiating																					
Terminating																					
Criticisms — Appearance																					
Violating rules																					
Skill level																					
Damaging property																					

Source: Schloss, P. J., and Smith, M. A. (1990). A matrix for social skill assessment and intervention priorities [Figure 2-2]. In *Social Skills Training Strategies for Hearing Impaired Children and Youth* (p. 19). Reprinted with permission of the Alexander Graham Bell Association for the Deaf and Hard of Hearing (www.agbell.org).

can also be completed for other concerned individuals (e.g., parents, school principal). When determining what training procedures would be most appropriate to accomplish a

Case for Action 14.1

Your students continue to show deficits in social competence and you would like to implement a structured program in your curriculum. To do this, you first must write a rationale and submit it to your principal. Describe your rationale.

specific goal, it is important to select the ones to be used with great care. Various researchers (Gresham, 1998; Mathur & Rutherford, 1996) have reported that specific procedures are significantly effective when training students in social skills. A review of the literature will aid the reader in selecting appropriate procedures.

Measuring the cost-effectiveness of a program will determine whether the program is worth the allocation of resources. This is conducted by establishing the actual cost of the program and then determining the cost of each objective achieved by the program. The relative value of the program can then be determined by those individuals concerned.

Assessing Social Competence

Consistent with the instructional model described in Chapter 4 of this text, social skill assessment serves three major purposes. First, assessment is conducted to describe the characteristics of the learner accurately and objectively. This information is subsequently used to establish annual goals and short-term objectives. Second, social skill assessment is conducted to determine the extent to which the goals and objectives are being achieved through instruction. Finally, social skill assessment is conducted to identify deficiencies in the instructional process. Assessment data may indicate to the teacher specific approaches that are ineffective and objectives that require more intensive intervention.

Hammill (1987) has recommended several general principles for assessing social skills:

1. Review all information currently available that relates to the student's characteristics. School records provide a historical perspective on any potential problems. They may be used to assess the origin of the difficulties as well as to suggest potentially effective intervention strategies.
2. Use existing information and your own observations to determine that the potential problem is of sufficient magnitude to warrant intervention. Many times what an individual teacher perceives to be a problem is not offensive to the student, his or her peers, and other teachers. If this is the case, the teacher's own attitudes or expectations may need to be altered as opposed to the student's behavior.
3. Conduct assessments under conditions as close to natural ones as possible. This guideline will ensure that results are not influenced by contrivances of the assessment situation. For example, a student may perform better under the one-to-one direction of an examiner than in a group performance situation.
4. Go beyond the evaluation of a student by evaluating the environment. It is widely recognized that responses do not occur in isolation. They are all motivated in part by attributes of the environment. In some cases, the learner may behave appropriately

and the environment may be defective. For example, a teacher might note, on the basis of subjective reports, that a student fights with others often. A close observation of the environment might reveal that he spends a substantial amount of time with aggressive youth in unstructured competitive situations. One might conclude that it is wrong for these situations to occur frequently throughout the school day and that remediation should be directed at this aspect of the environment.

5. Assess the learner and environment continually. It is important to recognize that social performance is not static. Just as students' academic skills improve or regress, so does their social functioning. Equally important, social skill performance for any individual is highly variable. A student might be highly glib one day and very sedate the next. Isolated observations may not be sensitive to these changes.

6. Collect multiple measures to ensure that intervention is effective. Simply noting a reduction in a target response may not indicate that an intervention was truly effective. Was the student pleased with the change to the extent that the improvement will be sustained following schooling? Were others pleased with the change to the extent that they are more willing to interact with the student?

7. Everyone's observations and conclusions are filtered through their own values, biases, and preferences. Educators must do more than substantiate that they are satisfied with the goals, objectives, and subsequent extent of the change. The learner, his or her parents, employers, and other significant individuals must contribute to the conclusion that the student is improving.

Five methods are commonly used to assess social skills: (1) self-reports, (2) self-monitoring, (3) reports and ratings by others, (4) direct observation, and (5) commercial instruments.

Self-Reports

Self-report techniques may be the most commonly used procedure in the assessment of social skills (Mathur & Rutherford, 1996; Schloss & Smith, 1998). These instruments are generally used to identify goals and objectives for a training program. They may also be used to determine whether the student is satisfied with the outcome of the training program.

Figure 14.2 illustrates a sample self-report instrument. The inventory is used by asking students to record the perception of their individual ability in each of the areas. The instructor may read items to less capable students. The inventory is scored by considering each response and looking for patterns of strengths and weaknesses as perceived by the student. These patterns should be corroborated through direct observation and reports of others. This approach helps the teacher identify specific intervention targets as opposed to looking for a total score indicative of generally low social performance.

Limited abstract thinking skills, memory deficits, time boundedness, and poor social perception problems of many youth with disabilities may reduce the usefulness of self-reports. Because of the complexity of social interactions, a student's self-appraisal may not be an accurate reflection of reality. Also, teachers' and students' expectations may alter their views of social performance. Moreover, questions and response options used on an inventory may not have the same meaning to all respondents.

FIGURE 14.2 *Self-Report Inventory*

Your response on this inventory will be used to identify possible objectives to be included in a social skills training program. Review each item and circle the number that best describes your ability.

1. Small talk: Initiating and terminating conversations with

Peers at school

1	2	3	4	5
Poor	Below average	Average	Above average	Excellent

Authority at school

1	2	3	4	5
Poor	Below average	Average	Above average	Excellent

Peers at work

1	2	3	4	5
Poor	Below average	Average	Above average	Excellent

Authorities at work

1	2	3	4	5
Poor	Below average	Average	Above average	Excellent

Peers at community sites

1	2	3	4	5
Poor	Below average	Average	Above average	Excellent

Authorities at community sites

1	2	3	4	5
Poor	Below average	Average	Above average	Excellent

Self-Monitoring

Self-monitoring is another frequently used procedure. Students are encouraged to monitor their activity of a specific target behavior and report their findings to the teacher (Grossi & Heward, 1998; Kellner, Bry, & Colletti, 2002; Mather & Rutherford, 1996; Schloss & Smith, 1998). This procedure may not be appropriate for evaluating a training program, because of its subjectivity and the possibly limited reliability of individuals recording their own performance. It is a useful method, however, for an adjunct data collection procedure.

Figure 14.3 illustrates a page from a standard daily calendar carried by many business executives. In this example, the calendar is marked as an interval recording device. Every half hour, the youth might indicate whether specific interpersonal skills were exhibited. The teacher can meet daily with the youth to discuss the self-monitoring log. He or she should initially reinforce the student for recording accurately. Later, the teacher might reinforce the student for correct recording and a desirable rate of the target behavior.

FIGURE 14.3   *Self-Monitoring*

March 23, 2007

8:00 _____ *Talked with friend on bus* _____

8:30 _____ *Greeted teacher* _____

9:00 _____ *Etc.* _____

9:30 _____

10:00 _____

10:30 _____

11:00 _____

11:30 _____

12:00 _____

12:30 _____

1:00 _____

1:30 _____

2:00 _____

2:30 _____

3:00 _____

3:30 _____

4:00 _____

An obvious advantage of this format is its age appropriateness. The daily calendar is a device carried by a large number of "high status" adults. Consequently, the student is unlikely to suffer pejorative reactions for the use of the recording device.

Aside from recording responses in school, self-monitoring can be used to assess a student's behavior in the community, at work, or at home. Once the behavior has been identified, the student can be asked to record his or her responses in other settings and to report back to the teacher. An adult daily calendar can again be used for this purpose. This procedure may allow the teacher to gain insight into the generalization of the skill or transfer of learning outside the school setting to community environments.

Reports and Ratings by Others

This procedure is similar to the self-report procedure. Instead of obtaining a student's self-perception, the professional obtains the perceptions of others (Schloss & Smith, 1998). For example, a teacher might ask the student's parent to complete the self-report inventory presented in Figure 14.2. Or, a less structured interview might be conducted with individuals who are in a position to evaluate the student's behavior (e.g., parents, siblings, peers).

Reports and ratings by others are subjective and based on individual perceptions. Information received should not be used as a basis for evaluating the effectiveness of a training program. Instead, this procedure can be used to gain additional insight into the appropriateness of training priorities and the general value to the individual and society of the training outcomes.

Direct Observation

Direct observation has been used frequently in applied skill training programs. High reliability and validity of behavior recordings can be achieved, and data can be used to evaluate the effectiveness of a training program. Chapter 5 describes observational methods that may be appropriate for this purpose.

One advantage of the procedure is that behavioral data can be recorded in an objective manner (Schloss, 2000). Two common observations used for data collection are in vivo and analogue. In vivo observations are those conducted during a specific period of time in the natural setting (e.g., conversation in the cafeteria during lunch). Analogue observations are those not conducted in a natural setting (e.g., conversation in a simulated cafeteria setting during class time) but instead through situation performance tests in a simulated setting.

Techniques used to record observations include (1) narrative recording, (2) event recording, (3) duration recording, (4) interval recording, and (5) time sampling. A description of each is found in Action Plan 14.1.

Commercial Instruments

Commercial publishing houses have marketed a number of instruments that may be useful in assessing social skills of youth who have disabilities. Many of these instruments can provide objective information to teachers (Masters et al., 1999). Unfortunately, they may have the same limitations that teacher-made instruments possess. First, they require either an accurate self-appraisal or an accurate appraisal by others. As noted earlier, students' self-

---

Action Plan 14.1   Recording Techniques

We recommend the following techniques when recording direct observations:

1. *Narrative recording:* Written record of student behaviors, time and duration of observation, environmental conditions, and actions of others present
2. *Event recording:* A tally of each occurrence for a specific target behavior
3. *Duration recording:* A recording of the length of time that a target behavior occurs
4. *Interval recording:* A method used to record one or more behaviors in a given specified time period
5. *Time sampling:* A recording of behavior that is exhibited after a predetermined time period lapses

appraisals may be limited by their cognitive abilities. The appraisal of others may be limited by their frame of reference. Parents may provide glowing reports not shared by teachers. Benevolent work supervisors may be highly positive, whereas the actual employer, concerned about the bottom line, may be more critical.

The principal limitation of these instruments is that they are marketed for a mass audience across the country. The questions and potential responses are not referenced to the demands of individual communities. For example, what may be described as being aggressive in Boone County, Missouri, may be considered assertive behavior in New York City. Commercial instruments are not sensitive to these regional and community differences. Furthermore, they solicit very general information that may not be sufficiently specific to suggest intervention priorities or to assess the effects of intervention. The Cain-Levine Social Competency Scale (Cain, Levine, & Elzey, 1963), for example, includes only 10 items used to measure interpersonal skills.

One feature recommending these scales is that a substantial amount of research and development has gone into their construction. Many have extensive national norms providing reliable comparisons between a student's performance and that of a national sample. The Adaptive Behavior Inventory (ABI) (Brown & Leigh, 1986), for example, provides detailed information for two separate normative groups (Normal Intelligence and Mentally Retarded), with over 1,000 individuals in each group. The ABI not only reports characteristics of these samples in terms of the usual demographic information such as age, sex, and geographic location, but also describes such categories as type of classroom placement, presence of other disabling conditions, urban/rural residential status, parent education and occupation, ethnicity, and language spoken in the home. Data extracted from the *Statistical Abstract of the United States* (U.S. Department of Commerce, 1980) are also published in the ABI manual to permit the reader to ascertain the representativeness of the sample. The percentages reported for the normative samples are similar to those reported for the population at large and thus provide credence to the claim for national representativeness.

With these strengths and limitations in mind, we encourage the reader to use commercial instruments as general screening devices. More highly focused teacher-made instruments are recommended for evaluating intervention effects. The commercial instruments commonly used are described in Action Plan 14.2.

General Principles of Social Skill Instruction

Social skill instruction is an approach aimed at increasing students' interpersonal skills in critical life situations (Grossi & Heward, 1998; Hartas & Donahue, 1997; Maag & Webber, 1997). It emphasizes the positive educational aspects of treatment rather than the elimination of maladaptive behaviors (Mathur & Rutherford, 1994; Walker et al., 1994). Social skill training follows the assumption that individuals perform select responses and choose the most effective ones in their repertoire when faced with demanding social situations. Owing to cognitive limitations and/or deficient learning histories, the best available response may be viewed by others as being maladaptive. The specific maladaptive behavior can be overcome or compensated for through appropriate training. This training is expected to lead the individual to replace the offensive behaviors with prosocial behaviors. Training generally consists of a variety of specific procedures, such as social reinforcement, modeling, behavior rehearsal, feedback, and homework.

Action Plan 14.2   Commercial Instruments

When considering the use of commercial instruments for assessment, you may wish to review one or more of the following for examples. These are just five of many available for your use.

1. Behavior Rating Profile (Brown & Hammill, 1990) provides an ecological assessment of social skill behaviors. Developed for use with children and youth in the age range of 6.6 to 18.6 years. Administered in a minimum amount of time.
2. Vineland Adaptive Behavior Scale (Sparrow, Cicchetti &, Balla, 2005) assesses social competence in four areas of adaptive behavior and one area of maladaptive behavior. Developed for use with individuals from birth to age 19. Designed to be completed by interviewing a knowledgeable informant such as the parent or teacher in approximately one hour.
3. AAMD Adaptive Behavior Scale: School Edition (Lambert, Windmiller, Tharinger, & Cole, 1993) assesses the extent to which the student meets social expectations in a school setting. Developed for use with students in the age range of 3.3 to 17.2 years. Observation of specific skills is recorded and scored in approximately 15 to 30 minutes.
4. Devereux Adolescent Behavior Rating Scale (Spivack, Spotts, & Haimes, 1967) assesses the social–affective skill development of youth 13 to 18 years of age. A behavior checklist is completed by an attendant or teacher in 10 to 15 minutes.

Case for Action 14.2

One of your students will not converse with peers in a community setting. How would you assess this social skill to get further information?

Social Reinforcement

Social reinforcement is defined as the use of interpersonal interactions to influence the future strength of an individual's behavior (Mathur, Kavale, Quinn, Forness, & Rutherford, 1998; Schloss & Smith, 1998). Social reinforcement is advocated in social skill programs because social interactions are motivators for prosocial behavior in natural settings (Kellner et al., 2002). Parents, peers, and authority figures tend to rely on social reinforcement, which emphasizes its importance to the student. Verbal praise, gestures, and physical contact are the primary social reinforcers used in social skill development. Schloss (1984) has suggested the guidelines presented in Action Plan 14.3 for increasing the effectiveness of social reinforcement.

Modeling

Modeling is defined as learning by imitation (Garff & Storey, 1998; Mathur et al., 1998; Moore et al., 1995). Modeling is an effective and reliable technique for teaching new behaviors and strengthening deficit behaviors (Smith & Travis, 2001). Learning through modeling

Action Plan 14.3   Social Reinforcement

The following guidelines are suggested for use when incorporating social reinforcement principles:

1. Define target behaviors.
2. In developing a new behavior, follow every occurrence of the behavior with social reinforcement. As the behavior occurs more consistently, social reinforcement should be reduced.
3. Verbally state the behavior likely to result in social reinforcement, using the youth's name when possible.
4. Verbally label process and product behaviors. For example, "Mark, I like the way you wrote your name (process). It is easy to read (product)."
5. Deliver social reinforcers enthusiastically.
6. Any time unnatural incentives are used, pair them with social praise. This will develop the reinforcement value of social praise.
7. Avoid socially reinforcing maladaptive responses.
8. Encourage significant others to socially reinforce the desired behavior(s) in a range of settings.

occurs by observing an individual's appropriate behavior and imitating the exact behavior. Depending on an individual's competence and ability to discriminate, preplanned observations may be necessary to promote social skill acquisition. Both prosocial and disruptive behaviors can be learned through modeling. A youth learns to be aggressive by observing others being reinforced for aggressive behavior. Conversely, a youth acquires assertive skills by observing others gain satisfaction from socially skillful interactions. Action Plan 14.4 suggests strategies for enhancing the value of peer models.

Behavior Rehearsal

Behavior rehearsal is defined as a situation in which an individual or group of individuals is asked to take a role, to enact a specific situation (Moore et al., 1995; Schloss & Smith, 1998). By acting out a situation, the students gain insight into specific social skill approaches. Kellner and colleagues (2002) suggested that teachers prepare scenes for students to role-play. As instruction progresses, students can identify situations they would like to role-play, based on provoking incidents in which they have been involved. Behavior rehearsals are an ideal way of developing behaviors to replace the disruptive responses targeted by punishment programs. For example, the youth can be asked to demonstrate a "better way" to act once a disruptive behavior has occurred. Action Plan 14.5 lists nine strategies for implementing behavior rehearsal principles.

Feedback

Feedback is defined as providing the student information on how well he or she performed (Garff & Storey, 1998; Schloss & Smith, 1998a). Providing students with frequent and

Action Plan 14.4   Modeling

The following strategies are suggested for use when implementing modeling principles:

1. Specify the behaviors to be influenced through modeling.
2. Arrange situations so that the individual is likely to observe others engaging in the specified (target) behaviors.
3. When another individual engages in the target behaviors, label it verbally, using the person's name (e.g., "You're dressed quite neatly today, Mae-Ling").
4. When the youth engages in an approximation of the target behavior, label it verbally, using his or her name (e.g., "You dressed nicely also, Joseph").
5. Expose the youth to a variety of models and settings to increase the likelihood that the behavior change will generalize to other settings.
6. Use high-status models when possible because they will have a stronger influence on the observer's behavior.
7. Avoid situations in which the youth observes maladaptive behavior produce satisfying consequences.

Remember, youth who are easily influenced are more likely to learn through observation.

Action Plan 14.5   Behavior Rehearsal

The following guidelines are suggested for use when implementing behavior rehearsal principles:

1. Determine the behavior to be developed.
2. Identify the natural antecedents or signals for the behavior.
3. Identify the natural consequences of the behavior.
4. Decide when to practice the desired response under the natural antecedent and consequent conditions.
5. Develop a plan for rehearsing the desired behaviors.
6. Verbally label the desired response, its antecedents, and its consequences.
7. Use other social learning techniques (e.g., modeling, shaping, and social reinforcement) with behavior rehearsal procedures when necessary.
8. Rehearse the desired behavior under a variety of conditions to enhance generalization (the extent to which the behavior will occur in other settings).
9. Socially reinforce the rehearsed behavior as it occurs naturally.

clear feedback during training will reinforce their behavior and encourage them to attend future training sessions. Feedback can be offered by the teacher/trainer or by other peers participating in the training. If it is implemented by the teacher/trainer, the student receives immediate social reinforcement after a specific activity and/or behavior by the teacher/trainer. During a training session, peers might provide spontaneous reinforcement (e.g.,

Action Plan 14.6   Feedback

The following examples are suggested feedback behaviors that can be used by teachers and peers during social skill training programs:

1. *Social reinforcement:* Verbal praise, gestures, physical contact
2. *Progress charts and graphs:* Noting behavior
3. *Material reinforcers:* Awards, points to earn awards, certificate of accomplishment
4. *Lights and buzzers:* Signaling when appropriate or inappropriate behaviors are exhibited
5. *Cue cards:* Identifying the response expected

cue cards, flashing lights) when a specific behavior is exhibited. If this did not occur or was not arranged, peers could then provide reinforcement following the behavior/activity. Action Plan 14.6 provides a list of examples that can be used for feedback by peers and teachers/trainers.

Homework

Homework provides students with frequent opportunities to practice social skills (Mercer & Mercer, 2005; Sugai & Lewis, 1998) outside of the training program. This technique may be structured, in that students are told the exact skill or procedure to practice and then asked to report back to the instructor. Homework can also be unstructured, in that students are asked to practice what they have learned and then to report back to the class. Action Plan 14.7 presents a sample structured homework assignment. Action Plan 14.8 provides a general unstructured recording form.

Promoting Generalization and Maintenance

Despite the availability of social skill development strategies and the data supporting their efficacy in initial skill development, concern has been expressed in the literature regarding limited maintenance and generalization of newly acquired skills (Gresham et al., 2001; Strain, 2001). Having invested the time and energy to develop and implement social skill instruction, it is only natural to want students to use these skills outside instructional settings with friends and family members. Maintenance and generalization may be limited for a variety of reasons. Some of the techniques used to promote social skill development may militate against maintenance and generalization (Gresham et al., 2001). For example, Kellner and colleagues (2002) suggested that using small group instruction limits opportunities to practice skills in more natural settings. Strain (2001) suggested that teachers may rely on criteria that are "based on some mythical, self-generated metric" such as "saying hello eight out of ten times or playing cooperatively 75% of the time" (p. 31). In addition, it is possible that students will continue to use inappropriate behaviors to get what they want, despite their participation in social skill instruction. It appears that although the student knows the socially appropriate skill and when to use it, other, less skillful behaviors are just as successful in getting the student what he or she wants. Gresham et al., (2001) suggested that these competing behaviors are more efficient and reliable than the socially skillful alternative.

Action Plan 14.7   Structured Homework

Structured homework assignments might be designed somewhat like this example:

HOMEWORK FORM

Accepting Praise

Name: _____   Date: _____

Directions: After someone praises you, answer these questions:

1. Who praised you?
2. What did they say?
3. Did you smile?
4. Did you say thank you?
5. What else did you say?
6. How did you do?   _____ Super   _____ OK   _____ Poor

Action Plan 14.8   Homework Recording

An example of a general unstructured homework recording is illustrated below:

HOMEWORK

Name: _____   Date: _____

A. Assignment: Steps to Follow:

1. _____
2. _____
3. _____
4. _____
5. _____
6. _____
7. _____
8. _____
9. _____
10. _____

B. Did you do all of the assignment steps?

C. Circle those you did not complete.

D. How did you do?   _____ Super   _____ OK   _____ Poor

We have already identified a few ways to promote maintenance and generalization of social skills. Specifically, teachers were encouraged to socially validate the skills they taught and the criterion they used to ensure the skills were important to the learners and significant others and actually made a qualitative difference in the lives of students. Homework activities were recommended to provide students with the opportunity to practice their skills in different settings with other people. Reinforcement from people in other settings allows students to see the benefits of choosing socially skillful behavior, increasing the likelihood that skills will continue to be used after instruction is completed. Finally, readers are referred to Chapter 6 for information on decreasing or eliminating inappropriate behaviors that compete with the application of socially skillful responses.

Additional Instructional Considerations

Numerous approaches can be used to teach social skills. They depend on a wide range of variables, from age and cognitive ability to communication skills. Improving social competence is a longitudinal process and should be conducted over a student's entire school career. Students must attain sufficient social affect and adequate social skills and exercise social cognition to become socially competent (Goldstein et al., 1997; Sugai & Lewis, 1998). Students who think better about themselves will tend to have a better social affect than those who do not. Affect is part of all social behavior and is best taught when integrated into all instructional areas, including academics, self-care, and vocational preparation. Inclusion alone is unlikely to improve social affect (Salend, 1999). A student's disposition can improve if specific socially enhancing activities are structured by the teacher. Cooperative learning, for example, has been shown to be effective in improving peer relations and affect (Prater et al., 1998). This instructional procedure has been reported to provide students who have disabilities with twice as much interaction as in competitive learning situations.

Cognitive behavior modification is another useful strategy (Kellner et al., 2002). Students are taught specific skills that alter the way they analyze and respond to a social problem. The teacher might provide a problem and the student might then be asked to verbalize an approach to solving the problem. Strategies are rehearsed and applied when needed. Various programs with a modified version of cognitive behavior modification have been found to have a significant effect on an individual's social affect (Goldstein et al., 1997; McGinnis, Goldstein, Sprafkin, & Gershaw, 1997; Polloway & Patton, 2004).

The practice of teaching specific social skills to individuals has consistently been reported in the literature (Clement-Heist, Seigel, & Gaylord-Ross, 1992; Garff & Storey, 1998; Grossi & Heward, 1998; Hartas & Donahue, 1997; Mace & Murphy, 1991; Mathur

---

Case for Action 14.3

You have a 12-year-old boy in your classroom who is high functioning although considered educationally disabled. He exhibits inappropriate social behaviors in the classroom, which annoy his peers. These include vocalizations when he wants the teacher's attention, tongue clicking when he is reading silently, and staring at peers when he wants to initiate a conversation. Are these behaviors deficient? What behaviors should be taught? What instructional procedures would you follow?

& Rutherford, 1994; McGinnis et al., 1997; Misra, 1992; Moore et al., 1995; Walker & Leister, 1994). Direct instruction is used for teaching specific social skills and relies heavily on social reinforcement, modeling, role-playing, feedback, and homework techniques.

Summary

Social skills continue to gain increasing attention among the teachers of students with disabilities. When these students are integrated into the community, intelligence, disability, and academic achievement are not as great a concern as social competence. Social skill deficits do appear to make a significant impact on the vocational success of individuals with disabilities. Students without such skills tend to be viewed negatively because they do not interact much with others. Instead, deficiencies become overgeneralized to unrelated competencies.

Deficits in social competence are defined as the discrepancy between the student's achieved skill level and what is expected. This discrepancy can be measured by both teacher-made and commercial assessment instruments. Once deficits are identified, objectives are prepared that reflect all information known about the student's learning and behavioral characteristics.

Social skill training is typically composed of a package of techniques most appropriate for the social skill to be taught. Social skills should be taught throughout a student's educational program and integrated into all areas of instruction, including academics, self-care, and vocational preparation.

15

Teaching in the Content Areas

Did you know that . . .

- The majority of secondary students with special needs will be educated in general high school classrooms?

- General education teachers will be held increasingly more responsible for teaching students with disabilities?

- Seventy-five percent of all special education students spend 40% or more of their school day in general education classrooms?

- Ninety-six percent of all general educators have taught students with special needs?

- The majority of secondary special educators have no specific training in the content areas?

- Instruction based on textbooks is particularly challenging for students with disabilities?

- The science curriculum is organized around themes or "big ideas"?

- There are two major approaches to teaching science?

- There are two goals in social studies education?

- Content enhancements improve learning for all students, not just those with disabilities?

- There are three types of mnemonics?

- Peer-mediated strategies enhance academic and social interaction skills?

Can you . . .

- Identify problems associated with the use of textbooks in the teaching of science and social studies?

- Differentiate between a content approach and a skills approach to secondary special education?

- Identify the two goals of social studies education?

- List the steps of project-based learning?

- Identify content enhancement techniques?

- Develop an advanced organizer?

- Develop a graphic organizer?

- Develop a study guide that uses short-answer questions?

- Develop a study guide that uses a framed outline?

- Develop a study guide that uses matching items?

- Develop a mnemonic device?

- Create your own mnemonic?

- Teach a mnemonic?
- Develop a set of guided notes?

- Teach students how to use guided notes?

As described in Chapter 1 and mentioned periodically throughout this text, there has been a greater move toward including students with disabilities in general education settings to allow access to the general curriculum and enhance opportunities for higher achievement on standardized tests (De La Paz & MacArthur, 2003). No longer is it automatically assumed that secondary students with disabilities can be served more appropriately in separate, self-contained classrooms. Rather, the majority of secondary students with special needs will receive their education in traditional classrooms alongside their nondisabled peers (Anderson, Yilmaz, & Wasburn-Moses, 2004). SPeNSE (2002) indicated that 75% of all students with special needs spend at least 40% of their day in general education settings; 96% of all general educators have taught students with disabilities. Undoubtedly, consultant teachers will be available to provide direct and indirect services; nonetheless, secondary teachers should expect and be prepared to meet the educational needs of students with disabilities for all or part of the school day. Chapter 4 presented instructional methods that secondary teachers can use to assist students with disabilities in mastering essential information. Subsequent chapters described specific applications of this information to enhance reading, mathematics, written language, listening and speaking, and social skill development. Suggestions for written language, listening and speaking, and social skills should be useful to all secondary educators, regardless of the content area. Recommendations offered in Chapters 10 and 11 should be useful to secondary educators whose content areas are related to literacy and mathematics. In this chapter, we turn our attention to other content areas addressed in typical high school programs—specifically, social studies and science. In addition to math and reading, these two content areas have been addressed in standards and assessments developed by all states (Jitendra, Edwards, Choutka, & Treadway, 2002).

McKenzie (1991) differentiated between two methods for providing secondary special education services: a content approach and a skills approach. A special educator using a content approach provides instruction in English, language, science, social studies, and other areas to students who it is believed will not profit from inclusion in secondary settings. The skills approach enhances basic reading, writing, computation, and social skills so that secondary students with disabilities can be more successful in general education settings. McKenzie (1991) reported that the content approach was used by 79% of the teachers surveyed; the skills approach was used by 19%. Nolet and Tindal (1993) and Jitendra and colleagues (2002) suggested that special educators have been more concerned with reducing basic skill deficits that secondary students may demonstrate in reading, writing, communication, and socialization than with what students are expected to do with these skills. They advised special educators to shift their instructional focus toward the acquisition and use of content knowledge. This shift will not be easy. As noted in Chapter 1, the special educator is more likely to have an undergraduate or graduate degree in special education, certification to teach special education, and no specific training in a content area. Because their teachers probably lack background in a content area, special education students may not receive instruction comparable to that of peers enrolled in general education content area classes (Nolet & Tindal, 1993). Secondary teachers generally have expertise and teacher certification in a content area (Jitendra et al., 2002). Therefore, it is more likely that secondary educators will possess a better understanding of the content they are supposed to teach, although they may have difficulty teaching that subject matter to students with special needs.

Fortunately, this circumstance may be changing. Some states, such as New York, are requiring graduates of teacher education programs who are interested in secondary special education to have a bachelor's degree that includes course work in secondary special education and at least 30 hours in an academic discipline such as mathematics, history, or one of the hard sciences. The benefit of this requirement includes the availability of teachers who have a solid understanding of the content they are supposed to teach and methods for presenting this information to students with disabilities. The disadvantage is that the increased time and financial resources required for degree completion act as disincentives for a college student to enroll in such a program. For the time being, it is likely that high school students with special needs who are educated in general education settings will have as their teachers individuals who are certified in secondary education, not special education.

Criticism has been directed at educational outcomes that focus primarily on the mastery of basic facts or the production of rote knowledge rather than on the development and application of concepts and skills that enable individuals to engage in higher-order thinking and problem solving (Jitendra et al., 2002). Another factor complicating the presentation of this subject matter is the reliance on textbook-based instructional approaches. Textbooks in science and social studies have been criticized for several reasons, including the lack of clarity of content goals, presumptions about the background knowledge students bring to the text, insufficient explanations, poor presentation of content, an emphasis on breadth of knowledge over depth of knowledge (Spencer, Scruggs, & Mastropieri, 2003), lack of interesting content, and reading levels that are too high (De La Paz & MacArthur, 2003). In response, the focus of instruction in science and social studies has shifted away from an emphasis on basic facts and skills presented through textbooks toward an emphasis on learning and using complex operations. To meet the ever-increasing demands of life in the twenty-first century, all students will need to think critically and solve problems. Students with disabilities are no exception; therefore, the question is not whether students with disabilities should be present and learning in content area classes but how best to make this happen (Nolet & Tindal, 1994).

In this chapter, we discuss science and social studies in more detail and offer suggestions to both general and special educators that will enhance the success experienced by secondary students with disabilities in typical high school classrooms.

Science Education

There is a heightened awareness that students in the United States do not compare favorably to students from other countries in their knowledge of science and technology (Blough & Schwartz, 1990). As a result, a great deal of national attention has focused on the quality of science education programs (Rutherford & Ahlgren, 1990). Problems associated with either the content or the methodology of science education programs and the measures developed to address them will affect students with disabilities because more than half receive instruction in science in general classes.

The Science Standards

The traditional science curriculum of the elementary school was spiral. It included several topics at each grade level that were repeated at subsequent grade levels, with more detailed and complex information being added. At the upper grades, the science curriculum focused on a single subject, such as biology or chemistry, that was taught for a year (Cawley, 1994). Out of concern that such a curricular model may have resulted in an emphasis on mastery of a series of disjointed facts, recent efforts to reform science instruction have called for the reconceptualization of science curricula into a series of "big ideas" or connected themes (Carnine, 1995; Cawley, 1994; Gurganus, Janas, & Schmitt, 1995; Mastropieri & Scruggs, 1994). The National Academy of Science (2005) developed the National Science Education Standards, which consists of eight categories of content standards. Rather than identify a curriculum, these eight standards specify outcomes—that is, what students should know, understand, and be able to do in natural science. Each standard includes underlying fundamental concepts. Standards and underlying concepts are listed in Action Plan 15.1 The purpose of these standards is to guide the development of scientific literacy. Several beliefs underlie the need for such knowledge. First, science can offer personal fulfillment and excitement. Second, the ability to use scientific judgment and a scientific way of thinking will enable Americans to make informed decisions about critical issues such as the environment. Third, individuals who understand and use science knowledge will have more meaningful and productive jobs. The availability of these standards should enable school district officials and community members to select or develop appropriate curriculum and assessment measures.

Approaches to Teaching Science

The diversity of curricula, the implications that a well-structured curriculum can have for the development of higher-order thinking skills, and the applicability of content to daily living make science a particularly useful content area for students with disabilities. Despite its importance, very little specific information is available regarding the appropriateness of the science instruction provided to students in either general or special education settings (Parmar & Cawley, 1993). If student grades can be used as indicators, however, then the picture is dismal. Cawley, Kahn, and Tedesco (1989) reported that between 50 and 70% of secondary students with disabilities received grades of D or lower.

Scruggs and Mastropieri (1993) classified approaches currently available for teaching science into two general categories: content-oriented approaches and activities-oriented approaches. Each approach is discussed separately.

The Content-Oriented Approach   The content-oriented approach is the most commonly used approach in general education settings. It relies heavily on the textbook as a primary medium of instruction. In addition, the content-oriented approach requires verbal communication skills. Specifically, students must be able to listen to a lecture, comprehend extensive vocabulary, discuss information, read the text, study, and complete written as-

Action Plan 15.1   Science Content Standards

The National Science Education Standards (National Academy of Science, 2005) include the following eight items for grades 9–12:

Unifying concepts in processes in science

    A. Systems, order, and organization
    B. Evidence, models, and explanations
    C. Change, constancy, and measurement
    D. Evolution and equilibrium
    E. Form and function

Science as inquiry

    A. Abilities necessary to do scientific inquiry
    B. Understandings about scientific inquiry

Physical science

    A. Structure of atoms
    B. Structure and properties of matter
    C. Chemical reactions
    D. Motions and forces
    E. Conservation of energy and increase in disorder
    F. Interactions of energy and matter

Life science

    A. The cell
    B. Molecular basis of heredity
    C. Biological evolution
    D. Interdependence of organisms
    E. Matter, energy, and organization in living systems
    F. Behavior of organisms

Earth and space science

    A. Energy of the earth system
    B. Geochemical cycles
    C. Origin and evolution of the earth system
    D. Origin and evolution of the universe

Science and technology

    A. Abilities of technical design
    B. Understandings about science and technology

Science in personal and social perspectives

    A. Personal and community health
    B. Population growth
    C. Natural resources
    D. Environmental quality
    E. Natural and human-induced hazards
    F. Science and technology in local, national, and global challenges

History and nature of science

    A. Science as a human endeavor
    B. Nature of scientific knowledge
    C. Historical perspectives

signments. These activities are occasionally supplemented with films, filmstrips, or videos. Many topics are covered in the content-oriented approach; however, few are addressed in detail. Progress is measured on the basis of responses to written test items that emphasize basic facts over in-depth mastery of material.

    Scruggs and Mastropieri (1993) identified the major disadvantage of the content-oriented approach for students with disabilities. Specifically, language deficits typically experienced by these students seriously undermine their abilities to listen, discuss, and read and write independently. In the absence of modifications or adaptation, secondary students with disabilities will perform poorly in science education classes dominated by the content-oriented approach.

Such modifications were described by Munk, Bruckert, Call, Stoehrmann, and Radandt (1998). First, they recommended that teachers prioritize the content that must be presented. They should preview text material, designate material that should be mastered, and eliminate less important information. Important text can be highlighted by photocopying only that information; highlighting the information so that it stands out from other, less relevant information; or using a marker to cross out sections the student can ignore. Second, Munk and colleagues (1998) suggested teachers preteach vocabulary before assigning students to read material or complete an activity. Third, teachers can encourage students to paraphrase or summarize after reading a paragraph or a page. Other recommendations included the use of study guides, graphic organizers, audiotapes, mnemonics, and guided notes, which are presented later in this chapter.

The Activities-Oriented Approach   Scruggs and Mastropieri (1994) argued that students with special needs will learn science more effectively by engaging in science activities rather than listening to lectures, reading science books, and completing worksheets. The result of their study (Mastropieri & Scruggs, 1994) indicated that students with disabilities who engaged in activities-oriented instruction were able to construct scientific knowledge that reflected a deeper level of understanding of science than the level achieved in a textbook-driven presentation.

This activities-oriented approach has also been referred to as the *discovery, inquiry,* or *constructivist* perspective (Roth, 1989) and, as discussed in Chapter 4, is based on the work of developmental theorists such as Piaget and Vygotsky. Although it allows for occasional teacher presentations, the activities-oriented approach highlights the use of small groups so that students can explore concepts. These explorations require students to ask questions, design experiments, observe, predict, manipulate materials, keep records, and learn from mistakes (Dalton, Morocco, Tivnan, & Mead, 1997) so that they can construct general rules about how the universe functions. Rather than reading about science, an activities-oriented approach provides students with the opportunity to work directly with science materials, using scientific methods (Mastropieri & Scruggs, 2002). Because explorations require more time to conduct, fewer topics are covered; however, they are studied in greater detail. In addition, students can develop their independent-thinking and problem-solving skills.

According to Salend (1998a), an activities-oriented approach typically occurs within the context of cooperative learning, which "can encourage the establishment of scientific classroom communities where students work in groups to communicate about and experiment with solutions to scientific problems" (p. 70). He described the activities-oriented approach as a learning cycle that consists of four phases: engagement, exploration, development, and extension. During *engagement,* the teacher presents a real-life activity, problem, or question that is motivating to students and encourages them to access their prior knowledge. During this phase, students should have access to hands-on manipulatives and concrete experiences that will enable them to learn more abstract concepts. For example, for a unit on simple machines, Salend suggested students should identify machines they use every day and take apart broken household appliances. During the *exploration* phase, students should share ideas, clarify thoughts, experiment, brainstorm, develop alternative solutions, and frame questions that will focus their work during subsequent phases. Students who are working in cooperative groups will have the opportunity to hear about others' perspectives and proposed solutions. Referring to Salend's example, having had the chance to examine the broken appliances, students can identify essential components, speculate about how these items worked, and hypothesize about how to fix them. In the *development* phase, students gather more information to increase their knowledge and draw conclusions about their observations. For example, students could arrange experiments that would give them more information about an appliance's power sources. During the *extension* phase, students extend what they have learned by applying it to unique situations. For example, they could apply what they learned about small household appliances to other, larger machines that serve different purposes.

The teacher's role in an activities-oriented approach is vastly different from that in a content-oriented approach. Rather than dispense information, the teacher facilitates, clarifies, and extends students' discovery experiences. He or she encourages students to think about questions, facilitates their ability to reason through alternatives, provides additional activities and resources, and assists with summarization. Student-centered, performance-based assessment measures are used to document the effect of an activities-oriented approach on the development of scientific knowledge. Students can make things, solve problems, produce a written project, give a presentation, or design and perform an experiment.

Dalton and colleagues (1997) described another constructivist approach to science called *supported inquiry science (SIS)* that may be particularly suited to students with disabilities. This approach includes eight interconnected principles:

1. Teachers should provide a learning environment in which students are comfortable expressing ideas. They should de-emphasize the need to find correct answers quickly, because many students with disabilities avoid such interactions.
2. Teachers need to base the instructional focus on one concept. Questions and challenges that arise during instruction should assist students in making clear connections between their experiences and the underlying concept.
3. Teachers should encourage students to share their existing beliefs, examine them in light of new evidence, clarify any misconceptions, and develop scientifically correct views.
4. Teachers should engage the entire group in conversation about their topic to help the students elaborate on and revise their understanding of the concept.
5. Teachers should provide opportunities for students to work with materials individually as well as in small and large groups. Such arrangements enable students to explore their own ideas and generate and test hypotheses individually and collaboratively, share their ideas with peers, and exchange knowledge and strategies.
6. Students should be able to express their ideas using a variety of modalities, such as drawings, diagrams, talking, and writing.
7. Teachers should embed hands-on assessment in the activity to gain a better understanding of students' strengths and difficulties.
8. Teachers may need to provide practice in collaborative science inquiry. Teachers can target the development of students' abilities to teach and learn from one another.

Some special considerations are in order when using an activities-oriented approach with students with disabilities. Scruggs and Mastropieri (1994) suggested that teachers may need to coach active reasoning in students with disabilities during activities-based instruction. For example, Scruggs, Mastropieri, and Sullivan (1994) presented students with the fact "An anteater has long claws on its feet" and coached them through an explanation with questions such as, "Why would it make sense that an anteater has long claws?"; "What does an anteater eat?"; and "Where do ants live?" Students exposed to coaching showed better immediate and delayed recall of facts and explanations. Subsequent work by Mastropieri, Scruggs, and Butcher (1997) showed that coaching was more useful for students with learning disabilities than for those with retardation. Secondary teachers may be concerned that such coaching will require more time than they have to devote to students with special needs during an instructional period. Perhaps the consultant teacher would be available to coach these students or others in the classroom who appear to need such assistance.

Salend (1998) advised that activities-oriented approaches could be made more appropriate for students with disabilities by choosing questions and problem-solving activities that address community-based problems, teaming students with nondisabled peers, distributing a checklist of steps students can consider as they complete a task, monitoring progress closely, and requiring students to maintain journals.

Many benefits are associated with the activities-oriented approach for students with disabilities. Tripp (1991) reported that science becomes more meaningful for students. They learn skills essential for mastery of *all* content areas, not just science. For example, students learn to observe, investigate, gather data, and report. Another benefit is that hypothesizing, creating new problems, and inventing and synthesizing new ideas all contribute to the development of creativity. Scruggs and Mastropieri (1994) noted that the de-emphasis on reading and vocabulary may relieve students with disabilities of many frustrating task demands. The use of performance-based assessment also allows students to show what they know about science rather than write about it.

Despite these benefits, there are some problems with constructivist approaches to science instruction for students with disabilities. First, Mastropieri, Scruggs, and Butcher (1997) noted that what may start out as a constructivist-based activity for the entire class may not end up that way for students with disabilities. When presented with a pendulum activity, normally achieving students "discovered" the principle more quickly than did students with learning disabilities, who required additional time and coaching to succeed. Students with retardation did not discover the principle at all. It is very likely that, because of the need to move on, some students would be told the rule or principle. Thus, the only instruction they would receive is when a teacher or another student called out the answer. Second, as Scruggs and Mastropieri (1993) noted, science is a vast and diverse content domain. Not all of the information students need to know can come from activities-based approaches. Material such as vocabulary cannot be constructed; rather, it must be learned and remembered. Practitioners are advised to examine carefully the goals and objectives students are expected to master and to select the instructional approach that will produce the most gains. Practitioners will probably find themselves using both activities-based approaches and teacher-directed techniques to enhance students' abilities to acquire and use scientific knowledge (cf. McCleery & Tindal, 1999).

Social Studies Education

Social Studies Goals and Curricula

A social studies education has two goals. First is the preparation of an informed and critical citizenry (De La Paz & MacArthur, 2003; Parker, 1991) who can participate in the democratic process. Second is the development of knowledge about problems that have historically confronted humanity, the solutions of which can assist society as it meets new challenges (Ferretti & Okolo, 1996). The National Council for the Social Studies (NCSS, 1994) has identified the following ten standards for social studies:

1. *Culture*: How people create, learn, and adapt culture
2. *Time, continuity, and change*: How people understand their historical roots and locate themselves in time
3. *People, places, and environments*: How people create their spatial views and geographical perspectives
4. *Individual development and identity*: How culture, groups, and institutions influence personal identity
5. *Individuals, groups, and institutions*: The role that institutions such as churches and governments play in a person's life
6. *Power, authority, and governance*: How to develop civic competence
7. *Production, distribution, and consumption*: Understanding the relations between wants and resources
8. *Science, technology, and society*: The advantages and challenges technology brings to resolving societal issues
9. *Global connections*: How to balance national interests with global issues
10. *Civic ideals and practices*: How to participate fully in society

Despite the importance of these goals and standards, social studies instruction has not been a priority for students with disabilities (Patton, Polloway, & Cronin, 1987). In fact, De La Paz and MacArthur (2003) noted that students with disabilities may not receive social studies instruction because their teachers are more focused on the development or remediation of basic skills. Mastropieri and Scruggs (2002) suggested that these students, as much as anyone else, need to know about the world around them. There is great diversity in the social studies curriculum, with topics of study including U.S. history, government, and geography; world history and geography; and political science. Mastropieri and Scruggs argued that a basic knowledge and understanding of history, geography, and government are essential to success in life. Although students are expected to analyze, synthesize, and evaluate major events in U.S. and world history, Mastropieri and Scruggs warned that historical facts are emphasized during instruction and on exams. Geography emphasizes the study of the earth's climate and natural land features as well as products and populations in different regions of the world. Study of the U.S. government focuses on the organizational structure, components, and functions of the executive, legislative, and judicial branches. Secondary teachers should be closely involved with a student's multidisciplinary and IEP teams and select carefully the most appropriate social studies goals and objectives.

Approaches to Teaching Social Studies

Horton, Lovitt, and Slocum (1988) warned that a typical instructional sequence of teacher lecture, silent reading, and group discussion is particularly inappropriate for students with disabilities. It is unlikely that students will be able to process large amounts of information that are transmitted by lecture. Because of reading deficits, many students with disabilities have difficulty learning information about history directly from texts. Passe and Beattie (1994) surveyed elementary and secondary social studies teachers to identify factors that undermined their ability to meet the needs of students with disabilities. Although the majority of the teachers indicated that the emphasis of the social studies curriculum should be the same for students with disabilities, they expressed concern about insufficient time, insufficient materials, and uncertainty about how best to meet needs.

Social studies teachers have been advised to incorporate visual materials—such as pictures, films, and videotapes—into their lessons (Mastropieri & Scruggs, 2002) and to use field trips and guest speakers (Passe & Beattie, 1994). Specialists in the areas of social studies have advocated the use of deductive or Socratic methods to teach social studies. Specifically, students are encouraged to use reasoning to arrive at relevant concepts, relationships, and ethical or moral principles (Mastropieri & Scruggs, 2002). Mastropieri and Scruggs (2002) noted that there is nothing wrong with the use of deductive methods if mastery of this technique is part of the social studies curriculum. They pointed out, however, that students will still be responsible for learning the facts, concepts, and rules associated with the social studies curriculum.

Ferretti and Okolo (1996) suggested that project-based instruction may be particularly well suited to the needs of students with disabilities and may enable them to meet the goals of a social studies curriculum. Project-based instruction has five features, beginning with an authentic question or problem that provides students with a framework for organizing concepts and principles. The topic should be broad so that students can study it for a period of time. It could also be a controversial topic so that groups of learners can take different positions. The second feature requires students to conduct investigations so that they can formulate and refine their research question, collect original data or locate data sources, analyze and interpret data, and draw conclusions. Ferretti and Okolo advised that more current issues and problems are well suited for project-based instruction because original data are easier to collect and data sources (such as interviews) are easier to access. Third, students develop artifacts to show their emerging understanding of the problem and how they would solve it. Fourth, students work in cooperative learning groups. They can collaborate with peers, teachers, and other community members so that they can share knowledge, divide tasks, make decisions, and construct an understanding of the topic through social mediation. Finally, students use cognitive tools, such as multimedia technology, "to extend and amplify [their] representational and analytic capacities" (p. 452). Multimedia technology allows students to combine the use of text, graphics, animation, sound, voice, music, and video to illustrate the results of their investigations and to demonstrate new knowledge and understanding. Throughout project-based learning, teachers provide students with assistance as needed, including teacher-directed instruction, modeling, and scaffolding.

Several advantages of project-based learning have been summarized by Ferretti and Okolo (1996), including increased motivation to learn and persist with a task, improved attention, the development and use of background knowledge, and greater opportunities to collaborate with peers. It is not without its disadvantages, however. Devoting extended periods of time to a few topics may be a concern to teachers who want to expose students to all the curriculum designed for a specific grade level or included on standardized tests.

Content Enhancements

As mentioned previously, secondary teachers have substantial expertise in their content area and are well versed in instructional techniques for presenting this information. Students with disabilities, however, may have difficulty learning content information using standard methods and could benefit from supplements to or adaptations of these techniques. Adaptations or techniques that help students identify, organize, understand, and remember information are called *content enhancements.* According to Platt (1996), content enhancements allow teachers to plan and establish routines for delivering content matter so that it can be organized, understood, and remembered by students. Using a content enhancement is based on the premise that students learn more when (1) they are actively involved, (2) abstract concepts are presented in concrete form, (3) information is organized, (4) relationships between pieces of information are made explicit, and (5) important information is differentiated from unimportant information.

Consultant teachers should have expertise in the development and use of content enhancements. Secondary teachers can collaborate with the consultant teacher to develop expertise in their use. It is acknowledged that secondary teachers are likely to feel overwhelmed just trying to meet the diverse needs of their typical learners. They are advised, however, that the time spent learning about, developing, and using content enhancements is an investment not only in students with special needs but also in all students in their classes, because all are likely to benefit (Anderson et al., 2004).

Anderson and colleagues (2004), Hudson, Lignugaris-Kraft, and Miller (1993), and Ellis and Sabornie (1990) identified several content enhancement techniques that have been used successfully with secondary students with disabilities. They are listed in Action Plan 15.2 and include advanced organizers, graphic organizers, study guides, mnemonic devices, guided notes, audio recordings, and peer-mediated strategies. Although we discuss these

---

Action Plan 15.2   Content Enhancement Techniques

Anderson, Yilmaz, and Wasburn-Moses (2004), Hudson and colleagues (1993), and Ellis and Sabornie (1990) described several content enhancement techniques, including the following:

1. Advanced organizers
2. Graphic organizers
3. Study guides
4. Mnemonic devices
5. Guided notes
6. Audio recordings
7. Peer-mediated instruction

FIGURE 15.1   *Advanced Organizer for a Social Studies Lesson in Global Studies*

THE CIVILIZATIONS OF AFRICA

I. Influence of Geography
    A. Rivers
        1. Limited navigability
    B. Savannahs
    C. Mountains and plateaus
    D. Lakes

II. Languages
    A. The role of linguists
    B. Bantu
    C. Nilotes

III. Oral Traditions
    A. Examples
    B. Importance to African clans, villages, and dynasties

IV. Music and Archeology

techniques separately, teachers may opt to combine several within a single lesson. Again, we advise careful evaluation of their effects on student performance.

Advanced Organizers

A teacher uses an advanced organizer at the beginning of a lesson to provide the secondary student with information about what is to be covered. This information can include the tasks that will be performed, topics or subtopics to be presented, background information, new vocabulary, or anticipated student outcomes. An advanced organizer can be written on the chalkboard, an overhead transparency, or a handout distributed to the class. The teacher may opt to use a verbal format, either by describing this information or by using questions to elicit it from the students. Figure 15.1 is a sample advanced organizer for a social studies lesson.

Graphic Organizers

Despite calls for change, textbooks still figure prominently in content area classes. Secondary teachers can use a visual display, such as a graphic organizer, to illustrate the relationship between two or more pieces of information contained in a content area lesson.

According to Doyle (1999) and Baxendell (2003), a graphic organizer (GO) is a visual representation of concepts that helps organize information, making it easier to learn. A GO can be a graph, chart, diagram (Guastello, 2000), time line, Venn diagram, concept map, flow chart (Doyle, 1999), semantic web, or genealogical tree (Dye, 2000). Because it does not rely as heavily on reading and language skills (Ives & Hoy, 2003), a GO can be useful for modifying complex, vocabulary-intensive materials and for making information more explicit to the reader (Woodward, 1994). The teacher can take material that is poorly organized and make it match the way it is stored in a person's memory. Thus, students do not appear to be learning a series of unrelated terms, facts, or concepts. DiCecco and Gleason (2002) reported that use of a GO increased the posttest scores on a multiple choice social studies test. Ives and Hoy (2003) described the use of GOs to facilitate understanding of higher-level mathematics for secondary students with disabilities.

Horton and Lovitt (1989) described a four-step procedure for constructing GOs. First, the teacher chooses a chapter that has proved difficult for students to master or that is, in the teacher's opinion, poorly written. The teacher breaks this chapter into passages of approximately 1,500 words. The text and the resulting GO can be completed by most students within a typical lesson. Next, the teacher outlines the main ideas contained in the passage. Third, the teacher selects an appropriate GO format. Two options include a hierarchical format and a compare–contrast format. A hierarchical format resembles an outline in that it presents major and minor points. A compare–contrast format illustrates similarities and differences. Completed sample graphic organizers are presented in Figures 15.2 and 15.3. Finally, the teacher prepares teacher and student versions of the GO. Ideally, the GO is clear and simple and can be presented on a single page. The teacher's version contains all the necessary information. The student's version has specific information deleted from it.

To use the GO in a lesson, the teacher first has the students mark the beginning and end of the relevant passage and then read it silently for 15 minutes. Books are then closed and student copies of the GO are distributed. The teacher presents his or her copy for 30 seconds (perhaps using a transparency on an overhead projector) and discusses the

FIGURE 15.2 *Sample Graphic Organizer in a Hierarchical Format for a Global Studies Lesson*

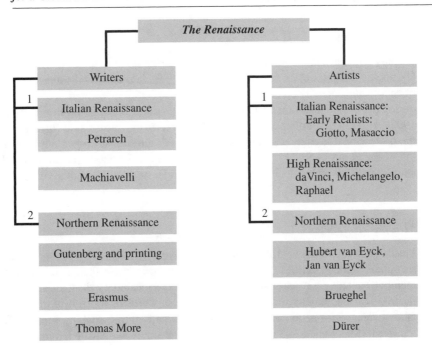

FIGURE 15.3 *Sample Graphic Organizer in a Compare–Contrast Format for Life Science*

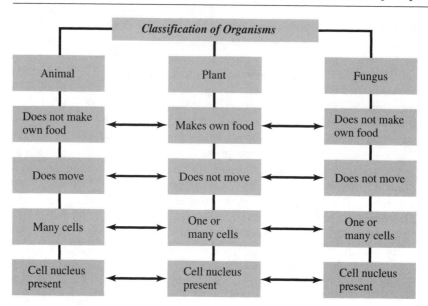

relationships among the items included on the GO. Items are then covered with pieces of paper. The teacher asks questions regarding the information that goes in each box, and students write correct answers on their copies of the GO.

Study Guides

A study guide is a set of statements or questions that relate directly to printed materials in textbooks (Horton, Lovitt, Givens, & Nelson, 1989). It highlights the most important points of an academic activity and can be used as a review before presentation of new information, during a lesson to maintain student engagement, or after a lesson as notes (Boyle & Yeager, 1997). Hudson and colleagues (1993) identified many study guide formats described in the professional literature, including short-answer questions, framed outlines, and matching items. Figures 15.4, 15.5, and 15.6 illustrate these formats. Procedures for developing study guides have been identified by Lovitt and Horton (1994) and are included in Action Plan 15.3.

Mnemonic Devices

Mastropieri and Scruggs (1998, 2002) have advocated the use of mnemonic devices with secondary students with disabilities, particularly to increase their ability to learn and remember content area material. Rather than teach vocabulary through verbal definitions, mnemonics link target words to carefully chosen words or illustrations. Mnemonics provide students with better ways to encode information, thus making it easier for them to retrieve it (Mastropieri & Scruggs, 1998). Teachers may already be familiar with the use of

FIGURE 15.4 *Study Guide Format Using Short-Answer Questions for Physical Science*

Answer these questions:

What are the properties of nonmetals? _____

_____

_____

Identify three nonmetals. _____

_____

How are nonmetals different from metals? _____

_____

_____

FIGURE 15.5 *Study Guide Using a Framed Outline for a Global Studies Lesson*

1. Copernicus argued against the _____ theory. He believed the _____
   was the center of the universe. (p. 137)

2. _____ was a great mathematician who proved Copernicus's theory. (p. 138)

3. Galileo used a _____ to study the planet and prove that Copernicus was
   correct. (p. 139).

FIGURE 15.6 *Study Guide Using Mathing Items*

Rocks	*Characteristics*
1. Igneous rocks	Fine-grained
2. Intrusive rocks	Form as a result of temperature and pressure changes
3. Extrusive rocks	The most common rocks on earth
4. Metamorphic rocks	Coarse-grained

mnemonics; perhaps their students use them now. For example, teachers may have noticed a word penciled in near a student's essay. While correcting, they may see that each letter in this word represented an item on a list, or the first letter of the first word in each of a series of sentences.

Types of Mnemonics Mnemonic techniques include the keyword method, the pegword method, and letter strategies. To use the keyword method, the teacher examines the word

Action Plan 15.3   Developing Study Guides

Teachers interested in developing study guides should follow these steps recommended by Lovitt and Horton (1994):

1. Analyze the material for subject matter and level of difficulty.
2. Select the content to be emphasized during the lesson.
3. Decide on the process students must use. Will students be responding to literal, interpretive, and/or applied items?
4. Consider students' abilities to read, write, listen, and organize.
5. Vary the structure of the study guide with question format and type.
6. Make the study guide as aesthetically pleasing as possible.

or phrase the students need to learn and uses it to create a visual image (Uberti, Scruggs, & Mastropieri, 2003). For example, to help them memorize the fact that Thomas Paine wrote *Common Sense,* students can visualize a picture of two characters. The first character is a man who has written so much that his hand is in pain. The second character tells the first that he would stop writing if he had any common sense.

The pegword method uses rhyming proxies for number. Each pegword rhymes with a number and is easily pictured. *One* is represented by a *bun, two* by *shoe, three* by *tree, four* by *door, five* by *hive, six* by *sticks, seven* by *heaven, eight* by *gate, nine* by *vine,* and *ten* by *hen.* The teacher can help students remember that a wheelbarrow is a second-class lever by telling them to picture a wheelbarrow with the wheel resting against a shoe. *Shoe* is the pegword for *two,* which is synonymous with *second.*

Letter strategies are popular with secondary students who need to remember lists or categories of information. A letter strategy can involve the creation of an acronym, in which each letter of the word represents a word on a list. For example, *TEENS* represents the sensory organs, including the tongue, ears, eyes, nose, and skin. Phrases and sentences can also be used. *ROY G. BIV* represents *red, orange, yellow, green, blue, indigo,* and *violet,* the colors of the light spectrum. The names of the notes in the lines of a treble clef can be represented by *Every Good Boy Does Fine.* As illustrated in Chapter 4, an acronym can also represent the first letter of each of a series of steps in a learning strategy. For example, in *ANSWER, A* stands for *analyze* the situation, *N* for *notice* requirements, *S* for *set* up an outline, *W* for *work* in details, *E* for *engineer* your answer, and *R* for *review* the answer.

Mnemonics need to be taught clearly to students with disabilities if they are to be effective. A teaching sequence is presented in Action Plan 15.4. Although several mnemonics have been described in the professional literature, it is possible that a mnemonic is not available for every group of facts a teacher wants to students to memorize. Heaton and O'Shea (1995) developed STRATEGY to help teachers create their own mnemonics. STRATEGY is presented in Action Plan 15.5.

Teachers should bear in mind that mnemonics will help students in the acquisition and retention of key terms, although this emphasis is not the sole focus of instruction in science and social studies. Also, just because students remember the information does not mean they comprehend it.

Action Plan 15.4   Teaching Mnemonics

If a mnemonic is to help students remember factual information, it will need to be taught clearly. Use the following steps:

1. Identify the purpose of the mnemonic.
2. Demonstrate how the mnemonic works.
3. Have the students memorize the mnemonic and/or its steps.
4. Provide opportunities for the students to use the mnemonic.
5. Provide feedback on their success.
6. Encourage independent application of the mnemonic.

Action Plan 15.5   Developing a Mnemonic

Heaton and O'Shea (1995) suggested STRATEGY for teachers who want to develop their own mnemonics:

S—Start by choosing a behavior or learning outcome that is required in the class and with which students are experiencing difficulty.

T—Task analyze the behavior or learning outcome.

R—Rearrange the wordings of the steps to see if a word can be formed that will facilitate retention.

A—Ask if you can make a word from the first letters of the steps.

T—Try to find a word that relates to the task. An acronym that relates to the anticipated outcome may facilitate student learning.

E—Examine possible synonyms to get the first letter.

G—Get creative. Creativity may reduce the amount of time it takes students to learn the mnemonics.

Y—Yes, a teacher can create a mnemonic!

Guided Notes

Notetaking abilities increase student engagement during lessons, provide students with the opportunity to clarify confusing information, enhance students' understanding of lecture material, and contribute to their ability to prepare for quizzes and exams (Boyle, 2005). Anderson and colleagues (2004) noted that notetaking can be problematic for students, especially students with disabilities. In his review of the literature, Boyle (2005) noted that students with disabilities may not be able to (1) identify information that should be included in notes, (2) write fast enough, or (3) make sense of the notes they do take. Limited notetaking skills can increase student frustration and off-task behavior. Because teachers may use class notes as the basis for items included on quizzes and tests, students with disabilities may score poorly and receive lower grades. Teachers who make a standard set of notes available to students can avoid these learning problems as well as increase the likelihood that students will perform better on quizzes and exams. Guided notes are prepared by the teacher and are intended to guide students through a lecture or a reading assignment. A set of guided notes follows the outline of the lecture or chapter and should contain at least the main ideas covered during a teacher presentation. The teacher can add key terms and phrases, definitions, related issues, and contrasting viewpoints (Lazarus, 1996), although spaces are left in which students write key terms or concepts.

Two types of formats exist for guided notes. The first is a columnar format, which allows students to use single words or phrases to record comparative types of information. The second type is the skeletal format, which contains main ideas and key concepts. Procedures for making guided notes are presented in Action Plan 15.6.

Lazarus (1996) offered some suggestions for using guided notes. First, students will need to be taught to use guided notes. Action Plan 15.7 lists steps teachers can use. Next, she recommended giving notes to all students, not just those with disabilities, because all students who have access to them can improve their grades. She suggested giving a set of guided notes to students before starting a new chapter so that it can serve as a reading guide. The guided notes should also include blanks or a series of letters or numbers to let students know how much information they should record. For example, listing *a, b, c, d,* and *e* lets students know there are five important points to record. At key points during a lecture, Lazarus suggested, teachers can reveal completed sections of a set of guided notes using an overhead projector or PowerPoint presentation. As the lecture continues, students will have access to accurate information. Finally, she recommended taking 5 to 10 minutes at the end of every class to review the notes completed by a randomly selected student and provide feedback. Students can also use this time to clarify the information in their notes.

It can take up to two hours to prepare a set of guided notes; however, the time is well invested (Lazarus, 1996). Guided notes allow the teacher to prioritize information. They can be used during lectures to assist students with notetaking, a task with which many students experience difficulty. Although they need to be modified over time, guided notes can be used in subsequent semesters with different students; thus, the initial investment of time can be worth the effort.

Action Plan 15.6   Making Guided Notes

Lazarus (1996) provided these steps teachers should follow to make guided notes:

1. Prepare the teacher lecture on a computer and save the full text.
2. Create another file in which the teacher's full text has been reduced to the text or notes students will need. This file then becomes the complete set of guided notes that will be revealed section by section during the lecture. Print out and make overheads or convert to a PowerPoint presentation.
3. Take the complete set of guided notes and delete information that students will eventually fill in during class. For example, leave a blank for a key word, but provide the definition. Conversely, provide the key word, but leave a blank so that students can write the definition. Use of an asterisk can signal students that they need to fill in information. Save this file in a separate location.
4. Make sure to use numbers or letters to indicate items on a list.
5. Number the pages in the guided notes. Print, make copies, and distribute to students.

Action Plan 15.7   Teaching Students to Use Guided Notes

To maximize achievement gains, students will need to be taught to use guided notes. Lazarus (1996) suggested the following teaching sequence:

1. Give each student a set of guided notes.
2. Use an overhead to show students their copy and a copy of a completed set of notes that is based on a short three- to five-minute presentation.
3. Present the three- to five-minute lecture live or through videotape. Highlight main ideas as they appear and point out that this information should be recorded on the notes.
4. Steps 1 through 3 can be repeated with material from a textbook.
5. Provide additional practice with another short presentation or piece of textbook material. Instruct students to copy at least the material from the complete set of notes still on display. Encourage them to add information that will help them understand the material.
6. Provide feedback. Peers can compare notes while the teacher circulates among the students.
7. Students can be quizzed. Hopefully, high scores will help them appreciate the value of guided notes.
8. Extend the length of the lecture and/or reading material.
9. For independent practice, give another set of guided notes and a homework assignment that requires reading.

Audio Recordings

Much of the information that secondary students are expected to master is gained by independently reading their textbooks. Obviously, a student with limited reading abilities is at a disadvantage. In Chapter 4, we suggested that secondary teachers tape record sections from textbooks that students with disabilities find difficult to read. Students can listen to these recordings as they follow along in their textbooks. We are familiar with a teacher who taught a normally achieving student to make recordings of chapters from textbooks for a peer with disabilities who is included in the general class. The two students developed their own schedule for making and exchanging recordings, leaving their teacher free to concentrate on other tasks.

Peer-Mediated Strategies

Peer-mediated strategies require that peers act as instructional agents for their fellow students. One example of a peer-mediated strategy is peer tutoring. Older students can tutor younger students, or students in the same class can tutor each other. The student who is acting as a tutor asks questions involving basic facts or details. The other student, the *tutee*, responds orally or in writing. If the tutee's answer is correct, the tutor provides reinforcement and proceeds to the next question. If the tutee is incorrect, the tutor provides the right answer and requires that it be written several times. Students who need extra motivation can earn points for their answers and can compete with other tutoring teams to see who has earned the most points.

Peer tutoring has been used successfully with secondary students with disabilities (Anderson & Yilmaz, 2002; Maheady, Sacca, & Harper, 1988). Its benefits include enhanced student performance, increased opportunities for student interaction, immediate feedback, an increase in on-task behavior, and accommodations for students' different ability levels (Anderson et al., 2004; Spencer et al., 2003); however, it requires careful teacher planning to maximize its effectiveness. All students will need to be taught how to ask questions, judge the accuracy of a response, record, praise, provide corrective feedback, and display materials.

Another peer-mediated strategy is cooperative learning. Cooperative learning is an organizational structure in which a small group of students collaborate to complete academic assignments and achieve academic goals. To use cooperative learning, the teacher first develops a task or a project for the students. This task needs to be clearly explained, with any necessary directions made explicit. Second, the students need to be assigned to groups of three to five individuals. Groups should be heterogeneous; that is, teachers should mix males and females and ensure that the group represents diverse ability levels and ethnic backgrounds. Third, students may need to be taught social skills prior to implementation of cooperative learning. Important social skills include listening, taking turns, complimenting, and giving and receiving constructive criticism. Fourth, the teacher should monitor the group to make sure everyone is participating and working cooperatively. Finally, the teacher should provide time for students to evaluate their work.

Ellis and Sabornie (1990) suggested that cooperative learning procedures can also include the use of a pause procedure. The teacher presents content area instruction for approximately eight minutes and then cues preestablished cooperative learning groups to engage in specific discussions. For example, the teacher might tell students to talk with other group members and identify the main idea and two important details in what was just taught. The teacher allows group discussion for two minutes and then selects a student to present the group's response.

Peer-mediated strategies do more than just increase the academic skill levels of secondary students with disabilities. They also increase the frequency of interactions between students with disabilities and their normally achieving peers. These interactions provide students with more opportunities to get to know one another better and to increase their appreciation for diversity. In addition, students with disabilities are provided with more direct models of appropriate interaction skills.

Hudson and colleagues (1993) identified numerous studies supporting the efficacy of content enhancement techniques for secondary students with disabilities. However, they also discussed some concerns associated with their use. For example, they pointed out that content enhancements have been used primarily to increase student mastery of factual information rather than higher-order skills. Secondary teachers are encouraged to provide stu-

---

Case for Action 15.1

You are preparing a series of lesson focusing on the Civil War. Develop several content enhancement techniques to assist your students.

dents with disabilities with the opportunity to analyze, synthesize, and apply content area information. In addition, Hudson and colleagues pointed out that some content enhancement techniques may require substantial investments of valuable teacher time. Teachers are encouraged to assess the effectiveness of the techniques they use, to work cooperatively to develop these techniques, to work jointly with consultant teachers, and to share their efforts with others. Finally, teachers are reminded that *all* students, not just those with disabilities, can benefit from the use of content enhancement techniques.

Summary

Major shifts in the science and social studies curricula have de-emphasized memorization of disjointed sets of facts and focused on an understanding of themes or "big ideas" and using them to solve problems. In addition to curricular changes, methods of instruction have moved away from teacher lecture, the reading of textbooks, and large-group discussion toward the use of student-oriented, hands-on approaches. Such changes have major implications for secondary students with disabilities. Using hands-on approaches to develop "big ideas" should foster a deeper understanding of important concepts and a better realization of how these themes can be used in students' everyday lives. This chapter described the curricular emphases of science and social studies and how activities-based approaches can be used with students who have disabilities.

Shifts in curricular and instructional approaches are also a source of concern for teachers responsible for developing content area knowledge. Students with disabilities may not have a level of background knowledge that is comparable to that of their peers. During activities-based instruction, they may take longer than their peers to develop the same level of understanding. Also, not all science and social studies content can be learned through activities-based instruction; there are still facts and important concepts that must be memorized.

Content enhancements are available to assist teachers with the delivery of content area instruction. These techniques help students identify, organize, understand, and remember information. Consultant teachers are available to assist secondary teachers in the development and use of content enhancements such as advanced organizers, graphic organizers, study guides, mnemonics, guided notes, audio recordings, and peer-mediated strategies. Although it is time consuming to collaborate with others, develop content enhancements, implement them, and document their effectiveness, it is more time consuming to present instruction from which students do not benefit. Secondary teachers are advised to share the workload with the consultant teacher and save permanent products for future use. Further, they are advised that content enhancements benefit all students in their classes, not just those with disabilities or who are low achieving.

References

Academy for Effective Instruction. (1987). *Working with mildly handicapped students: Design and delivery of academic lessons.* Reston, VA: Council for Exceptional Children.

Adams, T. L. (2003). Reading mathematics: More than words can say. *The Reading Teacher, 56,* 786–795.

Adelman, H. S. (1998). Involving teachers in collaborative efforts to better address the barriers to student learning. *Preventing School Failure, 42*(2), 55–60.

Ahrens, B. C. (2005). Finding a new way: Reinventing a sixth-grade reading program. *Journal of Adolescent & Adult Literacy, 48,* 642–654.

Alan Guttmacher Institute (AGI). (1994). *Testing positive: Sexually transmitted disease and the public health response.* New York: Author.

Alberto, P., & Troutman, A. (2003). *Applied behavior analysis for teachers* (6th ed.). Columbus, OH: Merrill.

Alberto, P. A., & Troutman, A. C. (2006). *Applied behavior analysis for teachers* (7th ed.). Columbus, OH: Pearson Prentice Hall.

Alfassi, M. (1998). Reading for meaning: The efficacy of reciprocal teaching in fostering reading comprehension in high school students in remedial reading classes. *American Educational Research Journal, 35,* 309–332.

Algozzine, B., O'Shea, D. J., Stoddard, K., & Crews, W. B. (1988). Reading and writing competencies of adolescents with learning disabilities. *Journal of Learning Disabilities, 21,* 154–160.

Allen, S., & Edwards-Kyle, D. (1995). Alternatives to expulsion: Houston's school of last resort. *Journal of Emotional and Behavioral Problems, 3,* 22–35.

Alper, S. (1985). The use of teacher questioning to increase independent problem solving in mentally retarded adolescents. *Education and Training of the Mentally Retarded, 20*(1), 83–88.

Alper, S. A., Schloss, P. J., & Schloss, C. N. (1994). *Families of students with disabilities.* Boston: Allyn and Bacon.

American Psychiatric Association. (1985). *Facts about teen suicide.* Washington, DC: Author.

American Psychiatric Association. (1994). *Diagnostic and statistical manual of mental disorders-IV* (4th ed.). Washington, DC: Author.

Anderson, D. M., & Christenson, G. M. (1991). Ethnic breakdown of AIDS related knowledge and attitudes from the national adolescent student health survey. *Journal of Health Education, 22*(1), 30–34.

Anderson, L. M., Evertson, C. M., & Brophy, J. E. (1979). An experimental study of effective teaching in first grade reading groups. *Elementary School Journal, 79,* 193–223.

Anderson, P. L. (1982). A preliminary study of syntax in the written expression of learning disabled children. *Journal of Learning Disabilities, 15,* 359–362.

Anderson, R. C., Hiebert, E. H., Scott, J. A., & Wilkinson, I. A. G. (1985). *Becoming a nation of readers: The report of the Commission on Reading.* Washington, DC: National Academy of Education.

Anderson, S., Yilmaz, O., Wasburn-Moses, L. (2004). Middle and high school students with learning disabilities: Practical academic interventions for general education teachers—A review of the literature. *American Secondary Education, 32*(2), 19–38.

Anderson, S. L., & Yilmaz, O. (2002). *A resource guide for teaching students with disabilities in secondary education classrooms.* Bloomington, IN: Tichenor Publishing.

Anderson-Inman, L. (1998). Electronic text: Literacy medium of the future. *Journal of Adolescent & Adult Literacy, 41,* 678–682.

Andrews, S. E. (1998). Using inclusion literature to promote positive attitudes toward disabilities. *Journal of Adolescent & Adult Literacy, 41,* 420–426.

Archambeault, B. (1992). Personalizing study skills in secondary students. *Journal of Reading, 35,* 468–472.

Archer, A., & Gleason, M. (1993). *Advanced skills for school success: Completing daily assignments* (Module 2). North Billerica, MA: Curriculum Associates.

Archer, A., & Gleason, M. M. (1998). *Power: A writing strategy applied to research reports.* Unpublished workshop materials.

Archer, A. L., Gleason, M. M., & Isaacson, S. (1995). Effective instructional delivery. In P. T. Cegelka & W. H. Berdine (Eds.), *Effective instruction for students with learning difficulties* (pp. 161–194). Boston: Allyn and Bacon.

Archer, A. L., Gleason, M. M., & Vachon, V. L. (2003). Decoding and fluency: Foundation skills for struggling older readers. *Learning Disability Quarterly, 26,* 89–101.

Armbruster, B. B., & Anderson, T. H. (1988). On selecting "considerate" content area textbooks. *Remedial and Special Education, 9*(1), 47–52.

Armbruster, B. B., Anderson, T. H., & Meyer, J. L. (1991). Improving content-area reading using instructional graphics. *Reading Research Quarterly, 26,* 393–416.

Armbruster, B. B., & Nagy, W. E. (1992). Vocabulary in content area lessons. *The Reading Teacher, 45,* 550–551.

Armstrong v. Kline. (1980). 476 F. Supp. 583 (E. D. Pa. 1979) aff'd CA 78-0172 (3rd Cir. July 15, 1980).

Artesani, A. J. (2001). *Understanding the purpose of challenging behavior: A guide to conducting functional assessments.* Upper Saddle River, NJ: Pearson.

Aseltine, R. H., & DeMartino, R. (2004). An outcome evaluation of the SOS Suicide Prevention program. *American Journal of Public Health, 94,* 446–451.

Aspel, N., Bettis, G., Test, D. W., & Wood, W. M. (1998). An evaluation of a comprehensive system of transition services. *CDEI, 21*(2), 203–222.

Atwell, N. (1987). *In the middle: Writing, reading, and learning with adolescents.* Portsmouth, NH: Heinemann.

Au, K. H. (1997). Literacy for all students: Ten steps toward making a difference. *The Reading Teacher, 51,* 186–194.

Austin, V. (2001). Teachers' beliefs about co-teaching. *Remedial and Special Education, 22,* 245–255.

Babbitt, B., & Miller, S. (1996). Using hypermedia to improve the mathematics problem-solving skills of students with learning disabilities. *Journal of Learning Disabilities, 29*(4), 391–401, 412.

Babbitt, B. C., & White, C. M. (2002). R U ready? Helping students assess their readiness for postsecondary education. *Teaching Exceptional Children, 35*(2), 62–66.

Babbitt, S., & Byrne, M. (1999/2000). Finding the keys to educational progress in urban youth: Three case studies. *Journal of Adolescent & Adult Literacy, 43,* 368–378.

Badian, N. A. (1999). Reading disability defined as a discrepancy between listening and reading comprehension: A longitudinal study of stability, gender differences, and prevalence. *Journal of Learning Disabilities, 32,* 138–148.

Baer, R. M., Flexer, R. W., Beck, S., Amstutz, N., Hoffman, L., Brothers, J., et al. (2003). A collaborative followup study on transition service utilization and post-school outcomes. *Career Development of Exceptional Individuals, 26,* 7–25.

Baker, L., & Wigfield, A. (1999). Dimensions of children's motivation for reading and their relations to reading activity and reading achievement. *Reading Research Quarterly, 34,* 452–477.

Baker, S., Gersten, R., & Graham, S. (2003). Teaching expressive writing to students with learning disabilities: Research-based applications and examples. *Journal of Learning Disabilities, 36,* 109–123.

Barnitz, J. G., & Speaker, R. B., Jr. (1999). Electronic and linguistic connections in one diverse 21st-century classroom. *The Reading Teacher, 52,* 874–877.

Barrett, T. C. (1968). Taxonomy of cognitive and affective dimensions of reading comprehension. In T. Clymer (Ed.), *Innovation and change in reading instruction.* Chicago: University of Chicago Press.

Barry, A. L. (1998). Hispanic representation in literature for children and young adults. *Journal of Adolescent & Adult Literacy, 41,* 630–637.

Battle v. Commonwealth. (1980). 79, 2158, 2188-90, 2568-70 (3rd Cir. July 18, 1980).

Baumann, J. F., Hooten, H., & White, P. (1999). Teaching comprehension through literature: A teacher-research project to develop fifth graders' reading strategies and motivation. *The Reading Teacher, 53,* 38–51.

Bauman-Waengler, J. (2000). *Articulatory and phonological impairments: A clinical focus.* Boston: Allyn and Bacon.

Baumgart, D., Filler, J., & Askvig, B. A. (1991). Perceived importance of social skills: A survey of teachers, parents, and other professionals. *Journal of Special Education, 25,* 236–251.

Baxendell, B. W. (2003). Consistent, coherent, creative: The 3 C's of graphic organizers. *Teaching Exceptional Learners, 35*(3), 46–53.

Baxter, J. A., Woodward, J., & Olson, D. (2005). Writing in mathematics: An alternative form of communication for academically low-achieving students. *Learning Disabilities Research & Practice, 20*(2), 119–135.

Beattie, J., & Algozzine, B. (1982). Improving basic academic skills of educable mentally retarded adolescents. *Education and Training of the Mentally Retarded, 17*(3), 255–258.

Beck, I. L., & McKeown, M. G. (1981). Developing questions that promote comprehension: The story map. *Language Arts, 58,* 913–918.

Beck, I. L., McKeown, M. G., Hamilton, R. L., & Kucan, L. (1997). *Questioning the author: An approach for enhancing student engagement with text.* Newark, DE: International Reading Association.

Beitchman, J. H., Wilson, B., Douglas, L., Young, A., & Adlaf, E. (2001). Substance use disorders in young adults with and without LD: Predictive and concurrent relationships. *Journal of Learning Disabilities, 34*(4), 317–332.

Bellamy, G. T., Rhodes, L. E., Bourdeau, P., & Mank, D. (1986). Mental retardation services in sheltered workshops and day activity programs: Consumer outcomes and policy alternatives. In F. R. Rusch (Ed.), *Competitive employment issues and strategies* (pp. 257–271). Baltimore, MD: Paul H. Brookes.

Bender, W. N. (1987). Secondary personality and behavioral problems in adolescents with learning disabilities. *Journal of Learning Disabilities, 20,* 280–285.

Bender, W. N., & Golden, L. B. (1988). Adaptive behavior of learning disabled and non-learning disabled children. *Learning Disability Quarterly, 11,* 55–61.

Bender, W. N., Shubert, T. H., & McLaughlin, P. J. (2001). Invisible kids: Preventing school violence by identifying kids in trouble. *Intervention in School and Clinic, 37*(2), 105–111.

Bennett, W. (1986). *What works: Schools without drugs.* Washington, DC: U.S. Department of Education.

Bennett, W. J. (1987). *What works: Research about teaching and learning* (2nd ed.). Washington, DC: U.S. Department of Education.

Benz, M. R., Lindstrom, L., & Yovanoff, P. (2000). Improving graduation and employment outcomes of students with disabilities: Predictive factors and student perspectives. *Exceptional Children, 66,* 509–529.

Bereiter, C., & Scardamalia, M. (1982). From conversation to composition: The role of instruction in a developmental process. In R. Glaser (Ed.), *Advances in instructional psychology* (Vol. 2, pp. 1–64). Hillsdale, NJ: Erlbaum.

Bernstein, D. A., & Borkovec, T. D. (1973). *Progressive relaxation training: A manual for the helping professions.* Champaign, IL: Research Press.

Bigge, J. (1988). *Curriculum based instruction for special education students.* Mountain View, CA: Mayfield.

Bigler, J. K. (1984). Increasing inferential comprehension scores of intermediate-age mildly retarded students using two direct teaching procedures. *Education and Training of the Mentally Retarded, 19*(2), 132–140.

Bintz, W. P. (1993). Resistant readers in secondary education: Some insights and implications. *Journal of Reading, 36,* 604–615.

Bintz, W. P. (1997). Exploring reading nightmares of middle and secondary school teachers. *Journal of Adolescent & Adult Literacy, 41,* 12–24.

Blachowicz, C. L. Z. (1985). Vocabulary development and reading: From research to instruction. *Reading Teacher, 38,* 876–881.

Black, R. S., & Rojewski, J. (1998). The role of social awareness in the employment success of adolescents with mild mental retardation. *Education and Training in Mental Retardation and Developmental Disabilities, 33*(2), 144–161.

Blackbourn, J. M. (1989). Acquisition and generalization of social skills in elementary-aged children with learning disabilities. *Journal of Learning Disabilities, 22,* 28–34.

Blackorby, J., & Wagner, M. (1996). Longitudinal postschool outcomes of youth with disabilities: Findings from the national longitudinal transition study. *Exceptional Children, 62*(5), 399–413.

Blanck, P. D., & Braddock, D. L. (1998). *The Americans with Disabilities Act and emerging workforce: Employment of people with mental retardation.* Washington, DC: American Association on Mental Retardation.

Bleile, K. M. (2004). *Manual of articulation and phonological disorders: Infants through adulthood* (2nd ed). Florence, KY: Thompson/Delmar Learning.

Block, C. C., & Israel, S. E. (2004). The ABCs of performing highly effective think-alouds. *The Reading Teacher, 58,* 154–167.

Bloodgood, J. W., & Pacifici, L. C. (2004). Bridging word study to intermediate classrooms. *The Reading Teacher, 58,* 250–263.

Bloodstein, D. (1995). *A handbook on stuttering.* San Diego, CA: Singular Publishing.

Blough, G. O., & Schwartz, J. (1990). *Elementary school science and how to teach it* (8th ed.). Fort Worth, TX: Holt, Rinehart and Winston.

Blum, R. W., & Rinehart, P. M. (1997). *Reducing the risk: Connections that make a difference in the lives of youth.* Minneapolis: University of Minnesota, Division of General Pediatrics and Adolescent Health.

Board of Education of Peoria v. Illinois State Board of Education. (1982). 1531 F. Supp. 56 148 (C. D. ILL. 1982).

Bolt, S. E., & Thurlow, M. L. (2004). Five of the most frequently allowed testing accommodations in state policy: Synthesis of research. *Remedial and Special Education, 25,* 141–152.

Bos, C. S., & Vaughn, S. (2002). *Strategies for teaching students with learning and behavioral problems* (5th ed). Boston: Allyn and Bacon.

Boswell, J., Fox, E., Hubbard, B., & Coyle, L. (1992). A comparison of HIV-related knowledge, attitudes, and behaviors among adolescents living in rural and urban areas of a southern state. *Journal of Health Education, 23*(4), 238–243.

Bouck, E. C. (2004). Exploring secondary special education mild mental impairment: A program in search of its place. *Remedial and Special Education, 25,* 367–382.

Bourdeau, P. E., Close, D. W., & Sowers, J. (1986). An experimental analysis of generalization of banking skills from classroom to bank settings in the community. *Education and Training of the Mentally Retarded, 21*(2), 98–107.

Boyle E. A., Rosenberg, M. S., Connelly, V. J., Washburn, S. G., Brinckerhoff, L. C., & Banjeree, M. (2003). Effects of audio texts on the acquisition of secondary-level content by students with mild disabilities. *Learning Disabilities Quarterly, 26,* 203–214.

Boyle, J. R. (2005). Enhancing the note-taking skills of students with mild disabilities. Retrieved July 26, 2005, from www.ldonline.org/ld_indepth/writing/notetaking.html.

Boyle, J. R., & Yeager, N. (1997). Blueprints for learning: Using cognitive frameworks for understanding. *Teaching Exceptional Children, 29*(4), 26–31.

Bradley D. F., & Calvin, M. B. (1998). Grading modified assignments: Equity or compromise. *Teaching Exceptional Children, 31*(2), 24–29.

Brandt, R. (1992). On performance assessment: A conversation with Grant Wiggins. *Educational Leadership, 49,* 35–37.

Brantlinger, E. A. (1984). *Teachers' perceptions of the sexual attitudes and knowledge of their mildly mentally handicapped secondary students.* Unpublished manuscript.

Brigance, A. (1980). *BRIGANCE® Diagnostic Inventory of Essential Skills.* North Billerica, MA: Curriculum Associates.

Brightbill, C. K. (1966). *Educating for leisure-centered living.* Harrisburg, PA: Stackpole.

Brinckerhoff, L. C. (1996). Making the transition to higher education: Opportunities for student empowerment. *Journal of Learning Disabilities, 29*(2), 118–136.

Briney, M. S., & Satcher, J. (1996). *The relationship between learning disabilities and delinquency and the vocational rehabilitation process regarding specific learning disabilities.* (ERIC Document Reproduction Service No. ED 405 682)

Brolin, D. (1992). *Life centered career education assessment batteries and competency units.* Reston, VA: Council for Exceptional Children.

Brolin, D. E. (1997). *Life centered career education: A competency based approach* (5th ed.). Reston, VA: Council for Exceptional Children.

Bromley, K., & Powell, P. (1999). Interest journals motivate student writers. *The Reading Teacher, 53,* 111–112.

Brook, J. S., Whiteman, M., & Gordon, A. S. (1985). Stages of drug use in adolescence: Personality, peer, and family correlates. *Developmental Psychology, 19,* 269–277.

Brooks-Gunn, J., Boyer, C. B., & Hein, K. (1988). Preventing HIV infection and AIDS in children and adolescents. *American Psychologist, 43,* 958–964.

Brophy, J. E. (1983). Classroom organization and management. *Elementary School Journal, 83,* 265–287.

Browder, D. M., & Grasso, E. (1999). Teaching money skills to individuals with mental retardation. *Remedial and Special Education, 10*(5), 297–308.

Browder, D. M., Spooner, F., Algozzine, R., Ahlgrim-Delzell, L., Flowers, C., & Karvonen, M. (2003). What we know and need to know about alternate assessment. *Exceptional Children, 70,* 45–61.

Brown, A. L., Campione, J. C., & Day, J. D. (1981). Learning to learn: On training students to learn from texts. *Educational Researcher, 10*(2), 14–21.

Brown, K. J. (1999/2000). What kind of text—For whom and when? Textual scaffolding for beginning readers. *The Reading Teacher, 53,* 292–307.

Brown, L., & Hammill, D. D. (1990). *Behavior rating profile.* Austin, TX: Pro-Ed.

Brown, L., & Leigh, J. E. (1986). *Adaptive behavior inventory.* Austin, TX: Pro-Ed.

Brown, M. R., Higgins, K., Pierce, T., Hong, E., & Thoma, C. (2003). Secondary students' perceptions of school life with regard to alienation: The

effects of disability, gender, and race. *Learning Disability Quarterly, 26,* 227–238.

Brozo, W. G., & Hargis, C. H. (2003). Taking seriously the idea of reform: One high school's efforts to make reading more responsive to all students. *Journal of Adolescent & Adult Literacy, 47,* 14–23.

Bryan, T., & Sullivan-Burstein, K. (1997). Homework how to's. *Teaching Exceptional Children 29*(6), 32–37.

Bryant, B., & Rivera, D. (1997). Educational assessment of mathematics skills and abilities. *Journal of Learning Disabilities, 30*(1), 57–68.

Bryant, D. P., Goodwin, M., Bryant, B. R., & Higgins, K. (2003). Vocabulary instruction for students with learning disabilities: A review of the research. *Learning Disability Quarterly, 26,* 117–128.

Bryant, D. P., Ugel, N., Thompson, S., & Hamff, A. (1999). Instructional strategies for content-area reading instruction. *Intervention in School and Clinic, 34,* 293–302.

Bui, Y. N. (2002). *The demand writing instructional model: Impacting the writing performance of students with learning disabilities and low-performing students from culturally and linguistically diverse backgrounds on the statewide writing assessment.* Unpublished doctoral dissertation, University of Kansas, Lawrence.

Buikema, J. L., & Graves, M. F. (1993). Teaching students to use context cues to infer word meanings. *Journal of Reading, 36,* 450–457.

Burbach, H. J., & Babbitt, C. E. (1988). Physically disabled students on the college campus. *Remedial and Special Education, 9*(2), 12–19.

Burns, B. (1998). Changing the classroom climate with literature circles. *Journal of Adolescent & Adult Literacy, 42,* 124–129.

Bursuch, W. D., Rose, E., Cowen, S., & Yahaya, M. A. (1989). Nationwide survey of postsecondary education services for students with learning disabilities. *Exceptional Children, 56,* 46–265.

Bursuck, W., Polloway, E. A., Plante, L., Epstein, M. E., Jayanthi, M., & McConeghy, J. L. (1996). Report card grading and adaptations: A national survey of classroom practices. *Exception Children, 62,* 301–318.

Byrom, E., & Katz, G. (Eds.). (1991). *HIV prevention and AIDS education: Resources for special educators.* Reston, VA: Council for Exceptional Children.

Cain, L., Levine, S., & Elzey, F. (1963). *Manual for the Cain-Levine School Competency Scale.* Palo Alto, CA: Consulting Psychologists Press.

Cairns, R. B., & Cairns, B. D. (1983). *Gender similarities and differences: A developmental perspective.* Paper presented at the Nags Head Conferences, Nags Head, NC.

Caldwell, J., & Leslie, L. (2003/2004). Does proficiency in middle school reading assure proficiency in high school reading? The possible role of think-alouds. *Journal of Adolescent & Adult Literacy, 47,* 324–335.

Calhoun, M. L. (1985). Typing contrasted with handwriting in language arts instruction for moderately mentally retarded students. *Education and Training of the Mentally Retarded, 20*(1), 48–52.

Camp, D. (2000). It takes two: Teaching with twin texts of fact and fiction. *The Reading Teacher, 53,* 400–408.

Campbell, J. R., Voelkl, K. E., & Donahue, P. L. (1998). *Report brief: NAEP 1996 trends in academic progress.* Washington, DC: National Center for Education Statistics.

Cantrell, R. P., & Cantrell, M. L. (1995). Recapturing a generation: The future of secondary programs for students with disabilities. *Preventing School Failure, 39*(3), 25–28.

Capital Publications. (1997). Special education dropout rate remains stagnant. *Special Education Law Reporter, 23*(1), 1–2.

Capuzzi, D. (1986). Adolescent suicide: Prevention and intervention. *Counseling and Human Development, 19*(2), 1–9.

Carl D. Perkins Vocational and Applied Technical Education Act Amendment of 1998, P.L. 105-332, Section 1b, Oct. 31, 1998, 112 Stat 3076.

Carl D. Perkins Vocational and Applied Technical Education Act of 1985, P.L. 98-524, Section 1, Oct. 13, 1984, 98 Stat 2437.

Carnine, D. (1989). Designing practice activities. *Journal of Learning Disabilities, 22,* 603–607.

Carnine, D. (1995, April). *The BIG accommodation for the middle grades.* Presentation at the annual meeting of the Council for Exceptional Children, Indianapolis, IN.

Carnine, D. (1997). Instructional design in mathematics for students with learning disabilities. *Journal of Learning Disabilities, 30*(2), 130–141.

Carpenter, C. D., Ray, M. S., & Bloom, L. A. (1995). Portfolio assessment: Opportunities and challenges. *Intervention in School and Clinic, 31*(1), 34–41.

Carr, E., & Wilson, K. K. (1986). Guidelines for evaluating vocabulary instruction. *Journal of Reading, 29,* 588–595.

Carrow-Woolfolk, E. (1998). *Comprehensive assessment of spoken language.* Circle Pines, MN: American Guidance Service.

Carson, S. A. (1999). A veteran enters the reading wars: My journey. *The Reading Teacher, 53,* 212–224.

Carter, J., & Sugai, G. (1988). Teaching social skills. *Teaching Exceptional Children, 54,* 68–71.

Carter, J. F. (1993). Self-management: Education's ultimate goal. *Teaching Exceptional Children, 25*(3), 28–32.

Carter, M. J., & Nelson, D. A. (1992). Leisure today: Leisure awareness in society. *Journal of Physical Education, Recreation and Dance, 63*(8), 25–55.

Cartledge G., & Kiarie, M. W. (2001). Learning social skills through literature for children and adolescents. *Teaching Exceptional Children, 34*(2), 40–47.

Cartwright, G. P., Cartwright, C. A., & Ward, M. E. (1995). *Educating special learners* (4th ed.). Belmont, CA: Wadsworth.

Cassady, J. K. (1998). Wordless books: No-risk tools for inclusive middle-grade classrooms. *Journal of Adolescent & Adult Literacy, 41,* 428–433.

Cassidy, J., & Wenrich, J. K. (1998/99). Literacy research and practice: What's hot, what's not, and why. *The Reading Teacher, 52,* 402–406.

Cavanaugh, R. A., Heward, W. L., & Donelson, F. (1996). Effects of response cards during lesson closure on the academic performance of secondary students in an earth science course. *Journal of Applied Behavior Analysis, 29,* 403–406.

Cawley, J., Parmar, R., Yan, W., & Miller, J. (1998). Arithmetic computation performance of students with learning disabilities: Implications for curriculum. *Learning Disabilities Research & Practice,* *13*(2), 68–74.

Cawley, J. F. (1994). Science for students with disabilities. *Remedial and Special Education, 15*(2), 67–71.

Cawley, J. F., Kahn, H., & Tedesco, A. (1989). Vocational education and students with learning disabilities. *Journal of Learning Disabilities, 22,* 630–634.

Cena, M. E., & Mitchell, J. P. (1998). Anchored instruction: A model for integrating the language arts through content area study. *Journal of Adolescent & Adult Literacy, 41,* 559–561.

Centers for Disease Control. (2002). *2001 STD prevention surveillance report.* Retrieved on July 20, 2004, from www.cdc.gov/std/stats00/2000SFAdol&Yadults.html.

Centers for Disease Control (2003). *National Vital Statistics Report, 52*(10). Retrieved on July 20, 2004, from http://cdc.gov/nchs/fastats/pdf/nvsr52_lotB.pdf.

Centers for Disease Control and Prevention. (1999). *HIV/AIDS surveillance report, 11*(1).

Centre for Addiction and Mental Health. (1996). People with disabilities. *Virtual Resources for the Addiction Treatment System.* Available www.sano.arf.org.

Chadsey, J. G., Linneman, D., Rusch, F. R., & Cimera, R. E. (1997). The impact of social integration interventions and job coaches in work settings. *Education and Training in Mental Retardation and Developmental Disabilities, 32*(4), 281–292.

Chadsey-Rusch, J. (1992). Toward defining and measuring social skills in employment settings. *American Journal on Mental Retardation, 96,* 405–418.

Chadsey-Rusch, J., & Rusch, F. R. (1996). Promising transition practices for youths with disabilities. *Contemporary Education, 68*(1), 9–12.

Chall, J. S. (1967). *Learning to read: The great debate.* New York: McGraw-Hill.

Chandler, K. (1997). The beach book club: Literacy in the "lazy days of summer." *Journal of Adolescent & Adult Literacy, 41,* 104–115.

Chandler, L. K., & Dahlquist, C. M. (2002). *Functional assessment: Strategies to prevent and remediate challenging behavior in school settings.* Upper Saddle River, NJ: Pearson.

Chilcoat, G. W. (1987). Teacher talk: Keep it clear! *Academic Therapy, 22,* 263–271.

Children's Literature and Reading Special Interest Group of the International Reading Association. (2000). 1999 notable books for a global society: A K–12 list. *The Reading Teacher, 53,* 374–380.

Chow, S. H. L. (1981). *A study of academic learning time of mainstreamed learning disabled students.* San Francisco: Far West Educational Laboratory for Educational Research and Development.

Christiansen, J., & Vogel, J. R. (1998). A decision model for grading students with disabilities. *Teaching Exceptional Children, 31*(2), 30–35.

Ciardiello, A. V. (1998). Did you ask a good question today? Alternative cognitive and metacognitive strategies. *Journal of Adolescent & Adult Literacy, 42,* 210–219.

Clark, G. M., Field, S., Patton, J. R., Brolin, D. E., & Sitlingon, P. L. (1994). Life skills instruction: A necessary component for all students with disabilities. A position statement of the Division on Career Development and Transition. *Career Development for Exceptional Individuals, 17,* 125–134.

Clary, L. M. (1991). Getting adolescents to read. *Journal of Reading, 34,* 340–345.

Cleland, J. V. (1999). We can charts: Building blocks for student-led conferences. *The Reading Teacher, 52,* 588–595.

Clement-Heist, K., Seigel, S., & Gaylord-Ross, R. (1992). Simulated and in situ vocational social skills training for youths with learning disabilities. *Exceptional Children, 58,* 336–345.

Clyde, J. A. (2003). Stepping inside the story world: The subtext strategy—A tool for connecting and comprehending. *The Reading Teacher, 57,* 150–160.

Cobb, R. G., & Larkin, D. (1985). Assessment and placement of handicapped pupils into secondary vocational education. In N. S. Bley & C. A. Thornton (Eds.), *Teaching mathematics to the learning disabled* (pp. 113–129). Rockville, MD: Aspen Systems.

Cohen, L., & Spenciner, L. J. (2005). *Teaching students with mild and moderate disabilities.* Columbus, OH: Pearson Prentice Hall.

Cohen, M., & Gies, S. V. (2002). *Specialized courts.* Washington, DC: U.S. Department of Justice.

Retrieved July 12, 2004, at www.dsgonline.com/ Documents/TAToolKits_SpecalizedCourts.pdf.

Cohen, S. (1986). Teaching new material. *Exceptional Children, 20,* 50–51.

Cohen, T. L. (1992). Utilizing the C-Zorloc instrument to determine locus of control for learning disabled children and associated levels of depression. *Dissertation Abstracts International,* 53-09B:4947. Order# AAI9302940.

Cole, M. L., & Cole, J. T. (1989). *Effective intervention with the language impaired child.* Rockville, MD: Aspen Systems.

Coleman, M., & Vaugh, S. (2000). Reading interventions for students with emotional/behavioral disorders. *Behavioral Disorders, 25,* 93–104.

Collet-Klingenberg, L. L. (1998). The reality of best practices in transition: A case study. *Exceptional Children, 65*(1), 67–78.

Colley, D. A., & Jamison, D. (1998). Post school results for youth with disabilities: Key indicators and policy implications. *CDEI, 21*(2), 145–160.

Colozzi, G. A., Coleman-Kennedy, M., Fay, R., Hurley, W., Magliozzi, M., Shackle, K., & Walsh, P. (1986). Data-based integration of a student with moderate special needs. *Education and Training of the Mentally Retarded, 21*(3), 192–199.

Colson, S. E., & Carlson, J. K. (1993). HIV/AIDS education for students with special needs. *Intervention in School and Clinic, 28,* 262–274.

Conderman, G., & Katsiyannis, A. (2002). Instructional issues and practices in secondary special education. *Remedial and Special Education, 23,* 169–179.

Conley, M. W., & Hinchman, K. A. (2004). No Child Left Behind: What it means for U.S. adolescents and what we can do about it. *Journal of Adolescent & Adult Literacy, 48,* 42–50.

Cordes, T. L., & Howard, R. W. (2005). Concepts of work, leisure and retirement in adults with an intellectual disability. *Education and Training in Developmental Disabilities, 40*(2), 99–108.

Cosden, M. (2001). Risk and resilience for substance abuse among adolescents and adults with LD. *Journal of Learning Disabilities, 34*(4), 352–358.

Council for Exceptional Children. (1994). Statistical profile of special education in the United States, 1994. *Teaching Exceptional Children, 26*(Suppl.), 1–4.

Courtney, A. M., & Abodeeb, T. L. (1999). Diagnostic-reflective portfolios. *The Reading Teacher, 52,* 708–714.

Cowen, J. E. (2003). *A balanced approach to beginning reading instruction.* Newark, DE: International Reading Association.

Cowen, S. E. (1988). Coping strategies of university students with learning disabilities. *Journal of Learning Disabilities, 21*(3), 161–164.

Crocker, A. C., Lavin, A. T., Palfrey, J. S., Porter, S. M., Shaw, D. M., & Weill, K. S. (1994). Supports for children with HIV infection in school: Best practices guidelines. *Journal of School Health, 64,* 32–34.

Crowe, T. (1995). *Youth crime and community safety.* Paper presented at a meeting of the Eugene City Club, Eugene, OR.

Crystal, D. (1981). *Clinical linguistics.* New York: Springer-Verlag Wien.

Csikszentmihalyi, M. (1990). *Flow: The psychology of optimal experience.* New York: Harper & Row.

Cullinan, D., Schloss, P. J., & Epstein, M. H. (1987). Relative prevalence and correlates of depressive characteristics among seriously emotionally disturbed and nonhandicapped students. *Behavioral Disorders, 12,* 90–98.

Daiute, C. A. (1986). Performance limits on writers. In R. Beach & L. S. Bridwell (Eds.), *New directions in composition research* (pp. 205–224). New York: Guilford.

Daley, C. E., & Onwuegbuzie, A. J. (1995). *Predictors of juvenile delinquency and violence.* (ERIC Document Reproduction Service No. ED 413 564)

Dalton, B., Morocco, C. C., Tivnan, T., & Mead, P. L. R. (1997). Supported inquiry science: Teaching for conceptual change in urban and suburban science classrooms. *Journal of Learning Disabilities, 30,* 670–684.

Daniels, H. (2002). *Literature circles: Voices and choice in book clubs and reading groups* (2nd ed.). Portland, ME: Stenhouse.

Darch, C., Carnine, D., & Gersten, R. (1984). Explicit instruction in mathematics problem solving. *Journal of Educational Research, 77,* 351–359.

Darling, S., & Lee, J. (2003/2004). Linking parents to reading instruction. *The Reading Teacher, 57,* 382–384.

Davies, D. K., Stock, E., & Wehmeyer, M. L. (2002). Enhancing independent time-management skills of individuals with mental retardation using a palmtop personal computer. *Mental Retardation,40*(5), 358–365.

Davies, D. K., Stock, E., & Wehmeyer, M. L. (2003a). Application of computer simulation to teach ATM access to individuals with intellectual disabilities. *Education and Training in Developmental Disabilities, 38*(4), 451–456.

Davies, D. K., Stock, E., & Wehmeyer, M. L. (2003b). Utilization of computer technology to facilitate money management by individuals with mental retardation. *Education and Training in Developmental Disabilities, 38*(1), 106–112.

Davis, C. L. (1997). The power of newsprint. *Journal of Adolescent & Adult Literacy, 41,* 136–137.

deBettencourt, L. U. (2002). Understanding the differences between IDEA and Secion 504. *Teaching Exceptional Children, 34*(3), 16–23.

deBettencourt, L. U., Bonaro, D. A., & Sabornie, E. J. (1995). Career development services offered to postsecondary students with learning disabilities. *Learning Disabilities Research & Practice, 10*(2), 102–107.

DeHotman, S. L., Hughes, A. G., & Green-Burns, W. B. (2000). "Gangstas" in your classroom: How to recognize them and what teachers should know. *Beyond Behavior, 10*(2), 24–27.

De Le Paz, S., & MacArthur, C. (2003). Knowing the how and why of history: Expectations for secondary students with and without learning disabilities. *Learning Disability Quarterly, 26,* 142–154.

Deno, E. (1970). Special education as developmental capital. *Exceptional Children, 37,* 229–237.

Deno, S. (1985). Curriculum-based assessment: The emerging alternative. *Exceptional Children, 52,* 219–232.

Deno, S., & Mirkin, P. (1977). *Data-based program modification: A manual.* Minneapolis: University of Minnesota, Leadership Training Institute.

Denton, D. R. (1999). Clarifying information in the reading wars. *The Reading Teacher, 53,* 93.

Deshler, D. D. (2005). Adolescents with learning disabilities: Unique challenges and a source for hope. *Learning Disability Quarterly, 28,* 122–124.

Deshler, D. D., Ellis, E., & Lenz, K. (1996). *Teaching the adolescent with learning disabilities: Strategies and methods* (2nd ed.) Denver: Love.

Deshler, D. D., Putnam, M. L., & Bulgren, J. A. (1985). Academic accommodations for adolescents with behavior and learning problems. In S. Braaten, R. B. Rutherford, & W. Evans (Eds.), *Programming for adolescents with behavioral disorders* (Vol. 2, pp. 20–30). Reston, VA: Council for Exceptional Children.

Deshler, D. D., Schumaker, J. B., & Lenz, B. K. (1984). Academic and cognitive interventions for LD adolescents: Part I. *Journal of Learning Disabilities, 17,* 108–117.

Deshler, D., Schumaker, J., Lenz, B., & Ellis, E. (1984). Academic and cognitive interventions for LD adolescents. *Journal of Learning Disabilities, 17,* 170–179.

Devlin, S. D., & Elliot, R. N. (1992). Drug use patterns of adolescents with behavioral disorders. *Behavioral Disorders, 17,* 264–272.

Dewitz, P., & Dewitz, P. K. (2003). They can read the words, but they can't understand: Refining comprehension assessment. *The Reading Teacher, 56,* 422–435.

Diana v. State Board of Education. (1970). No. C-70-37 RFR (District Court of Northern California Feb. 1970).

DiCecco, V. M., & Gleason, M. M. (2002). Using graphic organizers to attain relational knowledge from expository text. *Journal of Learning Disabilities, 35,* 306–320.

Dickson, S. (1999). Integrating reading and writing to teach compare-contrast text structure: A research-based methodology. *Reading & Writing Quarterly, 15,* 49–79.

Dieker, L. A. (2001). What are the characteristics of "effective" middle and high school co-taught teams for students with disabilities? *Preventing School Failure, 46,* 14–23.

Dielman, T. E., Butchart, A. T., & Shope, J. T. (1993). Structural equation model tests of patterns of family interaction, peer alcohol use, and intrapersonal predictors of adolescent alcohol use and misuse. *Journal of Drug Education, 23,* 273–316.

Diller, D. (1999). Opening the dialogue: Using culture as a tool in teaching young African American children. *The Reading Teacher, 52,* 820–828.

Dillner, M. (1993/1994). Using hypermedia to enhance content area instruction. *Journal of Reading, 37,* 260–270.

Dillon, D. R., O'Brien, D. G., & Heilman, E. E. (2000). Literacy research in the next millennium: From paradigms to pragmatism and practicality. *Reading Research Quarterly, 35,* 10–26.

Dole, J., Duffy, G., Roehler, L., & Pearson, P. D. (1991). Moving from the old to the new: Research on reading comprehension. *Review of Educational Research, 61,* 239–264.

Donahue, D. (2003). Reading across the great divide: English and math teachers apprentice one another as readers and disciplinary insiders. *Journal of Adolescent & Adult Literacy, 47,* 24–37.

Donahue, K., & Zigmond, N. (1990). Academic grades of ninth-grade urban learning disabled students and low-achieving peers. *Exceptionality, 1,* 17–27.

Dowhower, S. L. (1999). Supporting a strategic stance in the classroom: A comprehension framework for helping teachers help students to be strategic. *The Reading Teacher, 52,* 672–688.

Doyle, C. S. (1999). *The use of graphic organizers to improve comprehension of learning disabled students in social studies.* Unpublished Master's thesis, Kean University, Union, NJ.

Dreher, M. J. (1992). Searching for information in textbooks. *Journal of Reading, 35,* 364–371.

Dreher, M. J. (1998/1999). Motivating children to read more nonfiction. *The Reading Teacher, 52,* 414–417.

Dressman, M. (1999). On the use and misuse of research evidence: Decoding two states' reading initiatives. *Reading Research Quarterly, 34,* 258–285.

Duffy, G., & McIntyre, L. (1982). A naturalistic study of instructional assistance in primary grade reading. *Elementary School Journal, 83*(1), 15–23.

Duffy, G. G., & Hoffman, J. V. (1999). In pursuit of an illusion: The flawed search for a perfect method. *The Reading Teacher, 53,* 10–16.

Duffy-Hester, A. M. (1999). Teaching struggling readers in elementary school classrooms: A review of classroom reading programs and principles for instruction. *The Reading Teacher, 52,* 480–495.

Dukes, L. L., & Shaw, S. F. (1998). Not just children anymore: Personnel preparation regarding postsecondary education for adults with disabilities. *Teacher Education and Special Education, 21*(3), 205–213.

Dukes, R. L., & Lorch, B. (1989). The effects of school, family, self-concept, and deviant behavior on adolescent suicide ideation. *Journal of Adolescence, 12,* 239–251.

Dunn, C., Chambers, D., Rabren, K. (2004). Variables affecting students' decisions to drop out of school. *Remedial and Special Education, 25,* 314–323.

Dunn, L. M., & Dunn, L. M. (1997). *Peabody picture vocabulary test—III.* Circle Pines, MN: American Guidance Service.

Durand, V. M. (1990). *Severe behavior problems: A functional communication training approach.* New York: Guilford.

Duvdevany, I., Ben-Zur, H., & Amber, A. (2002). Self-determination and mental retardation: Is there an association with living arrangement and lifestyle satisfaction? *Mental Retardation, 40*(5), 379–389.

Dwyer, E. J., & Bain, S. (1999). Fostering good oral fluency. *The Reading Teacher, 52,* 538.

Dye, G. A. (2000). Graphic organizers to the rescue: Helping students link and remember information. *Teaching Exceptional Children, 32*(3), 72–76.

Dyer, W. (1978). Implications of the helping relationship between learning disabled students and their teachers. *Learning Disability Quarterly, 2,* 55–61.

Edens, R. M., Murdick, N. J., & Gartin, B.C. (2003). Preventing infection in the classroom: The use of universal precautions. *Teaching Exceptional Children, 35*(4), 62–65.

Edgar, E. (1987). Secondary programs in special education: Are many of them justifiable? *Exceptional Children, 53,* 555–561.

Edgar, E., Horton, B., & Maddox, M. (1984). Post school placements: Planning for public school students with developmental disabilities. *Journal for Vocational Special Needs, 6,* 15–18.

Edgar, E., & Polloway, E. A. (1994). Education for adolescents with disabilities: Curriculum and placement issues. *Journal of Special Education, 27*(4), 438–452.

Education for All Handicapped Children Act. (1975). Public Law 94-142, 42 U.S.C. 1401 et seq. (1975).

Egan, M. (1999). Reflections on effective use of graphic organizers. *Journal of Adolescent & Adult Literacy, 42,* 641–645.

Egelko, B. (2002, February 22). State must provide for disabled on test. *San Francisco Chronicle,* p. A21.

Eisenmann, R. (1991). Conduct disordered youth: Insights from a prison treatment program. *Beyond Behavior, 2*(1), 3–4.

Elbaum, B., Vaughn, S., Hughes, M., & Moody, S. W. (1999). Grouping practices and reading outcomes for students with disabilities. *Exceptional Children, 65,* 399–415.

Eldridge, B. H. (1998). The quick book share. *Journal of Adolescent & Adult Literacy, 41,* 473–474.

Ellett, L. (1993). Instructional practices in mainstreamed secondary classrooms. *Journal of Learning Disabilities, 26,* 57–64.

Elliot, S. N., Kratochwill, T. R., & Schulte, A. G. (1998). The assessment accommodation checklist. *Teaching Exceptional Children, 31*(2), 10–14.

Ellis, E., Lenz, B., & Sabornie, E. (1987). Generalization and adaptation of learning strategies to natural environments: Part I: Critical agents. *Remedial and Special Education, 8,* 6–20.

Ellis, E. S. (1994). An instructional model for integrating content-area instruction with cognitive strategy instruction. *Reading and Writing Quarterly: Overcoming Learning Difficulties, 1,* 63–90.

Ellis, E. S., Deshler, D. D., Lenz, B. K., Schumaker, J. B., & Clark, F. L. (1991). An instructional model for teaching learning strategies. *Focus on Exceptional Children, 26*(3), 1–24.

Ellis, E. S., & Sabornie, E. J. (1986). Effective instruction with microcomputers: Promises, practices, and preliminary findings. *Focus on Exceptional Children, 19*(4), 1–16.

Ellis, E. S., & Sabornie, E. J. (1990). Strategy-based adaptive instruction in content-area classes: Social validity of six options. *Teacher Education and Special Education, 13,* 133–144.

Elmquist, D. L. (1992). *Development and evaluation of a substance use prevention parent involvement program for parents of students with mild disabilities.* Unpublished doctoral dissertation, Utah State University, Department of Special Education.

Eng, T., & Butler, W. (Eds.). (1997). *The hidden epidemic: Confronting sexually transmitted diseases.* Washington, DC: National Academy Press.

Engelmann, S., Carnine, D., & Steely, D. (1991). Making connections in mathematics. *Journal of Learning Disabilities, 24,* 292–303.

Engelmann, S. E., & Carnine, D. W. (1991). *Theory of instruction: Principles and applications.* Eugene, OR: Association of Direct Instruction.

Englert, C. S., Raphael, T. E., Anderson, L. M., Anthony, H. M., Fear, K. L., & Gregg, S. L. (1988). A case for writing intervention: Strategies for writing informational text. *Learning Disabilities Focus, 3,* 98–113.

Englert, C. S., Raphael, T. E., Anderson, L. M., Anthony, H. M., & Stevens, D. D. (1991). Making strategies and self-talk visible: Writing instruction in regular and special education classrooms. *American Educational Research Journal, 28,* 337–372.

Epstein, M. H., Polloway, E. A., Foley, R. M., & Patton, J. R. (1993). Homework: A comparison of teachers' and parents' perceptions of the problems experienced by students identified as having behavioral disorders, learning disabilities, and no disabilities. *Remedial and Special Education, 14*(5), 40–50.

Erb, S., & Moore, N. (2003). A taste of Chautauqua: Historical investigation and oral presentation. *Journal of Adolescent & Adult Literacy, 47,* 168–175.

Espin, C. A., Busch, T. W., Shin, J., & Kruschwitz, R. (2001). Curriculum-based measurement in the content areas: Validity of vocabulary matching as an indicator of performance in social studies. *Learning Disabilities Research and Practice, 16,* 142–151.

Evans, E. D., Melville, G. A., & Cass, M. A. (1992). AIDS: Special educators' knowledge and attitudes. *Teacher Education and Special Education, 15,* 300–306.

Evertson, C. M., Emmer, E. T., Clements, B., Sanford, J., Worsham, M., & Williams, E. (1981). *Organizing and managing the elementary school classroom.* Austin: University of Texas, Research and Development Center for Education.

Evertson, C. M., Emmer, E. T., & Worsham, M. E. (2005). *Classroom management for elementary teachers* (7th ed.). Boston: Allyn and Bacon.

Family Planning Council of IA. (1991). *Sexually transmitted diseases.* Des Moines, IA: Author.

Farb, J., & Throne, J. M. (1978). Improving the generalized mnemonic performance of a Down's syndrome child. *Journal of Applied Behavior Analysis, 11*(3), 413–419.

Farey, J. W. (1986). An analysis of written dialogue of educable mentally retarded writers. *Education and Training of the Mentally Retarded, 21*(3), 181–191.

Farrington, D. P. (1980). Truancy, delinquency, the home, and the school. In L. Hersov & I. Berg (Eds.), *Out of school: Modern perspectives in school refusal and truancy.* New York: Wiley.

Farrington, D. P., Gallagher, B., Morley, L., St. Ledger, R. J., & West, D. J. (1986). Unemployment, school leaving, and crime. *British Journal of Criminology, 26,* 335–356.

Farris, P. J., & Downey, P. M. (2004/2005). Concept muraling: Dropping visual crumbs along the instructional trail. *The Reading Teacher, 58,* 376–380.

Ferretti, R. P., & Okolo, C. M. (1996). Authenticity in learning: Multimedia design projects in the social studies for students with disabilities. *Journal of Learning Disabilities, 29,* 450–460.

Fick, L. (1984). *Adolescent childbearing decisions: Implications for preventing.* St. Louis, MO: Danforth Foundation.

Fine, A. H., Welch-Burke, C. S., & Fondario, L. J. (1985). A developmental model for the integration of leisure programming in the education of individuals with mental retardation. *Mental Retardation, 23*(6), 289–296.

Fischbaugh, R. (2004). Using book talks to promote high-level questioning skills. *The Reading Teacher, 58,* 296–300.

Fischer, C. (1999/2000). An effective (and affordable) intervention model for at-risk high school readers. *Journal of Adolescent & Adult Literacy, 43,* 326–335.

Fisher, C., Berliner, D., Filby, N., Marliave, R., Cahen, L., & Dishaw, M. (1980). Teaching behaviors, academic learning time, and student achievement: An overview. In C. Denham & A. Liberman (Eds.), *Time to learn.* Washington, DC: National Institute of Education.

Fisher, C. W., Berliner, D.C., Filby, N. N., Marliave, R., Cahen, L. S., Dishaw, M. M., & Moore, J. E. (1978). *Teaching behaviors, academic learning time, and student achievement: Final report of Phase III-B Beginning Teacher Evaluation Study.* San Francisco: Far West Educational Laboratory for Educational Research and Development.

Fisher, D. (2004). Setting the "opportunity to read" standard: Resuscitating the SSR program in an urban high school. *Journal of Adolescent & Adult Literacy, 48,* 138–150.

Fisher, D., Flood, J., Lapp, D., & Frey, N. (2004). Interactive read-alouds: Is there a common set of implementation practices? *The Reading Teacher, 58,* 8–17.

Fisher, D., & Frey, N. (2003). Writing instruction for struggling adolescent readers: A gradual release model. *Journal of Adolescent & Adult Literacy, 46,* 396–405.

Fisher, G. L., & Harrison, T. C. (1992). Assessment of alcohol and other drug abuse with referred adolescents. *Psychology in the Schools, 29,* 172–178.

Fisk, C., & Hurst, B. (2003). Paraphrasing for comprehension. *The Reading Teacher, 57,* 182–185.

Fitzgerald, E. (1954). *Straight language for the deaf: A system of instruction for deaf children.* Washington, DC: Volta Bureau.

Fitzgerald, J. (1999). What is this thing called "balance?" *The Reading Teacher, 53,* 100–107.

Flynn, R. M. (2004/2005). Curriculum-based readers theatre: Setting the stage for reading and retention. *The Reading Teacher, 58,* 360–365.

Fokes, J. (1976). *Fokes sentence builder.* Boston: Teaching Resources.

Forbes, L. S. (2004). Using web-based bookmarks in K–8 settings: Linking the Internet to instruction. *The Reading Teacher, 58,* 148–153.

Forehand, R., McCombs, A., & Brody, G. H. (1987). The relationship between parental depressive mood states and child functioning. *Advances in Behavior Research and Therapy, 9,* 1–20.

Forness, S. R. (1988). School characteristics of children and adolescents with depression. In R. B. Rutherford, C. M. Nelson, & S. R. Forness (Eds.), *Bases of severe behavioral disorders of children and youth* (pp. 177–204). Boston: Little, Brown.

Forness, S. R., Horton, R. L., & Horton, A. A. (1981). Assessment of applied academic and social skills. *Education and Training of the Mentally Retarded, 16*(2), 104–109.

Frager, A. M. (1993). Affective dimensions of content area reading. *Journal of Reading, 36,* 615–622.

Francis, M. A., & Simpson, M. L. (2003). Using theory, our intuitions, and a research study to enhance students' vocabulary knowledge. *Journal of Adolescent & Adult Literacy, 47,* 66–78.

Frank, A. R., & McFarland, T. D. (1980). Teaching coin skills to EMR children: A curriculum study. *Education and Training of the Mentally Retarded, 15*(4), 270–277.

Fredericksen, E. (1999). Playing through: Increasing literacy through interaction. *Journal of Adolescent & Adult Literacy, 43,* 116–124.

Freedman, M. (1993). *The kindness of strangers.* San Francisco: Jossey-Bass.

Freppon, P. A., & Dahl, K. L. (1998). Balanced instruction: Insights and considerations. *Reading Research Quarterly, 33,* 240–251.

Fresch, M. J. (1999). Alice in computerland: Using the Internet as a resource for teaching reading. *The Reading Teacher, 52,* 652–653.

Frey, G. C., Buchanan, A. M., & Sandt, D. D. R. (2005). "I'd rather watch TV": An examination of physical activity in adults with mental retardation. *Mental Retardation, 43*(4), 241–254.

Friedland, E. S., & Truesdell, K. S. (2004). Kids reading together: Ensuring the success of a buddy reading program. *The Reading Teacher, 58,* 76–79.

Friedland, E. S., & Truscott, D. M. (2005). Building awareness and commitment of middle school students through literacy tutoring. *Journal of Adolescent & Adult Literacy, 48,* 550–562.

Friend, M., & Cook, L. (2003). *Interactions: Collaboration skills for school professionals* (4th ed.). White Plains, NY: Longman.

Friend, M., & McNutt, G. (1984). Resource room programs: Where are we now? *Exceptional Children, 51,* 150–155.

Fuchs, D., & Fuchs, L. (1994). Inclusive schools movement and the radicalization of special education reform. *Exceptional Children, 60,* 294–309.

Fuchs, D., Roberts, P. H., Fuchs, L., & Bowers, J. (1996). Reintegrating students with learning disabilities into the mainstream: A two-year study. *Learning Disabilities Research & Practice, 11*(4), 214–229.

Fuchs, L. S., & Deno, S. L. (1994). Must instructionally useful performance assessment be based in the curriculum? *Exceptional Children, 61*(1), 15–24.

Fuchs, L., & Fuchs, D. (1986). Effects of systematic formative evaluation: A meta-analysis. *Exceptional Children, 53*(3), 199–208.

Fuchs, L., & Fuchs, D. (1991). Curriculum-based measurements: Current applications and future directions. *Preventing School Failure, 35*(3), 6–11.

Fuchs, L., & Fuchs, D. (1998). General educators' instructional adaptation for students with learning disabilities. *Learning Disability Quarterly, 21,* 23–33.

Fuchs, L. S., Fuchs, D., Eaton, S. B., Hamlett, C., Karns, K. (2000). Supplementing teacher judgements about test accommodations with objective data sources. *School Psychology Review, 29,* 65–85.

Fulk, B. M., Brigham, F. J., & Lohman, D. A. (1998). Motivation and self-regulation: A comparison of students with learning and behavior problems. *Remedial and Special Education, 19*(5), 300–309.

Gable, R. A., Quinn, M. M., Rutherford, R. B., & Howell, K. (1998). Addressing problem behaviors in schools: Use of functional assessments and behavior intervention plans. *Preventing School Failure, 42,* 106–113.

Gajar, A., Goodman, L., & McAfee, J. (1993). *Secondary schools and beyond: Transition of individuals with mild disabilities.* New York: Macmillan.

Gambrell, L. B. (2005). Reading literature, reading text, reading the Internet: The times they are a'changing. *The Reading Teacher, 58,* 588–591.

Gardill, M. C., & Jitendra, A. K. (1999). Advanced story map instruction: Effects on the reading comprehension of students with learning disabilities. *Journal of Special Education, 33,* 2–17, 28.

Gardner, J., Wissick, E., Schweder, C., Canter, W., & Smith, L. (2003). Enhancing interdisciplinary instruction in general and special education. *Remedial and Special Education, 24*(3)*,* 161–172.

Gardner, M. (2000) *Expressive one word picture vocabulary test.* Novato, CA: Academic Therapy Publications.

Garff, J. T., & Storey, K. (1998). The use of self-management strategies for increasing the appropriate hygiene of persons with disabilities in supported employment settings. *Education and Training in Mental Retardation and Developmental Disabilities, 33*(2), 179–188.

Garmezy, N. (1991). *Resilience in children's adaptation to negative life events and stressed environments.* Paper presented at the Vulnerability and Resilience: A Focus on Children with Disabilities Symposium, Baltimore, MD.

Gartin, B.C., Rumrill, P., & Serebreni, R. (1996). The higher education transition model: Guidelines for facilitating college transition among college-bound students with disabilities. *Teaching Exceptional Children, 28,* 30–36.

Gartland, D. (1994). Content area reading: Lessons from the specialists. *LD Forum, 19*(3), 19–22.

Gartland, D. (1988). Educational service options. In P. J. Schloss, C. A. Hughes, & M. A. Smith (Eds.), *Mental retardation: Community transition* (pp. 57–113). San Diego: College-Hill.

Gary W. v. Louisiana. (1976). 437 F. Supp. 1209 (E. D. La. 1976).

Gaskins, I. W. (1998). There's more to teaching at-risk and delayed readers than good reading instruction. *The Reading Teacher, 51,* 534–547.

Gaskins, I. W. (1999). A multidimensional reading program. *The Reading Teacher, 53,* 162–164.

Geary, D.C. (2004). Mathematics and learning disabilities. *Journal of Learning Disabilities, 37*(1), 4–15.

Geisthardt, C., & Munsch, J. (1996). Coping with school stress: A comparison of adolescents with and without learning disabilities. *Journal of Learning Disabilities, 29*(3), 287–296.

Genaux, M., Morgan, D. P., & Friedman, S. G. (1995). Substance use and its prevention: A survey of classroom practices. *Behavioral Disorders, 20*(4), 279–289.

Gere, A. R. (1987). *Writing groups: History, theory, and implications.* Carbondale: Southern Illinois University Press.

Gersten, R., Darch, C., Davis, G., & George, N. (1990). Apprenticeship and intensive training of consulting teachers: A naturalistic study. *Exceptional Children, 57,* 226–237.

Gibbs, N. (1993, May 24). How should we teach our children about sex? *Time, 141,* 60–66.

Gierl, M. J., & Harnisch, D. L. (1995). *Estimating a model for dropping out for youth with disabilities: A latent variable analysis using data from the National Longitudinal Transition Study.* Paper presented at the annual meeting of the American Educational Research Association, San Francisco.

Gill, S. R. (2000). Reading with Amy: Teaching and learning through reading conferences. *The Reading Teacher, 53,* 500–509.

Gillespie, C. (1990). Questions about student-generated questions. *Journal of Reading, 34,* 250–257.

Gillespie, C. S. (1993). Reading graphic displays: What teachers should know. *Journal of Reading, 36,* 350–354.

Gipe, J., & Arnold, R. (1979). Teaching vocabulary through familiar associations and contexts. *Journal of Reading Behavior, 11*(3), 281–285.

Gitlin, T. (1990). On drugs and mass media in America's consumer society. In *Youth and drugs: Society's mixed messages* (pp. 31–52) (OSAP Monograph No. 6). Washington, DC: U.S. Department of Health and Human Services. (DHHS Publication No. ADM 90–1689)

Glatthorn, A. A. (1981). *Writing in the schools: Improvement through effective leadership.* Reston, VA: National Association of Secondary School Principals.

Goals 2000: The Educate America Act. (1994). Public Law 103-227 U.S.C. 5801 (1994).

Goldman, S., Hasselbring, T., & the Cognition and Technology Group at Vanderbilt. (1997). Achieving meaningful mathematics literacy for students with learning disabilities. *Journal of Learning Disabilities, 30*(2), 198–208.

Goldstein, A. P., Sprafkin, R. P., Gershaw, N. J., & Klein, P. (1997). *Skill-streaming the adolescent: A structured learning approach to teaching pro-social skills* (Rev. Ed.). Champaign, IL: Research Press.

Goleman, D. (1995). *Emotional intelligence: Why it can be better than IQ.* New York: Bantam Books.

Good, T. L., & Grouws, D. A. (1979). The Missouri Mathematics Effectiveness Project. *Journal of Educational Psychology, 71,* 355–362.

Goodman, K. S. (Ed.). (1998). *In defense of good teaching: What teachers need to know about the "reading wars."* York, ME: Stenhouse.

Gorman, C. (1995). Suicide check. *Time* (Online serial). Available: America Online, Health News.

Goss v. Lopez. (1975). 419 U.S. 565, 95 S. Ct. 729, 42 L. Ed. 2d 725 (1975).

Gould, M. S., Velting, D., Kleinman, M., Lucas, C., Thomas, T. G., & Chung, M. (2004). Teenagers' attitudes about coping strategies and help seeking behavior for suicidality. *Journal of the American Academy of Child and Adolescence Psychiatry, 43,* 1124–1133.

Graham, S., Harris, K. R., MacArthur, C. A., & Schwartz, S. (1991). Writing and writing instruction for students with learning disabilities: Review of a research program. *Learning Disability Quarterly, 14,* 89–114.

Grant, R. (1993). Strategic training for using text headings to improve students' processing of content. *Journal of Reading, 36,* 482–488.

Graves, M. F., & Philippot, R. A. (2002). High-interest, easy reading: An important resources for struggling readers. *Preventing School Failure, 46,* 179–182.

Green, M. (1997/1998). Rapid retrieval of information: Reading aloud with a purpose. *Journal of Adolescent & Adult Literacy, 41,* 306–307.

Greenspan, S., & Shoultz, B. (1981). Why mentally retarded adults lose their jobs: Social competence as a factor in work adjustment. *Applied Research in Mental Retardation, 2,* 23–38.

Greenwald, E. A., Persky, H. R., Campbell, J. R., & Mazzeo, J. (1999, September). *The NAEP 1998 writing report card for the nation and the states* (NCES 1999-462). Washington, DC: U.S. Department of Education, Office of Educational Research and Improvement, National Center for Education Statistics.

Gresham, F. M. (1981). Social skills training with handicapped children: A review. *Review of Educational Research, 51,* 139–176.

Gresham, F. M. (1982). Misguided mainstreaming: The case for social skills training with handicapped children. *Exceptional Children, 48,* 422–433.

Gresham, F. M. (1997). Social competence and students with behavior disorders: Where we've been, where we are, and where we should go. *Education and Treatment of Children, 20*(3), 233–249.

Gresham, F. M. (1998). Social skills training: Should we raze, remodel, or rebuild? *Behavioral Disorders, 24*(1), 19–25.

Gresham, F. M., & Elliott, S. N. (1989). Social skills deficits as a primary learning disability. *Journal of Learning Disabilities, 22,* 120–124.

Gresham, F. M., & MacMillan, D. L. (1997). Social competence and affective characteristics of students with mild disabilities. *Review of Educational Research, 67*(4), 377–415.

Gresham, F. M., Sugai, G., & Horner, R. H. (2001). Interpreting outcomes of social skills training for students with high incidence disabilities. *Exceptional Children, 67,* 331–344.

Griffith, L. W., & Rasinski, T. V. (2004). A focus on fluency: How one teacher incorporated fluency with her reading curriculum. *The Reading Teacher, 58,* 126–137.

Grigal, M., Neubert, D. A., & Moon, M. S. (2002). Postsecondary options for students with significant disabilities. *Teaching Exceptional Children, 35*(2), 68–73.

Grobe, C. (1981). Syntactic maturity, mechanics, and vocabulary as predictors of quality ratings. *Research in the Teaching of English, 15,* 75–85.

Grossi, T. A., & Heward, W. L. (1998). Using self-evaluation to improve the work productivity of trainees in a community-based restaurant training program. *Education and Training in Mental Retardation and Developmental Disabilities, 33*(3), 248–263.

Grossman, H. (2003). *Classroom behavior management in a diverse society* (3rd ed.). Mountain View, CA: Mayfield.

Guastello, E. F. (2000). Concept mapping effects on science content comprehension of low achieving inner city seventh graders. *Remedial and Special Education, 21,* 356–365.

Guetzloe, E. C. (1989). *Youth suicide: What the educator should know.* Reston, VA: Council for Exceptional Children.

Gupta, A. (2000). Ditto reading strategy. *The Reading Teacher, 53,* 370–371.

Gurganus, S., Janas, M., & Schmitt, L. (1995). Science instruction: What special education teachers need to know and what roles they need to play. *Teaching Exceptional Children, 27*(4), 7–9.

Gutkin, T. B. (1996). Core elements of consultation service delivery for special service personnel: Rationale, practice, and some directions for the future. *Remedial and Special Education, 17*(6), 333–340.

Guttmacher, S., et al. (1997). Condom availability in New York city public high schools: Relationships to condom use and sexual behavior. *American Journal of Public Health, 87*(90), 1427–1433.

Guzzetti, B. J., Hynd, C. R., Skeels, S. A., & Williams, W. O. (1995). Improving physics texts: Students speak out. *Journal of Reading, 38,* 656–663.

Haavik, S., & Menninger, K. A., II. (1981). *Sexuality, law, and the developmentally disabled person.* Baltimore: Paul H. Brookes.

Hadaway, N. L., & Mundy, J. (1999). Children's informational picture books visit a secondary ESL classroom. *Journal of Adolescent & Adult Literacy, 42,* 464–475.

Hagner, D., & Dileo, D. (1993). *Working together: Workplace culture, supported employment, and persons with disabilities.* Cambridge, MA: Brookline Books.

Hagood, B. F. (1997). Reading and writing with help from story grammar. *Teaching Exceptional Children, 29*(4), 10–14.

Hahn, A. (1987). Reaching out to America's dropouts: What to do? *Phi Delta Kappan, 69*(4), 256–263.

Halderman v. Pennhurst State School and Hospital. (1977). 446 F Supp. 1295 (E. D. Pa. 1977).

Hallahan, D., & Kauffman, J. (2000). *Exceptional learners: Introduction to exceptional children* (8th ed.). Boston: Allyn and Bacon.

Hallahan, D. P., & Kauffman, J. M. (2006). *Exceptional learners: Introduction to special education* (10th ed.). Boston: Allyn and Bacon.

Hallenbeck, M. J. (2002). Taking charge: Adolescents with learning disabilities assume responsibility for their own writing. *Learning Disability Quarterly, 25,* 227–246.

Halpern, A. (1985). Transition: A look at the foundations. *Exceptional Children, 51,* 479–486.

Halpern, A. (1993a). Quality of life as a conceptual framework for evaluating transition outcomes. *Exceptional Children, 59,* 486–498.

Halpern, A. S. (1993b). Transition: Old wine in new bottles. *Exceptional Children, 58,* 202–211.

Hammen, C., & Campas, B. E. (1994). Unmasking depression in children & adolescents: The problem of morbidity. *Clinical Psychology Review, 14,* 585–603.

Hammill, D. D. (1987). *Assessing the abilities and instructional needs of students.* Austin, TX: Pro-Ed.

Hammill, D. D. (1998). *Detroit tests of learning aptitude* (4th ed.). Austin: Pro-Ed.

Hammill, D. D. (2004). What we know about correlates of reading. *Exceptional Children, 70,* 453–468.

Hancock, M. R. (1993). Character journals: Initiating involvement and identification through literature. *Journal of Reading, 37,* 42–50.

Hanley-Maxwell, C., & Collet-Klingenberg, L. (1997). Curricular choices related to work: Restructuring curricula for improved work outcomes. In P. Wehman & J. Kregel (Eds.), *Functional curriculum for elementary, middle, and secondary age students with special needs* (pp. 155–183). Austin, TX: Pro-Ed.

Hanley-Maxwell, C., Wilcox, B., & Heal, L. W. (1982). A comparison of vocabulary learning by moderately retarded students under direct instruction and incidental presentation. *Education and Training of the Mentally Retarded, 17*(3), 214–221.

Hansen-Krening, N., & Mizokawa, D. T. (1997). Exploring ethnic-specific literature: A unity of parents, families, and educators. *Journal of Adolescent & Adult Literacy, 41,* 180–189.

Haring, N., Lovitt, T., Eaton, M., & Hansen, C. (1978). *The fourth R: Research in the classroom.* Columbus, OH: Merrill.

Haring, N. C., & Gentry, N. D. (1976). Direct and individualized instructional procedures. In N. G. Haring & R. L. Schiefelbusch (Eds.), *Teaching special children.* New York: McGraw-Hill.

Haring, N. G., & Schiefelbusch, R. L. (1976). *Teaching special children.* New York: McGraw-Hill.

Harmon, J. M. (1998). Vocabulary teaching and learning in a seventh grade literature-based classroom. *Journal of Adolescent & Adult Literacy, 41,* 518–529.

Harris Survey of Americans with Disabilities. (1998). [Electronic summary of findings]. Washington, DC: National Organization on Disabilities. Retrieved from www.nod.org/presssurvey.html#survey.

Harris, A., & Sipay, E. (1990). *How to increase reading ability* (9th ed.). White Plains, NY: Longman.

Harris, K. R., & Graham, S. (1985). Improving learning disabled students' composition skills: Self-control strategy training. *Learning Disability Quarterly, 8,* 27–36.

Harris, K. R., & Graham, S. (1992). *Helping young writers master the craft: Strategy instruction and self-regulation in the writing process.* Cambridge, MA: Brookline.

Harris, K. R., & Graham, S. (1994). Constructivism: Principles, paradigms, and integration. *Journal of Special Education, 28,* 233–247.

Harris, K. R., Graham, S., & Mason, L. H. (2003). Self-regulated strategy development in the classroom: Part of a balanced approach to writing instruction for students with disabilities. *Focus on Exceptional Children, 36*(7), 1–16.

Harris, R., & Robertson, J. (2001). Successful strategies for college-bound students with learning disabilities. *Preventing School Failure, 45,* 125–131.

Hart, D., Mele-McCarthy, J., Pasternack R. H., Zimbrich, K., & Parker, D. R. (2004). Community college: A pathway to success for youth with learning, cognitive, and intellectual disabilities in secondary settings. *Education and Training in Developmental Disabilities, 39,* 54–66.

Hartas, D., & Donahue, M. L. (1997). Conversational and social problem-solving skills in adolescents with learning disabilities. *Learning Disabilities Research & Practice, 12*(4), 213–220.

Hartwig, E. P., & Ruesch, G. M. (2000). Disciplining students in special education. *Journal of Special Education, 33,* 240–247.

Harvey, M. W. (2001). Vocational–technical education: A logical approach to dropout prevention for secondary special education. *Preventing School Failure, 45*(3), 108–113.

Hashey, J. M., & Connors, D. J. (2003). Learn from our journey: Reciprocal teaching action research. *The Reading Teacher, 57,* 224–232.

Hasselbring, T. S., & Goin, L. I. (1988). *Effective practices for computer use with mildly handicapped learners.* Paper presented at the 66th Annual Convention of the Council for Exceptional Children, Washington, DC.

Hatfield, E. M. (1975). Why are they blind? *Sight Saving Review, 45*(1), 3–22.

Hawton, K. (1986). Suicide in adolescents. In A. Roy (Ed.), *Suicide* (pp. 135–150). Baltimore: Waverly Press.

Hayes, J. R., & Flower, L. S. (1987). On the structure of the writing process. *Topics in Language Disorders, 7*(4), 19–30.

Heaton, S., & O'Shea, D. J. (1995). Using mnemonics to make mnemonics. *Teaching Exceptional Children, 28*(1), 34–36.

Heavy, C. L., Adelman, H. S., Nelson, P., & Smith, D. C. (1989). Learning problems, anger, perceived control, and misbehavior. *Journal of Learning Disabilities, 22,* 46–50, 59.

Heller, H. W. (1981). Secondary education for handicapped students: In search of a solution. *Exceptional Children, 47,* 582–583.

Henk, W. A., Moore, J. C., Marinak, B. A., & Tomasetti, B. W. (2000). A reading lesson observation framework for elementary teachers, principals, and literacy supervisors. *The Reading Teacher, 53,* 358–369.

Henwood, G. F. (1999/2000). A new role for the reading specialist: Contributing toward a high school's collaborative educational culture. *Journal of Adolescent & Adult Literacy, 43,* 316–325.

Hersen, M., & Bellack, A. (1986). Assessment of social skills. In A. R. Ciminero, K. S. Calhoun, & H. E. Adams (Eds.), *Handbook of behavioral assessment* (2nd ed., pp. 189–207). New York: Wiley.

Hester, P. (2002). What teachers can do to prevent behavior problems in school. *Preventing School Failure, 47,* 33–38.

Heward, W. L. (2003). Ten faulty notions about teaching and learning that hinder the effectiveeness of special education. *Journal of Special Education, 36*, 186–205.

Hibbing, A. N., & Rankin-Erickson, J. L. (2003). A picture is worth a thousand words: Using visual images to improve comprehension for middle school struggling readers. *The Reading Teacher, 56*, 758–770.

Hickson, L., Golden, H., Khemka, I., Urv, T., & Yamusah, S. (1998). A closer look at interpersonal decision-making in adults with and without mental retardation. *AJMR, 103*(3), 209–224.

Hiebert, E. H. (2002). Standards, assessment, and text difficulty. In A. E. Farstrup & S. J. Samuels (Eds.), *What research has to say about reading instruction.* Newark, DE: International Reading Association.

Hill, J. W., Seyfarth, J., Banks, P. D., Wehman, P., & Orelove, F. (1987). Parent attitudes about working conditions of their adult mentally retarded sons and daughters. *Exceptional Children, 54*, 9–23.

Hill, N. C., Parker, L. G., Corbett, A., & Miano, K. L. (1980). *Attending behavior commonalities and differences among educable retarded, learning disabled, and emotionally handicapped juvenile delinquents.* (ERIC Document Reproduction Service No. ED 197 569)

Hillocks, G., Jr. (1984). What works in teaching composition: A meta-analysis of experimental treatment studies. *American Journal of Education, 93*, 133–170.

Hinchman, K. A., Alvermann, D. E., Boyd, F. B., Brozo, W. G., & Vacca, R. T. (2003/2004). Supporting older students' in- and out-of-school literacies. *Journal of Adolescent & Adult Literacy, 47*, 304–310.

Hingsburger, D., & Tough, S. (2001). Healthy sexuality: Attitudes, systems, and policies. *Research and Practice for Persons with Severe Disabilities, 27*(1), 8–17.

Hitchcock, C., Meyer, A., Rose, D., & Jackson, R. (2002). Providing new access to the general curriculum: Universal design for learning. *Teaching Exceptional Children, 35*(2), 8–17.

Hobbs, T., & Westling, D. L. (1998). Promoting successful inclusion through collaborative problem-solving. *Teaching Exceptional Children, 31*(1), 12–19.

Hodapp, A. F., & Hodapp, J. B. (1992). Homework: Making it work. *Intervention in School and Clinic, 24*, 233–235.

Honig v. Doe. (1988). 484 U.S. 305, 108 S. Ct. 592, 98L. Ed. 2d 686 (1988).

Hoover, J. J., & Patton, J. R. (1995). *Teaching students with learning problems to use study skills.* Austin, TX: Pro-Ed.

Hoover, J. J., & Patton, J. R. (2004). Differentiating standards-based education for students with diverse needs. *Remedial and Special Education, 25*, 74–78.

Hopkins, C. J. (1998). "I'm here to help—What do you want me to do?": A primer for literacy tutors. *The Reading Teacher, 52*, 310–312.

Horton, S. (1985). Computational rules of educable mentally retarded adolescents with and without calculators in comparison to normals. *Education and Training of the Mentally Retarded, 20*(1), 14–24.

Horton, S. V., & Lovitt, T. C. (1989). Construction and implementation of graphic organizers for academically handicapped and regular secondary students. *Academic Therapy, 24*, 625–640.

Horton, S. V., Lovitt, T. C., & Bergerud, D. (1990). The effectiveness of graphic organizers for three classifications of secondary students in content area classes. *Journal of Learning Disabilities, 23*, 12–22, 29.

Horton, S. V., Lovitt, T. C., Givens, A., & Nelson, R. (1989). Teaching social studies to high school students with academic handicaps in a mainstreamed setting: Effects of a computerized study guide. *Journal of Learning Disabilities, 22*, 102–107.

Horton, S. V., Lovitt, T. C., & Slocum, T. A. (1988). Teaching geography to high school students with academic deficits. *Learning Disability Quarterly, 11*, 371–379.

Houck, C. (1987). Teaching LD adolescents to read. *Academic Therapy, 22*, 229–237.

Howell, K. W., & Morehead, M. K. (1987). *Curriculum-based evaluation for special and remedial education.* Columbus, OH: Merrill.

Hudley, C. A. (1992). Using role models to improve the reading attitudes of ethnic minority high school girls. *Journal of Reading, 36*, 182–188.

Hudson, P., Lignugaris-Kraft, B., & Miller, T. (1993). Using content enhancements to improve the performance of adolescents with learning disabilities in content classes. *Learning Disabilities Research and Practice, 8,* 106–126.

Hudson, R. F., Lane, H. B., & Pullen, P. C. (2005). Reading fluency assessment and instruction: What, why, and how? *The Reading Teacher, 58,* 702–715.

Huefner, D. S. (1988). The consulting teacher model: Risks and opportunities. *Exceptional Children, 54,* 403–414.

Hughes, C., Rodi, M. S., Lorden, S. W., Pitkin, S. E., Derer, K. R., Hwang, B., & Cai, X. (1999). Social interactions of high school students with mental retardation and their general education peers. *AJMR, 104*(6), 533–544.

Hughes, D., McGillivray, L., & Schmidek, M. (1997). *Guide to narrative language: Procedures for assessment.* Eau Claire, WI: Thinking Publications.

Hughes, M. T., Schumm, J. S., & Vaughn, S. (1999). Home literacy activities: Perceptions and practices of Hispanic parents of children with learning disabilities. *Learning Disability Quarterly, 22,* 224–235.

Hull, G. (1987). Current views of error and editing. *Topics in Language Disorders, 7*(4), 55–65.

Hunt, K. W., & O'Donnell, R. C. (1970). *An elementary school curriculum to develop better writing skills* (Cooperative Research Project No. 8–0903). Tallahassee: Florida State University. (ERIC Document Reproduction Service No. ED 050 108)

Hunt-Berg, M., Rankin, J. L., & Beukelman, D. R. (1994). Ponder the possibilities: Computer-supported writing for struggling writers. *Learning Disabilities Research & Practice, 9,* 169–178.

Huntington, D. D., & Bender, W. N. (1993). Adolescents with learning disabilities at risk? Emotional well-being, depression, suicide. *Journal of Learning Disabilities, 26*(3), 159–166.

Hutcherson, K., Langone, J., Ayres, K., & Clees, T. (2004). Computer assisted instruction to teach item selection in grocery stores: An assessment of acquisition and generalization. *Journal of Special Education Technology, 19*(4), 33–42.

Hutchins, M. P., & Renzaglia, A. (1998). Interviewing families for effective transition to employment. *Teaching Exceptional Children, 30*(4), 72–78.

Hynd, C. R. (1999). Teaching students to think critically using multiple texts in history. *Journal of Adolescent & Adult Literacy, 42,* 428–436.

Idol, L. (1988). A rationale and guidelines for establishing special education consultation programs. *Remedial and Special Education, 9*(6), 48–58.

Idol, L. (1997). Key questions related to building collaborative and inclusive schools. *Journal of Learning Disabilities, 30,* 384–394.

Idol, L., Paolucci-Whitcomb, P., & Nevin, A. (1994). *Collaborative consultation* (2nd ed.). Rockville, MD: Aspen Systems.

Individuals with Disabilities Education Act. (1990). Public Law 101-476, 602a, 20 U.S.C., 1401 (1990).

Individuals with Disabilities Education Act Amendments. (1997). Public Law 105-17, 20 U.S.C., 1400 (1997).

Individuals with Disabilities Education Act of 1997, 120 U.S.C. §1400 *et seq.*

Ingraham v. Wright. (1977). 430 U.S. 651 (1977).

International Reading Association. (2002). What is evidence-based reading instruction? A position statement of the International Reading Association. Newark, DE: Author.

Introduction: No Child Left Behind (2004). Retrieved August 4, 2004, from www.ed.gov/print/nclb/overview/intro/index.html.

Isaacson, S. (1984). Evaluating written expression: Issues of reliability, validity, and instructional utility. *Diagnostique, 9,* 96–116.

Isaacson, S. (1988). Assessing the writing product: Qualitative and quantitative measures. *Exceptional Children, 54,* 528–534.

Ives, B., & Hoy, C. (2003). Graphic organizers applied to higher-level secondary mathematics. *Learning Disabilities Practice, 18,* 36–51.

Ivey, G. (2003). "The teacher makes it more explainable" and other reasons to read aloud in the intermediate grades. *The Reading Teacher, 56,* 812–814.

Ivey, G. (1999). Reflections on teaching struggling middle school readers. *Journal of Adolescent & Adult Literacy, 42,* 372–381.

Jackson, L., Ryndak, D. L., & Billingsley, F. (2001). Useful practices in inclusive education: A preliminary view of what experts in moderate and severe disabilities are saying. In *Foundations of inclusive education* (pp. 184–196). (Original work published in 2000). Baltimore: TASH.

Jayanthi, M., Bursuck, W., Epstein, M. H., & Polloway, E. A. (1998). Strategies for successful homework. *Teaching Exceptional Children, 30*(1), 4–7.

Jessor, R., & Jessor, S. L. (1980). Adolescent development and the onset of drinking. In R. E. Muus (Ed.), *Adolescent behavior and society* (3rd ed.). New York: Random House.

Jewell, T. A., & Pratt, D. (1999). Literature discussions in the primary grades: Children's thoughtful discourse about books and what teachers can do to make it happen. *The Reading Teacher, 52,* 842–850.

Jitendra, A. K., Edwards, L. L., Choutka, C. M., & Treadway, P. S. (2002). A collaborative approach to planning in the content areas for students with learning disabilities: Accessing the general curriculum. *Learning Disabilities Research and Practice, 17,* 252–267.

Jitendra, A. K., Edwards, L. L., Sacks, G., & Jacobson, L. A. (2004). What research says about vocabulary instruction for students with learning disabilities. *Exceptional Children, 70,* 299–322.

Jitendra, A. K., Griffin, E., Deatline-Buckman, A., Dippi-Hoy, C., Sczesniak, E., Sokol, N. G. & Xin, Y. P. (2005). Adherance to mathematics professional standards and instructional design criteria for problem-solving in mathematics, *Exceptional Children, 71*(3), 319–337.

Johnson, A. P., & Rasmussen, J. B. (1998). Classifying and super word web: Two strategies to improve productive vocabulary. *Journal of Adolescent & Adult Literacy, 42,* 204–207.

Johnson, C. (1991). Developmental issues: Children infected with the human immunodeficiency virus. *Infants and Young Children, 6*(1), 1–10.

Johnson, D. D., Pittelman, S. D., & Heimlich, J. E. (1986). Semantic mapping. *The Reading Teacher, 39,* 779–782.

Johnson, D. R., Stodden, R. A., Emanuel, E. J., Luecking, R., & Mack, M. (2002). Current challenges facing secondary education and transition services: What research tells us. *Exceptional Children, 68,* 519–531.

Johnson, E. (2000). The effects of accommodations on performance assessments. *Remedial and Special Education, 21,* 261–267.

Johnson, E., Kimball, K., Olson Brown, S., & Anderson, D. (2001). A statewide review of the use of accommodations in large-scale, high-stakes assessments. *Exceptional Children, 67,* 251–264.

Johnston, F. R. (1993). Improving student response in DR-TAs and DL-TAs. *The Reading Teacher, 46,* 448–449.

Johnston, J. L., O'Malley, P. M., & Bachman, J. G. (1985). *Drug use among high school students, college students and other young adults: National trends through 1985.* Bethesda, MD: National Institute on Drug Abuse.

Johnston, P. (2003). Assessment conversations. *The Reading Teacher, 57,* 90–92.

Johnston, P. (2005). Literacy assessment and the future. *The Reading Teacher, 58,* 684–686.

Johnston, P., & Costello, P. (2005). Principles for literacy assessment. *Reading Research Quarterly, 40,* 256–267.

Jones, E., Wilson, R., & Bhojwani, S. (1997). Mathematics instruction for secondary students with learning disabilities. *Journal of Learning Disabilities, 30*(2), 151–163.

Jones, P. (2005). Inclusion: Lessons from the children. *British Journal of Special Education, 32*(2), 65–69.

Jones, V. F., & Jones, L. S. (2001). *Comprehensive classroom management: Creating communities of support and solving problems* (7th ed.). Boston: Allyn and Bacon.

Jongsma, K. (1999/2000). Vocabulary and comprehension strategy development. *The Reading Teacher, 53,* 310–312.

Kaiser Family Foundation (KFF). (1998a). *The Kaiser Family Foundation/Glamour 1998 survey of men and women on sexually transmitted diseases.* Press release. Retrieved July 12, 1999, from www.kff.org.

Kaiser Family Foundation (KFF). (1998b). *Sexually transmitted diseases in America: How many cases and at what cost?* Menlo Park, CA: Kaiser Family Foundation and American Social Health Association.

Kameenui, E. J. (1993). Diverse learners and the tyranny of time: Don't fix the blame; fix the leaky roof. *The Reading Teacher, 46,* 376–383.

Karacostas, D. D., & Fisher, G. L. (1993). Chemical dependency in students with and without learning disabilities. *Journal of Learning Disabilities, 26*(7), 491–495.

Karnes, F. A., & Riley, T. L. (1997). Enhancing reading and writing through competitions. *The Reading Teacher, 51,* 270–271.

Kasten, W. C., & Wilfong, L. G. (2005). Encouraging independent reading with ambience: The book bistro in middle and secondary classes. *Journal of Adolescent & Adult Literacy, 48,* 656–664.

Kastner, T. A., Nathanson, R. S., & Marchetti, A. G. (1992). Epidemiology of HIV infection in adults with developmental disabilities. In A. C. Crocker, H. J. Cohen, & T. A. Kastner (Eds.), *HIV infection and developmental disabilities: A resource for service providers* (pp. 127–132). Baltimore: Paul H. Brookes.

Katims, D. (2000). Literacy instruction for people with mental retardation: Historical highlights and contemporary analysis. *Education and Training in Mental Retardation and Developmental Disabilities, 35,* 3–15.

Katsiyannis, A., & Smith, C R. (2003). Disciplining students with disabilities: Legal trends and the issue of interim alternative education settings. *Behavioral Disorders, 28,* 410–418.

Katz, M. (1997). Overcoming childhood adversities: Lessons learned from those who have "beat the odds." *Intervention in School and Clinic, 32*(4), 205–210.

Kauffman, J., Lloyd, J., & McGee, K. (1989). Adaptive and maladaptive behavior: Teacher attitudes and their technical assistance needs. *Journal of Special Education, 23,* 185–200.

Kauffman, J. M. (2001). *Characteristics of emotional and behavioral disorders of children and youth* (7th ed.). Upper Saddle River, NJ: Merrill/Prentice-Hall.

Kaufman, L., Handl, P., & Thöny, B. (2003). Evaluation of numeracy intervention program focusing on basic numerical knowledge and conceptual knowledge: A pilot study. *Journal of Learning Disabilities, 36*(6), 564–573.

Kazdin, A. (1977). Assessing the clinical or applied significance of behavior change through social validation. *Behavior Modification, 1,* 427–452.

Kazdin, A. E. (1982). *Single-case research designs: Methods for clinical and applied settings.* New York: Oxford University Press.

Kazemek, F. E. (1998). The things they carried: Vietnam War literature by and about women in the secondary classroom. *Journal of Adolescent & Adult Literacy, 42,* 156–166.

Keefe, E. B., & Moore, V. (2004). The challenge of co-teaching in inclusive classrooms at the high school level: What the teachers told us. *American Secondary Education, 32,* 77–88.

Kellner, M. H., Bry, B. H., & Colletti, L. A. (2002). Teaching anger management skills to students with severe emotional or behavioral disorders. *Behavioral Disorders, 27,* 400–407.

Kellogg, R. T. (1988). Attentional overload and writing performance: Effects of rough draft and outline strategies. *Journal of Experimental Psychology: Learning, Memory, & Cognition, 14,* 355–365.

Kelly, J. B. (1982). *Leisure.* Englewood Cliffs, NJ: Prentice-Hall.

Keogh, B. K., & Weisner, T. (1993). An ecocultural perspective on risk and protective factors in children's development: Implications for learning disabilities. *Learning Disabilities Research and Practice, 8*(1), 3–10.

Kerr, M. M., & Nelson, C. M. (1998). *Strategies for managing behavior problems in the classroom* (3rd ed.). Columbus, OH: Merrill.

Kerr, M. M., Nelson, C. M., & Lambert, D. H. (1987). *Helping adolescents with learning and behavior problems.* Columbus, OH: Merrill.

King-Sears, M. E. (2001). Three steps for gaining access to the general education curriculum for learners with disabilities. *Intervention in School and Clinic, 37,* 67–76.

King-Sears, M. E., & Bonfils, K. A. (1999). Self-management instruction for middle school students with LD and ED. *Intervention in School and Clinic, 35,* 96–102.

Kirby, D. (1997). *No easy answers: Research findings on programs to reduce teen pregnancy.* Washington, DC: National Campaign to Prevent Teen Pregnancy.

Kirk, W. G. (1993). *Adolescent suicide: A school-based approach to assessment & instruction.* Champaign, IL: Research Press.

Klein, L. (1978). Antecedents of teenage pregnancy. *Clinical Obstetrics and Gynecology, 21*(4), 1151–1159.

Klein, T. W. (1990). *The Nevada Proficiency Examination Program results of the 1988–89 examinations. State evaluation report.* Carson City: Nevada State Department of Education: Planning, Research and Evaluation Branch. (ERIC Document Reproduction Service No. ED 323 265)

Kletzien, S. B., & Hushion, B.C. (1992). Reading workshop: Reading, writing, thinking. *Journal of Reading, 35,* 444–451.

Kliewer, C., & Landis, D. (1999). Individualizing literacy instruction for young children with moderate to severe disabilities. *Exceptional Children, 66,* 85–100.

Kluth, P., & Darmody-Latham, J. (2003). Beyond sight words: Literacy opportunities for students with autism. *The Reading Teacher, 56,* 532–534.

Knight, D., & Aucoin, L. (1999). Assessing job-readiness skills: How students, teachers, and employers can work together to enhance on-the-job training. *Teaching Exceptional Children, 31*(5), 10–17.

Kohler, P. D., & Field, S. (2003). Transition-focused education: Foundation for the future. *Journal of Special Education, 37,* 174–183.

Kokoszka, R., & Drye, J. (1981). Toward the least restrictive environment: High school learning disabled students. *Journal of Learning Disabilities, 14,* 22–23.

Kong, A., & Fitch, E. (2002/2003). Using book club to engage culturally and linguistically diverse learners in reading, writing, and talking about books. *The Reading Teacher, 56,* 352–362.

Kortering, L. J., & Braziel, P. M. (1999). School dropout from the perspective of former students: Implications for secondary special education programs. *Remedial and Special Education, 20*(2), 78–83.

Kortering, L. J., Braziel, P. M., & Tompkins, J. R. (2002). The challenge of school completion Among youths with behavorial disorders: Another side of the story. *Behavorial Disorders, 27*(2), 142–154.

Koskinen, P. S., Blum, I. H., Bisson, S. A., Phillips, S. M., Creamer, T. S., & Baker, T. K. (1999). Shared reading, books, and audiotapes: Supporting diverse students in school and at home. *The Reading Teacher, 52,* 430–444.

Koskinen, P. S., Wilson, R., Gambrell, L. B., & Neuman, S. B. (1993). Captioned video and vocabulary learning: An innovative practice in literary instruction. *The Reading Teacher, 47,* 36–43.

Kosky, R., Silburn, S., & Zubrick, S. R. (1990). Are children and adolescents who have attempted suicidal thought different from those who attempt suicide? *Journal of Nervous and Mental Disease, 178*(1), 38–43.

Kounin, J. (1970). *Discipline and group management in classrooms.* New York: Holt, Rinehart and Winston.

Kreuger, E., & Braun, B. (1998/1999). Books and buddies: Peers tutoring peers. *The Reading Teacher, 52,* 410–414.

Kroesbergen, E. H., Van Luit, J. E. H., & Naglieri, J. A. (2003). Mathematical learning difficulties and PASS cognitive processes. *Journal of Learning Disabilities, 36*(6), 574–582.

Kruger, L., & Wandle, C. (1992). A preliminary investigation of special needs students' global and mathematics self-concepts. *Psychology in the Schools, 29,* 281–289.

Kuhn, M. (2004/2005). Helping students become accurate, expressive readers: Fluency instruction for small groups. *The Reading Teacher, 58,* 338–344.

Kuper, D. J. (1991). Summary of the national conference on risk factors for youth suicide. In L. Davidson & M. Linniola (Eds.), *Risk factors for youth suicide* (pp. 27–143). New York: Hemisphere.

Kvaraceus, W. C. (1971). *Prevention and control of delinquency: The school counselor's role.* Hanover, NH: TSC.

Labbo, L. D. (2004). Author's computer chair. *The Reading Teacher, 57,* 688–691.

LaBerge, D., & Samuels, S. J. (1974). Toward a theory of automatic information processing in reading. *Cognitive Psychology, 6,* 293–323.

LaGreca, A. M., & Stone, W. L. (1990). LD status and achievement: Confounding variables in the study of children's social status, self-esteem, and behavioral functioning. *Journal of Learning Disabilities, 23,* 483–490.

Lakin, K. C., & Bruininks, R. H. (1985). Contemporary services for handicapped children and youth. In R. H. Bruininks & K. C. Lakin (Eds.), *Living and learning in the least restrictive environment.* Baltimore: Paul H. Brookes.

Lamarine, R. J. (1993). School drug education programming: In search of a new direction. *Journal of Drug Education, 23,* 325–331.

Lambert, N., Windmiller, M., Tharinger, D., & Cole, L. (1993). *Manual for AAMD Adaptive Behavior Scale: School edition* (2nd ed.). Washington, DC: American Association on Mental Deficiency.

Lambie, R. A. (1980). A systematic approach for changing materials instruction and assignments to meet individual needs. *Focus on Exceptional Children, 13*(1), 1–16.

Landrum, J. E. (1998/1999). Adolescent novels that feature characters with disabilities: An annotated bibliography. *Journal of Adolescent & Adult Literacy, 42,* 284–290.

Lange, C., & Ysseldyke, J. (1998). School choice policies and practices for students with disabilities. *Exceptional Children, 64,* 255–270.

Langone, C. A., Langone, J., & McLaughlin, P. J. (1991). Evaluating the impact of a secondary transitional teacher preparation program. *Teacher Education and Special Education, 14*(2), 94–102.

Langone, J. (1981). Curriculum for the trainable mentally retarded, or "What do I do when the ditto machine dies!" *Education and Training of the Mentally Retarded, 16*(2), 150–154.

Larrivee, B. (1986). Effective teaching for mainstreamed students is effective teaching for all students. *Teacher Education and Special Education, 9,* 173–179.

Larry P. v. Riles. (1981). 793 F.2d 969 (Ninth Circuit 1981).

Larry P. v. Riles, 343 F. Supp. 1306 (N. D. Cal. 1972), 502 F. 2d 963 (9th Cir. 1974), 495 F. Supp. 926 (N. D. Cal. 1979), aff'd. 9th Cir., Jan. 2 3 (EHLR 555: 304, Feb. 3, 1984).

Larson, P. J., & Maag, J. W. (1998). Applying functional assessment in general education classrooms: Issues and recommendations. *Remedial and Special Education, 19,* 338–349.

Larson, V. L., & McKinley, N. L. (2003). Communication solutions for older students: Assessment and intervention strategies. Eau Claire, WI: Thinking Publications.

Lazarus, B. D. (1996). Flexible skeletons: Guided notes for adolescents. *Teaching Exceptional Children, 28*(3), 36–41.

Leal, D., & Chamberlain-Solecki, J. (1998). A Newbery Medal-winning combination: High student interest plus appropriate readability levels. *The Reading Teacher, 51,* 712–715.

Leal, D. J. (1993). The power of literary peer group discussions: How children collaboratively negotiate meaning. *The Reading Teacher, 47,* 114–120.

Lehmann, J. P., Davies, T. G., & Laurin, K. M. (2000). Listening to student voices about postsecondary education. *Teaching Exceptional Children, 32*(5), 60–65.

Leinhardt, G., Zigmond, N., & Cooley, W. W. (1981). Reading instruction and its effects. *American Educational Research Journal, 18,* 343–361.

Lenihan, G. (2003). Reading with adolescents: Constructing meaning together. *Journal of Adolescent & Adult Literacy, 47,* 8–12.

Lenz, B., Alley, G., & Schumaker, J. (1987). Activating the inactive learner: Advance organizers in the secondary content classroom. *Learning Disability Quarterly, 10,* 53–67.

Lenz, B. K., & Hughes, C. A. (1990). A word identification strategy for adolescents with hearing disabilities. *Journal of Learning Disabilities, 23,* 149–158, 163.

Leone, P. E. (1991). *Alcohol and other drugs: Use, abuse, and disabilities.* Reston, VA: The Council for Exceptional Children.

Leone, P. E., Price, T., & Vitolo, R. K. (1986). Appropriate education for all incarcerated youth: Meeting the spirit of P.L. 94-142 in youth detention facilities. *Remedial and Special Education, 7*(4), 9–14.

Leslie, L., & Allen, L. (1999). Factors that predict success in an early literacy intervention project. *Reading Research Quarterly, 34,* 404–424.

Lesseliers, J., & Van Hove, G. (2001). Barriers to the development of intimate relationships and the expression of sexuality among people with developmental disabilities: Their perceptions. *Research and Practice for Persons with Severe Disabilities, 27*(1), 69–81.

Lester, J. H., & Cheek, E. H., Jr. (1997/1998). The "real" experts address textbook issues. *Journal of Adolescent & Adult Literacy, 41,* 282–291.

Leu, D. J., Jr. (2000). Our children's future: Changing the focus of literacy and literacy instruction. *The Reading Teacher, 53,* 424–429.

Leu, D. J., Jr., & Kinzer, C. K. (2000). The convergence of literacy instruction with networked technologies for information and communication. *Reading Research Quarterly, 35,* 108–127.

Levine, P., & Nourse, S. W. (1998). What follow-up studies say about postschool life for young men and women with learning disabilities: A critical look at the literature. *Journal of Learning Disabilities, 31*(3), 212–233.

Levinson, E. M., & Palmer, E. J. (2005). Preparing students with disabilities for school-to-work transition and postschool life. *Principal Leadership, 5*(8), 11–15.

Levy, S. R., Perhats, C., & Johnson, M. N. (1992). Risk for unintended pregnancy and childbearing among educable mentally handicapped adolescents. *Journal of School Health, 62,* 151–155.

Lewis, C. (1998a). Literary interpretation as a social act. *Journal of Adolescent & Adult Literacy, 42,* 168–177.

Lewis, C. (1998b). Rock'n'roll and horror stories: Students, teachers, and popular culture. *Journal of Adolescent & Adult Literacy, 42,* 116–120.

Ley, T. C., Schaer, B. B., & Dismukes, B. W. (1994). Longitudinal study of the reading attitudes and behaviors of middle school students. *Reading Psychology, 15,* 11–38.

Liang, L. A. (2002). On the shelves of the local library: High-interest, easy reading trade books for struggling middle and high school readers. *Preventing School Failure, 46,* 183–188.

Litow, L., & Pumroy, D. K. (1975). A brief review of classroom group-oriented contingencies. *Journal of Applied Behavior Analysis, 8,* 341–347.

Livdahl, B. S. (1993). "To read it is to live it, different from just knowing it." *Journal of Reading, 37,* 192–200.

Livingston, N., & Kurkjian, C. (2005). Circles and celebrations: Learning about other cultures through literature. *The Reading Teacher, 58,* 696–703.

Lloyd, R. J., & Brolin, D. E. (1997). *Life centered career education: Modified curriculum for individuals with moderate disabilities.* Reston, VA: Council for Exceptional Children.

Lloyd, S. L. (2004). Using comprehension strategies as a springboard for student talk. *Journal of Adolescent & Adult Literacy, 48,* 114–124.

Lock, R. H., & Layton, C. A. (2001). Succeeding in postsecondary ed through self-advocacy. *Teaching Exceptional Children, 34*(2), 66–71.

Locke, J. (1980). The inference of speech perception in the phonologically disordered child. Part II: Some clinically novel procedures, their use, some findings. *Journal of Speech and Hearing Disorders, 45,* 445–468.

Lodge Rogers, E., & Rogers, D. C. (2001). Students with E/BD transition to college: Make a plan. *Beyond Behavior, 10,* 42–45.

Lora v. Board of Education of City of New York, 456 F. Supp. 1211 (E. D. N. Y. 1978), 623 F. 2d. 248 (2d Cir. 1980), 587 F. Supp. 1572 (E. D. N. Y. 1984).

Lovie, B. (2005). Development of empathetic responses with multicultural literature. *Journal of Adolescent & Adult Literacy, 48,* 566–578.

Lovitt, T., & Haring, N. (1979). *Classroom application of precision teaching.* Seattle, WA: Special Child Publications.

Lovitt, T. C., & Horton, S. V. (1994). Strategies for adapting science textbooks for youth with learning disabilities. *Remedial and Special Education, 15,* 105–116.

Lubliner, S. (2004). Help for struggling upper-grade elementary readers. *The Reading Teacher, 57,* 430–437.

Maag, J. W. (1989). Assessment in social skills training: Methodological and conceptual issues for research and practice. *Remedial and Special Education, 10*(4), 6–15.

Maag, J. W. (2001). Rewarded by punishment: Reflections on the disuse of positive reinforcement in schools. *Exceptional Children, 67,* 173–186.

Maag, J. W. (2002). A contextually based approach for treating depression in school-age children. *Intervention in School and Clinic, 37*(3), 149–155.

Maag, J. W., & Forness, S. R. (1993). Depression in children and adolescents: Identification, assessment, and treatment. In E. L. Meyen, G. A. Vergason, & R. J. Whelan (Eds.), *Challenges facing special education* (pp. 341–367). Denver: Love.

Maag, J. W., & Katsiyannis, A. (1998). Challenges facing successful transition for youths with E/BD. *Behavioral Disorders, 23,* 209–221.

Maag, J. W., & Reid R. (1994). The phenomenology of depression among students with and without learning disabilities. *Learning Disabilities Research and Practice, 9,* 91–103.

Maag, J. W., & Webber, J. (1997). Cognitive therapies: Past trends, current practices, and future directions. *Journal of Emotional and Behavioral Problems, 6*(2), 70–74.

MacArthur, C. A. (1988). Computers and writing instruction. *Teaching Exceptional Children, 20*(2), 37–39.

MacArthur, C. A., Schwartz, S., & Graham, S. (1991). A model for writing instruction: Integrating word processing and strategy instruction into a process approach to writing. *Learning Disabilities Research & Practice, 6,* 230–236.

Maccini, P., McNaughton, D., & Ruhl, K. (1999). Algebra instruction for students with learning disabilities: Implications from a research review. *Learning Disability Quarterly, 22,* 113–126.

Mace, F. C., & Murphy, D. M. (1991). Training interactional behaviors of adults with developmental disabilities: A systematic replication and extension. *Journal of Applied Behavior Analysis, 24,* 167–174.

Macias, C. M., Best, S., Bigge, J., & Musante, P. (2001). Adaptations in physical education, leisure education, and recreation. In J. L. Bigge, S. J. Sherwood, & K. W. Heller (Eds.), *Teaching individuals with physical, health, or multiple disabilities* (4th ed., pp. 467–503). Columbus, OH: Merrill Prentice Hall.

Macy, L. (2004). A novel study through drama. *The Reading Teacher, 58,* 240–248.

Maguin, E., & Loeber, R. (1996). Academic performance and delinquency. In M. Tonry (Ed.), *Crime and justice: An annual review of research* (Vol. 20, pp. 145–264). Chicago: University of Chicago Press.

Maheady, L., Sacca, K., & Harper, G. (1988). Classwide peer tutoring with mildly handicapped high school students. *Exceptional Children, 55,* 52–59.

Malian, I. M., & Love, L. L. (1998). Leaving high school: An ongoing study. *Teaching Exceptional Children, 30*(3), 4–10.

Malmgren, K., Edgar, E., & Neel, R. S. (1998). Postschool status of youths with behavioral disorders. *Behavioral Disorders, 23*(4), 257–263.

Mancini, P., & Hughes, C. (1997). Mathematics interventions for adolescents with learning disabilities. *Learning Disabilities Research & Practice, 12*(3), 168–176.

Mandell, C. J., & Gold, V. (1984). *Teaching handicapped students.* St. Paul, MN: West.

Mangrum, C., & Strichart, S. S. (Eds.). (2003). *Peterson's colleges with programs for students with learning disabilities or attention deficit disorders* (7th ed.). Princeton, NJ: Peterson's.

Manset-Williamson, G., & Nelson, J. M. (2005). Balanced, strategic reading instruction for upper-elementary and middle school students with reading disabilities: A comparative study of two approaches. *Learning Disability Quarterly, 28,* 59–75.

Manzo, A. (1969). The ReQuest procedure. *Journal of Reading, 13,* 123–127.

Marchetti, A., Nathanson, R. S., Kastner, T., & Owens, R. (1990). AIDS and state developmental disabilities agencies: A national survey. *American Journal of Public Health, 80,* 54–56.

Marchisan, M. L., & Alber, S. R. (2001). The write way: Tips for teaching the writing process to resistant writers. *Intervention in School and Clinic, 36,* 154–162.

Margolis, H., & McGettigan, J. (1988). Managing resistance to instructional modifications in mainstreamed environments. *Remedial and Special Education, 9*(4), 15–21.

Markell, M. C., & Deno, S. L. (1997). Effects of increasing oral reading: Generalization across reading tasks. *Journal of Special Education, 31,* 233–250.

Marquis, M. A. (1990). *Pragmatic-language trivia for thinking skills.* Tucson, AZ: Communication Skill Builders.

Martin, A., Ruchkin, V., Caminis, A., Vermeiren, R., Henrich, C. C., Schwab-Stone, M. (2005). Early to bed: A study of adaptation among sexually active urban adolescent girls younger that age sixteen. *Journal of the American Academy of Child and Adolescent Psychiatry, 44,* 358–367.

Martin, E. J., Tobin, T. J., & Sugai, G. M. (2002). Current information on dropout prevention: Ideas from practitioners and the literature. *Preventing School Failure, 47*(1), 10–17.

Martinez, M., Roser, N. L., & Strecker, S. (1998/1999). "I never thought I could be a star": A readers theatre ticket to fluency. *The Reading Teacher, 52,* 326–334.

Martinez-Roldan, C. M., & Lopez-Robertson, J. M. (1999/2000). Initiating literature circles in a first-grade bilingual classroom. *The Reading Teacher, 53,* 270–281.

Mascari, B. G., & Forgnone, C. (1982). A follow-up study of EMR students four years after dismissal from the program. *Education and Training of the Mentally Retarded, 17*(4), 288–292.

Massey, D. D., & Heafner, T. L. (2004). Promoting reading comprehension in social studies. *Journal of Adolescent & Adult Literacy, 48,* 26–40.

Masters, L. F., Mori, B. A., & Mori, A. A. (1999). *Teaching secondary students with mild learning and behavior problems.* Austin, TX: Pro-Ed.

Mastropieri, M. A., Leinart, A., & Scruggs, T. E. (1999). Strategies to increase reading fluency. *Intervention in School and Clinic, 34,* 278–283, 292.

Mastropieri, M. A., & Scruggs, T. E. (1994). Text versus hands-on science curriculum: Implications for students with disabilities. *Remedial and Special Education, 15,* 72–85.

Mastropieri, M. A., & Scruggs, T. E. (1998). Enhancing school success with mnemonic strategies. *Intervention in School and Clinic, 33,* 201–208.

Mastropieri, M. A., & Scruggs, T. E. (2002). *Effective instruction for special education* (3rd ed.). Austin, TX: Pro-Ed.

Mastropieri, M. A., Scruggs, T. E., & Butcher, K. (1997). How effective is inquiry learning for students with mild disabilities? *Journal of Special Education, 31,* 199–211.

Mastropieri, M. A., Scruggs, T. E., & Graetz, J. E. (2003). Reading comprehension instruction for secondary students: Challenges for struggling students an teachers. *Learning Disability Quarterly, 26,* 103–116.

Mastropieri, M. A., Scruggs, T. E., Graetz, J., Norland, J., Gardizi, W., & McDuffie, K. (2005). Case studies in co-teaching in the content areas: Successes, failures, and challenges. *Intervention in School and Clinic, 40,* 260–270.

Mathes, P. G., Francis, D. J., Denton, C. A., Fletcher, J. M., Anthony, J. L., & Schatschneider, C. (2005). The effects of theoretically different instruction and student characteristics on the skills of struggling readers. *Reading Research Quarterly, 40,* 148–183.

Mathes, P. G., Howard, J. K., Allen, S. H., & Fuchs, D. (1998). Peer-assisted learning strategies for first-grade readers: Responding to the needs of diverse learners. *Reading Research Quarterly, 33,* 62–94.

Mathur, S. R., Kavale, K. A., Quinn, M. M., Forness, S. R., & Rutherford, R. B. (1998). Social skills interventions with students with emotional and behavioral problems: A quantitative synthesis of single-subject research. *Behavioral Disorders, 23*(3), 193–201.

Mathur, S. R., & Rutherford, R. B. (1994). Teaching conversational social skills to delinquent youth. *Behavioral Disorders, 19*(4), 294–305.

Mathur, S. R., & Rutherford, R. B. (1996). Is social skills training effective for students with emotional or behavioral disorders? Research issues and needs. *Behavioral Disorders, 22*(1), 21–28.

Matson, J. L., & DiLorenzo, T. M. (1986). Social skills training and mental handicap and organic impairment. In C. R. Hollin & P. Trower (Eds.), *Handbook of social skills training* (Vol. II, pp. 67–90). Elmsford, NY: Pergamon.

Mattes, J. A., & Amsell, L. (1993). The Dexamethasane Suppression Test as an indication of depression in patients with mental retardation. *American Journal on Mental Retardation, 98,* 354–359.

Matthews, M. W., & Kesner, J. E. (2000). The silencing of Sammy: One struggling reader learning with his peers. *The Reading Teacher, 53,* 382–390.

Mattie T. v. Holladay. (1979). No. DC-75-31 (N. D. Miss. Jan. 26, 1979) (EHLR 551-109, Apr. 1, 1979).

McBride, H. E. A., & Siegel, L. S. (1997). Learning disabilities and adolescent suicide. *Journal of Learning Disabilities, 30*(6), 652–659.

McCabe, P. P. (1992). *The attitude toward school of secondary special education students with high, moderate, and low attendance rates.* (ERIC Document Reproduction Service No. ED 371 149)

McCleery, J. A., & Tindal, G. A. (1999). Teaching the scientific method to at-risk students and students with learning disabilities through concept anchoring and explicit instruction. *Remedial and Special Education, 20,* 7–18.

McConnell, M. E. (2001). *Functional behavioral assessment: A systematic process for assessment and intervention in general and special education classrooms.* Denver: Love.

McConnell, M. E., Hilvitz, P. B., & Cox, C. J. (1998). Functional assessment: A systematic process for assessment and intervention in general and special education classrooms. *Intervention in School and Clinic, 34,* 10–20.

McDonnell, J., & Wilcox, B. (1983). *Issues in the transition from school to adult services: A survey of parents of secondary students with severe handicaps.* Unpublished manuscript, University of Oregon.

McDonnell, J., Wilcox, B., & Boles, S. M. (1986). Do we know enough to plan for transition? A national survey of state agencies responsible for services to persons with severe handicaps. *Journal of the Association for Severe Handicaps, 11*(1), 53–60.

McGaughey, M. J., Kiernan, W. E., McNally, L. C., Gilmore, D. S., & Keith, G. R. (1995). Beyond the workshop: National trends in integrated and segregated day and employment services. *JASH, 20*(4), 270–285.

McGee, K., & Guetzloe, E. (1998). Suicidal emotionally handicapped students: Tips for the classroom teacher. *The Pointer, 32,* 7–10.

McGinnis, E., Goldstein, A., Sprafkin, R. P., & Gershaw, N. J. (1997). *Skill-streaming the elementary child* (Rev. Ed.). Champaign, IL: Research Press.

McIntosh, P. I., & Guest, C. L. (2000). Suicidal behavior: Recognition and response for children and adolescents. *Beyond Behavior, 10*(2), 14–17.

McKenna, M. C., Kear, D. J., & Ellsworth, R. A. (1995). Children's attitudes toward reading: A national survey. *Reading Research Quarterly, 30,* 934–955.

McKenzie, R. G. (1991). Content area instruction delivered by secondary learning disabilities teach-

ers: A national survey. *Learning Disabilities Quarterly, 14,* 467–470.

McKeown, M. G. (1993). Creating effective definitions for young word learners. *Reading Research Quarterly, 28,* 17–31.

McLaughlin, M., & DeVoogd, G. (2004). Critical literacy as comprehension: Expanding reader response. *Journal of Adolescent & Adult Literacy, 48,* 52–62.

McLaughlin, S. (1998). *Introduction to language development.* San Diego, CA: Singular Publishing.

McLeskey, J. (1982). Procedures for ameliorating attentional deficits of retarded children through instructional medial design. *Education and Training of the Mentally Retarded, 17*(3), 227–233.

McLeskey, J., & Waldron, N. (1995). Inclusive elementary programs: Must they cure students with learning disabilities to be effective? *Phi Delta Kappan, 77*(5), 300–303.

McLoughlin, J. A., & Lewis, R. B. (1994). *Assessing special students* (4th ed.). New York: Macmillan.

Meadows, N. B., Neel, R. S., Scott, C. M., & Parker, G. (1994). Academic performance, social competence, and mainstream accommodations: A look at mainstreamed and nonmainstreamed students with serious behavioral disorders. *Behavioral Disorders, 19,* 170–180.

Mechling, L., & Gast, D. (2003). Multi-media instruction to teach grocery word associations and store location: A study of generalization. *Education and Training in Mental Retardation and Developmental Disabilities, 38,* 62–76.

Meehan, K. A., & Hodell, S. (1986). Measuring the impact of vocational assessment activities upon program decisions. *Career Development for Exceptional Individuals, 9,* 106–112.

Meese, R. L. (1992). Adapting textbooks for children with learning disabilities in mainstreamed classrooms. *Teaching Exceptional Children, 24*(3), 49–51.

Mellard, D. F., & Lancaster, P. E. (2003). Incorporating adult community services in students' transition planning. *Remedial and Special Education, 24,* 359–368.

Mellon, J. (1979). Issues in the theory and practice of sentence combining: A twenty year perspective. In D. A. Daiker, A. Kerek, & M. Morenburg (Eds.), *Sentence combining and the teaching of writing* (pp. 1–38). Akron, OH: Brooks.

Mellon, J. (1981). *Sentence-combining skills: Results of the sentence combining exercises in the 1978–79 National Writing Assessment* (Special Paper No. 10-W-65 prepared for the National Assessment of Educational Progress). (ERIC Document Reproduction Service No. ED 210 696)

Mellon, J. C. (1969). *Transformational sentence-combining: A method for enhancing the development of syntactic fluency in English composition* (Research Report No. 10). Urbana, IL: National Council of Teachers of English.

Menchetti, B. M., & Piland, V. C. (1998). The personal career plan: A person-centered approach to vocational evaluation and career planning. In F. R. Rusch & J. Chadsey (Eds.), *Beyond high school: Transition from school to work* (pp. 319–339). Belmont, CA: Wadsworth.

Menchetti, B. M., & Piland V. C. (2000). Assessment for the transition from school to adult life. In S. Alper, D. L. Ryndak, & C. N. Schloss (Eds.), *Alternate assessment of students with disabilities in inclusive settings.* Boston: Allyn and Bacon.

Menon, M. B., & Mirabito, J. (1999). Ya' mean all we hafta do is read? *The Reading Teacher, 53,* 190–196.

Mercer, C. D., Jordon, L., & Miller, S. P. (1994). Implications of constructivism for teaching math to students with mild to moderate disabilities. *Journal of Special Education, 28,* 290–306.

Mercer, C. D., & Mercer, A. R. (2005). *Teaching students with learning problems* (7th ed.). Columbus, OH: Merrill.

Mercer, C. D., & Pullen, P. C. (2004). *Students with learning disabilities.* Englewood Cliffs, NJ: Prentice-Hall.

Merkley, D. (1997). Modified anticipation guides. *The Reading Teacher, 50,* 365–368.

Mesmer, H. A. E. (1999). Scaffolding a crucial transition using text with some decodability. *The Reading Teacher, 53,* 130–142.

Meyen, E. L., Vergason, G. A., & Whelan, R. J. (1998). *Educating students with mild disabilities: Strategies and methods* (2nd ed.). Denver: Love.

Miles, D., & Forcht, J. (1995). Mathematics strategies for secondary students with learning disabilities or mathematics deficiencies: A cognitive approach. *Intervention in School and Clinic, 31*(2), 91–96.

Miller, D. (1994). Suicidal behavior of adolescents with behavior disorders and their peers without disabilities. *Behavioral Disorders, 20*(1), 61–68.

Miller, L., & Downer, A. (1988). AIDS: What you and your friends need to know—A lesson plan for adolescents. *Journal of School Health, 58*(4), 137–141.

Miller, S., Strawser, S., & Mercer, C. (1996). Promoting strategic math performance among students with learning disabilities. *LD Forum, 21*(2), 34–40.

Miller, S. R., Sabatino, D. A., & Larsen, R. P. (1980). Issues in the professional preparation of secondary school special educators. *Exceptional Children, 46,* 344–350.

Miller, T. (1998). The place of picture books in middle-level classrooms. *Journal of Adolescent & Adult Literacy, 41,* 376–381.

Mims, A., Harper, C., Armstrong, S. W., & Savage, S. (1991). Effective homework instruction for students with disabilities. *Teaching Exceptional Children, 24*(1), 42–44.

Miner, C. A., & Bates, P. E. (1997). Person-centered transition planning. *Teaching Exceptional Children, 30*(1), 66–69.

Minton, C. A., & Dodder, R. A. (2003). Participation in religious services by people with developmental disabilities. *Mental Retardation, 41*(6), 430–439.

Misra, A. (1991). Behavior management: The importance of communication. *LD Forum, 11,* 26–28.

Misra, A. (1992). Generalization of social skills through self-monitoring by adults with mild mental retardation. *Exceptional Children, 58,* 495–507.

Misra, A. (1994). Partnership with multicultural families. In S. K. Alper, P. J. Schloss, & C. N. Schloss (Eds.), *Families of students with disabilities: Consultation and advocacy.* Boston: Allyn and Bacon.

Mitchell, J. P., Abernathy, T. V., & Gowans, L. P. (1998). Making sense of literacy portfolios: A four-step plan. *Journal of Adolescent & Adult Literacy, 41,* 384–389.

Montague, M. (1997). Cognitive strategy instruction in mathematics for students with learning disabilities. *Journal of Learning Disabilities, 30*(2), 164–177.

Moore, D. W., Bean, T. W., Birdyshaw, D., & Rycik, J. A. (1999). Adolescent literacy: A position statement. *Journal of Adolescent & Adult Literacy, 43,* 97–112.

Moore, D. W., Moore, S. A., Cunningham, P. M., & Cunningham, J. W. (1986). *Developing readers and writers in the content areas.* White Plains, NY: Longman.

Moore, R. J., Cartledge, G., & Heckaman, K. (1995). The effects of social skill instruction and self-monitoring on game-related behaviors of adolescents with emotional or behavioral disorders. *Behavioral Disorders, 20*(4), 253–266.

Morado, C., Koenig, R., & Wilson, A. (1999). Mini-performances, many stars! Playing with stories. *The Reading Teacher, 53,* 116–123.

Morgan, D. P., Cancio, E., & Likins, M. (1992). *Preventing substance use: What special educators need to know.* Logan: Department of Special Education, Utah State University.

Morgan, D. P., & Jenson, W. R. (1988). *Teaching behaviorally disordered students: Preferred practices.* Columbus, OH: Merrill.

Morrison, T. G., & Chilcoat, G. W. (1998). The "Living Newspaper Theatre" in the language arts class. *Journal of Adolescent & Adult Literacy, 42,* 104–115.

Moustafa, M., & Maldonado-Colon, E. (1999). Whole-to-parts phonics instruction: Building on what children know to help them know more. *The Reading Teacher, 52,* 448–458.

Muccigrosso, L., Scavarda, M., Simpson-Brown, R., & Thalacker, B. E. (1991). *Double jeopardy: Pregnant and parenting youth in special education.* Reston, VA: Council for Exceptional Children.

Mull, C. A., & Sitlington, P. L. (2003). The role of technology in transition to postsecondary education of students with learning disabilities. *The Journal of Special Education, 37,* 26–32.

Munk, D. D., Bruckert, J., Call, D. T., Stoehrmann, T., & Radandt, E. (1998). Strategies for enhancing the performance of students with LD in inclusive science classes. *Intervention in School and Clinic, 34,* 73–78.

Munk, D. D., & Bursuck, W. D. (2001). What report card grades should and do communicate: Perceptions of parents of secondary students with and without disabilities. *Remedial and Special Education, 22,* 280–287.

Murphy, S. T., & Rogan, P. M. (1995). *Developing natural supports in the workplace: A practioner's guide.* St. Augustine, FL: Training Resource Network.

Murray, P., & Penman, J. (2000). *Telling our own stories—Reflections on family life in a disabling world.* United Kingdom: Sheffield IBK Initiatives.

Nagle, J. P. (1999). Histories of success and failure: Working class students' literacy experiences. *Journal of Adolescent & Adult Literacy, 43,* 172–185.

Nagy, W. E., & Anderson, R. C. (1984). How many words are there in printed school English? *Reading Research Quarterly, 19,* 304–330.

NARAL Foundation. (1995). *Sexuality education in America: A state-by-state review.* Washington, DC: Author.

National Academy of Science (2005). National Science Education Standards. Retrieved August 9, 2005, from www.nap.edu/readingroom/books/nses/html.

National Center for Education Statistics. (2001). *Digest of educational statistics.* Washington, DC: U.S. Department of Education.

National Center for Education Statistics. (2003). *Digest of educational statistics.* Washington, DC: U.S. Department of Education.

National Commission on AIDS. (1994). Preventing HIV/AIDS in adolescents. *Journal of School Health, 64,* 7.

National Council for the Social Studies. (1994). *Expectations of excellence: Curriculum standards for social studies.* Waldorf, MD: Author.

National Council of Teachers of Mathematics. (2000). *Principles and standards for school mathematics.* Reston, VA: Author.

National Institute of Child Health and Human Development. (2000). *The report of the National Reading Panel. Teaching children to read: An evidence-based assessment of the scientific re-*

search literature on reading and its implications for reading instruction. Washington, DC: U.S. Government Printing Office.

National Joint Committee on Learning Disabilities. (2004). State and district-wide assessments and students with learning disabilities: A guide for states and school districts. *Learning Disability Quarterly, 27,* 67–76.

National Organization on Adolescent Pregnancy, Parenting, and Prevention (NOAPPP). (1995). *Pregnancy, poverty, school and employment.* Bethesda, MD: Author.

National Research Council. (1987). *Risking the future: Adolescent sexuality, pregnancy, and childbearing.* Washington, DC: National Academy Press.

National Research Council. (1989). *Everybody counts.* Washington, DC: National Academy Press.

Nelson, C. M., & Rutherford, R. B. (1989, September). *Impact on the Correctional Special Education Training (C/SET) Project in correctional special education.* Paper presented at the CED/CCBD National Topical Conference in Behavioral Disorders, Charlotte, NC.

Neubert, D. A., & Moon, M. S. (2000). How a transition profile helps students prepare for life in the community. *Teaching Exceptional Children, 33*(2), 20–25.

Neubert, D. A., Moon, M. S., & Grigal, M. (2004). Activities of students with significant disabilities receiving services in postsecondary settings. *Education and Training in Developmental Disabilities, 39,* 16–25.

Neuman, S. B. (1999). Books make a difference: A study of access to literacy. *Reading Research Quarterly, 34,* 286–311.

Neuman, S. B., Caperelli, B. J., & Kee, C. (1998). Literacy learning, a family matter. *The Reading Teacher, 52,* 244–252.

Newcomer, P. L., & Barenbaum, E. M. (1991). The written composition ability of children with learning disabilities: A review of the literature from 1980–1990. *Journal of Learning Disabilities, 24,* 578–593.

Newcomer, P. L., Borenbaum, E., & Pearson, N. (1995). Depression and anxiety in children and adolescents with learning disabilities, conduct disorders, and no disabilities. *Journal of Emotional and Behavioral Disorders, 3,* 17–39.

Nietupski, J., Welch, J., & Wacker, D. (1983). Acquisition, maintenance, and transfer of grocery item purchasing skills by moderately and severely handicapped students. *Education and Training of the Mentally Retarded, 18*(4), 279–286.

Nilsson, N. L. (2005). How does Hispanic portrayal in children's books measure up after 40 years? The answer is "It depends." *The Reading Teacher, 58,* 534–548.

No Child Left Behind Act of 2001, P.L. 107-110. Stat 1425 (2002).

Nolet, V., & Tindal, G. (1993). Special education in content area classes: Development of a model and practical procedures. *Remedial and Special Education, 14*(1), 36–48.

Nolet, V., & Tindal, G. (1994). Instruction and learning in middle school science classes: Implications for students with disabilities. *Journal of Special Education, 28,* 166–187.

Norman, M. E., & Bourexis, P. S. (1995). *Including students with disabilities in school-to-work opportunities.* Washington, DC: Council of Chief State School Officers.

Norton, B. (2003). The motivating power of comic books: Insights from Archie comic readers. *The Reading Teacher, 57,* 140–147.

Norton, D. E. (1992a). Modeling inferencing of characterization. *The Reading Teacher, 46,* 64–67.

Norton, D. E. (1992b). Understanding plot structures. *The Reading Teacher, 46,* 254–258.

Norton-Meier, L. A. (2005). Trust the fungus: Lessons in media literacy learned from movies. *Journal of Adolescent & Adult Literacy, 48,* 608–611.

Nunnally, J. C., & Bernstein, I. H. (1994). *Psychometric theory* (3rd ed.). New York: McGraw-Hill.

O'Bryne, B. (2003). The paradox of cross-age, multicultural collaboration. *Journal of Adolescent & Adult Literacy, 47,* 50–63.

Odom, S. L., Brantlinger, E., Gersten, R., Horner, R. H., Thompson, B., & Harris, K. (2005). Research in special education: Scientific methods and evidence-based practices. *Exceptional Children, 71,* 137–148.

Office of National Drug Control Policy (2000). National drug control strategy: 2000 annual report. Washington, DC: U.S. Government Printing Office.

Ohtake, Y., & Chadsey, J. G. (1999). Social disclosure among coworkers without disabilities in supported employment settings. *Mental Retardation, 37*(1), 25–35.

Olive, M. L., & McEvoy, M. A. (2004). Issues, trends and challenges in early intervention. In A. M. Sorrells, H. J. Rieth, & P. T. Sindelar, (Eds.), *Critical issues in special education: Access, diversity and accountability* (pp. 92–106). Boston: Pearson Education.

Oliver, D. (2005). *ESL idiom page.* Retrieved July 3, 2005, from www.eslcafe.com/idioms.

Oliver, M. N., Anthony, A., Leimkuhl, T. L., & Skillman, G. D. (2002). Attitudes toward acceptable socio-sexual behaviors for persons with mental retardation: Implications for normalization and community integration. *Education and Training in Mental Retardation and Developmental Disabilities, 37*(2), 193–201.

Olson, M. R., Chalmers, L., & Hoover, J. H. (1997). Attitudes and attributes of general education teachers identified as effective inclusionists. *Remedial and Special Education, 18,* 28–35.

O'Melia, M., & Rosenberg, M. (1994). Effects of cooperative homework teams on the acquisition of mathematics skills by secondary students with mild disabilities. *Exceptional Children, 60*(6), 538–548.

O'Neill, R., Horner, R., Albin, R., Sprague, J., Storey, K., & Newton, J. S. (1997). *Functional assessment and program development for problem behavior* (2nd ed.). Pacific Grove, CA: Brooks/Cole.

Opitz, M. (1998). Text sets: One way to flex your grouping—In first grade, too! *The Reading Teacher, 51,* 622–623.

Oppenheim, J. (1989). *The elementary school journal: Making the most of your child's education.* New York: Pantheon.

Orellana, M. F., & Hernandez, A. (1999). Talking the walk: Children reading urban environmental print. *The Reading Teacher, 52,* 612–619.

Osterag, B. A., & Rambeau, J. (1982). Reading success through rewriting for secondary LD students. *Academic Therapy, 18,* 27–32.

Owens, R. E. (1996*). Language development: An introduction* (4th ed.). Boston: Allyn and Bcaon.

Owens, R. E. (2005). *Language development: An introduction* (6th ed.). Boston: Allyn and Bacon.

Owens-Johnson, L., & Johnson, J. (1999). The local employer survey project: An effective school-to-work curriculum. *Teaching Exceptional Children, 31*(5), 18–23.

Palmer, B.C., & Brooks, M. A. (2004). Reading until the cows come home: Figurative language and reading comprehension. *Journal of Adolescent & Adult Literacy, 47,* 370–379.

PARC, Bowman et al. v. Commonwealth of Pennsylvania. (1971). 334 F. Supp. 279 (1971).

Paris, S. G., & Carpenter, R. O. (2003). FAQs about IRIs. *The Reading Teacher, 56,* 578–580.

Parker, W. C. (1991). Achieving thinking and decision-making objectives. In J. P. Shaver (Ed.), *Handbook of research on social studies teaching and learning* (pp. 345–356). New York: Macmillan.

Parmar, R. S., & Cawley, J. F. (1993). Analysis of science textbook recommendations provided for students with disabilities. *Exceptional Children, 59,* 518–531.

Passe, J., & Beattie, J. (1994). Social studies instruction for students with mild disabilities: A progress report. *Remedial and Special Education, 15,* 227–233.

Patton, J., Cronin, M., Bassett, D., & Koppel, A. (1997). A life skills approach to mathematics instruction: Preparing students with learning disabilities for the real-life math demands of adulthood. *Journal of Learning Disabilities, 30*(2), 178–187.

Patton, J. R., Cronin, M. E., & Jairrels, V. (1997). Curricular implications of transition: Life skills instruction as an integral part of transition education. *Remedial and Special Education, 18*(5), 294–306.

Patton, J. R., Polloway, E. A., & Cronin, M. E. (1987, May/June). Social studies instruction for handicapped students: A review of current practices. *The Social Studies,* pp. 131–135.

Patton, J. R., Polloway, E. A., Smith, T. E., Edgar, E., Clark, G., & Lee, S. (1996). Individuals with mild mental retardation: Postsecondary outcomes and implications for educational policy. *Education and Training in Mental Retardation and Developmental Disabilities, 31*(2), 75–84.

Paulson, F. L., Paulson, P. R., & Meyer, C. A. (1991). What makes a portfolio a portfolio? *Educational Leadership, 48,* 60–63.

Peck, A., & Scarpati, S. (2003). Functional matters in behavioral assessment. *Teaching Excpetional Children, 35*(5), 7.

Perkins, V., & Cullinan, D. (1985). Effects of direct instruction intervention for fraction skills. *Education and Treatment of Children, 8*, 41–50.

Perl, S. (1983). How teachers teach the writing process: Overview of an ethnographic research project. *Elementary School Journal, 84*, 19–24.

Peterson, M. (1986). Work and performance samples for vocational assessment of special students: A critical review. *Career Development for Exceptional Individuals, 9*, 69–76.

Pfeffer, C. R. (1989). Studies of suicidal preadolescent and adolescent inpatients: A critique of research methods. *Suicides and Life-Threatening Behavior, 19*(1), 58–77.

Phelps-Gunn, T., & Phelps-Terasaki, D. (1982). *Written language instruction: Theory and remediation.* Rockville, MD: Aspen Systems.

Piaget, J. (1970). *Science of education and the psychology of the child.* New York: Orion.

Pikulski, J. J., & Chard, D. J. (2005). Fluency: Bridge between decoding and reading comprehension. *The Reading Teacher, 58*, 510–519.

Piletic, C. K. (1998). Transition: Are we doing it? *Journal of Physical Education, Recreation, and Dance, 69*(9), 46–51.

Pisha, B., & Coyne, P. (2001). Smart from the start: The promise of universal design for learning. *Remedial and Special Education, 22*, 197–203.

Planned Parenthood Federation of America. (1999). *Fact sheet: Sexually transmitted infections.* New York: Katharine Dexter McCormick Library.

Platt, J. (1996, April). *Could this be magic? Instructional approaches for students with mild disabilities within regular education settings.* Presentation at the annual meeting of the Council for Exceptional Children, Orlando, FL.

Polder, D. D. (2000). Schoolwide literacy days. *The Reading Teacher, 53*, 371–373.

Polloway, E. A., & Epstein, M. H. (1985). Current research issues in mild mental retardation: A survey of the field. *Education and Training of the Mentally Retarded, 20*(3), 171–174.

Polloway, E. A., Epstein, M. H., Bursuck, W. D., Jayanthi, M., & Cumblad, C. (1994). Homework practices of general education teachers. *Journal of Learning Disabilities, 27*, 500–509.

Polloway, E. A., Epstein, M. H., Bursuck, W. D., Roderique, T. W., McConeghy, J. L., & Jayanthi, M. (1994). Classroom grading: A national survey of policies. *Remedial and Special Education, 15*, 162–170.

Polloway, E. A., & Patton, J. R. (1993). *Strategies for teaching learners with special needs* (5th ed.). New York: Merrill/Macmillan.

Polloway, E. A., & Patton, J. R. (2004). *Strategies for teaching learners with special needs* (8th ed.). New York: Prentice Hall.

Powell-Brown, A. (2003/2004). Can you be a teacher of literacy if you don't love to read? *Journal of Adolescent & Adult Literacy, 47*, 284–288.

Powers, A. R., & Wilgus, S. (1983). Linguistic complexity in the written language of hearing-impaired children. *Volta Review, 85*, 201–210.

Prater, M. A., Bruhl, S., & Serna, L. A. (1998). Acquiring social skills through cooperative learning and teacher-directed instruction. *Remedial and Special Education, 19*(3), 160–172.

Prater, M. A., & Dyches, T. T. (2005). Books about children with special needs. *The Reading Teacher, 58*, 791–793.

Prater, M. A., & Sileo, N. M. (2001). Using juvenile literature about HIV/AIDS: Ideas and precautions for the classroom. *Teaching Exceptional Children, 33*(6), 34–45.

Pressley, M., Hogan, K., Wharton-McDonald, R., Mistretta, J., & Ettenberger, S. (1996). The challenges of instructional scaffolding: The challenges of instruction that supports student thinking. *Learning Disabilities Research and Practice, 11*, 138–146.

Purdy, M. (1997). What is language? In M. Purdy & D. Borisoff (Eds.), *Listening in everyday life: A personal and professional approach* (2nd ed.). New York: University Press of America.

Purnell, K. N., & Solman, R. T. (1991). The influence of technical illustrations on students' comprehension in geography. *Reading Research Quarterly, 26*, 277–299.

Putnam, M. L. (1995). Crisis intervention with adolescents with learning disabilities. *Focus on Exceptional Children, 28*(2), 3–24.

Questions and Answers on No Child Left Behind. (2004). Retrieved August 4, 2004, from www.

ed.gov/print/nclb/accountability//schools/accountability.html.

Rabren, K., Darch, C., & Eaves, R. C. (1999). The differential effects of two systematic reading comprehension approaches with students with learning disabilities. *Journal of Learning Disabilities, 32,* 36–47.

Ramos, F., & Krashen, S. (1998). The impact of one trip to the public library: Making books available may be the best incentive for reading. *The Reading Teacher, 51,* 614–615.

Raphael, T. E., Kirschner, B. W., & Englert, C. S. (1986). *Text structure instruction within process-writing classrooms: A manual for instruction* (Occasional Paper No. 104). East Lansing: Michigan State University, Institute for Research on Teaching.

Readence, J. E., Bean, T. W., & Baldwin, R. S. (1989). *Content area reading: An integrated approach* (3rd ed.). Dubuque, IA: Kendall/Hunt.

Rekrut, M. D. (1999). Using the Internet in classroom instruction: A primer for teachers. *Journal of Adolescent & Adult Literacy, 42,* 546–557.

Renzaglia, A., & Hutchins, M. (1988). A community referenced approach to preparing persons with disabilities for employment. In P. Wehman & M. S. Moon (Eds.), *Vocational rehabilitation and supported employment* (pp. 91–110). Baltimore: Paul H. Brookes.

Resnick, M. D., Bearman, P. S., Blum, R. M., Bauman, K. E., Harris, K. M., Jones, J., et al. (1997). Protecting adolescents from harm: Findings from the national longitudinal study on adolescent health. *Journal of the American Medical Association, 278*(10), 823–832.

Retherford, K. S. (1993). *Guide to analysis of language transcripts* (2nd ed.). Eau Claire, WI: Thinking Publications.

Reutzel, D. R., & Mitchell, J. (2005). High-stakes accountability themed issue: How did we get here from there? *The Reading Teacher, 58,* 606–608.

Reynolds, C. R., & Brown, R. T. (1984). *Perspectives on bias in mental testing.* New York: John Wiley & Sons.

Reys, R. E., Lindquist, M. M., Lambdin, D. V., Suydam, M. N., & Smith, N. L. (2003). *Helping children learn mathematics* (7th ed.). Boston: Allyn and Bacon.

Rhode, G., Jenson, W., & Reavis K. (1993). *The tough kid book.* Longmont, CO: Sopris West.

Rice, K. G., & Meyer, A. L. (1994). Preventing depression among young adolescents: Preliminary process results of a psycho-educational intervention program. *Journal of Counseling and Development, 73,* 145–152.

Richards, J. C., & Anderson, N. A. (2003). How do you know? A strategy to help emergent readers make inferences. *The Reading Teacher, 57,* 290–293.

Richards, P. O., Thatcher, D. H., Shreeves, M., Timmons, P., & Barker, S. (1999). Don't let a good scare frighten you: Choosing and using quality chillers to promote reading. *The Reading Teacher, 52,* 830–840.

Richardson, J. S., & Boyle, J. (1998). A read-aloud for discussing disabilities. *Journal of Adolescent & Adult Literacy, 41,* 684–686.

Riedesel, C. A., Schwartz, J. E., & Clements, D. H. (1996). *Teaching elementary school mathematics* (6th ed.). Boston: Allyn and Bacon.

Riggs, S., Alario, A. J., & McHorney, C. A. (1990). Health risk behavior and attempted suicide in adolescents who report prior maltreatment. *Journal of Pediatrics, 116*(5), 815–820.

Roeber, E., Bond, L., & Braskamp, D. (1997). *Annual survey of state student assessment programs.* Washington, DC: Council of Chief State School Officers.

Rogan, J., LaJeunesse, C., McCann, P., McFarland, G., & Miller, C. (1995). Facilitating inclusion: The role of learning strategies to support secondary students with special needs. *Preventing School Failure, 39,* 35–39.

Rojewski, J. W. (2002). Career assessment for adolescents with mild disabilities: Critical concerns for transition planning. *Career Development of Exceptional Individuals, 25,* 73–95.

Rollins, S. P., & Unruh, A. (1964). *Introduction to secondary education.* Chicago: Rand-McNally.

Romeo v. Youngberg. (1982). 451 U.S. 982 (1982).

Rose, T. L. (1988). Current discipline practices with handicapped students: Suspensions and expulsions. *Exceptional Children, 55,* 230–239.

Rosenberg, M. (1986). Maximizing the effectiveness of structured classroom management programs:

Implementing rule-review procedures with disruptive and distractible students. *Behavioral Disorders, 11,* 239–248.

Rosenshine, B. (1983). Teaching functions in elementary school programs. *Elementary School Journal, 83,* 335–352.

Rosenshine, B., Meister, C., & Chapman, S. (1996). Teaching students to generate questions: A review of the intervention studies. *Review of Educational Research, 66,* 181–221.

Roth, K. J. (1989). Science education: It's not enough to "do" or "relate." *American Educator, 13,* 16–48.

Rubin, D. L. (1987). Divergence and convergence between oral and written communication. *Topics in Language Disorders, 7*(4), 1–18.

Rupley, W. H., Logan, J. W., & Nichols, W. D. (1998/1999). Vocabulary instruction in a balanced reading program. *The Reading Teacher, 52,* 336–346.

Rusch, F. R. (1979). Toward the validation of social vocational survival skills. *Mental Retardation, 17,* 143–145.

Rusch, F. R., & Chadsey, J. G. (1998). *Beyond high school: Transition from school to work.* Belmont, CA: Wadsworth.

Rusch, F. R., & Phelps, L. A. (1987). Secondary special education and transition from school to work: A national priority. *Exceptional Children, 53,* 487–492.

Rusch, R., Schutz, R., Mithaug, D., Steward, J., & Mar, D. (1982). *The vocational assessment and curriculum guide.* Seattle, WA: Exceptional Children.

Rutherford, F. J., & Ahlgren, A. (1990). *Science for all Americans.* New York: Oxford.

Rutherford, R. B., Nelson, C. M., & Wolford, B. I. (1985). Special education in the most restrictive environment: Correctional/special education. *Journal of Special Education, 19,* 59–71.

Ryan, A. L., Halsey, H. N., & Matthews, W. J. (2003). Using functional assessment to promote desirable student behavior in schools. *Teaching Excpetional Children, 35*(5), 8–15.

Rylance, B. J. (1997). Predictors of high school graduation or dropping out for youth with severe emotional disturbances. *Behavioral Disorders, 23*(1), 5–17.

Ryndak, D. L., & Alper, S. (2003). *Curriculum and instruction for students with significant disabilities in inclusive settings* (2nd ed.). Boston: Allyn and Bacon.

Ryndak, D. L., Alper, S., Stuart, C., & Clark, D. (in press). Identifying curriculum content for students with severe disabilities in inclusive settings. Boulder, CO: PEAK.

Ryndak, D. L., Jackson, L., & Billingsley, F. (2000). Defining school inclusion for students with moderate or severe disabilities: What do experts say? *Exceptionality, 8*(2), 101–116.

Sabornie, E. J., & deBettencourt, L. U. (1997). *Teaching students with mild disabilities at the secondary level.* Columbus, OH: Merrill.

Sacca, K. C., & Raimondi, S. (1996). *Ten terrific teaching techniques for active engagement.* A presentation at the Annual Conference of the New York State Council for Exceptional Children, Niagara Falls, NY.

Salembier, G. B. (1999). SCAN and RUN: A reading comprehension strategy that works. *Journal of Adolescent & Adult Literacy, 42,* 386–394.

Salend, S. J. (1998a). Using an activities-based approach to teach science to students with disabilities. *Intervention in School and Clinic, 34,* 67–72.

Salend, S. J. (1998b). Using portfolios to assess student performance. *Teaching Exceptional Children, 31*(2), 36–41.

Salend, S. J. (1999). So what's with our inclusion program? Evaluating educators' experiences and perceptions. *Teaching Exceptional Children, 32*(2), 46–54.

Salend, S. J. (2004). *Creating inclusive classroom: Effective and reflective practices for all students* (5th ed.). Columbus, OH: Prentice Hall.

Salend, S. J., & Garrick Duhaney, L. M. (2002). Grading students in inclusive settings. *Teaching Exceptional Children, 34*(3), 8–15.

Salend, S. J., & Schliff, J. (1989). An examination of the homework practices of teachers of students with learning disabilities. *Journal of Learning Disabilities, 22,* 621–623.

Salvia, J., & Ysseldyke, J. (2003). *Assessment in special and inclusive education* (9th ed.). Boston: Houghton Mifflin.

Sammons, R. B., & Davey, B. (1993/1994). Assessing students' skills in using textbooks: The Textbook Awareness and Performance Profile (TAPP). *Journal of Reading, 37,* 280–286.

Sample, P. L. (1998). Postschool outcomes for students with signifiant emotional disturbance following best-practice transition services. *Behavioral Disorders, 23*(4), 231–242.

Samuels, J. (1979). The method of repeated readings. *The Reading Teacher, 32,* 403–408.

Sanacore, J. (1992). Encouraging the lifetime reading habit. *Journal of Reading, 35,* 474–477.

Sanacore, J. (1998). Responding proactively to criticisms of literacy-learning practices. *Journal of Adolescent & Adult Literacy, 41,* 574–578.

Santogrossi, D., O'Leary, K., Romanczyk, R., & Kaufman, K. (1973). Self-evaluation by adolescents in a psychiatric hospital school program. *Journal of Applied Behavior Analysis, 6,* 227–287.

Sargent, L. R. (1998). *Systematic instruction of social skills (Project SISS)* (2nd ed.). Des Moines, IA: Iowa Department of Education, Bureau of Special Education.

Sarkees-Wircenski, M. D., & Scott, J. L. (1995). *Vocational special needs* (3rd ed.). Homewood, IL: American Technical Publishers.

Sattler, J. M. (2001). *Assessment of children: Cognitive applicatons* (4th ed.). San Diego: Jerome M. Sattler.

Schalock, R. L. (1985). Comprehensive community services: A plea for interagency collaboration. In R. H. Bruininks & K. C. Lakin (Eds.), *Living and learning in the least restrictive environment.* Baltimore: Paul H. Brookes.

Schloss, C. N. (2000). Measuring responses through direct observation. In S. Alper, D. Ryndak, & C. N. Schloss (Eds.), *Alternate assessment of students with disabilities in inclusive settings.* Boston: Allyn and Bacon.

Schloss, P. J. (1984). *Social development of handicapped children and adolescents.* Rockville, MD: Aspen.

Schloss, P. J. (1985). Postsecondary opportunities: The role of secondary educators in advocating handicapped young adults. *Journal for Vocational Special Needs, 7,* 15–19.

Schloss, P. J. (1986). Sequential prompt instruction for mildly handicapped learners. *Teaching Exceptional Children, 18,* 181–184.

Schloss, P. J., McEwen, D., Lang, E., & Schwab, J. (1986). PROGRESS: A model program for promoting school to work transition. *Career Development for Exceptional Individuals, 9,* 16–23.

Schloss, P. J., & Schloss, C. N. (1985). Contemporary issues in social skills research with mentally retarded people. *Journal of Special Education, 19,* 269–282.

Schloss, P. J., & Schloss, C. N. (1987). A critical review of social skills research in mental retardation. In R. P. Barrett & J. L. Matson (Eds.), *Advances in developmental disorders.* Greenwich, CT: JAI Press.

Schloss, P. J., & Sedlak, R. A. (1986). *Instructional methods for students with learning and behavioral problems.* Boston: Allyn and Bacon.

Schloss, P. J., & Smith, M. A. (1990). *Social skills development of hearing impaired youth.* Washington, DC: Alexander Graham Bell Association for the Deaf.

Schloss, P. J., & Smith, M. A. (1998). *Applied behavior analysis in the classroom* (2nd ed.). Boston: Allyn and Bacon.

School-to-Work Opportunities Act. (1994). Public Law 103-239, 20 U.S. C., 6101 (1994).

Schulte, A. C., Osborne, S. S., & Erchul, W. P. (1998). Effective special education: A United States dilemma. *School Psychology Review, 27*(1), 66–76.

Schumaker, J., Deshler, D., Alley, G., & Warner, M. (1983). Toward the development of an intervention model for learning disabled adolescents: The University of Kansas Institute. *Exceptional Education Quarterly, 4,* 45–74.

Schumaker, J. B., & Deshler, D. D. (2003). Can students with LD become competent writers? *Learning Disability Quarterly, 26,* 129–142.

Schumaker, J. B., Deshler, D. D., Bulgren, J. A., Davis, B., Lenz, B. K., & Grossen, B. (2002). Access of adolescents with disabilities to general education curriculum: Myth or reality? *Focus on Exceptional Children, 35*(3), 1–16.

Schumaker, J. B., Nolan, S., & Deshler, D. D. (1985). *Learning strategies curriculum: The error monitoring strategy.* Lawrence: University of Kansas, Institute for Research in Learning Disabilities.

Schumm, J. S., & Mangrum, C. T., II. (1991). FLIP: A framework for content area reading. *Journal of Reading, 35,* 120–124.

Schumm, J. S., & Strickler, K. (1991). Guidelines for adapting content area textbooks: Keeping teachers and students content. *Intervention in School, 27,* 798.

Schumm, J. S., & Vaughn, S. (1991). Making adaptations for mainstreamed students: Classroom teachers' perspectives. *Remedial and Special Education, 12*(4), 18–27.

Schwartz, R. M. (1988). Learning to learn vocabulary in content area textbooks. *Journal of Reading, 32,* 108–118.

Schwartz, S. E., & Budd, D. (1981). Mathematics for handicapped learners: A functional approach for adolescents. *Focus on Exceptional Children, 13*(7), 1–12.

Scotti, J. R., Nangle, D. W., Masia, C. L., Ellis, J. T., Ujcich, K. J., Giacoletti, A. M., et al. (1997). Providing an AIDS education and skills training program to persons with mild developmental disabilities. *Education and Training in Mental Retardation and Developmental Disabilities, 32*(2), 113–128.

Scotti, J. R., Speaks, L. V., Masia, C. L., & Drabman, R. S. (1996). The educational effects of providing AIDS-risk information to persons with developmental disabilities: An exploratory study. *Education and Training in Mental Retardation and Developmental Disabilities, 31*(2), 115–122.

Scruggs, T. E., & Laufenberg, R. (1986). Transformational mnemonic strategies for retarded learners. *Education and Training of the Mentally Retarded, 21*(3), 165–173.

Scruggs, T. E., & Mastropieri, M. A. (1993). Current approaches to science education: Implications for mainstream instruction of students with disabilities. *Remedial and Special Education, 14*(1), 15–24.

Scruggs, T. E., & Mastropieri, M. A. (1994). The construction of scientific knowledge by students with mild disabilities. *Journal of Special Education, 28,* 307–321.

Scruggs, T. E., Mastropieri, M. A., & Sullivan, G. S. (1994). Promoting relational thinking skills: Elaborative interrogation for students with mild disabilities. *Exceptional Children, 60,* 450–457.

Secretary's Commission of Achieving Necessary Skills (SCANS). (1991). *What work requires of schools: A SCANS report for America 2000.* Washington, DC: U.S. Department of Labor.

Sedlak, R. A., & Sedlak, D. M. (1985). *Teaching the educable mentally retarded.* Albany: State University of New York Press.

Sedlak, R. A., & Sedlak, D. M. (1985). *Teaching the educable mentally retarded.* Albany: State University of New York Press.

Sedlak, R. A., & Weener, P. (1973). Review of research on the Illinois Test of Psycholinguistic Abilities. In L. Mann & D. A. Sabatino (Eds.), *The first review of special education.* Philadelphia: Journal of Special Education Press.

Seegers, G., Van Putten, C. M., & Vermeer, H. J. (2004). Effects of causal attributions following mathematics tasks on student cognitions about a subsequent task. *The Journal of Experimental Education, 72*(4), 307–328.

Seidal, J., & Vaughn, S. (1991). Social alienation and the learning disabled school dropout. *Learning Disabilities Research, 6,* 152–157.

Semel, E., Wiig, E. H., & Secord, W. A. (2003). *Clinical evaluation of language fundamentals* (4th ed.). San Antonio, TX: Psychological Corporation.

Shaffer, D., Vieland, V., Garland, A., Rojas, M., Underwood, M., & Busner, C. (1990). Adolescent suicide attempters: Response to suicide-prevention programs. *Journal of the American Medical Association, 264,* 3151–3155.

Shaftel, J., Pass, L., & Schnabel, S. (2005). Math games for adolescents. *Teaching Exceptional Children, 37*(3), 25–26.

Shames, G. H., & Anderson, N. (2002). *Human communication disorders: An introduction* (6th ed.). Boston: Allyn and Bacon.

Shanahan, T., & Shanahan, S. (1997). Character perspective charting: Helping to develop a more complete conception of story. *The Reading Teacher, 50,* 668–677.

Shannon, J. (1986). In the classroom stoned. *Phi Delta Kappan, 66*(1), 60–62.

Shannon, P. (2000). We gotta get out of this place: The politics of what works. *The Reading Teacher, 53,* 394–396.

Shaughnessy, L., Doshi, S. R., & Jones, S. E. (2004). Attempted suicide and associated health risk behaviors among Native American high school students. *Journal of School Health, 74,* 177–182.

Shavelson, R. J., & Stern, P. (1981). Research on teachers' pedagogical thoughts, judgements, decisions, and behavior. *Review of Educational Research, 51*(4), 455–498.

Shaw, S. F. (1997). Professional standards and a code of ethics for postsecondary disability personnel. *Journal of Postsecondary Education and Disability, 12*(3), 3–4.

Sheppard-Jones, K., Prout, H. T., & Kleinert, H. (2005). Quality of life dimensions for adults with developmental disabilities: A comparative study. *Mental Retardation, 43*(4) 281–291.

Shiflett, A. C. (1998). Marketing literature: Variations on the book talk theme. *Journal of Adolescent & Adult Literacy, 41,* 568–570.

Shippen, M. E., Simpson, R. G., & Crites, S. A. (2003). A practical guide to functional behavioral assessment. *Teaching Exceptional Children, 35*(5), 36–44.

Shores, R. E., Gunter, P. L., & Jack, S. L. (1993). Classroom management strategies: Are they setting events for coercion? *Behavioral Disorders, 18,* 92–102.

Shriner, J. G., Ysseldyke, J. E., & Thurlow, M. L. (1994). Standards for all American students. *Focus on Exceptional Children, 26*(5), 1–19.

Shutes, R., & Peterson, S. (1994). Seven reasons why textbooks cannot make a curriculum. *NASSP Bulletin, 78*(565), 11–20.

Sikorski, M. F., Niemiec, R. P., & Walberg, H. J. (1996). A classroom checkup: Best teaching practices in special education. *Teaching Exceptional Children, 29*(1), 27–29.

Silbert, J., Carnine, D., & Stein, M. (1990). *Direct instruction mathematics* (2nd ed.). Columbus, OH: Merrill.

Sinatra, R., & Dowd, C. A. (1991). Using syntactic and semantic clues to learn vocabulary. *Journal of Reading, 35,* 224–229.

Sindelar, P., Rosenberg, M., Wilson, R., & Bursuck, W. (1984). The effects of group size and instruction method on the acquisition of mathematical concepts by fourth-grade students. *Journal of Educational Research, 77,* 178–183.

Sindelar, P. T., Smith, M. A., Harriman, N. E., Hale, R. L., & Wilson, R. J. (1986). Teacher effectiveness in special education programs. *Journal of Special Education, 20,* 195–207.

Sitlington, P. L., & Clark, G. M. (2006). *Transition education and services for students with disabilities* (4th ed.). Boston: Allyn and Bacon.

Skillings, M. J., & Ferrell, R. (2000). Student-generated rubrics: Bringing students into the assessment process. *The Reading Teacher, 53,* 452–455.

Skinner, M. E., & Lindstrom, B. D. (2003). Bridging the gap between high school and college: Strategies for the successful transition of students with learning disabilities. *Preventing School Failure, 47,* 132–137.

Small, L. H. (2005). *Fundamentals of phonetics.* Boston: Allyn and Bacon.

Smith v. Robinson. (1984). 468 U.S. 992, 104 S. Ct. 3457 (1984).

Smith, K. (1990). Suicidal behavior in school aged youth. *School Psychology Review, 19,* 186–195.

Smith, M., & Schloss, P. (1986). A "superform" for enhancing competence in completing employment applications. *Teaching Exceptional Children, 18,* 277–280.

Smith, M. A., & Misra, M. (1994). Using group contingencies with students with learning disabilities *LD Forum, 19*(4), 17–20.

Smith, S. W., & Travis, P. C. (2001). Conducting social competence research: Considering conceptual frameworks. *Behavioral Disorders, 26,* 360–369.

Smith, T. E., Polloway, E. A., Patton, J. R., & Dowdy, C. A. (2004). *Teaching students with special needs in inclusive settings* (4th ed.). Boston: Allyn and Bacon.

Smith, T. M., Desimone, L. M., & Ueno, K. (2005). "Highly qualified" to do what? The relationship between NCLB teacher quality mandates and the use of reform oriented instruction in middle school mathematics. *Educational Evaluation and Policy Analysis, 27,* 75–109.

Smolin, L. I., & Lawless, K. A. (2003). Becoming literate in the technological age: New responsibilities and tools for teachers. *The Reading Teacher, 56,* 570–577.

Smolowe, J. (1995). The downward spiral. *Time* (Online serial). Available: America Online, Education.

Snarr, R., & Wolford, B. (1995). *Introduction to corrections.* Columbus, OH: McGraw-Hill.

Snow, C. E., Burns, M. S., & Griffin, P. (1998). *Preventing reading difficulties in young children.* Washington, DC: National Academy Press.

Sorrentino, A., & Zirkel, P. A. (2004). Is NCLB leaving special education students behind? *Principal, 83,* 26–29.

Sparrow, S. S., Cicchetti, D. V., & Balla, D. A. (2005). *Vineland Adaptive Behavior Scales* (2nd ed). Circle Pines, MN: American Guidance Service.

Speaker, R. B., Jr., & Speaker, P. R. (1991). Sentence collecting: Authentic literacy events in the classroom. *Journal of Reading, 35,* 92–96.

Spencer, V. G., Scruggs, T. E., & Mastropieri, M. A. (2003). Content area learning in middle school social studies classroom and students with emotional or behavioral disorders. *Behavioral Disorders, 28,* 77–93.

SPeNSE. (2002). *General education teachers' role in special education: Study of personnel needs in special education.* Retrieved March 31, 2003, from the www.spense.org.

Spires, H. A., Williams, J. B., Jackson, A., & Huffman, L. E. (1998/1999). Leveling the playing field through autobiographical reading and writing. *Journal of Adolescent & Adult Literacy, 42,* 296–304.

Spivack, C., Spotts, J., & Haimes, P. E. (1967). *Devereux Adolescent Behavior Rating Scale Manual.* Devon, PA: Devereux Foundation.

Stallings, J. A., Needles, M., & Stayrook, N. (1979). *How to change the process of teaching basic reading skills in secondary schools.* Menlo Park, CA: SRI International.

Stanovich, K. E. (1986). Matthew effects in reading: Some consequences of individual differences in the acquisition of literacy. *Reading Research Quarterly, 21,* 360–407.

Stanovich, P. J., & Stanovich, K. E. (2003). *Using research and reason in education: How teachers can use scientifically based research to make curricular and instructional decisions.* Washington, DC: U.S. Department of Education.

Stark, K. (1990). *Childhood depression: School-based intervention.* New York: Guilford.

Starlin, C., & Starlin, A. (1973). *Guides for continuous decision making.* Bemidji, MN: Unique Curriculums.

Steere, D. E., & Cavaiuolo, D. (2002). Connecting outcomes, goals, and objectives in transition planning. *Teaching Exceptional Children, 34*(6), 54–59.

Stein, M., Carnine, D., & Dixon, R. (1998). Direct instruction: Integrating curriculum design and effective teaching practice. *Intervention in School and Clinic, 33,* 227–234.

Stein, M., Johnson, B., & Gutlohn, L. (1999). Analyzing beginning reading programs. *Remedial and Special Education, 20,* 275–287.

Stern, M., Northman, J., & Van-Slyck, M. (1984). Father absence and adolescent "problem behaviors." Alcohol consumption, drug use and sexual activity. *Adolescence, 19,* 302–312.

Sternberg, R. J. (1991). Are we reading too much into reading comprehension tests? *Journal of Reading, 34,* 540–545.

Stevens, R., & Rosenshine, B. (1981). Advances in research on teaching. *Exceptional Education Quarterly, 2,* 1–9.

Stevens, T. (1977). *Teaching skills to children with learning and behavior disorders.* Columbus, OH: Merrill.

Stinson, J., Christian, L., & Dotson, L. A. (2001). Overcoming barriers to the sexual expression of women with developmental disabilities. *Research and Practice for Persons with Severe Disabilities, 27*(1), 18–26.

Stodden, R. A. (1986). Vocational assessment: An introduction. *Career Development for Exceptional Individuals, 9,* 67–68.

Stodden, R. A., & Whelley, T. (2004). Postsecondary education and persons with intellectual disabilities: An introduction. *Education and Training in Developmental Disabilities, 39,* 6–15.

Stodden, R. A., Galloway, L. M., & Stodden, N. J. (2003). Secondary school curricula issues: Impact on postsecondary students with disabilities. *Exceptional Children, 70,* 9–25.

Stokeld, C. L. (1995). *The adult sequelae of a childhood diagnosis of attention-deficit/hyperactivity disorder: A review of the literature for the past decade.* (ERIC Document Reproduction Service No. ED 389 131)

Storey, K. (1997). Quality of life issues in social skills assessment of persons with disabilities. *Education and Training in Mental Retardation and Developmental Disabilities, 32,* 197–200.

Stotsky, S. (1975). Sentence combining as a curricular activity: Its effect on written language development and reading comprehension. *Research in the Teaching of English, 9,* 30–71.

Strain, P. S. (2001). Empirically based social skill intervention: A case for quality-of-life improvement. *Behavioral Disorders, 27,* 30–36.

Strassman, B. K., & D'Amore, M. (2002). The write technology. *Teaching Exceptional Children, 34*(6), 28–31.

Straw, S. B. (1981). Grammar and teaching of writing: Analysis versus synthesis. In V. Froese & S. B. Straw (Eds.), *Research in the language arts: Language and schooling* (pp. 147–161). Baltimore: University Park Press.

Strommen, L. T., & Mates, B. F. (2004). Learning to love reading: Interviews with older children and teens. *Journal of Adolescent & Adult Literacy, 48,* 188–200.

Strong, W. (1983). *Sentence combining: A composing book* (2nd ed.). New York: Random House.

Stumbo, N. J., & Peterson, C. A. (1998). The leisurability model. *Therapeutic Recreation Journal, 32*(2), 82–96.

Sturm, J. M., Rankin, J. L., Beukelman, D. R., & Schutz-Muehling, L. (1997). How to select appropriate software for computer-assisted writing. *Intervention in School & Clinic, 32,* 148–161.

Sugai, G., & Lewis, T. J. (1998). Preferred and promising practices for social skills instruction. In E. L. Meyen, G. A. Vergason, & R. J. Whelan (Eds.), *Educating students with mild disabilities: Strategies and methods* (2nd ed., pp. 137–162). Denver: Love.

Swanson, H. L. (2000). Issues facing the field of learning disabilities. *Learning Disability Quarterly, 23,* 37–50.

Swanson, H. L., & Howard, C. B. (2005). Children with reading disabilities: Does dynamic assessment help in classification? *Learning Disability Quarterly, 28,* 17–34.

Swanson, P. N., & De La Paz, S. (1998). Teaching effective comprehension strategies to students with learning and reading disabilities. *Intervention in School and Clinic, 33,* 209–218.

Swicegood, P. (1994). Portfolio-based assessment practices. *Intervention in School and Clinic, 30*(1), 6–15.

Swiderek, B. (1997). Full inclusion—Making it work. *Journal of Adolescent & Adult Literacy, 43,* 234–235.

Swift, K. (1993). Try reading workshop in your classroom. *The Reading Teacher, 46,* 366–371.

Swindall, V., & Cantrell, R. J. (1999). Character interviews help bring literature to life. *The Reading Teacher, 53,* 23–25.

Taber, T. A., Alberto, P. A., Hughes, M., & Seltzer, A. (2002). A strategy for students with moderate disabilities when lost in the community. *Research and Practice for Persons with Severe Disabilities, 27*(2), 141–152.

Taylor, R. L. (2006). *Assessment of exceptional students: Educational and psychological procedures* (7th ed.). Boston: Allyn and Bacon.

Taymans, J. M., West, L. L., Sullivan, M., & Scheiber, B. (2000). *Unlocking potential: College and other choices for people with LD and ADHD.* Bethesda, MD: Woodbine, House.

Teacher Quality: Frequently Asked Questions. (2004). Retrieved August 4, 2004, from http://www.ed.gov/print/nclb/accountability//schools/accountability.html.

Terban, M. (1998). *Scholastic dictionary of idioms.* New York: Scholastic.

Test, D. W., Keul, P. K., & Grossi, T. (1988). Transitional services for mildly handicapped youth: A cooperative model. *Journal for Vocational Special Needs, 10,* 7–11.

Thoma, C. A. (1999). Support student voice in transition planning. *Teaching Exceptional Children, 31*(5), 4–9.

Thorn-Gray, B. E., & Kern, L. H. (1983). Sexual dysfunction associated with physical disability: A treatment guide for the rehabilitation practitioner. *Rehabilitation Literature, 44,* 138–144.

Thorum, A. (1986). *Fullerton language test for adolescents* (2nd ed.). Chicago: Riverside.

Thurlow, M. L., Ysseldyke, J. E., & Anderson, C. L. (1995). *High school graduation requirements: What's happening for students with disabilities?* Minneapolis: National Center on Education Outcomes, University of Minnesota. (ERIC Document Reproduction Service No. ED385 056)

Tierney, R. J., Clark, C., Fenner, L., Herter, R. J., Simpson, C. S., & Wiser, B. (1998). Portfolios: Assumptions, tensions, and possibilities. *Reading Research Quarterly, 33,* 474–486.

Tilton, L. (2000). *Inclusion: A fresh look.* Stenhouse, ME: Covington Cove Publications.

Timothy W. v. Rochester School District. (1989). 875 F. 2d 954 (1st Cir. 1989).

Tindall, G., McDonald, M., Tedesco, M. Glasgow, A., Almond, P., Crawford, L., & Hollenbeck, K. (2003). Alternate assessments in reading and math: Development and validation for students with significant disabilities. *Exceptional Children, 69,* 481–494.

Tindall, G., Shinn, M. R., & Rodden-Nord, K. (1990). Contextually based school consultation: Influential variables. *Exceptional Children, 56,* 324–336.

Tompkins, G. E., & Friend, M. (1988). After your students write: What's next? *Teaching Exceptional Children, 20,* 4–9.

Towell, J. (1997/1998). Fun with vocabulary. *The Reading Teacher, 51,* 356–358.

Towell, J. T. (1999/2000). Motivating students through music and literature. *The Reading Teacher, 53,* 284–289.

Tripp, A. (1991). The scientific method: It works. *Teaching Exceptional Children, 23*(2), 16–20.

Turkewitz, H., O'Leary, K., & Ironsmith, M. (1975). Generalization and maintenance of appropriate behavior through self-control. *Journal of Consulting and Clinical Psychology, 43,* 577–583.

Turnbull, A. P., Turnbull, H. R. III., Erwin, E. J., & Soodak, L. C. (2005). *Families, professionals, and exceptionality: Positive outcomes through partnership and trust* (5th ed.). Columbus, OH: Prentice Hall.

Tyner, B. (2004). *Small-group reading instruction.* Newark, DE: International Reading Association.

Uberti, H., Scruggs, T. E., & Mastropieri, M. A. (2003). Keywords make the difference! Mnemonic instruction in inclusive classrooms. *Teaching Exceptional Children, 35*(3), 56–61.

U.S. Department of Commerce. (1980). *Statistical abstract of the United States.* Washington, DC: Department of Commerce, Bureau of the Census.

U.S. Department of Education. (1997). National Center for Education Statistics. Principal/School disciplinarian survey on school violence. *Fast Response Survey System, 63.*

U.S. Department of Education. (1998). *Twentieth annual report to Congress on the implementation of the Individuals with Disabilities Education Act.* Washington, DC: Author.

U.S. Department of Education. (2002). *Twenty-third annual report to Congress on the implementation of Public Law 101-476: The Individuals with Disabilities Education Act.* Washington, DC: Author.

U.S. Department of Education. (2003a). *The nation's report card: Reading 2002.* Washington, DC: Author.

U.S. Department of Education. (2003b). *No Child Left Behind: A parents guide.* Washington, DC: Author.

U.S. Department of Education. (2004). *No Child Left Behind: A toolkit for teachers.* Washington, DC: Author.

U.S. Department of Health and Human Services. (1997). *1995 national survey of family growth.* Washington, DC: U.S. Government Printing Office.

U.S. Department of Health and Human Services. (2002). Monitoring the Future Survey.

U.S. Department of Health and Human Services. (2003). *Substance use disorder treatment for people with physical and cognitive disabilities. #29 Treatment improvement protocol (TIP) series.* (DHHS Publication No. SMS 03-3809.) Rockville, MD: Author.

U.S. Department of Labor. (1991). *Dictionary of occupational titles.* Washington, DC: Author.

U.S. Department of Labor. (2006). *Occupational outlook handbook, 2006–2007.* Washington, DC: Author.

U.S. Public Law 93-112 (Rehabilitation Act of 1973). (1973). Section 504. 29 U.S.C. 794.

Vacca, R. (1998). Let's not marginalize adolescent literacy. *Journal of Adolescent & Adult Literacy, 41,* 604–609.

Vacca, R., & Alvermann, D. (1998). The crisis in adolescent literacy: Is it real or imagined? *NASSP Bulletin, 82,* 4–9.

Vacca, R., & Vacca, J. (1999). *Content area reading* (6th ed.). New York: Longman.

Valdes, K. A., Williamson, C. L., & Wagner, M. M. (1990). *The national longitudinal transition study of special education students (Vol. 1).* Menlo Park, CA: SRI International.

Van Luit, E., & Naglieri, J. (1999). Effectiveness of the MASTER program for teaching special children multiplication and division. *Journal of Learning Disabilities, 32*(2), 98–107.

Vaughn, S., & Klingner, J. K. (1999). Teaching reading comprehension through collaborative strategic reading. *Intervention in School and Clinic, 34,* 284–292.

Vaughn, S., Ridley, C., & Cox, J. (1983). Evaluating the efficacy of an interpersonal skills training program with children who are mentally retarded. *Education and Training of the Mentally Retarded, 18,* 191–196.

Villaume, S. K., & Brandt, S. L. (1999/2000). Extending our beliefs about effective learning environments: A tale of two learners. *The Reading Teacher, 53,* 322–330.

Vyas, S. (2004). Exploring bicultural identities of Asian high school students through the analytic window of a literature club. *Journal of Adolescent & Adult Literacy, 47,* 168–175.

Vygotsky, L. (1978). *Mind in society.* Cambridge, MA: Harvard University Press.

Wagner, M., Blackorby, J., Cameto, R., Hebbeler, K., & Newman, L. (1993). *What makes a difference? Influences on post-school outcomes of youth with disabilities: The third comprehensive report from the national longitudinal transition study of special education students.* Menlo Park, CA: SRI International. (ERIC Document Reproduction Service No. ED 365 085)

Walker, B. J. (2003). Instruction for struggling readers contains multiple features. *The Reading Teacher, 57,* 206–207.

Walker, D. W., & Leister, C. (1994). Recognition of facial affect cues by adolescents with emotional and behavioral disorders. *Behavioral Disorders, 19*(4), 269–276.

Walker, H. M., Schwarz, I. E., Nippold, M. A., Nippold, M. A., Irvin, L. K., & Noell, J. W. (1994). Social skills in school-age children and youth: Issues and best practices in assessment and intervention. *Topic in Language Disorders, 14*(3), 70–82.

Walker, H. M., & Sprague, J. R. (1999). The path to school failure, delinquency, and violence: Casual factors and some potential solutions. *Intervention in School and Clinic, 35*(2), 67–73.

Wallace, G., Cohen, S. B., & Polloway, E. A. (1987). *Language arts: Teaching exceptional students.* Austin: Pro-Ed.

Wallace G., & Hammill, D. D. (1994). *CREUT-2: Comprehensive receptive and expressive test* (2nd ed.). Austin, TX: Pro-Ed.

Walpole, S. (1998/1999). Changing texts, changing thinking: Comprehension demands of new science textbooks. *The Reading Teacher, 52,* 358–369.

Walters, A. S. (1995). Suicidal behavior in children and adolescents with mental retardation. *Research in Developmental Disabilities, 16*(2), 85–96.

Ward, K. M., Trigler, J. S., & Pfeiffer, K. T. (2001). Community services, issues, and service gaps for individuals with developmental disabilities who exhibit inappropriate sexual behavior. *Mental Retatdation, 39*(1), 11–19.

Warner, M. M., Cheney, C. O., & Pienkowski, D. M. (1996). Guidelines for developing and evaluating programs for secondary students with mild disabilities. *Intervention in School and Clinic, 31*(5), 276–284.

Washburn-Moses, L. (2003). What every special educator should know about high stakes testing. *Teaching Exceptional Children, 35*(4), 12–15.

Wasik, B. A. (1998). Volunteer tutoring programs in reading: A review. *Reading Research Quarterly, 33,* 266–292.

Wasik, B. A. (1999). Reading coaches: An alternative to reading tutors. *The Reading Teacher, 52,* 653–656.

African American youth. *Adolescence, 39,* 653–667.

Wright-Strawderman, C., Lindsey, P., Navarette, L., & Flippo, J. R. (1996). Depression in students with disabilities: Recognition and intervention strategies. *Intervention in School and Clinic, 31*(5), 261–275.

Wyatt v. Aderholt. (1971). 334 F. Supp. 1341 (1971).

Xin, Y. P., Grasso, E., Dippi-Hoy, C. M., & Jitendra, A. (2005). The effects of purchasing skill instruction for individuals with developmental disabilities: A meta-analysis. *Exceptional Children, 71*(4), 379–400.

Yavas, M. (1998). *Phonology, development and disorders.* San Diego, CA: Singular Publishing.

Yell, M. L. (1990). The use of corporal punishment, suspension, expulsion, and time-out with behaviorally disordered students in public schools: Legal considerations. *Behavioral Disorders, 15,* 100–109.

Yell, M. L., & Katisyannis, A. (2001). Legal issues. *Preventing School Failure, 45,* 82–88.

Yell, M. L., Rozalski, M. E., & Drasgow, E. (2001). Disciplining students with disabilities. *Focus on Exceptional Children, 33*(9), 1–16.

Yopp, R. H., & Yopp, H. K. (2003). Time with text. *The Reading Teacher, 57,* 284–287.

Ysseldyke, J., & Olsen, K. (1999). Putting alternative assessments into practice: What to measure and possible sources of data. *Exceptional Children, 65*(2), 175–185.

Yu, D. C. U., Spevack, S., Hiebert, R., Martin, T. L., Goodman, R., Martin, T., et al. (2002). Happiness indices among persons with profound and severe disabilities during leisure and work activities: A comparison. *Education and Training in Developmental Disabilities, 78*(4), 421–426.

Zabel, R. H., & Nigro, F. A. (1999). Juvenile offenders and behavioral disorders, learning disabilities, and no disabilities: Self-reports of personal, family, and school characteristics. *Behavioral Disorders, 25*(1), 22–40.

Zafft, C., Hart, C., & Zimbrich, K. (2004). College career connection: A study of youth with intellectual disabilities and the impact of postsecondary education. *Education and Training in Developmental Disabilities, 39,* 45–53.

Zarkowska, E., & Clements, J. (1988). *Problem behavior in people with severe learning disabilities: A practical guide to a constructional approach.* London: Croom Helm.

Zigmond, N., Jenkins, J., Fuchs, L., Deno, S., Fuchs, D., Baker, J., et al. (1995). Special education in restructured schools: Findings from three multiyear studies. *Phi Delta Kappan, 76*(7), 531–540.

Zirpoli, T. J. (2005). *Behavior management: Applications for teachers* (4th ed.). Upper Saddle River, NJ: Pearson.

Zoellner, R. (1969). Talk-write: A behavioral pedagogy for composition. *College English, 30,* 267–320.

Author Index

Abernathy, T., 237, 385
Abodeeb, R., 237, 365
Academy for Effective Instruction, 83, 358
Adams, T. L., 245, 358
Adelman, H. S., 318, 319, 358, 374
Adlaf, E., 48, 360
Ahlgren, A., 339, 391
Ahlgrim-Delzell, L., 111, 362
Alan Guttmacher Institute (AGI), 61, 69, 358
Alario, A. J., 57, 390
Alber, S. R., 214, 215, 216, 222, 382
Alberto, P., 173, 260, 268, 274, 298, 358, 387, 396
Albin, R., 388
Alfassi, M., 249, 358
Algozzine, B., 17, 111, 214, 230, 274, 358, 360, 362, 399
Allen, L., 254, 380
Allen, S., 44, 358
Allen, S. H., 245, 383
Alley, G., 221, 270, 380, 392
Almond, P., 111, 397
Alper, S., 23, 23, 273, 297, 304, 306, 307, 308, 358, 391
Alverman, D. E., 235, 375, 398
Amber, A., 310, 367
American Psychiatric Association, 56, 358
Amsell, L., 53, 383
Anderson, C. L., 18, 397
Anderson, D., 109, 377
Anderson, D. M., 62, 358
Anderson, L. M., 78, 86, 216, 358, 368
Anderson, N., 203, 393
Anderson, N. A., 247, 390
Anderson, P. L., 223, 358
Anderson, R. C., 242, 247, 386

Anderson, S., 338, 347, 353, 356, 358
Anderson, T. H., 148, 242, 247, 359
Anderson-Inman, L., 248, 358
Andrews, S. E., 254, 358
Anthony, A., 64, 388
Anthony, H. M., 216, 368
Archambeault, B., 249, 359
Archer, A., 229, 235, 260, 270, 359
Armbruster, B. B., 148, 242, 247, 359
Armstrong, S. W., 90, 358
Armstrong v. Kline, 8, 359
Arnold, J., 243, 371
Aseltine, R. H., 56, 359
Askvig, B. A., 318, 360
Aspel, N., 278. 359
Atwell, N., 253, 359
Au, K. H., 236, 254, 359
Aucoin, L., 278, 279, 379
Austin, V., 178, 179, 193, 359
Ayres, K., 261, 376

Babbitt, B., 261, 376
Babbitt, B. C., 29, 359
Babbitt, C. E., 27, 362
Babbitt, S., 240, 359
Bachman, J. G., 63, 377
Badian, N. A., 235, 359
Baer, R. M., 279, 359
Bain, S., 245, 367
Baker, L., 252, 259
Baker, S., 215, 219, 359
Baker, T. K., 244, 379
Baldwin, R. S., 249, 390
Balla, D. A., 330, 395
Banjeree, M., 75, 361
Banks, P. D., 23, 375
Barenbaum, E. M., 214, 387
Barrett, T. C., 234, 256, 359
Barry, A. L., 253, 360

Bassett, D., 259, 388
Bates, P. E., 283, 385
Battle v. Commonwealth, 8, 360
Bauman, K. E., 53, 390
Baumann, J. F., 249, 360
Bauman-Waengler, J., 196, 208, 360
Baumgart, D., 318, 360
Baxendell, B. W., 348, 360
Baxter, J. A., 263, 360
Bean, T. W., 235, 249, 385, 386, 390
Bearinger, L. H., 53
Bearman, P. S., 53, 390
Beattie, J., 274, 346, 360, 388
Beck, I. L., 247, 251, 360
Beitchman, J. H., 48, 360
Bellamy, G. T., 3, 23, 360, 400
Bender, W. N., 42, 44, 46, 54, 56, 318, 319, 360, 376
Bennett, W. J., 62, 260, 360
Benz, M. R., 278, 279, 360
Ben-Zur, H., 210, 367
Bereiter, C., 220, 360
Bergerud, D., 148, 346, 375
Berliner, D. C., 78, 369
Bernstein, D. A., 154, 360
Bernstein, I. H., 108, 387
Best, S., 303, 382
Bettis, G., 278, 359
Beuhring, T., 53
Beukelman, D. R., 222, 225, 376, 396
Bhojwani, S., 260, 377
Bigge, J., 14, 303, 360, 382
Biggler, J. K., 260, 360
Billingsley, F., 297, 376
Bintz, W. P., 245, 252, 253, 360
Birdyshaw, D., 235, 249, 386

Bisson, S. A., 244, 379
Blachowicz, C. Z., 243, 361
Black, R. S., 289, 319, 361
Blackburn, J. M., 319, 361
Blackorby, J., 23, 279, 361, 398
Blanchette, W. J., 63, 69, 400
Blanck, P. D., 23, 361
Bleile, K. M., 196, 203, 208, 361
Block, C. C., 246, 361
Bloodgood, J. W., 241, 361
Bloodstein, D., 196, 361
Bloom, L. A., 129, 363
Blough, G. O., 339, 361
Blum, I. H., 244, 379
Blum, R. M., 53, 56, 390
Board of Education of Peoria, 17, 361
Boles, S. M., 23, 384
Bolt, S. E., 108, 110, 11, 361
Bond, L., 108, 390
Bonero, D. A., 27, 366
Bonfils, K. A., 166, 378
Borenbaum, E., 51, 387
Borkovec, T. D., 154, 360
Bos, C. W., 96, 361
Boswell, J., 62, 361
Bouck, E. C., 14, 19, 361
Bourdeau, P., 23, 276, 360, 361
Bourexis, P. S., 2, 387
Bowers, B., 258, 370
Boyd, F. P., 235, 375
Boyer, C. B., 62, 362
Boyle, E. A., 75, 76, 350, 353, 361
Boyle, J., 254, 390
Boyle, J. R., 353, 361
Braddock, D. L., 23, 361
Bradley, D. F., 100, 361
Brandt, R., 241, 361
Brant, R., 105, 361
Brantlinger, E. A., 69, 361, 388

Braskamp, D., 108, 390
Braziel, P. M., 47, 379
Brigance, A., 263, 361
Brigham, F. J., 320, 370
Brightbill, C. K., 298, 361
Brinckerhoff, L. C., 23, 75, 361
Briney, M. S., 42, 362
Brody, G. H., 56, 370
Brolin, D. E., 18, 283, 284, 287, 362, 364, 381
Brook, J. S., 48, 362
Brookes-Gunn, J., 62, 362
Brooks, M. A., 248, 388
Broomley, K., 248, 249, 362
Brophy, J. E., 78, 92, 358, 362
Browder, D. M., 111, 260, 362
Brown, A. L., 258, 362
Brown, B., 254, 379
Brown, K. J., 246, 352
Brown, L., 329, 333, 362
Brown, M. R., 42, 362
Brown, V., 189, 399
Brozo, W. G., 235, 252, 362
Bruckert, J., 342, 386
Bruhl, S., 321, 389
Bruininks, R. H., 23, 380
Bry, B. H., 326, 378
Bryan, T., 91, 362
Bryant, B., 262, 362
Bryant, B. R., 242, 245, 362
Bryant, D. P., 242, 245, 362
Buchanan, A. M., 297, 370
Budd, D., 259, 393
Bui, Y. N., 214, 362
Buickema. J. M., 240, 362
Bulgren, J. A., 75, 144, 366, 392
Burbach, H. J., 27, 362
Burns, M. S., 235, 246, 362, 395
Bursuck, W. D., 23, 90, 100, 101, 102, 109, 267, 362, 386, 394
Busch, T. W., 100, 368
Butchart, A. T., 51, 366
Butcher, K., 344, 383
Butler, W., 60, 368
Byrne, M., 240, 359

Byrom, E., 63, 363

Cahen, K. S., 78, 369
Cairns, B. D., 41, 363
Cairns, R. B., 41, 363
Caldwell, J., 246, 363
Calhoun, M. L., 259, 363
Call, D. T., 342, 386
Calvin, M. B., 88, 363, 368
Cameto, R., 279. 398
Caminis, A., 60, 382
Camp, D., 254, 363
Campas, B. E., 51, 373
Campbell, J. R., 21, 232, 363, 372
Campione, J. C., 250, 363
Cancio, E., 49, 386
Canter, W., 314, 371
Cantrell, M. L., 15, 363
Cantrell, R. P., 15, 363
Caperelli, B. J., 254, 387
Capuzzi, D., 58, 363
Carlson, J. K., 62, 365
Carnine, D., 77, 88, 260, 268, 340, 363, 368, 394, 395
Carpenter, C. D., 129, 363
Carpenter, R. O., 237, 388
Carr, E., 243, 363
Carrow-Woolfolk, E., 200, 202, 363
Carson, S.A., 240, 363
Carter, J., 319, 363
Carter, J. F., 165, 363
Carter, M. J., 295, 298, 363
Cartlegde, G., 318, 319, 363
Cartwright, C. A., 290, 319, 363
Cartwright, G. P., 290, 319, 363
Cass, M. A., 62, 368
Cassady, J. K., 255, 363
Cassidy, J., 241, 252, 363
Cavaiulo, D., 280, 281, 285, 395
Cavanaugh, R. A., 142, 363
Cawley, J., 258, 340, 363, 364, 388
Cena, M. E., 246, 364
Center for Disease Control and Prevention, 61, 364

Centers for Disease Control, 56, 61, 65, 364
Centre for Addiction and Mental Health, 296, 364
Chadsey, J. G., 2, 13, 319, 320 391
Chadsey-Rusch, J., 3, 259, 364
Chall, J. S., 240, 364
Chalmers, L., 187, 388
Chamberlain-Solecki, J., 247, 380
Chambers, D., 2, 45, 367
Chandler, L. K., 173, 364
Chapman, S., 247, 391
Chard, D. J., 244, 389
Cheek, E. H., 250, 381
Cheney, C. O., 19, 398
Chilcoat, G. W., 87, 364
Chilcoat, M., 255, 364, 386
Children's Literacy and Reading Specialization of the International Reading Association, 253, 364
Choutka, C. M., 338, 377
Chow, S. H. L., 78, 364
Christian, L., 64, 395
Christiansen, J., 101, 102, 103, 364
Christianson, G. M., 62, 358
Chung, M., 56, 372
Ciardiello, V. A., 247, 364
Cicchetti, D. V., 30, 395
Clark, D., 297, 391
Clark, F. L., 96, 368
Clark, G., 23, 388
Clark, G. M., 3, 17, 18, 364, 394
Clary, L. M., 253, 364
Clees, T., 261, 376
Clement, D., 97, 390
Clement-Heist, K., 335, 364
Clements, J., 15, 401
Close, D. W., 276, 361
Clyde, J. A., 255, 364
Cohen, L., 260, 364
Cohen, M., 41, 364
Cohen, S., 75, 83, 365
Cohen, T. L., 51, 365
Cole, J. T., 198, 203, 365
Cole, M. L., 198, 203, 365

Coleman, M., 254, 365
Coletti, L. A., 326, 378
Collet-Klingenberg, L. L., 278, 289, 365, 373
Colley, D. A., 278, 365,
Colson, S. E., 62, 365
Conderman, G., 3, 19, 74, 365
Conley, M., 237, 365
Connelly, V. J., 75, 361
Connors, D. J., 246, 374
Cook, L., 178, 179, 180, 182, 193, 370
Cooley, W. E, 78, 380
Corbett, A., 42, 375
Cordes, T. L., 297, 298, 365
Cosden, M., 48, 49, 365
Costello, P., 246, 377
Costenbader, A., 24, 29, 30, 31
Council for Exceptional Children, 45, 365
Courtney, A. M., 237, 365
Cowen, J. E., 236, 365
Cowen, S., 23, 27, 362, 365
Cox, C. J., 173, 384
Cox, J., 321, 398
Coyle, L., 62, 361
Coyne, P., 75, 389
Crawford, L., 111, 399
Creamer, T. S., 244, 379
Crews, W. B., 214, 258
Cronin, M., 258, 388
Cronin, M. E., 285, 287, 345, 388
Crowe, T., 44, 365
Crystal, D., 198, 365
Csikszentmihalyi, M., 294, 365
Cullinan, D., 51, 276, 365, 389
Cumblad, C., 90, 389
Cunningham, J. W., 235, 386
Cunningham, P. M., 235, 386

Dahl, K. L., 240, 370
Dahlquist, C. M., 173, 364
Daiute, C. A., 223, 365
Daley, C. E., 41, 42, 365
Dalton, B., 342, 365
D'Amore, M., 215, 396
Daniels, H., 246, 365

Darch, C., 182, 249, 371, 390

Darling, S., 254, 366

Darmody-Latman, J., 255, 379

Davies, D. K., 303, 366

Davies, T. G., 29, 380

Davis, B., 75, 392

Davis, G., 182, 371

Day, J. B., 258, 362

deBettencourt, L. U., 5, 11, 14, 27, 366, 391

DeHotman, S. L., 42, 366

De La Paz, S., 249, 338, 339, 345, 366, 396

DeMartino, R., 56, 359

Deno, E., 8, 9, 366

Deno, S., 105, 245, 264, 275, 366, 370, 382

deSaman, L., 259, 399

Deshler, D. D., 15, 16, 18, 75, 94, 95, 96, 144, 145, 195, 214, 221, 241, 258, 366, 392

Desimone, L. M., 6, 394

Devlin, S. D., 48, 366

DeVoogd, G., 235, 366

DeWitz, P. K., 236, 366

Diana v. State Board of Education, 8, 366

Dicecco, V. M., 349, 366

Dieker, L. A., 178, 366

Dielman, T. E., 51, 366

Dileo, D., 281, 373

Diller, D., 253, 367

Dillner, M., 248, 367

Dillon, D. R., 240, 367

DiLorenzo. T. M., 322, 383

Dippi-Hoy, C. M., 260, 401

Dishau, M. M., 78, 369

Dusmukes, B. W., 252, 387

Dixon, R., 77, 395

Dodden, R. A., 303, 385

Dole, J., 246, 367

Donahue, D., 101, 235, 367

Donahue, M. L., 320, 329, 335, 372

Donahue, P. L., 252, 363

Donelson, F., 142, 363

Doshi, S. R., 56, 57, 394

Dotson, L. A., 64, 395

Douglas, L., 48, 360

Dowd, C. A., 243, 394

Dowdy, C. A., 17, 18, 315, 394

Dowhower, S. L., 249, 376

Doyle, C. S., 348, 367

Drasgow, E., 133, 401

Dreher, M. J., 251, 254, 367

Dressman, M., 240, 367

Drye, J., 18, 379

Duffy, G., 240, 246, 268, 367

Duffy-Hester, A., 236, 367

Dukes, L. L., 23, 28, 367

Dukes, R. L., 57, 367

Dunn, C., 2, 3, 45, 46, 47, 367

Dunn, L. M., 202, 367

Durand, V. M., 173, 367

Duvdevany, I., 310, 311, 367

Dwyer, E. J., 245, 367

Dyches, T. T., 254, 389

Dye, G. A., 348, 367

Dyer, W., 258, 367

Egan, M., 247, 368

Eaton, M., 264, 373

Eaton, S. B., 58, 110, 264, 370, 371

Eaves, R. C., 249, 390

Edens, R. M., 62, 367

Edgar, E., 3, 17, 23, 24, 367, 368, 382, 388

Edgar, E. B., 43, 399

Edwards, L. L., 241, 338, 377

Edwards-Kyle, D., 44, 358

Egelko, B., 214, 368

Eisenmann, R., 41, 368

Elbaum, B., 240, 368

Eldridge, B. H., 248, 368

Ellett, L., 188, 368

Elliot, S. N., 48, 110, 366

Elliot, S. V., 318, 372

Ellis, E., 18, 95, 96, 195, 251, 275, 347, 356, 366, 368

Ellsworth, R. A., 252, 384

Elmquist, D. L., 50, 51, 368

Emanuel, E. J., 278, 377

Emmer, E. T., 138, 369

Eng, T., 60, 368

Englemann, S., 77, 266, 368

Englert, C. S., 216, 219, 224, 226, 368, 390

Epstein, M. H., 51, 90, 259, 365, 368, 384, 389

Erb, S., 255, 368

Erchul, W. P., 177, 392

Erwin, E. J., 22, 397

Espin, C. A., 100, 109, 112, 114, 368

Evans, E. D., 62, 368

Evertson, C. M., 78, 138, 358, 369

Family Planning Council, 61, 369

Farb, J., 273, 369

Farey, J. W., 259, 369

Farrington, D. P., 41, 46, 369

Ferretti, R. P., 345, 369

Fick, L., 68, 369

Field, S., 18, 279, 280, 364, 379

Filby, N. N., 78, 369

Filler, J., 318, 360

Fine, A. H., 272, 369

Fischbaugh, L. R., 249, 369

Fischer, C., 235, 369

Fisher, C. W., 78, 86, 260, 266, 268, 369

Fisher, D., 224, 252, 369

Fisher, G. L., 48, 49, 369, 378

Fisher, L., 254, 369

Fisk, C. 247, 369

Fitch, E., 253, 379

Fitzgerald, E., 210, 369

Fitzpatrick, K. M., 48, 400

Flippo, J. R., 57, 401

Flower, L. S., 215, 219, 220, 374

Flowers, C., 111, 362

Fokes, J., 210, 369

Foley, R. M., 90, 368

Fondario, L. J., 272, 369

Forbes, L. S., 240, 369

Forcht, J., 261, 385

Forehand, R., 56, 370

Forgnone, C., 274, 383

Forness, S. R., 51, 52, 330, 370, 381, 383

Fortmeyer, D. J., 259, 399

Fox, E., 62, 361

Francis, M. A., 241, 370

Frank, A. R., 263, 370

Freedman, M., 45, 370

Freidman, S. G., 49, 371

Freppon, P. A., 240, 370

Fresch, M. J., 248, 370

Frey, G. C., 297, 299, 370

Frey, N., 240, 369

Friedland, E. S., 245, 370

Friend, M., 178, 179, 180, 182, 220, 221, 377

Fuchs, D., 19, 110, 177, 254, 258, 275, 276, 370, 383, 399, 400

Fuchs, L. S., 19, 105, 110, 177, 258, 275, 276, 370, 399, 400

Fulk, B. M., 320, 370

Gable, R. A., 173, 174, 370

Gajar, A. 23, 27, 370

Gallagher, D. P., 46, 369

Galloway, L. M., 18, 396

Gambrell, L. B., 244, 248, 370, 379

Gardill, M. C., 235, 371

Gardner, J., 314, 371

Gardner, M., 202, 317

Garff, J. T., 330, 331, 335, 371

Garmezy, N., 54, 371

Garrick Duhaney, L. M., 100, 391

Gartin, B. C., 24, 27, 62, 367, 371

Gartland, D., 11, 245, 359, 371

Gary W. v. Louisiana 159, 371

Gaskins, I. W., 240, 371

Gast, D., 261, 384

Gaylord-Ross, R., 335, 364

Geary, D. C., 258, 371

Geisthardt, C., 53, 371

Genaux, M., 49, 371

Gentry, N. D., 78, 86, 373

George, N., 182, 371

Gere, A. R., 220, 224, 371

Gershaw, N. J., 318, 319, 335, 372, 384

Gersten, R., 182, 215, 262, 359, 371, 387, 400

Gibbs, N., 62, 68, 371

Gierl, M. J., 45, 371

Gies, S. V., 41, 364

Gilbertson, D., 137, 400

Gill, S. R., 247, 371

Gillespie, C. S., 247, 251, 371
Gilmore, D. S., 23, 384
Gipe, J., 243, 371
Gitlin, T., 48, 371
Givens, A., 350, 375
Glascow, A., 111, 397
Gleason, M. M., 229, 230, 235, 260, 349, 359, 366
Goals 2000, 2, 16, 46, 371
Goin, L. I., 274, 374
Gold, V., 201, 382
Golden, L. B., 319, 321
Goldman, S., 260, 371
Goldstein, A., 318, 319, 335, 372
Goleman, D., 53, 55, 372
Good, T. L., 78, 86, 372
Goodman, K. S., 240, 372
Goodman, L., 23, 370
Goodwin, M., 242, 362
Gordon, A. S., 48, 362
Gorman, C., 51, 53, 372
Goss v. Lopez, 170, 372
Gould, M. S., 56, 372
Gowan, L. P., 237, 385
Graetz, J. E., 249, 383
Graham, S., 97, 98, 99, 214, 215, 216, 222, 223, 228, 359, 374
Grant, R., 250, 372
Grasso, E., 260, 362, 401
Graves, M. F., 243, 247, 362
Green, M., 245, 372
Green-Burns, W. B., 42, 366
Greenspan, S., 319, 372
Greenwald, L. A., 214, 372
Gresham, F. M., 318, 320, 321, 324, 333, 372
Griffen, P., 235, 372
Griffith, L. W., 244, 372
Grigal, M., 25, 26, 27, 280, 372, 387
Grobe, C., 223, 372, 382
Grossen, B., 75, 392
Grossi, T., 24, 57, 384, 396
Grossi, T. A., 326, 329, 335, 372
Grossman, H., 137, 372
Grouws, D. A., 78, 86, 372
Guastello, E. F., 340, 372
Guest, C. L., 56, 384
Guetzloe, E. C., 58, 373
Gunter, P. L., 44, 394

Gupta, A., 254, 373
Gurganus, S. 340, 373
Gutkin, T. B., 181, 184, 186, 373
Gutlohn, L., 235, 395
Guttermacher, S., 69, 373

Haavik, S., 70, 373
Hadaway, N. L., 253, 373
Hagner, D., 281, 373
Hagood, B. F., 247, 337
Hahn, A., 46, 373
Haimes, P. E., 330, 395
Halderman v. Pennhurst, 8, 373
Hale, R. L., 78, 268, 394
Hallahan, D. P., 18, 108, 318, 319, 373
Hallenbeck, M. J., 214, 221, 373
Halpern, A., 4, 279, 373
Hamff, A., 242, 362
Hamilton, R. L., 251, 360
Hamlett, C., 110, 373
Hammen, C., 51, 373
Hammill, D., 189, 201, 202, 204, 235, 324, 362, 373, 398, 399
Hancock, M. R., 248, 373
Handl, P., 261, 378
Hanley-Maxwell, C., 289, 373
Hansen, C., 264, 373
Hanson-Krening, N., 253, 373
Haring, N. C., 78, 264, 275, 373, 374, 400
Harmon, J. M., 241, 374
Harnish, D. L., 45, 371
Harper, C., 90, 395
Harper, G., 274, 356, 394
Harriman, N. E., 78, 334
Harris, A., 240, 374
Harris, K. R., 97, 98, 99, 215, 219, 220, 374, 387
Harris, R., 24, 30, 374
Harrison, T. C., 49, 369
Harris Survey of Americans with Disabilities, 278, 374
Hart, C., 24, 401
Hart, D., 24, 25, 26, 29, 374
Hartas, D., 320, 329, 335, 374
Hartwig, E. P., 171, 372

Harvey, M. W., 45, 47, 374
Hashey, J. M., 246, 374
Hatfield, E. M., 108, 374
Hawton, K., 56, 57, 374
Hayes, J. R., 215, 219, 220, 374
Heafner, T. L., 245, 383
Heal, L. W., 266, 373
Heaton, S., 353, 374
Heavy, L. L. 319, 374
Hebeler, K., 279, 398
Heckaman, K., 319, 386
Heilman, E. E., 240, 367
Heimlich, J. E., 244, 377
Hein, K., 62, 362
Heller, H. W., 4, 18, 374
Henk, W. A., 240, 374
Henwood, G. F., 246, 374
Hernandez, A., 254, 382
Hester, P., 134, 136, 137, 138, 174, 374
Heward, W. L., 88, 112, 142, 326, 329, 335, 368, 371, 372, 374
Hibbing, A. N., 247, 375
Hickson, L., 321, 375
Hiebert, E. H., 249, 375
Higgins, K., 42, 241, 362
Hill, J. W., 23, 24, 375
Hill, N. C., 42, 375
Hillocks, G., 216, 228, 375
Hilvitz, P. B., 173, 384
Hinchman, K. A., 235, 237, 365, 375
Hingsburger, D., 64, 375
Hitchcock, C., 375
Hobbs, T., 184, 196, 375
Hodapp, A. F., 90, 375
Hodapp, J. B., 90, 375
Hodell, S., 107, 384
Hoffman, J. G., 240, 367
Hogan, K., 98, 389
Hollenbeck, K., 111, 397
Hong, E., 42, 362
Honig v. Doe, 8, 170, 375
Hooten, H., 249, 360
Hoover, J. H., 187, 388
Hoover, J. J., 5, 18, 375
Hopkins, C. J., 254, 375
Horner, R., 173, 388
Horner, R. H., 318, 372, 387
Horton, B. 24, 368
Horton, S. V., 259, 273, 346, 349, 350, 352, 375
Houck, C., 79, 375

Howard, C. B., 235, 396
Howard, J. K., 235, 383
Howard, R. W., 297, 298, 365
Howell, K., 173, 376
Hoy, C., 349, 376
Hubbard, B., 62, 361
Hudson, P., 245, 347, 350, 356, 376
Huefner, D. S., 177, 182, 376
Huffman, L. E., 254, 395
Hughes, A. G., 42, 366
Hughes, C., 258, 319, 320, 376, 382
Hughes, C. A., 93, 380
Hughes, D., 204, 376
Hughes, M., 298, 396
Hull, G., 220, 376
Hunt, K. W., 227, 376
Hunt-Berg, M., 223, 226, 228, 359
Huntington, D. D., 56, 376
Hurst, B., 247, 369
Hushion, B. C., 253, 379
Hutcherson, K., 261, 376
Hutchins, M. P., 290, 376
Hynd, C. R., 246, 250, 376

Idol, L., 178, 179, 181, 182, 183, 184, 187, 376, 399
Ingraham v. Wright, 159, 376
International Reading Association, 236, 376
Ireland, M., 53
Ironsmith, M., 275, 397
Irvin, L. K., 318, 398
Isaacson, S., 223, 226, 228, 260, 359
Israel, S. E., 246, 361
Ives, B., 348, 349, 376
Ivey, G., 246, 252, 255, 376

Jack, S. L., 44, 394
Jackson, A., 254, 395
Jackson, L. 297, 376
Jackson, R. F., 75, 375
Jacobson, L. A., 241, 377
Jairrels, V., 285, 289, 388
Jamison, D., 278, 365
Janas, M., 340, 373
Jayanthi, M., 90, 91, 389
Jenson, W., 137, 258, 386, 390

Jessor, R., 48, 377
Jessor, S. L., 48, 377
Jewell, T. A., 246, 377
Jitnedra, A. K., 235, 241, 259, 260, 266, 338, 339, 371, 377
Johnson, A. P., 241, 377
Johnson, B., 235, 395
Johnson, C., 65, 377
Johnson, D. D., 235, 377
Johnson, D. R., 278. 377
Johnson, E., 5, 109, 110, 377
Johnson, J., 278, 289
Johnson, M. N., 68, 381
Johnston, J. L., 63, 377
Johnston, P., 236, 246, 377
Jones, E., 260, 377
Jones, J., 53, 57, 390
Jones, L. S., 139, 377
Jones, P., 296, 377
Jones, S. E., 56, 394
Jones, V. F., 139, 377
Jongsma, K., 249, 377
Jordan, L., 98, 385

Kahn, H., 340, 364
Kaiser Family Foundation, 60, 377
Kameenui, E. J., 235, 378
Karacostas, D. D., 48, 378
Karns, K., 110, 370
Karvonen, M., 111, 362
Kasten, W. C., 247, 378
Kastner, T., 62, 382
Katims, D., 240, 378
Katsiyannis, A., 3, 11, 19, 44, 74, 75, 133, 172, 378, 382, 401
Katz, G., 63, 363
Katz, M., 54, 378
Kauffman, J. M., 18, 42, 108, 261, 263, 318, 319, 373, 378
Kaufman, K., 275, 392
Kavale, K. A., 330, 383
Kazdin, A. E., 126, 265, 378
Kazemek, F. E., 254, 378
Kear, D. J., 252, 384
Kee, C., 244, 387
Keefe, E. B., 177, 178, 179, 180, 184, 378
Keith, G. R., 23, 384
Kellner, M. H., 326, 330, 331, 333, 335, 378
Kellog, R. T., 216, 378

Kelly, J. B., 299, 378
Keogh, B. K., 60, 378
Kern, L. H., 68, 397
Kerr, M. M., 65, 166, 167, 168, 169, 376
Kesner, J. E., 254, 383
Keul, P. K., 24, 396
Khemka, I., 321, 375
Kiarie, M. W., 318, 363
Kiernan, W. E., 23, 384
Kimball, K., 109, 110, 377
King, R., 275, 399
King-Sears, M. E., 19, 75, 165, 166, 378
Kinzer, J. K., 248, 381
Kirby, D., 69, 378
Kirk, W. G., 57, 379
Kirschner, B. W., 219, 390
Klein, L., 65, 379
Klein, P. 318, 372
Klein, T. W., 214, 379
Kleinert, H., 298, 394
Kleinnman, M., 56, 372
Kletzien, S. B., 253, 379
Kliewen, C., 240, 379
Klutn, P., 255, 379
Knight, D., 278, 279, 379
Koenig, C., 255, 386
Kohler, P. D., 279, 280, 379
Kokoszka, R., 18, 379
Kong, A., 253, 379
Koppel, A., 259, 388
Kortering, L. J., 47, 379
Koskihen, P. S., 244, 254, 379
Kosky, R., 57, 379
Kounin, J., 932, 379
Krashen, S., 254, 390
Kratochwill, T. R., 110, 368
Kregel, L., 278, 285, 399
Kreuger, E., 254, 379
Kroesbergen, E. H., 263, 379
Kruger, L., 259, 379
Kruschwitz, R., 100, 109, 368
Kucan, L., 251, 360
Kuhn, M., 244, 379
Kuper, D. J., 69, 379
Kurkjian, C., 246, 387
Kvararceus, W. C., 41, 379

Labbo, L. D., 246, 379
LaBerge, D., 245, 379
LaFleur, L., 137, 400

LaGreca, A. M., 49, 379
LaJeunesse, C., 94, 390
Lakin, K. C., 23, 380
Lamarine, R. J., 49, 380
Lambdin, D. V., 97, 390
Lambert, D. H., 65, 330, 378, 380
Lambie, R. A., 266, 380
Lancaster, P. E., 280
Landis, D., 240, 379
Landrum, J. E., 254, 380
Lang, E., 288, 392
Lange, C., 17, 380
Langone, C. A., 19, 239, 376, 380
Langone, J., 19, 380
Larrivee, B., 258, 261, 380
Larry P. v. Riles, 8, 107, 380
Larsen, R. P., 4, 385
Larson, P. J., 173, 380
Larson, V. L., 195, 201, 202, 203, 205, 380
Laufenberg, R., 273, 393
Laurin, K. M., 29, 380
Lawless, K. A., 248, 395
Layton, C. A., 29, 381
Lazarus, B. D., 354, 355, 380
Leal, D. J., 246, 247, 380
Lee, J., 254, 366
Lee, S., 23, 388
Lehmann, J. P., 29, 380
Leigh, J. E., 329, 362
Leimkuhl, T. L., 64, 388
Leinhardt, G., 78, 380
Leinhart, A., 222, 283
Lenihan, G., 246, 380
Lenz, B. K., 15, 18, 75, 94, 95, 96, 195, 258, 270, 366, 380, 392
Leone, P. E., 42, 48, 49, 380
Leslie, L., 246, 363, 380
Lesseliers, J., 64, 380
Lester, J. H., 250, 381
Levine, P., 278, 381
Levinson, E. M., 281, 289, 290, 381
Levy, S. R., 68, 381
Lewis, C., 246, 381
Lewis, R. B., 107, 108
Ley, 252, 381
Liang, L. A., 247, 381
Lignugaris-Kraft, B., 347, 376
Likins, M., 49, 386

Lillywhite, H., 198, 399
Lindorom, L., 278, 360
Lindquist, M. M., 97, 390
Lindsey, P., 57, 401
Lindstrom, B. D., 23, 24, 29, 30, 394
Linneman, D., 319, 364
Litow, L., 163, 381
Livingston, N., 246, 381
Lloyd, J., 318, 378
Lloyd, R. J., 284, 381
Lloyd, S. L., 246, 381
Lock, R. H., 29, 381
Locke, J., 202, 381
Lodge Rogers, E., 29, 279, 381
Loeber, R., 42, 44, 382
Logan, J. W., 242, 391
Lohman, D. A., 320, 370
Lopez-Robertson, J. M., 246, 383
Lora v. Board of Education, 107, 381
Lorch, B., 57, 367
Love, L. L., 278, 382
Lovitt, T., 264, 275, 373, 381
Lovitt, T. C., 148, 346, 349, 350, 352, 375
Lubliner, S., 241, 381
Lucas, C., 56, 372
Luecking, R., 278, 377

Maag, J. W., 44, 51, 52, 54, 133, 173, 255, 322, 329, 380, 381, 382, 383
MacArthur, C. A., 214, 223, 338, 339, 345, 366, 382
Maccini, P., 271, 382
Mace, F. C., 335, 382
Macias, C. M., 303, 382
Mack, M., 278, 377
Maddox, M., 24, 43, 368, 399
Maguin, E., 42, 44, 382
Maheady, L., 274, 356, 382
Maher, M., 17, 399
Maldonado-Colon, E., 240, 386
Malian, I. M., 278, 382
Malmgren, K., 23, 382
Mancini, P., 258, 382
Mandelbaum, L., 274, 399
Mandell, C. J., 211, 382
Mandy, J., 255, 373

Mangrum, C., 3, 250, 382
Mank, D., 23, 360
Manset-Williamson, G., 240, 382
Mar, D., 290, 391
Marchetti, A. 62, 382
Marchisan, M. L., 214, 215, 216, 222, 382
Margolis, H., 188, 382
Marinak, L., 240, 374
Markell, M. C., 245, 392
Marliave, R., 78, 369
Marquis, M. A., 211, 382
Martin, A., 60, 382
Martin, E. J., 46, 50, 383
Martin, J. E., 281, 399
Martinez, M., 255, 383
Martinez-Roldan, C. M., 246, 383
Mascari, B. G., 274, 383
Mason, C. H., 214, 374
Massey, D. D., 245, 383
Masters, L. F., 319, 328, 383
Mastropieri, M. A., 178, 182, 183, 184, 193, 244, 249, 339, 340, 341, 342, 344, 345, 348, 350, 352, 383, 395, 398
Mates, B. F., 240, 396
Mathes, P. E., 234, 245, 383
Mathur, S. R., 320, 322, 324, 325, 326, 329, 330, 339, 383
Matson, J. L., 322, 383
Mattes, J. A., 53, 383
Matti T. v. Halladay, 107, 383
Mazzeo, J., 214, 372
McAfee, J., 23, 370
McBride, H. E. A., 57, 383
McCabe, P. P. 46, 383
McCann, P., 94, 369
McCleery, J. A., 344, 384
McCombs, A., 56, 370
McConeghy, J. L., 90, 389
McConnell, M. E., 173, 384
McDonald, M., 11, 397
McDonnell, J., 23, 384
McEvoy, M. A., 296, 388
McEwen, D., 288, 392
McFarland, G., 94, 390
McFarland, T. D., 263, 370
McGaughey, M. J., 23,

36, 384
McGee, K, 318, 378
McGettigan, J., 188, 382
McGilivray, L., 204, 376
McGinnis, E., 335, 336, 384
McHorney, C. A., 57, 390
McIntosh, P. I., 56, 384
McIntyre, L., 268, 367
McKenna, M. C., 252, 384
McKenzie, R. G., 338, 384
McKinley, N. L., 195, 201, 202, 203, 205, 380
McKoewn, M. G., 243, 247, 251, 360, 384
McLaughlin, J. A., 107, 108, 384
McLaughlin, M., 233, 384
McLaughlin, P. J., 19, 42, 360, 380
McLaughlin, S., 198, 203, 209, 384
McLeskey, J., 19, 384
McMillan, D. L., 320, 372
McNally, L. C., 23, 384
McNaughton, D., 271, 382
McNutt, G., 187, 370
Mead, P. L. R., 342, 365
Meadows, N. B., 46, 384
Mechliong, L., 261, 384
Meehan, K. A.,107, 384
Meese, R. L., 147, 384
Meister, C., 247, 391
Mele-McCarthy, J., 24, 374
Mellon, J., 227, 228, 384
Melville, G. A., 62, 368
Menchetti, B. M., 281, 282, 283, 385
Mendez, D., 259, 399, 385
Menninger, K. A, 70, 373
Menon, M. B., 253, 385
Mercer, A. R., 84, 147, 149, 228, 333, 385
Mercer, C. D., 84, 108, 147, 149, 228, 261, 333, 385
Merkley, D., 251
Mesmer, H. A. E., 246, 385
Meyen, C. A. 108, 388
Meyen, E. L., 3, 19, 385
Meyer, A., 75, 375
Meyer, A. L., 55, 390
Meyer, J. L., 247, 359
Miano, K. L., 42, 375
Miles, D., 261, 385

Miller, C., 94, 390
Miller, J., 258, 363
Miller, S., 261, 385
Miller, S. D., 98, 385
Miller, S. R., 4, 385
Miller, T., 255, 347, 376, 385
Mills v. Board of Education, 8
Mims, A., 90, 91, 385
Miner, C. A., 283, 385
Minton, C. A., 303, 385
Mirabito, J., 253, 385
Mirkin, P., 275, 366
Misra, A., 45, 159, 160, 163, 198, 326, 385, 394
Misretta, J., 98, 389
Mitchell, J. P., 236, 246, 385
Mithaug, D., 290, 391
Mizokawa, D. T., 253, 373
Montague, M., 261, 386
Moody, S. W., 240, 368
Moon, M. S., 25, 26, 34, 280, 372, 387
Moore, D. W., 229, 235, 321, 330, 331, 336, 386
Moore, J. C., 235, 240, 24, 243, 245, 252, 374
Moore, J. E., 78, 369
Moore, N. M., 255, 368
Moore, S. A., 235, 386
Moore, V., 177, 178, 180, 184, 378
Moorman, M., 255, 400
Morado, C., 255, 386
Morgan, D. P., 49, 258, 371, 386
Mori, A. A., 319, 383
Mori, B. A., 319, 383
Morley, L., 46, 369
Morocco, C. C., 342, 363
Morrison, G., 255, 368
Moustata, M., 240, 386
Muccigrosso, L., 65, 70, 386
Mull, C. A., 23, 31, 386
Munk, D. D., 100, 342, 386
Munsch, J., 53, 371
Murdick, N. J., 62, 367
Murphy, D. M., 335, 382
Murphy, S. T., 283, 386
Murray, P., 296, 386
Musante, P., 303, 382

Nagle, J. P., 254, 386
Nagliera, J. A., 261, 263, 379
Nagy, W. E., 242, 386
Naquin, G., 137, 400
NARAL Foundation, 61, 386
Nathanson, R. S., 62, 382
National Academy of Science, 340, 386
National Center for Educational Statistics, 45, 48, 386
National Commission on AIDS, 62, 65, 386
National Council of Teachers of Mathematics, 266, 386
National Institute of Child Health and Human Development, 245, 386
National Joint Commission on Learning Disabilities, 236, 387
National Organization on Adolescent Pregnancy, 69, 387
National Research Council, 69, 98, 387
Navarette, L., 57, 401
Needles, M., 78, 395
Neel, R. S., 46, 382, 384
Nelson, C. M., 41, 65, 166, 167, 168, 169, 378, 381, 391
Nelson, D. A., 295, 298, 363
Nelson, J. M., 240, 382
Nelson, R., 350, 375
Neubert, D. A., 25, 26, 34, 280, 372, 387
Neuman, S. B., 244, 254, 379, 387
Nevin, A., 198, 376
Newcomer, P. L., 51, 214, 387
Newman, L., 278, 398
Newton, J. S., 173, 388
Nichols, W. D., 242, 387, 391
Niemic, R. P., 86, 394
Nietupski, J., 276, 387
Nigro, F. A., 41, 44, 401
Nilsson, N. L., 253, 387
Nippold, M. A., 318, 398
Nippold, M. A., 318, 398
Noell, J. W., 318, 398

Nolan, S., 221, 393
Nolet, V., 338, 339, 387
Nomran, M. E., 2, 387
Northman, J., 48, 395
Norton, B., 246, 247, 387
Norton, D. E., 246, 247, 387
Nourse, S. W., 278. 381
Nunnally, J. C., 108, 387

O'Brien, D. G., 240, 367
O'Byrne, B., 246, 387
Odom, S. L., 387
O'Donnell, R. C., 227, 376
Office of National Drug Control Policy, 48, 388
Okolo, C. M., 345, 369
O'Leary, K., 275, 392, 397
Olive, M. L., 296, 388
Oliver, D., 209, 388
Oliver, M. N., 64, 388
Olsen, K., 107, 112, 401
Olson, D., 263, 360
Olson, M. R., 187, 388
Olson-Brown, S., 109, 377
O'Malley, P. M., 63, 377
O'Melia, M., 388
O'Neill, R., 173, 388
Onwuegbuzie, A. J., 41, 42, 365
Opitz, M., 254, 388
Oppenheim, J., 91, 389
Orellana, M. F., 254, 388
Orelove, F., 23, 375
Osborne, S. S., 177, 392
O'Shea, D. J., 214, 353, 358, 374
Osterag, B. A., 149, 388
Otis-Wilborn, A., 240, 400
Owens, R., 62, 382
Owens, R. E., 203, 209, 211, 388
Owens-Johnson, L., 278, 284, 388

Pacifici, L. C., 241, 361
Palmer, B. C., 248, 388
Palmer, E. J., 281, 287, 290, 381
Paolucci-Whitcomb, P., 178, 376
PARC, 8, 388
Paris, S. L., 277, 388
Parker, D. R., 24, 374
Parker, G., 46, 384
Parker, L. G., 42, 375
Parker, W. C., 345, 388

Parmar, R., 258, 340, 363, 388
Pass, L., 259, 393
Passe, J., 346, 388
Pasternack, R. H., 24, 374
Patton, J. R., 5, 17, 18, 23, 90, 259, 285, 289, 318, 319, 320, 335, 345, 364, 368, 375, 388, 389, 389
Paulson, F. L., 128, 388
Paulson, P. R., 128, 388
Pearson, N., 51, 387
Pearson, P. D., 246, 367
Peck, A., 172, 389
Penman, J., 296, 386
Perhats, C., 68, 381
Perkins, V., 276, 389
Perl, S., 224, 389
Persky, H. R., 214, 372
Peters, D. J., 16, 400
Peterson, C. A., 299, 301, 302, 396
Peterson, M., 107, 389
Pfeffer, C., 57, 389
Pfeiffer, K. T., 68, 398
Phelps, L. A., 9, 391
Phelps-Gunn, T., 227, 389
Phelps-Teraski, D., 227, 389
Philippot, R. A., 247, 372
Phillips, S., M., 244, 379
Piaget, J., 97, 389
Pienkowski, D. M., 19, 398
Pierce, T., 42, 362
Pikulski, J. J., 241, 389
Piland, V. C., 281, 282, 283, 385
Piletic, C. K., 303, 389
Pisha, B., 75, 389
Pittelman, S. D., 244, 377
Platt, J., 347, 389
Polden, D. D., 255, 389
Polloway, E. A., 3, 17, 18, 23, 90, 91, 101, 259, 285, 318, 319, 320, 335, 345, 368, 388, 389, 394
Powell, P., 248, 249, 362
Powell-Brown, A., 252, 389
Powers, A. R., 226, 389
Prater, M. A., 63, 254, 321, 389
Pratt, D., 246, 377
Pressley, M., 98, 389
Price, T., 42, 380
Prout, H. T., 298, 394

Pullen, P. C., 108, 245, 376 385
Pumroy, D. K., 163, 381
Purdy, M., 195, 389
Putnam, M. L., 50, 144, 366, 389

Quinn, M. M., 173, 330, 370, 383

Rabren, K., 2, 45, 249, 367, 390
Radandt, E., 342, 386
Raimondi, S., 142, 391
Rambeau, J., 149, 388
Ramos, F., 254, 390
Rankin, J. L., 222, 223, 376, 396
Rankon-Erickson, J. L., 247, 375
Raphael, T. E., 216, 219, 368, 390
Rasinski, T. V., 244, 372
Rasmussen, J. B., 241, 377, 390
Ray, M. S., 129, 363
Readence, J. E., 249, 390
Reavis, K., 137, 390
Reid, R., 51, 382
Rekrut, M., 248, 390
Renzaglia, A., 290, 376
Resnick, M. D., 53, 56, 390
Retherford, K. S., 204, 390
Reynolds, C. R., 107, 390
Reys, R. E., 97, 98, 99, 389, 390
Rhodes, G., 137, 163, 390
Rhodes, L. E., 23, 360
Rice, K. G., 55, 390
Richards, J. C., 247, 390
Richards, P., 255, 390
Richardson, S. S., 254, 390
Ridley, C., 321, 398
Riedesel, C. A., 97, 390
Riggs, S., 57, 390
Rinehart, P. M., 56, 361
Rivera, D., 262, 362
Roberston, J., 24, 30, 374
Robert, P. H., 258, 370
Rodden-Nord, K., 192, 397
Roderique, T. W., 91, 100, 101, 389
Roeber, E., 129, 363
Roehler, L., 246, 367
Rogan, J., 94, 390, 395
Rogan, P. M., 283, 386

Rogers, D. C., 29, 279, 381
Rojewski, J., 281, 292, 289, 319, 361
Rollins, S. P., 15, 390
Romanczyk, R., 275, 392
Romeo v. Youngberg, 159, 380
Rose, D., 75, 375
Rose, E., 23, 362
Rose, T. L., 169, 171, 390
Rosen, N. L., 255, 383
Rosenberg, M. S., 75, 267, 361, 388, 391, 394
Rosenshine, B., 247, 260, 267, 268, 391, 395
Roth, K. J., 342, 391
Rozalski, M. E., 133, 401
Rubin, D. L., 216, 391
Ruchkin, V., 60, 382
Ruesch, G. M., 171, 374
Ruhl, K., 271, 382
Rumrill, P., 24, 27, 371
Rupley, W. H., 242, 243, 391
Rusch, F., 290, 319, 320, 364, 391
Rusch, F. R., 2, 3, 9, 13, 364, 391
Rutherford, F. J., 339, 391
Rutherford, R. B., 41, 173, 320, 322, 324, 325, 326, 329, 330, 335, 370, 383, 387, 391
Ryan, A. L., 172, 391
Rycik, J. A., 235, 386
Rylance, B. J., 46, 391
Ryndak, D. L., 277, 304, 306, 307, 308, 376, 391

Sabatino, D. A., 4, 385
Sabornie, E. J., 14, 27, 223, 273, 336, 343, 366, 368, 391
Sacca, K. C., 142, 274, 351, 382, 390
Sacks, G., 241, 377
St. Ledger, R. J., 46, 369
Salembier, G. B., 235, 391
Salend, S., 91, 100, 129, 318, 335, 342, 344, 391
Salvia, J., 107, 391
Sample, P. L., 23, 392
Samuels, S. J., 245, 379
Sanacone, J., 253, 254, 392
Sands, D. J., 281, 399

Sandt, D. D. R., 297, 370
Santagrossi, D., 275, 392
Sargent, L. R., 321, 392
Sarkees-Wircenski, M. D., 13, 292, 392
Satcher, J., 42, 362
Sattler, J. M., 107, 392
Savage, S., 90, 385
SCANS, 278, 279, 393
Scardamalia, M., 220, 360
Scarpati, S., 172, 389
Scavarda, M., 65, 70, 386
Schaer, B. B., 252, 381
Scheiber, B., 27, 396
Schiefelbusch, R. L., 78, 374
Schloss, C. N., 23, 318, 319, 328, 358, 392
Schloss, P. J., 15, 23, 37, 51, 74, 79, 80, 88, 89, 92, 114, 133, 134, 136, 137, 140, 149, 152, 154, 155, 158, 165, 211, 268, 273, 275, 282, 285, 289, 318, 319, 321, 322, 323, 325, 326, 327, 330, 331, 358, 365, 392
Schmid, R., 17, 399
Schmidek, M., 204, 376
Schmitt, L., 340, 373
Schnabel, J. B., 258, 393
Schulte, A. C., 177, 392
Schulte, A. G., 110, 368
Schumaker, J., 15, 366, 392
Schumaker, J. B., 3, 5, 17, 18, 75, 93, 96, 214, 230, 392
Schumm, J. J., 101, 393
Schumm, J. S., 147, 177, 250, 254, 393
Schutz, R., 290, 391
Schutz-Muehling, L., 23, 396
Schwab, J., 285, 392
Schwartz, J., 339, 361
Schwartz, J. E., 97, 390
Schwartz, M., 288, 399
Schwartz, S., 214, 223, 382
Schwartz, S. E., 259, 393
Schwarz, I. E., 318, 398
Schweder, C., 314, 371
Scott, C. M., 46, 384
Scott, J. L., 13, 292, 392
Scruggs, T. E., 244, 249, 273, 339, 340, 341, 342,

344, 345, 346, 350, 352, 383, 393, 398
Secord, W. A., 200, 393
Secretary's Commission of Achieving Necessary Skills, 2, 393
Sedlak, D. M., 208, 237, 238, 393
Sedlak, R. A., 74, 79, 80, 88, 89, 92, 107, 114, 149, 208, 237, 238, 282, 393
Seegers, G., 258, 393
Seidel, J., 46, 393
Seigel, S., 335, 364
Seiving, R. E., 53
Seltzer, A., 298, 396
Semel, E., 200, 393
Serebreni, R., 24, 27, 371
Serna, L. A., 321, 389
Sevcik, B., 275, 399
Seyfarth, J., 23, 375
Shaftel, J., 259, 393
Shalock, R. L., 23, 392
Shames, G. H., 203, 393
Shanahan, S., 248, 394
Shanahan, T., 248, 394
Shannon, P., 49, 394
Shaughnessy, L., 56, 57, 394
Shavelson. R. J., 250, 394
Shaw, S. F., 23, 27, 28, 367
Sheppard-Jones, K., 298, 299, 394
Shew, M., 53
Shiflett, A. C., 255, 394
Shin, J., 100, 109, 368
Shinn, M. R., 182, 397
Shope, J. T., 51, 366
Shores, R. E., 44, 394
Shoultz, B., 319, 372
Shriner, J. G., 18, 394
Shubert, T. H., 42, 360
Siegel, L. S., 57, 383
Sikorski, M. F., 86, 88, 394
Silbert, J., 260, 267, 274, 394
Silburn, S., 57, 379
Sileo, N. M., 63, 389
Simpson, M. L., 241, 370
Simpson-Brown, R., 65, 70, 386
Sinatra, R., 243, 394
Sindelar, P., 78, 267, 268, 270, 384, 394
Sipay, E., 251, 374
Sitlington, P. L., 3, 17, 18,

23, 31, 364, 386, 394
Slocum, T. A., 346, 375
Skiba, R., 275, 399
Skillman, G. D., 64, 388
Skinner, M. E., 23, 24, 29, 30, 394
Small, L. H., 205, 394
Smith, C. R., 172, 378
Smith, D. L., 318, 375
Smith, L., 314, 371
Smith, M., 235, 400
Smith, M. A., 15, 78, 133, 134, 136, 140, 152, 154, 155, 163, 165, 198, 268, 321, 322, 323, 325, 326, 327, 331, 392, 394
Smith, N. L., 97, 390
Smith, S. W., 318, 319, 320
Smith, T. E., 315, 394
Smith, T. M., 6, 17, 18, 23, 388, 394
Smith v. Robinson, 8, 394
Smolin, L. I., 240, 395
Smolowe, J., 53, 395
Snarr, R., 41, 395
Snow, C. E., 235, 395
Soodak, L. C., 22, 397
Sorrentino, A., 5, 6, 109, 111, 395
Sowers, J., 276, 364
Sparrow, S. S., 330, 395
Speaker, P. R., 253, 395
Speaker, R. B., 253, 395
Spencer, V. G., 339, 356
Spenciner, L. J., 260, 364
SPeNSE, 338, 395
Spines, H. A., 254, 393
Spivak, C., 330, 384, 395
Spooner, F., 111, 362
Spotts, J., 330, 395
Sprafkin, R. P., 318, 335, 372
Sprague, J., 173, 388
Sprague, J. R., 44, 398
Stallings, J. A., 78, 86, 87, 395
Stanovich, P. J., 236, 395
Stanovich, V. E., 236, 244, 395
Starlin, A., 266, 395
Starlin, C., 266, 395
Stayrock, N., 78, 395
Steely, D., 266, 368
Steere, D. E., 280, 281, 395
Stein, M., 77, 235, 260,

394, 395
Stern, M., 48, 395
Stern, P., 258, 394
Sternberg, R. J., 236, 395
Stevens, D. O., 216, 368
Stevens, R., 87, 264, 395
Steward, J., 290, 391
Stinson, J., 64, 395
Stock, E., 303, 366
Stoddard, K., 214, 358
Stodden, N. J., 18, 396
Stodden, R. A., 18, 23, 29, 107, 278, 377, 395, 396
Stoehrmann, T., 342, 386
Stokeld, C. L., 48, 396
Stone, W. L., 49, 379
Storey, K., 173, 320, 330, 331, 388
Stotsky, S., 228, 396
Strain, P. S., 333, 396
Strassman, B. K., 215, 396
Strecker, S., 255, 383
Strichart, S. S., 3, 382
Strickler, K., 147, 393
Strommen, L. T., 240, 396
Strong, W., 227, 396
Stuart, C., 297, 391
Stumbo, N. J., 299, 301, 302, 396
Sturm, J. M., 223, 396
Sugai, G. M., 46, 318, 319, 333, 335, 363, 372, 383
Sullivan, G. S., 344, 393
Sullivan, M., 27, 396
Sullivan-Burnstein, K., 91, 362
Suydam, M. N., 97, 390
Swanda, J. R., 195, 399
Swanson, H. L., 235, 240, 376
Swanson, P. N., 249, 396
Swiegood, P., 128, 396
Swift, K., 253, 396
Swindall, V., 248, 396

Taber, T. A., 298, 396
Tabor, J., 53
Taylor, R. L., 107, 396
Taymans, J. M., 27, 396
Teacher Quality, 6, 396
Tedesco, A., 340, 364
Tedesco, M., 11, 397
Terban, M., 209, 396
Test, D. W., 24, 278, 359, 396
Thalacker, B. E., 65, 70, 386

Tharmayer, D., 330, 380
Thoma, C., 42, 278, 362, 396
Thomas, T. G., 56, 372
Thompson, B., 387
Thompson, S., 242, 362
Thoram, A., 201, 202, 397
Thorn-Gray, B. E., 68, 397
Thorny, B., 261, 378
Throne, J. M., 273, 369
Thurlow, M. L., 18, 108, 110, 111, 361, 397
Tierney, R. J., 237, 397
Tilton, L., 297, 397
Timothy v. Rochester, 8, 397
Tindall, C., 111, 112, 397
Tindall, G., 182, 338, 339, 344, 387, 397
Tivnant, T., 342, 365
Tobin, J. T., 46, 383
Tomasetti, B. W., 240, 374
Tompkins, G. E., 220, 221, 397
Tough, S., 64, 375
Towell, T., 244, 255, 397
Travis, P. C., 318, 319, 320, 322, 330, 394
Treadway, P. S., 338, 377
Trigler, J. S., 68, 398
Tripp, A., 338, 397
Troutman, A., 155, 161, 260, 268, 274, 358
Truesdale, K. S., 245, 370
Truscott, D., 254, 370
Turkewitz, H., 275, 397
Turnbull, A. P., 22, 397
Turnbull, H. R., 22, 397
Turner, M., 255, 400
Tyner, B., 241, 397

Uberti, H., 352, 397
Udrv, J. R., 53
Ueno, K., 6, 394
Ugel, N., 242, 362
Unruh, A., 15, 390
Urv, T., 321, 375
U.S. Department of Commerce, 329, 397
U.S. Department of Education, 17, 45, 397
U.S. Department of Health and Human Services, 51, 296, 397

U.S. Department of Labor, 291, 397

Vacca, J., 245, 398
Vacca, R. T., 235, 241, 245, 375, 398
Vachon, V. L., 235, 359
Valdes, K. A., 100, 398
Van Hove, G., 64, 380
Van Luit, J. E. H., 261, 379
Van Putten, L. M., 258, 393
Van-Slyck, M., 48, 395
Vaughn, S., 46, 96, 100, 177, 240, 247, 251, 254, 321, 361, 365, 368, 393, 398
Velting, D., 56, 372
Vergason, G. A., 3, 385
Vermeer, H. J., 258, 393
Vermeiren, R., 60, 382
Vitolo, R. K., 42, 380
Voelkl, K. E., 251, 363
Vogel, J. R., 101, 102, 103, 364
Vyas, S., 253, 398
Vygotsky, L., 97, 398

Wacker, D., 276, 387
Wagner, M., 23, 279, 361
Wagner, M. M., 100, 398
Walberg, H. J., 86, 394
Waldron, N., 19, 384
Walker, B. J., 254, 396
Walker, H. M., 44, 318, 319, 320, 329, 336, 398
Wallace, G., 201, 202, 205, 206, 209, 398
Walters, A. S., 57, 398
Wandle, C., 259, 379
Ward, K. M., 68, 398
Ward, M. E., 290, 319, 363
Warner, M., 221, 392
Warner, M. M., 19, 398
Washburn, S. G., 75, 361
Washburn-Moss, L., 109, 110, 338, 347, 358, 398
Wasik, B. A., 254, 396
Watts, S., 242, 399
Webb, S. L., 43, 399
Webber, J., 329, 382
Wechsler, D., 108, 399
Weener, P., 107, 393
Wehman, P., 3, 15, 17, 23, 278, 285, 375, 399
Wehmeyer, M. L., 303, 366

Weiderholt, J., 189, 399
Weigle, K. L., 172, 399
Weinberg, N. Z., 48, 399
Weiner, I., 6, 58, 399
Weinrauch, J. D., 195, 399
Weir, C., 30, 399
Weisner, T., 60, 378
Weiss, C., 198, 399
Welch, J., 276, 387
Welch-Burke, C. S., 272, 369
Welker, W. A., 249, 399
Wells, D., 17, 399
Wenner, M. V., 51, 399
Wenrich, J. K., 252, 363
West, D. J., 46, 369
West, J. F., 178, 182, 187, 399
West, L. L., 27, 396
Westerling, D. L., 184, 186, 375
Wharton-McDonald, R., 98, 389
Whelan, R. J., 3, 259, 385, 399
Whelley, T., 24, 29, 395
Whinnery, K. W., 177, 275, 399, 400
White, C. M., 29, 359
White, O., 275. 400
White, P., 249, 360
Whiteman, M., 48, 362
Wigfield, A., 252, 359
Wiig, E. H., 200, 400
Wilcox, B., 3, 23, 260, 384, 400
Wilfong, L. G., 247, 378
Wilgus, S., 226, 389
Wilhelm, J. D., 235, 400
Will, M., 177, 400
Williams, B. T., 240, 400
Williams, J. B., 250, 254, 395
Williams, K., 202, 400
Williamson, C. L., 100, 398
Willis, A. I., 240, 363, 400
Wilson, B., 48, 360
Wilson, K. K., 243, 363
Wilson, R., 78, 244, 267, 268, 377, 379, 400
Wilson, R. J., 78, 394
Wimmer, D., 20, 400
Windmiller, M., 330, 380
Winn, J., 240, 400

Wissick, E., 314, 371
Witt, J., 137, 400
Wolf, M. M., 322, 400
Wolf, S. A., 237, 255, 400
Wolfe, P. S., 63, 69, 400
Wolford, B., 41, 395
Wolford, B. I., 41, 391
Wood, W. M., 278, 359
Wood v. Strickland, 400
Woodward, D. M., 16, 400
Woodward, J., 261, 263, 348, 360, 400
Worsham, H. E., 138, 369
Worthy, J., 252, 255, 400
Wright, D. R., 48, 400
Wright-Strawderman, C., 57, 401
Wyatt v. Aderholt, 8, 401

Xin, Y. P., 260, 401

Yahaya, M. A., 23, 362
Yamasah, S., 321, 375
Yan, W., 253, 363
Yavas, M., 196, 208, 401
Yeager, N., 350, 361
Yell, M. L., 11, 133, 134, 136, 137, 161, 168, 169, 170, 173, 174, 401
Yilmaz, O., 338, 347, 356, 358
Yopp, H. K., 245, 401
Yopp, R. H., 245, 401
Young, A., 48, 360
Yovanoff, P., 278, 360
Ysseldyke, J., 17, 18, 107, 112, 380, 391, 397, 401
Yu, D. C. U., 296, 401

Zabel, R. H., 41, 44, 401
Zafft, C., 24, 26, 30, 401
Zarkowska, E.,15, 401
Zigmond, N., 19, 78, 100, 367, 380, 401
Zimbrich, K., 24, 374, 401
Zirkel, P. A., 5, 6, 109, 111, 395
Zirpoli, T. J., 155, 401
Zoellner, R., 219, 401
Zubrick, S. R., 57, 379

Subject Index

A-B-C recording, 174
Academic learning time, 142
Accommodations, 12, 24, 29, 76,
    102, 110–111
Activities-oriented approach
    benefits, 344
    disadvantages, 344
    phases, 342, 343
    special considerations
    teacher role, 343
Activity reinforcers, 157
Adequate Yearly Progress (AYP), 6
Advanced organizers, 348
Advanced planning, 82
AIDS, 61–65
Alcohol abuse. *See* Substance abuse
Allocated time, 141, 142–143
Americans with Disabilities Act
    (ADA), 12, 23, 24, 28
ANSWER, 94
Antecedent, 174
Antecedent control techniques
    functional activities, 144–149
    functional materials, 144–149
    interactions with peers, 151
    modeling, 151–152
    physical arrangement, 135
    rates of success, 149–150
    review of IEP, 152
    routines, 137–138
    schedules, 138–140
    systematic instruction, 144
    teacher–student interactions,
        150–151
    time management, 141–144
Anticipation grid, 251
Antonym chart, 228
Articulation, 197, 203, 208
Assessment
    alternate, 105, 111–112
    criterion-referenced
        measurement, 79, 112–119,
        263
    curriculum-based assessment,
        79, 105
    curriculum-based vocational
        assessment, 282
    goals, 264–265

identifying learner
    characteristics, 79
listening skills, 200–202
mathematics, 263–264
norm-referenced assessment, 79,
    106–112
paper-and–pencil tests, 114–119
reading, 236–240
social skills, 324–329
speech, 202–205
statewide assessment, 109–112
systematic observation, 79
vocational, 281–283
written language, 216
Assistive technology, 31, 32
Association on Higher Education
    and Disability Standards, 27
Audio recordings, 355

Balanced reading, 241–242
Battle v. Commonwealth, 8
Behavior intervention plan
    (BIP), 174
Behavior rehearsal, 331
Bidialectalism, 211
Big idea, 77, 340
Bilingualism, 212
BIP. *See* Behavior intervention
    plan
Brigance, 263
Bureau of Vocational Rehabilitation,
    34
Business and industry, 33–34

Captions, 244
Career Ability Placement Survey,
    281
Career education, 12, 283–284
Career Education Incentive Act of
    1977, 12
Career Occupational Performance
    System, 281
Carl D. Perkins Vocational and
    Applied Technology Act of
    1985, 282
Carl D. Perkins Vocational and
    Applied Technology Act of
    1990, 13

Cascade of service, 8, 9
CETA. *See* Comprehensive
    Employment and Training Act
    of 1978
Character interviews, 248
Choral reading, 245
*Clinical Evaluation of Language
    Fundamentals*, 200, 202
Cloze procedure, 239, 243
College Career Connection, 26
Community college. *See* Two-year
    college
Compare/contrast, 218, 226
Comprehension
    appreciation, 235
    evaluation, 235
    inferential, 235
    instruction in, 244–249
    literal, 234
    taxonomy, 234–235
*Comprehensive Assessment of
    Spoken Language*, 200, 202
Comprehensive Employment and
    Training Act of 1978, 12–13,
    32
*Comprehensive Receptive and
    Expressive Vocabulary Test*,
    200, 202
Computer-assisted instruction,
    243, 269
Concept map, 244
Confidentiality, 8
Consequence, 155
Consequence control techniques
    contracts, 157, 158
    extinction, 157
    group contingencies, 162–163
    positive reinforcement,
        156–157
    punishment, 158
    reprimands, 159
    school wide systems, 166–172
    self-management, 164–166
    time out, 161–162
Constructivism
    criticisms of, 99
    premises, 97–98
    teaching science, 342

Consultant teacher
  characteristics, 182–184
  responsibilities, 181–187
Consultation
  advantages, 181–182
  barriers, 181–182
  defined, 178–179
  development, 182
  factors undermining, 187
  goals of, 179
  principles of, 179–181
  steps in, 184–187
Content approaches
  disadvantages, 341–342
  general education, 340–342
  modifications, 342
Content enhancements
  advanced organizers, 348
  audio recording, 353
  definition, 347
  graphic organizers, 348, 351
  guided notes, 353, 354
  mnemonics, 350
  peer mediated, 355
  study guides, 350, 351
Context clue instruction, 244
Contingency contract, 157, 158
Contingency planning, 83, 85
Continuity, 92
Conventions (writing), 226
Cooperative learning, 356
COPS, 221
CRAM, 94
Criterion-referenced assessment,
  79, 263
Curriculum
  defined, 75
  design, 77–78
  functional, 14, 82, 229, 285,
    288–289
  written language, 215
  types, 14, 76
Curriculum-based measurement, 79
  defined, 112
  selection, 114
  types, 105
Curriculum-based vocational
  assessment, 282

DEAR, 253
Decoding, 234
Depression
  causes, 52–53
  identification of, 54–55
  incidence, 51

intervention needs, 53–54
  parental involvement, 56
  prevention, 55–56
  teacher responsibilities, 54–56
Desensitization, 154–155
Detroit Tests of Learning Aptitude,
  201, 202
Detention, 166–168
Diagnostic evaluation, 113
Diagnostic and Statistical Manual of
  Mental Disorders, 54
Diana v. State Board of Education, 8
Dictionary of Occupational Titles,
  291
Direct instruction
  assessment procedures, 105
  criticisms of, 97
  curriculum design, 77–78
  defined, 76–77, 78, 79
  implementation, 92–93
  instructional procedures, 86–92
  mathematics instruction, 267
  phases, 78
  reading, 240
  sequence, 79–93
Directed reading activity, 246
Direct observation, 328
Direct services, 179, 191–192
Discipline, 133
Discourse, 200
Discrete cue, 141
Discussion group, 246, 247
DRAW, 95
Dropouts
  causes, 45–46
  identification of, 6–47
  incidence, 45
  intervention needs, 46
  parental involvement, 47
  prevention, 47
  teacher responsibilities, 46–47
Drug abuse. *See* Substance abuse
Due process, 9
Duration recording, 122, 123
Dysfluent, 196

Echo reading, 245
Editing, 219, 220–221
Educational coaches, 26
Education Amendments of
  1974, 12
Education of All Handicapped
  Children Act, 7
Education of the Handicapped
  Amendments, 9–10

Elementary and Secondary Education
  Act, 5
Emotional learning, 154
Enclaves in industry, 35–36
Enforced leisure, 298–299
Engaged time, 141
Ethnic-specific literature, 253
Expressive One Word Picture
  Vocabulary Test, 202
Expressive Vocabulary Test, 202
Expulsion, 44, 170–171
Extinction, 157

FAPE. *See* Free appropriate public
  education
FAST, 95
FBA. *See* Functional behavior
  assessment
Feedback, 331, 332, 333
Fitzgerald Key, 210
FLIP, 250
Fluency
  mathematics, 273–274
  reading, 244–245
  writing, 223, 224,
Following directions, 206
Formative evaluation, 112–113
Four-year colleges
  academic support services, 27
  advantages, 28, 29
  assistive technology, 31, 32
  choosing, 29, 30
  disadvantages, 28–29
  noncompletion, 29
  success strategies, 30–31
Frame, 248
Free appropriate public education
  (FAPE), 18
Frequency recording, 120–121
Fullerton Language Test for
  Adolescents, 201, 202
Functional academic instruction, 259
Functional activities, 144–149, 259
Functional behavior assessment
  (FBA), 10, 144–149
Functional curriculum, 14, 82, 229,
  285, 288–289
Functional instruction, 240
Functional materials, 144–149

Generalization, 276, 333, 35
Goals
  instructional, 81
  mastery, 264–265
  mathematics, 261

social validation, 265
vocational, 285
Goals 2000, 2, 16
Grading
    accommodations, 102
    determining, 103
    effective practices, 101–102
    purposes, 100
    responsibility for, 102
    types, 101
Grammar, 199
Graphic organizers
    constructing, 349
    defined, 348
    purpose, 348–349
    reading, 244, 247
    use, 349–350
Graphs
    graphing data, 126
    interpreting, 126–127
Great Debate, 240
Group contingencies, 162–164
Guided notes
    making, 334
    teaching, 353
    types, 354
    using, 354
Guided practice, 88–89
Guided reading, 245

Halderman v. Pennhurst, 8
High interest, low vocabulary, 247
High-stakes testing, 108
HIV, 61–65
Homework, 90–91, 333, 334
Honig v. Doe, 8
HOW, 230

IDEA. *See* Individuals with
    Disabilities Act
IEP. *See* Individualized Education
    Plan
Inclusion
    consultation, 177, 178
    content area instruction, 338
    leisure education, 296–297
Independent practice, 90
Indirect services, 179, 192
Individualization, 87
Individualized Education Plan (IEP)
    components, 7, 14
    goals, 81
    leisure education, 297, 298
Individualized written rehabilitation
    plan, 34, 35

Individuals with Disabilities Act
    (IDEA)
    amendments to, 4, 10, 109
    consultant teacher, 177
    discipline, 152, 171, 172, 173
    leisure education, 296
    mathematics, 279, 281
    postsecondary education, 29
    student placement, 73
    transition, 24, 279, 281
    written language, 214
Individuals with Disabilities
    Improvement Act, 10
Inferences, 247
Informal reading inventory, 237–238
In-school suspension (ISS), 168–170
Interactions with peers, 151
Interval measurement, 122–124
Inventories
    environmental, 206–207
    family, 307
    peer, 308
ISS. *See* In-school suspension

Job search skills, 290
Job Training and Partnership Act
    (JTPA), 12–13, 32
Journals, 248–249
JTPA. *See* Job Training and
    Partnership Act
Juvenile Corrections Interagency
    Transition Model, 43
Juvenile delinquency
    causes, 41–42
    identification of, 44
    incidence, 41
    intervention needs, 42–43
    parental involvement, 45
    prevention, 44–45
    teacher responsibilities, 43–45

Kernel sentences, 226–227
Keystone of Postsecondary
    Placements Model, 37–38
Keyword method, 351, 352

Language, 196–197
Language sample, 204
Latency, 128
Latency recording, 122, 123
Larry P. v. Riles, 8
Learning standards. *See* Standards
Learning strategies
    characteristics, 95
    curriculum, 14, 18, 81

defined, 94
reading, 249
samples, 94, 95
teaching, 96
Least restrictive environment (LRE),
    8
Legislation
    No Child Left Behind, 5–7, 13–14,
        297
    Special education, 7–11, 13–14
    Vocational education, 11–14,
        32–33
Leisure
    activity skills, 300
    awareness, 300
    defined, 298, 299
    education, 299
    enforced, 298–299
    opportunities, 301–303
    options, 304
    prioritizing options, 309–314
    resources, 300–3
Letter strategy, 351, 352
Level, 127
Life Centered Career Education,
    284, 286–287, 288
LINKS, 94
Listening
    assessment, 200–202
    defined, 195–196
    improving, 205–208
Litigation, 107

Maintenance, 333, 335
Manifest determination, 171, 172
Materials, 19–20, 84, 86, 144–149,
    247, 266
Mathematics
    assessment, 263–264
    materials, 266
    principles of instruction, 258–261
    transition-oriented instruction,
        261–262
Mean, 127
Mills v. Board of Education, 8
Mnemonics
    developing, 353
    teaching, 353
    types, 351–352
Modeling
    antecedent control, 151–152
    social skills, 332
    written language, 216
Momentary-interval recording,
    124–125

Momentum, 92
Morpheme, 198
Morphology, 197–198

NCLB. *See* No Child Left Behind
    Act
No Child Left Behind Act (NCLB)
    adequate yearly progress, 6
    highly qualified paraprofessionals,
        6
    highly qualified teachers, 6,
        10–11, 19
    leisure education, 297
    pillars, 5–7
    purpose, 5
    report cards, 7
    statewide assessment, 108–112
Nondiscriminatory testing, 8
Norm-referenced assessment, 79
    characteristics, 106
    criticisms, 106–107
    defined, 105
Notetaking, 206–207, 353

Objectives, 82, 115–116, 285,
    321, 323
Occupational Aptitude Survey and
    Instructional Schedule, 282
Occupational Outlook Handbook,
    291
Office of Special Education and
    Rehabilitation Services
    (OSERS), 4
Office of Vocational
    Rehabilitation, 34
Omissions, 197
Oral reading error analysis, 239
OSERS. *See* Office of Special
    Education and Rehabilitation
    Services
Overlapping, 92

Paired reading, 245
Pairing, 154
Paper-and-pencil tests, 114–119
Parallel curriculum, 14
*PARC, Bowman et al. v.
    Commonwealth of PA,* 8
Parent rights, 8
Partial interval recording, 123–124
PARTS, 251
Peabody Picture Vocabulary Test,
    202, 204
Peer buddies, 245
Peer-mediated strategies, 355

Peer tutoring, 356
Pegword method, 351, 352
Permanent product recording, 121
Personal care skills, 289–290
Person-centered planning, 282–283
Phonemes, 197
Phonetic analysis, 234, 243
Phonology, 197, 203, 208
Physical arrangement, 135
PIC. *See* Private industry council
Placement evaluation, 107–108
Planned ignoring, 157
PLISST, 70
Portfolio assessment
    advantages, 128–129
    content, 129
    defined, 128
    evaluation of content, 129–130
    reading, 237
    reliability of, 130
    validity of, 130
Positive reinforcement, 156–157
Postsecondary education
    benefits, 24
    choosing, 29
    enrollment problems, 24
    four-year colleges, 27–31
    Keystone of Postsecondary
        Placements Model, 37–38
    sheltered rehabilitation centers,
        35–36
    supported employment, 36–37
    technical programs, 32–33
    two-year colleges, 24–26
    vocational rehabilitation, 34–35
POWER, 217
Practical curriculum, 14
Pragmatics, 197, 200, 205, 211
Pregnancy. *See* Teenage pregnancy
Premack principle, 140, 157
Prerequisite vocabulary, 242
Presenting new information, 86–88
Previewing, 245
Prewriting, 215
Private industry council (PIC), 12
Procedural facilitation, 224
Process (writing), 215
Product (writing)
    assessment, 223–228
    components, 223–228
Project-based instruction
    advantages, 346–347
    features, 346
    premise, 347
Project PROGRESS, 285

Prompts
    defined, 88
    hierarchy, 88
    increasing effectiveness of,
        88–89
    manual, 268
    verbal, 268
    visual, 268–269
Proofreader's marks, 221
Public Law 93-112, 11
Public Law 93-380, 12
Public Law 94-142
    amendments, 9, 100
    provisions, 7–8
Public Law 95-207, 12
Public Law 97-300, 12
Public Law 98-199, 9
Public Law 98-523, 282
Public Law 99-457, 10
Public Law 101-336, 12
Public Law 101-476, 4, 10
Public Law 105-17, 10
Public Law 105-202, 32
Punishment, 158
Purposes (writing), 215

Questioning, 207–208

Rapid retrieval of information, 245
Rate of success, 149–150
Ratings by others, 327–328
Reading
    assessment, 235
    defined, 234
    formal assessment, 236
    informal assessment, 236–240
    principles of instruction, 240–241
    students with disabilities, 2
        35–236
Reading workshop, 253
Real leisure, 298–299
Reduced reading rate, 244
REI. *See* Regular Education Initiative
Regular Education Initiative (REI),
    177
Rehabilitation Service
    Administration, 34
Related personal characteristics
    academic skills, 153
    social skills, 153
Reliability, 117, 125, 130
Repeated reading, 245
Report cards, 109
Reports by others, 327–328
Reprimands, 159

Resource room
  advantages, 189
  definition, 189
  staffing, 190
  teacher, 191–193
Response cards, 141, 142
Response cost, 160–161
Review and reteach, 91–92
Revising, 215, 219
Routines, 137–138
Rules, 136–137, 139, 148

Scaffolding
  defined, 88
  reading instruction, 246
SCANS, 2
Schedule, 138–140
School-to-Work Opportunities Act, 2, 13
Science
  standards, 340
  teaching, 340
SCROL, 250
Secondary reinforcers, 156–157
Secondary special education
  curricular approaches, 14
  development of, 17–20
  goals of, 15–16
  legislative foundations, 4–14
  outcomes, 3
Section 503, 11
Section 504, 11
Self-determination
  assessment, 281
  defined, 280
Self-management, 164–166
Self-monitoring, 326–327
Self-report, 325–326
Semantic maps, 218
Semantics, 198, 204, 205, 209–210
Sentence combining, 227–228
Setting variables, 27
Sexually transmitted disease (STD)
  causes, 62
  identification of, 63
  incidence, 60–61
  intervention needs, 62–63
  parental involvement, 51
  prevention, 63–64
  teacher resources, 66–68
  teacher responsibilities, 63–65
Sheltered rehabilitation centers, 35–36
Sight words, 234, 213

Skill assessment, 202
Skills approach, 38
Smith v. Robinson, 8
Social coach, 304
Social competence, 318, 320
Social reinforcement, 156, 330, 331
Social skills
  assessment, 324–329
  community integration, 31
  curriculum, 18
  definition, 319–321
  employment, 319
  instruction, 329–336
  objectives, 321–332
  pragmatics, 205
  related personal characteristic, 153
  social validation
  transition, 289
Social studies
  curriculum, 345
  goals, 345
  standards, 345
  teaching, 346–347
Social validation, 265, 322–324
Special education, 178
Speech
  assessment, 202
  defined, 196
  improving, 208–212
SPIN, 165–166
Standards
  characteristics, 75
  purpose, 75
  science, 340, 341
  social studies, 345
Standards-based curriculum, 5, 14
Statement PIE, 226
Statewide assessments
  alternate, 111–112
  accommodations, 110–111
  concerns, 109
  exclusion of students with disabilities, 109
  purpose, 108–109
  results, 109
STD. *See* Sexually transmitted disease
Story map, 247
Strategies Intervention Model, 94–95
STRATEGY, 352, 353
Structural analysis, 234, 243
Study guides, 350, 351
Stuttering, 196
Substance abuse
  categories of drugs, 49, 50

  causes, 48
  identification of, 49–50
  incidence, 48
  intervention needs, 49
  parental involvement, 51
  prevention, 50–51
  prevention curricula, 52, 53
  signs of drug use, 50
  teacher responsibilities, 49–51
Substance abuse disorder (SUD), 48
Substitution, 197
Suicide
  causes, 57
  incidence, 56–57
  intervention needs, 57–58
  parental involvement, 60
  prevention, 58–59
  prevention curricula, 52, 53
  teacher responsibilities, 58–60
  warning signs, 58
Summative evaluation, 108
Supported employment services, 36–37
Suspension, 44, 170–171
Sustained silent reading, 252–253
Synonym chart, 205
Syntax
  speech, 197, 199, 210
  written language, 226
Systematic instruction, 144
Systematic observation, 79
  interobserver agreement, 125
  methods, 120–125
  selecting procedures, 119–120

Talk–write model, 219–220
Target vocabulary, 242
Teacher qualifications, 6, 10–11,19
Teacher student interactions, 150–151
Technical programs, 32–33
Teenage pregnancy
  causes, 65–66, 68
  incidence, 65
  intervention needs, 68–69
  parental involvement, 70
  prevention, 70
  teacher responsibilities, 69–70
Telegraphic speech, 199
Testing accommodations, 110–111
Textbook
  instruction, 249–250
  science, 339
Think-pair-share, 141, 142

Time management
  academic learning time, 142–143
  allocated time, 141
  engaged time, 141
  transition time, 143
*Timothy W. v. Rochester School
  District,* 8
Token reinforcement, 157
Transfer of training, 14–15
Transition
  defined, 4, 10
  difficulties with, 278–279
  funds for, 9–10
  IDEA, 279–280
  planning, 10, 24, 29–30, 279–280
Transition time, 143
Trend, 128
Two-year colleges
  advantages, 25
  assistive technology, 31, 32
  choosing, 30
  dual enrollment, 25–26
  goals, 26
  mission, 24–25
  models, 25
  success strategies, 30–31
  versus technical schools, 32

Undue hardship, 12
Universal design, 75–76
Universal precautions, 62
Universities. *See* Four-year colleges

Validity, 117, 130
Visual imagery, 247
Vocabulary
  development, 199
  instruction, 241–244
  prerequisites, 242
  reading, 234
  target, 242
  written language, 228
Vocational assessment
  aptitude tests, 281–282
  defined, 281
  curriculum based, 282
  goal of, 281, 285
  guidelines, 282
  person-centered planning
*Vocational Assessment and
  Curriculum Guide,* 290
Vocational education
  legislation, 11–14
Vocational instruction, 292
Vocational rehabilitation, 34–35

Vocational Rehabilitation Act, 11–12,
  23, 24, 28
Voice disorders, 196

Webbing, 247–248
Whole interval recording, 123
WIA. *See* Workplace Investment Act
With-it-ness, 92–93
Word processors, 222–223
Word recognition, 234
Workplace Investment Act (WIA),
  13, 32–33
Written language
  assessment, 214
  curriculum, 215–216
  performance of students, 214
  phases, 216
  process, 216
  product, 223–228
  purposes, 229–231
  teaching, 216–223
Wyatt v. Aderholt, 8

Zone of proximal development, 98